W9-CQZ-944

Normal Aging III

Normal Aging III

Reports from the Duke Longitudinal Studies, 1975–1984

Edited by Erdman Palmore, Ewald W. Busse,
George L. Maddox, John B. Nowlin, and Ilene C. Siegler

Duke University Press Durham 1985

Printed in the United States of America
Library of Congress Cataloging in Publication Data
Main entry under title:
Normal aging III.
Includes index.
1. Aged—Mental health—Longitudinal studies.
2. Aging—Psychological aspects—Longitudinal studies.
3. Aging—Social aspects—Longitudinal studies.
4. Aging—Longitudinal studies. I. Palmore, Erdman
Ballagh, 1930–. II. Duke University. [DNLM:
1. Aging. 2. Longitudinal Studies. WT 104 N842]
RC451.4.A5N64 1985 618.97 85-1598
ISBN 0-8223-0624-7

Foreword

Ewald W. Busse

Two long-term multidisciplinary longitudinal studies of "normal" aging have been conducted at the Duke University Center for the Study of Aging and Human Development. The vast amount of longitudinal data that have been collected will continue to be analyzed for a number of years. Related investigations are continuing and new work is emerging.

The Duke First Longitudinal Study began in 1955 after five years of cross-sectional research on normal aging. Several years of preliminary research were necessary in order to develop the research design, select the observations, and decide on methods of storage, retrieval, and analysis of the longitudinal data. The first longitudinal study was officially known as "The Effect of Aging upon the Nervous System—A Physiological, Psychological, and Sociological Study of Aging." The second longitudinal study was begun in 1968 and was designated "The Adaptation Study." The history of these two studies is necessarily complex. Attention was given to communication within the interdisciplinary team. Procedures were established by the team to control the investigation. Consequently, these studies provided some important information about the effective organization and administration of interdisciplinary research on aging,[1] as well as many important observations regarding the processes of aging.

The two longitudinal studies are different in a number of ways—the sample, the hypotheses to be tested, the measurement procedures, the duration of the study, and so forth.[2] As indicated by its title, the first longitudinal study focused on understanding the aging nervous system. The emphasis of the second longitudinal study was on adaptation to change over time as well as response to important life events. The observations selected were based upon the best available knowledge at the time of the study, and it is unfortunate that certain procedures were not developed until a later date. Attempts were made to include useful new procedures, such as cerebral blood flow, without jeopardizing the longitudinal aspect of the study.

The development of the longitudinal studies was fortuitous and logical. Beginning in 1948, the principal investigator (Busse) was engaged in research ac-

Correction: Ewald Busse's Foreword was inadvertently printed as the Introduction to Section B on pages 77–80. The proper Introduction to Section B begins on page 81. The Editors and the Publisher regret the error.

1. Busse, E. W. Administration of the interdisciplinary research team. *Journal of Medical Education*, 40:832–839, 1965.

2. Maddox, G. L. (Ed.). The Duke multidisciplinary longitudinal studies of normal aging. Vol. 6, no. 1, Center Reports of Advances in Research, Duke University Center for the Study of Aging and Human Development, Durham, N.C., July 1982.

tivity concerned with epileptic seizures and temporal lobe functioning in adults. An observation was made that many elderly persons referred for clinical diagnostic EEGs showed focal electrical disturbances arising from the temporal region of the brain. The focal disturbance found in the elderly who were free of epileptic seizures could not be distinguished from those individuals with focal epileptogenic focus. Consequently; for those individuals who were free of seizures but had a focal abnormality, the EEG interpretations included the notation, "The focal abnormality present in the record does not appear to be related to the patient's complaint or to the diagnosis." The possible cause and clinical significance of this focal abnormality provided an important investigational challenge.

In the spring of 1952, a paper was read at the annual meeting of the American Medical Association reporting the observation that a significant number of apparently normal elderly persons had EEG temporal lobe focal activity. The following year, additional data were presented to the meeting of the American Psychiatric Association. This paper confirmed that "the cortical activity of persons over the age of sixty shows a definite change as measured by the EEG. A high percentage (37.3 percent) have focal dysrhythmias which are primarily found in the left temporal lobe."[3] These early studies were supported by funds from the National Institute of Mental Health. However, in subsequent years, the funding was derived from various components of the National Institutes of Health. First support was received in the fall of 1951 (Research Grant No. MH 434) and terminated in the fall of 1953. The progress report submitted to the granting agency included the following summary statement: The specific aims of this project were:

> 1. The Standardization of the Normal Electroencephalogram in the Age Group of Subjects 60 Years of Age and Over. 2. The Evaluation of Central Nervous System Functioning in (*a*) Individuals of 60 and Over with Uncomplicated (that is, Normal) Aging, (*b*) Individuals of 60 and Over with Senile and Arteriosclerotic Changes (Pathological Aging).
>
> A total of 332 subjects have been studied. These subjects have been separated into various groups which were determined by social and economic status and their medical condition. Information on these subjects is derived from careful physical and neurological examination, medical and social history, psychiatric examination, psychological testing, EEGs, laboratory studies, and critical flicker fusion for light. Our original observations indicated a high percentage of focal EEG changes in our subjects that were primarily in the temporal areas. This finding has continued as our series has expanded. The focal dysrhythmias are not accompanied by defect of specific functioning; in fact, there is evidence which suggests that those with focal changes function at a somewhat better level than those with 'normal' EEGs. However subjects with diffused disturbances show definite declines in psychological abilities which include such things as facility of communi-

3. Busse, E. W., et al. Studies of processes of aging: VI. Factors that influence the psyche of elderly persons. *American Journal of Psychiatry*, 110:896–903, 1954.

cation, clarity of perception, and abstract thinking. No correlation can be made between these changes and the status of the cardiovascular system or with cerebral dominance.

In 1953, three members of the research team (Busse, Barnes, and Silverman) moved to Duke University School of Medicine in Durham, North Carolina. The research activity continued in this new setting, and grant support was awarded (Research Grant No. 900C). In the fall of 1956, a summary statement was submitted to the granting agency. This statement reads as follows: "Broadly stated, our objectives under this project have been to define and investigate further specific psychological, physiological, and social factors as they relate to human aging. During two years of preliminary work in this field at the University of Colorado School of Medicine, we made certain observations concerning the electroencephalogram, the types of tracing seen in people of 60 and over and correlations between these tracings and measurements of psychological and social functioning. We have now continued these studies in a different cultural and geographical setting looking for the influence of these variables on the various aspects of the aging process. Further, we have attempted to improve our evaluation or measuring technique in both the social and psychological areas and have also added new evaluation tools within the physiological area (cf. Photographs of the ocular fundi and microscopic observations of the bulbar conjunctiva). In the fifteen months spent to date on the current project, the major effort has gone into (1) selecting and training research personnel, (2) selection and mastery of additional evaluation techniques, (3) the establishment of community relationships to allow for the obtaining of volunteer elderly subjects, and (4) the collection of desired evalution data on these subjects. (The schedule as developed accommodates 4–5 subjects per week.) Only now are we able to devote time to ordering an analysis of our data."

This was the beginning of the first longitudinal study. In 1957, the longitudinal research project was incorporated into a program project grant (RG H MH A B 5385) which provided the core support for the development of the Center for the Study of Aging at Duke.

Long-term interdisciplinary research requires that all participants have a clear understanding of the objectives and that the effort is creative and has a careful research design. Equally important is the selection of members of the team. The team should be guided by administrative principles and procedures which are easily understood and equitable. Efforts must be given to the maintenance of a team concept, with frequent and congenial methods of communication and cooperation. Responsibility for the collection of data in specific areas as well as other activities must be clearly assigned. Continuing attention must be given to data management, including data reduction, cleaning, storage, and retrieval. Statistical consultation must be readily available and review procedures of publications are necessary to ensure quality and to avoid any adverse effect that would result from a scientific report of questionable quality published by a member of the team. These features and procedures of the longitudinal studies have been reported in some detail in *Normal aging* (Busse, "Administration of the Interdisciplinary Research Team") and in the report of the Duke longitudinal studies edited by Busse and Maddox.[4]

Individuals and combinations of various members of the team have been recognized for their outstanding scientific contributions to the study of aging. The team was recently recognized as a highly productive, interdisciplinary effort when it received the Sandoz Award. The announcement of July 22, 1983, from Basel, Switzerland, is presented below:

> The International Association of Gerontology has announced that the Duke Longitudinal Study of Normal Aging is one of the recipients of the Sandoz Prize. The co-recipient is a research team based in The Netherlands headed by Dr. Carel Hollander. The award will be presented to Dr. E. W. Busse representing the Duke Research Team on September 3, 1983, in Budapest, Hungary.
>
> The Sandoz Prize for Gerontology is not limited to any specific area of gerontology or geriatrics, but has a special emphasis on multidisciplinary programs. The Duke Longitudinal Studies are composed of two major efforts. The first was initiated in 1955 and the second in 1968. Both studies focused on the biomedical, physiological, psychological, and social aspects of normal aging. The subjects were followed into 1980. Analysis of the data collected continues. "These studies produced some important insights into the complex processes of normal aging, but more than this these studies illustrated and strengthened the commitment to multidisciplinary research" and "generated laboratories and programs that provided natural sites for research training." The Sandoz Prize that will be received by the Duke investigators is 10,000 Swiss francs. These funds will be utilized to promote research and training in the Center for the Study of Aging and Human Development of Duke University. Dr. E. W. Busse was the principal investigator of the Duke Longitudinal Studies and Dr. George Maddox assisted and participated in the research.
>
> Since 1955 many investigators have participated in these studies, including current faculty: Ilene Siegler, Erdman Palmore, John Nowlin, Linda George, Dietlof Ramm, Hsioh-Shan Wang, Edward Buckley III, Gail Marsh, Stephen Vogel, Peter Burger, Max Woodbury, David Madden, Carol Hogue, Alan Whanger, Daniel Gianturco.

The core data from these two studies are now available for further analysis by other qualified investigators. We hope that further analysis of this rich store of data will continue to yield better understanding of the processes of aging.

4. Busse, E. W., and Maddox, G. L. (Eds.). Final report: The Duke longitudinal studies—an integrated investigation of aging and the aged, ancillary studies, and research support services—1955–1980. Submitted from the Center for the Study of Aging and Human Development, Duke University, November 30, 1980.

Contents

Section A. Physical Aging

Section B. Mental Health and Mental Illness

Section C. Psychological Aging

Section D. Social Aging

List of Figures

List of Tables

Preface

This volume is a sequel to *Normal aging*, *Normal aging II*, and *Social patterns in normal aging*. Its purpose is to bring together and summarize the main findings which build upon and extend those presented in the first three volumes. It contains all the articles from the Duke longitudinal studies published since 1973 and in addition almost as many papers presented at professional meetings or written especially for this volume.

All four of these volumes deal with "normal aging" in two senses: healthy aging and typical aging. The aged and middle-aged persons studied were relatively healthy in that they were noninstitutionalized, ambulatory community residents who were willing and able to come to the Duke Medical Center for one or two days of tests and examinations periodically. Second, the more common or typical patterns and problems of aging are focused upon rather than the unusual abnormalities. This volume deals with the typical physical changes which accompany aging; typical patterns of mental health and mental illness; typical patterns of psychological aging; and the normal social roles, self concepts, satisfactions, and adjustments to retirement.

As pointed out in earlier volumes, investigations of normal aging are of crucial importance in advancing the science of gerontology and in helping aged persons develop and enjoy a richer and longer life. When we can distinguish normal and inevitable processes of aging from those which may accompany aging simply because of accident, stress, maladjustment, or disuse, we can better focus our attention and efforts on those factors which can be changed and corrected.

All four volumes also emphasize the theoretical and methodological advantages of the longitudinal and interdisciplinary methods used in these studies. Since aging is by definition a process of change over time, it would seem that the best way to study aging is longitudinally, by repeated observations over time. This is not to deny the value of cross-sectional studies, nor to deny the technical and methodological problems connected with longitudinal study; it is meant to reassert the unique advantages of longitudinal studies such as the following: each panel member can be used as his own control, consistent trends can be distinguished from temporary fluctuations, errors due to retrospective distortion are minimized, early warning signs of disease or death can be studied, cohort differences can be distinguished from age changes, and the effects of one kind of change on another kind of change at a later time period can be studied.

The interdisciplinary nature of the studies is useful because aging affects many interrelated types of behavior and functioning. When specialists from different disciplines work together, the mutual stimulation, correction, and combination of perspectives can result in a more accurate, thorough, and comprehensive understanding of the aging process.

This volume differs from the others in format: it has as editor for each of the four sections the staff member primarily responsible for the investigations in his or her area. Each section editor reviews and comments on the thoretical implications of the papers in that section. We believe this format provides a more meaningful framework for interpreting the diverse findings of the specific papers.

The reader who is interested in detailed description and discussion of the first longitudinal study of aging is referred to chapter 1 of *Normal aging*. Suffice it to say here that the first longitudinal study began in 1955 with 271 persons sixty to ninety years of age. The subjects were not a probability sample but were selected from a pool of volunteers who lived in the community, so that the overall sample reflected the age, sex, ethnic, and socioeconomic characteristics of the older population in Durham, North Carolina. Each panelist was brought in to the Medical Center for a two-day long series of medical, psychiatric, psychological, and social examinations. These examinations were repeated every three or four years until 1965, every two years until 1972, and each year between 1972 and 1976. In 1976, the eleventh and final round of examinations on the survivors of this study was completed.

The second longitudinal study, or adaptation study, began in 1968 with 502 persons forty-six to seventy years of age. These panelists were a probability sample of the members of the local health insurance association, stratified by age and sex. The sample and study were designed so that at the end of five years there would remain approximately forty persons in each of ten five-year age-sex cohorts. This design makes possible various kinds of cross-sequential types of analyses in order to separate the effects of aging from cohort differences and from changes in the environment over time. Each subject was brought in for a day-long series of physical, mental, and social examinations. The panelists were reexamined at two-year intervals, and in 1976 the fourth and final round of examinations was completed. For more details and discussion of the second longitudinal study design, the reader is referred to Appendix A of *Normal aging II*.

The articles which are reprinted from various journals appear with no deletions except for duplicate passages such as those which repeat the description of the panelists. Since most of the reports are interdisciplinary, the placement of some reports in one section rather than another was somewhat arbitrary, but an attempt was made to group reports by the type of central variable under investigation. The book closes with an overall summary of the main findings and themes. The reader may wish to start with the introductions or summary in order to decide which reports to read for more detail.

We thank the many authors, journal editors, and publishers for their permission to reprint articles. Special thanks are due to Ms. Pamela Kay Bailey for her help in preparing the manuscript. Most of this research was partially supported by the U.S. Public Health Service, National Institute of Child Health and Human Development, Grant HD-00668.

Erdman B. Palmore
Coordinating Editor

Contributors

Chris P. Averett, Ph.D., Instructor of Sociology, Duke University, Durham, North Carolina.

Kurt W. Back, Ph.D., Professor of Sociology, Duke University, Durham, North Carolina.

Dan G. Blazer, M.D., Ph.D., Professor of Psychiatry, Duke University, Durham, North Carolina.

Jack Botwinick, Ph.D., Professor of Psychology, Washington University, St. Louis, Missouri.

Linda B. Bourque, Ph.D., Associate Professor of Sociology, University of California, Los Angeles, California.

C. Edward Buckley, III, M.D., Professor of Medicine, Duke University, Durham, North Carolina.

Ewald W. Busse, M.D., Professor of Psychiatry, Duke University, Durham, North Carolina.

William P. Cleveland, Jr., Ph.D., Bureau of the Census, Washington, D.C.

Stephen J. Cutler, Ph.D., Professor of Sociology, Oberlin College, Oberlin, Ohio.

Elizabeth B. Douglas, Ph.D., Executive Director, Association for Gerontology in Higher Education, Washington, D.C.

Carl Eisdorfer, Ph.D., M.D., Director, Montefiore Hospital and Medical Center, Bronx, New York.

Charles W. Erwin, M.D., Professor of Psychiatry, Duke University, Durham, North Carolina.

Judith H. Fox, Ph.D., Professor of Nursing, Duke University, Durham, North Carolina.

Margaret Gatz, Ph.D., Associate Professor of Psychology, University of Southern California, Pasadena, California.

Linda K. George, Ph.D., Associate Professor of Medical Sociology, Duke University, Durham, North Carolina.

Daniel T. Gianturco, M.D., Professor of Psychiatry, Duke University, Durham, North Carolina.

Jacquelyne J. Jackson, Ph.D., Associate Professor of Medical Sociology, Duke University, Durham, North Carolina.

Vira R. Kivett, Ph.D., Professor of Home Economics, University of North Carolina, Greensboro, North Carolina.

Patrick E. Logue, Ph.D., Associate Professor of Medical Psychology, Duke University, Durham, North Carolina.

Janet H. Lowry, Ph.D., Professor of Sociology, Austin College, Sherman, Texas.

George L. Maddox, Ph.D., Professor of Sociology, Duke University, Durham, North Carolina.

Sarah M. McCarty, Ph.D., Assistant Professor of Rehabilitative Medicine, Tufts New England Medical Center, Boston, Massachusetts.

David Mechanic, Ph.D., Professor of Sociology, Rutgers University, New Brunswick, New Jersey.

John B. Nowlin, M.D., Assistant Professor of Community Health Sciences, Duke University, Durham, North Carolina.

Morris A. Okun, Ph.D., Associate Professor of Education, Arizona State University, Tempe, Arizona.

Erdman B. Palmore, Ph.D., Professor of Medical Sociology, Duke University, Durham, North Carolina.

Patricia N. Prinz, Ph.D., Professor of Psychiatry, University of Washington, Seattle, Washington.

Dietolf Ramm, Ph.D., Associate Professor of Computer Science, Duke University, Durham, North Carolina.

Michele J. Rusin, Ph.D., Clinical Psychologist, Houston, Texas.

Ilene C. Siegler, Ph.D., Associate Professor of Medical Psychology, Duke University, Durham, North Carolina.

Deborah A. Sullivan, Ph.D., Assistant Professor of Sociology, Arizona State University, Tempe, Arizona

Richard C. Tessler, Ph.D., Professor of Sociology, University of Massachusetts, Amherst, Massachusetts.

James W. Thompson, M.D., Evans, Georgia.

H. Shan Wang, M.B., Professor of Psychiatry, Duke University, Durham, North Carolina.

Stephen J. Weiler, M.D., Assistant Professor of Psychiatry, University of Wisconsin, Madison, Wisconsin.

Alan D. Whanger, M.D., Professor of Psychiatry, Duke University, Durham, North Carolina.

Frances Wilkie, M.A., Research Associate, University of Washington, Seattle, Washington.

Rosemary W. Wilson, Ph.D., Research Associate, Dallas Geriatric Research Institute, Dallas, Texas.

Section A. Physical Aging

Introduction

John B. Nowlin

One of the many strengths of the two Duke longitudinal studies of aging is their broad-based availability of health data. This health information is made up of three major components: (1) a careful review of past medical events which preceded participation in the longitudinal study, along with ongoing updates at the time of each participant's return; (2) a tightly structured general medical examination; and (3) laboratory information useful in defining health status (for example, routine hematology, blood chemistry procedures, electrocardiogram, etc.). The primary purpose underlying this extensive health data collection was to derive some objective indicators of the older individual's state of physical well-being. However, there was also the participant "payoff factor" to consider. Longitudinal studies, in general, are at the mercy of the "dropout phenomenon." An incentive such as a free medical examination is of great value in reducing the attrition so often characteristic of long-term longitudinal follow-up. While the two Duke studies are not unique among longitudinal studies of aging in possessing a wide-ranging bank of medical data, the health information accessible spans a far greater time interval than any other longitudinal undertaking. Moreover, there is one unusual feature of the two Duke studies: a number of global physician ratings which provide summary statements of various body systems in terms of impairment. In addition, an overall estimate of health is provided by the examining physician. For the interdisciplinary team of investigators who work with these data, largely unfamiliar with the complexities and jargon surrounding health information, availability of such a set of "summary scores" has proven most helpful.

One of the strong attractions for researchers involved with the two Duke longitudinal studies is specifically the interdisciplinary nature of the research team. Although it is frequently mentioned, the richness of ideas stemming from the hybridization of research disciplines cannot be overemphasized. Many of the papers in this section reflect a mingling of two seemingly disparate areas of research interest. Nonetheless, there are also specialized realms of research which need to be developed; these also are represented by papers in this section. Perhaps the happiest aspect of interdisciplinary research is this blending of collegial and "solitary" investigative endeavors.

Following is a precis of the papers included in this section. Except that they are all concerned with physical aspects of aging found among two ambulatory older populations, no common theme unites these papers, which reflect the catholic range of interests characteristic of this interdisciplinary team of researchers.

In a superficial overview, the enterprise of medicating the older patient would seem to be straightforward. To ameliorate or cure illness, the health care provider devises a medication regimen to deal with pathophysiological derangement. By following this regimen, the patient would presumably improve. In reality, the medication process proves far more complex. Many factors influence the outcome of medication prescription. For the older person, age-related physiological changes, use of other concurrent medications, and comprehension of instructions all pose major issues. Perhaps less frequently considered, attitudes about medication also influence compliance among older individuals. The Back and Sullivan paper explores this issue and looks at the attitudes of the older individual toward use of the so-called "social drugs," alcohol and tobacco.

One of the more noteworthy contributions of the first longitudinal study was the demonstration that expression of sexuality extends far into the later years, contrary to conventional notion. Sexual behavior among middle-aged and older individuals as seen among study participants of the second longitudinal study is described in the paper by George and Weiler. Particular emphasis is placed upon change in self-report of sexual activity over the six-year interval encompassed by the study. Both aggregate and intraindividual changes in this important aspect of human behavior are features of this paper. Stability in the frequency of sexual intercourse is the general finding from both vantage points.

Factors relating to length of life were examined by establishing a "longevity difference" score (the difference between age actually attained by first longitudinal study participants and the age at death expected from actuarial tables). Palmore found that a number of characteristics, physical, mental, and social, were significant predictors of the longevity difference. In a regression analysis, however, independent factors predicting longevity tended primarily to involve health, particularly among women.

Two related papers in this section deal with the concept of successful aging using data derived from the first longitudinal study. Definitions of successful aging were based, in both articles, upon attainment of age seventy-five in good health. The article by Palmore also included a happiness scale as part of the definition of successful aging. Study variables from early rounds of the first longitudinal study were employed as predictors of subsequent successful aging. The Nowlin paper, emphasizing primarily health predictors, found that the extent of cardiovascular disease, serum cholesterol, level of intelligence, and educational level were significant predictors of successful aging. The Palmore article noted that level of physical activity and extent of social contact were strongly predictive of successful aging.

The ubiquity of cardiovascular disease and the well known prevalence of decrement in intellectual function and psychomotor task performance among older populations has generated interest in the potential relationship between these two aspects of aging. A pair of papers by Siegler and Nowlin deal with this issue, employing data collected from the second longitudinal study. Such associations are indeed apparent when study participants are carefully segregated by cardiovascular disease status (i.e., "no clinical disease," presence of atherosclerosis, or presence of hypertension). Older individuals with evidence of atherosclerosis often present reduced intellectual and psychomotor performance, particularly when performance speed is at issue. Also, the nature of the cardiovascular disease has relevance, with the hypertensive older individual presenting less performance decrement than age peers with atherosclerotic disease. A primary issue which arises in evaluating these data is the question of cause-and-effect relationship. A differential pattern of response over time among cardiovascular disease groups, which would have suggested such a relationship, is not evident in these or in other investigations of this issue. The possibility remains that intrinsic central nervous system changes occurring in parallel with, but independent of, cardiovascular disease might explain the decrease in psychological performance accompanying the aging process.

The impact of aging upon a sensory modality, vibratory sense, is examined in a paper by Nowlin and Whanger. Employing a quantitative measure of this sensory modality, age and sex, as well as health factors were evaluated within the second longitudinal study population. The long-established difference between upper and lower extremities was clearly evident: sensation at the ankles was far less acute than that at the wrist. Evidence of cardiovascular disease and systolic blood pressure was associated with lower vibratory sense. Also, over the comparatively short measurement-remeasurement interval of two years, there was a significant decrease in vibratory sense in both upper and lower extremities.

Although a somewhat technical paper, the Thompson and Buckley article evaluates a key component of the immune system, the complement system, which is one mechanism by which the human body manages foreign antigens (such as proteins occurring in bacteria). The effectiveness of a particular constituent of the complement system seems unimpaired by the aging process.

To conclude, I offer a few personal observations regarding my involvement with the two longitudinal studies. Not only was I afforded the opportunity to work within the context of a stimulating interdisciplinary setting, but also, as the examining physician for over ten years in both of the two projects, I was the senior research investigator who experienced an "in vivo" relationship with the participants who took part in these two studies. I had anticipated that this association would be wearisome and tedious; it proved instead to be informative and all too short.

A few other general observations are worth mention. First, the more usual consensus holds that the older person is confronted with broad-based attrition of health status. From my exposure to the older individuals comprising the two longitudinal studies, I have been impressed, to the contrary, with the stability of health over long periods of time. When health decrement occurs, rather than being gradual the pattern is instead abrupt and fairly profound. Only among the group of much older individuals, in their eighties or nineties, does decline in physical well being appear to assume a more gradual slope. Another impressive characteristic of the older person is resilience in the face of health or personal loss. Even with the occasional remarkable loss of health resources, the elderly seem to maintain a healthy, functional equilibrium. Beyond a certain critical level of resource loss, however, this equilibrium gives way, with a profound loss of function, possibly death. In many ways, then, the response of the older individual to resource loss resembles the pattern proposed in the so-called "catastrophe theory" of human physiologic functioning.

Perhaps the most lasting impression I carry away from this immersion in geriatrics is the immense wealth of information available from the older individual, singly and collectively. Not for a moment to denigrate the scope of inquiry encompassed by the two longitudinal studies, I nevertheless recognize the limitations of the questions raised when compared to the extensive information the older individual can offer.

Self-Image, Medicine, and Drug Use

Kurt W. Back and Deborah A. Sullivan

The problems associated with drug use can range from a physician's attempt to obtain a patient's acceptance of a regime of prescribed medicines to the prevention of frivolous or even dangerous drug abuse. The variation among individuals in their use of drugs depends on both their willingness to be changed and their acceptance of a chemical means of inducing this change. Some types of drugs are more socially acceptable than others. In fact, one could propose a spectrum of drugs which includes, at one end, those prescribed to treat acute infectious diseases or physiological disorders and, at the other end, those prohibited drugs used for "recreational" purposes. Motivation for the use of a drug may depend on the specific situation or the specific effect of the drug to be used. However, a predisposition to use or not to use drugs in any situation also may explain some of the variation in drug use patterns among individuals.

Previous studies (Brehm and Back, 1968; Brehm and Davis, 1971), have shown that the use of drugs is related to general personality tendencies, such as a "great desire to be changed, devaluation of the self-image, belief in the beneficial influence of somatic means, and even a positive reaction and curiosity about the effects of physical agents" (Brehm and Back, 1968). A questionnaire, devised to investigate this area, led to the identification of five factors which represent several different personality traits related to a preference for drug use, particularly the use of drugs with strong psychological effects such as opiates, energizers, and hallucinogens.

Reprinted by permission from *Addictive Diseases*, 3:373–382, 1978.

These previous studies principally include young subjects who were conscious of stimulating or recreational drug use. Moreover, the drugs listed in the questionnaire were mainly psychotropic, mood-changing drugs, and the setting of the data collection may have encouraged the subjects to interpret "drugs" in this sense. In the current study we focus on middle-aged and elderly subjects and shift the attention more toward drugs used for medicinal purposes, thereby looking at the general conditions of drug use.

Method

The data are derived from a multidisciplinary study of middle-aged and elderly population (Duke Second Longitudinal Study). This research uses data collected in two separate parts of the program. One source is the medical history section of the physical examination, where the respondents were asked to check the amount of drugs and medicines which they had taken in the preceding year. This list includes both prescription and nonprescription drugs and those used for specific physical ailments, as well as those used for general onerous conditions. In addition, the use of alcohol and tobacco was checked. Table A—1 shows the extent

Table A—1. *Extent of use of different kinds of drugs.*

Drugs being used at present	Yes	No	Percentage of Use
A. Medicines			
High blood pressure medicine	51	451	10.2
Digitalis pills for the heart	14	488	2.8
Nitroglycerin tablets for chest pain	20	482	4.0
Diabetes medicine (insulin shots or pills)	18	482	3.6
Cortisone pills	4	498	.8
Pills to make one lose water or salt	33	469	6.6
Blood thinner medicine (anticoagulant)	10	492	2.0
Other kinds of medicine	101	401	20.1
B. Medical drugs			
Tranquilizers (nerve medicine)	79	423	15.7
Sleeping pills (more than one a month)	44	458	8.8
Vitamin or iron pills	88	414	17.5
Laxatives (more than three times a week)	30	472	6.0
Thyroid pills	21	481	4.2
Female hormone pills	49	453	9.8
Pills to cut back appetite	11	491	2.2
Pain-killer medicine (more than two or three times a week)	56	446	11.2
C. Social drugs			
Alcohol	234	268	46.6
Tobacco	251	251	50.0

of use of the different drugs. They are classified into those which deal with specific ailments (medicines), with nonspecific complaints (medicinal drugs), and with nonmedical social use (social drugs).

The rest of the data are taken from the social history questionnaire. Besides the thirty-five statements that yielded the drug-use personality factors in the previously mentioned studies, a number of standard personality scales are used. These include the sick-role index (Mechanic and Volkart, 1961), the internal-external scale (I-E scale) (Rotter, 1966), the positive-negative affect indices (Bradburn and Caplovitz, 1965), and a series of semantic differentials. In these semantic differentials the concepts "myself," "how I would like to be," and "how I appear to others" are rated on seven bipolar scales. The Euclidian distance between these concepts (the square root of the means of the squared difference between the scale scores) gives an impression of the discrepancies between the three concepts. The distance between "myself" and "how I would like to be" is termed self-evaluation, that between "myself" and "how I appear to others" is termed persona, and that between "how I would like to be" and "how I appear to others" is termed ideal persona.

Results

Factors

Five factors emerge from the principal components analysis of the thirty-five statements related to sickness and drug use among the middle-aged and elderly sample (table A—2). Items related to a dissatisfaction with oneself (e.g., seeing oneself as too nervous, anxious, self-conscious, or tired) and a desire for some physical action to overcome personal limitations dominate the first factor. As in previous studies, this factor is labeled "insecurity." The second factor accounts for 10.5 percent of the total variance and loads highly on those items related to seeking medical attention and showing concern about health. These items appear to measure the degree of willingness on the part of the respondents to accept a sick role. In contrast, the third factor loads highly on items related to fear of medicine or drugs. Paradoxically, curiousness about the personal effect of a "mind-expanding" drug also loads highly on this factor. The fourth factor also indicates a fear of medicine or drugs. However, the fear embodied in this factor is related more directly to a fear of the loss of personal control that might result from medicine or drugs rather than the medicine or drugs themselves. The final factor deals with curiosity about mind-changing drugs. The five factors together account for 44.2 percent of the total variance.

A comparison of this factor structure with that found in the previous studies of young subjects reveals several striking similarities. The insecurity and sick-role factors are almost identical. The difference in the insecurity factor consists of a high loading on the statement "In the past I faked illness to get out of something I haven't wanted to go do" for the older sample and high loadings on three other statements for the student sample ("I get very afraid if I don't know what is

Table A—2. *Factor structure of attitudes toward drugs.*

Item Loading	Factor 1 (insecurity)
.64	Sometimes I feel I have to take something to make me relax.
.59	Sometimes I feel I have to take something to stimulate me.
.56	Sometimes I feel I have to take something to make me less self-conscious.
.50	If there were a drug that would make me feel less anxious, I would take it.
.46	In the past, I have faked illness to get out of doing something I haven't wanted to do.
.45	I wish I could help to achieve the real me.
	Factor 2 (sick role)
.84	I would see a doctor if I had a temperature of about 100 degrees.
.77	I would see a doctor if I had a temperature of about 101 degrees.
.59	I would see a doctor if I had been feeling poorly for a few days.
.45	I am more concerned than most people about my health.
	Factor 3 (fear of medicine and drugs)
.58	I would avoid taking drugs when I'm sick for as long as I could.
.57	In general, I tend to avoid taking medicine and drugs.
.56	Even though a drug might not be physically habit-forming I would be afraid of becoming dependent on it psychologically.
.48	I would be curious to know what effect a "mind-expanding" drug would have on me.
	Factor 4 (fear of loss of control)
.66	I might do something under the influence of drugs that I would not normally do.
.66	People sometimes do things when under the influence of drugs that they would not normally do.
.55	I would be worried if I had to take a drug whose effects I know little about.
.51	I would be afraid of losing personal control under drugs.
	Factor 5 (curiosity)
.84	"Personal Curiosity" (see note).
.66	Most people would be curious to know what effect a "mind-expanding" drug would have on them.

Note: "Personal curiosity" is defined as the difference in score between the questions, "I would be curious to know what effect a 'mind-expanding' drug would have on me" and "Most people would be curious to know what effect a 'mind-expanding' drug would have on them."

happening to me," "I am more concerned than most people about my bodily feelings," and "I wish that all my problems could be solved by taking a pill").

The only difference in the composition of the sick-role factor is a high loading on the relative concern about personal health statement in the older sample that was not found in the younger sample. However, the higher order of the sick-role factor in the older group, compared to the younger group where it was the third factor, suggests the greater importance of health for older respondents.

The "fear of loss of control" factor was second in importance for the younger sample, although it is the fourth factor in the older sample. This reflects the greater concern with mind-changing drugs in the younger sample. The lesser interest in nonmedicinal aspects of drugs in the older sample is further supported by the smaller number of statements heavily weighted in the fifth, curiosity, factor.

The major difference in the factor structure between the two samples is the appearance of a factor suggesting a general fear of medicine or drugs in the older group. In contrast, two of the statements in this factor ("I would avoid taking drugs when I'm sick for as long as I could" and "In general, I tend to avoid taking medicine and drugs") loaded with two of the statements from the "fear of loss of control" factor ("I might do something under the influence of drugs that I would not normally do" and "In general, I tend to avoid taking medicine and drugs"), forming a factor that was labeled as "denial of effects" for the younger sample. This "denial of effects" factor does not emerge in the older sample.

Drug Use

Table A—3 shows the relationship between the five personality factors and the indicators of drug and medicine use. For women, use of medicine is significantly correlated with three of the personality factors: insecurity, sick role, and fear of medicine. For men, none of the personality factors is significantly correlated with use of medicine, although acceptance of a sick role is just below the significance-level cutoff. This may indicate that the use of specific and usually prescribed medicines relates to an acceptance of a clearly defined sick role and that this definition is more salient among women than men. The importance of the definition of the sick role may partially explain the curious positive correlation factor 3 (fear of medicine) with taking medicine among women: the fear of the possible effects of medicines may be just the impulse which makes women consult a physician and, therefore, have medicines prescribed. This is further supported by the relationship between insecurity and the use of medicine among women.

It is interesting that there is no significant relationship between insecurity and use of medicines for men, although insecurity is strongly related to use of medical drugs (many of which do not require a prescription) for both sexes. This suggests that insecurity in general is related to a desire for change and an acceptance of a chemical means of inducing change. However, men appear more reluctant than women to seek a physician's aid.

None of the personality factors was significantly associated with the social drugs tobacco and alcohol; however, the negative correlation with sick role for women and the positive correlation with fear of medicine for men are just below the significance level. This might suggest tentatively viewing tobacco and alcohol, especially the latter, as an alternative to acceptance of the sick role, but this relation is different in the two sexes, corresponding to their differences in the willingness to accept a sick role and consult a physician.

Table A—3. *Correlations of attitude factors with type of drug use by sex.*

Males $N = 258$ Factor	Medicines	Drug use Medical drugs	Social drugs
1. Insecurity	.09	.34**	.04
2. Sick role	.11	.00	−.05
3. Fear of medicine and drugs	.02	.06	.12
4. Fear of loss of control	−.06	−.07	.03
5. Curiosity	−.05	.02	.02
Females $N = 237$			
1. Insecurity	.24**	.31**	−.07
2. Sick role	.21**	.06	−.10
3. Fear of medicine and drugs	.14*	.08	.04
4. Fear of loss of control	−.01	.00	.09
5. Curiosity	.01	−.01	.04

*Significant at .05 level.

**Significant at .01 level.

Further tests of the relationships are provided by multiple regression analyses of the different kinds of drug consumption. Several other variables which measure similar dimensions of self-acceptance, some of which have been shown to be important in previous drug studies (Brehm and Back, 1968; Brehm and Davis, 1971), are added to the five factors as predictor variables. These include the I-E scale, the positive-negative affect indices and the self-evaluation, persona, and ideal persona concepts formed from semantic differentials of "myself," "how I would like to be," and "how I appear to others."

Table A—4 shows the results for men and women. The predictor variables are added in a step-wise program down to an F-level of 1.00. Variables with lower F values are eliminated; their inclusion would not change the multiple correlation to any appreciable degree.

The multiple correlations are consistently higher for women than for men and highest for medical drugs, followed by medicines and social drugs. This, then, is the rank order of the predictive capacity of our personality variables for the different dependent variables.

The regression analysis adds further insights to the influence of personality traits on drug use. Use of medical drugs in both sexes depends on general unhappiness-insecurity, negative feelings, and the difference between how one appears to others and how one would like to be (ideal persona). These strong relationships are the most important results of the study.

For medicines, sex differences are important. Men are influenced mainly by ideal persona and positive affect (i.e., having had positive feeling during the preceding week). Several other variables have only a minor effect. Women, however, are influenced to take medicines mainly by the fear of medicines, acceptance of sick role, insecurity, and fear of loss of control, as well as by the

Table A—4. *Regression analysis of medicine-drug use.*

Sex	Dependent variable	Multiple r	F value	Independent variables in order of significance (all F's > 1.00) 1	2	3
M	Use of medicine	.31	4.03	Ideal persona**	Positive affect*	Sick role
M	Use of medical drugs	.41	12.90**	Insecurity**	Negative affect	Ideal persona**
M	Use of social drugs	.15	2.96	Fear of medicine**	Positive affect	
F	Use of medicine	.36	6.81**	Fear of medicine**	Sick role*	Insecurity*
F	Use of medical drugs	.43	12.63**	Negative affect**	Insecurity	Ideal persona(−)
F	Use of social drugs	.21	2.21	I-E scale	Ideal persona(−)	Sick role(−)

Sex	Dependent variable	Independent variables in order of significance (all F's > 1.00) 4	5	6
M	Use of medicine	Curiosity(−)	Insecurity	Ideal Persona
M	Use of medical drugs	Persona(−)		
M	Use of social drugs			
F	Use of medicine	Fear of loss of control*	Persona*	
F	Use of medical drugs	Sick role		
F	Use of social drugs	Positive affect(−)	Persona*	

*Significant at .05 level.

**Significant at .01 level.

difference between how they are and how they appear to others (persona). Although there is some similarity between men and women, men seem to have a more positive approach to medicines than women have. Women seem to be influenced mainly by fear.

A similar sex difference occurs in the prediction of the use of the social drugs tobacco and alcohol. For men, fear of medicine is important; for women, a variety of variables show some effect, although none is significant. This finding provides further support for the contention that men who fear medicines or mental drugs may be using alcohol as a substitute.

Discussion

The results of this study lend some support to the hypothesis that personal attitudes and disposition are important factors in the use of medicines and medical drugs as well as of mood-changing drugs. Measures which had been shown to be related to mind-expanding drug use among young adults in a previous study are also related to the use of drugs for medicinal purposes in an elderly population both to treat a specific psychological disorder and to treat nonspecific symptoms.

While similarities in predispositions toward drug use among young and old justify this kind of approach, we must also note the differences. The original scale factored in a slightly different way, leading to clusters of items concerned with illness and the use of medicine and not with the search for stimulation and curiosity. Further, the clearest pattern was found with the medical drugs; medicines seem to be more closely connected with the demands of the illness, and the social drugs alcohol and tobacco may be determined by social influences.

The middle-aged and elderly respondents try to obtain a balance between their general anxiety and mood, their feelings about illness and medicine, the way they see themselves, their impression on others, and how they would like to be. These personal preferences lead to consumption of drugs, depending on the availability and use of medical and pharmaceutical services. The different patterns exhibited indicated the alternatives that are possible for accepting a rational relationship between medical care and the reasons, fears, or alternative attractions which might interfere with a purely rational use of health care. Thus, the data give an indication of the social-psychological determinants of drug use.

References

Bradburn, N. M., and Caplovitz, D. *Reports on happiness*. Chicago: Aldine, 1965.

Brehm, M. L., and Back, K. W. Self-image and attitudes toward drugs. *Journal of Personality*, 36:299–314, 1968.

Brehm, M. L., and Davis, G. C. Juvenile prisoners: Motivational factors in drug use (Abstract). *Proceedings, seventy-ninth annual convention, American Psychological Association*, 1971.

Mechanic, D., and Volkart, E. Stress, illness and the sick role. *American Sociological Review*, 26:51–58, 1961.

Palmore, E. Appendix A. Design of the adaptation study. In *Normal aging II*. Palmore, E. B. (Ed.), Durham, N.C.: Duke University Press, 1974.

Rotter, J. B. Generalized expectancies for internal versus external control of reinforcement. *Psychological Monographs*, 80, whole no. 609, 1966.

Sexuality in Middle and Late Life

Linda K. George and Stephen J. Weiler

Sexuality in late life is a relatively recent but increasingly popular topic of scientific discussion and systematic research. The natural history of this area of inquiry has consisted largely of dispelling a variety of myths that surround the topic of sexuality in late adulthood. The first myth was that of the asexual older person. As numerous studies have demonstrated, sexual interest and activity typically persist well into late life, although they are reported to decline in the last half of adulthood. A second myth suggested that impotence and other sexual problems typically are irreversible when experienced at older ages. Detailed clinical studies of sexuality in late life, particularly the work of Masters and Johnson, have now demonstrated that restoration of sexual function is possible at later as well as earlier stages of the life cycle.

Since the myth of the asexual older person has been dispelled, it has been commonly assumed that sexual interest and activity decline over the course of middle and late adulthood. The purpose of this report is to present longitudinal data which suggest that patterns of sexual activity tend to remain more stable over middle and late life than previously suggested. We also demonstrate that it is crucial to distinguish between aggregate trends and intraindividual change. Although stable levels of sexual activity are typical, aggregate statistics can mask or blur distinct patterns of change and stability exhibited by individuals.

The ideal data set for examining the effects of age on sexual activity would (1) include subjects who span a considerable proportion of the adult age range, (2) be longitudinal in design, and (3) be analyzed using appropriate statistical controls of confounding factors. The data used in this study meet these criteria.

The data used in this analysis are those from the Duke Second Longitudinal Study. Unlike previous reports from that study, however, this analysis examines both aggregate and intraindividual longitudinal patterns of sexual activity.

Research Design

The research design includes four test dates at two-year intervals. The data reported here are based on those subjects who (1) completed all four rounds of data collection and (2) remained married throughout the study. A total of 348 persons completed all four rounds of data collection; most sample attrition was due to death. Analysis was restricted to those who remained in the study to preserve the panel design. To examine the effects of age per se, the sample for this analysis was further limited to the 278 persons who remained married throughout the study. The unmarried persons who completed the four rounds of data collection

Reprinted from *Archives of General Psychiatry*, 38:919–923, 1981.

Table A—5. *Age-cohort-gender groups* (N = *278*).

Age at start of study, year	Number of participants M (N = 170)	F (N = 108)
≤ 55	63	57
55–65	74	36
≤ 66	33	15

were distributed as follows: ten were never-married, six were separated or divorced throughout the study, thirty-four were widowed throughout the study, and twenty became widowed during the study. It also is important to note that only one unmarried person answered any questions about sexuality. The remaining widowed and unmarried subjects reported that such questions were not applicable. This pattern suggests that the reports of unmarried persons may be influenced by social desirability issues and, if provided, would be less reliable than those of married persons.

Table A—5 gives the six age-cohort-gender groups in the sample. The lower numbers of women reflect increased widowhood among women over the course of the study rather than disproportionate numbers of women in the original sample or differential attrition.

Measures

Data on sexual behavior and interest were gathered as part of a self-administered medical history questionnaire. The questionnaire included self-reports of sexual enjoyment, sexual feelings, frequency of sexual relations, awareness or perception of decline in sexual interest or activity, and age or time at which sexual activity stopped (if appropriate) and for cessation of sexual activity (if appropriate). These questions were repeated at each of the four test dates.

The data reported in this study are primarily reports of the frequency of sexual relations and of the decline or cessation of sexual activity. The specific question involving frequency of sexual relations is: "How often, on the average, do you have sex relations at the present time? (0) Never; (1) Less than once a week, but some sexual relations; (2) Once or twice a week; (3) Three times a week; (4) More than three times a week." In subsequent analyses, reports of sexual frequency refer to the coded value (0 through 4) of the respondents' self-reports of sexual activity.

Results

Mean Levels of Activity

The initial analysis suggested that the mean levels of sexual activity for the sample as a whole remained remarkably stable over the six-year course of the

study ($\overline{X}$ = 1.57, 1.49, and 1.47). This pattern of stability contrasts with previous reports of decline in sexual activity over middle and late life; however, this analysis was restricted to study participants who were married throughout the course of the study, thus precluding any spurious effects of widowhood on reports of sexual activity over time. As demonstrated, however, optimal analysis required attention to the following two additional factors: (1) disentangling age-related changes in sexual activity from differences among cohorts and (2) distinguishing among distinct patterns of sexual activity, patterns that are masked by aggregate statistics.

Table A—6 gives mean levels of sexual activity in the six age-gender groups at the four test dates. These data show several patterns. First, for each of the four test dates, a two-factor analysis of variance (ANOVA) was performed to examine the effects of gender and age-cohort on sexual activity. At each test date, the results indicate significant effects ($p < .05$) for gender (F = 3.78, 3.57, 4.58, and 6.96) and age-cohort (F = 5.59, 3.82, 6.89, and 10.45). Men consistently reported higher levels of sexual activity than women, and younger age-cohort groups reported higher levels of sexual activity than older groups. The interactions between age and gender were not significant. In these cross-sectional comparisons, of course, the effects of age are inherently confounded with cohort.

Using the means given in table A—6, age-related changes in sexual activity over time also were examined. For each of the six age-gender groups, a repeated-measures ANOVA was performed to determine whether levels of sexual activity significantly changed over the course of the study. The results indicate a significant difference only for the men who were initially aged fifty-six to sixty-five years (F = 4.14, p = .04). The means of the other five age-gender groups did not significantly differ during the course of the study. These findings suggest stability in sexual activity over time within the age-cohort-gender groups.

Table A—6. *Mean (SDs) of levels of sexual activity over four rounds of study.**

Age at start of study year	Men			
	1969	1971	1973	1975
46–55	2.03 (0.87)	1.98 (0.81)	1.95 (0.92)	1.94 (0.93)
56–65	1.47 (0.86)	1.54 (0.85)	1.45 (0.91)	1.32 (0.81)
66–71	1.18 (0.81)	1.21 (0.96)	1.19 (0.91)	1.17 (0.81)
Age at start of study year	**Women**			
	1969	1971	1973	1974
46–55	1.70 (0.92)	1.71 (0.90)	1.69 (0.88)	1.66 (0.86)
56–65	1.23 (1.00)	1.24 (0.89)	1.20 (1.02)	1.16 (1.04)
66–71	0.79 (0.83)	0.77 (0.83)	0.76 (0.91)	0.67 (1.00)

*Sexual activity was coded on a five-point scale (range 0 to 4 points). At any given round, data collection required approximately ten months. The years reported here represent the primary year of data collection at each round.

Activity Patterns

A second way of examining changes in sexual activity is to classify subjects' intraindividual patterns over the four test dates into a discrete set of patterns. Seven patterns of sexual activity were found for the entire sample. Examination of these patterns reveals that stable activity (i.e., reporting exactly the same level of sexual activity at all four test dates) was the pattern exhibited by a majority of subjects (58.27 percent, or 162). An additional 7.19 percent of the subjects (twenty) reported no sexual activity at all four test dates. About 5 percent of the sample reported increases in sexual activity; approximately half of this (2.88 percent, or eight subjects) signified resumption of sexual activity after some period of cessation and approximately half (2.16 percent, or six subjects) signified increased activity. Almost 20 percent reported a decrease in sexual activity; more than half of this (10.79 percent, or thirty subjects) is the result of cessation of sexual activity and less than half (8.27 percent, or twenty-three subjects) is the result of decreased activity. The remaining 10.43 percent (twenty-nine subjects) showed other patterns of sexual activity (i.e., fluctuation).

Absolute Levels

Since the group reporting stable sexual activity is the largest and includes a variety of absolute levels of sexual activity, we will describe this group in somewhat more detail. Of the 162 subjects in this group, sixty-two reported sexual intercourse levels of less than once a week at all four test dates; eighty-five reported engaging in sexual intercourse once or twice a week at all four test dates; and fifteen reported sexual relations three times a week at all four test dates. No subject consistently reported engaging in sexual intercourse more than three times a week.

Activity Patterns and Gender

Table A—7 gives the sexual activity patterns for the six age-cohort-gender groups. Compatible with earlier findings, the patterns differ across groups. Men were more likely to report stable or increasing sexual activity than their female peers. Conversely, in each cohort, women were more likely to report cessation of or decreases in sexual activity. For both men and women, older cohorts exhibited greater proportions of subjects with cessation or decline in sexual activity, while members of younger cohorts more often reported stable or increasing sexual activity.

These patterns of sexual activity over time, like the ANOVA results, suggest stability in the frequency of sexual relations during middle and late life. For all six age-gender groups, stable sexual activity was the modal pattern. While the ANOVA results suggest that cohort differences influence levels of sexual activity more than age-related changes, the intraindividual patterns of change and sta-

Table A—7. *Distribution of sexual activity patterns over six years of study.**

	Age at start of study year		
	<56	56–65 (percentages)	<65
Men			
Stable activity	66.6	63.5	42.4
No activity to some activity	1.6	2.7	9.1
Increasing activity	3.2	1.4	0.0
Some activity to no activity	4.8	6.8	18.2
Decreasing activity	11.1	8.1	3.0
Continuously absent	0.0	9.5	12.1
Other	12.7	8.1	15.2
Women			
Stable activity	61.4	55.6	33.3
No activity to some activity	1.8	2.8	0.0
Increasing activity	1.8	0.0	0.0
Some activity to no activity	5.3	22.2	33.3
Decreasing activity	10.5	8.3	0.0
Continuously absent	5.3	5.5	33.3
Other	14.0	5.5	0.0

*The percentages are rounded to one decimal place; consequently, the column totals may depart slightly from 100 percent.

bility show substantial evidence of age-related change. For all six age-gender groups, reports of decreasing sexual activity or a cessation of sexual activity are considerably more frequent than either reports of increasing sexual activity or a resumption of sexual relations after a period of cessation. Furthermore, the older the cohort, the more likely is a decline in or cessation of sexual activity. Among the oldest cohort, for example, 18.2 percent of the men and 33.3 percent of the women reported a total cessation of sexual activity during the course of the study. In contrast, in the youngest cohort 4.8 percent of the men and 5.3 percent of the women reported a cessation of sexual relations over time.

Interest and Reasons for Cessation

Finally, although the data will not be described in detail, a series of analyses were performed to examine patterns of sexual interest and the reported reasons for cessation of sexual activity. The patterns of sexual interest closely paralleled those of sexual activity: (1) levels of sexual interest remained highly stable over time, (2) men reported higher levels of sexual interest than their female age peers, and (3) younger cohorts reported higher levels of sexual interest than older cohorts. In giving their reasons for stopping sexual activity, both men and women overwhelmingly attributed the cessation of sexual relations to the attitudes or physical condition of the male partner.

Comment

Limitations of the Study

Before we discuss the contributions and implications of these findings, it is prudent to acknowledge two limitations of this study. First, our examination of sexual activity is restricted to sexual intercourse. The data set included no information on other forms of sexual activity. Forms of sexual activity other than intercourse should be studied and may exhibit different patterns of change and stability. Sexual intercourse by itself, however, is an important focus for research and clinical purposes. In addition, given that our analysis is limited to married persons, patterns of sexual intercourse are likely to be related to the broader topics of marital adjustment and gender-spouse roles. Second, this longitudinal study included only four test dates covering a total time period of six years. Ideally, one would like to have a longer-term study which permits examination of interindividual patterns of change and stability over a broader segment of adulthood. However, given the clear superiority of longitudinal to cross-sectional data and the fact that this study included longitudinal observations of multiple cohorts, these data make important contributions to our understanding of sexual activity in middle and later life.

Comparisons with Previous Studies

The data presented in this report both support and diverge from findings reported in previous studies. This analysis, like the results of other studies, indicates that (1) women report significantly lower levels of sexual interest and activity than their male age peers and (2) both sexes attribute the responsibility for cessation of sexual activity to the male partner. As speculated by previous authors, the first pattern undoubtedly reflects the fact that women in our society tend to be somewhat younger than their husbands. The second finding testifies to the importance of the man's role as initiator of sexual behavior among current cohorts of middle-aged and older adults.

Contrary to previous studies, the data presented in this study suggest that levels of sexual activity tend to remain stable over middle and later life. This was demonstrated by both the age-gender means over the course of the study and by the distribution of intraindividual patterns of change and stability exhibited by study participants. There are at least two reasons why previous studies overestimate the degree of age-related decline in sexual activity. First, most previous studies were based on cross-sectional, rather than longitudinal, data; consequently, cohort and age effects were inherently confounded. Our data suggest that part of the differences between age groups reflects the effects of cohort-related rather than age-related change. Second, previous studies have neglected to control important confounding variables, especially marital status. Because marital status is correlated with age, inclusion of unmarried and widowed subjects confounds cohort differences and age-related changes in sexual activity with loss of a sexual partner.

One might still question the importance of these findings. For example, it might be pointed out that, in the older population as a whole, sexual activity is less frequent than among younger persons regardless of the particular factors that account for that difference. However, it is important to distinguish the effects of aging per se from those of cohort differences or other factors. The fact that there are apparent cohort differences in the frequency of sexual activity suggests that in the future older persons may not present the same pattern that older persons do today. Thus, our current knowledge of sexuality in late life may be specific to that group of persons who are currently old. In addition, our findings suggest that as the number of intact couples surviving to old age increases (as is the current trend), there will be concomitant increases in the number of older people reporting continuity in sexual behavior.

Group Versus Individual Patterns

Our analysis also emphasizes the distinction between group or aggregate statistics and discrete patterns of intraindividual change and stability in levels of sexual activity. Thus, statistics that describe groups of persons often are misleading when extrapolated to estimate the sexual activity patterns of individuals. This issue is especially important when one considers the clinical implications of this study. Although a majority of the study participants showed stable levels of sexual activity over time, notable minorities of subjects reported decreases in and cessation of sexual activity over time. The fact that 8.3 percent of the men and 14.8 percent of the women in this sample of married middle-aged and older persons reported cessation of sexual activity over a six-year time interval is an important, although minor, pattern. It is this group of persons who are perhaps most likely to seek and profit from clinical services. However, evidence from this study (i.e., the group of study participants who reported resumption of sexual activity after some period of cessation), as well as the clinical evidence of Masters and Johnson, suggest that sexual dysfunction in later life often is reversible. Examining the common patterns of sexual activity over the course of adulthood helps us to better understand the role of age and social change (i.e., cohort effects) on sexual behavior and can help service providers to better anticipate the kinds of problems couples are likely to experience.

References

Finkle, A. L., et al. Sexual potency in aging males. *Journal of the American Medical Association*, 207:113–115, 1969.

Freeman, J. T. Sexual capacities in the aging male. *Geriatrics*, 16:37–43, 1961.
Kinsey, A. C., Pomeroy, W. B., and Martin, C. E. *Sexual behavior in the human male*. Philadelphia: W. B. Saunders, 1948.
Kinsey, A. C., et al. *Sexual behavior in the human female*. Philadelphia: W. B. Saunders, 1953.
Masters, W. H., and Johnson, V. E. *Human sexual response*. Boston: Little, Brown, 1966.
Masters, W. H., and Johnson, V. E. *Human sexual inadequacy*. Boston: Little, Brown, 1970.
Newman, G., and Nichols, C. R. Sexual activities and attitudes in older persons. *Journal of the American Medical Association*, 173:117–119, 1960.
Palmore, E. B. Adaptation study design. In Palmore, E. B. (Ed.), *Normal aging II*. Durham, N.C.: Duke University Press, 1974, 291–296.
Pfeiffer, E., and Davis, G. C. Determinants of sexual behavior in middle and old age. *Journal of the American Geriatrics Society*, 20:151–158, 1972.
Pfeiffer, E., Verwoerdt, A., and Wang, H. S. The natural history of sexual behavior in a biologically advantaged group of aged individuals. *Journal of Gerontology*, 24:193–198, 1969.
Pfeiffer, E., Verwoerdt, A., and Davis, G. C. Sexual behavior in middle life. *American Journal of Psychiatry*, 128:82–87, 1972.
Verwoerdt, A., Pfeiffer, E., and Wang, H. S. Sexual behavior in senescence: Changes in sexual activity and interest of aging men and women. *Journal of Geriatric Psychiatry*, 2:163–180, 1969.
Verwoerdt, A., Pfeiffer, E., and Wang, H. S. Sexual behavior in senescence: II. Patterns of sexual activity and interest. *Geriatrics*, 24:137–154, 1969.

Predictors of the Longevity Difference

Erdman B. Palmore

Just as actuaries can predict longevity on the basis of age, sex, and race, several studies have found that various physical, mental, and social characteristics can also predict longevity (Palmore and Jeffers, 1971; Rose and Bell, 1971). The Duke First Longitudinal Study of aging is the only set of data allowing analysis of the predictors of longevity among a cohort of older persons over a period of twenty-five years. Previous analyses of these data found that the strongest predictors of longevity (when age, sex, and race are controlled) were physical function, nonsmoking, work satisfaction, and happiness (Palmore, 1969a; Palmore, 1969b; Palmore and Jeffers, 1971). This paper reports the results of a new analysis with several advantages over the previous ones: (1) Most of the panelists have now died, so their exact longevity is known; in the previous analysis about one-third were still living, so their longevity had to be estimated. (2) The present analysis uses a new measure of longevity, the Longevity Difference (LD), which controls for the effects of age, sex, and race, while allowing estimates of the years of added longevity each predictor provides. (3) In addition to the variables

Reprinted by permission from *Gerontologist*, 22:513–518, 1982.

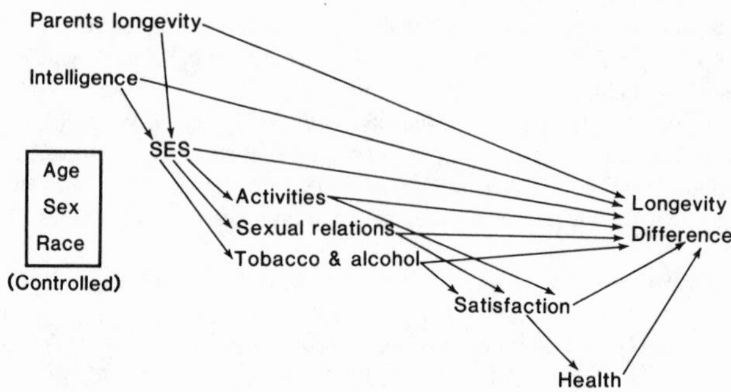

Figure A—1. *Simplified model for predictors of LD.*
From: E. B. Palmore, Predictors of the longevity difference, *Gerontologist* 22:513–518, 1982.

previously tested, fourteen new variables were tested as possible predictors of longevity.

The purpose of this analysis is to test theoretical predictors of longevity, to estimate how many years each predictor adds to or subtracts from expected longevity, and to test which predictors remain significant in a stepwise multiple regression analysis.

A simplified theoretical model of possible predictors of the LD is shown in figure A—1. Age, sex, and race are controlled in the LD (as explained below). Parents' longevity is hypothesized to have a direct effect on the LD through the transmission of genes favorable to longevity and an indirect effect through the social inheritance of healthy life-styles and environments which contribute to longevity. Intelligence is hypothesized to have a direct effect on longevity through greater problem-solving ability which contributes to survival, and an indirect effect through its contribution to other factors favorable to longevity.

Activities are hypothesized to have a direct effect on longevity through greater physical, mental, and social stimulation, and an indirect effect through their contribution to greater satisfaction and general health. Sexual relations are also hypothesized to have a direct effect on longevity through psychosomatic processes and an indirect effect through their contribution to satisfaction and general health. Excessive tobacco and alcohol use are hypothesized as having a direct effect on longevity through their well-known effects on lung cancer, cardiovascular diseases, etc., and possible indirect effects through a reduction of satisfaction and general health.

Satisfaction is hypothesized as having direct effects on longevity through various psychosomatic processes, and indirect effects through its contribution to general health.

Finally, health is hypothesized as having direct effects on longevity. It should be understood that this is a simplified model which does not show possible interaction effects, nonlinear relationships, etc. This research will not attempt to separate these various possible effects, but will focus on total effects as indicated (1) by bivariate significant associations between the predictors and the LD and (2) through the associations which remain significant in a multiple regression analysis that controls for the effects of other significant predictors.

The Duke First Longitudinal Study

Volunteers (270) in a longitudinal, interdisciplinary study of aging were examined the first time during 1955–59. All predictors in this analysis were taken from the 1955–59 examinations. At that time the panelists ranged in age from sixty to ninety-four, with a median age of seventy. All were ambulatory, noninstitutionalized residents of central North Carolina. They were not a random sample, but were selected so their sex, racial, and socioeconomic distributions approximated that of the area. Forty-eight percent were males (52 percent females), 67 percent were white (33 percent black), and 60 percent were manual worker class (40 percent nonmanual). However, the average panelists were somewhat above the average area residents in several respects, as reflected by the fact that the average panelists had LD scores of 1.6, which means that they lived 1.6 years longer than expected.

Although the sample was not random, tests of statistical significance are used in this analysis in order to eliminate those correlations which were so small that they probably would not be significant even if this were a random sample. It should be kept in mind that we are not attempting to generalize beyond samples similar to ours: a sample of volunteers from the Durham, North Carolina, area.

The LD is the difference between the number of years the panelists lived after initial testing and the actuarially expected number of years remaining based on their age, sex, and race (1959–61 tables). For the twenty-six persons still alive at the time of the analysis (spring 1981), estimates of the number of years they will have lived after initial testing were made by adding the present number of years since initial testing to the actuarially estimated number of years now remaining, based on their present age. Since the LD equals actual minus expected years, a positive LD means that the person lived longer than expected and a negative LD means the person lived a shorter time than expected. Thus, the LD controls for the well-known effects on longevity of age (older people have higher mortality rates), sex (women have lower mortality than men), and race (white men have lower mortality than nonwhite men up to age sixty-four; white women have lower mortality than nonwhite women up to age seventy; and, after seventy, nonwhites have lower mortality).

Since the LD controls for the effects of age, it is not significantly correlated with the age of the respondent at the beginning of the study. It is also normally distributed around the mean of 1.6, with a few persons dying fourteen years before expected and a few living fifteen years longer than expected. There were mortality improvements in the 1970s, but they were about equal for all age groups in this sample and so should not affect the validity of our findings. This analysis is based on the 252 panelists with complete information on the LD and its predictors.

The Significant Predictors

There were fifty variables that fit into the eight categories of possible predictors. Of these, twenty-two turned out to be significant (zero-order) predictors of longevity for men or women or both (table A—8).

1. Parents' longevity. Only the father's age at death was a significant predictor.

2. There were two significant intelligence predictors. The performance score was the performance weighted sub-score on the Wechsler Adult Intelligence Scale (Wechsler, 1955). The verbal score was the verbal weighted sub-score on the WAIS.

3. There were three significant socioeconomic predictors. Education was based on the number of years of formal education completed. Finances was based on the panelist's rating of his/her present financial position ranging from 1 (can't make ends meet) to 4 (wealthy or well-to-do). Occupation was a coding of the panelist's major lifetime occupation ranging from 1 (operatives and unskilled laborers) to 3 (professionals and managers). This and several of the other variables are ordinal scales, not equal interval scales that are the preferred type scale for regression analysis. However, research has shown that regression analysis can be used with ordinal scales, without producing serious bias.

4. There were five significant activity predictors. Locomotor was the number of activities reported which involved physical mobility either in its performance or in getting to the place to do it. Secondary activity was a score based on the number of organizations belonged to, number of meetings attended, time spent reading, and number of leisure activities reported. It could range from 0 (low) to 10 (high). (Secondary activity is in contrast to primary group activities such as with family and friends.) Club activity was a count of the number of different types of organizations belonged to. Secondary activity rating was a rating by the interviewing social worker of the amount of formal group or specialized contacts the panelist was involved in, ranging from 0 (in no groups, no reading, complete social isolation) to 9 (time filled with many groups, much reading). Nongroup was a rating by the social worker of the panelist's activities outside groups ranging from 0 (nothing to do) to 9 (time filled with daily activities and hobbies to the exclusion of group activities).

5. Three indicators of sexual relations were significant. Frequency of intercourse was the panelist's report of present frequency of intercourse, ranging from 0 (none) to 4 (more than once a week). Past enjoyment of intercourse was the panelist's rating of his/her enjoyment of intercourse in younger years, and could range from 0 (none) to 2 (very much). Present enjoyment of intercourse was a similar rating for their enjoyment of intercourse at present.

6. *Tobacco use* was a score reflecting the reported frequency of tobacco use

Table A—8. *Significant*[a] *predictors of longevity difference: bivariate correlations* (r) *and regression coefficients* (b).

Predictors	Men (*N* = 122) *r*	Men (*N* = 122) *b*	Women (*N* = 130) *r*	Women (*N* = 130) *b*
1. *Father's age at death*	.15	.39	—	—
2. *Intelligence*				
Performance	.29	.14	.21	.11
Verbal	.22	.07	.19	.06
3. *Socioeconomic status*				
Education	.14	.13	—	—
Finances	.29	2.38	—	—
Occupation	.15	1.13	—	—
4. *Activities*				
Locomotor	—	—	.22	.75
Secondary	—	—	.20	.64
Clubs	—	—	.14	.64
Secondary rating	.19	.79	.20	.80
Nongroup	.22	.76	.17	.80
5. *Sexual relations*				
Frequency of intercourse	.15	.72	—	—
Past enjoyment of intercourse	—	—	.22	1.98
Present enjoyment of intercourse	—	—	.14	2.79
6. *Tobacco use*	−.15	−.62	−.17	−.81
7. *Satisfaction*				
Work	.28	1.30	—	—
Religious	−.24	−1.36	—	—
Usefulness	.16	.84	—	—
Happiness	.18	.86	.17	.80
8. *Health*				
Physical function rating	.31	1.47	.30	1.84
Health self-rating	.33	1.86	.21	1.49
Health satisfaction	—	—	.36	2.20

[a] All values shown were statistically significant at the .05 level except for present enjoyment of intercourse, which had a *p* value of .12. Each pair of correlations and coefficients represent a separate bivariate regression equation between one predictor and the LD.

ranging from 0 (never use) to 4 (heavy use: eleven cigarettes or more per day, cigar and/or pipe five or more times per day, or constant use of snuff or chewing tobacco).

7. There were four significant satisfaction predictors. Work satisfaction was based on agreement or disagreement with six statements from the Chicago Inventory of Activities and Attitudes such as "I am satisfied with the work I do" and "I can no longer do any useful work," and could range from 0 (low) to 6 (high). Religious satisfaction was based on agreement or disagreement with six statements such as "Religion is fairly important in my life" and "I have no use for religion," and could range from 0 (low) to 6 (high). Usefulness was based on agreement or disagreement with six statements such as "My life is still busy and useful" and "I feel now that my life is not very useful," and could range from 0 (low) to 6 (high). Happiness was based on agreement or disagreement with six statements such as "These are the best years of my life" and "This is the saddest time of my life," and could range from 0 (low) to 6 (high).

8. There were three significant health predictors. The physical function rating was a score given by the examining physician for the level of physical function ability in everyday activities, on the basis of the medical history, the physical and neurological examination, audiogram, electroencephalogram, electrocardiogram, and laboratory studies of the blood and urine. For the present analysis the scores ranged from 1 (total disability) to 6 (no pathology). The health self-rating was the panelist's own rating of his/her health, ranging from 1 (poor) to 5 (excellent). The health satisfaction score was based on the panelist's agreement or disagreement with six statements, from the Chicago Inventory of Activities and Attitudes (Burgess et al., 1949) such as "I feel just miserable most of the time" and "I am perfectly satisfied with my health." The score could range from 0 (least satisfied) to 6 (most satisfied).

The Strongest Predictors

1. Parents' longevity. Mother's age at death was not a significant predictor, but father's age at death was. The bivariate regression coefficient (*b* column in table A—8) indicates that each additional year the father lived determined about a third of a year longer life for the men. This finding contrasts with our earlier analyses, in which no relationship was found between longevity of the panelists and longevity of the father or mother. However, this predictor is fairly weak and it may reflect the social inheritance of healthy habits as much as or more than any direct genetic inheritance of longevity. Note that neither father's nor mother's longevity significantly predicted longevity among the women.

2. Intelligence. The two measures of intelligence were weak to moderately strong predictors, performance somewhat stronger than verbal. This fits with other research that shows that performance measures of intelligence are more likely to show decrements with old age than are verbal measures. Higher intelligence may contribute to greater longevity through greater problem-solving ability and better coping mechanisms.

3. SES. The measures of socioeconomic status were moderate to strong predictors for men. The finances regression coefficient indicates that for each point increase on this four-point scale there was a two and one-third-year increase in longevity. These variables also predict longevity among women, but the relationship was not strong enough to be significant. There has been substantial research to show that persons from higher socioeconomic groups have lower mortality, probably because they get better nutrition, housing, medical care, and other things that contribute to longer life.

4. Activity. Among the activity predictors, locomotor activities were fairly strong predictors of longevity among the women; each additional locomotor activity predicted an increase of three-fourths of a year in longevity. This may indicate the importance of staying physically active. More active men also lived longer, but the association was not statistically significant.

Three moderately strong predictors were alternate measures of formal group activities: secondary activities, club, and secondary rating. They all indicate that participation in formal groups outside the family and neighborhood may contribute to longevity, probably through the physical and mental stimulation they provide, as well as through their psychological gratifications and contributions to mental health. Nongroup activities also were moderately predictive of longevity among both men and women. All these activity predictors probably reflect the importance of staying active.

5. Sexual relations. Frequency of intercourse was a significant predictor of longevity for men. This may simply reflect the fact that healthier men tend to be more sexually active, or it may be that intercourse contributes to greater longevity indirectly through its physical stimulation and emotional gratification.

For women, frequency of intercourse was not significant, but past enjoyment of intercourse was a significant and moderately strong predictor of longevity. Present enjoyment of intercourse was a weaker predictor with only borderline significance. This may reflect the fact that past enjoyment represents a lifetime of healthy sexual activity, while present enjoyment represents only recent activity, which may be influenced by recent widowhood or the sexual partner's recent loss of potency or interest, both of which may be unrelated to the panelist's longevity. In any case, it is worth noting that frequency of intercourse is the significant predictor for men, but enjoyment of intercourse is the significant predictor for women. This may indicate that the quantity is more important for men and the quality is more important for women. This is not to imply that sexual activity is necessary for longevity (many celibate groups have normal longevity), but that in this population sexual activity *may* have enchanced longevity.

6. Tobacco and alcohol. Use of tobacco had a significant negative relationship with longevity. This supports the well established fact that use of tobacco is "dangerous to your health" and increases mortality. Drinking alcohol was not a significant predictor, probably because there was little or no heavy drinking in this sample.

7. *Satisfaction*. Among the satisfaction predictors, work satisfaction was the strongest predictor for men. Usefulness was a similar predictor. These predictors may indicate the importance for men to maintain a useful and satisfying role in society. It is curious that religious satisfaction was a negative predictor of longevity for men. Religious satisfaction had strong negative correlations with physical function rating, intelligence, education, and other socioeconomic measures. Thus, it may be that the poorer health and lower socioeconomic status of men with higher religious satisfaction scores are the factors making it a negative predictor of longevity. This interpretation is supported by the fact that it was not a significant independent predictor in the multiple regression analysis (table A—9). For men as well as women, happiness was a moderately strong predictor, indicating that a positive or optimistic view of life may contribute to longevity through its effects on mental health.

8. *Health*. As expected, the strongest group of predictors were the health variables. For men the strongest predictor of all was the health self-rating, whose regression coefficient indicates that for each point increase in this five-point scale, there was an increase of almost two years in longevity. For women the strongest predictor of all was the health satisfaction scale, and its regression coefficient of 2.2 indicates that for each point increase in this seven point scale, there was an increase of more than two years in longevity. There was a similar association for men, but it was not statistically significant. It is not surprising that better health predicts longer life, but it is interesting that the subjective measures of health predict longer life somewhat better than the objective measure (physical function rating). This indicates that how a person reacts to his/her health is more important than their objective health itself. It may be that persons

Table A—9. *Multiple regression of the longevity difference by sex.*

Predictors	b	Multiple R	Adjusted R^2
Men (N = 121)			
Health self-rating	1.31	.33	.10
Work satisfaction	.84	.38	.13
Performance intelligence	.09	.42	.16
Constant: −9.46			
Women (N = 127)			
Health satisfaction	1.93	.36	.12
Past enjoyment of intercourse	2.14	.44	.18
Physical function rating	1.36	.49	.22
Constant: −11.14			

Note: All predictors included increased variance explained by an amount significant at the .05 level.

who learn to compensate and to minimize health impairments live longer than those who do not.

Simultaneous Predictors

In order to determine which variables had independent predictive power when other strong predictors were controlled simultaneously, we did a stepwise multiple regression analysis (table A—9). The intercorrelations between the significant predictors in the multiple regression were all below .30, which indicates that multicollinearity did not significantly affect the results. We did a stepwise multiple regression rather than a simultaneous entry of all independent variables for two reasons. First, we wanted to develop the most parsimonious and efficient model possible. That is, we wanted to maximize the variance explained and minimize the number of variables included in the equation. Simultaneous entry of all variables would include many variables not significantly related when others are controlled. Simultaneous entry also would not show which combination of variables would produce the most variance explained. Second, we wanted to find out which variable was the most important one and enter that one first, then which variable was second in importance net of the first, etc. This is best done with stepwise regression.

For men there were three independently significant predictors: health self-rating, work satisfaction, and performance intelligence (table A—9). This may indicate that the three most important ways men can increase their longevity are to maintain health, maintain a satisfying useful role, and maintain problem-solving abilities.

Women also had three independently significant predictors: health satisfaction, past enjoyment of intercourse, and physical function rating. This may indicate that the three most important ways women can increase their longevity are to maintain health, maintain a lifetime of sexual enjoyment, and maintain physical functioning.

It should be kept in mind that prediction does not necessarily prove causation. Controlled experiments are required to prove causation. However, these predictions do provide evidence that there *may* be a causal relationship between them and longevity.

To illustrate how much difference in longevity these simultaneous predictors can make, if we compared a man with the lowest possible score on health self-rating (1) with a man with the highest possible score (5), there would be a predicted difference of over five years in their longevity (range times $b = 4 \times 1.31 = 5.24$). Similarly, work satisfaction could make a difference of five years ($6 \times .84 = 5.04$), and performance intelligence could make a difference of five and a half years ($62 \times .09 = 5.58$). Adding these differences, we find that the three simultaneous predictors could make a combined difference of almost sixteen years between the men with the highest and lowest scores.

Similarly, for women, health satisfaction could make a difference of 11.58 years (6 × 1.93), past enjoyment of intercourse could make a difference of 4.28 years (2 × 2.14), and physical function rating could make a difference of 6.8 years (5 × 1.36). Adding these, we find that the three simultaneous predictors could make a combined difference of 22.7 years between the women with the highest and lowest scores.

Nonpredictors

There were several variables which we had expected would be significant predictors of longevity but which turned out to be nonsignificant. We had thought that obesity and malnutrition would predict shorter longevity. We found that there was a tendency in that direction (correlations around −.10), but they did not reach statistical significance. We think this is because there were relatively few very obese or malnourished panelists in our study.

Other research indicates that being married reduces mortality, but in our study there was almost no relationship between marriage and longevity. This, combined with the findings that sexual activity and satisfaction are predictors of longevity, suggests that it is not marriage as such but the sexual activity and satisfaction associated with marriage which may contribute to longevity.

None of the measures of contacts with family and friends (primary groups) was a significant predictor. This, combined with the finding that several measures of secondary or organizational activities were significant predictors, suggests that interactions outside the neighborhood are more important for longevity than interactions with family and friends. It may be that most of our panelists had adequate relationships with family and friends, but those who had substantial involvement outside the neighborhood were an above-average group who benefited from the extra stimulation and gratifications of organizational activities.

Previous Analyses

Our previous analyses, using different measures of longevity and with less complete data, found that health, nonsmoking, intelligence, education, work satisfaction, usefulness, secondary group activities, nongroup activities, and happiness were significant predictors of longevity. The present analysis confirms the significance of these predictors and generally shows them to be even stronger than previously estimated. In addition, several previously untested variables were found to be significant predictors of longevity: finances (for men), locomotor activities (for women), frequency of intercourse (for men), and past enjoyment of intercourse (for women). Another new finding was that independently significant predictors could make a combined difference of almost sixteen years for men and almost twenty-three years for women.

References

Burgess, E., et al. *Your activities and attitudes*. Chicago: Science Research Associates, 1948.

Palmore, E. B. Physical, mental, and social factors in predicting longevity. *Gerontologist*, 9: 103–108, 1969a.

Palmore, E. B. Predicting longevity: Follow-up controlling for age. *Gerontologist*, 247–250, 1969b.

Palmore, E. B. Predictors of longevity. In S. Haynes, and M. Feinleib (Eds.), *Proceedings, Second Conference on the Epidemiology of Aging, 1977*. Bethesda, Md.: National Institutes of Health, 1980.

Palmore, E. B. (Ed.), *Normal aging*. Durham, N.C.: Duke University Press, 1970.

Palmore, E. B. (Ed.), *Normal aging II*. Durham, N.C.: Duke University Press, 1974.

Palmore, E. B., and Jeffers, F. (Eds.), *Prediction of life span*. Lexington, Mass.: Heath Lexington Books, 1971.

Rose, C., and Bell, B. *Predicting longevity*. Lexington, Mass.: Heath Lexington Books, 1971.

Wechsler, D. *Manual for the Wechsler Adult Intelligence Scale*. New York: Psychological Corp., 1955.

Predictors of Successful Aging

Erdman B. Palmore

The concept "successful aging" has sometimes been equated with life satisfaction or morale (Havighurst, 1961; Williams and Wirth, 1965), and sometimes with survival and good health (Nowlin, 1985). A more comprehensive definition of successful aging would combine all three of these elements: survival (longevity), health (lack of disability), and life satisfaction (happiness).

The purpose of this paper is to find the strongest predictors of successful aging and to analyze the strongest explanatory factors for successful aging among a panel of normal community residents. The findings will be related to the controversy between activity and disengagement theories.

There have been numerous studies of factors associated with mortality and a few predicting longevity (Palmore and Jeffers, 1971). Predictors of longevity include being female, being physically active, not smoking, having good cognitive functioning, having higher socioeconomic status, having more social activity, having greater life satisfaction, having greater work satisfaction, and having a higher happiness rating. In the Duke First Longitudinal Study, work satisfaction

Reprinted by permission from *Gerontologist*, 19:427–431, 1979. (Editor's Note: The reader should understand that Palmore's definition of successful aging includes a measure of life satisfaction, while Nowlin's definition in the following article does not. These differences in definition, combined with the different methods of analysis, account for the differences in findings.)

and the happiness rating were the two best predictors of age-sex standardized longevity. In general, the predictors of longevity also predict better health among the survivors.

There have also been numerous studies of factors associated with life satisfaction among the aged (Larson, 1978). The factors include better health, higher socioeconomic status, being single or married (as opposed to widowed, divorced, or separated), and more social activity (especially organizational activity). There has usually been little or no relationship found between life satisfaction and age, race, sex, and employment once controls are made for health and income. There have been few studies of predictors of life satisfaction. In the second longitudinal study, the strongest predictors of life satisfaction were health, social activity, and sexual enjoyment (Palmore and Kivett, 1977). Note that there is considerable overlap in these sets of predictors; health, higher SES, and activity predict both longevity and satisfaction.

The Duke First Longitudinal Study

Sample. The sample includes the 155 persons in the first longitudinal study of aging who were aged sixty to seventy-four at the initial examination.

Successful aging. We defined successful aging persons as those who met three criteria: (1) survival to age seventy-five; (2) a physical-function rating indicating less than 20 percent disability (see next section); and (3) a happiness rating indicating generally or always happy, contented and unworried (see next section). There were seventy persons who met these three criteria and so were classified as successful aging. The other eighty-five were classified as not successful. Thus, successful aging was treated as a dichotomy. Of the not successful, thirty-six did not survive to seventy-five; fifteen were both unhealthy and unhappy at age seventy-five; thirteen were unhealthy but happy; and twenty-one were healthy but unhappy. The 155 persons included seventy-two males and eighty-three females, 100 whites, and fifty-five blacks. The average number of years of survivors between first examination and the examination past age seventy-five was 8.7. Thus, the predictors of successful aging were measured about nine years prior to the determination of the outcome (successful or not successful).

Predictors. On the basis of previous research and theory, eighteen variables from the first examination were selected for testing as predictors of successful aging: age, sex, marital status, physical-function rating, happiness rating, cigarette smoking, intelligence (WAIS verbal and performance), activities ratings (primary group, secondary group, physical, and solitary), attitude scales (usefulness, work satisfaction, and emotional security), and socioeconomic status (education, financial status, and prestige rating).

The physical-function rating was a rating given by the examining physician, ranging from 0 for total disability to 5 for "no pathology."

The happiness rating was part of the Cavan Adjustment Rating (Havighurst and Albrecht, 1953), given by the interviewing social worker, and it ranged from

0 for "unhappy, discontented, worried, fearful, frustrated" to 9 for "very happy, exultant, great contentment."

Three of the activities ratings were also part of the Cavan Adjustment Rating: primary group, secondary group, and solitary activities. The primary-group activities rating ranged from 0 for "alone in the world; no family, relatives, or friends" to 9 for "daily contacts; closely incorporated into group life." The secondary-group activities rating ranged from 0 for "in no groups, no reading, no radio or television, complete social isolation," to 9 for "time filled with many groups, much reading, always on the go or occupied with reading, etc."

The solitary activities rating ranged from 0 for "nothing to do" to 9 for "time filled with daily activities, hobbies, plans, to the exclusion of group activities."

The number of physical activities was the number of different physical or locomotor activities the person mentioned in response to the question "What do you do with your free time?"

The usefulness and work satisfaction scales were part of the Chicago Inventory of Activities and Attitudes (Cavan et al., 1949; Havighurst, 1951). The usefulness scale was based on agreement or disagreement with six statements such as "My life is still busy and useful" and "I feel now that my life is not very useful." The scale ranged from 0 for no answers indicating usefulness, to 6 for six answers indicating usefulness. The work satisfaction scale was based on agreement or disagreement with six statements such as "I am satisfied with the work I now do" and "I have no work to look forward to." It ranged from 0 for no work satisfaction to 6 for the maximum work satisfaction. Work was broadly defined to include all useful activities, not just paid employment.

The emotional security rating was also part of the Cavan Adjustment Rating and it ranged from 0 for "feels unwanted, nobody cares, pushed aside," to 9 for "feels greatly beloved, wanted, gets lavish attention."

Three measures of socioeconomic status were used. Years of education was coded as 0 for no formal education to 10 for Ph.D. or other doctoral degrees. The financial status variable was based on responses to the question "How would you describe your present financial position in life?" The responses were scored as ranging from 1 for "can't make ends meet" to 4 for "well-to-do" or "wealthy." The prestige rating was also part of the Cavan Adjustment Rating and ranged from 0 for "feels looked down on, low status, feels disrespect on the part of others," to 9 for "feels in a position of high status; opinion sought and followed."

Missing scores. Forty-four of the 155 persons in this analysis had one or more scores in these predictors missing. Most had only one score missing, and the total number of missing scores was only 4 percent of the total scores. In order to save these cases for the overall analysis, a program, developed at the Duke center by Max Woodbury and Larry Dowdy, was used to estimate the value of the missing score based on recursive linear regressions on all of the other variables. The effect of estimating these missing scores was less than 0.1 on any mean value.

What Makes the Difference?

Significant predictors. We first tested all eighteen variables to find which had significant zero-order correlations with successful aging (scored 0 for not successful, 1 for successful). Since previous research has shown that the strength of predictors of longevity and life satisfaction vary between men and women (Palmore, 1974; Palmore and Kivett, 1977), the main analysis was done separately for men and women. Ten variables had significant correlations (.05 level) with successful aging among men or women or both (table A—10). Eight variables did not have significant correlations with successful aging: age, sex, marital status, education, WAIS performance, WAIS verbal, cigarette smoking, and primary group activities.

The two strongest predictors among both men and women were the physical-function rating and the happiness rating (at first examination). This was expected, because both of these ratings are used as criteria for successful aging when the person reaches age seventy-five. In longitudinal research, a general finding is that the best single predictor of a score at a later point in time is usually the person's scores on that variable at an earlier point in time. This reflects the basic consistency of people's behavior and attitudes over time. In this case it means that the best predictor of successful aging (at age seventy-five) is whether the person was successfully aging at the beginning of the study. A discriminant

Table A—10. *Significant predictors of successful aging.*

	Simple correlation with successful aging	
Predictor	Women (N = 83)	Men (N = 72)
Physical function	.46**	.31*
Happiness	.44**	.38**
Activities		
Secondary group	.42**	.30*
Physical	.41**	.22*
Solitary	.20**	.19*
Attitudes		
Usefulness	.33*	.08
Work satisfaction	.08	.25*
Emotional security	.27*	.14
Socioeconomic status		
Prestige	.37**	.04
Financial Status	.17	.21*

* = $p < .05$.

** = $p < .01$.

function analysis with just these two predictors correctly classified 74 percent of the cases as to their later successful and unsuccessful aging.

Of more interest are the other eight significant (zero-order) predictors. The strongest of these among both men and women, were secondary group activity (table A—10). This had correlations with successful aging almost as strong as did the physical-function rating and the happiness rating. The second strongest of these other variables was physical activities for women and work satisfaction for men. Women seemed less affected by work satisfaction (probably because few women were employed even though work was broadly defined to include nonpaid work), but were more affected by usefulness. Solitary activities had smaller, but still significant, correlations with successful aging among both men and women.

Emotional security had a moderate relationship to successful aging among women but not among men. Among the socioeconomic indicators, prestige had a strong predictive value among women but not among men, while financial status had a significant relationship among men but not among women.

The strong predictive values of secondary group activities, physical activities, usefulness, and work satisfaction seem to point to the predominant influence of such activities and attitudes on successful aging.

Multiple regression. In order to test the relative importance of the significant predictors, especially the explanatory predictors, we next did a two-stage, stepwise multiple-regression analysis of the ten significant predictors of successful aging. Since the strongest predictors (physical function and happiness) were also part of the criteria of later successful aging, they do not help explain what contributes to successful aging. In order to examine the relative strength of the explanatory variables, we entered in the first stage only those significant explanatory variables which increased the variance explained in successful aging by 1 percent or more. Table A—11 shows that there were three such explanatory variables for each sex: for women they were, in order of importance, secondary-group activity, physical activity, and solitary activity; for men they were secondary-group activity, work satisfaction, and physical activity.

When physical functioning and happiness were added in the second stage, both variables provided statistically significant increases in the variance explained for women, but only happiness provided a significant increase for men. The total regression equations (corrected for degrees of freedom) explained about one-fourth of the variance in successful aging among women and one-eighth among the men.

In order to test whether the eight variables without significant (zero-order) correlations might show some significant association in a multiple regression, we entered them one at a time after the variables discussed above, in a third stage of the analysis. None of these eight variables increased the variance explained by a statistically significant (.05) amount among women or men.

Table A—11. *Multiple regression of strongest predictors of successful aging.*

Predictor	Slope (B)	Multiple correlation (R)	Variance explained (R^2)
Women (N = 83)			
Secondary group activity	.002	.419	.176[a]
Physical activity	.057	.464	.215[a]
Solitary activity	.027	.502	.252[a]
Physical function	.158	.546	.300[a]
Happiness	.087	.585	.342[a]
R^2 corrected for degrees of freedom			.243
F value of equation = .802; $p < .001$			
Men (N = 72)			
Secondary group activity	.016	.300	.082[a]
Work satisfaction	.021	.334	.112[a]
Physical activity	.026	.354	.125
Physical function	.097	.381	.145
Happiness	.110	.467	.218[a]
R^2 corrected for degrees of freedom			.121
F value of equation = 3.67; $p < .01$			

[a]Increase in variance explained is statistically significant at .05 level.

Discussion. The fact that neither verbal nor performance intelligence, nor years of education had significant correlations with successful aging suggests that intelligence and education by themselves contribute little to successful aging; rather it is more important what one does with one's intelligence or education.

The fact that primary group activities had almost no relationship to successful aging may be explained by the fact that most of the participants in this study had fairly high levels of primary group activity, and so had enough to allow successful aging. Secondary group activity was much lower on the average, and thus represents a more critical factor in successful aging. In other words, it appears that most of the participants had sufficient family and friend contacts, but only the more active and involved belonged to several groups and participated in them regularly enough for their participation to contribute to successful aging. This seems to support activity theory and contradict disengagement theory, but only in regard to secondary group activity, not in primary group activity.

Greater participation in secondary groups probably contributes to successful aging on three levels: physical, psychological, and social. Group participation usually involves some physical activity that helps maintain physical health. On the psychological level, group activity helps mental stimulation, maintenance of interaction skills, reality orientation, and general mental health. On the social level, group activity gives a sense of belonging, morale, purpose, and social gratification. All these processes contribute toward better mental and physical health and, in short, toward successful aging. This interpretation is supported by several previous studies which found group participation to be related to longevity (Palmore and Jeffers, 1971) and to life satisfaction (Larson, 1978).

The relationship of physical activity to successful aging seems fairly clear; greater physical activity contributes directly to better health; inactivity leads to atrophy of muscles, bones, circulatory system, etc. In addition, there may be an indirect effect of physical activity and health on greater mental health and feelings of life satisfaction. Thus, activity theory is also supported in regard to physical activity.

Conclusions

Conclusions based on these findings should be considered tentative due to the limited sample and the problem of imputing causality to predictors. However, these findings do support the activity theory of aging (Havighurst, 1961), in that two of the strongest explanatory predictors of successful aging among both men and women were secondary group activity and physical activity, with work satisfaction also being important for men. This indicates that men and women who are more active in organizations and who engage in more physical activity are more likely to age successfully.

There is probably a reciprocal causal relationship between these variables; those who are healthy and happy are also more likely to remain active in organizations and remain more physically active, and vice versa. However, the prospective design of this study ensures that successful aging (the outcome) did not cause the earlier activity (the predictor). Thus, these findings do suggest that secondary group and physical activity contribute to successful aging.

It remains to be tested whether increasing group and physical activity would increase successful aging. A careful experimental study with long-term follow-up would be required to test this theory. In the meantime, the practical implication for practitioners and older persons seems to be that secondary group and physical activity may help prolong healthy and happy aging.

References

Cavan, R., et al. *Personal adjustment in old age*. Chicago: Science Research Associates, 1949.

Havighurst, R. Validity of the Chicago Attitude Inventory as a means of personal adjustment in old age. *Journal of Abnormal and Social Psychology*, 46:24–29, 1951.

Havighurst, R. Successful aging. *Gerontologist*, 1:4–7, 1961.

Havighurst, R., and Albrecht, R. *Older people*. New York: Longmans, 1953.

Larson, R. Thirty years of research on the subjective well-being of older Americans. *Journal of Gerontology*, 33:109–129, 1978.

Nowlin, S. Successful aging. In Palmore, E. B., et al. (Eds.), *Normal aging III*. Durham, N.C.: Duke University Press, 1985.

Palmore, E. B. (Ed.), *Normal aging*. Durham, N.C.: Duke University Press, 1970.

Palmore, E. B. (Ed.), *Normal aging II*. Durham, N.C.: Duke University Press, 1974.

Palmore, E. B., and Jeffers, F. *Prediction of life span*. Lexington, Mass.: Heath Lexington Books, 1971.

Palmore, E. B., and Kivett, V. Change in life satisfaction. *Journal of Gerontology*, 32:311–316, 1977.

Williams, R., and Wirths, C. *Lives through the years*. New York: Atherton Press, 1965.

Successful Aging

John B. Nowlin

An informal concept currently prevalent among gerontologists is that of "successful aging." A healthy contrast to the more usual focus upon age-associated attrition of personal resources, this notion has been primarily a talking point. There has been, for example, no precise attempt at any definition of what might comprise successful aging. Formulation of a substantive definition for this concept has practical merit as well as intrinsic interest. A workable, concise definition would permit evaluation of factors which, in turn, might serve as guidelines for the attainment of successful aging.

This paper proposes a tentative definition of successful aging and examines data collected from an older population in the context of this definition. Any specific definition of successful aging will necessarily be, at least in part, arbitrary. Two criteria, both with prima facie validity, would be chronological age and health status. With respect to chronological age, the older person, by virtue of remaining alive and accruing years, reflects some degree of success in dealing with the vicissitudes of aging. The particular age at which an individual can be considered successful in coping with these vicissitudes is moot. Yet another gerontologic talking point, at present as informal as that of successful aging, is consideration of later life in terms of "younger old age" and "older old age"; the age of seventy-five has been suggested as the dividing point between these two age groups. Attainment of age seventy-five then could serve as a reasonable age criterion for definition of successful aging. Other than chronological age, it is difficult to conceive of a factor more fundamental to any notion of successful aging than health status. For any age group, the pervasive role of health in all aspects of coping needs little emphasis. Since senescence itself often is associated with loss of physiological resources, health status seems an obvious second criterion for successful aging.

The population considered in this paper provides an excellent source for examination of successful aging defined in these terms. Involved in a long-term

Reprinted by permission from *Black Aging*, 2:4–6, 8–17, 1977.

longitudinal study of aging with an initial minimal age of sixty, this population has been seen periodically over a subsequent twenty-year time span with careful medical, psychological evaluation at each visit. One feature of this project has been a physician rating of health based upon health data collected from each of the study participants at the time of his or her return visits. Access to this rating provides a clear health criterion of the definition of successful aging. Moreover, since many of the individuals in this study group were seen both before and after reaching age seventy-five, there is the opportunity to examine successful aging in a prospective fashion.

In this evaluation of successful aging, sex and race characteristics of the study population were given prominence. Because of the well-known effects of both factors upon many parameters of health, psychological, and socioeconomic status regardless of age, they would seem likely to influence, as well, any later life outcome such as successful aging. Thus, the potential interplay of race and sex status with successful aging was examined using a number of specific health, psychological, and socioeconomic parameters.

Materials and Methods

Study population. The sample for this analysis is the participants in the Duke First Longitudinal Study.

Definition of successful aging categories. As described earlier in this report, definition of successful aging was based upon two criteria: (1) the attainment of age seventy-five and (2) status of good health upon reaching that age. The second criterion was defined by use of a physician health rating formulated at the conclusion of a thorough medical examination provided to each study participant. In addition to a physical examination, medical evaluation included routine hematologic studies, urinalysis, chest x ray, and electrocardiogram. With this information in hand, the physician rated health on a 0–5 scale, 0 and 1 representing essentially good health; values of 2–5 indicated progressively poorer health. Those individuals whose health rating, when they attained age seventy-five, was 0 or 1 made up the group that might be thought of as representing successful aging ($N = 51$). For convenience of reference, these individuals are designated "group A." Persons reaching age seventy-five with health rating of 2–5 were considered an unhealthy older group ($N = 103$), and designated "group B." A third group compromised of individuals who did not survive to age seventy-five made up the third or nonsurvivor group ($N = 99$), designated "group C." Of the original population of 270, seventeen persons were not considered because of insufficient follow-up information.

Parameters examined for differences among successful aging groups. Selected variables collected at the time of the second visit of this population in 1960 were employed to evaluate differences between the three successful aging categories. Variables were chosen to reflect characteristics of health and psychological function as well as socioeconomic status. Specific health parameters considered included systolic and diastolic blood pressure, Quetelet Index (a person's weight divided by the square of his height, considered a reasonable estimate of the extent of adiposity), serum cholesterol level, a physician rating of cardiovascular impairment (ranging from 0 to 9, with 9 indicative of a terminal bedridden state arising from cardiovascular disease). Also evaluated were visual acuity as rated by an ophthalmologist, denoted again by a 0–9 scale (0 reflecting excellent vision, 9 indicating total blindness), auditory acuity, expressed in percentage of hearing loss as defined by the American Standards Association. Intellectual function was evaluated for the successful aging categories by full scale Wechsler Adult Intelligence Scale (WAIS) scores. Also evaluated was the Cavan Activity Scale, a general summation of the number of an individual's interpersonal contacts. As a reflection of socioeconomic status, educational level was employed, defined as the number of school attendance years.

Results

Distribution of Sex and Race Groups among Successful Aging Categories

Table A—12 presents sex and race of the study population sorted among the three successful aging categories. The number (N) of individuals in each sex-race successful aging category is provided, along with the percentage (in parentheses) of the entire population each cell contains. Evaluation of the distribution of race and sex groups among the successful aging categories, using chi square technique, indicates no statistical significance in distributional pattern (chi square = 8.5, df = 6, p = .21). Therefore, race and sex status can be said to be distributed in random fashion with respect to the aging outcome defined by the successful aging categories.

Table A—12. *Sex and race distribution among successful aging groups.*

	Group A	Group B	Group C
White males	19 (7.5%)	26 (10.3%)	38 (15.0%)
White females	13 (5.1%)	41 (16.2%)	26 (10.3%)
Black males	6 (2.4%)	17 (6.7%)	17 (6.7%)
Black females	13 (5.1%)	19 (7.5%)	18 (7.1%)
Total N = 253			
Chi square = 8.5 (df = 6, p = .21)			

Group A—healthy at age 75 (successful aging group).

Group B—unhealthy at age 75.

Group C—nonsurvivors at age 75.

Health, Psychological, and Socioeconomic Variables in 1960 Compared among Sex, Race, and Successful Aging Groups

Variable scores, collected at the time of the second longitudinal population visit in 1960, were considered on the basis of sex, race, and successful aging categories. A three-factor analysis of variance was the statistical technique employed to apprise the significance of the differences in mean values between the various population subgroups. Table A—13 presents mean values for each variable with the population segregated on the bases of age, sex, and successful aging categories. *F*-values, indicating the statistical significance of between-group mean differences, are also provided.

Chronological age, at the time of the 1960 visit, poses a problem in terms of other variable analyses. As seen in table A—13, age differed in statistically significant fashion between successful aging and sex categories. Since chronological age itself is often highly correlated with many of the other variables under consideration in this study, any apparent between-category differences might instead derive from a substantial correlation with age. Therefore, in analyses of variance evaluating other study parameters, age at the time of the 1960 visit was used as a covariate, mitigating this potentially confounding effect.

Analyses of variance for other measures recorded at the 1960 longitudinal visit presented statistically significant mean differences for cardiovascular rating, serum cholesterol level, educational level, Cavan Activity Scale, and full-scale WAIS scores. The 1960 (or visit 2) cardiovascular ratings were lowest (i.e., indicating less cardiovascular impairment) among group A, intermediate among group B, and highest among group C. Serum cholesterol levels were lowest among the group A population and roughly the same among the other two successful aging categories. Educational level is clearly distinguished by successful aging category with more school attendance found among group A, slightly less among group B, and least among the nonsurvivors to age seventy-five (group C). The Cavan Activity Scale score is highest among group A persons and approximately equivalent among the other two groups. Finally, intellectual function, as reflected by WAIS scores, parses out so that group A scores highest, with group B intermediate in level, and group C presenting the lowest scores.

Statistically significant between-sex mean differences for the visit 2 measures are found between systolic and diastolic blood pressures (men with higher blood pressure readings), Quetelet Index (men with more body bulk than women), cholesterol level (women with far higher level than men), and Cavan Activity Scale (women presenting a greater degree of interpersonal-related activity than men). These findings have all been noted in earlier studies of aging.

Time 2 racial differences, statistically significant, include systolic blood pressure (blacks with higher levels than whites), cardiovascular rating (blacks with higher—i.e., more cardiovascular impairment—than whites), hearing loss (greater among whites than blacks), hemoglobin level (lower levels among blacks), educational level (fewer years of education among blacks), and WAIS scores (lower among blacks).

No statistically significant interactions were noted between the successful aging categories and race or sex.

Variables distinguished in statistically significant fashion between the three successful aging groups were considered separately in a stepwise discriminant analysis. This secondary analysis evaluates each variable as it distinguishes between the three successful aging categories independent of any interrelatedness with other variables. Summarized results of the discriminant analysis are shown

Table A—13. *Mean for 1960 health, socioeconomic, and psychological variables: successful aging, race, and sex groups.*

	Groups							*F*-Value	*F*-Value	*F*-Value
Variable	A	B	C	Blacks	Whites	Men	Women	A–C	Race	Sex
Age (1960)	70.1	71.8	68.1	68.1	71.4	71.5	70.6	8.1**	<1	4.1*
Systolic pressure	154	156	160	160	164	164	150	<1	6.4*	9.4*
Diastolic pressure	81.7	81.0	84.8	84.6	80.7	81.2	83.0	1.2	1.9	5.1*
Cardio-vascular rating	1.1	1.7	2.0	2.2	1.3	1.6	1.6	3.8*	12.2**	<1
Quetelet index	3.6	3.5	3.6	3.4	3.6	3.7	3.4	<1	1.2	4.2*
Serum cholesterol	230	260	254	252	240	227	262	5.2*	2.9	14.1**
Vision	1.9	2.6	2.0	2.4	2.3	2.3	2.3	1.7	<1	<1
Hearing loss (%)	13.4	16.5	13.9	14.1	19.8	17.4	18.3	<1	5.2*	<1
Hemoglobin	14.3	14.0	14.1	13.4	14.5	14.6	13.6	<1	13.6**	19.8**
Educational level	11.7	10.3	9.2	7.6	11.9	10.1	10.8	3.6*	11.2**	<1
Cavan Activity Scale	31.3	28.3	28.7	29.2	29.2	28.0	30.5	3.9*	<1	5.8*
WAIS intellectual function	93.0	84.3	79.4	62.2	97.5	83.4	87.9	3.4*	46.3**	1.6

Group A—Healthy at age 75 (Successful Aging Group).
Group B—Unhealthy at age 75.
Group C—Nonsurvivors to age 75.
*$p < .05$.
**$p < .01$.

Table A—14. *Significant variables in discriminate analysis of successful aging groups.*

	F at entry
(1) Cavan activity	3.9
(2) Serum cholesterol	4.9
(3) Cardiovascular rating	3.9

Wilks lambda = 0.84 (F = 4.0, df = 6, 266, $p < .001$).

in table A—14. Cavan Activity Scale, cardiovascular rating, and serum cholesterol level enter the discriminant analysis in statistically significant fashion. With these variables considered simultaneously in this manner, the statistical significance of the overall between-category differences are available. With the three variables, serum cholesterol, Cavan Activity Scale, and cardiovascular rating considered simultaneously, group A differed significantly from group B (F = 5.1, df = 3/132, $p < .01$), and group C (F = 4.9, df = 3/132, $p < .01$). Groups B and C did not differ in statistically significant fashion (F = 0.8, df = 3/132, p = ns).

Discussion

The concept of successful aging has been formally defined, in this paper, as the attainment of age seventy-five in good health. This concept, so defined, was apprised among an older population followed longitudinally over two decades. With use of age and health criteria in defining successful aging, there are three groups of persons within the longitudinal population: a group who attained age seventy-five in good health (and who could be called the successful agers), a group who attained age seventy-five but with significant health impairment and, finally, a group who died before age seventy-five. Grouping of the study population on these criteria allowed further characterization of the successful aging concept with respect to health, socioeconomic status, and psychological factors.

The first finding of note involves racial and sex makeup of the three successful aging subgroups. Distribution of blacks and whites, and men and women within the three successful aging categories did not exceed the proportional expected by chance alone. Therefore, within this particular older population, the characteristics of race or gender seem irrelevant to the attainment of successful aging. By tradition, older blacks are thought to experience poorer health generally and, therefore, might have been expected to cluster within the two study subgroups representative of more health compromise. At least within this study population, it appears that racial status does not hold that association.

Evaluation of the successful aging categories in terms of health, psychological, and socioeconomic factors, as noted at the 1960 visit of this study group, offers some predictive power to the relationship found between these categories.

That is—since the 1960 observations were made at a point in time before the study participants attained the age of seventy-five—these findings are prospective in nature, possibly reflecting some degree of cause and effect.

Among the health factors which distinguished between the three successful aging categories is that of cardiovascular function. This finding is, of course, predictable; extent of cardiovascular compromise has long been accepted as a major health issue for the geriatric population. The association of lesser degree of cardiovascular impairment with subsequent successful aging is certainly to be anticipated. The other 1960 health parameter which is significantly differentiated on the bases of successful aging categories is that of serum cholesterol. Generally viewed as holding a relationship to subsequent development of the atherosclerotic disease process, level of serum cholesterol in this study is lowest among the individuals subsequently included within the successful aging group and higher but equivalent within the other two population subgroups. The preponderance of illness that developed after 1960 within this group was cardiovascular in nature; therefore, level of cholesterol, as a precusor to atherosclerosis, seems to hold continuing relevance even for older populations. Among non-health factors differentiating between the three study groups is that of educational level. Educational level, generally considered a strong indicator of socioeconomic status, is clearly differentiated among the three successful aging categories. Study individuals who ultimately are included within the successful aging group present the highest degree of educational attainment. Socioeconomic factors are well known to hold association with health outcomes and, in this instance, are seemingly predictive of successful aging, defined, to a large extent, on the bases of health criteria. Extent of interpersonal dealings, as suggested by the 1960 Cavan Activity Scale scores, is highest among persons subsequently comprising the successful aging group. Such a relationship provides an emphasis to the relevancy, for this population, of sociability to subsequent well-being. Finally, intellectual function, as defined by the 1960 WAIS scores, is likewise indicative of future successful aging categorization, higher degree of intellectual functioning being associated with inclusion in the successful aging group. Overall, this sampling of health, socioeconomic status, and psychological characteristics demonstrates the broad range of influences bearing on attainment of successful aging.

Sex and race characteristics of this population, noninfluential in the makeup of the successful aging categories, likewise appear irrelevant as influences upon the various health, socioeconomic status, and psychological variables employed to characterize successful aging. While many between-sex and between-race differences were apparent in the three-factor analysis of variance, there was no statistically significant interaction between sex, race groups, and the successful aging categories. Such a finding provides a reemphasis of the finding that race and sex of the individual seemingly bear little pertinence to successful aging as defined in this study.

Discriminate function analysis of the 1960 parameters which demonstrated statistically significant mean differences between the successful aging categories points up the relevant independence of predictive value provided by the Cavan Activity Scale, cholesterol level, and cardiovascular rating scale. Moreover, the discriminate analysis suggests, on the bases of the five variables considered, that the successful aging category is distinct from the other two categories, while the latter present little between-category differences. This relationship implies that successful aging might be considered unique, while there is little to distinguish between individuals who do not attain that status when older (i.e., those individuals who reach seventy-five unhealthy or those who succumb before that age).

Finally, a caveat is in order concerning broad generalization of the findings described in this report. The original longitudinal study group which served as the basis for the findings about successful aging were not randomly selected; they tended to be healthier, more socially involved and of higher socioeconomic status than the older population in the community at large. Further, arbitrary selection of the variables employed to characterize the successful aging categories raises the possibility of chance rather than meaningful association. Nevertheless, this report provides some substance to the notion of successful aging and proposes hypotheses for future evaluation of this concept.

Psychomotor Performance and Cardiovascular Disease

John B. Nowlin and Ilene C. Siegler

Age-related impairment in cognitive task performance among older people—particularly those tasks which require speed—is a well-known and frequently observed phenomenon. One of the more often cited hypotheses relates this performance decrement to concurrent degenerative cardiovascular changes known to accompany aging (Birren, 1965; Birren et al., 1980; Eisdorfer and Wilkie, 1977). Specifically, atherosclerosis and hypertensive vascular disease are the two cardiovascular entities usually considered in this context. Some elegant research has examined this potential relationship, usually detecting more compromised cognitive performance among older groups defined as having cardiovascular pathology (Speith, 1965; Botwinick and Storandt, 1974; Hertzog et al., 1978). One consistent difficulty in much of this research, however, has been the lack of a stringent operational definition of cardiovascular status. No doubt an exact definition of cardiovascular status will always remain elusive. Even so, one solution

Paper presented at the 23nd Annual Meeting of the Gerontological Society, Toronto, Canada, November 1981.

to this dilemma might be availability of careful documentation of health status coincident in time with the testing of cognitive function. Such an approach could at least provide reasonably objective grounds to make valid judgements about cardiovascular status and its relationship to cognitive work outcomes among older people. This current report is based upon data collection that approaches these criteria. Information was gathered from a large middle-aged and elderly community based population carefully apprised for health status who also performed a complex cognitive task. With this older age group defined as to cardiovascular status, three issues relating to cognitive performance were examined. First, the impact of presence or absence of cardiovascular disease was evaluated, regardless of type of cardiovascular pathology. Second, the relationship between performance and specific type of degenerative cardiovascular disease was examined. Third, the influence of cardiovascular status and change in cognitive performance measures over time was examined.

Method

Subjects. The population under study in this report is that of the Duke Second Longitudinal Study. Only individuals present at all four study rounds are included in this particular report.

Definitions of disease. Presence or absence of degenerative cardiovascular disease was established in this population, using extensive health information provided by a detailed medical history and physical examination, with laboratory as well as ancillary clinical information. Definition of a group of hypertensive persons was based response to an item in the written medical history questionnaire which inquired into presence or absence of physician diagnosed high blood pressure. Participants were included in the hypertensive group if they reported hypertension at least during three of the four biennial visits. Individuals disclaiming hypertensive disease for all four project visits were defined as being free of the disorder. Participants who indicated presence of this disorder once or twice during project involvement were denoted as ambiguous and were excluded from analysis. For two reasons, actual blood pressure recordings were not employed for the definition of the hypertension subgroup. First, the marked variability of this physiological parameter renders it somewhat unreliable. Second, blood pressure readings might be influenced by antihypertensive therapy.

Presence or absence of atherosclerosis was defined on the basis of electrocardiographic findings. Presence of coronary artery atherosclerosis was defined by usual electrocardiographic criteria: i.e., evidence of new or old myocardial infarction, pattern of left ventricular ischemia or injury, left bundle branch block, atrial fibrillation, or flutter. Individuals with normal biennial electrocardiograms for all four visits were defined as being free of atherosclerosis; individuals with cardiograms indicative of significant atherosclerosis in three out of four biennial visits were included in the atherosclerotic group. The individual with only one or two electrocardiograms indicative of coronary atherosclerosis were defined as ambiguous and were excluded from analysis.

Further exclusion included the subject who met criteria for one form of cardiovascular disease yet was ambiguous for the other. For example, the person with three out of four electrocardiograms indicative of coronary atherosclerosis but also with one or two self-reports of hypertension would be among individuals not included in the analysis. Individuals with no self-report of hypertension and with normal electrocardiograms for all of their four visits were designated as a group free of cardiovascular disease.

Measure. The cognitive task employed was that of a continuous performance task, abbreviated as CPT (see Harkins et al., 1974). In the paradigm used in this study, known as the odd-even task, participants were exposed to a successive series of single digit numbers at a presentation rate of one per second. Duration of stimulus presentation was one second. With presentation of two consecutive even or two consecutive odd numbers, the subjects were instructed to depress a key as quickly as possible. Study participants were confronted with no overlap of appropriate stimulus events. Each test session lasted for ten minutes; number paired appropriate for response occurred randomly on an average of every six seconds. Behavioral measures considered for this report include correct responses, reaction time required for the correct response, and commission errors. Correct responses were defined as subject-produced signals presented between 200 and 1,200 milliseconds after appearance of the second number of an appropriate number pair. Responses that occurred outside this interval were considered commission errors.

Test schedule. CPT testing was available to each participant on alternate longitudinal project visits. Hence, at the most, participants had two exposures to the CPT. Only those persons with both exposures to the CPT were included in this present evaluation. Moreover, a number of these middle-aged and older people involved in the CPT testing performed quite erratically, suggesting that they were not fully task-engaged. To exclude data arising from this type of non-engaged behavior, all participants were excluded whose correct responses numbered less than two standard deviations below the mean or whose total commission errors numbered greater than two standard deviations above the mean.

Results

The final study population for this evaluation was made up of individuals with consistent evidence of either presence or absence of cardiovascular degenerative disease along with evidence of appropriate engagement in the setting of the cog-

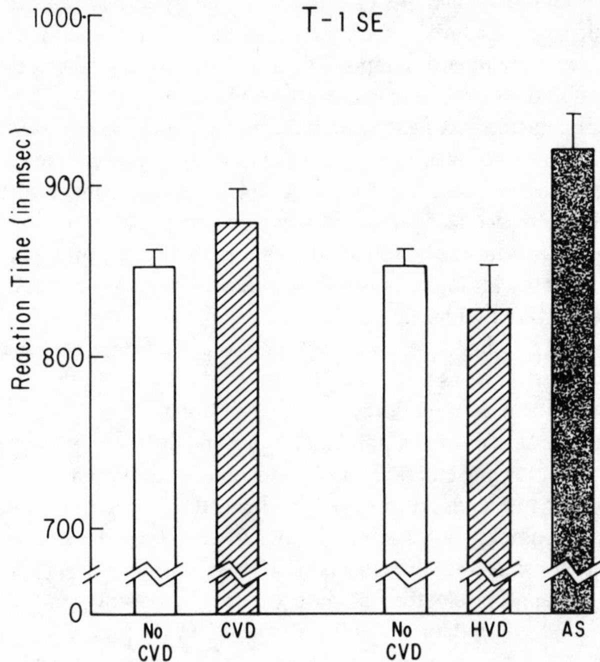

Figure A—2. *Correct responses among cardiovascular disease groupings.*

nitive task. After subject exclusion based upon CPT behavioral response criteria, cardiovascular disease categorization, there was a residual study group made up of 141 individuals. One hundred and two individuals were defined as free of cardiovascular disease. In the cardiovascular disease group, twelve were defined as hypertensive and twenty-one as demonstrating electrocardiographic evidence of coronary artery disease. The group presenting no cardiovascular disease is younger than their counterparts defined as having that disease. When the cardiovascular disease is segregated into either hypertensive or atheroscleortic subgroups, the latter subgroup proves to be the older of the three groups. Hypertensive persons were intermediate in age, with disease-free individuals the youngest. When tested in an analysis of variance, the between-group differences in mean age were statistically significant beyond the .05 level of confidence. Finally, there was no difference in distribution by sex within the various cardiovascular status groups.

Measures of behavioral response in the CPT experimental format are shown in the next several figures. Values presented are two-trial averages, i.e., averaged over the initial trial and the second trial performed four years later. Figure A—2 presents total number of CPT correct responses among the cardiovascular disease groupings. On the left, individuals free of cardiovascular disease are contrasted with persons having either hypertensive or atherosclerotic disease. Number of correct responses is clearly greater among the disease-free individuals. An analysis of variance indicates that this between-group mean difference attains statistical significance beyond the .01 confidence level. On the right, the disease-free group is contrasted with individuals falling into each of the two cardiovascular disease groups. Again, of course, the group without evidence of cardiovascular disease differs from the pair of groups with CVD. However, each of the two CVD subgroups differs from each other so that the atherosclerotic group produces fewer CPT correct responses than does the hypertensive group. An analysis of variance confirms the statistical significance of these apparent mean differences between groups. Since a significant age difference exists between the atherosclerotic and other two subgroups, there is the possibility that the age difference itself might explain the performance differential between the three groups. However, when chronological age is included in the analysis of variance as a covariant, the between-group difference still proves to be statistically significant beyond the .01 confidence level.

Number of commission errors were not significantly different among groups, although individuals with cardiovascular disease produce more commission errors than do those in the disease-free group.

Reaction time, as recorded for CPT correct responses, is presented in figure A—3. As seen on the left portion of that figure, disease-free individuals were slightly quicker in response than were individuals with either hypertension or electrocardiographic evidence of atherosclerosis. However, in an analysis of variance, this difference was not statistically significant. With the atherosclerotic and

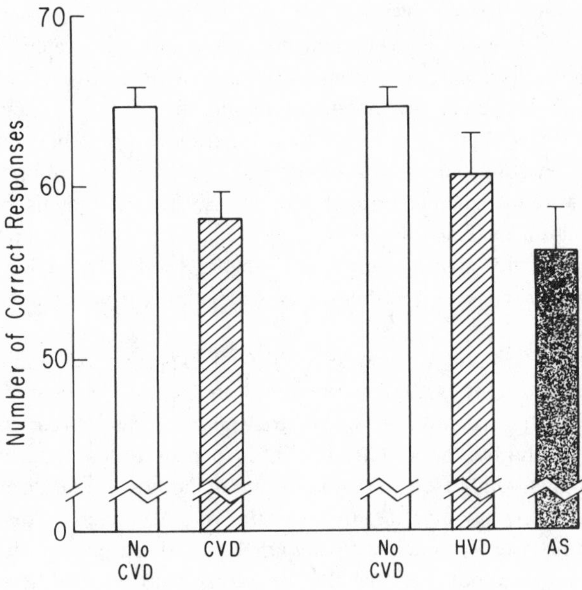

Figure A—3. *Reaction time to correct responses among cardiovascular disease groupings.*

hypertensive groups considered separately and compared to the disease-free group, greater mean differences in reaction time were apparent. The atherosclerotic group presented more prolonged reaction times than did the hypertensive and disease-free groups. This apparent difference proved to be statistically significant beyond .01 confidence level when evaluated by an analysis of variance. With the analysis of variance repeated using chronological age as a covariant, this relationship between the three cardiovascular status groups still proved statistically significant.

If cardiovascular disease status exerts influence on overall performance scores of a cognitive task, one might also anticipate an impact upon pattern of change in these measures over time. The next figure examines such a possibility. Visits averaged four years apart. As is evident, there is a slight increase in number of correct responses and shorter reaction times at the second visit regardless of cardiovascular disease status. Using a repeated measures analysis of variance, these changes were found to be statistically significant. The between-visit differences in number of commission errors seems minimal, a lack of trend confirmed by the analysis of variance. More germane to this report, however, between-group change in CPT measures over time appears similar for all three cardiovascular disease categories. The disease group-by-visit interaction terms in the repeated measures analysis of variance proved statistically insignificant for all CPT scores. Thus, it seems that the relatively stable cardiovascular disease status holds little relationship to the pattern of test-retest change among CPT behavioral measures.

Discussion

Before we discuss the significance of these findings, there are a pair of issues which merit special comment. First, the population evaluated is comprised of a basically healthy group of older people. All were ambulatory and most were fully capable of coping well with the usual daily contingencies. Had they been less

Figure A—4. *Pattern of change in performance scores of a cognitive task, over time.*

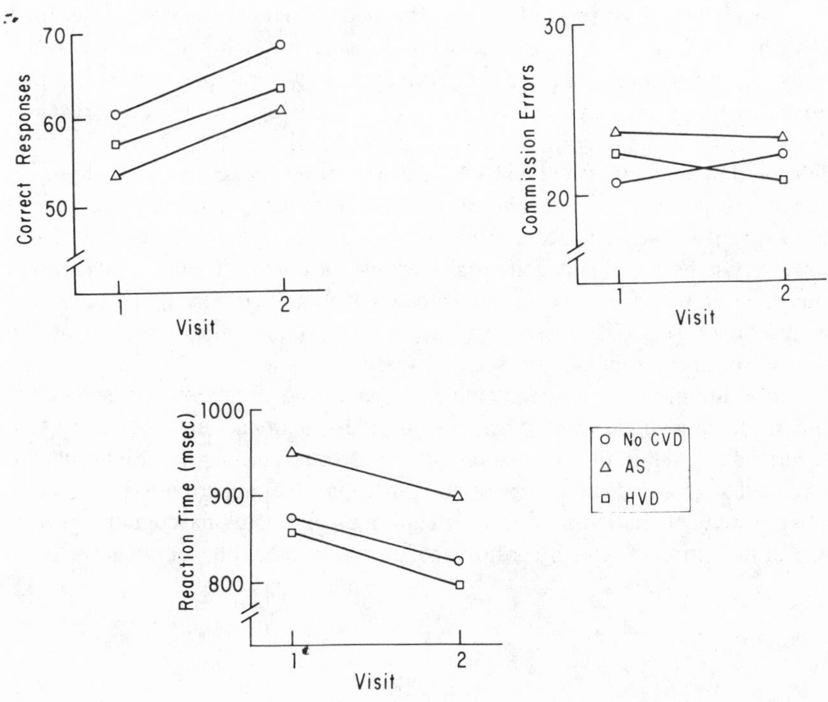

healthy individuals, perhaps differences in CPT performance would have been more striking between groups. Moreover, the relatively healthy state of this population posed a problem by generating a pronounced inequality in the size of the various cardiovascular disease groups. The two disease groups were quite small in number as compared to the group defined as free of cardiovascular disease. The difference in size between the groups could possibly confound statistical evaluation. To evaluate the effect produced by the unequal group sizes, secondary analyses were performed in which each member of the two disease groups was matched by age and sex with one disease-free individual. With group sizes then rendered approximately equal, between-group differences emerged similar to those just reported. Statistical evaluation turned up the same patterns of statistical significance.

A second issue raised by this report pertains to the criteria employed to define atherosclerosis. There is an underlying tacit assumption that electrocardiographic changes associated with coronary artery atherosclerosis also reflect a more generalized vascular involvement with this disease process. Presumably, if the coronary arteries are compromised by atherosclerosis to the extent of producing electrocardiographic change, then other areas of arterial vasculature would likely be similarly involved. Relevant to this report, one would assume cerebrovascular involvement as well as that of the coronary arteries. Such a notion is generally supported by clinical and pathologic observation.

These data which reflect CPT performance seem to corroborate earlier findings which indicate that, for middle-aged and elderly individuals, cardiovascular status is pertinent to cognitive task performance. In general, performance of cognitive work appears impaired among individuals with cardiovascular disease. Moreover, these data permit speculation as to the nature of such a relationship. One could maintain that the two CPT measures, number of correct responses and length of response time, reflect degree of attention to the task at hand. Presence of cardiovascular disease appears to be associated with partial impairment of this capacity. On the other hand, commission errors, the third CPT behavioral measure considered in this report, reflect not so much degree of attentiveness as criterion for response. This CPT response measure seems minimally influenced by the presence or absence of cardiovascular disease.

In addition, this study clearly indicates that cardiovascular disease should not be considered a single entity when one considers its impact upon cognitive task performance. Within this population, atherosclerotic vascular disease appears to be related to greater decrement in performance than does hypertension. Certainly, in future study of relationships between cardiovascular status and cognitive performance, definition of type of cardiovascular disease should be a critical factor.

References

Birren, J. E. Age changes in speed of behavior: Its central nature and physiological correlates. In A. T. Welford and J. E. Birren (Eds.), *Behavior, aging, and the nervous system*. Springfield, Ill.: Charles C. Thomas, 1965.

Birren, J. E., Woods, A. M., and Williams, M. V. Behavioral slowing with age: Causes, organization, and consequences. In L. W. Poon (Ed.), *Aging in the 1980s: Psychological issues*. Washington, D.C.: American Psychological Association, 1980.

Botwinick, J., and Storandt, M. Cardiovascular status, depressive affect and other factors in reaction time. *Journal of Gerontology*, 29:543–548, 1974.

Eisdorfer, C. E., and Wilkie, F. L. Stress, disease, aging and behavior. In J. E. Birren and K. W. Schaie (Eds.), *Handbook of the psychology of aging*. New York: Van Nostrand Reinhold, 1977.

Harkins, S. W., et al. Effects of age, sex, and time-on-watch on a brief continuous performance task. In Palmore, E. B. (Ed.), *Normal aging II*. Durham, N.C.: Duke University Press, 1974.

Hertzog, C., Schaie, K. W., and Gribbin, K. Cardiovascular disease and change in intellectual functioning from middle to old age. *Journal of Gerontology*, 33:872–883, 1978.

Speith, W. Slowness of task performance and cardiovascular disease. In W. T. Welford and J. E. Birren (Eds.), *Behavior, aging, and the nervous system*. Springfield, Ill.: Charles C Thomas, 1965.

Cardiovascular Disease, Intellectual Function, and Personality

Ilene Siegler and John B. Nowlin

The relationship between cardiovascular disease and psychological function has long been a focus of gerontologic research. Speith (1965) suggested an association between cardiovascular disease and cognitive performance decrement among an older population evaluated in a cross-sectional design. Data collected from the Duke First Longitudinal Study population indicated that more pronounced levels of hypertension were related to intellectual decline (as measured by the Wechsler Adult Intelligence Scale—WAIS), while less severe hypertension was associated with maintenance of intellectual function in later life (Wilkie and Eisdorfer, 1971, 1974). Light (1975, 1978) cites findings indicating that hypertension might exert a less baneful effect upon cognitive function than atherosclerosis. Hertzog et al., (1978) evaluated the impact of cardiovascular disease upon intellectual function, highlighting the importance of dealing with effects of mortality when interpreting longitudinal data collected among older persons. Possible links between personality traits and occurrence of major atherosclerotic disease events such as myocardial infarction are well recognized, at least among middle-aged men (Jenkins et al., 1974). Also, earlier work with the second longitudinal study (Nowlin et al., 1973) demonstrated that not only more elevated first visit systolic blood pressure, higher serum cholesterol, and lower resting heart rate, but also higher anxiety (as measured by Cattell Primary Order Factor 0), was predictive of heart attack occurrence in men.

Taking advantage of the extensive health assessment available from second longitudinal study participants, the present report describes the effects of cardiovascular disease or intellectual function and personality factors.

Methods

Subjects. The population under study was selected from the 375 second longitudinal study participants who had full data available at all four rounds of study. Previous analysis of personality predictors (Rusin and Siegler, 1985) suggest that the dropout and deceased groups differed from the long-term survivors only in that the former were more anxious. Only subjects with complete information on cardiovascular status, intellectual function, and personality status were included in the present analyses.

Hypertension and atherosclerosis. Presence of hypertension was defined as participant self-report of this disease at three of four visits. A diagnosis of atherosclerosis was based upon consistent electrocardiographic evidence of coronary heart disease. Individuals with electrocardiographic evidence of coronary heart disease at three of four visits were included within the atherosclerotic group. Participants who met the criteria for both hypertension and atherosclerosis were put in a fourth group. Participants with either hypertension or coronary heart disease at only one or two of the possible four occasions were defined as an inconsistent subgroup. Because of the ambiguous nature of their cardiovascular status, these individuals were not included in this analysis. For more detail regarding assignment to the cardiovascular disease status groups, the reader is referred to the previous paper by Nowlin and Siegler in this section. Final group sizes were: (1) individuals with no evidence of cardiovascular disease, $N = 120$; (2) individuals with hypertension alone, $N = 18$; (3) individuals with atherosclerosis alone, $N = 22$; and (4) individuals with both hypertension and atherosclerosis, $N = 7$.

Intellectual function and personality. Intellectual function was assessed by weighting the scores of four subtests from the Wechsler Adult Intelligence Scale (verbal = 3 times sum of vocabulary and information; performance = 2.5 times sum of picture arrangement and digit symbol; Wechsler, 1958). Personality was assessed by two second-order factors derived from the Form C Cattell 16 Personality Factor (16 PF) questionnaire: Q_I (introversion-extroversion) and Q_{II} (anxiety-adjustment) (Cattell et al., 1970).

Results

Group means for the dependent variables are presented in table A—15. For evaluation of associations, a repeated-measures analysis of variance was employed.

The specific format of statistical analysis was a multifactorial, multivariate repeated-measure analysis of variance (the University of Rochester Weighted ANOVA System). The independent variable was cardiovascular disease status. Hypertensives had slightly higher total WAIS scores than the other CVD groups. However, as determined by the repeated-measures analysis of variance, this main effect proved statistically insignificant ($p = .22$). Likewise, no between-group differences were apparent for WAIS verbal scores. The influence of CVD is most apparent on the WAIS performance scores; those with no cardiovascular disease and those with only hypertension had higher scores than the atherosclerotic groups ($p = <.05$).

Over the three retest sessions, there were slight improvements in scores for the total and verbal WAIS scores (table A—16). These changes were statistically significant ($p = <.0001$). Performance WAIS values were fairly stable throughout the retest sessions and presented no statistically significant changes ($p = .06$).

Differences between CVD groups in WAIS change over time would be of special interest. However, none of these differences was statistically significant.

Table A—15. *Mean WAIS and personality scores for CVD status groups.**

	No CVD (N = 120)	HVD (N = 18)	AS (N = 22)	HAS (N = 7)
Total WAIS	112.8 (26.4)**	123.2 (23.6)	104.7 (23.0)	115.6 (23.1)
Verbal WAIS	70.3 (17.6)	76.7 (17.2)	66.8 (17.9)	75.3 (21.2)
Performance WAIS	42.6 (11.3)	46.5 (9.6)	37.9 (8.0)	40.3 (11.8)
Extroversion	4.6 (1.5)	5.9 (1.9)	4.6 (1.8)	4.4 (1.2)
Anxiety	5.6 (1.5)	6.0 (1.7)	5.9 (1.5)	6.3 (1.9)

*Values cited are those averaged over the four subject visits.

**Standard deviations are in parentheses.

Table A—16. *Mean WAIS and personality scores by round.*

	Round 1	Round 2	Round 3	Round 4
Total WAIS	109.2 (25.5)*	113.3 (26.0)	115.2 (26.7)	114.3 (27.0)
Verbal WAIS	67.9 (17.4)	71.0 (17.6)	72.0 (18.1)	72.1 (18.3)
Performance WAIS	41.3 (10.5)	42.4 (11.2)	43.3 (11.1)	42.2 (11.0)
Extroversion	4.8 (1.5)	4.7 (1.8)	4.7 (1.6)	4.7 (1.6)
Anxiety	5.7 (1.5)	5.8 (1.5)	5.7 (1.6)	5.8 (1.5)

*Standard deviations are in parentheses.

The personality factor, introversion-extroversion, was significantly higher in the hypertensive group than in the others. There was no significant differences in introversion-extroversion between the other three groups. There was no significant change over time, nor was change over time in this factor influenced by cardiovascular disease status.

The anxiety-adjustment factor also showed no significant differences between groups, no significant changes, and no significant differences between groups in amount of change.

Discussion

The sample used in this analysis is a select one because it included only participants present at all four rounds. The dropout phenomenon, a problem in all longitudinal studies, is generally associated with poorer health status and more psychologic dysfunction (Rusin and Siegler, 1985). Nevertheless, this sample provided two strong advantages: (1) a more careful delineation of cardiovascular disease, status and (2) measurement of change over three intervals. Since consistency over time is often necessary to establish presence or absence of cardiovascular disease, the four biennial sets of health data available in this sample make for a more accurate assessment of these illnesses.

Birren et al. (1965, 1980) attribute much of the decline in cognitive behavior to a slowing of central nervous system (CNS) function; moreover, they consider this slowing to be a primary process in aging. There exists an impressive array of evidence to support such a contention, well summarized by those authors (Birren et al., 1980). However, this theory is somewhat confounded by the high prevalence among older individuals of cardiovascular disease (i.e., hypertension and generalized atherosclerotic arterial disease). The generalized involvement of the arterial vascular system, characteristic of these disease entities, raises the possibility that an impediment of blood flow to key CNS structures might play an important role in the decline of cognitive function. A minimal hypotheses would propose at least some degree of interaction between an intrinsic aging influence upon cognition and that superimposed by coincident vascular disease.

The data presented in this report indicate that older individuals with cardiovascular disease present evidence of decline in intellectual function when compared to their disease-free age peers. As suggested by Birren et al. (1980), such a decline is more evident in testing situations where speed of response is involved. The WAIS performance subtests are examples of this type of cognitive testing. The actual role played by cardiovascular disease in the older person's cognitive performance decrement is ambiguous; these data cannot indicate whether the phenomenon is primary or simply additive to the normal aging process. Greater decline in WAIS scores over the six years among the disease group would have implied a more primary role for cardiovascular disease. However, with results similar to those recorded by Hertzog et al. (1978), the present study found no significant differences in changes among groups defined on the basis of cardiovascular disease.

The introversion-extroversion factor also reflects some impact of cardiovascular disease status. The hypertensive older individuals had higher scores on this factor than did either older persons without evidence of cardiovascular disease or those with atherosclerosis. The outgoing, striving nature of the hypertensive individual has drawn frequent comment in the past; the current finding seems to indicate that this trait persists into late middle age.

In most previous research on the relationship between cardiovascular disease and psychological functioning, vascular illness has been treated as a single entity (for example, Hertzog et al., 1978). Pathophysiologically, hypertension and atherosclerosis are quite different illnesses, even though there is often some interplay between the two. Findings from this study suggest some differential effects of hypertension and atherosclerosis upon psychological functioning. The highest WAIS scores were found among hypertensives, while the lowest were noted among individuals defined as having atherosclerosis. Future investigators of the interaction between cardiovascular disease and psychological function would be well advised to make a clear distinction between these two most common forms of vascular illness.

References

Birren, J. E. Age changes in speed of behavior: Its central nature and physiological correlates. In A. T. Welford and J. E. Birren (Eds.), *Behavior, aging, and the nervous system*. Springfield, Ill.: Charles C. Thomas, 1965, 191–216.

Birren, J. E., Woods, A. M., and Williams, M. V. Behavioral slowing with age: Causes, organization, and consequences. In L. W. Poon (Ed.), *Aging in the 1980s: Psychological issues*. Washington, D.C.: American Psychological Association, 1980.

Cattell, R., et al. *Handbook for the 16 personality factor questionnaire*. Champaign, Ill.: Institute for Personality, 1970.

Hertzog, C., Schaie, K. W., and Gribbin, K. Cardiovascular disease and change in intellectual functioning from middle to old age. *Journal of Gerontology*, 33:872–883, 1978.

Jenkins, C. D., Rosenman, F. H., and Zyzanski, S. J. Predictions of clinical coronary heart disease by a test for the coronary prone behavior pattern. *New England Journal of Medicine*, 290: 1271–1275, 1974.

Light, K. C. Slowing of response time in young and middle-aged hypertensive patients. *Experimental Aging Research*, 1:209–227, 1975.

Light, K. C. Effects of mild cardiovascular and mild cerebrovascular disorders on serial reaction time performance. *Experimental Aging Research*, 4:3–22, 1978.

Nowlin, J. B., Williams, R., and Wilkie, F. Prospective study of physical and psychologic factors in elderly men who subsequently suffer acute myocardial infarction. *Clinical Research*, 21:465, 1973.

Russin, M., and Siegler, I. Personality, dropout, and death. In this volume, 1985.

Speith, W. Slowness of task performance and cardiovascular disease. In A. T. Welford and J. E. Birren (Eds.), *Behavior, aging and the nervous system*. Springfield, Ill.: Charles C. Thomas, 1965.

Wechsler, D. *The measurement and appraisal of adult intelligence*. 4th ed. Baltimore: Williams & Wilkins, 1958.

Wilkie, F., and Eisdorfer, C. E. Intelligence and blood pressure in the aged. *Science*, 172:959–962, 1971.

Wilkie, F., and Eisdorfer, C. E. Intelligence and blood pressure in the aged. In Palmore, E. B. (Ed.), *Normal aging II*, Durham, N.C.: Duke University Press, 1974.

Vibratory Threshold and Health

John B. Nowlin, Alan D. Whanger, and William D. Cleveland, Jr.

The aging process has been often associated with decline in acuity of peripheral sensation (Kenshalo, 1977). With the advent of instrumentation that makes possible quantitative appraisal of a modality such as vibratory sense, the potential interrelationships between aging, individual characteristics, and peripheral sensory decrement have become more accessible to scrutiny. With regard to vibratory sense, qualitative evaluation with use of the tuning fork had frequently documented a relationship between aging and decline in that peripheral sensory modality. Moreover, the age-related decrement in vibratory sense was recognized as more prominent in the lower extremities (Calne and Pallis, 1966; Skre, 1972; Kenshalo, 1977). Using quantitative measuring techniques, which permit a more precise definition of this sensory modality in terms of numeric threshold values, these earlier findings have been often reaffirmed (Steiness, 1957a; Rosenberg, 1958; Perret and Regli, 1970; Whanger and Wang, 1974; Nielsen, 1972; Daniel et al., 1977). Generally, however, quantitative assessments of vibratory sense, among groups of all ages, have been small in number; only now are other attributes of this sensory modality coming to light. Between-sex differences, not earlier appreciated, have been detected, with women presenting more acute vibratory sense than men, at least in the lower extremities (Nielsen, 1972). Whanger and Wang (1974), appraising a population of older hospitalized psychiatric patients, reported a racial difference: blacks presented higher vibratory sense in the lower extremities as compared to whites.

To date, there have been no follow-up vibrometry measurements among older individuals; earlier appraisal of age-related change in vibratory sense was exclusively cross-sectional in nature. Specifically, follow-up evaluation can provide an estimate both of extent of time-related change in this modality and degree of stability in the between-extremity and between-sex differences previously observed. Moreover, since some degree of health compromise is commonplace among older individuals, it seems logical to propose that physiological impairment might bear some relationship to the well-established age-associated decline in vibratory sense. This report examines these issues, employing quantitative vibratory threshold data and health information collected from a large middle-aged and older population with a two year follow-up.

Materials and Methods

Study population. Vibratory threshold values were recorded during a longitudinal study of aging sponsored by the Duke Center for the Study of Aging and Human Development (Duke Second Longitudinal Study). Vibratory threshold data were collected at the third and fourth return visits (1972–76). Only participants who were present at both visits with valid vibratory threshold data (i.e., vibratory threshold values from all of the four measurement sites to be described later), were included in data analysis. Also, those individuals with known diabetes or neurologic illness were excluded from consideration. All told, 320 persons made up the vibratory threshold group, 172 men and 148 women. The average age of the group under study was sixty-two years at the first vibratory threshold testing session.

Vibratory threshold recording. An estimate of vibratory threshold was provided by use of the Biothesiometer (Biomedical Instrument Company, Chagrin Falls, Ohio), an instrument that provides vibration to the body surface by a tactor button one cm in diameter. Vibratory frequency was delivered at a constant 120 hz; the amplitude of vibration was controlled by a manually operated rheostat. Vibratory sense was recorded bilaterally at the styloid process of the wrist and at the tibial plateaux immediately below the knees. In determining vibratory threshold, the instrument is held in such a manner as to permit it to rest on the recording site on its own weight. Recordings were made in the ascending mode; that is, the rheostat was initially set at zero, then gradually increased until the participant reported perception of vibration. In this manner, a vibratory threshold was determined. Each testing site was appraised three times; vibratory threshold for each site was an average of these three readings. With variation between any of the three readings of greater than 20 percent, no value was reported for that measurement area. Measurement values are reported in terms of micra of motion presented to each recording area.

Measurement of vibratory threshold in the lower extremities posed a problem of potential bias among older members of the study population. Even with the vibratory source set at maximal amplitude, a number of participants reported no perception of vibration in the lower extremity. These individuals, numbering twenty-six, were assigned a maximum vibratory threshold score (27.25 micra). Such an artifact introduces the possibility of ceiling effect when evaluating the response of those older individuals.

Health variables. A number of biomedical parameters were selected to evaluate the potential relationship between health factors and vibratory threshold within this middle-aged and older population. These health-related measures represent values found coincident with determinations of vibratory threshold at the third and fourth second longitudinal study visits. Measures related to these threshold values include first chronological age then sex. Another factor evaluated was that of adiposity as reflected by the Quetelet Index—that is, the weight divided by the square of height. There has been some speculation that fatty tissue might muffle vibratory sense (Calne and Pallis, 1966). Used as still another correlate with vibratory threshold was an overall physician health rating of each study participant, with a graduated scale ranging from 1–9; higher scores represent increasing compromise of health. Study participants were so rated by the examining physician on the basis of both physical examination and laboratory findings. In the past, the age-associated decrement in vibratory sense has been attributed, in part, to coincident occurrence of cardiovascular disease (Rosenberg, 1958; Magladery, 1959). A number of variables reflecting cardiovascular function were therefore considered in this evaluation. First, an estimate of extent of cardiovascular disease, as rated by the examining physician, was included as one factor. In a fashion similar to the overall health rating just mentioned, there was a 0–9 rating scale, with higher scores corresponding to more evidence of cardiovascular disease. Likewise, systolic and diastolic blood pressures and serum cholesterol levels were considered as potential cardiovascular correlates with vibratory threshold. Since the blood glucose level in diabetes mellitus can be often related to presence or absence of peripheral neuropathy, fasting blood sugar values were examined among this nondiabetic group for any potential relationship to vibratory threshold. Previous assessment of vibratory threshold among diabetics has indicated that only duration, not severity, of illness has a relationship to decrease in this modality (Steiness, 1957b); however, there was no attempt to correlate blood sugar directly with vibratory threshold values. Decrease in renal function has been demonstrated to be associated with decreased vibratory sense (Nielsen, 1974; Daniel et al., 1977). Hence, blood urea nitrogen level, as a reflection of renal status, is included as a correlate. Finally, Whanger and Wang's study clearly implicates Vitamin B-12, folic acid, deficiency as a potential contributor to vibratory sense decrease within their institutionalized elderly population (Whanger and Wang, 1974). Hemoglobin level, as a rough index of such a deficiency, is examined for its relationship to vibratory threshold.

Results

Mean vibratory threshold values for both extremities at the two times of measurement are presented in figure A—5; the population is grouped on the basis of five-year categories as defined at the time of the first vibratory threshold assessment. The long recognized between-extremity difference in vibratory threshold is evident. Also apparent is the lower vibratory threshold among younger age groups as compared to older. These relationships were clear cut at both threshold assessments, two years apart. A slight, but consistent, increment in vibratory threshold is also evident over the two year between-test intervals. Moreover, between-sex differences are also apparent for upper and lower extremities; as

Table A—17. *Repeated-measures analysis of variance: vibratory threshold.*

	df	*F*-value	Significance level
Age group	4	22.9	$p < .0001$
Sex	1	11.7	$p < .001$
Extremity	1	141.5	$p < .0001$
Time	1	71.0	$p < .0001$
Age group * sex	4	1.2	$p =$ ns
Age group * extremity	4	92.3	$p < .0001$
Age group * time	4	0.0	$p =$ ns
Sex * extremity	1	26.1	$p < .0001$
Sex * time	1	0.4	$p =$ ns
Extremity * time	1	21.3	$p < .0001$

Note: Analysis of variance factors include: Age group (based upon 5-year categories at time of first VT measurement), extremity (upper and lower), sex groups, and times of measurement. Only analysis of variance main effects, first-order interactions are presented. All higher order interactions are statistically nonsignificant.

shown in figure A—5, men demonstrated higher vibratory threshold than did women. Also, the between-extremity differences were less among women than men. These relationships likewise held over the pair of testing occasions two years apart.

These relationships and potential interactions were evaluated in a repeated-measures analysis of variance (ANOVA) for vibratory threshold with visit, extremity (upper and lower), sex, and five-year age category serving as factors. Results are presented in table A—17. Vibratory threshold differed in statistically

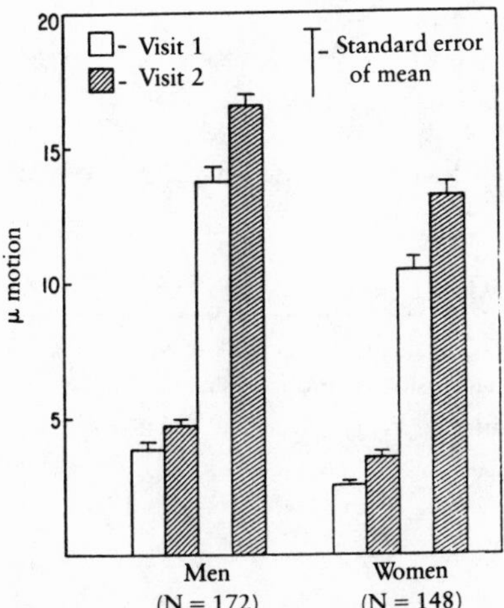

Figure A—5. Mean vibratory threshold by sex, visit.

Table A—18. *Health variable means, standard deviations, and first-order correlations with vibratory threshold (VT).*

	Mean	Std. dev.	Upper extremity VT correlations	Lower extremity VT correlations
Age	62.0	7.0	.43	.45
	(64.0)	(7.0)	(.32)	(.49)
Sex*			−.32	−.23
			(−.24)	(−.25)
Physician health rating	1.8	0.7	.11	.21
	(1.9)	(0.7)	(.32)	(.30)
Cardiovascular disease rating	0.34	0.7	.32	.21
	(0.39)	(0.7)	(.26)	(.20)
Quetelet Index	25.3	3.1	.13	.07
	(25.4)	(3.8)	(.11)	(.13)
Systolic blood pressure mmHg	135.5	21.4	.17	.16
	(131.6)	(18.6)	(.18)	(.20)
Diastolic blood pressure mmHg	75.9	12.4	.04	−.02
	(72.0)	(11.8)	(.02)	(.00)
Serum cholesterol (mgm %)	234.7	46.1	−.08	−.03
	(248.1)	(44.3)	(−.13)	(.00)
Blood urea nitrogen (mgm %)	15.6	5.6	.12	.19
	(16.4)	(4.8)	(.13)	(.18)
Fasting blood sugar (mgm %)	97.1	28.2	.18	.07
	(105.1)	(31.3)	(−.02)	(.02)
Hemoglobin level (gm %)	14.8	1.4	.20	.08
	(14.5)	(1.4)	(.06)	(.09)

Numbers in parentheses indicate second measurement period means, standard deviations, first-order correlations. All correlations are positive unless indicated with a minus sign ("−").

*Sex is used as a "dummy variable" ("1" = males; "2" = females).

$p < .05$: $r = .13$; $p < .01$: $r = .19$; $p < .001$: $r = .31$.

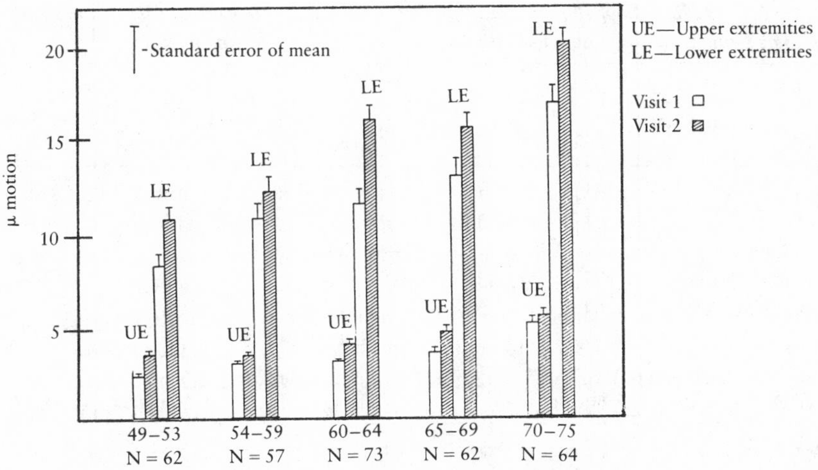

Figure A—6. *Mean vibratory threshold by 5-year age categories, visit.*

significant fashion with respect to all main effects: time, extremity, sex, and five-year age categories. First order ANOVA interactions evaluating the age group-extremity difference (suggested by figure A—6) and the sex-extremity difference (suggested by figure A—6) proved to be statistically significant. The time-extremity interaction factor is also statistically significant, reflecting a greater change among lower extremity threshold values than among upper extremity values over the two-year between-assessment interval.

Potential relationships of vibratory threshold to selected health variables was also evaluated, using correlational techniques. Table A—18 presents means, standard deviations, and the first-order correlation coefficients which reflect the degree of association between health variables and vibratory threshold. Sex was employed as a dummy variable: 1 denoting men and 2 denoting women. Variables presenting a statistically significant correlation (at least at the .05 level of confidence) consistently over time and at each extremity include age, sex, overall physician health rating, physician rating of extent of cardiovascular disease, systolic blood pressure, and blood urea nitrogen level.

Since the health variables correlated with vibratory threshold are themselves highly interrelated, a multiple stepwise regression technique was employed to evaluate the association of health factors with vibratory threshold, independent of any degree of interrelatedness. Results of the multiple regression analyses for each extremity at each testing session are presented in table A—19. These analyses reveal that sex and chronological age are consistently the most potent correlates with vibratory threshold in both extremities at both times of vibratory threshold assessment. Except for the vibratory threshold recorded in the lower extremities at the first testing, more general indicators of health (physician overall health rating, cardiovascular disease status) proved to have the strongest relationship with vibratory threshold.

Table A—19. *Results of stepwise multiple regression analysis with vibratory threshold (VT) as dependent variable and health factors as independent variables.*

Time 1			Time 2		
Upper extremity VT			Upper extremity VT		
Variable	F at entry	R^2	Variable	F at entry	R^2
Age	65.1	.19	Age	30.7	.09
Sex	34.6	.28	Sex	21.7	.15
Cardiovascular disease rating	27.6	.34	Physician health rating	12.9	.18
Quetelet Index	4.2	.35	Cardiovascular disease rating	3.9	.19
Lower extremity VT			Lower extremity VT		
Variable	F at entry	R^2	Variable	F at entry	R^2
Age	64.5	.19	Age	93.7	.23
Sex	26.4	.25	Sex	26.9	.29
Systolic blood pressure	4.9	26	Physician health rating	7.2	.31
Diastolic blood pressure	5.1	.27	Quetelet Index	4.6	.32
Blood urea nitrogen	3.9	.28			

Health variables are reported in order of their entry into the regression analysis. Only variables attaining a significance level of $p < .05$ at entry are included.

A final set of multiple regression analyses were employed to gauge the influence which health variables might have exerted on change in vibratory threshold over the two-year interval between the test sessions. In this instance, all time 1 values (including vibratory threshold, chronological age, sex, and health factors) were considered first en bloc (as so-called forced variables) for their overall relationship to the second vibratory threshold value; time 2 variables entering into the regression analysis after this simultaneous consideration of time 1 values presumably relate to the change in vibratory threshold between the two test occasions. For the upper extremity vibratory threshold, as appraised in this second regression analysis format, only time 2 physician overall health rating was related to the change in vibratory threshold (F-value at entry = 9.7, $p < .01$, R^2 increase from .38 to .41). In the lower extremities, the Quetelet Index entered the regression formula first, after the forced variables (F-value at entry = 6.5, $p < .01$, R^2 increase from .50 to .52) followed by time 2 physician overall health rating (F-value at entry = 5.5, $p < .05$, R^2 increase from .52 to .53), then followed by time 2 cholesterol (F-value at entry = 5.9, $p < .05$, R^2 increase from .53 to .54).

Discussion

Findings from this study are in agreement with those of earlier investigations of vibratory sense. The association of chronological age, as demonstrated in previous cross-sectional analysis, with increasing vibratory threshold is again documented. Likewise, the well-established between-extremity differences in vibratory threshold are apparent among this middle-aged and older population. Previous observations of sex differences in this sensory modality are also corroborated, but with lower vibratory threshold among women noted not only in the lower but also in the upper extremities. The magnitude of sex differences, while consistent, is small and probably evident only when large populations are appraised. The follow-up vibratory thresholds, determined after a two-year interval, present evidence of a slight but statistically significant decline in this modality over time. Moreover, the second set of vibratory threshold measurements indicate consistency in the sex, age, and extremity differences. However, the lack of significant age and sex higher-order interaction with time in a repeated-measures ANOVA suggests that these factors have little bearing on the degree of time-related change.

Not surprisingly, health variables presented substantial first-order correlations with vibratory threshold values. The direction of the relationship was such that evidence of increasing compromise of health factors was associated with increasing vibratory threshold, or decreasing vibratory sense. Moreover, these correlations presented little between-extremity difference. Such a finding is somewhat unexpected; the pronounced between-extremity difference in absolute threshold values would lead to expectation of a differential effect in relationships with health factors. The approximate equivalence of health factor correlations with upper and lower extremity threshold values suggests that common physiological mechanisms are determinants of vibratory sense in both sets of extremities.

The age-related decrement in vibratory sense has been, at least partly, attributed to concurrent atherosclerotic disease (Rosenberg, 1958; Magladery, 1959). In terms of first order correlations, two variables indicative of circulatory system function (cardiovascular disease rating and systolic blood pressure) present consistent statistically significant relationships with vibratory threshold: higher systolic pressure readings and more evidence of cardiovascular disease are accompanied by higher threshold values. Since cardiovascular disease in this age group is likely to be atherosclerotic in nature and since higher systolic pressure readings are likewise commonly found with this disease process, these findings would offer credence to the theory that decreased vibratory threshold attendant to aging is related to associated atherosclerotic vascular disease. A prominent relationship between the cardiovascular disease status and vibratory threshold in the multiple regression analysis statistical format adds more strength to such a contention.

The first-order correlations between blood urea nitrogen, an indicator of kidney function, and decline in vibratory threshold are also noteworthy. Clinicians working in the area of renal dialysis have long found vibratory threshold to be a sensitive reflector of the status of renal function (Nielsen, 1974; Daniel et al, 1977). First-order correlations in this study between blood urea nitrogen and vibratory threshold levels suggest that such a relationship might hold, even in the absence of obvious renal disease. Decrease in vibratory threshold with renal compromise has generally been considered the effect of the disease-related alteration in both intracellular and extracellular electrolyte composition so as to interfere with transmission of nerve impulses generated at vibratory sensors (Nielsen, 1974). The relationship between blood urea nitrogen levels and decreased vibratory threshold in this group might be reflective of very subtle electrolyte composition shifts with secondary damping of efferent impulses from vibratory sensors. Unfortunately, specific determination of serum electrolyte levels was not available in this population.

Within the multiple regression statistical format, age and sex assumed major importance again in the relationship with vibratory threshold in both extremities and at both testing occasions two years apart. The more global health factors tended also to be more associated with absolute vibratory threshold levels than with more specific health parameters. The comparative prominence of the more general health ratings in the regression analysis probably stems from the likelihood that more specific health parameters are themselves constituent determinants of those ratings. The multiple regression analysis examining the two-year change in vibratory threshold confirms the suggestion from the repeated analysis of variance that chronological age and sex are little related to the extent of difference between the two test occasions. Between-testing change in threshold generally seemed more related to global health ratings.

Summary

Vibratory threshold and its relationship to health parameters was examined among 320 white middle-aged and elderly individuals with a two-year follow-up. Within this population, vibratory threshold for both upper and lower extremities increased significantly over the two-year, between-test interval. Between-extremity threshold differences (lower extremity greater than upper extremity) and between-sex threshold differences (men with greater threshold values than women) were consistent at both initial and follow-up testing. First-order correlations between vibratory threshold and health parameters between chronological age, sex, systolic blood pressure, overall physician health rating, cardiovascular disease status, and blood urea nitrogen were statistically significant in both upper and lower extremities at both test occasions. Stepwise multiple regression revealed age and sex as consistent correlates with upper and lower extremity threshold values, along with medical parameters reflecting more global health functions. In a separate stepwise multiple regression to estimate influences upon over-time change, the more general health indicators again proved to be the most potent correlates.

References

Calne, D. B., and Pallis, C. A. Vibratory sense: A critical review. *Brain*, 89:723–746, 1966.

Daniel, C. R., III, et al. Vibrometry and uremic peripheral neuropathy. *Southern Medical Journal*, 70:1311–1313, 1977.

Kenshalo, D. R. Age changes in touch, vibration, temperature, kinesthesis, and pain sensitivity. In J. E. Birren and K. W. Schaie (Eds.), *Handbook of the psychology of aging*. New York: Van Nostrand Reinhold, 1977, 562–579.

Magladery, J. W. Neurophysiology of aging. In J. E. Birren (Ed.), *Handbook of aging and the individual*. Chicago: University of Chicago Press, 1959, 173–186.

Nielsen, V. K. Peripheral nerve function in chronic renal disease IV: An analysis of vibratory perceptive threshold. *Acta Medica Scandinavica*, 191:287–296, 1972.

Nielsen, V. K. The peripheral nerve function in chronic renal failure. *Acta Medica Scandinavica*, 195:155–162, 1974.

Palmore, E. B. (Ed.), *Normal aging II*. Durham, N.C.: Duke University Press, 1974, 258.

Perret, E., and Regli, C. Age and perceptual threshold for vibratory stimuli. *European Neurology*, 4:65–76, 1970.

Rosenberg, G. Effect of age on peripheral vibratory sensation. *Journal of the American Geriatrics Society*, 6:471–481, 1958.

Skre, H. Neurological signs in a normal population. *Acta Neurologica Scandinavica*, 48:575–606, 1972.

Steiness, I. Vibratory perception in normal subjects. *Acta Medica Scandinavica*, 158:315–325, 1957a.

Steiness, I. Vibratory perception in diabetics. *Acta Medica Scandinavica*, 158:327–335, 1957b.

Whanger, A. D., and Wang, H. S. Clinical correlates of the vibratory sense in elderly psychiatric patients. *Journal of Gerontology*, 29:39–45, 1974.

Serum B_{1A} Levels in Older Humans

James Thompson and C. Edward Buckley, III

Although altered immune function is thought to have a role in the aging process (Walford, 1969), relatively little attention has been directed toward immune mechanisms which might lead to age-dependent deterioration of physiological function. Complement-fixing antibodies to infectious agents are decreased (Schwick and Becker, 1969) and autoantibodies increased in serums from older humans (Svec and Veit, 1967). Complement-fixing antibodies activate complement, a powerful accessory system responsible for immunological injury. In addition to

Reprinted by permission from *Journal of Gerontology*, 28:434–440, 1973.

its role in the elimination of foreign antigens, complement can participate in autoaggressive tissue destruction. The complement system is composed of nine different serum proteins and at least three inhibitors or inactivator proteins (Muller-Eberhard, 1969). Complement can be activated by the action of complement-fixing antibodies on the first component of the system. In addition, the complement system can be nonspecifically activated through the properdin pathway (Mayer and Nelson, 1971) by foreign natural products such as endotoxins. The third discovered complement component, C3, is a key component of the system. C3 is the fourth component activated by antigen-antibody complexes, but it can also be activated directly by the shunt pathway. Therefore, serum C3 concentrations provide a measure of the specific and nonspecific destructive capacity of the complement system in aging subjects.

C3 levels can be measured immunochemically as the serum B_{1C}/B_{1A} antigen. The active form of C3 in blood is called B_{1C} antigen. Activation of the complement system results in conversion of B_{1C} to an inactive electrophoretically different form of the same molecule, which is called B_{1A} (Muller-Eberhard, 1969). Serum C3 concentrations correlate closely with the hemolytic complement activity of fresh serum (Klemperer et al., 1965; West et al., 1965). We identified sources of technical and analytical error in the use of single radial diffusion measurements of B_{1A}. An optimal method was identified and used to quantify B_{1A} levels in sera from 129 apparently healthy subjects aged twenty to ninety years. Changes observed were interpreted in relation to serum immunoglobulin levels measured in the same subjects (Buckley and Dorsey, 1970) in order to deduce whether or not the C3 component of the complement system might limit the function of the immune system in order persons.

Materials and Methods

Serum was obtained from apparently healthy volunteers. These included older persons followed periodically by the Duke University Center for the Study of Aging and Human Development, professional and paramedical hospital personnel, and blood donors to the Duke Medical Center blood bank. Serum was separated within one hour of phlebotomy and aliquots stored at $-20°$ C. or $4°$ C. during periods of analysis. Sera studied were stored not longer than five years and no less than one year before immunochemical determinations of B_{1A} levels.

Single radial diffusion. Serum concentrations of B_{1A} were measured by single radial diffusion (Fahey and McKelvey, 1965; Mancini et al., 1965) using commercially prepared antibody-agar plates and standards (Hyland Laboratories, 3300 Hyland Ave., Box 2214, Costa Mesa, Calif.). Antigen wells were loaded with 5 ± 0.12 of serum with a microliter pipette (Eppendorf pipette, Brinkmann Instruments Inc., Cantiague Rd., Westbury, N.Y.). Equilibrium time for the development of maximum ring size was determined in preliminary experiments and found to be twenty-eight hours with a serum reference standard containing 2.8 mg/ml B_{1A} (Hyland Laboratories, 3300 Hyland Ave., Box 2214, Costa Mesa, Calif.). Precipitin rings in all antibody-agar plates were measured at thirty hours. Diffusion diameters were measured on the moist agar gel plate in two perpendicular directions with a comparator microscope (Nikon microscope, Preiser Scientific Co., S. Miami Blvd., Durham, N.C.) having a precision of $\pm$ 0.002 mm. The area of the precipitin ring was calculated from the average of measured diameters. Concentrations of B_{1A} in unknown sera were determined by computation from a least-squares regression of the known concentrations and areas observed with dilutions of the reference standard (Hyland Laboratories, 3300 Hyland Ave., Box 2214, Costa Mesa, Calif.). All comparisons were accomplished with a small programmable calculating machine (Wang Laboratories Inc., Tewksbury, Mass.). Sera yielding ring diameters in excess of the diameter of undiluted reference standard were diluted to one-half strength prior to quantitation.

Correlated serum levels of IgG, IgA, and IgM were measured by single radical diffusion and have been previously reported (Buckley and Dorsey, 1970). The hemolytic activity of complement was assayed by a semimicro method described and used in prior studies (Dowell and Buckley, 1970).

Statistical analyses were by methods detailed by Mather (1947) and by multivariate analysis (Starmer and Grizzle, 1968).

Results

Sources of analytical variation. The analytical precision of single radial diffusion was evaluated in a series of experiments designed to measure variation associated with various technical components of the method. Table A—21 presents an example of one of these experiments. An analysis of variance suggests variation due to pipetting error was twice the standard error of estimate of the experiment. Analytical precision was not limited by the reproducibility with which precipitate diameters could be measured with a comparator microscope. Differences between measurements made on the same precipitate ring in two directions ninety degrees apart resulted in variation quantitatively similar to the standard error of estimate of the experiment (table A—20).

In similar experiments, variation associated with replicate pipetting ranged up to 4.4 percent of total variation and was dependent upon the care with which the automatic pipette was used to load serum in the agar wells. When larger serum wells were punched over those in the commercial agar plate, the standard error of estimate increased threefold and variation related to differences in the direction in which the precipitating ring was measured increased ninefold. Analytical variation resulting from measurements of the same serum sample on different plates or on different rows of the same antibody agar plates was similar to the standard error of estimate. However, when measurements were made on the same serum sample on different days of the same plate (i.e., radial diffusion of

Table A—20. *Analysis of sources of variation in measurement of serum* B_{IC}/B_{IA} *concentrations.*

B_{IC}/B_{IA} concentration mg/ml	Replicate pipetting	Direction of measurement: Horizontal, Readings first	Horizontal, Readings second	Vertical, Readings first	Vertical, Readings second
		mm			
50	First	4,372	4,357	4,295	4,289
	Second	4,411	4,391	4,361	4,363
140	First	5,795	5,795	5,742	5,745
	Second	5,745	5,754	5,673	5,685
280	First	7,354	7,361	7,432	7,429
	Second	7,236	7,248	7,257	7,250

Analysis of variance

Treatment	Sum of squares	F	Mean square	Variance ratio	$p <$	Variation SD	Variation %
Concentrations	35.237904	2	17.618952	5600.1330	0.01	±4.197	70.4
Pipettings	0.014602	1	0.014602	4.6413	0.05	±0.120	2.0
Directions	0.003700	1	0.003700	1.1760	n.s.	±0.060	1.0
Readings	0.000001	1	0.000001	0.0004	n.s.	±0.001	<0.1
Error	0.056631	18	0.003146			±0.056	0.9
Total	35.312839	23					

Note: Immunoplate human complement C3 test (Control No. 7051MO25A1), Hyland Division, Travenol Laboratories, Inc., Los Angeles, Calif. 90039.

antigen in an unknown serum on a previously partially used plate without simultaneous assay of an appropriate reference standard) observed variation was almost four times as great as the standard error of estimate.

These preliminary experiments indicate that carefully pipetted replicate samples of serum can be used to measure B_{1A} with a precision of ± 1.3 percent. Replicate measurements are necessary; the precision of a single measurement was ± 2.8 percent. When unknown and standards were not measured simultaneously, the precision of the method was ± 6.8 percent.

Differences related to conversion of B_{IC} *to* B_{IA}. Only B_{1A} is found in sera stored beyond several months. Since it is possible to compare observations of B_{1A} with similar measurements made on fresh sera, we evaluated apparent differences in C3 concentration in plasma and serum during conditions equivalent to the analytical manipulation and trivial activation of the complement system. Conversion of the B_{1C} form of C3 to B_{1A} is expected during activation of the complement system. Quantities of minimally sensitized sheep red blood cells were used (one to five H_{50} units of hemolysin per 1.67×10^8 cells). When equal volumes of cells and aliquots of fresh serum were mixed and maintained at 37° C. for varying periods of time, hemolytic complement activity decreased. Table A—21 presents the results of an experiment of this type. Replicate measurements of plasma separated from blood and diluted with an equal volume of sensitized sheep red blood cells yielded a precipitin diameter equivalent to 1.26 mg/ml. Fresh serum obtained from the same phlebotomy diluted with an equal volume of buffer and also maintained at 4° C. for three hours had 31.1 CH_{50} of hemolytic complement activity but only 0.90 mg/ml measurable antigen. Serum maintained three hours at 4° C. in a water bath with an equal volume of sensitized sheep cells had 27.4 CH_{50} units of complement and 1.05 mg/ml of measurable B_{1C}/B_{1A}. Similarly prepared replicate tubes were transferred to a 37° C. water bath at 0, 30, 60, 90, 120, and 150 minutes after initiation of the experiment. All estimates of B_{1C}/B_{1A} and hemolytic complement activity were made at the end of the experiment. Table A—21 shows a 3.7 CH_{50} unit decrease in complement activity associated with activation of complement at 4° C. and a further 5.2 CH_{50} unit decrease in hemolytic activity over the three-hour period of incubation. The apparent concentration of B_{1C}/B_{1A} during this period of marginal activation of the complement system decreased and then increased slightly. B_{1C}/B_{1A} levels measured after three hours of incubation at 37° C. were equivalent to those measured in the same serum incubated at 4° C. with antibody-coated red cells.

Age-dependent normal variation. Figure A—7 presents the cumulative frequency distribution of B_{1A} levels in 129 apparently healthy adults. The probit (Mather, 1947) derived from this distribution of subjects was regressed, first against measured B_{1A} concentrations and then against the log of B_{1A} concentrations. The standard error of the slope of the geometric distribution was 2.8-fold

Table A—21. *Variation in measurable* B_{IC}/B_{IA} *induced by trivial activation of the complement system.*

Sequential incubation Times, 4°C	Minutes 37°C	Treatment	Hemolytic activity CH$_{50}$	%	B_{1C}/B_{1A} mg/ml	%
180	0	Buffer control	31.1	100	—	
180	0	EA + EDTA	—		1.26	100
180	0	EA	27.4	88	1.05	83
150	30	EA			1.08	86
120	60	EA	25.6	82	1.05	83
90	90	EA			.98	77
60	120	EA	22.2	71	.96	76
30	150	EA			.99	79
0	180	EA	22.2	71	1.06	84

Note: Equal volumes containing 1.87×10^8 minimally sensitized sheep red blood cells (EA) were added to aliquots of the same fresh serum maintained in a water bath at 4°C. Aliquots were removed to a 37°C. water bath at indicated times, centrifuged at the end of the incubation period, cooled to 4°C., and the treated supernatant serum used for assay of hemolytic complement and B_{1C}/B_{1A}. Values presented represent the average of duplicate measurements. Dried EDTA (ethylendeiaminetetraacetic acid) was used to prepare plasma and retard conversion of B_{1C} to B_{1A}.

greater than the standard error of the slope of the arithmetic progression. This suggests B_{1A} levels in sera of healthy adults are not log normally distributed. The mean B_{1A} concentration was 1.72 mg/ml and the interval bounding 95 percent of all observations was .87 to 2.59 mg/ml. Table A—22 presents the age distribution and numbers of male and female subjects studied in each decade of life along with the age-sex group average B_{1A} concentrations. Age differences were highly significant ($p = 0.0016$). Differences related to sex among all age groups were not significant ($p = 0.1515$), but contrasts based on sex within the fifth and eighth decades of life were significant. Table A—22 presents the average B_{1A} level and standard deviation for all subjects within each decade of adult life.

Serum B_{1A} concentrations reached a maximum in the middle of the seventh decade of life and decreased in the declining years of life. During early adult life, average serum B_{1A} concentrations increased by approximately 0.14 mg/ml per decade from a mean of 1.39 mg/ml in the third decade to a mean of 2.00 mg/ml by the middle of the seventh decade of life. Variation about the mean was slightly greater during early adult life and beyond the seventh decade.

Correlations with antibody globulin levels. Comparisons of serum B_{1A} concentrations and IgG, IgA, and IgM levels in the same subjects yielded the partial correlation matrix presented in table A—23. Serum levels of B_{1A} correlated significantly with levels of IgG and less well with IgA but not with IgM. The correlation between IgA and IgG was greater than with C3, suggesting that this association may account for the apparent relation of IgA levels with C3. High serum levels of C3 are maintained in aging subjects who maintain relatively high levels of IgG, a complement-fixing antibody. Serum levels of C3 were not correlated with levels of IgM, the other complement-fixing antibody found in serum.

Table A—22. *Comparison of age and sex differences in serum* B_{IC}/B_{IA} *levels.*

Age range (years)	No. of subjects Male	Female	B_{1A}/B_{1C}(C3) Male mean	Female mean	Both sexes mean ± S.E.M.
			mg/ml		
20–29	9	11	1.50	1.29	1.39 ± 0.49
30–39	9	9	1.72	1.44	1.59 ± 0.38
40–49**	8	9	2.16	1.51	1.82 ± 0.82
50–59	12	11	1.80	1.70	1.75 ± 0.23
60–69	10	10	2.02	1.98	2.00 ± 0.34
70–79*	6	9	1.65	2.14	1.97 ± 0.48
80–89	8	7	1.80	1.81	1.81 ± 0.33
Age differences $p = 0.0016$					
Sex differences $p = 0.1515$					

Significant within age range univariate contrasts of sex differences: $*p < 0.05$; $**p < 0.005$.

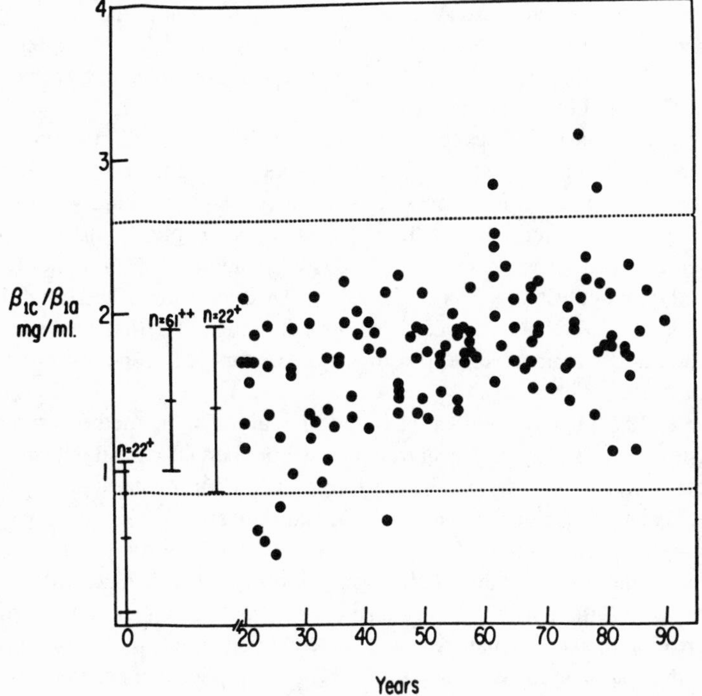

Figure A—7. *The age dependence of observed serum* B_{1C}/B_{1A} *concentrations throughout adult life are shown in relation to estimates of the 95% confidence interval for all adults (dotted line). Note the highly significant age-dependent changes (table A—22). Estimates of serum* B_{1C}/B_{1A} *levels in paired maternal and cord serums (+) derived from the report of Adinolfi (1970) and in children and young adults (++) derived from the studies of West et al. (1965) are presented for comparison.*

Discussion

C3 has been biochemically isolated (Muller-Eberhard et al., 1960) and characterized as a B-migrating plasma molecule called B_{1C}/B_{1A}. C3 is the most abundant component of human plasma (Lundh, 1964) and has a molecular weight of approximately 185,000 daltons (Muller-Eberhard, 1969). The intact B_{1C} molecule contains three distinct antigens, A, B, and D (West et al., 1966). It can be converted to a hemolytically inactive product, C3i, by antigen-antibody complexes treated with the first, fourth, and second components of the complement system (Pondman and Peetoom, 1964). The C3i fragment lacks the B antigenic determinant, but contains a new antigen, Dd, not present on the intact C3 molecule. C3i in serum undergoes further degradation to a B_{1A} protein with the loss of another antigen containing fragment a_2D. The B_{1A} fragment is electrophoretically different from B_{1C} and contains the A antigenic determinant while the a_2D fragment contains the D and Dd fragments (Pondman and Peetoom, 1964). Numerous allotypic antigenic differences in the C3 component of complement have been described (Alper and Prapp, 1968).

These relationships between the molecular and antigenic structure of C3 and its unique correlation with levels of hemolytic complement activity have led to its use in the evaluation of patients with disorders of immunity. Decreased levels have been described in children with hypocomplementemic nephritis (Klemperer et al., 1965; West et al., 1965) and in adults with immune diseases associated with nephritis (Lewis et al., 1971). An assessment of the reliability of measurements of B_{1A} and characterization of the range of serum levels in older healthy adults is also important prior to use of similar measurements in the evaluation of older patients.

Berne (1972) has recently emphasized limitations in the methods suggested for measurement of antigen concentration with commercially available antibody-agar plates. The area of the precipitate formed is proportionate to concentration only after each precipitin ring has reached maximum size. We circumvented this problem by demonstrating no further increase in the area of the precipitate rings of antigen standards under the conditions used to assay B_{1A}. Unknown sera were measured within the concentration range of the standard. Other sources of analytical error were also evaluated. Under the conditions used, pipetting error limited the precision of measurements of B_{1A}. The replicate measurements presented in this report have an expected precision of 1.3 percent. This level of precision compares favorably with $\pm$ 5 percent (Buckley and Dorsey, 1970) level of single radial diffusion measurements made with shorter diffusion times and based on the apparent linear relationship between log concentration and precipitin ring diameter. A fourfold or greater difference in analytical uncertainty may exist between the two techniques—possibly a consequence of the subtle curvature of the relationship between log concentration and diameter when shorter diffusion times are used (Berne, 1972).

West et al. (1965) observed changes in the measurability of C3 during conversion of B_{1C} to B_{1A} and suggested that measurements be made after conversion to B_{1A}. Depletion of antibodies to B_{1A} required 1.8-fold more fresh than aged serum. We evaluated variation in measurability during the process of generation of B_{1A} (table A—21) and found that trivial activation of the complement system could account for 20 percent variation in detectable antigen. This magnitude of change is much greater than the precision of the method. Assay of C3 after conversion to B_{1A}, as suggested by West et al. (1965), provides more reliable measurements. Only sera containing B_{1A} were evaluated in this study. Since serum B_{1A} was less than B_{1C} measured in the same EDTA treated sample, differences related to conversion of C3 to B_{1A} do not provide a reasonable explanation for the higher range of values observed in these studies.

The optimal techniques and diffusion times used to quantify B_{1A} levels in 129 twenty- to ninety-year-old apparently healthy white adult males and females suggested a normal range of 0.87–2.59 mg/ml with a mean of 1.73 mg/ml (fig. A—7). These levels are more than 20 percent greater than prior estimates of serum B_{1C}/B_{1A} levels (Klemperer et al., 1965; Lewis et al., 1971; West et al., 1965). Age-dependent changes in the hemolytic activity of complement occur early in life and in older adults. Hartman (1957–58) reported 1.5-fold more hemolytic activity in sera from persons aged seventy to ninety years than in sera from twenty- to forty-six-year old subjects and suggested C3 as the complement component primarily responsible for this observation. Papanoyiotou et al. (1969) observed similar variation in the hemolytic activity of complement with age. In contrast, West et al. (1965) measured B_{1A} levels in children aged eight to eighteen years and in adults and found that differences related to age were not significant. At the other extreme of life, Adinolfi (1970) reported the appearance of B_{1C}/B_{1A} in fetal sera at midgestation; levels increased steadily until birth, when cord serum levels were approximately half the levels observed in paired maternal sera.

We tested the hypothesis that age differences or possibly sex differences could account for the differences between this and prior studies. Table A—22 suggests that overall sex differences were not significant; minor sex-related differences in B_{1A} levels may occur in the fifth and eighth decades of life. In contrast, age-related changes in serum B_{1A} levels were highly significant. Serum B_{1A} levels in adults during the third and fourth decades of life (fig. A—7) closely approximate previously reported studies (Klemperer et al., 1965; Lewis et al., 1971; West et al., 1965). A mean and standard deviation of 1.72 ± 0.43 mg/ml probably provides a better estimate of the adult range of normal B_{1A} values. Figure A—7 suggests that the confidence interval of normal serum B_{1A} concentrations may remain relatively constant and the mean serum B_{1A} level changes with age. An age adjustment of the confidence interval with values presented in table A—22 would likely provide the best estimate of normal B_{1A} levels. In experimental studies, contrasts of observations in patients with age-matched and possibly sex-matched controls seems requisite for demonstration of meaningful differences.

Despite a small decrease in average B_{1A} levels in individuals surviving to the eighth and ninth decades of life (table A—22), C3 levels in older adults remain adequate throughout adult life. In contrast, geometric mean serum levels of IgG and IgM, immunoglobulins responsible for the activity of complement-fixing antibodies, begin to decline during the fourth decade of life (Buckley and Dorsey, 1970). The correlations presented in table A—23 suggest that serum B_{1A} levels in this smaller sample of subjects correlated with the serum IgG levels. This means that despite the age-dependent abiotrophy of IgG and IgM, subjects with higher levels of IgG also had higher levels of B_{1A}. In contrast, the relative level of B_{1A} had no predictable correlation with high or low levels of IgM. An association may exist between mechanisms responsible for maintenance of serum levels of C3 and IgG. Older persons who maintain relatively high levels of IgG are also able to maintain high levels of a component of the accessory immune

Table A—23. *Correlation coefficients between serum immunoglobulins and* B_{IC}/B_{IA}.

	IgG	IgA	IgM
		r	
IgA	0.3626[a] $p = 0.0002$		
IgM	0.0629	0.1290	
B_{1C}/B_{1A}	0.2431[a] $p = 0.0089$	0.2329[a] $p = 0.0121$	0.0204

system activated by the same immunoglobulin class. The lack of correlation between IgM and B_{1A} levels suggests a possible disparity between complement activity and the availability of intravascular complement-fixing antibodies in the sera of older persons (Waldman et al., 1971). This relationship could be important in the distribution of complement-induced tissue injury. Serum levels of C3 do not limit specific and nonspecific activation of the destructive influence of the complement system in older persons.

Summary

Sources of analytical error in the immunochemical quantitation of C3 by single radial diffusion were evaluated and used to select an analytical method having a precision of ± 1.3 percent. Quantification of the level of C3 as B_{1A} was accomplished in sera from 129 adults aged twenty to ninety years. Serum concentrations of B_{1A} correlated significantly with serum concentrations of IgG but not IgM. Concentrations in older adults were significantly higher than levels of B_{1A} based on prior studies of children and adults. Significant age variation was observed; mean serum levels of B_{1A} increased from 1.39 mg/ml in the third decade to 2.00 mg/ml in the seventh decade of life and were slightly lower in subjects seventy to ninety years of age. A normal range of 0.87–2.59 mg/ml is more applicable to older adults. Adequate levels of C3 for specific and nonspecific activation of the complement system are maintained throughout adult life.

References

Adinolfi, M. Levels of two components of complement (C′4 and C′3) in human fetal and newborn sera. *Developmental Medicine and Child Neurology*, 12:306–308, 1970.

Alper, C. A., and Prapp, R. P. Genetic polymorphism of the third component of human complement (C′3). *Journal of Clinical Investigation*, 47:2181–2191, 1968.

Berne, B. H. Discrepant equations derived from the single radial diffusion technique. *Immunochemistry*, 9:1256–1259, 1972.

Buckley, C. E., III, and Dorsey, F. C. The effect of aging on human serum immunoglobulin concentrations. *Journal of Immunology*, 105:964–972, 1970.

Dowell, A. R., and Buckley, C. E., III. Arteriovenous complement activity differences across the human lesser circulation. *American Review of Respiratory Disease*, 102:213–220, 1970.

Fahey, J. L., and McKelvey, E. M. Quantitative determination of serum immunoglobulins in antibody-agar plates. *Journal of Immunology*, 94:84–90, 1965.

Hartman, J. Complement determination. 2. Determination of hemolytic complement activity in human serum as a function of age. *Acta Pathologica et Micro-biologica Scandinavica*, 42: 164–172, 1957–58.

Klemperer, M. R., et al. Estimation of the serum *beta* lc globulin concentration: Its relation to the serum hemolytic complement titer. *Pediatrics*, 35:765–767, 1965.

Lewis, E. J., Carpenter, C. B., and Schur, P. H. Serum complement levels in human glomerulonephritis. *Annals of Internal Medicine*, 75:555–560, 1971.

Lundh, B. A method for quantitative determination of B_{1C}-globulin, a component of the human serum complement system. *Scandinavian Journal of Clinical and Laboratory Investigation*, 16:108–114, 1964.

Mancini, G., Carbonara, A. O., and Heremans, J. F. Immunochemical quantitation of antigens by single radial immunodiffusion. *Immunochemistry*, 2:235–248, 1965.

Mather, K. *Statistical analysis in biology*. New York: Interscience Publishers, 1947.

Mayer, M. M., and Nelson, R. A. Biochemistry of complement. In D. B. Amos (Ed.), *Progress in immunology*. New York: Academic, 1971, 1429.

Muller-Eberhard, J. H. Complement. *Annual Review of Biochemistry*, 38:389–414, 1969.

Muller-Eberhard, J. H., Nilsson, U., and Aronsson, T. Isolation and characterization of two B_1-glycoproteins of human serum. *Journal of Experimental Medicine*, 111:201–215, 1960.

Pondman, K. W., and Peetoom, F. The significance of the antigen antibody complement reaction. IV. The plement system. *Immunochemistry*, 1:65–90, 1964.

Papanoyiotou, P., et al. Variations physiologiques du complement serique. Influence de l'age et du sex sur le taux C'H50. *Annales de l'Institut Pasteur*, 117:796–800, 1969.

Schwick, H. G., and Becker, W. Humoral antibodies in older humans. In O. Westphal, H. E. Beck, and F. Brundmann (Eds.), *Current problems in immunology*. Berlin: Springer, 1969, 253–257.

Starmer, C. F., and Grizzle, J. E. *A computer program for analysis of data by general linear models*, Institute of Statistics Mimeo Series No. 560. Chapel Hill, N.C.: Institute of Statistics, 1968.

Svec, K. H., and Viet, B. C. Age-related anti-nuclear factors: Immunologic characteristics and associated clinical aspects. *Arthritis and Rheumatism*, 10:509–516, 1967.

Waldman, T. A., Strober, W., and Blaese, R. M. Metabolism of Immunoglobulins. In D. B. Amos (Ed.), *Progress in immunology*. New York: Academic, 1971, 891.

Walford, R. L. *The immunologic theory of aging*. Copenhagen: Munksgaard, 1969.

West, C. D., et al. Hypocomplementemic and normocomplementemic persistent (chronic) glomerulonephritis; clinical and pathologic characteristics. *Journal of Pediatrics*, 64:1089–1109, 1965.

West, C. D., et al. Antigenic determinants of human B_{1C} and B_{1G}-globulins. *Journal of Immunology*, 96:650–658, 1966.

Section B. Mental Health and Mental Illness

Introduction

Ewald W. Busse

Two long-term multidisciplinary longitudinal studies of "normal" aging have been conducted at the Duke University Center for the Study of Aging and Human Development. The vast amount of longitudinal data that have been collected will continue to be analyzed for a number of years. Related investigations are continuing and new work is emerging.

The Duke First Longitudinal Study began in 1955 after five years of cross-sectional research on normal aging. Several years of preliminary research were necessary in order to develop the research design, select the observations, and decide on methods of storage, retrieval, and analysis of the longitudinal data. The first longitudinal study was officially known as "The Effect of Aging upon the Nervous System—A Physiological, Psychological, and Sociological Study of Aging." The second longitudinal study was begun in 1968 and was designated "The Adaptation Study." The history of these two studies is necessarily complex. Attention was given to communication within the interdisciplinary team. Procedures were established by the team to control the investigation. Consequently, these studies provided some important information about the effective organization and administration of interdisciplinary research on aging,[1] as well as many important observations regarding the processes of aging.

The two longitudinal studies are different in a number of ways—the sample, the hypotheses to be tested, the measurement procedures, the duration of the study, and so forth.[2] As indicated by its title, the first longitudinal study focused on understanding the aging nervous system. The emphasis of the second longitudinal study was on adaptation to change over time as well as response to important life events. The observations selected were based upon the best available knowledge at the time of the study, and it is unfortunate that certain procedures were not developed until a later date. Attempts were made to include useful new procedures, such as cerebral blood flow, without jeopardizing the longitudinal aspect of the study.

The development of the longitudinal studies was fortuitous and logical. Beginning in 1948, the principal investigator (Busse) was engaged in research ac-

1. Busse, E. W. Administration of the interdisciplinary research team. *Journal of Medical Education*, 40:832–839, 1965.

2. Maddox, G. L. (Ed.). The Duke multidisciplinary longitudinal studies of normal aging. Vol. 6, no. 1, Center Reports of Advances in Research, Duke University Center for the Study of Aging and Human Development, Durham, N.C., July 1982.

tivity concerned with epileptic seizures and temporal lobe functioning in adults. An observation was made that many elderly persons referred for clinical diagnostic EEGs showed focal electrical disturbances arising from the temporal region of the brain. The focal disturbance found in the elderly who were free of epileptic seizures could not be distinguished from those individuals with focal epileptogenic foçus. Consequently; for those individuals who were free of seizures but had a focal abnormality, the EEG interpretations included the notation, "The focal abnormality present in the record does not appear to be related to the patient's complaint or to the diagnosis." The possible cause and clinical significance of this focal abnormality provided an important investigational challenge.

In the spring of 1952, a paper was read at the annual meeting of the American Medical Association reporting the observation that a significant number of apparently normal elderly persons had EEG temporal lobe focal activity. The following year, additional data were presented to the meeting of the American Psychiatric Association. This paper confirmed that "the cortical activity of persons over the age of sixty shows a definite change as measured by the EEG. A high percentage (37.3 percent) have focal dysrhythmias which are primarily found in the left temporal lobe."[3] These early studies were supported by funds from the National Institute of Mental Health. However, in subsequent years, the funding was derived from various components of the National Institutes of Health. First support was received in the fall of 1951 (Research Grant No. MH 434) and terminated in the fall of 1953. The progress report submitted to the granting agency included the following summary statement: The specific aims of this project were:

> 1. The Standardization of the Normal Electroencephalogram in the Age Group of Subjects 60 Years of Age and Over. 2. The Evaluation of Central Nervous System Functioning in (*a*) Individuals of 60 and Over with Uncomplicated (that is, Normal) Aging, (*b*) Individuals of 60 and Over with Senile and Arteriosclerotic Changes (Pathological Aging).
>
> A total of 332 subjects have been studied. These subjects have been separated into various groups which were determined by social and economic status and their medical condition. Information on these subjects is derived from careful physical and neurological examination, medical and social history, psychiatric examination, psychological testing, EEGs, laboratory studies, and critical flicker fusion for light. Our original observations indicated a high percentage of focal EEG changes in our subjects that were primarily in the temporal areas. This finding has continued as our series has expanded. The focal dysrhythmias are not accompanied by defect of specific functioning; in fact, there is evidence which suggests that those with focal changes function at a somewhat better level than those with 'normal' EEGs. However subjects with diffused disturbances show definite declines in psychological abilities which include such things as facility of communi-

3. Busse, E. W., et al. Studies of processes of aging: VI. Factors that influence the psyche of elderly persons. *American Journal of Psychiatry*, 110:896–903, 1954.

cation, clarity of perception, and abstract thinking. No correlation can be made between these changes and the status of the cardiovascular system or with cerebral dominance.

In 1953, three members of the research team (Busse, Barnes, and Silverman) moved to Duke University School of Medicine in Durham, North Carolina. The research activity continued in this new setting, and grant support was awarded (Research Grant No. 900C). In the fall of 1956, a summary statement was submitted to the granting agency. This statement reads as follows: "Broadly stated, our objectives under this project have been to define and investigate further specific psychological, physiological, and social factors as they relate to human aging. During two years of preliminary work in this field at the University of Colorado School of Medicine, we made certain observations concerning the electroencephalogram, the types of tracing seen in people of 60 and over and correlations between these tracings and measurements of psychological and social functioning. We have now continued these studies in a different cultural and geographical setting looking for the influence of these variables on the various aspects of the aging process. Further, we have attempted to improve our evaluation or measuring technique in both the social and psychological areas and have also added new evaluation tools within the physiological area (cf. Photographs of the ocular fundi and microscopic observations of the bulbar conjunctiva). In the fifteen months spent to date on the current project, the major effort has gone into (1) selecting and training research personnel, (2) selection and mastery of additional evaluation techniques, (3) the establishment of community relationships to allow for the obtaining of volunteer elderly subjects, and (4) the collection of desired evalution data on these subjects. (The schedule as developed accommodates 4–5 subjects per week.) Only now are we able to devote time to ordering an analysis of our data."

This was the beginning of the first longitudinal study. In 1957, the longitudinal research project was incorporated into a program project grant (RG H MH A B 5385) which provided the core support for the development of the Center for the Study of Aging at Duke.

Long-term interdisciplinary research requires that all participants have a clear understanding of the objectives and that the effort is creative and has a careful research design. Equally important is the selection of members of the team. The team should be guided by administrative principles and procedures which are easily understood and equitable. Efforts must be given to the maintenance of a team concept, with frequent and congenial methods of communication and cooperation. Responsibility for the collection of data in specific areas as well as other activities must be clearly assigned. Continuing attention must be given to data management, including data reduction, cleaning, storage, and retrieval. Statistical consultation must be readily available and review procedures of publications are necessary to ensure quality and to avoid any adverse effect that would result from a scientific report of questionable quality published by a member of the team. These features and procedures of the longitudinal studies have been reported in some detail in *Normal aging* (Busse, "Administration of the Interdisciplinary Research Team") and in the report of the Duke longitudinal studies edited by Busse and Maddox.[4]

Individuals and combinations of various members of the team have been recognized for their outstanding scientific contributions to the study of aging. The team was recently recognized as a highly productive, interdisciplinary effort when it received the Sandoz Award. The announcement of July 22, 1983, from Basel, Switzerland, is presented below:

> The International Association of Gerontology has announced that the Duke Longitudinal Study of Normal Aging is one of the recipients of the Sandoz Prize. The co-recipient is a research team based in The Netherlands headed by Dr. Carel Hollander. The award will be presented to Dr. E. W. Busse representing the Duke Research Team on September 3, 1983, in Budapest, Hungary.
>
> The Sandoz Prize for Gerontology is not limited to any specific area of gerontology or geriatrics, but has a special emphasis on multidisciplinary programs. The Duke Longitudinal Studies are composed of two major efforts. The first was initiated in 1955 and the second in 1968. Both studies focused on the biomedical, physiological, psychological, and social aspects of normal aging. The subjects were followed into 1980. Analysis of the data collected continues. "These studies produced some important insights into the complex processes of normal aging, but more than this these studies illustrated and strengthened the commitment to multidisciplinary research" and "generated laboratories and programs that provided natural sites for research training." The Sandoz Prize that will be received by the Duke investigators is 10,000 Swiss francs. These funds will be utilized to promote research and training in the Center for the Study of Aging and Human Development of Duke University. Dr. E. W. Busse was the principal investigator of the Duke Longitudinal Studies and Dr. George Maddox assisted and participated in the research.
>
> Since 1955 many investigators have participated in these studies, including current faculty: Ilene Siegler, Erdman Palmore, John Nowlin, Linda George, Dietlof Ramm, Hsioh-Shan Wang, Edward Buckley III, Gail Marsh, Stephen Vogel, Peter Burger, Max Woodbury, David Madden, Carol Hogue, Alan Whanger, Daniel Gianturco.

The core data from these two studies are now available for further analysis by other qualified investigators. We hope that further analysis of this rich store of data will continue to yield better understanding of the processes of aging.

4. Busse, E. W., and Maddox, G. L. (Eds.). Final report: The Duke longitudinal studies—an integrated investigation of aging and the aged, ancillary studies, and research support services—1955–1980. Submitted from the Center for the Study of Aging and Human Development, Duke University, November 30, 1980.

Mental Health and Mental Illness

Ewald W. Busse

Papers in this section have been modified by deleting repetitious descriptions of the two longitudinal studies; two papers are expanded versions of original presentations. This introduction focuses on selected areas of investigation with an elaboration of relevant information and discussion of issues and theories.

An issue is a conclusion that has been reached after investigation and careful consideration but, because of its complex nature, is debatable. A gerontological theory offers a plausible explanation for a phenomenon associated with aging and the aged. A theory is not proven scientifically; hence, a theory invites argument and disagreement that hopefully result in further investigation and clarification.

The elderly are often afflicted with certain common mental illnesses that can be seriously incapacitating (e.g., organic brain disease, depression, and hypochondriasis). To understand the cause and to develop preventive and treatment methods are critical to improving the health and well-being of the elderly. Many elderly persons are able to avoid serious mental problems and maintain a healthy mental status. This discussion emphasizes new information, theories, and issues generated by the papers included in this section. Some of these theories and issues are relevant to clinical investigation but others are concerned with the basic sciences: biological, sociological, or psychological.

Psychiatric Problems in Later Life

There are a number of issues in the Gianturco and Busse paper which are of utmost interest to the clinician, and important information on these issues has come from both longitudinal studies. Issues in this paper deal with depression, organic brain syndrome, hypochondriasis, psychoneurotic reactions, and attitudes toward death.

The terminal drop hypothesis has existed for more than two decades, and contends that a decline in intellectual performance heralds an early death and that the decline is associated with physical health deterioration, and therefore decline in mental ability should not be considered a normal aging process. Most data derived from the longitudinal studies support this hypothesis (see section C), but there is conflicting evidence as to whether there are substantial differences in the survival time of those diagnosed as having organic brain disease and those free of mental deterioration. An earlier investigation (Wang and Busse, 1974) found that those with brain impairment had slightly shorter longevity than others, controlling for age and sex; but the Gianturco and Busse paper reports no difference in longevity of those with organic brain disease and others. This discrepancy may be due to different methods used.

As to organic brain disease, the term brain impairment was preferred in reports from the longitudinal studies to designate loss of brain function based on a number of laboratory procedures including EEG, measures of cerebral blood flow, and cerebral oxygen metabolism. Furthermore, brain impairment was determined by psychological tests, clinical measures of intellectual performance, and observation of emotional status. At the beginning of the first longitudinal study, when the average age of the subjects was 70.8 years, only 3 percent were judged to have moderate to severe manifestation of brain impairment. Approximately twenty-five years later the number of subjects had declined, but the average age had increased to eighty-five years, and 12 percent were judged to have moderate to severe clinical evidence of brain impairment. An extremely important observation made in the longitudinal studies is that from one point in time to another there is a fluctuation in the degree of impairment in those believed to have organic brain disease. There appear to be varying degrees of remissions and exacerbations. The loss of mental ability (what one does) and capacity (what is possible) are influenced by changes not only within the brain but the health status of the entire body, habitual behavior patterns, and socioeconomic determinants. A particularly impressive statistic is that 59 percent of the subjects in the first longitudinal study before death or dropout were evaluated at some time as having evidence of brain impairment.

The term depression, when utilized clinically, is an imprecise diagnosis that places the disorder in a category of affective reactions. The specific subcategories of depression are gradually emerging and are usually based upon responsiveness to medication. This in turn suggests a biological etiology. The emerging diagnoses are to a lesser extent influenced by symptom and duration. For many years a depressive episode that was believed to be precipitated by an external event was labeled reactive, while those depressions that were not associated with an external event were assumed to be endogenous. An endogenous diagnosis was strengthened if the affective episode was recurrent and if a family history of serious depressions was elicited.

The depressive periods given attention in the longitudinal subjects were frequent, usually recurrent, and of short duration. Such depressive episodes can hardly be considered other than a feature of everyday living and should not be treated with antidepressants or other medication. Rather, supportive measures and the utilization of restorative activity which returns the individual self-esteem to an acceptable level is the best procedure to bring relief and reduction in frequency. Depressive episodes were reported by the subjects in the first longitudinal study to have increased in old age. However, it is to be noted that objective observation of depressions did not increase over the years in the survivors. Hence these conflicting observations deserve further study. An issue remains—do depressive episodes increase throughout later life?

The two biologically determined affective disorders are unipolar and bipolar psychoses. The unipolar type is characterized by recurrent depressions or manias without phases of the opposite polarity. The bipolar type is characterized by the occurrence of both depression and manic phases. The median age of onset for unipolar psychosis is forty-five years of age, but for bipolar it is thirty years (Zung, 1980). The appearance of major affective disorders did not seem to be related to episodic depressions of the elderly. This area also needs further investigation.

Among the psychiatric diagnostic categories that are relevant to the longitudinal studies, perhaps the diagnosis of hypochondriasis has been the most variable. Three "official" diagnostic systems have appeared during the course of the longitudinal studies. Much of the work was done while DSM II was in clinical use. For many years, prior to DSM II, hypochondriasis was considered a syndrome rather than a distinct disease entity, but the second edition of the *Diagnostic and Statistical Manual of Mental Disorders* of the APA (DSM II) established hypochondriasis neurosis as a separate neurotic condition.[1] DSM III placed hypochondriasis into a group of four somatoform disorders. These four categories include (1) somaticization disorder (Briquet's syndrome), (2) conversion disorders, (3) psychogenic pain disorders, and (4) hypochondriasis. The longitudinal studies have generally adhered to the following definition: "Hypochondriasis is an anxious preoccupation (high bodily concern) with one's own body or a portion of one's own body which the patient believes to be either diseased or functioning improperly." The fears or worries about the body are grossly exaggerated and apparently without explanation and not based on medical information and examination. Depression feelings frequently are present (Busse and Pfeiffer, 1977:179).

The fact that the longitudinal studies utilized consistent and sensitive measures to determine hypochondriasis that were not always consistent with the prevailing diagnostic system did produce some misunderstandings. Many of the subjects experienced periods of hypochondriasis.

EEG Changes in Late Life

There are numerous unresolved questions surrounding the electroencephalographic changes in late life. Slowing of the alpha frequency is the most common change in awake EEGs recorded after the age of sixty-five years. Little is known of the behavioral significance of sex differences. Males have a lower mean alpha frequency than do females of comparable age. Another sex difference involves the appearance and gradual increase in the amount of fast waves during the lifespan of approximately 20 percent of females. Fast waves do not increase in males.

A question regarding EEG. Another question: does age or disease change the wave form and distribution of alpha rhythms? Monomorphic alpha rhythm is

1. "300.7 Hypochondrical Neurosis. This condition is dominated by preoccupation with the body and with fear of delusional quality as in psychotic depressions they persist despite reassurance. The condition differs from hysterical neurosis in that there are no active losses or distortions of function."

very stable in frequency and constant in amplitude; polymorphic alpha is irregular and stable. Monomorphic alpha rhythm is common among patients with demonstrated cerebral vascular insufficiency, yet the same type of alpha occasionally appears in normal elderly. This observation deserves additional attention.

A major contribution of the EEG analyses was recognition and confirmation that a relatively high percentage (30–40 percent) of elderly people were found to have focal EEG abnormalities predominantly over the temporal area of the brain. As indicated by the papers in this section, the focal temporal abnormalities are predominantly on the left side of the brain. When this focal slow activity is discrete and confined to the anterior temporal area, it is compatible with a good social adjustment and does not impair mental processes. However, when it involves adjacent areas of the brain (i.e., midtemporal and posttemporal) and/or when it is associated with more diffuse slowing of the brain waves, organic brain impairment is probable.

What is the explanation for this phenomenon? Does the confined focal EEG represent an insidious process which at a certain level or threshold passes beyond the level of control or compensation? When the EEG abnormality spreads posteriorly, it is associated with organic symptomatology. Investigation cannot ignore the possibility that the observations are not properly directed or are insensitive and require redirection and increased sensitivity before further advances are made.

Two of the diagnostic procedures utilized in the longitudinal studies (electroencephalography and cerebral blood flow) were the best noninvasive diagnostic tools (investigational psychological) available during this era of scientific investigation. These technologies, particularly EEG/EP, will continue to be useful; however, the biologically oriented behavioral scientist will, of necessity, become much involved with rapidly emerging new scientific instruments: positron emission tomography (PET) and nuclear magnetic resonance (NMR).

Cerebral Blood Flow

The use of a noninvasive method for measuring cerebral blood flow was introduced into the longitudinal studies and conducted in the laboratory of Obrist and Wang. The examination utilized the Xe-133 inhalation method. This study indicated that normal aged subjects had a significantly lower blood flow than young controls. These elderly normal subjects had a mean age of eighty years. Demented patients showed a greater decline in cerebral blood flow. This was despite the fact that the demented patients were twenty years younger than the elderly normal subjects. When compared to young subjects, there was a 28 percent reduction in cerebral blood flow at age eighty, while the cerebral blood flow of the demented subjects was 39 percent of the younger controls (Obrist et al., 1967).

The normal aged subjects were divided into two groups according to whether their cerebral blood flow was above or below the medium value of the sample.

The groups differed significantly in the Wechsler Adult Intelligence Scale and in the dominant alpha EEG frequency. This difference in WAIS was heavily influenced by the decline in the performance scale as opposed to the verbal scale. The deterioration quotient was .30 for the low flow cerebral blood flow as compared to .19 for the high flow subjects. The cerebral blood flow and EEG findings were consistent with each other. A slower alpha frequency was found in subjects with reduced blood flow. The alpha index was 9.3 (high flow), as compared to 8.5 (low flow) (Obrist et al., 1971).

The Xe-133 inhalation technique of measuring brain metabolism and blood flow added much needed knowledge of the aging brain. However, over the next five years, the Xe-133 inhalation will be replaced by use of nuclear magnetic resonance (NMR) and positron emission tomography (PET).

Sleep Patterns

The total sleep requirement in the normal human appears to decrease gradually over the entire life span. Although the time in bed, not necessarily sleeping, tends to increase, sleep latency, the time needed to fall asleep, also increases with age. Furthermore, the sleep of the elderly is lighter and is associated with more frequent awakening during the night. These increased awakenings are often remembered by the elderly person and noted as a definite change from sleep earlier in life. It is true that some normal aging persons distribute their sleep differently across the twenty-four-hour cycle. Some sleep for varying periods during the day, but their total sleep requirement does not seem to be affected. These normal changes in sleep with aging can be disturbing to some elderly persons. Many older people are concerned that poor sleep will lead to serious illness and there are many who complain of difficulty in going to sleep, of restlessness or insufficient sleep, and of the previously mentioned frequent awakenings. Sleep does occupy about one-third of the life of most adults, and there is little doubt that the physiological changes that transpire during sleep are very important to the functioning of a human. It is essential that investigators such as Prinz continue to study this rapidly emerging new area of scientific investigation.

Prinz conducted an ancillary study on sleep patterns and intellectual performance. Sleep EEGs were recorded at the homes of the subjects and were done in proximity to the eighth examination (1973). The subjects were divided into two groups representing high and low REM periods. Time spent in REM sleep was found to be positively correlated with the WAIS performance score measured in proximity to the EEG. Those with a lesser amount of sleep showed a decline in their WAIS scores, while the opposite was true of those with more REM sleep time. In contrast, the verbal score was not related to REM sleep. Of the measures available from the Wechsler Memory Scale, only the change in the performance of the hard paired associates task was related to REM sleep.

Clinical Correlates of Vibratory Sense

The issue over the relationship of adequate nutrition and vitamin intake to disease and disability in late life appears to be destined for continuing debate. Vitamin B_{12} (cyanocobalamin) has received considerable attention from geriatricians for many years. According to Whanger (personal communication) a deficiency of vitamin B_{12} is present in 35 percent of elderly with organic mental impairment. There are some physicians who say that the injection of B_{12} is a placebo. When given by injection, B_{12} solution is a bright red color.

Pernicious anemia, which is relatively common in late life, is caused by a malabsorption of B_{12} (extrinsic factor), which is, in turn, due to the failure of the gastric mucosa to secrete adequate and potent intrinsic factor. It is also associated with elderly people who have a histamine-fast achlorhydria.

Whanger and Wang provide a succinct review of the anatomic and physiological basis of vibratory perception in the extremities. Vibratory threshold "is raised in a number of diseases as well as in the course of aging." Sex apparently does not influence the vibratory threshold, but black females seem to have a more sensitive vibratory sense. Higher thresholds were found among those who were judged to be on inadequate diet, but heavy users of alcohol did not seem to be affected. As would be expected, diabetes mellitus and syphilis do impair vibratory perception. The use of tobacco also has a negative affect. The ingestion of vitamin supplements lacking B_{12} does not enhance the vibratory threshold. When B_{12} is included there is a favorable influence on the capacity to recognize vibration. The authors conclude, "The elevation of vibratory threshold among the elderly has some relationship to aging per se, but is much more related to disease and nutritional factors." The authors imply that the massive use of vitamin supplementation in our society using preparations that do not contain B_{12} may be a detrimental rather than a positive influence.

Stress and Coping in Later Life

The issues of stress and coping are central to the main thrust of the second longitudinal study (adaptation to change). George and Siegler recognize the importance of definition of terms and the scientific interpretation of these findings. Consequently, it was their decision that "to define stress in terms meaningful to them (older persons) leads to a greater understanding of life in old age." A life event can be labeled as a stress when the reaction to the event is a maladaptative response. George and Siegler define maladaptive experience as one in which an individual is unable to meet the demands of the environment, is unable to maintain a sense of well being, or both. The opposite (i.e., adaptation or adjustment) is held to be a state of congruence between the individual and the environment. Individuals experience certain life events such as the death of a spouse in quite different ways. In late life such an event as the death of a spouse with far advanced organic brain disease can contribute to the alleviation of a maladaptative situation. The response, not the event, is critical and it emphasizes the value of the George and Siegler approach of allowing older persons to define stress in terms meaningful to them.

The authors did not elect to follow this same approach of subject participation in the definition of coping. Coping is defined as the overt and covert behavior individuals use to prevent, alleviate, or respond to stressful situations. To measure and study coping, the authors elected to utilize the typological approach. This model utilizes four major coping modes: (1) information seeking, (2) direct action, (3) inhibition of action, and (4) intrapsychic modes.

The authors, in allowing the elderly to define stress, utilized a common framework, asking the subject to identify periods of problems during his or her life. Adaptation was asked about in terms of the best time in whole life, the best time in the past ten years, and the best aspects of the current situation. Maladaptation was asked about in terms of the worst time experienced during these periods. The next step was to identity the event or events experienced by the subject that were perceived as the major influences in the living experience. The worst aspects of the present are emphasized in their analysis, since it focuses on stress.

A cross-coding scheme of domain and context was devised that resulted in a two-dimensional matrix. A dimension called domain included five categories that identified the sources of stress. These categories include: self, family, health, work, and economics. A second dimension labeled context had two groupings: personal and interpersonal. The context was considered to be interpersonal when the event affected other persons as well as the subject.

In the first domain, the category of self represented interpsychic conflict such as issues of morality, social values, and religion. At times this self-conflict would not be contained within the individual, but could affect other persons close to the individual. Therefore, it could be self-interpersonal. In rank order, the domain of stress was 31 percent health, 21 percent family, 20 percent self, 16 percent economics, and 12 percent work.

The possibility that imposed unexpected events were more traumatic than chosen events was not substantiated. Chosen events emerged as more stressful, hence maladaptative, than unexpected experiences. A positive event was never perceived as a stress, although it, at times, involved a disruption of customary patterns of living.

As to methods of coping, again, a two-dimensional approach was utilized. There were four modes: information seeking, direct action, inhibition of action, and intrapsychic coping. Coping orientation was broken into two components: instrumental and palliative. It is my interpretation that instrumental coping is an action that was intended to eliminate or reduce the stressful experience, while a palliative orientation was intended to help the respondent feel better about the situation. The question of how effective are the modes and orientations of coping is almost impossible to measure; not only do different individuals use different techniques more or less successfully, but the domain and context of the stress and the subsequent maladaptative response may pose limitations on coping responses.

Three factors were closely related to coping effectiveness: self-rated perceptions of coping effectiveness is rated most favorably if (1) the individual does not attribute the occurrence of the stress to himself or herself, (2) the individual perceives that he or she was in control of how the stress was handled, and (3) if both instrumental and palliative coping strategies were employed. Interestingly, if only one coping orientation is pursued, palliative coping strategies are associated with higher rates of effectiveness than instrumental strategies. This, in my opinion, may mean that the event could not have been controlled or prevented. At least the palliative technique buffers the experience of stress.

Sex Differences in Coping and Perception in Life Events

The authors refer to previous work which affirmed that there was stable sex differences seen in personality traits. There was no evidence to suggest an increasing homogeneity between the sexes in later life. Most of the sex differences are consistent with those which are traditionally considered gender personality features. An important question is, do older men and women have to cope with the same set of life events? There are other assumptions about life events that were tested: (1) that stress is a function of the degree of change generated by an event, (2) that stress is independent of whether the event is perceived as positive or negative, (3) that individual differences in perception of events are not important, and (4) that stress is cumulative and additive, with a high degree of stress producing negative health outcomes.

In testing the effectiveness of instrumental and palliative coping orientation, no sex differences were found. However, there were differences if the events were considered to be personal or nonpersonal. Palliative coping was effective for 62 percent of the nonpersonal events and 38 percent of the personal; however, instrumental strategies were effective for 62 percent of the personal events. In my opinion, these differences may closely relate to the amount of control the individual has over the event. Much more control and the instrumental strategy can be exerted when it is personal rather than nonpersonal.

When stressful events take place during the life span is of considerable interest. The timing of events across the life cycle did not vary significantly by sex. There appears to be no particular phase of life where the best or worst events are likely to begin (note the subjects' age range was fifty-five to seventy-eight years). The mean age at the beginning and the mean age at the end of an event showed that the starting age for the best event was thirty-one years, and the ending age was forty-three years. For the worst event in the whole life, the age at the beginning was forty, and the age at the ending was forty-one. As to event differences, men were more likely to report experiences that were work-related personal or health-related personal. Women were more likely to report health/interpersonal events, particularly the illness of the husband and family events. However, family troubles occurred for all of the subjects.

There were also differences in self-descriptions. Men described themselves as more internal in their locus of control, and more active copers. Women described themselves as more nervous, having more psychosomatic symptoms, and having more negative affect during the previous week. There were no gender differences on measures of life satisfaction, self-esteem, trust, affect balance, social desirability, or anomie. Contrary to one of the four assumptions tested, this study indicates that events perceived positively or negatively have different consequences. Most of the respondents did not perceive that they had a coping task to accomplish when the event was perceived as a positive one.

It has often been assumed that major historical events such as wars and economic depressions have a predominantly negative impact upon the lives of people. These data suggest that sociohistorical events have relatively little impact upon events in the family life cycle. It is my assumption that this is likely to hold true unless the major historical event is associated with a personal catastrophe such as the death of a husband or the loss of family in an enemy attack. Since the United States is relatively free of this type of historical trauma, it is quite possible that this finding would not apply to other nations.

Psychological Distress and Perceived Health

Tessler and Mechanic deal with a subject that has been frequently examined in both longitudinal studies. The terms employed by Tessler and Mechanic are appropriate, but they are sometimes inconsistent with those used by other investigators. The terms psychological distress and distress usually describe acute reactions, but in this presentation they cover both acute and prolonged adverse psychological reactions. A major strength of this paper is that it utilizes four different health surveys. The four surveys contrast sharply with one another in respect to the characteristics of the population studied. The authors note that the items forming the basis of perceived health status, physical health status, and psychological distress all could be questioned. For example, the psychological distress measures are varied, while the perceived health measures could be influenced by a number of uncontrolled factors. The authors emphasize that the association between psychological distress and perceived health status is in all likelihood reciprocal in character. This is the long-standing basis of psychosomatic medicine and it is the view of many studies conducted in the longitudinal investigations. Tessler and Mechanic also recognize that perceived health status is only a proxy for more objectively measured health status. In 1964, Maddox reported that only two out of three subjects in the first longitudinal study displayed a reality orientation in their subjective evaluations of health status. When the objective and the perceived health statuses were incongruous, some were pessimistic and others optimistic. The pessimistic group were preoccupied with their health, while the optimistic group probably were utilizing the mechanism of denial. Both optimism and pessimism were related to social placement and attitudinal factors. The social placement factors included age, sex, major lifetime occupation of subject or spouse, type and level of activity maintained, and extent of change in work role. The attitudinal factors were morale and preoccupation with health. Maddox's study has influenced many of the subsequent investigations and reports.

Drivers, Ex-Drivers, and Drowsiness

It is suspected that at least part of the difference between male and female drivers in drowsiness and driving can be accounted for by driving habits. The men averaged 12,000 miles yearly and the women averaged 7,000 miles. Only 7 percent of the males drove fewer than 6,000 miles per year, whereas 54 percent of the females drove fewer than 6,000 miles. Only 3 percent of the women as compared to 30 percent of the men reported driving more than 15,000 miles per year. Cattell personality testing revealed no consistent group of personality traits which correlate with getting drowsy while driving. However, for drivers who actually fell asleep, testing indicated that they were prone to worry, they would give up responsibilities, and they evaded responsibilities more frequently. Numerous physical factors, including vision, corrected vision, etc., were examined, but all failed to reveal any consistent pattern of physical defect that was more prevalent in the group which reported drowsiness while driving.

The contribution by Gianturco, Ramm, and Erwin is the second paper to appear in the normal aging series. The first paper, "The Elderly Driver and Ex-Driver" appeared in *Normal aging II*. This earlier publication utilized a number of measures including the physical functioning rating (PFR), vision and hearing, attitudes toward driving, and an activities inventory. Of the elderly subjects who continued to drive, the average age was seventy-eight years and the physical functioning rating was 1.2. This was on a scale of 0 to 5. Therefore, in spite of their advanced age, there was little limitation in their physical functioning. However, some of the drivers had visual restrictions, which limited their driving. Of those continuing to drive, a very small percent had severe hearing impairment. As to mean reaction time, there were some elderly drivers who had reaction times comparable to young subjects. However, many did not. The slower reactions of the elderly driver did not result in a higher rate of automobile accidents. Apparently, although reaction times are slowed they are sufficient for ordinary driving. Those who discontinued driving were somewhat older than the drivers, and their physical functioning was poorer (2.1). Visual problems were by far the most common physical infirmity, but a frequent reason for discontinuing driving was the expense of maintaining an automobile. Total activities and life satisfactions were markedly different in drivers as compared to ex-drivers. Drivers were definitely happier and more satisfied than ex-drivers. Many of the ex-drivers had reduced their social activities and contacts. The loss of mobility was a detriment for many elderly.

Older drivers do not have a higher accident rate than drivers under age sixty-five, apparently because they drive more carefully than younger drivers.

Elderly drivers appear to have a realistic appreciation of their limitations and to restrict their driving accordingly.

References

Busse, E. W., and Pfeiffer, E. Functional psychiatric disorders in old age. In E. W. Busse and E. Pfeiffer (Eds.), *Behavior and adaptation in late life*. 2d Ed. Boston: Little, Brown, 1977, 158–211.

Obrist, W. D., et al. Determination of regional cerebral blood flow by inhalation of 133-Xenon. *Circulation Research*, 10:125–235, 1967.

Obrist, W. D., et al. A simplified procedure for determining fast compartment rCBFs by 133 xenon inhalation. In R. W. R. Russel (Ed.), *Brain and blood flow*. London: Pitman Medical, 1971, 11–15.

Wang, H. S., and Busse, E. W. Brain impairment and longevity. In Palmore, E . B. (Ed.), *Normal aging II*. Durham, N.C.: Duke University Press, 1974.

Zung, W. K. Affective disorders. In E. W. Busse and D. G. Blazer (Eds.), *Handbook of geriatric psychiatry*. New York: Van Nostrand Reinhold, 1980, 338–367.

Psychiatric Problems in Later Life

Daniel T. Gianturco and Ewald W. Busse

The psychiatric observations in the Duke First Longitudinal Study focus on aspects of mental status including affect, recent and remote memory, orientation, intellectual function, anxiety, and hypochondriasis. Particular attention was given to the assessment of mood and other associated symptoms of depression. Later sections will review selected psychiatric findings from the initial data and present a longitudinal analysis of follow-up data to clarify further the course of the initial psychiatric observations.

The Prevalence of Mental Illness in Late Life

Evidence from hospitalization rates and community surveys demonstrates clearly that older age groups have a substantial amount of mental illness (Kay, 1964). Prevalence rates of 10–20 percent have been suggested (Shepherd, 1966). These high rates among the aged, coupled with the fact that an extremely high proportion (50 percent) of hospital and nursing home beds in the United States are filled

Reprinted by permission from *Studies in Geriatric Psychiatry*, edited by A. Isaacs and F. Post. Chichester, Sussex: Wiley, 1978.

with psychiatrically ill elderly people underscore the seriousness of this problem for the elderly (Stotsky, 1973). Psychiatric services have been largely confined to the institutionalized elderly, who now comprise two percent of the sixty-five to seventy-four and over age group (Reddick, et al., 1973). The number of aged in need of psychiatric services is expected to increase with the size of the elderly population at risk. Such high rates of illness have understandably stimulated research into the nature of mental illness in the later years. However, very little longitudinal research has been done on psychiatric problems of older people who live more or less adequately in the community. Most research has been cross-sectional in nature, which would be a satisfactory method if psychiatric disorders were fixed and immutable entities. The longitudinal method certainly has its deficiencies, but it is an invaluable technique for the study of process. The nature and course of psychiatric disorders is one such example of process.

Depression

A common clinical syndrome encountered in old age is depression. A review of our inpatient experience with geriatric patients at Duke Hospital indicated that, in over one-half of the admissions in this age group, depression was the major disorder (Gianturco, 1974). There is indirect evidence that rates of depression, among elderly males at least, increase after age sixty-five. One very impressive statistic is that of suicides in white males. The base rate for white males aged fifteen to twenty-four is 7.4 per 100,000. This rate increases steadily with age, so that for the sixty-five to seventy-four age group, the rate is 45.5 (Resnik and Kantor, 1970).

Many of the psychiatric investigations into the initial panel data focused upon the problem of depression in old age. Evidence was found that indicates that depressive episodes increase in frequency and depth in the advanced years of life. In one of the early investigations (Busse et al., 1955), the researchers found that elderly subjects were aware of more frequent and more annoying depressive periods than they had experienced earlier in life. The subjects reported that during such episodes they felt so discouraged, worried, and troubled that they often saw no reason to continue their existence. However, only a small number admitted entertaining suicidal ideas, although a larger percentage did state that during such depressive periods they would welcome a painless death.

The vast majority of the depressed subjects were able to trace the onset of most of these depressive episodes to specific stimuli. Previous research by Busse et al. (1954), related these depressions of old age to the loss of self-esteem which results from the aged individual's inability to supply his needs or drives (loss of narcissistic supplies) or to defend himself against threats to his security. The pathologic mechanism of introjection, or the turning inward of hostile impulses that are unacceptable to the superego, is relatively common in the depression of younger adults, but seldom present, to the same degree, in elderly people. Thus, the depressions of old age may be relatively guilt free, with self-accusatory tendencies absent. Since these early studies, additional data on prevalence of depression have accumulated, and in the next section of this paper we present those findings.

Longitudinal Evaluation of Depression

Table B—1 presents an overall statistical summary of the prevalence of depression during the entire course of the study to date. These data document the high likelihood of depression throughout. With one exception (study IV), the proportion of people rated depressed remained remarkably constant at approximately 20 percent to 25 percent. These data demonstrate that depression is exceedingly common in well-functioning elderly who live in the community. This point is further emphasized in table B—2, which summarizes the data according to the number of times the panelists were seen prior to death or dropout. Since the surviving panel has had ten periods of evaluation, it was decided to collapse the table into five categories for which the proportion rated depressed was enumerated. This clearly demonstrates the increasing proportion rated depressed over time. The cumulative effect is such that by seven or eight periods of evaluation, only 30 percent of the people who remained had no depressive episode, 40 percent had at least one such episode, and 30 percent had two or more episodes. This longitudinal analysis of data demonstrates rather clearly that very few, even well-functioning, elderly escape depression. The legacy of a long life appears to be a confrontation and struggle with the value of living. The issue for older people may well be not just survival but meaningful and purposeful existence.

Old age has been described as a season of loss, and depressive reactions are responses to losses. The theme of loss is cited by a number of authors (Pfeiffer and Busse, 1973; Shock, 1962; Kreps, 1960; Heyman and Gianturco, 1973), to include inevitable declines in physical vigor, mental agility, income, loss of loved one, and, finally, one's own impending demise. The ubiquitous nature of loss at this time of life may be one factor to explain the high frequency of depression.

The high prevalence of depression in old age is apparently not confined to the United States, which has a culture that does not treat its elderly in a kindly fashion (Palmore, 1975). In a particularly noteworthy cross-cultural study utilizing participants from many countries with different cultural traditions, an extremely high incidence of depression in the sixty-five and older age group was found (Zung, 1972). Loss of self-esteem was the most predominant depressive factor uncovered. This study corroborates our findings and demonstrates that, regardless of cultural attitudes, depression is the price which must be paid for the privilege of survival.

Recurrent Nature of Depression

Table B—3 classifies people according to whether or not they were depressed at round one and then whether they returned at least once more during a following

Table B—1. *Prevalence of depression.*

	Study period									
Number	I	II	III	IV	V	VI	VII	VIII	IX	X
Evaluated	264	174	136	110	89	87	48	37	19	16
Not evaluated	6	24	12	8	14	4	7	6	10	248
Died/dropped out		72	122	152	167	179	215	227	246	
Rated depressed	55 (21%)	38 (22%)	39 (29%)	17 (15%)	18 (20%)	20 (23%)	7 (15%)	9 (24%)	3 (21%)	4 (25%)

Table B—2. *Frequency of depression.*

Number of depressive episodes	Number of times evaluated					
	1–2	3–4	5–6	7–8	9–10	Total
0	84 (66%)	26 (48%)	20 (47%)	10 (30%)	3 (43%)	143
1	39 (31%)	16 (30%)	23 (30%)	13 (40%)	1 (14%)	92
2+	4 (3%)	12 (22%)	10 (23%)	10 (30%)	3 (45%)	39
Total	127	54	53	33	7	274

Table B—3. *Recurrence of depression.*

	Depressed	
Round	Yes	No
I	31	163
II/III	6/16 (38%)	17/71 (24%)
IV/X	13/15 (87%)	49/92 (53%)

round. The table also presents the frequency of depression during later rounds for these two groups. Thirty-one people who were depressed at round one and 163 who were not depressed at round one were examined at least one more time. For the sake of clarity, the data are collapsed into those seen two or three times and those seen four or more times. This table clearly demonstrates that, while there is a high frequency of depression for both groups, those rated depressed at round one had a much higher recurrence rate of depressive episode in the later rounds. The recurrent nature of depression is illustrated since almost 90 percent of those depressed at round one had at least one other depressive episode. One must wonder whether such recurrences are not preventable with proper intervention. The extremely high recurrence rate mandates a strategy not only of treatment but of prevention.

Age

Table B—4 presents a cross-sectional analysis of all the depression evaluations based on age. All of the data, regardless of when collected, were categorized by subject age. The number of patients rated depressed and not depressed were grouped into age decades.

There appears to be no relationship between the proportion of people rated depressed and age category within the elderly group. This suggests that depressive episodes are based upon factors other than simple chronological age. This finding is in agreement with a previous study on round-one data. This early study tested the affect of age on the incidence of depression (Dovenmuehle and

Table B—4. *Depression and age.*

Age	Not depressed	Depressed
60–69	145 (74%)	51 (26%)
70–79	403 (81%)	96 (19%)
80–89	208 (78%)	58 (22%)
90+	14 (78%)	4 (22%)
Total	770 (79%)	209 (21%)

McGough, 1965). Age differences within the elderly group were not significant for incidence of depression.

Health and depression

The technique of stepwise multiple regression analysis was used to examine the correlation between a number of different variables and episodes of depression. The initial analysis on first-round data related depression to financial situation and physical condition. However, analysis of the subsequent data in the following rounds made clear that there exists a sex difference in these related variables. Repeated episodes of depression in women is significantly associated with their financial state, whereas in men physical function is the most significant variable. These findings do not mean that other variables such as age, sex, race, marital status, nearness to death, education, etc. are unimportant but that no consistent pattern of association can be ascertained. The finding that there is an association between depression and the older person's health status (i.e., declining physical function is positively related to increased incidence of depression) is not a new observation.

In a previous study it was found that depressed subjects had significantly more physical pathology than normals (Busse and Dovenmuehle, 1959). This suggests that decline in physical function increases the likelihood of depression. Physical pathology often disrupts mobility, which can lead to social isolation. It also interrupts many other pursuits and activities which ordinarily contribute to self-esteem (Pfeiffer and Busse, 1973).

Nowlin (1974) analyzed the relationship between depression and health in the longitudinal population over a ten-year period of observation. He found an association between depression and limitation of activity, lower self-health ratings, concern about health, higher systolic blood pressure, and more abnormal cardiovascular ratings. He speculated that "poor health with its attendant discomforts and limitations may invoke the feeling state of depression."

It is tempting to speculate why such sex differences exist. Certainly the elderly men in the study grew to manhood in a culture where performance, either in work or athletics, is a highly valued trait among men. Decrements in physical abilities would be viewed as a greater threat to self-esteem. Also, men have shorter longevity than women, and decrements in health may be viewed with greater fears about survival. Women, on the other hand, may worry about finances since they do have a longer life span. Both men and women place a high premium on their independence, and such factors as poverty and ill health usually mean that, to survive, the older person must become more dependent. This is a prospect which all older people view with intense distaste.

Organic Brain Syndrome

The elderly are particularly prone to organic brain syndrome. The extensive epidemiological survey of old age mental disorders in Newcastle upon Tyne (Kay et al., 1964), estimated that 5.6 percent of all the elderly over age sixty-five have chronic brain syndrome. The increasing duration of life among the elderly raises the prevalence of this group of disorders, requiring society to make an increasing commitment to provide for the care of such persons.

What symptoms constitute an organic brain syndrome has been clearly defined: according to the second edition of *Diagnostic and Statistical Manual* of the American Psychiatric Association (DSM II), the symptoms of organic brain syndrome include: impairment of orientation, impairment of memory, impairment of intellect, impairment of judgment, and lability and shallowness of affect.

The technique of assessment for organic brain syndrome was the standard mental status examination. This method frequently revealed a discrepancy between the elderly person's subjective self-assessment of his abilities and the more objective tests. Many elderly subjects will admit to memory decline or intellectual impairment yet perform adequately on tests of these mental functions. For example, during the first series of observations, 26 percent of the volunteers admitted to poor memory for recent events; 6 percent said they had poor memory for remote events; and 10 percent considered themselves to have had a decline in intellectual function; yet only 14 percent of the volunteers had evidence of disorientation and only 3 percent demonstrated confusion. This discrepancy may reflect the insensitivity of our tests which were unable to discriminate the fine differences appreciated by the volunteers. Clearly our subjects complained more extensively about declining abilities than the objective testing demonstrated.

Prevalence of Organic Brain Syndrome

Table B—5 presents a round-by-round tabulation of the prevalence of dementia in the community volunteers. Clinically, 26 percent of these volunteers were judged to have a mild organic brain syndrome and 3 percent were considered to have objective signs and symptoms severe enough for the diagnosis of organic brain syndrome (moderate to severe) in round one. This latter figure is more similar to the prevalence of organic brain syndrome reported in the epidemiological literature (Kay et al., 1964).

Table B—5. *Prevalence of organic brain syndrome.*

Round	No disability	Mild disability	Moderate to severe disability
I (N = 263)	71%	26%	3%
II (N = 180)	78%	17%	4%
III (N = 129)	79%	18%	4%
IV (N = 106)	62%	33%	8%
V (N = 89)	63%	29%	8%
VI (N = 81)	60%	31%	9%
VII (N = 45)	48%	46%	3%
VIII (N = 37)	62%	30%	8%
IX (N = 15)	77%	23%	
X (N = 16)	50%	38%	12%

In eight of these mentally impaired volunteers, there was an associated psychosis predominantly organic in origin (Busse et al., 1960). These eight subjects all had recent and remote memory defects. The finding that these subjects were maintaining a satisfactory adjustment in the community despite psychotic illness leads one to conclude that the other factors which permit a person to maintain a satisfactory community role need investigation.

The proportion rated mildly disabled (less than 20 percent disability) varies from a low of 17 percent to a high of 46 percent. There is a tendency, though not marked, for the percentage in this category to increase. This tendency is more apparent in the moderate to severe category of disability (greater than 20 percent), where the increase is from 3 percent in round one to 12 percent in round ten. These figures indicate that dementia of varying degree is quite common among elderly persons living in the community. Since the average age of the sample gradually increases with each successive round (average age eighty by round nine), there is a gradual increase in the prevalence of this disorder in our sample, though not so dramatic as to be obvious.

Course of Organic Brain Syndrome

Seventy-six people (26 percent of total) were rated impaired at round one. In round two, thirty-two of them were rated impaired. Sixteen were rated unimpaired, eighteen were dead and ten did not return. Subsequent analysis revealed that there were an additional thirty-nine subjects in the later rounds who received an impaired rating which was followed by unimpaired ratings. These findings reveal the high variability of the course of organic brain syndrome. Unlike the popular conception of this disorder as a fixed entity, organic brain symptoms are frequently characterized by varying degrees of remission and exacerbation.

This finding can be confirmed by clinical observation of impaired elderly individuals in institutions. Dramatic improvement of the mental state can often be achieved when underlying physical problems are adequately treated or the patient's milieu is altered so as to receive a satisfactory degree of interaction with others. Such programs as reality-orientation, occupational therapy, recreation, singing, and physical therapy are highly desirable alternatives to the usual practice of allowing brain syndrome patients to vegetate. Findings from the first longitudinal study support the activity theory: that the most satisfying pattern of aging is to maintain as high a level of physical, mental, and social activity as is consistent with the person's life-style (Palmore, 1970).

Longitudinal analysis of all subjects revealed that 154 (59 percent) of the subjects eventually received a rating of organic brain syndrome with disability prior to death or dropout. This is a much higher frequency than any cross-sectional analysis of single-round data on dementia (see table B—5). An episode of brain impairment can therefore be expected to occur in roughly half the elderly who survive their sixty-fifth birthday. This is a rather frightening prospect, particularly for the elderly, many of whom report that they fear dependence and disability far more than death. Long-term survival can be viewed as both a blessing and a burden. Life is sweet and enjoyable but the end of the road becomes increasingly fraught with perils of the worst sort.

Fortunately, despite the high prevalence of this syndrome in this sample, only one subject required hospitalization in a psychiatric institution. So, despite impaired brain function and the associated intellectual deterioration, these subjects were capable of living a community life. Clearly, many factors other than brain impairment play a role in determining whether a person with organic brain syndrome may remain in the community. Adaptation to these changes as well as stresses from the environment may play a crucial part in the psychological deterioration often associated with these disorders. Such complications as depression, regression, agitation, and paranoid symptoms may well be determined more by the person's personality and environment than by the brain impairment. For this reason, the clinical syndrome associated with this disorder has been described as a sociopsychosomatic disorder (Wang and Busse, 1970). The following example is illustrative of this view.

After the death of her husband, a seventy-nine-year old white female lived with her eldest daughter for two years. Over the last several months of her life, she manifested confusion, nocturnal restlessness, agitation, incontinence, and delusions of poisoning. The daughter was extremely devoted to her mother and painfully attentive to all her needs. She never displayed anger, irritation or resentment over her enormous sacrifices of ministering to this elderly woman, who required almost constant nursing. During her mother's hospitalization, the daughter refused to even consider placement and instead planned to take her mother home as soon as improvement could be affected. With the staff, the mother remained calm and collected and even occasionally manifested periods of lucidity. She ate and slept well and was no longer incontinent. However, whenever the daughter visited, her behavior quickly deteriorated. She would become visibly agitated, clutch at the bed rails and try to raise herself stating, "I've got to get out of here." Thereafter, she would spend a restless night and would wet the bed. The contrast in the woman's behavior was most striking.

Related Factors

The factors contributing to organic brain syndrome have been previously studied in this population of subjects (Busse and Wang, 1974). Many factors were found to be related including decompensated heart disease, low socioeconomic status, and inactivity. Mild elevation of blood pressure was positively correlated with preserved brain function. The authors speculated that the relatively high blood pressure may be necessary to maintain sufficient blood supply to the brain for adequate cerebral function.

There was no relationship found between the amount of social contacts and organic brain syndrome. This finding was confirmed by the San Francisco project (Lowenthal, 1965), where it was concluded that isolation may well be a consequence rather than a factor in organic mental illness of old age.

Much remains to be uncovered by future research. Promising research directions include studies of cerebral blood flow, neurochemical studies, effects of new drugs on mentation, and neuropathologic investigations.

EEG

An excellent review of the EEG findings during the longitudinal studies has recently appeared (Busse, 1973). The major findings are summarized as follows:

Progressive slowing of the dominant alpha frequency and the appearance of slow waves in the theta or delta range is characteristically found in organic brain syndrome (Wang and Busse, 1970). Furthermore, there is a highly positive correlation between EEG frequency and cerebral oxygen consumption or blood flow (Obrist, 1963). Focal abnormalities of the EEG, largely over the left temporal areas of the brain, have been repeatedly observed in a high percentage of apparently healthy older people (Busse et al., 1955). The origin of these foci and their significance is unclear. In any event the occurrence of focal EEG abnormalities has little or no prognostic or diagnostic value among the aged (Busse and Obrist, 1963) and are not related to transient ischemic attacks. An incidental finding, the significance of which is unclear, is that fast activity and temporal foci are much more common in elderly women than men.

Hypochondriasis

The neurotic disorder of hypochondriasis is defined by the second edition of *Diagnostic and Statistical Manual* of the American Psychiatric Association (DSM-II) as "a condition dominated by preoccupation with the body and with fear of presumed diseases of various organs. The fears persist despite reassurance . . . and there are no losses or distortion of function." This condition is encountered in

many elderly people who attend medical clinics and this pattern of illness frequently precipitates a request for psychiatric consultation. Such patients may be considered to have a psychotic disturbance if the hypochondriacal symptoms are of delusional quality or if the functional incapacity is total.

Hypochondriacal reactions do occur in elderly people and interfere with their health and happiness. This category of reaction is usually considered a neurosis.

Psychoneurotic reactions were found to be extremely common among the volunteers. The psychoneurotics were found to differ markedly from the other elderly subjects (Busse et al., 1960). They had a much lower evaluation of their own happiness and contentment, fewer friends, and fewer wholesome attitudes toward their friends. The authors pointed out that the vast majority of the severe neurotics were in fact hypochondriacs. Despite no difference in overall physical function, they showed a marked difference in health attitudes (a clear result of their neurotic overconcern with body functions). There was no discernible difference between the neurotic and normal groups in work attitudes. They argue that this may be an important finding, since a socially acceptable attitude toward work may be one of the major factors in maintaining an individual in the community in spite of neurotic processes. These elderly differed from typical hypochondriacs in that they did not seek excessive medical attention.

The psychodynamics of hypochondriasis are considered a defensive operation against the loss of self-esteem by withdrawal from other persons and concentration on the self; the hypochondriacal symptoms may be viewed by the person as punishment and atonement for feelings of hostility; and the symptom can serve the purpose of shifting anxiety away from interpersonal issues to a less threatening concern with bodily function (Busse, 1975).

The first longitudinal study has provided an opportunity to serve hypochondriacal tendencies in elderly subjects who reside in the community. For the first six rounds of observations, a global rating of hypochondriasis was made after the psychiatric interview. In the initial round, 33 percent were found to have hypochondriasis. This percentage declined over the course of the study to roughly half the initial percentage. Table B—6 compares the ratings over the initial two rounds. The general direction is for hypochondriasis to remit. For example, of the fourteen people who were rated in the severe category initially, all received improved ratings in round two; eighteen people who were rated moderate initially improved. These findings indicate that hypochondriasis is not the constant tendency so frequently described in the literature as a lifelong pattern. Rather it appears to remit or exacerbate, depending on numerous factors but most noticeably the phenomenon of depression. Statistical analysis revealed that there was no consistent pattern of association between hypochondriasis and sex, race, physical health, nearness to death, or financial condition. Depression appeared to be the only consistent associated variable. This is not surprising in view of the similarity in the psychodynamics of both disorders. The phenomenon of depressive equivalent reactions is well known to clinicians: painful symptoms

Table B—6. *Hypochondriasis.*

	Round 1			
Round 2	None	Mild	Moderate	Severe
None	103	14	5	2
Mild	8	16	13	8
Moderate	1	1	1	4
Severe	0	0	0	0

which express the person's underlying depressive state yet conceal it since energy and attention are directed elsewhere. This ailment is another example where hypochondriacal tendencies and depressive reactions are interwoven into the same fabric.

Longitudinal analysis of the first six rounds of data reveal that ultimately over half of the survivors receive a rating of hypochondriasis.

Terminal Drop

The terminal drop hypothesis states that a decline in intellectual performance may be associated with impending mortality and that this decline may be detected several years prior to the death of the person (Kleemeir, 1962). This suggests that factors such as health deterioration are associated with intellectual decline rather than with normal aging. Since the diagnosis of organic brain syndrome implies intellectual deterioration, an analysis of the survival patterns in the longitudinal study should provide a test of this hypothesis.

The test was completely negative and it questions the hypothesis of terminal drop. Statistical analysis of survival patterns after the onset of organic brain syndrome, controlled for age and sex, showed no substantive differences from other volunteers. The average survival time was roughly 120 months for both groups. This is a rather surprising result in view of the previously reported positive relationship between physical disability, particularly of the cardiovascular system, and organic brain syndrome (Busse and Wang, 1974), as well as between brain impairment and earlier death (Wang and Busse, 1974). Several plausible explanations exist. First, the number of volunteers in the study may have been too small to reveal the difference in mortality. Sound actuarial statistics are usually comprised from the mortality of thousands of persons. Second, it is entirely possible that the genuine difference in physical disability between the organic and the nonorganic groups may have been too small to exert a deleterious impact on mortality. Third, since the organically disabled volunteers remained in the community until their terminal illness, the favorable impact of supportive relationships and continued familiar physical surroundings may have been considerable.

The Newcastle studies (Savage et al., 1973), found significant differences in mortality between community residents with organic brain syndrome and other elderly.

The terminal drop hypothesis has been recently reviewed (Siegler, 1975). Siegler conceptualized two components: the relationship between the level of cognitive performance and survival, and the relationship between the level of cognitive performance and death. She cited five longitudinal studies in support of the hypothesis and three against. Clearly, the issue has not been resolved, but the author concludes that the concept has stimulated sharper evaluation of the effects of health status and correlates of survival into studies of cognitive functioning.

Attitudes toward Death

The first section of this chapter concludes with a review of the Duke longitudinal study reports on age and death. Since attitudes toward death may have an effect on psychological adjustment in the later years, an exploration of the feelings and thoughts associated with physical death, either of the self or of loved ones, is an entirely appropriate topic in a psychiatric paper.

During the first round of the study, two questions about death were included. The responses contradicted the idea that most aged persons are fearful about death (Jeffers et al., 1961). Only 10 percent of the volunteers admitted to fear of death; 35 percent said they had no fear; and the rest said no, but with qualifications suggesting ambivalent feelings. Factors associated with no fear of death include frequent Bible reading, belief in a future life, religious conceptions of death, fewer feelings of depression, and higher IQ scores. Seventy-seven percent of the volunteers were convinced that a personal life after death exists. Very few (only 2 percent) denied such a belief outright.

A related investigation reported on the frequency of death thoughts by the volunteers (Jeffers and Verwoerdt, 1966). Most of the volunteers believed that people their age thought about death more often than in earlier years. Forty-two percent stated that they thought of death daily, and 7 percent stated that death thoughts were a constant accompaniment to their life. Almost half thought that the enjoyment of life was marred by death thoughts. During the interviews, the majority of subjects were extremely willing to speak about death and most did so with an accepting, comfortable affect.

These findings can lead one to speculate that denial is an important mechanism for dealing with the anxiety associated with death. The mental mechanism of denial is therefore an important adaptive mechanism in personality adjustment associated with old age. This concept has recently received strong support from Becker (1975), who argues that terror of death is natural and is present in everyone—the "worm at the core" of man's pretensions to happiness. Man must therefore use defensive mechanisms (denial systems) or else face overwhelming anxiety.

A discussion of death would not be complete without some comments on bereavement. Actually, while widowhood is one of the most significant events in life, the repercussions over time for the older person are not as dramatic as might be expected. Studies of the elderly persons who have been widowed during the course of the longitudinal study conclude that the normal elderly adapt to the death of the spouse in fashion characterized by (1) emotional stability supported by deep religious faith and (2) relatively few life changes. Several women did show a trend in the direction of increased depressed feelings, and lowered feelings of usefulness (Heyman and Gianturco, 1973).

In addition to the factors enumerated previously, the reasonable adaptation to bereavement in the elderly may be accounted for by "death rehearsal." This is an important psychological mechanism which enables people to prepare intellectually and emotionally for bereavement. The opportunity for death rehearsal permits gradual identification with the widowhood role before the actual event. Such events as decline in health, a lingering illness, deaths of contemporaries, making of wills, reading the obituary column, and frequent thoughts of death permit rehearsal at a leisurely pace.

References

Becker, E. *The denial of death*. New York: MacMillan, 1975.

Busse, E. W., Barnes, R. H., and Silverman, A. J. Studies of the processes of aging: Factors that influence the psyche of elderly persons. *American Journal of Psychiatry*, 110:897–903, 1954.

Busse, E. W., et al. Studies of the processes of aging: X. The strengths and weaknesses of psychic functioning in the aged. *American Journal of Psychiatry*, 111:896–901, 1955.

Busse, E. W., and Dovenmuehle, R. H. Neurotic symptoms and predisposition in aging people. Paper read at the Annual Orthopsychiatric Meeting, San Francisco, April, 1959.

Busse, E. W., Dovenmuehle, R. H., and Brown, R. G. Psychoneurotic reactions in the aged. *Geriatrics*, 15:97–105, 1960.

Busse, E. W., and Obrist, W. D. Significance of focal electroencephalographic changes in the elderly. *Postgraduate Medicine*, 34:179–182, 1963.

Busse, E. W., Schlagenhauff, R. E., and Carney, A. L. Round table discussion: EEG in gerontology. *Clinical Electroencephalography*, 4:152–184, 1973.

Busse, E. W., and Wang, H. S. The multiple factors contributing to dementia in old age. In Palmore, E. B. (Ed.), *Normal aging II*. Durham, N.C.: Duke University Press, 1974, 151–159.

Busse, E. W. Aging and psychiatric diseases of late life. In M. F. Reiser (Ed.), *American handbook of psychiatry IV*. New York: Basic Books, 1975, 67–89.

Cobb, S., King, S., and Chen, E. Differences between respondents and non-respondents in a morbidity survey involving clinical examination. *Journal of Chronic Diseases*, 6:95–108, 1957.

Dovenmuehle, R. H., and McGough, W. E. Aging, culture and affect: Predisposing factors. *International Journal of Social Psychiatry*, 11:19, 1965.

Eisdorfer, C., and Wilkie, F. Intellectual change with advanced age. In L. F. Jarvik, C. Eisdorfer, and J. E. Blum (Eds.), *Intellectual functioning in adults*. New York: Springer, 1973.

Gianturco, D. T. The older psychiatric patient at Duke Hospital. In W. E. Fann and G. L. Maddox (Eds.), *Drug issues in geropsychiatry*. Baltimore: Williams & Wilkins, 1974, 73–76.

Heyman, D. K., and Gianturco, D. T. Long-term adaptation by the elderly to bereavement. *Journal of Gerontology*, 28:359–362, 1973.

Jeffers, F. C., Nichols, C. R., and Eisdorfer, C. Attitudes of older persons towards death. *Journal of Gerontology*, 16:53–56, 1961.

Jeffers, F. C., and Verwoerdt, A. Factors associated with the frequency of death thoughts. In *Elderly community volunteers; Proceedings of the Seventh International Congress of Gerontology*, 1966, 149–152.

Kay, D. W. K., Beamish, P., and Roth, M. Old age mental disorders in Newcastle-upon-Tyne. Part I: A study of prevalence. *British Journal of Psychiatry*, 110:146–158, 1964.

Kleemeier, R. W. Intellectual changes in the senium. *Proceedings of the American Statistical Association, Social Statistics Section*, 1:290–295, 1962.

Kreps, J. M. Economics of retirement. In E. W. Busse and E. Pfeiffer (Eds.), *Behavior and adaptation in late life*. Boston: Little, Brown, 1969.

Lowenthal, M. F. Antecedents of isolation and mental illness in old age. *Archives of General Psychiatry*, 12:245–250, 1965.

Maddox, G. L. Selected methodological issues. *Proceedings of The American Statistical Association, Social Statistics Section*, 1962, 280–285.

Nowlin, J. Depression and health. In Palmore, E. B. (Ed.), *Normal aging II*. Durham, N.C.: Duke University Press, 1974, 168–172.

Obrist, W. D., et al. Relation of EEG to cerebral blood flow and metabolism in old age. *Electroencephalography and Clinical Neurophysiology*, 15:610–619, 1963.

Palmore, E. B. (Ed.), *Normal aging*. Durham, N.C.: Duke University Press, 1970.

Palmore, E. B. *The honorable elders*. Durham, N.C.: Duke University Press, 1975.

Pfeiffer, E., and Busse, E. W. Affective disorders. In E. W. Busse and E. Pfeiffer (Eds.), *Mental illness in later life*. Washington, D.C.: American Psychiatric Association, 1973, 107–144.

Redick, R. W., Kramer, M., and Taube, C. A. Epidemiology of mental illness and utilization of psychiatric facilities among older persons. In E. W. Busse and E. Pfeiffer (Eds.), *Mental illness in later life*. Washington, D.C.: American Psychiatric Association, 1973, 199–232.

Resnik, H. L. P., and Kantor, J. M. Suicide and aging. *Journal of the American Geriatrics Society*, 7:152–158, 1970.

Savage, R. D., et al., *Intellectual functioning in the aged*. London: Methuen, 1973.

Shepherd, M., et al. *Psychiatric illness in general practice*. London: Oxford University Press, 1966, 1–21.

Shock, N. W., The physiology of aging. *Scientific American*, 206:100–110, 1962.

Siegler, I. C. The terminal drop hypothesis: Factor artifact. *Experimental Aging Research*, 1:169–185, 1975.

Stotsky, B. A. Extended care and institutional care: Current trends, methods, and experience. In E. W. Busse and E. Pfeiffer (Eds.), *Mental illness in later life*. Washington, D.C.: American Psychiatric Association, 1973, 167–178.

Wang, H. S., and Busse, E. W. Dementia in old age. In Wells, C. E. (Ed.), *Dementia*. Philadelphia: F. A. Davis, 1970, 151–162.

Wang, H. S., and Busse, E. W. Brain impairment and longevity. In Palmore, E. B. (Ed.), *Normal aging II*. Durham, N.C.: Duke University Press, 1974, 261–268.

Zung, W. W. K. How normal is depression? *Psychosomatics*, 13:174–178, 1972.

Senescence and Senility

Ewald W. Busse

To attempt to separate the aging processes from acquired disease or trauma-induced pathology, it is necessary to use certain definitions. The biological processes of aging are usually associated with a decline of efficiency and faulty integration of physiological functions or structural alteration that eventually result in death. Some investigators prefer to define biologic aging as a progressive loss of functional capacity after an organism has reached maturity, while others insist that aging processes can be identified with the onset of differentiation. Still others contend that an attempt to separate aging processes and to identify them is not useful or possible. For operational purposes, I prefer to separate declines in functioning into primary aging (senescence) and secondary aging (senility). Primary aging is biological processes which are apparently rooted in heredity. They are inborn and inevitable detrimental changes that are time related but are etiologically relatively independent of stress, trauma, or acquired disease (infection, toxication, or hostile environment). Not all of the aging processes are recognizable in all people, and those that are present do not progress at the same rate. This operational definition clearly has limitations. For example, it does not adequately distinguish between the aging processes and the diagnostic entities related to inborn errors of metabolism. For me, the ultimate question is, can medical science provide the diagnostic skills and the techniques for prevention and intervention which will control the aging processes? Intermediate steps may be possible.

If one assumes that the first cause of senile dementia is an inherent biological defect that is initiated or exacerbated when the human organism is in a vulnerable physiological condition and that this condition has been produced by external insults including trauma, infections, toxic disease, or psychosocial stress, then the avoidance or removal from the environment of such negative factors will permit a degree of prevention or restoration in the individual who is at risk as it pertains to senile dementia.

This complex concept of many of the mental losses associated with aging and senile dementia has existed at Duke for some years (Wang and Busse, 1971). As one would expect, there is no unanimity regarding the accuracy of certain observations and their role in precipitating or aggravating the pathological condition in a vulnerable person.

Reprinted by permission from *Alzheimer's Disease, Senile Dementia, and Related Disorders*. Vol. 7: *Aging*. Edited by R. Katzmann, R. Terry, and K. Bick. New York: Raven Press, 1978.

EEG Changes

EEG changes in adulthood, particularly those which occur in late life, have occupied a substantial part of my interest and work. I will briefly review certain observations which are pertinent to Alzheimer's disease and related disorders.

A common characteristic of EEG changes after the age of sixty-five years is the progressive slowing of the dominant frequency involving the alpha frequency and the appearance of slow waves in the theta or delta range. Elderly subjects in good health are found to have a mean occipital frequency which is almost a full cycle slower than that found in healthy young adults. A slight slowing of the alpha index is not pathognomonic for any particular brain disorder. However, a nonspecific moderate-to-severe slowing is characteristically found in brain disorders whether they are classified as degenerative or vascular in origin. Since a good correlation has been demonstrated between EEG frequency and cerebral oxygen consumption or blood flow, the slowing of the dominant frequency in the majority of elderly people may indicate a depression of cerebral metabolism.

Residents of institutions for the aged are found to have EEG slowing that highly correlates with measures of psychological impairment. Unfortunately, this correlation is not nearly as consistent in subjects who remain in the community. It is possible that those who live in the community are actually adjusting at a borderline level and may be vulnerable to stress which would precipitate the appearance of organic brain disease. Throughout adult life, fast waves are more frequent in women than in men and tend to increase in females. Fast activity is present in 23 percent of females age sixty to seventy-nine but in only 4 percent of elderly males.

Focal abnormalities of EEG, slow waves, and sharp waves over the temporal areas of the brain have been repeatedly observed in 30 percent to 40 percent of apparently healthy elderly people. The left anterior temporal area is primarily involved (75–80 percent). In approximately 25 percent of temporal foci the mid and posterior temporal leads are active. Bilateral focal patterns are found in 18–20 percent and in 4–5 percent the disturbance is found on the right. This finding was first reported by Busse et al. in 1955. Since that date, the observation of the frequent occurrence of a left-temporal focus in old people has been reported by other investigators. A study of healthy volunteers between the ages of twenty and sixty reveals that only 3 percent of normal adults under the age of forty have temporal lobe EEG changes. This increases so that in the twenty years between ages forty and sixty, 20 percent of the subjects show temporal lobe irregularities. After age sixty, severity of the focal disturbance tends to stabilize, but new foci are more likely to appear in women; hence a higher percentage of women have the change as compared to men (Busse, 1973).

In spite of twenty-plus years of attention, the exact origin of these foci, as well as their significance, is not clear. The localized EEG abnormality is usually episodic in nature and is composed of high-voltage waves in the delta and theta range, occasionally accompanied by focal short waves. The disturbance is found in the waking record, is maximum in the drowsy state, and disappears in sleep (Busse and Obrist, 1963). In 75 to 80 percent of the cases, the abnormality is at a maximum or completely confined to the left side of the brain. It is not related to handedness and, although it is evidently episodic in nature, it is unrelated to seizures. Numerous attempts have been made to relate temporal foci to localized cerebral vascular insufficiency and transient ischemic attacks. No consistent relationship has been established. Furthermore, the anterior temporal focal disturbances in senescent EEG's have not been consistently correlated with any clear alteration in psychological function, social adjustment, chronic disease, or longevity. However, Obrist (1976) indicates that when a focal alteration involves adjacent areas or is associated with a more diffuse disturbance, organic brain syndrome is probable.

Clinical Course of Dementia—Influence of Various Factors

Clinicians report that depressive symptoms are not unusual in patients with organic brain disease. The majority of clinical studies indicate that depressive symptoms are more common in cerebral arteriosclerosis and cerebral vascular brain disease disturbances than in senile dementia. One explanation is that insight is less frequently observed in senile dementia.

Some years ago depression in the elderly was often considered prodromal depression or the neuroasthenic stage of cerebral arteriosclerosis or senile dementia. Felix Post and other investigators have demonstrated that elderly depressives do not subsequently develop cerebral degeneration any more than do elderly people in general (Post, 1962).

The Duke longitudinal studies clearly confirm the increase in depressive episodes in the latter part of middle life. However, our studies suggest that the depressive episodes increase in frequency and in depth until approximately the age of seventy, at which time they become relatively constant.

Depressed elderly patients occasionally present a clinical picture of pseudodementia. Obviously the proper recognition of the depressive disorder is essential for clinical purposes but has relatively little importance to organic brain disease.

In 1971, Wang and Busse reported in some detail observations regarding dementia in old age. In that study the term brain *impairment* was utilized to designate measures of loss of brain function based upon a number of laboratory procedures including EEG, cerebral blood flow, cerebral metabolism, etc. The manifestations of possible brain impairment were determined by psychological tests, clinical measures of intellectual performance, and emotional variations. It was found that often there is a poor correlation between these two types of evaluation, i.e., laboratory procedures versus qualified person-to-person observations. Of particular concern is the discrepancy of as much as 25 percent (Busse and Wang, 1974b) found in patients and subjects with a precipitous decline in clinically observable mental signs and symptoms which were not paralleled by evidence of physiologically measured brain changes. Careful consideration of factors such as general physical health, economic status, social environment, and previous living habits led to the conclusion by Wang that dementia in late life is a social sociopsychosomatic disorder.

The technique of assessment for organic brain syndrome in the first longitudinal study was a systematized mental status examination that includes two sections specifically rating the presence or absence and degree of organic signs and symptoms. The evaluator completes a six-point OBS rating scale utilizing all observations made during the mental examination. This method of evaluation frequently revealed discrepancy between the elderly person's subjective self-assessment of his abilities and the more objective structured evaluations. A paper by Gianturco and Busse (1978) reports many elderly subjects will complain of memory decline or intellectual impairment yet perform adequately on tests of these mental functions. For example, during the first series of observations, 20 percent of the volunteers admitted to poor memory for recent events. In addition, 6 percent said they had a poor memory for remote events, and 10 percent considered themselves to have had a decline in intellectual function, particularly in such things as problem solving. However, only 14 percent of the volunteers were recorded to have problems of orientation, particularly with time and date, and only 3 percent demonstrated some confusion. Evaluations for organic disability as demonstrated in table 4 (Busse and Gianturco), indicate that 26 percent were considered to show evidence of possible-to-mild organic signs and symptoms, while 3 percent were rated as having moderate-to-serious disability. This discrepancy, which actually has become more apparent during the longitudinal studies, shows that our subjects complain more extensively about declining abilities than the structured evaluations could demonstrate. It is of interest to note that those classified as moderate-to-severe represent 3 percent of the sample, and this percentage is not remarkably different from the prevalence of organic brain syndrome reported in the epidemiological literature.

Again, referring to table 5, one notes that the rate of mildly disabled (less than 20 percent disability) varies from a low of 17 percent to a high of 46 percent. There is a slight tendency for the percentage in this category to increase over time. This trend is more apparent in the moderate-to-severe category of disability that is greater than 20 percent, where the increase is from 3 percent in round one to 12 percent in round ten (span of twenty years). The average age of the sample gradually increases with each successive round: 70.8 to 85.25 years. There is a gradual increase in the prevalence of this disorder in our longitudinal sample.

There were seventy-six people who were rated mildly impaired in round one. In the next round, thirty-two of them were rated impaired; sixteen were rated unimpaired; eighteen were dead and ten did not return. Longitudinal analysis revealed that there was an additional thirty-nine subjects in the later rounds who received an impaired rating who in a subsequent year had unimpaired ratings. These findings point to a high variability in the course of organic brain syndrome. Obviously these observations indicated that the signs and symptoms of organic brain disease are not persistent but rather are characterized by varying degrees of remission and exacerbations.

Longitudinal analysis of all subjects revealed that 154 (59 percent) eventually receive evaluation indicating the presence of organic brain syndrome with some degree of disability prior to death or dropout. This is a much higher frequency than would be indicated by any cross-sectional analysis of the presence or absence of dementia. To state it another way, an episode of brain impairment can therefore be expected to incur in roughly half the elderly who survive their sixtieth birthday.

Factors contributing to the appearance of organic brain signs and symptoms have been previously studied in this population of subjects (Busse and Wang, 1974b). The major contributors appeared to be decompensated heart disease, low socioeconomic status, and decreased physical and mental activity. One should be aware that Lowenthal in 1965 reported that there was no relationship between the amount of social contacts and organic brain disease. The findings from this San Francisco project led to the conclusion that isolation may well be a consequence of original mental disease rather than a factor in the development of organic mental illnesses of old age.

The relationship to cardiovascular pulmonary disease has been looked at very carefully. Mild elevation of blood pressure was positively correlated with preserved brain function. It is our speculation that the relatively high blood pressure may be necessary to maintain sufficient blood supply to the brain for adequate cerebral function (1974a).

Summary

Utilizing the electroencephalogram as the measure of physiological functioning of the aging brain, it is evident that there is a distinct sex difference in the aging process in that a large number (26 percent) of the elderly women reveal an increase in diffuse fast activity. There is some suggestion that fast activity is related to the preservation of intellectual functioning.

Two other age changes are seen in the EEG. The first is slowing of the dominant alpha and the appearance of theta waves. Slowing of the EEG does tend to correlate with a decline in mental capacities. The third age change is the gradual development of foci in the anterior temporal area, particularly on the left in more than one-third of elderly men and women. This change has not consistently shown an effect on mental capacities or behavior. The fact that these changes occur in a broad spectrum of noninstitutionalized elderly people confirms that they must be given attention as part of the aging processes.

The loss of mental ability in late life is not usually the result of solely a pathologic brain change. Incapacitating dementia is not an inevitable consequence within the limited life span of most elderly Americans. The loss of mental ability (what one does) and capacity (what is possible) is influenced by changes within the brain, the health status of the entire body, behavioral patterns, and socioeconomic determinants. Consequently, the clinical course is often found to be one of periodic exacerbation and remissions or recovery and recurrence.

References

Busse, E. W. Administration of the interdisciplinary research team. *Journal of Medical Education*, 40:832–839, 1965.

Busse, E. W. Physiological, psychological, and sociological study of aging. In E. B. Palmore (Ed.), *Normal aging*. Durham, N.C.: Duke University Press, 1970, 3–6.

Busse, E. W. Brain wave changes in late life. *Clinical Electroencephalography*, 4:153–163, 1973.

Busse, E. W., et al. Studies of processes of aging. X: Strengths and weaknesses of psychic functioning in the aged. *American Journal of Psychiatry*, 111:896–901, 1955.

Busse, E. W., and Obrist, W. D. Significance of focal electroencephalographic changes in the elderly. *Postgraduate Medicine*, 34:179–182, 1963.

Busse, E. W., and Wang, H. S. Heart disease and brain impairment among aged persons. In E. B. Palmore, (Ed.), *Normal aging II*. Durham, N.C.: Duke University Press, 1974a, 160–167.

Busse, E. W., and Wang, H. S. Multiple factors contributing to dementia in old age. In E. B. Palmore, (Ed.), *Normal aging II*. Durham, N.C.: Duke University Press, 1974b, 151–160.

Gianturco, E., and Busse, E. W. Psychiatric problems encountered during a long term study of normal aging volunteers. In A. D. Isaacs and F. Post (Eds.), *Studies in geriatric psychiatry*. Chichester, Sussex: Wiley, 1978.

Lowenthal, M. F. The relationship between social factors and mental health in the aged. In A. Simon and L. S. Epestein (Eds.), Aging in modern society. Psychiatric Research Report 23, 187–197. American Psychiatric Association, Washington, D.C., 1968.

Maddox, G. L. A longitudinal multidisciplinary study of human aging: Selected methodological issues. *Proceedings of the American Statistical Association, Social Statistics Section*. 1962, 280–285.

Obrist, W. D. Problems of aging. In Antoine Redmond (Ed.), *Handbook of Electroencephalography and Clinical Neurophysiology*, Vol. 6. Section V. Amsterdam: Elsevier, 1976, 6:6A275–6A292.

Palmore, E. B. Appendix A. Design of the adaptation study. In E. B. Palmore (Ed.), *Normal aging II*. Durham, N.C.: Duke University Press, 1974, 291–296.

Post, F. *The significance of affective symptoms in old age*. London: Oxford University Press, 1962.

Ramm, D., and Gianturco, D. Appendix B. Data processing in longitudinal studies. In E. B. Palmore, (Ed.), *Normal aging II*. Durham, N.C.: Duke University Press, 1974, 297–307.

Wang, H. S., and Busse, E. W. Dementia in old age. In C. Wells (Ed.), *Dementia*. Philadelphia: F. A. Davis, 1971, 151–162.

Electroencephalographic Changes in Late Life

Ewald W. Busse and H. S. Wang

Introduction

This review is concerned with characteristics of the human electroencephalograms commonly found for persons in late life. The review is based upon the Duke longitudinal studies of normal aging which have occupied much of the attention of the authors. Included is a brief description of the methodology and the criteria for interpretation of the EEGs. Elsewhere in this volume is a description of the two longitudinal research studies.

EEG Methodology and Criteria

This EEG research was started prior to the development of the international standards for electrode placement, recording standards, and classification. Twelve scalp electrodes were placed symmetrically over the major areas of each hemisphere (frontal, precentral, parietal, occipital, anterior temporal, and posterior temporal), with reference leads on the vertex and ears. Particular attention was given to the location of the anterior temporal electrodes, placed 1.5 cm above the zygomatic arch at a point one-third of the distance between the auditory meatus and external canthus of the eye. EEGs were recorded on a Grass instrument by means of both monopolar and bipolar techniques. A sufficient length of tracing was obtained to ensure an adequate evaluation of the waking state. When possible, drowsiness and natural sleep were also recorded. The possible effects of medication taken by a few of the subjects were considered in evaluating the EEGs. Interpretation of the records was based upon adult standards (Gibbs and Gibbs, 1950) and was carried out independently by both of the authors and their associates. Comparisons of interpretations on the same subjects revealed 88 percent agreement between investigators. Discrepancies were resolved by joint review and consultation.

Waking EEGs were rated as follows (the original Gibbs system was used for classification with some elaboration. Details are available in Technical Report Type I, EEG longitudinal studies, Duke University, Center for the Study of Aging and Human Development): (1) *normal*: variable amounts of 8–12 c/sec alpha rhythm mixed with low-voltage fast-activity in the absence of other features noted below. Beta activity (low-voltage fast [LVF]), a type of normal activity, can be the dominant activity. LVF is composed of brain waves with a frequency above the alpha range, usually between 18–30 cps and does not exceed twenty microvolts; (2) *diffuse slow*: generalized appearance of theta ($4/7$ through c/sec) or delta ($1/3$ through c/sec) waves composing the dominant activity of a record; (3) *excess fast*: occurrence of rhythmic activity above alpha frequency (beta waves) exceeding fifteen microvolts and present 50 percent of the time in one or more leads; (4) *focal disturbance*: either (*a*) focal slow waves, (*b*) amplitude asymmetry, or (*c*) focal sharp waves. *Focal slow* is defined as theta or delta waves, localized to a given cortical region, which appear and are classified as either unilateral or bilateral. *Amplitude asymmetry* denotes a persistence of or numerous runs of alpha or beta (LVF) activity in which there is a 50 percent difference in voltage between homologous areas of the two hemispheres. *Focal sharp waves* refer to localized potentials of less than 100 milliseconds that have a spike-like configuration, usually standing out above the background activity. Except for the normal tracings, which are separate, the above categories are not mutually exclusive.

The Normal EEG

The human electroencephalogram undergoes progressive changes with age from birth through senescence. There are two distinct components of the normal adult EEGs recorded while awake. The relatively regular alpha rhythm changes with advancing age in both males and females. Aging does not seem to have a clear impact upon beta rhythm (low voltage fast activity). Alpha activity is seen as physiological evidence of the maturing process as it appears after three and a half to four years of age and progressively reaches its adult characteristics between twelve and sixteen years. Both alpha and beta activity will be discussed in some detail.

Alpha Activity

Slowing of the alpha frequency is the most common change in EEGs recorded after the age of sixty-five. By limiting the range of alpha to waves between 8 and 13 c/sec, such slowing by definition remains within the alpha range. Cross-sectional and longitudinal studies have demonstrated a decline in mean alpha frequencies in normal control groups. Utilizing the results of several investigators, the frequency declines approximately 0.5 to 0.75 c/sec each decade after age sixty. Many EEG changes seem to reflect the health status of the individual. Therefore it is plausible that alpha slowing found in apparently healthy elderly subjects is influenced by minimal, perhaps subclinical, pathology.

Males were found to have a significant lower mean alpha frequency than females of comparable age. We found no difference between white Americans and black Americans, suggesting that age changes in alpha frequency are approximately the same for the two races living in America. The alpha slowing within the normal range of 8 to 13 c/sec found in elderly community subjects is not paralleled by changes in intellectual performance. In comparison with the young adult average of 10.0 to 10.5 c/sec., the mean alpha frequency of mentally normal old subjects is significantly lower reaching 9.0 to 9.5 s/sec around age seventy and 8.5 to 9.0 c/sec after age eighty. This decline is greater among institutionalized-aged patients, particularly those with cerebral vascular disease or neurologic disorders where the frequency is often 8 c/sec or less. Those with obvious dementia usually have frequencies of 7 c/sec or less.

Individuals vary widely in the degree to which their EEGs manifest senescent changes. It does appear, however, that vascular disease is an important contributing factor. Patients with arteriosclerotic brain disease show not only a slowing of alpha but also a decline in cerebral blood flow and cerebral metabolism. In this type of patient, a number of investigators have reported the degree of slowing as quantitatively related to impaired memory and to other aspects of intellectual functioning. As mentioned, this correlation is not nearly as consistent in subjects who remain in the community. It is possible that those who survive in the community are actually adjusting at a borderline level and may be vulnerable to stress which would precipitate the appearance of organic brain disease. There is some evidence that this is true, but the vulnerability of such elderly people deserves greater attention.

A related matter that needs study is the hypothesis that the speed of information processing is dependent upon brain wave frequencies. This possibility primarily stems from the work of Surwillo (1963), who found a correlation between the stimulus response interval of a simple auditory reaction time and average duration of alpha waves.

There are other alpha changes with aging. In normal young adults the frequency varies about one-tenth of the mean value. If the variation is greater, the rhythm is said to be unstable. If this criterion is applied to older subjects, many of them have unstable EEGs. This apparently has no demonstrated significance.

Several studies indicate that there is a relationship between alpha slowing and decreased longevity. This is not surprising when one recognizes the relationship between vascular disease and alpha slowing. Obrist and associates (1979) showed that over a span of five to seven years the alpha slowing in those who died was double that found in the survivors. This result has been confirmed by Wang and Busse and Muller and co-workers.

An important aspect of the senile EEG is its reaction to sensory stimulation. An alpha-blocking response to light or eye opening has been found to decrease with age in both psychiatric patients and normal subjects. Also it is claimed that the habituation of the blocking response with repeated stimulation is faster and more complete in elderly community volunteers than in young controls. The magnitude of alpha attenuation, however, is apparently unrelated to motor response speed in normal elderly subjects (Thompson and Botwinick, 1968).

Slowing—Theta and Delta

Another common feature of EEG changes in late life, in addition to alpha slowing, is the appearance of scattered slow waves. A slight slowing of the alpha index with scattered 6 to 8 c/sec waves is not pathognomonic for any particular disorders. A moderate amount of slowing within the theta range with rate delta or severe slowing (i.e., the appearance of delta activity approximately 10 percent or more of the time), is characteristically found in brain disorders whether they are classified as degenerative or vascular in origin. As previously stated, we have demonstrated that elderly subjects in good health are found to have a mean alpha occipital frequency which is almost a full cycle slower than that found in healthy young adults. Furthermore, about 7 percent of the EEGs in the elderly subjects manifest a dominant frequency of 6 to 8 c/sec waves. A good correlation has been demonstrated between EEG frequency and cerebral oxygen consumption and/or cerebral blood flow (Obrist et al., 1963). Therefore the slowing of the dominant frequency in the majority of elderly people is associated with a decline of cerebral metabolism. Diffuse slow activity, more than any other EEG variable, is related to senile intellectual deterioration. It is important to recall that institutionalized elderly subjects manifest a good correlation between diffuse EEG slowing and tests of cognitive function. This relationship, however, does not hold true in community volunteers, particularly those with borderline or mild slowing, as they do not demonstrate clear intellectual impairment. It is possible that psychological tests are not sufficiently sensitive to early mental changes (Wang and Busse, 1975).

In spite of these unanswered questions, EEG slowing is used to differentiate functional psychiatric disorders from organic mental diseases in old age. This distinction was first emphasized by Luce and Rothschild (1953), by Frey and Sjogren (1959), and by Obrist and Henry (1958). Obrist and Henry found that 79 percent of cases with diffuse slow activity were found to have organic brain syndrome, while 88 percent of those with normal EEGs had functional disorders consisting primarily of depressions and paranoid reactions. These same authors found that a majority of elderly people with diffuse slow activity required hospitalization or died within one year after the slow EEG record was demonstrated.

EEG, Blood Pressure, and Heart Disease

In 1961, a publication appeared linking electroencephalographic changes to blood pressure in elderly persons (Obrist et al., 1961). This study included a total of 233 hospitalized psychiatric patients age sixty or above and 261 of the subjects of the first longitudinal study. An average blood pressure was obtained by computing the geometric mean of the systolic and diastolic readings as determined by routine physical examination. When several EEG categories were plotted separately against mean blood pressure in the hospitalized group, it was found that the incidence of normal electroencephalograms increased markedly as the blood pressure rose, while the number of diffuse slow and mixed abnormal electroencephalograms was maximum with the lower blood pressure readings.

A similar correlation did not hold for the subjects in the first longitudinal study. The findings in this study of normal subjects suggested that a mild elevation of blood pressure may tend to preserve a normal electroencephalogram by maintaining adequate circulation to the brain, thus compensating for cerebral arteriosclerosis. It was speculated that the diffuse slow activity in many aged psychiatric patients results from the combination of a relatively low blood pressure and cerebral arteriosclerosis.

Wang and Busse (1974a) divided subjects from the first longitudinal study into four groups: those without heart disease, those who possibly had heart disease, those with definite and compensated heart disease, and those with definite and decompensated heart disease. This study revealed that EEG changes were significantly higher in the subjects with decompensated heart disease when compared to those with compensated heart disease and those without heart disease. It was concluded that the brain impairment as evidenced by the EEG changes is probably due to a profound reduction of cerebral blood flow which is shown to be proportional to the reduction in cardiac output. Subjects with compensated heart disease also had a mild hypertension. These findings suggest that mild hypertension in some elderly patients may help to maintain the blood flow to the brain and hence to preserve the status of the brain, perhaps at the expense of the heart. Sustained severe hypertension, however, is often associated with intellectual decline (Wilkie and Eisdorfer, 1961).

Focal EEG Abnormalities

The recognition that a relatively high percentage of elderly people had focal EEG abnormalities predominantly over the temporal areas of the brain was first observed in 1949 and 1950. In 1951, with the support of the National Institutes of Health, a research project was undertaken, specifically directed toward EEG changes in late life. The first complete report from this study was made in May 1953 at a meeting of the American Psychiatric Association. This report was published in Busse et al. (1954). Since that date, the observation that such foci are common in older people and appear gradually throughout adulthood has been reported by other investigators.

A paper presented in 1953 utilized three series of community subjects, separated according to socioeconomic criteria. A correlation was found between increased incidence of EEG disturbance and socioeconomic status. This finding is probably influenced by health variables. It has been repeatedly observed that 30 percent to 40 percent of apparently healthy people have temporal focal abnormalities predominantly on the left side of the brain. An even higher incidence of focal slowing, 50 percent, was reported by Mundy-Castle in 1962. His subjects were residents of an old age home. This report was in agreement with the prior observation, as it indicated that maximum involvement was in the anterior temporal area and 75 percent of these foci were found on the left side. Furthermore, the most prominent foci occurred among normal old people with an adequate social adjustment. A high incidence of temporal lobe EEG alterations has been noted in a number of other studies involved with elderly hospitalized subjects (Harvald, 1958; Frey and Sjogren, 1959).

In a study parallel to the first longitudinal study, Barnes et al. (1956) contrasted community subjects with aged psychiatric patients. Elderly mentally ill patients are found to have a wider distribution of the temporal abnormality extending into the posterior and midtemporal areas. Among patients with organic brain syndrome, the focal changes often took the form of localized accentuated diffuse low activity. Those initial observations and conclusions, that is, that focal slow activity in the anterior temporal area is compatible with a good social adjustment in old age, have not been altered over the years. However, when it involves adjacent areas or is associated with a more diffuse disturbance, organic brain syndrome is probable.

A 1982 publication that also addresses the possible significance of temporal slowing in the EEG in old age reported a study involving 2,085 inpatients sixty to ninety-two years of age (Kazis et al., 1982). Twenty-seven percent of those studies were found to have temporal abnormalities and 66% were on the left side. Note that all those studied were patients and no normal controls were included. Consequently, the percentage of disturbances increased with vascular disease.

Some studies have not observed such a high incidence of temporal foci in elderly people. For example, Obrist (1954), using a midtemporal placement with an ear reference, failed to demonstrate foci in more than a small percentage of aged subjects. Obrist believes that this points to the importance of electrode placement.

Temporal Abnormalities and Age on Onset

Kooi and associates reported (1964) similar findings related to electroencephalographic patterns of the temporal region in normal adults. These investigators studied 218 neurologically normal subjects who ranged in age from twenty-six to eighty-one years. They found an increasing incidence of temporal lobe irregularities with advancing age. In addition, Kooi stated: "Detailed review of the comprehensive clinical data including analysis combining various medical findings reveals no evident medical factors responsible for the common type of temporal transients." Shortly thereafter, Busse and Obrist (1965) made a similar report. This study was based on 424 normal white volunteer subjects, including those derived from the longitudinal studies, with an age span of twenty to eighty years. It was found that foci occurred in 3.4 percent of subjects twenty to twenty-nine years of age, 8 percent between thirty and thirty-nine, 20 percent between forty and forty-nine, 22 percent between fifty and fifty-nine, and 36 percent between sixty and sixty-nine years of age, with a very gradual increase thereafter.

The Dominant Background Activity and Foci

Based upon cross-sectional study early in the first longitudinal study, it was found that an EEG with dominant alpha was found in 61 percent of the subjects. Sixteen percent had low-voltage fast activity; 15 percent were diffuse fast; and

7 percent diffuse slow. The average age of these subjects was slightly less than seventy years. As to age distribution and dominant activity, subjects under the age of seventy account for 75 percent of the diffuse fast but were not represented in the diffuse slow group. The mean age of subjects in the diffuse fast group was 66.7 years but in the diffuse slow group it was 77.7 years. Subjects with dominant alpha and low-voltage fast frequencies were found throughout the age range and were equally divided between those over seventy and those under that age.

As to those with foci, 75 percent of subjects with diffuse slow EEGs have foci, as do 38 percent of those with alpha and 25 percent of the diffuse fast group. Of particular importance is that none of the low-voltage fast EEGs (normal) contained focal disturbances (Wang and Busse, 1969).

Activitation of Temporal Foci

Hyperventilation tends to exacerbate temporal slowing that is already present, but it does not elicit new unsuspected foci. Passive tilting of the subject, starting from a prone position, does not exacerbate foci or elicit new ones. EKG monitoring and blood pressure readings taken during this procedure indicate relatively little hypotensive effect. Five percent inhalation of CO_2 does not eliminate or reduce the severity of a temporal foci. Temporal foci are not reduced or eliminated while the subject is exposed to hyperbaric conditions, and there is no evidence of a change following hyperbaric exposure.

Drowsiness does influence the appearance of foci, as 25 percent of foci appear in a drowsy condition, thus increasing the usual percentage from 30 percent to 40 percent of subjects. In addition, existing foci become more evident during drowsiness (Busse and Obrist, 1963).

The Origin of Foci

During the first longitudinal study, electrodes were placed in some cases in the Fp location (international system) just above the supraorbital ridge. A high proportion of subjects with temporal lobe foci revealed similar discharges of about equal magnitude from this electrode, suggesting that the inferior frontal region may also be involved. However, attempts utilizing nasopharyngeal leads were not well tolerated by the volunteer subjects, and no further information was established. It has been speculated that temporal foci may originate either from a lesion, possibly in the hippocampal region, or from a remote area outside the temporal lobe. Gershwind and Levitsky (1968) reported that marked anatomic asymmetries exist between upper surfaces of the left and right temporal lobe in the human brain: the left temporal lobe is usually larger and longer than the right. There is also evidence to suggest that the temporal lobes, particularly the left one, are susceptible to vascular insufficiency.

Psychological Implications

Psychological deficiencies have been suspected but have not been unequivocally confirmed. In one study involving the longitudinal subjects, the EEG focus predominantly in the left temporal region was significantly associated with a decline in verbal but not in performance ability. This decline in verbal ability over a span of approximately two and half years was greater in the focal group than in the nonfocal group (Wang et al., 1970). However, in another study, again involving subjects in the first longitudinal study, Davis and Obrist selected twenty subjects with severe temporal foci and compared them with twenty aged matched cases having normal EEGs. No difference could be found in learning or memory, and survival twelve years later was approximately equal in the two groups (Obrist, 1975).

Low-Voltage Fast Activity

Some electroencephalographers do not believe that the beta activity is synonymous with low-voltage fast activity (LVF). Chatrian and Lairy (1976) believe that the definition they utilize excludes the LVF described by Gibbs, which is characterized most by nonrhythmic amorphous fast activity usually not exceeding 20 microvolts in amplitude. The longitudinal studies utilized as the criteria for normal low-voltage fast, all fast waves below 20 microvolts with no countable frequency. Low-voltage fast activity is considered synonymous with beta activity and is distinguished from F1 and F2 records which are considered synonymous with gamma activity. Gamma is now considered an obsolete classification; consequently, low-voltage fast or beta activity is a type of normal brain wave which includes frequencies above the alpha range usually between 18 to 30 c/sec with diminished voltage. LVF activity is more often found in the anterior regions of the brain. When it periodically appears in posteriors of the brain, it is disrupting an alpha rhythm and is usually associated with an attention response. The amount of LVF activity appears to be a reflection of the state of arousal in the longitudinal subjects who are the basis of this paper. It is evident that in the early part of the routine recording in the longitudinal study, LVF is much more in evidence. As the examination progresses, alpha not only becomes more prominent in the posterior leads but spreads anteriorly, replacing varying amounts of LVF.

Complicating the distinction of LVF from beta activity is the separation of beta into two or three types. These types of beta activity are said to occur in some unmedicated, apparently normal adult human subjects. Chatrian and Lairy (1976) separate beta into three types: a central or frontal central rhythm of frequency as high as 30 c/sec that is selectively blocked by contralateral movement or touch of moderate intensity; a diffuse beta rhythm frequently between 20 and 25 c/sec that is not selectively blocked by any stimulus; and a posterior beta rhythm of 14 to 19 c/sec that is selectively blocked by visual stimulus of moderate intensity and mental activity. The diffuse beta potentials can be produced or enhanced by a wide variety of drugs. Chatrian and Lairy are convinced that none of the three beta rhythms correlates with any psychological variable or personality traits in normal adults.

Dondey and Gaches (1977) recognize two types of beta activity. The first is referred to as either diffuse or frontal beta activity and is usually under 30 microvolts in amplitude and between 25 and 40 c/sec with a larger amplitude. It is symmetrical although often not synchronous, and it is distinguished from frontal and diffuse beta activity by the fact that it is blocked by voluntary movement or imaginary voluntary movement and also by tactile stimuli. The rolandic beta activities are related to rolandic cortical activities. The frontal and diffuse beta are increased by drugs, as noted by the previously mentioned authors. W. A. Cobb (1976) is another writer who supports the idea of three types of beta activity. Cobb believes, however, that the occipital beta or fast rhythm is actually a type of fast alpha rhythm as it is usually in the range between 14 to 18 c/sec.

Chatrian and Lairy (1976) conclude that there is no adequate evidence of any relationship between normal and excessive beta activity in any psychiatric or neurologic disorder. They speculate that it might be of use when it does not appear in a localized area as the result of a usually drug-induced type of beta activity. Similarly, in another type of drug (for example, Thorazine), the appearance of fast potentials, particularly unilaterally, may give some evidence of a pathological process in the brain. The Greek letter Mu is used to designate an apparent subharmonic variant of rolandic beta rhythm. It differs from beta activity in that its frequency is usually between 7 and 11 c/sec, and it has an arched form (Duterte, 1977). Chatrian and Lairy (1976) conclude that no convincing proof has been conducted so far "suggesting that the presence of 'Mu' waves correlates with psychological variables and personality traits, or normal or mentally ill subjects of psychiatric diagnosis."

Fast Activity

In the Duke longitudinal studies, fast waves above the alpha range are distinguished from low voltage fast activity on the basis of amplitude and to some degree by regularity. The frequency of fast activity is confined to a relatively narrow spectrum, and its amplitude usually exceeds 25 microvolts. It is to be recalled that in our longitudinal studies the original Gibbs classification was the initial basis for all interpretations. Hence fast activity included F1 and F2. Evaluation of F1 included determination of amplitude and frequency, the percent of time it is present, and the number of leads in which it appears. F2 was considered an excessive amount of diffuse fast activity. In the first longitudinal study, as well as in cross-sectional investigations, it was found that the amount of fast activity present in normal females increases in young adulthood, reaches a peak at late middle life, and then gradually declines. This fast activity appears predominantly over the precentral areas of both hemispheres and is rarely associated with Mu rhythms (Busse and Obrist, 1965). Busse and Obrist report that women between the ages of twenty to thirty-nine years have an incidence of 8 percent fast activity. Between the ages of forty and fifty-nine, this increases to 26 percent, and thereafter it does not increase. From age sixty until age seventy-nine, there is a decrease to 23%. After the age of eighty, in females the amount of fast activity appears to begin a gradual decline. That hormonal changes may play a role in the development of fast rhythms in middle-aged females have been suggested by McAdam and Robinson (1956), who observed a significantly greater amount of beta activity in postmenstrual as opposed to premenstrual women. It is evident, however, that the increase in females previously described would suggest that if it is hormonally related, it is not directly tied to the menopause.

Thompson and Wilson (1966) believe that fast activity is associated with superior learning. Obrist (1975) adds that the presence of fast activity in the EEGs of elderly persons can probably be regarded as a favorable sign, affecting both longevity and mental capacity. In contrast, fast activity is rarely found in deteriorated senile patients.

Roubicek made a study of the frequency and amount of fast activity in elderly women. He divided the whole beta band into two parts: 12 to 25 c/sec and 25 to 45 c/sec. With advancing age, the lower portion of the band, 12 to 25 c/sec, continually decreased in abundance, while the percentage of the waves above 25 c/sec did not change or slightly increased. Roubicek believes that the different patterns of change found in these fast waves is probably a sign of diverse physiological meaning of the waves under and above 25 c/sec. He believes that there are at least two generating sites which influence these different spectra of fast activity.

A greater incidence of fast tracings in females was reported by Mundy-Castle in 1951 and by Vogel in 1965.

Summary

Major changes found in the awake EEG of relatively normal elderly persons living in the community are progressive slowing of the alpha rhythm, appearance of fast rhythms in aging females, and development of foci, predominantly in the left anterior temporal region, in approximately one-third of the subjects. Neither the slowing of the alpha frequency within the normal range of 8 through 12 c/sec nor the temporal lobe foci can be consistently correlated with intellectual decline, health, or longevity. The increase in fast waves in females, however, may be related to better learning abilities.

References

Barnes, R. H., Busse, E. W., and Friedman, E. L. The psychological functioning of aged individuals with normal and abnormal electroencephalograms: A study of hospitalized individuals. *Journal of Nervous and Mental Disease*, 124:585–593, 1956.

Busse, E. W. Brain wave changes in late life. *Clinical Electroencephalography*, 4:152–163, 1973.

Busse, E. W., and Obrist, W. D. Significance of focal electroencephalographic changes in the elderly. *Postgraduate Medicine*, 34:179–182, 1963.

Busse, E. W., and Obrist, W. D. Presenescent electroencephalographic changes in normal subjects. *Journal of Gerontology*, 20:315–320, 1965.

Busse, E. W., et al. Studies of the processes of aging: Factors that influence the psyche of elderly persons. *American Journal of Psychiatry*, 110:897–903, 1954.

Chatrian, G. E., and Lairy, G. C. Typical normal rhythms and significant variants. In Antoine Remond (Ed.), *Handbook of Electroencephalography and Clinical Neurophysiology*. Vol. 6, Section I. Amsterdam: Elsevier, 1976, 6A–32.

Cobb, W. A. EEG interpretation in clinical medicine. In Antoine Remond (Ed.), *Clinical EEG handbook of EEG and clinical neurophysiology*. Vol. 11, Section II. Amsterdam: Elsevier, 1976, 11B16–25.

Dondey, M., and Gaches, J. Semiology in clinical EEG. In Antoine Bedmond (Ed.), *Handbook of electroencephalography and clinical neurophysiology*. Vol. 11, Part A. Amsterdam: Elsevier, 1977, 1A–111.

Duterte, F. Catalogue of the main EEG patterns. In Antoine Redmond (Ed.), *Handbook of EEG and clinical neurophysiology*. Vol. 11, Part A. Amsterdam: Elsevier, 1977, 11A–57.

Frey, T. S., and Sjogren, H. The electroencephalogram in the elderly persons suffering from neuropsychiatric disorders. *Acta Psychiatrica Scandinavica*, 34:438–450, 1959.

Gershwind, N., and Levitsky, W. Human brain: Left right asymmetries in temporal speech region. *Science*, 161:186–187, 1968.

Gibbs, F. A., and Gibbs, E. L. *Atlas of electroencephalography: Methodology and controls*. Vol. 1. Cambridge, Mass.: Addison-Wesley, 1950.

Harvald, B. EEG in old age. *Acta Psychiatrica Scandinavica*, 33:193–196, 1958.

Kazis, A., Karlovasitou, A., and Xafenias, D. Temporal slow activity of the EEG in old age. *Archiv fuer Psychiatrie und Nervenkrankheiten*, 231:547–554, 1982.

Kooi, D. A., et al. Electroencephalographic patterns of the temporal region in normal adults. *Neurology*, 14:1029–1035, 1964.

Luce, R. A., and Rothschild, D. The correlation of electroencephalographic and clinical observations in psychiatric patients over 65. *Journal of Gerontology*, 8:167–172, 1953.

McAdam, W., and Robinson, R. Senile intellectual deterioration and the electroencephalogram. *Journal of Mental Science*, 102:819–825, 1956.

Muller, H. F., Grad, B., and Engelsmann, F. Biological and psychological predictors of survival in a psychogeriatric population. *Journal of Gerontology*, 30:45–52, 1975.

Mundy-Castle, A. C. Theta and Beta rhythm in the electroencephalograms of normal adults. *Electroéncephalography and Clinical Neurophysiology*, 3:477–486, 1951.

Mundy-Castle, A. C. Central excitability in the aged. In H. T. Blumenthal (Ed.), *Medical and clinical aspects of aging*. New York: Columbia University Press, 1962, 575–595.

Obrist, W. D. The electroencephalogram of normal aged adults. *Electroencephalography and Clinical Neurophysiology*, 6:235–244, 1954.

Obrist, W. D. Cerebral physiology of the aged: Relation to psychological function. In N. Burch and H. L. Altshuler (Eds.), *Behavior and brain electrical activity*. New York: Plenum, 1975, 421–430.

Obrist, W. D. Cerebral blood flow and EEG in normal aging and dementia. In E. W. Busse and D. Blazer (Eds.), *Handbook of geriatric psychiatry*. New York: Van Nostrand Reinhold, 1980.

Obrist, W. D., and Henry, C. Electroencephalographic findings in aged psychiatric patients. *Journal of Nervous and Mental Disease*, 126:254–267, 1958.

Obrist, W. D., Busse, E. W., and Henry, C. E. Relation of electroencephalograms to blood pressure in elderly persons. *Neurology*, 2:151–158, 1961.

Obrist, W. D., et al. Relationship of EEG to cerebral blood flow and metabolism in old age. *Electroencephalography and Clinical Neurophysiology*, 15:610–619, 1963.

Roubicek, J. The electroencephalogram in the middle-aged and the elderly. *Journal of the American Geriatric Society*, 25:145–152, 1977.

Surwillo, W. W. The relation of simple response time to brain wave frequency and the effects of aging. *Electroencephalography and Clinical Neurophysiology*, 15:105–111, 1963.

Thompson, L. W., and Botwinick, J. Age differences in the relationship between EEG arousal and reaction time. *Journal of Psychology*, 68:167–172, 1968.

Thompson, L., and Wilson, S. Electrocardial reactivity and learning in the elderly. *Journal of Gerontology*, 21:45–51, 1966.

Vogel, F. Genetic aspects of the EEG. *Electroencephalography and Clinical Neurophysiology*, 19:196–197, 1965.

Wang, H. S., and Busse, E. W. EEG of healthy old persons: A longitudinal study, dominant background activity and occipital rhythm. *Journal of Gerontology*, 24:419–426, 1969.

Wang, H. S., and Busse, E. W. Brain impairment and longevity. In E. B. Palmore (Ed.), *Normal aging II*. Durham, N.C.: Duke University Press, 1974a, 263–268.

Wang, H. S., and Busse, E. W. Heart disease and brain impairment among aged persons. In E. B. Palmore (Ed.), *Normal aging II*. Durham, N.C.: Duke University Press, 1974b, 160–167.

Wang, H. S., and Busse, E. W. Correlates of regional cerebral blood flow in elderly community residents. In A. M. Harper et al. (Eds.), *Blood flow and metabolism in the brain*. Edinburgh: Churchill Livingstone, 1975, 8.17–8.18.

Wang, H. S., Obrist, W. D., and Busse, E. W. Neurophysiological correlates of the intellectual function of elderly persons living in the community. *American Journal of Psychiatry*, 126:39–46, 1970.

Wilkie, F. L., and Eisdorfer, C. Intelligence and blood pressure in the aged. *Science*, 172:959–962, 1961.

Cerebral Blood Flow Changes with Age

Ewald W. Busse and H. S. Wang

In 1951, a study appeared (Freyhan et al.) that advanced the now generally accepted observation that cerebral blood flow is significantly reduced in patients with organic dementias and that there is a correlation between intellectual test scores and measurements of global cerebral flow.

In 1956, Seymour Kety, using an invasion nitrous oxide technique, concluded that cerebral blood flow progressively decreases with age. Kety's studies, as well as others, included hospitalized patients with chronic illnesses, but excluded individuals with neurological and circulatory disorders.

In a subsequent study, Dastur et al. (1963) attempted to rule out the effects of disease by selecting elderly subjects who were in excellent health. This study concluded that age per se cannot account for the decline in cerebral blood flow, since it was found that a significantly lower cerebral blood flow in elderly subjects was accompanied by mild asymptomatic disease. These authors concluded that pathology is primarily responsible for the disease in cerebral blood flow in old age.

The nitrous oxide technique was replaced by the radioisotope method which permitted the study of cerebral blood flow on a regional basis.

Obrist et al. (1970) focused upon senile and presenile dementia and found that prefrontal and anterior temporal regions underwent greater blood flow reductions than other critical areas. Obrist believes that blood flow reductions are consistent with the increased incidence of EEG abnormalities in the frontal temporal region with advancing age. Bauer et al. (1966) reported a significant relationship between regional cerebral blood flow measures and a battery of psychological tests in elderly patients with dementia. The frontal and temporal areas gave consistently higher correlations than the parietal and occipital areas, again suggesting greater pathological involvement of the region.

The development of a noninvasive method for measuring cerebral blood flow was particularly useful to the longitudinal studies, as subjects are very willing to participate in a nonpainful, nonthreatening research experience. It is of particular interest that the healthy volunteers, although they functioned quite normally in their home environments, showed a decrease in cerebral blood flow. In fact, at age eighty there was a 28 percent reduction as compared to young, healthy adults.

The Inhalation Method—Xenon 133

This noninvasive method of measuring cerebral blood flow was used in the longitudinal studies as well as in many other investigations. Details of how this was carried out have been published (Obrist et al., 1967; Obrist et al., 1971).

In brief, the procedure is to request the subject to breathe normal air with a tracer amount of Xe^{133} gas for one minute through an anesthesia mask. Blood flow to the brain is then detected from eight detectors or probes placed bilaterally over the frontal, central, parietal, and temporal regions of the brain. Expired isotope and end-tidal CO_2 values, along with the head detectors, are followed for fifteen minutes. Arterial blood pressure is obtained from the brachial artery and four samples of blood gases are taken over the fifteen-minute period. Electroencardiographic measurements are carried out throughout the test period. The CO_2 reactivity test is given after a one-hour period. The test is identical with the above, except for the addition of 5 percent CO_2 to the inspired gas mixture beginning five minutes before the cerebral blood flow measures are initiated.

Blood flow to gray matter and white matter in the various brain areas can be obtained by computation from a model of known parameters governing brain blood flow. There are two features of interest. The first is called F_1. This compartment measures regional blood flow of the gray matter. It is known as the fast compartment. F_2 is the slow compartment, representing flow through white matter. Many of these studies are concerned primarily with the flask clearing component (F_1).

Correlates of Cerebral Blood Flow

The 133-xenon inhalation method using two-compartmental analysis (Obrist et al., 1971) was employed to study the regional cerebral blood flow of forty-eight elderly community volunteers (mean age 79.9, SD 6.9 years) from an ongoing longitudinal project. Blood flow to the brain was measured by eight detectors placed bilaterally over the cranium.

The mean value of average gray matter flow over the bilateral parietal regions (rCBF) was 47.4 ml/100gm/min (SD 10.2), about 24 percent lower than the value obtained from a group of young healthy adults by the same method. Females consistently had a higher flow than males. There was a steady decline of flow with advanced age in both sexes. For the entire group, combining males and females, the correlation coefficient between blood flow and age was $-.34$ ($p < 0.05$), and the regression line had a slope of -0.7 ml/100gm/min per year.

Using the median (47.3 ml), these forty-eight elderly subjects were divided into a high-flow and a low-flow group. These two groups did not differ significantly in race, education, socioeconomic background, cardiovascular disease, or arteriosclerotic retinopathy. Significant differences were observed in several measures between the high-flow and low-flow groups. Serum cholesterol was 256.4 (high flow) and 231.3 mg/100 (low flow) $p < 0.05$. The EEG occipital dominant frequency was 9.33 + 6.4 (high flow) and 8.53 + 0.73 (low flow). Both the Wechsler performance and verbal scores were better for the high-flow subjects as compared to the low-flow group—hence a significant difference in the Wechsler deterioration quotient (see table B—7).

The mean arterial blood pressure (MABP) was slightly, but not significantly, higher in the high-flow group than in the low-flow group. When these two flow groups were combined, those having a high MABP (115 mm Hg) had a significantly higher gray matter flow than those having a low MABP (94 mm Hg) (table B—8).

In summary, the reduction of rCBF in our community residents was associated with low WAIS performance scores, high deterioration quotient and slow EEG occipital frequency. This was most likely due to a depressed metabolic activity of the brain. The role of cerebrovascular disease in the reduction of rCBF

Table B—7. *Comparison of subjects with high and low rCBF.*

	High flow (N = 24) Mean ± SD	Low flow (N = 24) Mean ± SD
WAIS		
Scaled scores		
Verbal	60.3 ± 20.9	52.5 ± 21.3
Performance	31.8 ± 13.7	23.7 ± 11.4*
Full	92.1 ± 33.7	76.9 ± 32.2
Deterioration quotient	.195 ± .106**	.305 ± .163**
EEG frequency (Hz)	9.33 ± .64**	8.53 ± .73**

*$p < .05$.

**$p < .01$.

Table B—8. *MABP and rCBF.*

MABP (mm Hg)	94	95–114	115
Number cases	10	29	9
rCBF (ml/100gm/min)			
mean	42.3*	47.5	52.5*
SD	4.4	10.0	11.5

*$t = 2.565$.
$p < .02$.

and MABP may indicate an impairment of the autoregulatory mechanism in many of our elderly subjects.

Due to its noninvasiveness, we found the xenon inhalation method a practical and safe procedure for the determination of rCBF. It is our opinion that the reduction of rCBF in elderly community residents most likely reflects structural or functional changes in the brain.

References

Bauer, H., Apfeldorf, M., and Hoch, H. Relationship between alpha frequency, age, disease, and intelligence. *Proceedings of the Seventh International Congress of Gerontology*, 2:341–349, 1966.

Busse, E. W., and Wang, H. S. The electroencephalographic changes in late life: A longitudinal study. *Journal of Clinical and Experimental Gerontology*, 1:145–158, 1979.

Dastur, D. K., et al. Effects of aging and cerebral circulation and metabolism in man. In Birren, J. E., et al. (Eds.), *Human aging: A biological and behavioral study*. PHS Pub. No. 986. Washington, D.C.: U.S. Government Printing Office, 1963, 57–76.

Freyhan, F. A., Woodford, R. B., and Kety, S. S. Cerebral blood flow and metabolism in psychoses of senility. *Journal of Nervous and Mental Disorders*, 113:449–496, 1951.

Kety, S. S. Human cerebral blood flow and oxygen consumption as related to aging. *Research Publications* (Association for Research in Nervous and Mental Disease), 35:31–45, 1955.

Obrist, W., et al. Determination of regional cerebral blood flow by inhalation of 133-xenon. *Circulation Research*, 20:124–135, 1967.

Obrist, W. D., et al. Regional cerebral blood flow in senile and presenile dementia. *Neurology*, 20:315–322, 1970.

Obrist, W., et al. A simplified procedure for determining fast compartment rCBFs by 133-xenon inhalation. In R. W. R. Russell (Ed.), *Brain and blood flow*. London: Pitman Medical, 1971.

Sleep Patterns in the Aged

Patricia N. Prinz

It has long been known that human sleep patterns undergo changes with advancing age. Overall, sleep becomes more fragmented and awakenings during the night are longer and more frequent (Feinberg et al., 1967). All-night electroencephalographic (EEG) measurements of the stages of sleep generally indicate that with advancing age there is a significant reduction in rapid eye movement (REM) sleep (Feinberg et al., 1967; Kales et al., 1967). Furthermore, the nightly amount of REM sleep correlates well with performance scores on the Wechsler Adult Intelligence Scale (WAIS) in both normal elderly groups and in groups with evidence of organic brain impairment (Feinberg et al., 1967). For this reason, REM sleep decrements have been considered by some investigators to reflect normal age-related as well as pathological changes in the functional integrity of the brain (Feinberg and Carlson, 1968; Kahn and Fisher, 1969).

A second major change with age seen in EEG measurements of sleep is the sharp decline in stage 4 (S4) sleep, which is entirely absent in some older individuals. Stage 4 refers to sleep periods in which delta waves (slow waves between 0.5 and 2.0 Hz) are the predominant activity in a given epoch (Rechtschaffen and Kales, 1968). It has also been observed that the amplitude of EEG delta waves during sleep is notably reduced in the elderly (Feinberg et al., 1967; Kales et al., 1967). The implications of changes in S4 sleep are not entirely clear. Like REM sleep, it is homeostatically regulated in young normal subjects, in the sense that compensatory increases follow S4 sleep deprivation (Agnew et al., 1964). Similarly, as with REM, S4 sleep is reduced not only in normal aged but in patients with chronic brain syndrome and in mental retardation (Feinberg et al., 1967; Feinberg et al., 1969).

Previous studies of sleep involving elderly individuals have been conducted in the laboratory or in a hospital setting away from home, where subjects are constrained to sleep only at night. In view of the potential disruption in sleep patterns which can occur in unfamiliar surroundings, particularly for the elderly (Kales et al., 1967), it would seem that monitoring sleep (including nap times) in the home might yield a more reliable, stable estimate of true sleep pattern characteristics. Accordingly, in this study all sleep recordings were obtained in the subjects' homes, according to the scheduling typical for each subject, including daytime naps.

Finally, earlier studies correlated sleep measures with single intelligence measures obtained near the time of the sleep study. The present study affords the opportunity to examine the relation of sleep variables to repeated assessments of intellectual functioning over the preceding eighteen years. Thus, it is possible to

Reprinted by permission from *Journal of Gerontology*, 32:179–186, 1977.

determine whether change in intellectual functioning rather than a single measure of intelligence is better correlated with sleep pattern variables.

Method

Subjects. This study used participants in the Duke First Longitudinal Study. Three male and nine female healthy volunteer participants were selected on the basis of personal interviews from a panel of fifty subjects who had been routinely evaluated for social, psychological, and physical functioning during the past eighteen years. The subjects were between the ages of seventy-six and ninety ($x = 82$), socially outgoing and free of any temporary stress or drug influence at the time of the sleep recordings. All subjects were in reasonably good health; complete physical examinations showed them to be relatively free of appreciable cardiovascular or pulmonary disease. Blood pressures were in a relatively normal range for their age levels (between 120/80 and 160/95).

Procedure. Sleep patterns were recorded using a portable Beckman EEG machine (type T dynograph) for three or, in cases of questionable recordings, four consecutive nights in the volunteer's own home. Previously established daily schedules were adhered to, including any routine daytime naps. All naps were recorded on days 2 and 3. Individuals who napped at irregular times were excluded from the study. Those who generally did not nap refrained from napping during this study. EEG, muscle, and eye movement electrodes (Rechtschaffen and Kales, 1968) were fed through a Grass electrode collar with a receptacle into which the recording cable could be easily inserted by the subject himself. This allowed him mobility at any time during the night without need of assistance. The technicians who performed the recording duties were familiar to the elderly volunteers due to their prior experience in a larger longitudinal study. EEG electrodes were positioned as for conventional sleep recordings at C3 and C4 and referred to the contralateral mastoid. Electrode resistances were maintained between 3K to 4K ohms by use of punctured skin contacts sealed with collodion. Time constants were 0.3 seconds.

The sleep patterns obtained during the last two consecutive all-night recordings were scored blindly for all stages of sleep and waking according to conventional EEG, EOG, and EMG criteria (Rechtschaffen and Kales, 1968) for young normal subjects. However, for elderly subjects, criteria for the EEG delta wave were relaxed to include waves of lower amplitude (50 μV peak-to-peak or greater) between 0.5 Hz and 2 Hz, since the conventional 75 μV criterion reduced stage 4 values so greatly that the range of individual differences was sharply curtailed. The sleep stage analysis included only the time spent when the subjects were in bed with room lights turned off. For both nighttime and nap sleep, prolonged periods of wakefulness occurring before the subject's routine retiring time or after his established rising time were excluded from the analysis. Sleep latency is the time between retiring and sleep onset. Number of wakenings are subsequent periods of one or more minutes of wakefulness. Time awake includes sleep latency as well as all subsequent awakening prior to arising. For the three elderly subjects who napped routinely, mean naptime values from days 2 and 3 have been combined with the mean values from the last two nights, in order to include in subsequent analyses the total sleep experiences by these elderly.

The WAIS and the Wechsler Memory Scale had been administered to these subjects eight times at periodic intervals over the preceding eighteen years. Both the verbal and performance scales were analyzed for the slope of the regression line over time, using the method of least squares. The hard paired-associate scores from the Wechsler Memory Scale were averaged across the first and last nine-year period, and a different score between the two periods was derived.

All analyses of the intellectual function data were carried out independently of the analyses of the sleep data by different personnel. The amount of time spent in REM and S4 sleep was correlated with both the change measures and with single scores of intellectual function obtained within six months of the sleep measurement using the Spearman's rank order correlation test for levels of significance (Siegel, 1956).

Results

Table B—9 shows the sleep pattern variables for the last two all-night recordings. It can be seen that the values remain fairly stable across the two nights. The reproducibility of each subject's data across nights is indicated by the Spearman rank order correlation, which was significant ($p < .05$) for all stages except S4 sleep. This suggests that these values reliably reflect the typical sleep patterns for these individuals. Night 1 data were excluded from these analyses because they displayed typical first night alteration in sleep variables.

Table B—9. *Comparison of average sleep data for 12 elderly subjects taken from each of the last two consecutive all-night recordings (N2 and N3) in the home environment.*

	N2	N3	rho, N2/N3	Mean
Sleep latency (minutes)	14.1	11.1	.705*	12.6 ± 8.6
Number of wakenings	7.0	6.7	.802*	6.8 ± 3.3
Time awake (minutes)	53.0	62.8	.762*	61.5 ± 40.0
Stage 1 + 2	222.9	232.5	.803*	237.6 ± 52.0
Stage 3	69.1	72.0	.834*	75.4 ± 21.3
Stage 4 sleep	24.9	23.3	.385*	25.3 ± 7.9
REM sleep	70.1	80.7	.692*	75.8 ± 13.5
Total time in bed	440.0	471.3	.772*	475.6 ± 52.0

Note: Reproducibility of individual N2 vs. N3 data is indicated by the Spearman rank order correlation, RHO. The mean ± 1 SD represents the average for N2 and N3 plus mean values during naps for the three subjects who routinely napped.

*$p \geq .05$.

Only three of the twelve subjects obtained additional sleep during established naptimes. For these subjects there were: seventy-nine, eighty-seven, and seventy-five total minutes, of which only 5.9 percent and 1.8 percent, on the average, was spent in S4 and in REM sleep, respectively. In order to include all sleep experienced by each subject for use in subsequent analyses, the mean nap time values have been combined with the mean nighttime values for these three subjects. The mean nighttime values for the various sleep stages are also shown in table B—9. It can be seen that the inclusion of naptime data did not appreciably change these group means. In addition, the relationship between sleep variables and measures of cognitive function reported below were essentially unchanged by this inclusion of nap values.

The results of the present study indicate that aged individuals experience significant changes in their sleep patterns. As summarized in table B—10, wakefulness occupied a mean of 62 min of the total time in bed. Young adults, in contrast, typically spent significantly less time awake; 10 and 26 min have been reported in two sleep laboratory studies, and 11 min was observed in a home study of all-night sleep recordings. Accompanying the increase in wakefulness in these elderly, there were more awakenings during the night (group mean = 6.8 min) for longer periods of time (group mean = 7.1 min) than reported in studies of young adults.

The amount of S4 and REM sleep obtained in this elderly group was also observed to differ from young adult norms. Only 25 and 76 min were observed, corresponding to 6.0 percent and 18.4 percent of total sleep time spent in S4 and REM sleep, respectively. Young adults normally obtain greater amounts of both

Table B—10. *Sleep pattern variables observed in studies of aged normal (AN) compared with young normal (YN) subjects.*

	Time awake (minutes)	Number of awakenings	Time in bed (minutes)	Time in S4 sleep (minutes)	Time in REM sleep (minutes)
AN. present study	61.5[a] ± 40.0	6.8	475 ± 52	25.3 ± 7.9	75.8 ± 13.5
AN. Kales et al., 1967	76.0	10.0	457	5.3	75.0
AN. Feinberg et al., 1967	84.0 ± 30.0	5.4	469 ± 38	27.0 ± 26.0	81.0 ± 17.0
YN. Prinz, present study	11.0 ± 5.0	2.8	480 ± 22	63.0 ± 20.0	106.0 ± 15.0
YN. Kales et al., 1967	10.0	2.5	457	50.0	107.0
YN. Feinberg et al., 1967	26.0 ± 13.0	3.1	421 ± 27	52.0 ± 26.0	90.0 ± 16.0

Note: The present results obtained from all-night recordings in the home environment were in general agreement with previous studies carried out in sleep laboratories.

[a]Includes sleep latency and night time awakenings ≥ one minute.

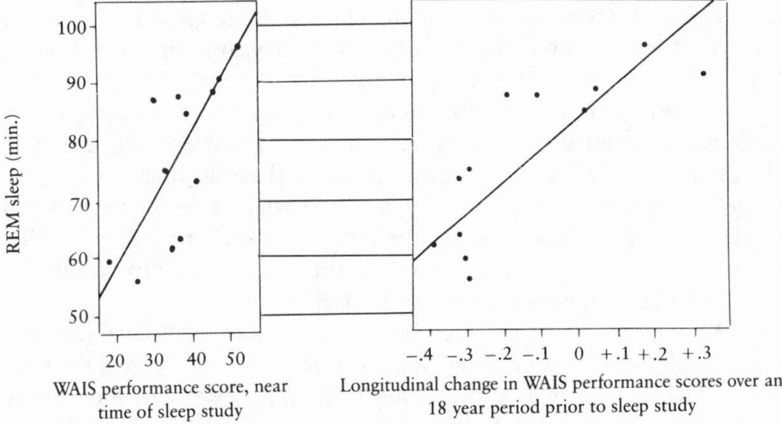

Figure B—1. *Relationships between sleep variables and cognitive function in healthy, aged individuals. Each point represents a single subject's scaled score on the WAIS performance test and his time spent in REM sleep (the mean value taken from the last two all-night sleep recordings, including naps). WAIS scores are also expressed as the yearly change during the 9th and 10th decades of life (slope of the linear regression and 8 separate testings).*

S4 and REM sleep; group means of 50 and 52 min of S4 were observed in two laboratory studies (Feinberg et al., 1967; Kales et al., 1967) while 63 min was observed in this home study. Similarly, group means from REM sleep time were 107, 90, and 105 min in these young adult studies (see table B—10).

As shown in figure B—1, a wide range of cognitive function test scores were observed to accompany the changes in sleep patterns in these elderly subjects; WAIS performance scores (unadjusted for age) near the time of sleep assessment ranged from 18 to 52, with a mean of 38.8 and SD of 7.2. The corresponding mean score for young adults aged twenty-five to thirty-four is 49.5 ± 11.8. This difference reflects the fact that WAIS performance scores are generally lower for groups of aged subjects (Wechsler, 1955). Preexisting change in cognitive function for these aged subjects was usually, although not always, in a decreasing direction, as indicated by longitudinal change in WAIS performance scaled scores over the preceding eighteen years, calculated as the slope of the least squares regression line. The mean yearly change was −0.14 ± 0.22. Corresponding scores for younger adults between the ages of sixteen and thirty-four years are generally stable (Wechsler, 1955).

The hard paired-associates task from the Wechsler Memory Test was selected as an additional measure of longitudinal change for further study because it appeared to be a reliable measure that was consistently affected by age factors. Hard paired-associate scores in these subjects ranged from 2 to 12 near the time the sleep recordings were obtained. An examination of scores obtained in earlier periodic testing indicated that, for most subjects, there was a decline over time in this measure. The group mean of all measurements made in the earlier nine-year period was 7.0 ± 2.2, while for the later nine-year period it was 6.6 ± 2.3.

Such declining scores are not seen in young adult groups, who typically retain their level of functioning (group mean for twenty to twenty-nine year olds = 7.15 ± 2.6) over time (Wechsler, 1945).

In contrast to the trends toward declining cognitive functioning in these elderly subjects, verbal functioning was maintained at stable levels, as indicated by WAIS verbal scaled scores. Single verbal scores near the time of the sleep study ranged from 41 to 88 ($x = 73 \pm 15$) with the change, as reflected in the slope of regression, being -0.08 ± 0.07. The lack of consistent change in WAIS verbal scores in these subjects is in accord with the greater stability in this measure throughout the later life-span (Wechsler, 1955).

When sleep pattern variables were compared with intellectual function measures, some significant interrelationships were observed. The nightly amount of REM sleep correlated positively with both single WAIS performance scaled scores (Spearman's rank order rho = .764; $p < .05$) and with change in this score over time (slope of linear regression) (rho = .841; $p < .05$) (see table B—11). The time spent in stage 4 sleep was also positively, but not significantly, related to both these measures. The other sleep stages failed to correlate with these measures of mental function.

An analysis of the subjects' scores from the hard paired-associates task of the Wechsler Memory Task revealed an additional positive correlation with sleep. When the change score from this task was compared with time spent in REM sleep, a significant correlation was observed (rho = .605; $p < .05$). How-

Table B—11. *Rank order (Spearman's rho) correlations between the sleep variables that are age-sensitive (time awake and in REM and S4 sleep) and intellectual function scores, measured both singly and longitudinally.*

	WAIS scaled performance score Change per year/ (single score)	WAIS scaled verbal score Change per year/ (single score)	Wechsler memory hard paired-associates task change/ (single score)
Time spent in REM sleep	0.841 */ (0.764 *)	0.334/ (0.101)	0.605 */ (0.129)
	−0.661/ (−0.488)	−0.052/ (−0.065)	−0.629/ (−0.390)
	0.288/ (0.264)	0.329/ (0.374)	0.421/ (0.147)

Note: WAIS scores obtained eight times during the preceding 18 years were analyzed for the slope of the linear regression over time (least squares fit). Single psychometric scores were obtained near the time of the sleep assessments (shown in parentheses). Sleep variables represent the averaged score of three 24-hour measurement periods.

* $p < .01$, two-tailed.

$N = 12$ for all comparisons.

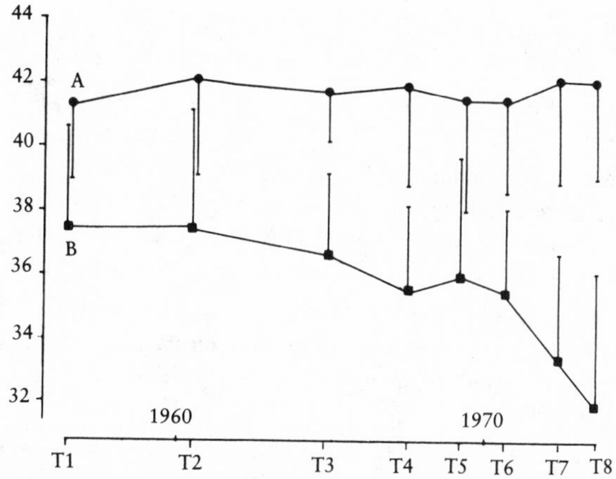

Figure B—2. *Longitudinal change in intellectual function for the 6 elderly subjects with the greater (Group A) and the 6 with the lower (Group B) REM sleep times. Group means ± SD for WAIS performance scores are shown at periodic intervals. Sleep assessments were made near the time of the 8th testing (T8), when the group A and B mean ages were 80.7 and 83.8, respectively. This age difference was not statistically significant.*

ever, as summarized in table B—11, no correlation was observed when single scores were used or when sleep stages other than REM sleep were examined.

WAIS verbal scores were not found to correlate with any of the sleep stage measures, as shown in table B—11. This was the case, regardless of whether single scores or yearly change in preexisting scores were used for comparison.

The elderly subjects were divided into two equal groups on the basis of the amount of REM sleep they obtained, in order to examine preexisting psychometric scores more carefully. The group with the greater REM sleep (x = 89 min) was found to have enjoyed a stable level of intellectual functioning, as shown in figure B—2. In contrast, the group showing the lower amount of REM sleep time (x = 64.6 min) was found to have sustained significant loss in intellectual function over the preceding ten years. This indicates that the diminished REM sleep of these elderly may serve as a sensitive indicator of a preexisting condition of moderately declining mental function.

The positive correlations between REM sleep and WAIS performance score in the present study could not be attributed to age per se, since in this selected sample population neither time in REM sleep nor time in S4 sleep were correlated with chronological age (rho = −.172 and −.136, respectively).

As discussed below, it is possible that underlying age-dependent biological alterations may account for changes in sleep and in mental functioning.

Discussion

The senescent sleep patterns recorded here in a home environment are comparable with those recorded in the sleep laboratories of Agnew et al. (1964), Feinberg et al. (1967), Kahn and Fisher (1969), and Kales et al. (1967). The present data indicate that the differential effects of a home versus laboratory environment on sleep are minor for healthy aged subjects. All studies agree in finding evidence of impaired sleep as indicated by an increased wakefulness and a decrease in both S4 and REM sleep stages. Moreover, since the present study did not constrain subjects to sleep only at nighttime as in the laboratory studies, the present findings also indicate that naptime sleep in the elderly may not compensate for impaired sleep.

The significance of these sleep changes in senescence are not clearly understood. The human brain undergoes many other alterations with advancing age, including declines in neuronal population number, metabolic rate, and blood flow (Brody et al., 1975; Obrist, 1972; Thompson and Marsh, 1973). In addition, alterations in synchronous rhythmic activities, during waking as well as during sleep, have been observed in the senescent EEG (Prinz, 1976b). Declines in certain measures of cognitive function also occur in senescence (reviewed by Thompson and Marsh, 1973). Some of these neurobiological changes have been observed to intercorrelate, particularly among groups of subjects who are very advanced in age or who have an impaired health status. Cognitive function measures, in particular, have been found to intercorrelate with neurobiological measures only when some evidence of health impairment is present (Birren et al., 1963).

The present subjects, although in relatively good health for their age, could be regarded as having some health impairments based on their blood pressure range. In addition, these subjects showed a wide range of neurobiological test scores: waking EEG rhythmic frequencies in the alpha range (known to slow with age) ranged from 8.0 Hz to 9.7 Hz, and cerebral blood flow levels (considered to reflect brain metabolic rate) were between 0.26 and 0.53 ml/gm/min. These values are generally lower than the typical levels seen in young adults, for whom a mean alpha frequency of 10.5 ± 0.9 Hz (Brazier and Finesinger, 1944) and a mean cerebral blood flow (gray matter) of 0.75 ± 0.8 ml/gm/min (Obrist et al., 1975) have been reported. These measures indicate that some degree of neurobiological impairment is present for each subject in this elderly group, although to varying degrees. To the extent that this is the case, one can argue that both sleep and WAIS performance may be influenced by underlying age-dependent biological changes occurring in the clinically impaired or the aged nervous system. Some support for this interpretation comes from more extensive observation using this same study population in which physiological measures (alpha frequency and cerebral blood flow levels) were found to correlate positively with REM sleep variables (Prinz et al., 1975).

Age-related changes such as diffuse cortical neuron depopulation (Brody,

1955) and the loss of dendritic ramifications (Scheibel and Scheibel, 1975), together with associated reductions in cerebral metabolic rate (Sokoloff, 1975) could well influence the neural systems controlling the onset and maintenance of sleep stages. The recent findings of Brody (1975) are of particular interest in any consideration of possible neurobiological bases for age-related sleep changes. He observed a sizeable (40 to 50 percent) age-related depopulation of neurons in the locus coeruleus, a brain stem site involved in the control of sleep and wakefulness behavior. The loss of neurons here could exert a particularly important influence on the sleep of the elderly (reviewed in Prinz, 1976b).

Feinberg et al. (1967) have extensively examined the relationships between REM sleep and intellectual function, both across the human life span and across a spectrum of clinical conditions characterized by impaired cognitive function. Significant correlations between REM sleep variables and psychometric test scores have been reported for normal elderly groups and for patient groups having organic brain syndrome or mental retardation of mixed etiologies (Feinberg et al., 1967; 1969). Such findings have encouraged many investigators to postulate that sleep phenomena are integrally involved in the maintenance of adequate levels of cognitive functioning (the "sleep cognition hypothesis") (Feinberg et al., 1969; Feinberg and Carlson, 1968). Viewed from a biological standpoint, the sleep cognition hypothesis poses the issue of whether sleep losses sustained in advanced age, or in any clinical condition, might impede ongoing neurobiological processes resulting in, among other things, impaired cognition.

The biological implications of age-related changes in sleep and wakefulness remain unclear. Among young adult subjects, both REM and S4 sleep are considered to be homeostatically regulated, since experimentally induced sleep losses are followed by compensatory increases in stage 4, followed by REM sleep on recovery nights (Agnew et al., 1964; Berger and Oswald, 1962). It is not clear whether such homeostatic influences on sleep are diminished in the aged. While short-term loss of REM or stage 4 sleep appear to be tolerated by the organism without notable pathological change (Feinberg, 1974; Freemon, 1972), prolonged total sleep losses have been reported to be accompanied by neuronal degenerative changes and ultimate death in animals (Karadzic, 1973; Kleitman, 1963).

The time-honored notion that sleep serves restorative functions for the organisms has been reexamined (Oswald, 1973) in the light of recent findings that human growth hormone, known to promote protein synthesis in many body tissues, is released into the plasma in large amounts during slow-wave sleep stages (Honda et al., 1969), and could presumably influence processes of tissue maintenance and repair. In a recent study by Prinz et al. (1976), sleep alterations in elderly males were accompanied by attenuated growth hormone release in eight of eleven cases tested, indicating that biological consequences of sleep impairments with advanced age may exist. To the extent that sleep does serve a restorative function, the sleep losses sustained in advanced age may be a contributing factor in the other neurobiological systems under decline with age. Further studies will be needed in order to evaluate this possibility.

Stage 4 sleep is known to be altered to a greater extent than the REM sleep stage in the senescent sleep pattern (Feinberg, 1967; Kales et al., 1967; Prinz, 1976a). In fact, stage 4 is often entirely absent in old subjects. As noted by Feinberg and associates (1967), S4 decreases may reflect the generally lower amplitude of the EEG slow wave in the senescent recording, since S4 is characterized by a predominance of slow waves meeting a fixed amplitude criterion (Rechtschaffen and Kales, 1968). The amplitude of the slow wave was generally less than 150 μV in the present study, while young normal adults often exceed this level.

Although age-related change in REM sleep time is relatively smaller than the S4 alteration, REM sleep has been much more extensively examined, perhaps because this stage can be more reliably and accurately assessed than stages 2 through 4 (Monroe, 1969). The scoring variability associated with slow-wave sleep assessments could account for the failure to find significant correlations between stage 4 and intellectual function measures, as well as the lower reproducibility of S4 levels across nights in the present study.

It is possible that the use of a more rigidly defined slow-wave sleep variable, such as the time spent in slow-wave sleep activity, as determined by computer analysis, could reveal a positive correlation between the slow-wave EEG during sleep and intellectual function measures. A preliminary evaluation of the time spent in sleep-related EEG has been undertaken using the present sleep data. Slow waves between 0.5 and 2.5 Hz and of 50 μV or larger amplitude were summed over time by a blind rating procedure using a map distance measuring device. The resultant values, when compared with REM sleep levels in each individual, indicated a strong correlation between these two sleep variables (rho = .816; $p < .01$) and an additional correlation between the slow wave variable and WAIS performance score (rho = .932; $p < .01$). Further studies will be required in order to establish this relationship more clearly.

Summary

Sleep pattern variables were monitored on nine females and three male elderly community volunteers in the home. Measures of intellectual functioning were also obtained over a preceding eighteen-year period. Both sleep pattern variables and intellectual function measures were found to be altered in elderly subjects compared with young adult normals. Individual differences among these elderly subjects were such that REM sleep time and WAIS performance score correlated positively. Moreover, greater amounts of REM sleep were found in subjects who had maintained stable intellectual function over the preceding eighteen years, while lower REM sleep levels occurred in subjects with a prior history of cognitive decline. The present findings can be interpreted to indicate that the senescent sleep pattern contains at least some variables which are highly sensitive to age-related alterations in the integrity of brain function, as inferred from mental performance test scores.

References

Agnew, H., Webb, W., and William, R. The effect of stage four sleep deprivation. *Electroencephalography and Clinical Neurophysiology*, 17:68–70, 1964.

Berger, R., and Oswald, I. Effects of sleep deprivation on behavior, subsequent sleep and dreaming. *Journal of Mental Science*. 108:457–465, 1962.

Birren, J. E., et al. Interdisciplinary relationships: Interrelations of physiological, psychological and psychiatric findings in healthy elderly men. In J. E. Birren et al. (Eds.), *Human aging: A biological and behavioral study* (PHS Pub. No. 986). Washington, D.C.: U.S. Government Printing Office, 1963.

Brazier, M. A. B., and Finesinger, J. E. Characteristics of the normal electroencephalogram. I. A study of the occipital cortical potentials in 500 normal adults. *Journal of Clinical Investigation*, 23:303–311, 1944.

Brody, H. Organization of the cerebral cortex. III. A study of aging in the human cerebral cortex. *Journal of Comparative Neurology*, 102:511–556, 1955.

Brody, H. Structural changes in the aging nervous system. Paper presented at a symposium on the Neurobiology of aging, New York University Medical Center, 1975.

Brody, H., Harmon, D., and Ordy, J. (Eds.), *Aging*. Vol. 1. New York: Raven Press, 1975.

Feinberg, I. Changes in sleep cycle patterns with age. *Journal of Psychiatric Research*, 10:283–306, 1974.

Feinberg, I., Braun, M., and Shulman, E. EEG sleep patterns in mental retardation. *Electroencephalography and Clinical Neurophysiology*, 27:477–505, 1969.

Feinberg, I., and Carlson, R. Sleep variable as a function of age in man. *Archives of General Psychiatry*, 18:239–250, 1968.

Feinberg, I., Koresko, R., and Heller, N. EEG sleep patterns as a function of normal and pathological aging in man. *Journal of Psychiatric Research*, 5:107–144, 1967.

Freemon, F. *Sleep research: A critical review*. Springfield, Ill.: Charles C. Thomas, 1972.

Honda, Y., et al. Growth hormone secretion during nocturnal sleep in normal subjects. *Journal of Clinical Endocrinology*, 29:20–29, 1969.

Kahn, E., and Fisher, C. The sleep characteristics of the normal aged male. *Journal of Nervous and Mental Disease*, 148:477–505, 1969.

Kales, A., et al. Measurements of allnight sleep in normal elderly persons: Effects of aging. *Journal of the American Geriatrics Society*, 15:405–414, 1967.

Karadzic, V. Physiological changes resulting from total sleep deprivation. In W. Koella and P. Levin (Eds.), *Sleep: Physiology, biochemistry, psychology, pharmacology, clinical implications*. Basel: S. Karger, 1973.

Kleitman, N. *Sleep and wakefulness*. (Rev. ed.) Chicago: University of Chicago Press, 1963.

Monroe, L. Inter-rater reliability and the role of experience in scoring EEG sleep records: Phase I. *Psychophysiology*, 5:376–384, 1969.

Obrist, W. D. Cerebral physiology of the aged: Influence of circulatory disorders. In C. M. Gaitz (Ed.), *Aging and the brain*. New York: Plenum, 1972.

Obrist, W., et al. The xenon-133 inhalation method: Assessment of CBF in carotid endarterectomy. In T. Langfitt et al. (Eds.), *Cerebral circulation and metabolism*. New York: Springer, 1975.

Oswald, I. Is sleep related to synthetic purpose? In W. Koella and P. Levin (Eds.), *Sleep: Physiology, biochemistry, psychology, pharmacology, clinical implications*. Basel: S. Karger, 1973.

Palmore, E. B. (Ed.), *Normal aging*. Durham, N.C.: Duke Univeristy Press, 1970.

Prinz, P. N. Sleep patterns of healthy elderly subjects: Changes in EEG slow wave activity and REM sleep. *Special review of experimental aging research*, 1976a.

Prinz, P. N. EEG during sleep and waking states. In B. Eleftheriou and M. Elias (Eds.), *Special review of experimental aging research*. Bar Harbor, Me.: EAR, Inc., 1976b, 135–163.

Prinz, P., et al. Growth hormone levels during sleep in elderly males. In M. H. Chase, W. C. Stern, and P. L. Walter (Eds.), *Sleep Research*. Vol. 4. Los Angeles: Brain Information Service/Brain Research Institute, University of California, 1975.

Prinz, P., Obrist, W., and Wang, H. Sleep patterns in healthy elderly subjects: Individual differences as related to other neurobiological variables. In M. H. Chase, W. C. Stern, and P. L. Walter (Eds.), *Sleep Research*. Vol. 4. Los Angeles: Brain Information Service/Brain Research Institute, University of California, 4:132, 1975.

Rechtschaffen, A., and Kales, A. (Eds.), *A manual of standardized terminology, techniques, and scoring system for sleep stages of human subjects*. PHS Pub. No. 204. Washington, D.C.: U.S. Government Printing Office, 1968.

Scheibel, M., and Scheibel, A. Structural changes in the aging brain. In D. Harman and J. M. Ordy (Eds.), *Aging*. Vol. 1. New York: Raven Press, 1975.

Siegel, S. *Nonparametric statistics for the behavioral sciences*. New York: McGraw-Hill, 1956.

Sokoloff, L. Cerebral circulation and metabolism in the aged. In S. Gershon and A. Raskin (Eds.), *Aging*. Vol. 2. New York: Raven Press, 1975.

Thompson, L. W., and Marsh, G. R. Psychophysiological studies of aging. In C. Eisdorfer and M. P. Lawton (Eds.), *The psychology of adult development and aging*. Washington, D.C.: American Psychological Association, 1973.

Wechsler, D. A standardized memory scale for clinical use. *Journal of Psychology*, 19:87–95, 1945.

Wechsler, D. *Manual for the Wechsler Adult Intelligence Scale*. New York: Psychological Corp., 1955.

Clinical Correlates of the Vibratory Sense

Alan D. Whanger and H. Shan Wang

Interest in the ability of a person to perceive vibration as a tool in neurological diagnosis began when Rumpf introduced the tuning fork in 1889 in evaluating a case of syringomylelia (Fox and Klemperer, 1942). The nature and significance of this peculiar perceptual ability have been discussed in the literature over the years, and they were recently reviewed by Calne and Pallis (1966), who feel that vibratory sensibility represents a temporal modulation of tactile sense, similar to the relationship between flicker and vision. The peripheral receptors are the pacinian corpuscles, which are innervated by large afferent nerve fibers. In the spinal cord the relevant impulses ascend in both the dorsal and lateral columns. How these impulses are synthesized and interpreted in the brain is still not certain, but the parietal lobe is involved, and subcortical lesions of the brain may impair vibratory perception (Fox and Klemperer, 1942).

It was noted early that the vibratory threshold (VT) is raised in a number of disease states as well as in the course of aging. Presumably, the higher the VT the worse the nervous system is functioning. Several studies have been done on groups of normal aging persons (Cosh, 1953; Fox and Klemperer, 1942; Pearson, 1928; Perret and Regi, 1970; Rosenberg, 1958; Steiness, 1957). There are conflicting opinions, but in general the threshold begins increasing in the fourth or

Reprinted by permission from *Journal of Gerontology*, 29:39–45, 1974.

fifth decade, is higher in the lower extremities, is more impaired at higher frequencies, and possibly becomes higher on the dominant side of the body.

Vitamin deficiencies, especially those of thiamine and vitamin B_{12}, are known to impair vibratory perception, and Vatassery and others recently wrote of neuroaxonal dystrophy in the posterior column nuclei in vitamin E deficiency (Vatassery et al., 1971). Our primary interest in studying vibratory perception was as a modality in a study of vitamin B_{12} deficiencies in elderly psychiatric patients. There are few reports of its use among psychiatric patients. Detre et al. (1962) reported elevated vibratory threshold in schizophrenic patients. Dovenmuehle et al. (1960) reported on the physical functioning ratings of the Duke First Longitudinal Study subjects and some patients similar to ours; they reported that a higher disease frequency was invariably associated with lower socioeconomic status. We report in this paper the results of our experience and findings in using the vibratory threshold as a parameter in evaluating a large number of relatively unselected elderly hospitalized patients, and we compare them to community controls.

Method

Subjects. In this study, four groupings of subjects were used. One group of ten healthy males and females aged fifteen to forty-five were used to measure the perceptuaLVT of younger persons, and no further studies were done with them. All of the rest of the subjects were over age sixty-five.

The control subjects were from the geriatric longitudinal study groups at the Duke University Center for the Study of Aging and Human Development. They are volunteers living in the community who have been followed at intervals since 1954 for extensive testing which has been reported elsewhere (Palmore, 1970, 1974). They were tested for the vibratory study on a consecutive basis during the sixth round of investigations.

The acute psychiatric patients were new admissions to a state hospital having a catchment area of about one-fourth of the state of North Carolina. All new patients over age sixty-five were admitted to the geropsychiatry service and they were studied on the basis of consecutive admissions.

The chronic psychiatric patients were those in a state hospital who had been hospitalized for at least six months continuously, were ambulatory, were able to feed themselves from the ordinary hospital diets, and who had not lost over ten pounds of weight in the past six months. They were otherwise selected randomly using an alphabetical basis.

Examinations. Detailed psychiatric, social, and medical histories were obtained to the extent possible, with particular attempts to ascertain the previous drug and vitamin use. The general adequacy of the diet was estimated in gross terms of adequate, doubtfully adequate, and inadequate on the basis of food type and quantity intake, regularity of meals, and the estimation of the examining physician on the appearance of the subject. Batteries of tests and examinations were carried out, including physical neurologic examination, evaluation of the degree of papillary atrophy of the tongue, serum vitamin B_{12} and folic acid studies on many, psychiatric evaluation, and evaluation of the VT. Enough consecutive subjects were seen in each group originally to make up twelve subgroups of ten each, matched for age (over and under seventy-five) and for sex. Demographic and other data indicated that those who were not included in that study (Whanger and Wang, 1974) were basically similar to the matched groups, so they were included in this study, accounting for the unequal *N* in the groups.

Apparatus. The vibratory stimuli were generated by a Bio-thesiometer (Bio-Medical Instrument Company, Newbury, Ohio), which is a standardized electronic device delivering vibration at 120 cycles per second (HZ) by a button 1 cm. in diameter. A rheostat varies the intensity of the vibration, which can be read either in terms of voltage or in microns (10^{-4} cm) of motion perpendicular to the body surface. All readings in this report are in terms of microns of vertical motion. The maximum displacement of this device is 25 μ, and all figures are rounded off to the nearest micron. The pressure or weight on the button is held relatively constant by using the weight of the vibratory head held lightly in the fingers.

Procedure. Each subject was seated in a quiet, warm room for several minutes. The general procedure was explained to each subject, and then the operator demonstrated upon himself first, in order to alleviate the possible fear of pain or shock that the subject might have. Then the vibratory button was applied over the styloid process of the radius at the wrist and turned high enough initially for the subject to distinctly perceive the nature of the sensation. The voltage was then returned to zero. The patient was then instructed to say "Now" as soon as he first felt the vibration as the rheostat was slowly raised, and then at least three readings were taken at each site and were recorded. If there was a question about accurate perception, an off-on switch on the Bio-thesiometer was used without altering the voltage to check the subjects' reliability. Each wrist was checked, and then the same procedure was repeated by applying the vibrator button to the tibial tuberosity at the knee of the partially extended leg on each side. The reasons for these sites were: (1) to check the upper and lower extremities, (2) to utilize easily accessible sites not requiring the subject to disrobe, (3) to minimize variations due to differing thickness of subcutaneous tissue since these sites are prominent bony landmarks, and (4) to avoid the ankles because such a high number of subjects are unable to perceive any vibration there. The VT was recorded in the ascending mode only. Perret reported the VT to be lower in the desending mode (i.e., when the vibratory sensation was at a high level and decreased until the subject reported its disappearance), but we found this to produce much more erratic results, and so abandoned it. Perret also made the observation that the VT increased more in the aged on the preferred (dominant) side of the body, rather than equally on each side as reported by others (Goff et al., 1965; Perret and Regli, 1970). We noted considerable variation between the right and left in many subjects but, because of the reported incidence of such things as strokes, fractures, and thrombophlebitis affecting these limbs, we used the lesser value of the VT in the calculations, whichever side that was on, feeling that this represented the subjects' best and most realistic capacity for perception and least likely the effects of incidental disease (Birren, 1947).

Results

Only a portion of the results and correlations will be reported in this paper, with emphasis on those with some clinical importance or implications.

A total of 164 subjects were examined for this study, with a mean age of seventy-seven years. Only two of these refused to have the vibrator applied. Of the rest, however, a number were either unable to comprehend the task, were unable to cooperate well, or gave such inconsistent results (over 3 μ variation on three trials) that they were excluded from the calculations. The percentage of these in each of the three groups were as follows: control, 4 percent, acute, 32 percent, and chronic, 25 percent. The remaining *N* is 122. A surprising number of quite disoriented patients were able to cooperate well and give very consistent answers at each site. We were unable to get other accurate data about some items among a number of subjects, but did not exclude them from the study on this basis. This varied the *N* in different calculations, and it obviously makes the statistics less neat.

We calculated the percentage of each grouping who had a difference of more than 2 μVT between the right and left sides. At the wrist this was 16 percent of the controls, 16 percent of the acute patients, and 9 percent of the chronic patients. At the knees this was 26 percent of the controls, 19 percent of the acute, and 24 percent of the chronic patients.

Among those who were able to cooperate with the test, there were a number who were unable to perceive the vibratory stimulation at the knee even at maximal intensity. Among those with minimal or no organic brain syndromes, this constituted 15 percent of the subjects, while, among those rated with severe organic brain syndromes, this was 24 percent. For purposes of calculations, however, these were rated at 25 μ, the maximal capacity of the testing instrument. All of these were able to perceive and report vibration consistently in the wrists.

The mean VT values for the total group are noted in figure B—1, subdivided on the basis of five-year age increments. The mean values for the normal under age forty-five group are noted as well. There is no age decrement in the values for the knee by age above age sixty-five. Mean values at the wrist show a very high value for the sixty-five to sixty-nine age group, and then a gradual rise with age is noted. It is to be noted that there was a lack of control subjects with VT tested under age seventy.

When the means for each of the subgroups are separated, however, as in figure B—2 for the wrist, then we find a highly significant difference between the control group and the psychiatric patients. The VT's are lower for the controls, who also show a steadily increasing threshold with age. It is noted that the

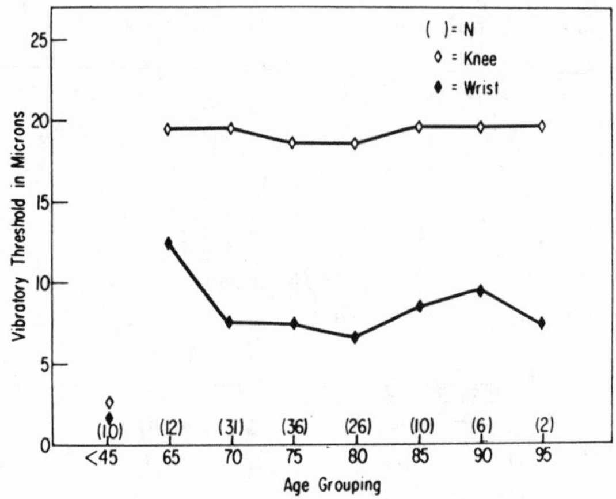

Figure B—3. *Mean vibratory thresholds at wrist and knee of total group of* N = *122 by 5-year age groupings.*

VT of the psychiatric patients over age ninety closely approximates that of the control group, however.

In figure B—3, the same pattern, with a lesser degree of significance is noted in the knees.

The racial composition of the total group was 63 percent white and 37 percent nonwhite (or essentially black, as otherwise it included only one Indian). This approximates the racial makeup of this geographic area. The mean values were subdivided on the basis of race and sex. In table B—12 it is noted that there is no difference in the mean value at the wrist between all of the men and women. There is a lower VT at both the wrist and the knee among the nonwhite subjects, which is highly significant at the knee, as seen in table B—13.

Those with doubtfully adequate or grossly inadequate diets were 14 percent among the controls, 71 percent among the acute, and 5 percent among the chronically hospitalized psychiatric patients. As noted in figure B—4, there are significantly higher thresholds for those on inadequate diets. Surprisingly, there was no significant difference in VT between the nonusers and the heavy users of alcohol.

Among those subjects with diabetes mellitus, there was a significant increase in the VT as noted also on figure B—4.

Table B—12. *Mean vibratory threshold of wrist by sex and race in microns of vibration (N = 89).*

Group	White	Nonwhite	Total
Male	9	7	8
Female	8	7	8
Total	9	7	8

Note: Analysis of trends in various groupings does not reach significance.

Table B—13. *Mean vibratory threshold of knee by sex and race in microns of vibration (N = 89).*

Group	White	Nonwhite	Total
Male (M)	20	18	19
Female (F)	21	16	19
Total	21	17	19

Note: Analysis of variance (chi square) *P*.
(1) White M vs. nonwhite M, NS; (2) White M vs. white F, NS; (3) White F vs. nonwhite F, .05; (4) Nonwhite M vs. nonwhite F, NS; (5) All M vs. all F, NS; (6) All white vs. all nonwhite, .02.

While there was accurate tobacco use data on only eighty-one of the subjects, of whom thirty-one used tobacco in some form at the time of the interview, there was a lower VT in the nonusers at both the wrist and the knee, but the difference was significant only at the wrist.

Among those with syphilis, or at least with a positive serological test, there was a significant elevation of the threshold at the wrist but not at the knee.

As part of our original study of the prevalence of low levels of vitamin B_{12} among elderly psychiatric patients, we obtained detailed histories of supplemental vitamin intakes (i.e., in addition to enriched foods). During the preceding year those known to have taken supplemental vitamins were 42 percent of the controls, 20 percent of the acute group, and forty-eight percent of the chronic subjects. Of this group, those who had taken oral vitamin B_{12} were 22 percent of the controls, 12 percent of the acute, and 10 percent of the total chronic. Five percent of the total group had received vitamin B_{12} by injection within the previous year. In figure B—4, the mean VT values for the groups with different types of vitamin intakes are noted, with emphasis on the significantly elevated VT of those taking some type of single or multiple vitamin without B_{12}.

No significant differences in VT were noted among those subjects taking barbiturates, tranquilizers, phenothiazines, steroids, or thyroid. There was an in-

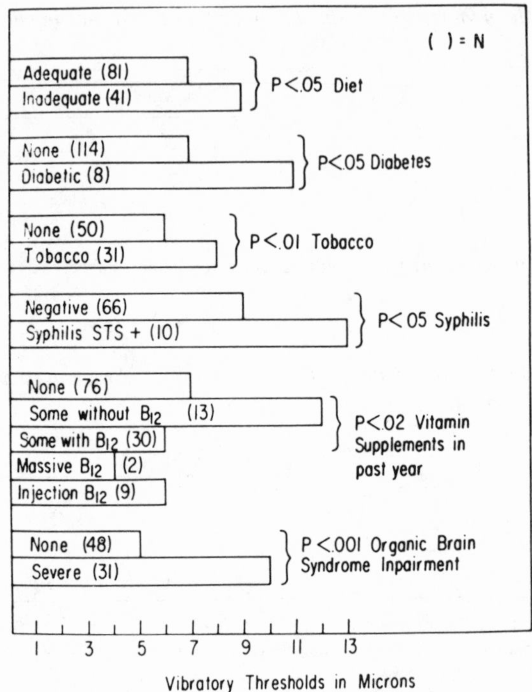

Figure B—4. *Mean vibratory thresholds at the wrist in a variety of states. Analysis is by the* t-*test.*

crease of the VT at the wrists of those on anticonvulsant drugs (mostly diphenylhydantoin) significant at the .05 level, however. It is not clear whether this is an effect of the drug or the underlying disease.

All of the subjects were rated by a psychiatrist as to the degree of organic brain syndrome (OBS), ranging from none to total disability on a six-point scale. The VT of those with absent or nondisabling OBS as compared to those with severe disability (over 50 percent) from OBS is tabulated in figure B—4, and there is a highly significant elevation among the organically impaired who were still able to give accurate reports.

Discussion

Elderly psychiatric patients are perhaps the most complicated group of patients to work with because of the multiplicity of physical and psychological disorders, the difficulty of obtaining accurate history, and our remaining ignorance about many of the processes of aging. There are so many etiologies and variables that it is impossible not to overgeneralize or to oversimplify. We used the measurement of the vibratory threshold as a relatively objective and easily obtained measurement of the functioning of the nervous system among ill patients. How valid a measure the VT is of the general state of the nervous system is not determined, and it would be interesting to correlate with the EEG. The VT does have a marked correlation with the degree of organic brain syndrome. Perhaps related is an observation by Newman of a marked relationship between a low VT of the penis of elderly men and the frequency of their sexual activity (Newman, 1970).

The increasing levels of perceptual thresholds for vibratory stimuli (VT) start after age forty-five, and our relatively normal elderly controls did show a progressive elevation of VT by age. The psychiatric patients showed significantly higher levels of VT, with wider mean fluctuations noted at the wrists. The wrist readings are more useful clinically in that there is less variability between the two sides, and a substantial number of the elderly are unable to perceive strong vibratory stimuli at the knee. The high VT levels in the acute patients at age sixty-five and again at age eighty-five may reflect patients in severely ill states, especially with organic brain disease, and who may be in terminal declines. This study does not include this information, but we are presently continuing sequential studies to determine this. The return of the mean VT of those psychiatric patients over age ninety to levels comparable to those of the normal controls may reflect either the superior nervous system of someone surviving that long or that they may have been hospitalized more for social reasons than for psychiatric reasons.

The significantly lower VTs among the black subjects had not been noted previously, but may possibly reflect the same type of preservation mechanisms which account for blacks retaining their hearing better and longer than whites. Interestingly, we had also observed the nearly identical pattern in our vitamin B_{12} studies, in which blacks had significantly higher mean serum B_{12} levels than whites. It is not clear whether this is a genetic difference or reflects a state with better survival value, since the average life-span of the black person is substantially less than the white, although if he survives into old age he has a longer remaining life expectancy than the white (Whanger and Wang, 1974).

There are several interesting relationships between the VT and vitamins as we observed them. The observation that those taking vitamin supplements without B_{12} have a much higher VT may reflect multiple vitamin deficiencies which are being aggravated, as far as damaging the nervous system is concerned, by partial treatment. It is well known that folic acid supplementation in the face of vitamin B_{12} deficiency will aggravate neurologic symptoms and signs, and an analogous process may be taking place. We know from our recent studies that nearly 50 percent of acute elderly psychiatric patients have borderline or definitely low serum levels of folic acid. Obviously this should be studied further as it has considerable possible implication for the types of vitamin supplementation that should or should not take place in the elderly, and possibly in the young (Whanger, 1973).

The elevated VT of those using tobacco may suggest nerve damage by the cyanide arising from smoking (Matthews and Wilson, 1971). Vitamin B_{12} is a major detoxifying agent for cyanide in the human.

A considerable number of the elderly have good preservation of the VT at the wrists, and sometimes at the knees. We looked at those with a VT of the wrist of 3 μ or less, which is near the threshold of young people. These made up 49 percent of the controls, 7 percent of the acutes, and 3 percent of the chronics. Of those with these low levels, about 50 percent were taking oral vitamin B_{12}. This could reflect the better care that some take of themselves, even to the point of taking unnecessary vitamins, rather than vitamin B_{12} (or possibly other related untested factors) having a protective value. Another interesting observation not previously reported from a study of ours of all patients over age ninety in two state psychiatric hospitals ($N = 11$) showed a mean vitamin B_{12} level of 560 picograms, while the mean for the whole group in the study reported in this paper was 366 picograms. The one individual in this over-ninety group who had a VT at the wrist of 3 μ was a spry gentleman who was both the oldest man in the whole study (age 100) and also had the highest B_{12} level (1450 picograms). We are not suggesting that vitamin B_{12} or any other vitamin or compound is a magic elixir for aging, but it certainly warrants further and more careful study. The elevation of VT among the elderly has some relation to aging per se, but is much more closely related to disease and nutritional factors. The VT can possibly be used as a measure of the progress of a disease, the effectiveness of drugs and treatments, and, possibly, as a predictor of mortality and morbidity.

Summary

The vibratory threshold (VT) was measured quantitatively at the wrists and knees of acutely-admitted and chronically hospitalized elderly psychiatric patients and compared with a cohort of elderly persons living in the community. The VT was markedly elevated in all groups as compared with a young control group. The VT of the psychiatric patients was significantly higher, hence implying neurologic impairment, than that of the community volunteers. The measurement at the wrists was the more useful one clinically. The VT of black subjects was significantly lower than that of white subjects. Those on inadequate diets had a significantly elevated VT, as did those using tobacco, when compared to nonusers. Subjects with diabetes, syphilis, and severe organic brain syndromes also had significantly elevated VT.

Interesting observations were made on some relationships of the vibratory sense and vitamin levels and usage. Most important is that those subjects who were taking vitamin supplements (either single vitamins or multiple preparations) which did not contain vitamin B_{12} had a markedly elevated VT over both those taking no vitamin supplements at all and those taking supplements containing vitamin B_{12}. The implications of this are enormous in view of the massive use of incomplete vitamin supplementation in our society. We offer these data, incomplete and preliminary as they are, in hopes that the study will be replicated under better controlled situations with more elaborate vitamin and dietary information. It may be that the vibratory sense will be a useful tool in measuring the effects of nutritional factors and disease states on the nervous system.

References

Birren, J. E. Vibratory sensitivity in the aged. *Journal of Gerontology*, 2:267–268, 1947.

Calne, D. B., and Pallis, C. A. Vibratory sense: A critical review. *Brain*, 89:723–746, 1966.

Cosh, J. A. Studies on the nature of vibration sense. *Clinical Science*, 12:131–150, 1953.

Detre, T. P., et al. Vibration perception in normal and schizophrenic subjects. *Journal of Neuropsychiatry*, (supp. 1.), 3:145–150, 1962.

Dovenmuehle, R. H., Busse, E. W., and Newman, E. G. Physical problems of psychiatrically hospitalized elderly persons. *Journal of the American Geriatrics Society*, 8:838–846, 1960.

Fox, J. C., and Klemperer, W. W. Vibratory sensibility. *Archives of Neurology and Psychiatry*, 48:622–645, 1942.

Goff, G. D., et al. Vibration perception in normal man and medical patients. *Journal of Neurology, Neurosurgery, and Psychiatry*, 28:503–509, 1965.

Matthews, D. M., and Wilson, J. Cobalamins and cyanide metabolism in neurological diseases. In H. R. V. Arnstein and R. J. Wrighton (Eds.), *The cobalamins*. Edinburgh: Churchill Livingstone, 1971.

Newman, H. F. Vibratory sensitivity of the penis. *Fertility and Sterility*, 21:791–793, 1970.

Palmore, E. B. (Ed.), *Normal aging*. Durham, N.C.: Duke University Press, 1970.

Palmore, E. B. (Ed.), *Normal aging II*. Durham, N.C.: Duke University Press, 1974.

Pearson, G. H. J. Effect of age on vibratory sensibility. *Archives of Neurology and Psychiatry*, 20:482–496, 1928.

Perret, E., and Regli, F. Age and perceptual threshold for. vibratory stimuli. *European Neurology*, 4:65–76, 1970.

Rosenberg, G. Effect of age on peripheral vibratory perception. *Journal of the American Geriatrics Society*, 6:471–481, 1958.

Steiness, I. Vibratory perception in normal subjects. *Acta Medica Scandinavica*, 158:315–325, 1957.

Vatassery, G. T., Alter, M., and Stadlan, E. M. Serum tocopherol levels and vibratory threshold changes with age. *Journal of Gerontology*, 26:481–484, 1971.

Whanger, A. D. Vitamins and vigor at 65 plus. *Post-graduate Medicine*, 53:167–172, 1973.

Whanger, A. D., and Wang, H. S. Vitamin B_{12} deficiency in normal aged and elderly psychiatric patients. In Palmore, E. B. (Ed.), *Normal aging II*. Durham, N.C.: Duke University Press, 1974.

Stress and Coping in Later Life

Linda K. George and Ilene C. Siegler

It is perhaps a sign of the times that both the mass media and scholarly journals are devoting substantial space to issues of stress and coping. Scholarly works, however, are less likely to promise information about successful coping or stress management. Despite the intuitive appeal and obvious significance of the topic, social scientists have only begun to understand the nature of stress and coping. The development of intervention strategies lags even further behind.

In this paper we will describe (1) the common stresses and problems reported by a sample of community-dwelling older adults, (2) the coping strategies employed in response to those stresses, and (3) the relationships among types of stresses, coping strategies, and perceptions of coping effectiveness. The data reported in this paper are part of a larger study of stress and coping during adulthood.

Background

The use of adaptation as an indicator of life quality during old age has a long history in gerontological literature (Maddox and Wiley, 1976). Adjustment may be defined as a state of congruence between the individual and the environment (George, 1980). In such a state the individual is able to successfully meet environmental demands and is able to experience a sense of personal well-being. Maladaptation can occur if the individual is unable to meet the demands of the environment, is unable to maintain a sense of well-being, or both.

For the past two decades, most studies of late life adjustment have emphasized demographic and social variables such as sex, race, and education to predict and explain differences in adjustment among individuals (George, 1978; Palmore and Luikart, 1972). Now, research investigators are considering the effects of stress and coping upon late life adjustment. Available evidence suggests that links among stress, coping, and adjustment during later life may increase our knowledge about the quality of life in old age (George, 1980).

Following the lead of Holmes and Rahe, stress typically is measured in terms of life events such as marriage, widowhood, and illness, and the degree to which such events disrupt established patterns of behavior or degree of change. Therefore, greater amounts of change are expected to increase the likelihood of adaptive problems. From this perspective, events that are presumably experienced as positive or pleasant—marriage or a job promotion—as well as those that are typically negative—widowhood—are viewed as stressful because both

Reprinted by permission from *Educational Horizons*, 60:147–154, 1982.

types of events disrupt established behavior patterns (Holmes and Rahe, 1967; Lieberman, 1975).

A central problem with the conventional stress perspective is the assumption that a given experience has the same impact on everyone. We prefer to examine the conditions under which life events do and do not have negative effects on adjustment or personal well-being. If one adopts this approach, one must also question the assumption that degree of change is the sole underlying component of stress. First, change may not be inevitably stressful. For example, failing to obtain a desired promotion may be more stressful than receiving the promotion and adapting to the behavior changes that accompany it. This example illustrates that the meaning of the event to the individual must be incorporated in the study of stress and its impact (House, 1981; Lowenthal et al., 1975).

We collected considerable data about the meaning of the events experienced by participants in the study. In addition to eliciting general information about the meaning of events, we focused on three specific characteristics of events that we felt would be related to the impact of stress upon personal well-being. First, we hypothesized that events that are chosen are less stressful than those that are imposed by others or by external forces. For example, being fired is likely to be more stressful than resigning. Similarly, Schulz and Brenner note that involuntary residential relocation has a more negative effect upon health, mortality, and life satisfaction of older people than moving by choice (Schulz and Brenner, 1977). Second, we hypothesized that unexpected events are perceived as more stressful than expected or anticipated events. Glick, Weiss, and Parkes, report, for example (1974), that widowhood is more likely to lead to long-term adjustment problems when the spouse's death was unexpected than when the spouse died after a long illness. Moreover, unpleasant events seem to be significantly easier to cope with if they are expected or predictable, because the individual has time to plan a response to the event and mobilize available resources. Third, it seemed plausible to hypothesize that negative events will pose greater threats to adjustment than positive events. Therefore, we expected to explain differences in individuals' responses to life events in terms of personal meaning and its accompanying stress.

Individuals differ in the ways they react to stressful situations. Some people are unable to cope with the slightest problem; others appear to handle even the most difficult situations with grace and competence. Thus, coping skills also may affect significantly the relationship between stress and problems of adaptation. Behavioral scientists have only begun to describe and understand coping, perhaps because of the many ways that coping has been defined. Some scientists distinguish between intrapsychic responses and behavioral responses to stressful situations and view only the latter as coping (French et al., 1974; Mechanic, 1970). Others define coping as only those efforts explicitly intended to alter the stressful situation. They prefer to view attempts to reduce anxiety or secure comfort as defenses or stress management techniques rather than as coping. In practice, such distinctions are almost impossible to make. When an individual alters a stressful situation, perceptions of stress are altered also. In this study, coping is defined as the overt and covert behaviors individuals use to prevent, alleviate, or respond to stressful situations. This definition encompasses behaviors directed toward altering perceptions of stress and accompanying emotional states as well as efforts to directly alter the source of stress.

Two major approaches have been used to measure and study coping: process and typological. Process approaches attempt to abstract the elements that best capture the coping process. These models emphasize an active stance toward the environment, a rational process of information gathering, and an organized form of behavioral implementation. Other theorists have developed typologies of different coping strategies that frequently include the distinction between active strategies intended to alter directly the stressful situation and passive strategies which modify perceptions of stress or the affective consequences of stress. Lazarus and Launier (1978) classify the orientation of coping strategies as either (1) instrumental—intended to modify the stressful situation—or (2) palliative—intended to regulate emotion. They further describe four major coping modes: (1) information seeking, (2) direct action, (3) inhibition of action, and (4) intrapsychic modes. Coping mode is assumed to be independent of coping orientation; thus, each coping mode may be either instrumental or palliative in terms of its intended purpose or actual effect. We found the typological measures based on the Lazarus and Launier typology of coping mode and orientation most useful; thus, these are the measures discussed in this paper.

Sample and Methods

The sample for this study consisted of 100 men and women aged 55–80. All study participants were white, noninstitutionalized older adults living in central North Carolina. The sample included equal numbers of men and women drawn from a sample of older persons who had completed a six-year longitudinal study conducted by the Duke University Center for the Study of Aging and Human Development. The primary data for the study were collected from indepth, semi-structured interviews, averaging about two and a half hours in length. The interview was supplemented by a fairly lengthy questionnaire which included standard social and demographic variables as well as a variety of standardized social-psychological measures. The interview data, however, comprised the major source of information about stress and coping. Interviews obtained detailed information about six life events or periods: best time in whole life; worst time in whole life; best time in past ten years; worst time in past ten years; best aspects of the present; and worst aspects of the present. Within these time referents, participants were asked to identify the specific good and bad experiences most meaningful to them. Using this respondent-selected experience as the event context, interviewers elicited a standard set of information about that experience including: nature of the experience; characteristics of the event or experience (e.g., chosen versus imposed); perceptions of the stress; other people involved in the experience; impact of the experience on the respondent; specific ways that the respondent coped with or handled the situation; how the participant evaluated his or her coping efforts; and perceptions of control and efficiency.

This article emphasizes stress commonly reported by older persons. Consequently, results reported are based on respondents' descriptions of the worst aspect of the present, although comparisons with other time referents are occasionally noted.

Stress during Later Life

Because we wanted to focus the interview on those problems of most concern to respondents rather than impose our definitions of stress upon them, study participants defined the problems discussed in the interviews. As one might expect, a wide range of specific problems and issues were volunteered by the one hundred respondents. Consequently, we devised a classification system that would do justice to the richness of individual experience and permit an organized and readily understood classification system. Ultimately, we developed the classification system presented in table B—14. The coding scheme takes the form of a matrix with events cross-classified in terms of two dimensions. The first dimension is called domain and is represented by the rows of the matrix. We found that all the stresses reported could be coded into one of the five domain categories: self, family, health, work, and economics. The second dimension, which we call context, forms the columns of the matrix. Context refers to the scope of the stress in terms of the people involved, and it has two categories. Personal stresses affect only the respondent, and interpersonal stresses are those in which people other then the respondent play a major role. It took us a long time to realize the existence of two dimensions. Once that realization was made, however, coding became straightforward and highly reliable.

Table B—14 presents the distribution of stresses reported by the older persons in our sample as the worst experience in the present. Because there are one hundred participants in the study, the numbers may be interpreted as either frequencies or percentages.

Table B—14. *Matrix of stressful life experiences.*

	Context		
Domain	Personal	Interpersonal	Frequency
Self	15	5	20
Family	0	21	21
Health	25	6	31
Work	8	4	12
Economics	12	4	16
Total	60	40	

The self/personal events covered a substantial variety of specific experiences including feelings of boredom, fear of the future, loneliness, and lack of sufficient time to devote to preferred activities. The self/interpersonal stresses fell into two types: three respondents reported disagreements or discomfort in important friendships, two other respondents reported considerable concern with issues of morality, social values, and spiritual life. There was an interesting sex difference in the self-events. All but one of the respondents reporting self/personal events were women; all five of the respondents reporting self/interpersonal events were men.

The twenty-one respondents who reported family/interpersonal events as the most difficult aspects of the present formed three groups. Eleven respondents indicated that they were having disagreements with or were concerned about their children and/or grandchildren. Nine participants described problems with their spouses as the worst aspect of the present. One respondent described her mother's residence in her home as the most unpleasant aspect of the present. Seventeen of the twenty-one family events were reported by women; all four men who described family events reported marital problems as the worst aspect of the present.

The largest category of stressors was health/personal events, reported by one-fourth of the respondents. The health problems described were relatively straightforward: chronic, limiting conditions, problems following prescribed diets or medication regimens; and complaints about a lack of energy. Health/interpersonal events, reported by six participants, referred to health problems experienced by respondents' family members. In some cases, the stressful aspect of a family member's illness was worry and concern; in other cases, the family member's need for care and service from the respondent was viewed as difficult. Men were significantly more likely than women to report health events as the worst aspect of the present.

Eight participants described work/personal experiences as the worst aspect of the present. Four respondents, evenly split by gender, described excessive pressures at work as the worst aspect of the present. Three men reported fear that they would not accomplish all they would like. These men were in their seventies and had no desire or plans to retire, but feared that a lifetime of work would not be sufficient to accomplish all they hoped. One woman was having difficulty deciding whether or not to retire. Four work/interpersonal experiences were described as the worst aspect of the present. Two men and one woman reported unpleasant relationships with co-workers. One woman described her maid's retirement as the worst part of the present. She admitted that loss of a maid would not be viewed as a serious problem by many people, but she had employed the maid for nearly fifty years and was not enjoying the resumption of housework. It is interesting to note, in light of common stereotypes, that work is more important for men than women and that there were no significant gender differences in work events, either personal or interpersonal.

Twelve respondents described economics/personal experiences as the worst thing about the present. Four of these respondents were men and eight were women; all described general financial insecurity as their greatest problem. All of the men were in their seventies. Some of the women were considerably younger than this, but all except one were widows. Four respondents described economics/interpersonal experiences as the worst aspect of the present. One man, a seventy-six-year-old farmer still working full-time, worried about a drought that threatened the local farming industry. Two women were concerned about their children's financial difficulties. One man worried about the economic security of the country as a whole and the implications for future generations. Women were significantly more likely than men to report economics/interpersonal problems.

Space limitations preclude a detailed comparison of the distribution of events described as the worst aspect of the present with the distributions generated for the other five event contexts mentioned previously. Two comparisons will be briefly highlighted, however, because they have implications for our understanding of later life. First, the older the respondent at the time an event occurred, the more likely it was that the event was personal than interpersonal. A similar pattern was found for domain; the frequency of self-events increased dramatically across the age ranges reported by study participants. This pattern was true for all six event contexts examined in the study. The age-related increase in reports of events in the self domain and/or personal context appears compatible with the narrowing social and psychological spheres that Neugarten and others have described as typical of later life (1973). A second interesting finding is that economic problems were rarely reported for any period except the present. This is especially dramatic in light of the fact that all the study participants lived through the economic depression and, although many mentioned that period of their early adulthood, serious worries about economic security were most frequently reported for later life.

We also examined the effects of specific event characteristics upon perceptions of stress. The distinction between positive and negative events was, of course, built into the structure of the interview. Respondents could understand coping, perceptions of stress, and handling situations only in the context of negative events. The notion that both positive and negative change pose adaptive challenges was flatly rejected by study participants. Within the negative event contexts, including the worst aspect of the present, one of our initial hypotheses was supported: increased perceptions of stress were associated with perceptions that the event was unexpected rather than expected. The hypothesis that imposed events are perceived as more stressful than chosen events was not supported. In fact, it appears that, for negative events, perceptions that the event was chosen are associated with increased perceptions of stress. The underlying issue appears to be attribution of responsibility, a topic discussed in more detail in the context of coping.

Coping during Later Life

Because the Lazarus and Launier mode is central to our examination of coping, it is important to understand the two dimensions. Table B—15 shows an eight-cell matrix in which the two coping orientation categories form the columns of the matrix and the four coping mode categories form the rows.

Information seeking is a process whereby the individual seeks out specific information relevant to the stress or problem at hand. Consider the case in which a man who is ill goes to the doctor and learns all he can about his illness: how to prevent recurrence, how to handle its limitations, etc. This form of information seeking is instrumental in that it is directed toward obtaining information useful in treatment and management of the illness. In contrast, consider the case of a recently widowed woman who goes to her former husband's physician to assure herself that everything possible was done to save her husband's life. In this case, the information cannot change the stressor, but it can help the woman to handle the emotional consequences of widowhood. Such information is palliative.

Direct action may be either instrumental or palliative. Consider the hypothetical example of a woman who has had a serious disagreement with her boss. She may confront her employer, attempting to settle the issue to their mutual satisfaction, in which case her direct action is instrumental in orientation. On the other hand, she may decide to become involved in a hobby in order to get her mind off the unpleasantness at work; in this case, the woman's coping is direct action in mode and palliative in orientation.

Inhibition of action is a coping mode in Lazarus and Launier's model (1978), although other theorists have frequently viewed it as noncoping. There are situations in which inhibition of action is instrumental in that the stress dissipates or is righted more quickly in the absence of action. Parents, for example, occasionally suggest that children correct behavior problems more quickly if ignored rather than confronted. Inhibition of action also can be palliative in that one thereby avoids unpleasant tasks, and precludes the depletion of resources.

Finally, intrapsychic coping behavior refers to the emotional and cognitive strategies that individuals use to respond to stressful situations. If an individual can use denial or some other form of reappraisal to decide that what appears as a

Table B—15. *Matrix of coping responsibilities.*

Coping mode	Coping orientation: Instrumental	Palliative	Frequency
Information seeking	28	0	28
Direct action	68	22	90
Inhibition of action	21	5	26
Intrapsychic	2	52	54
Total	119	79	

stress is in fact benign, such intrapsychic coping is instrumental in orientation. More frequently, intrapsychic strategies are used to regulate the affective consequences of stress. Reports of relying on faith or looking on the bright side are ways of dissipating some of the distress that accompanies a problem or worry.

Table B—2 presents the frequencies of respondents' descriptions of the coping strategies they employed to respond to the worst aspects of the present. The frequencies sum to more than one hundred because respondents often reported using multiple coping strategies for a given problem. Turning first to coping mode, the rows of the matrix, direct-action coping strategies were reported most frequently, followed by intrapsychic coping responses. Smaller and approximately equal numbers of coping responses were classified as information-seeking and inhibition-of-action strategies. In terms of coping orientation, the majority of coping responses were instrumental in orientation—intended to alleviate, modify, or eliminate the stressful event. A significant minority of coping responses, however, were palliative—directed toward making the person feel better about the situation.

The cells of the matrix indicate that coping orientation and coping mode were not independent in this sample. Intrapsychic coping responses were overwhelmingly palliative in orientation. The other three coping modes—direct action, inhibition of action, and information seeking—were employed primarily for instrumental reasons.

One of the goals of our study was to determine the factors associated with the use of particular coping strategies. Does choice of a coping strategy reflect personal predispositions to respond to stress in a characteristic manner? Or do constraints, resources, and other characteristics of a situation better predict the type of coping strategy employed? Our findings suggest that the type of event is a significant predictor of the type of coping strategy used. In particular, there was a strong relationship between event context and coping orientation. In the worst present, for events that were personal rather than interpersonal in context, 63 percent of the coping responses were instrumental in orientation and only 37 percent were palliative. Conversely, for events that were interpersonal in context, a majority (55 percent) were palliative in orientation and a minority (45 percent) were instrumental. Thus, it appears that respondents were more active and instrumental in responding to personal events. Interpersonal events may pose more constraints and lead to increased frequency of the more passive palliative coping strategies. This general relationship between event context and coping orientation held true for all three time referents that required respondents to describe negative events.

Finally, we examined the general question of coping effectiveness. This is a very difficult issue and one we were reluctant to tackle for several reasons. The issue of coping effectiveness is difficult because there are no adequate criteria (i.e., no criteria based on either rigorous research evidence or professional consensus) by which to evaluate coping effectiveness. Without adequate criteria, we simply do not know which personal or situational factors to take into account or how such factors should be included in the evaluation of coping effectiveness. A few examples may help to illustrate the thorny nature of this issue. First, at what point should coping effectiveness be evaluated? Should the immediate consequences of coping be evaluated, or should we await some long-term impact before rendering judgment? Second, should coping effectiveness be evaluated solely in terms of its impact on the individual most directly involved or should we examine the effects of coping behaviors on the entire network of individuals affected by the stressful experience? One can imagine circumstances in which an individual preserves his or her own well-being by making life miserable for everyone else involved in the situation. Do such self-protective, but interpersonally destructive strategies represent effective or ineffective coping? A third issue concerns how one takes into account the severity or difficulty of the stress. If one person does a moderately effective job of eliminating a severely stressful situation and another person does an excellent job of eliminating a relatively minor annoyance, who is the more successful coper? People obviously confront stressors of varying severity, and these differences matter. But how can an evaluation of coping effectiveness take such differences into account? Finally, how should we take account of the differential resources available to individuals? If two people face the same stressful experience (e.g., mandatory retirement) but differ substantially in health, income, number of friends, etc., can we reasonably attribute the better adjustment of the resource-rich individual to superior coping? Obviously, all of these issues are important elements of the stress-coping-adaptation transaction and the eventual effectiveness of the coping strategy employed. At this point, however, this complex set of factors cannot easily be integrated into a method of evaluating coping effectiveness.

Because of the difficulties that preclude objective ratings of coping effectiveness, we relied upon respondents' evaluations of the effectiveness of their coping strategies. Respondents were asked to judge how well they had handled the stressful situations they described to us. In general, most respondents felt that they had coped fairly effectively. A minority rated their efforts as excellent, but most felt their efforts were adequate or better. About 30 percent felt that they had done a less than adequate job, but only 9 percent rated themselves as coping failures. It is interesting to note that, in explaining their coping effectiveness self-ratings, respondents frequently commented upon precisely the issues noted above (e.g., the severity of the stressor, the resources available to them) indicating that they took such factors into account in making their self-evaluations.

Perceptions of coping effectiveness were strongly related to two factors: perceptions of control and coping orientation. Perceptions of control refer to whether respondents felt responsible for the occurrence of the event and whether they had been in control of the ways they responded to the event. Both aspects of control, but especially perceptions of being in control of how the event was handled, were related to self-evaluations of coping effectiveness. In terms of control over occurrence of event, 78 percent of those respondents who perceived themselves to be responsible for the event rated themselves as having been less than effective in coping with the event, compared to only 22 percent of those who perceived themselves as not responsible for the event. Even more dramatic, only 6 percent of those who felt they were in control of how the event was handled rated their coping as less than adequate compared to 94 percent of those who felt that they were not in control of how the event was handled. In addition, comments volunteered throughout the interviews indicated that respondents generally felt that, although some problems cannot be avoided, one does have a choice of how to respond to problems regardless of whether those problems are self-initiated or imposed by external forces.

Perceptions of coping effectiveness also were related to coping orientation. As we might expect, those persons who reported using both instrumental and palliative coping strategies reported the highest self-ratings of coping effectiveness. Those respondents who employed both coping orientation strategies covered all the bases: they directed some efforts toward altering the sources of stress but also devoted some energy toward alleviating the emotional distress that accompanies problems. Even more interesting, however, are the results of comparing those respondents who reported using only instrumental coping strategies with those participants who reported using only palliative coping strategies. Comparison of these groups indicated that those persons who used only palliative coping strategies rated their coping effectivenes higher than those who used only instrumental coping strategies. Indeed, those who employed only palliative strategies were almost as high in self-ratings of coping effectiveness as those respondents who used both instrumental and palliative coping strategies. Apparently those persons who felt better about how they cope also are those individuals who cope by using behavioral and/or intrapsychic strategies intended to make them feel better. In general, we were impressed with the degree to which the findings support the importance of palliative coping strategies for personal well-being. Such findings are at odds with some of the previous literature on coping, which emphasizes the active, planned, and rational nature of effective coping (Janis, 1974; Tyler, 1978). Our study participants suggest that effective coping involves at least as much effort on behalf of maintenance of the self as toward altering external circumstance.

Discussion

This article presents a limited number of findings from our study of stress and coping during adulthood and focuses on the stresses and problems which study participants were experiencing at the time of the interviews. The findings reported are beginning efforts to identify the links between stress and coping during later life.

Our findings suggest that older people confront a wide variety of stressful or problematic situations, although the stresses reported typically were not viewed as overwhelming. Most previous studies of stress have used checklists of life events to elicit information about problems. Comparison of the stresses reported by study participants with conventional checklist measures suggests that at least a third of the stresses described by our respondents would have been missed if a checklist had been used. This finding illustrates the importance of permitting older persons to define stress in terms meaningful to them.

Respondents also described a wide array of specific coping strategies that they employed to handle the stresses or problems they confronted. The Lazarus and Launier typology proved to be a useful way of summarizing and understanding those coping strategies. We were particularly interested in identifying factors associated with choice of a particular coping strategy. The results suggested that there is a strong relationship between event context and coping orientation. Respondents were more likely to employ instrumental coping strategies in response to stresses or events that were personal in context.

The final issue examined was coping effectiveness, which was measured by respondents' self-evaluations. Two factors were found to be closely related to self-ratings of coping effectiveness: perceptions of control, especially control over how the stress was handled, and coping orientation. Coping effectiveness is rated most favorably if (1) the individual does not attribute the occurrence of the stress to himself or herself, (2) the individual perceives that he or she was in control of how the stress was handled, and (3) both instrumental and palliative coping strategies were employed. Additionally, if only one coping orientation is pursued, palliative coping strategies are associated with higher ratings of effectiveness than instrumental strategies. These findings again illustrate the importance of permitting respondents to define and describe the meaning of their life experiences, rather than having such decisions imposed on them by research investigators.

The semistructured interviews utilized in this study generated a rich data set. Although the findings reported are significant and meaningful, in many ways the richness of the data remains immersed in the interview transcripts. Each of our respondents had an interesting story to tell, and we became convinced that older people have much to teach us about the good and bad times of life. If stress and coping research can be conducted so that the study participants are able to convey the meaning and richness of their experiences, such research can perhaps provide an opportunity for all of us to learn some important lessons about life.

References

French, J. R. P., Jr., Rodgers, W., and Cobb, S. Adjustment as person-environment fit. In G. V. Coelho, D. A. Hamburg, and J. E. Adams (Eds.), *Coping and adaptation*. New York: Basic Books, 1974.

George, L. K. The impact of personality and social status factors upon levels of activity and psychological well-being. *Journal of Gerontology*, 33:840–847, 1978.

George, L. K. *Role transitions in later life*. Monterey, Calif.: Brooks/Cole, 1980.

Glick, I. O., Weiss, R. D., and Parkes, C. M. *The first year of bereavement*. New York: Wiley, 1974.

Holmes, T. H., and Rahe, R. H. The social readjustment rating scale. *Journal of Psychosomatic Research*, 11:213–218, 1967.

House, J. S. *Work stress and social support*. Reading, Mass.: Addison-Wesley, 1981.

Janis, I. L. Vigilance and decision making in personal crises. In G. V. Coelho, D. A. Hamburg, and J. E. Adams (Eds.), *Coping and adaptation*. New York: Basic Books, 1974.

Lazarus, R. S., Launier, R. Stress related transactions between persons and environment. In L. A. Pervin and M. Lewis (Eds.), *Perspectives in interactional psychology*. New York: Plenum, 1978.

Lieberman, M. A. Adaptive processes in later life. In N. Datan and L. H. Ginsberg (Eds.), *Life-span developmental psychology: Normative life crisis*. New York: Academic, 1975.

Lowenthal, M. F., Thurnher, M., and Chiriboga, D. *Four stages of life*. San Francisco: Jossey-Bass, 1975.

Maddox, G. L., and Wiley, J. Scope, concepts, and methods in the study of aging. In R. H. Binstock and E. Shanas (Eds.), *Handbook of aging and the social sciences*. New York: Van Nostrand Reinhold, 1976.

Mechanic, D. Some problems in developing a social psychology of adaptation to stress. In J. E. McGrath (Ed.), *Social and psychological factors in stress*. New York: Holt, Rinehart and Winston, 1970.

Neugarten, B. L. Personality change in late life: A developmental perspective. In C. Eisdorfer and M. P. Lawton (Eds.), *The psychology of adult development and aging*. Washington, D.C.: American Psychological Association, 1973.

Palmore, E. B., and Luikart, C. Health and social factors related to life satisfaction. *Journal of Health and Social Behavior*, 13:68–80, 1972.

Schulz, R., and Brenner, G. Relocation of the aged: A review and theoretical analysis. *Journal of Gerontology*, 32:323–333, 1977.

Tyler, F. B. Individual psychosocial competence: A personality configuration. *Educational and Psychological Measurement*, 38:309–323, 1978.

Sex Differences in Coping and Perceptions of Life Events

Ilene C. Siegler and Linda K. George

In this paper we explore the question of sex differences in coping and perceptions of life events. An important question is: do older men and women have the same set of life events to cope with?

In our previous work with the Duke Second Longitudinal Study data set (Siegler et al., 1979), stable sex differences were seen in personality traits. We found no evidence for a view that would suggest an increasing unisex in later life. Our findings essentially replicate the biosocial trait view of Schaie and Parham (1976). Most of the differences were traditional sex differences. Thus it will be interesting to explore whether these personality differences are related to the efficacy of coping.

In many longitudinal studies concerned with personality and social develop-

Reprinted by permission from *Journal of Geriatric Psychiatry*, 16:197–209, 1983.

ment that include data from both men and women, related but different patterns of development were identified for men versus women. Such findings can be found in various reports from Berkeley/Oakland studies, the Terman studies, and the Fels studies (see Siegler, 1980 for review). Similarly, findings from the Human Development and Aging Program at the University of California, San Francisco, have consistently reported sex differences in the ways that men and women respond to the transitions present in middle and later life (Chiriboga and Cutler, 1980; Lowenthal et al., 1975).

Method

Our work on stress and coping grew out of the second longitudinal study, which began in 1968. The present study is essentially a fifth examination point for 100 of the respondents from the second longitudinal study. A structured interview was designed to assess individuals' perceptions of the life events they experienced as well as their view of their own coping processes. The data were collected in two phases. The first seventy-two respondents were interviewed in 1978 and an additional twenty-eight were added in 1980 for a total of 100. Only those individuals who had complete data on the psychological measures during the four previous times of measurement were considered for inclusion in the present study. The sample had equal numbers of men and women and was reasonably distributed across the age range available (fifty-five to seventy-eight), with half of the sample under sixty-six and half over, and it was balanced in terms of current economic well-being.

Once someone agreed to be in the study, they were sent a package of self-report instruments and demographic information sheets to fill out at home and bring with them when they came in for the interview part of the study. Respondents drew a life graph as an orienting technique to focus on the best and worst times of their lives. They were then asked to describe in detail the best and worst events within three time periods: their whole lives, the past ten years, and the present. They were asked the same set of questions each time. The interviewer first assessed the characteristics of the event, then the individuals involved in the event, and then the individual's coping with the event.

Studies of stressful life events have often used events checklists. In these lists, individuals check the events that have happened during a specified period of time. For example, a popular scale is the Social Readjustment Rating Scale (Holmes and Rahe, 1967), which makes certain assumptions about life events that we felt were worth testing: (1) that stress is a function of the degree of change generated by an event; (2) that stress is independent of whether the event is perceived as positive or negative; (3) that individual differences in perceptions of events are not important, as weightings derived from large samples can be assumed to be appropriate for many persons; and (4) that stress is cumulative and additive, with high degrees of stress producing negative health outcomes (see George, 1980 for a more detailed discussion of these issues).

Events were coded for amount of impact and direction (positive or negative), degree of expectedness, whether the event was chosen or imposed, and whether the effect of the event was enriching, sustaining (e.g., neutral) or debilitating. Additionally, the nearly 600 different event contexts were categorized in a matrix which cross-classified the domain of the event with the context of the event. Events were rated as in the contexts of personal, interpersonal, or community and in the domains of self, family, work, economics, or health. The deciding factor in classification was the individual's description of the event. Thus a promotion at work could have been classified as self/personal if the major meaning was as a mark of self-esteem, as work/personal if the major theme was achievement in career, or both if both were present.

Coping was first assessed with a process model developed by Tyler (1978). In this model, successful coping is indexed by rational, active, and intentional processing similar to problem solving. Also, the good coper was predicted to have an internal locus of control and a high degree of trust and autonomy and to preserve the self while solving the problem. Our later analyses (George and Siegler, 1982) indicated that the typological model developed by Lazarus and his colleagues gave a much better fit to our data. The Lazarus model is also a matrix with two independent dimensions of coping: coping orientation (either instrumental—something that modifies the situation; or palliative—something that regulates the emotions), cross-classified by modes of coping (information seeking, direct action, inhibition of action, and intrapsychic). We recoded the data thematically in order to test Lazarus' model and explore sociohistorical events and family themes in the data. In our study, effectiveness of coping was an assessment made by the respondent. Overall, there were no sex differences in the effectiveness of coping. Type of event was related to type of effective coping, so that, for negative events, palliative coping techniques that dealt with regulation of the emotions were effective in 62 percent of the cases if the events were nonpersonal (in the domains of family, work, economics, and health) and in 38 percent of the personal events. The reverse was true for the effectiveness of instrumental strategies where, if the event was a personal event, 62 percent of the time instrumental coping was effective and only 38 percent of the time palliative coping was effective. For all types of events, however, perceived coping effectiveness was highest if the respondent reported using both instrumental and palliative coping strategies.

Results and Discussion

Comparisons with Second Longitudinal Study Population

The 100 subjects in the coping study were compared with the 402 second longitudinal study participants who were not included in the coping study. These comparisons were made with data collected at the first time of measurement, approximately ten years earlier. The coping study participants were younger, had better self-perceived health, and were brighter. There were no differences in measures of psychological well-being, life satisfaction, locus of control, or self-concept. As the coping study respondents represent a selection from the surviving participants, it is not surprising that they were drawn from those who were originally younger, healthier, and brighter. More importantly, there were no differences in the major sociopsychological variables of interest.

Timing of Events

The timing of events across the life cycle did not vary significantly by sex. An initial question of interest is: do the best and worst events happen during the same phase of life? Our data suggest that the answer is no. The correlation between age at the beginning of the best and worst events was −.06 and nonsignificant. The next question is: were the events evenly distributed across the life cycle? As can be seen in table B—16, no decade was left out. Remember, our subjects range in age from fifty-five to seventy-eight. Even more interesting are the data on the duration of events, presented in table B—17.

Note that discrete events are relatively rare, and that positive events last longer than negative events. These durations were calculated by asking the person his or her age at the beginning and at the end of the event. If we look at the mean age at beginning and the mean age at end for the events for the best whole life (excluding ongoing events), the starting age was 30.86 and the ending age 34.40; for the worst event in the whole life, the ages were 40.03 and 40.90.

The timing of events appears to be influenced by the retrospective nature of our study. For example, a death was rarely described as the date of death, but rather as the time interval from the start of the terminal diagnosis or the feeling of ill health until some time after the funeral when equilibrium was reestablished. Most events were described in similar ways, so that the decisions or signs leading

Table B—16. *Timing of events in best and worst whole life.*

Event context		Childhood	Adolescence	20s	30s	40s	50s	60s	70s
Best, bounded,	M	1	3	16	12	3	6	1	1
	F	4	4	18	10	2	7	1	1
Worst, bounded,	M	2	4	11	9	8	7	0	2
	F	2	1	7	9	11	11	6	0
Best, ongoing,	M	—	—	—	—	1	4	2	1
	F	—	—	—	2	—	2	3	2
Worst, ongoing,	M	—	—	—	1	1	0	3	2
	F	—	—	—	—	—	2	0	1
Best total		5	7	34	29	6	19	7	5
Worst total		4	5	18	19	19	20	9	5

Table B—17. *Duration of events in best and worst whole life.*

	Best whole life		Worst whole life	
Length of event	Men	Women	Men	Women
Discrete < 1 year	6	7	21	22
1 year	0	2	4	5
2 years	2	2	3	5
3 years	5	1	3	1
4 years	4	1	3	1
5 years	6	6	4	3
6–10 years	9	10	5	6
11–15 years	3	8	3	1
16–19 years	1	0	0	0
20–29 years	5	4	0	1
30–39 years	1	2	0	0
Ongoing	8	7	4	5

up to the event, as well as the sequelae of the event, were included by our respondents as characteristic of the event itself.

Cohorts and Sociohistorical Time

Figure B—5 shows the major sociohistorical events experienced by our cohorts. This figure helps to fix in time the ages at which our respondents experienced major life events.

The major sex differences among the cohorts are shown in table B—18.

The cohorts differed in the reporting of sociohistorical events. Historical events conveniently seen as negative were often reported by respondents as the "best times of life." This is because the sociohistorical event served as the context in which the event happened, for example, marriage or birth of first child during the economic depression. The context changed the details and often the magnitude of the problems and issues that the individual had to cope with but generally not the individual's coping style.

The majority of the women reported family life cycle events and thus the depression and world wars were mentioned primarily if and only if they were the times of courtship, early marriage and/or childrearing. Men also mentioned these times but, in addition to family events, they included the impact of events on their career development.

We often assume that cohort effects should be linear, assuming that each cohort, for example, has more education than the previous. If, however, we instead conceptualize a cohort effect as a specific age by time of measurement effect that has happened in the past, we can see that the particular age or life stage does not suggest linearity at all. Our data suggest that cohorts who are spread out by about a generation may have somewhat similar effects; this appears

Figure B—5. *Ages of cohorts in study and major sociohistorical events.*

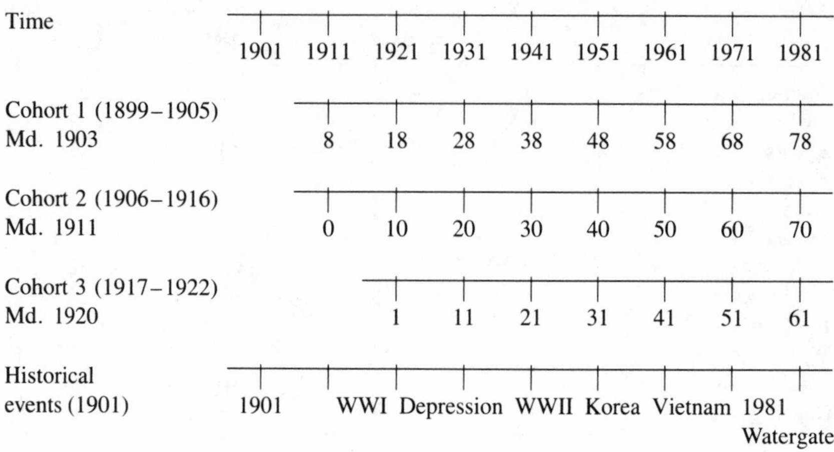

Table B—18. *Mentions of major events by sex and by cohort group.*

	Men					
Event	Cohort A (1917–22)	Cohort B1 (1911–16)	B2 (06–10)	Total B (06–16)	Cohort C (1899–05)	All men
WWI					1 5%	1 2%
WWII	8 57%	4 36%	1 17%	5 29%	4 21%	17 34%
Depression	8 57%	7 64%	3 50%	10 59%	10 53%	28 56%
N	14	(11)	(6)	17	19	50
	Women					
Event	Cohort A (1917–22)	Cohort B1 (1911–16)	B2 (06–10)	Total B (06–16)	Cohort C (1899–05)	All women
WWI					2 18%	2 4%
WWII	5 38%	5 33%		5 19%	3 27%	13 26%
Depression	4 30%	5 33%	3 27%	8 31%	5 45%	17 34%
N	13	(15)	(11)	26	11	50
	Men and Women					
Event	Cohort A (1917–22)	Cohort B1 (1911–16)	B2 (06–10)	Total B (06–16)	Cohort C (1899–05)	All
WWI					3 10%	3 3%
WWII	13 48%	9 35%	1 67%	10 23%	7 23%	39 39%
Depression	12 44%	12 46%	6 35%	18 42%	15 50%	45 45%
N	27	(26)	(17)	43	30	100

to be true for wars where children are affected if parents are in the war, and parents if their children are in the war. Adjacent cohorts may not be similarly affected at all.

Sex Differences in Self-Descriptions and Events

On the set of social-psychological constructs assessed by questionnaire there were some differences between men and women. Men described themselves as more internal in their locus of control and as more active copers. Women described themselves as more nervous, having more psychosomatic symptoms, and having more negative affect during the past week. Men and women did not differ on measures of life satisfaction, self-esteem, trust, affect balance, social desirability, and anomie.

The types of events mentioned by the fifty men were quite different from those mentioned by the fifty women. The men were more likely to report events that were work-related and personal or health-related and personal. Women were more likely to report health interpersonal events (often illness of the husband) and family events. However, family as a context was mentioned by all one hundred subjects. These family issues fell into five major categories: marriage and courtship, establishing a home (at three phases of the life-cycle: first home, dream home, and retirement home), parenting with own kids (including emptying and refilling the nest), relationships with own parents across the life-cycle, and alcoholism in the family. Relatively few events were mentioned by a large enough number of persons for calculations of sex differences.

The interview provided data about both event and coping constructs. Most striking is the difference in the type of event given salience across the life cycle by the men and by the women. For the men, personal events were mentioned significantly more often than interpersonal or community events. On the other hand, women disproportionally filled their stories with content in the domains of interpersonal events and often in the family context. This selection of events may be partially responsible for differences observed in descriptions of coping. When events described are those that happen to others (illness of husband or children and divorce or remarriage in children's lives) the controllability of those events and the active nature of the coping process possible may well have been reduced.

While positive events cause change, they do not generally require the same level of coping. Men and women most often picked marriage and childrearing as the most common positive events; however, they differed in that men were more involved in work-related personal achievements and women were more involved in the lives of their children. Men described themselves as more autonomous and more likely to be internal in their orientations to both causing the event to happen and in managing the event than did women. Women reported experiencing more emotion during the event and in feeling a greater sense of trust. Men and women did not differ in the ways they actually managed the events, active nature of the coping strategies they employed, and their feelings of self-esteem and life satisfaction. The differences appear to be related to the differences in the types of events reported. With the negative events, where much more coping is required, the men were clearly more active in their styles of coping, which also related to the differences in types of events. Men's events were personal and in the domains of work and health. Women's events were interpersonal and involved family and health. Our analyses of the interview material from the coping study suggest that it is because of differential life experiences that such large sex differences are perceived by the individuals themselves as well as by others.

Summary and Conclusions

These data illustrate some important methodological considerations about the study of life events and the study of developmental data. As data on the distribution of life events indicate, when individuals retell their life stories, events are rarely discrete. Psychologically, an event expands to include those predictors that later became apparent and the time taken to put the event into perspective. This calls into question the interpretation given to many life-event questionnaires which seek to consider an event within a narrow time framework. Positive and negative events appear to have differential consequences. Our exploration of coping with positive events was an interesting one. Most of our respondents did not perceive that they had a coping task to accomplish when the event was perceived as a positive one. Many of the events reported by our respondents were events in the lives of others. While this was more often the case for women than for men, interpersonal events and events in which the major impact fell on a family member were quite common in later life.

In attempting to understand the impact of sociohistorical events as a context for development, it has often been assumed that overall negative events such as wars and economic depressions will have predominantly negative impacts. Our data suggest that sociohistorical events form the context for events in the family life cycle that happen pretty much independently of what is happening in the larger society. Events related to family formation happened against different backgrounds of sociohistorical events. These data also suggest that we should look for cohort effects in nonlinear ways that reflect generational communality of an event.

This study also has limits. Our sample was small and, as the respondents had maximal freedom to pick the events to be discussed, we know only that we had a sample of three positive and three negative event contexts. We did not ask individuals how many positive and negative events they had had during their lives and how the events mentioned fit into that ranking. The interviews were rich in the individuals' perceptions of the important aspects of their lives and indicated a realistic group of persons who had managed to cope reasonably well with the events in their lives.

The cohorts in the study are of the age that traditional sex differences are founded on. The content of the issues to be coped with and the requirements of the situation suggest that life experience is what is predictive of coping skills. To the extent that men and women of certain cohorts have tended to have different life experiences, their resulting coping skills will reflect these differences.

References

Chiriboga, D. A., and Cutler, L. Stress and adaptation: Life span perspectives. In L. W. Poon (Ed.), *Aging in the 1980s: Psychological issues*. Washington, D.C.: American Psychological Association, 1980, 347–362.

George, L. K. *Role transitions in later life*. Belmont, Calif.: Brooks/Cole, 1980.

George, L. K., and Siegler, I. C. Stress and coping in later life. *Educational Horizons*, 60:147–154, 1982.

Holmes, T., and Rahe, R. The social readjustment rating scale. *Journal of Psychosomatic Research*, 11:213–218, 1967.

Lowenthal, M. F., et al. *Four stages of life*. San Francisco: Jossey-Bass, 1975.

Palmore, E. B. Design of the adaptation study. In E. B. Palmore (Ed.), *Normal aging II*. Durham, N.C.: Duke University Press, 1974, 291–296.

Schaie, K. W., and Parham, I. A. Stability of adult personality: Fact or fable? *Journal of Personality and Social Psychology*, 34:146–158, 1976.

Siegler, I. C. Psychological aspects of the Duke longitudinal studies. In K. W. Schaie (Ed.), *Longitudinal studies of adult psychological development*. New York: Guilford Press, 1983.

Siegler, I. C. The psychology of adult development and aging. In E. W. Busse and D. G. Blazer (Eds.), *Handbook of geriatric psychiatry*. New York: Van Nostrand Reinhold, 1980, 169–221.

Siegler, I. C., George, L. K., and Okun, M. A. A cross-sequential analysis of adult personality. *Developmental Psychology*, 15:350–351, 1979.

Tyler, F. B. Individual psychosocial competence: A personality configuration. *Educational and Psychological Measurement*, 38:309–323, 1978.

Psychological Distress and Perceived Health

Richard Tessler and David Mechanic

A typical problem in the provision of medical care is the tendency for physicians and patients to view health status in fundamentally different ways. When the patient seeks the doctor's assistance, the physician tries to identify specific problems or diseases underlying the reported symptoms. Frequently, physicians are unable to locate a specific cause of the patient's sense of distress and complaints,

Reprinted by permission from *Journal of Health and Social Behavior*, 19:254–262, 1978. (Editor's Note. Because this article uses data from three other sources in addition to data from the Duke Second Longitudinal Study, it is a good example of how secondary analysis of our data can be compared with analysis of other data to test how representative and generalizable our data are.) We are grateful to the Duke University Center for the Study of Aging and Human Development for allowing us to make use of the North Carolina data.

and they may characterize the problems of such patients as trivial or the patients as neurotic. Physicians have been trained to manage in specific ways and are frustrated by diffuse complaints which cannot be readily classified.

Patients, in contrast, view their health status in a somewhat more global fashion. Not having the physician's more detailed perspective of disease processes, they react more experientially to their overall sense of well-being and to the extent to which the symptoms they experience disrupt their ability to function or interfere in some fashion with their life activities (Mechanic, 1968; Twaddle, 1974). The discordance in perspective between the physician and patient may result in breakdowns in communication, physician frustration, and patient dissatisfaction (Mechanic, 1976; Svarstad, 1976).

Various studies suggest that feeling-states tend to influence people's judgements of their physical health, and vice versa (DiCicco and Apple, 1958; Apple, 1960; Baumann, 1961; Schulman and Smith, 1963; Hennes and Warton, 1970). For instance, when respondents in Baumann's (1961:40) study were asked to indicate what people mean when they say they are in good physical condition, a typical response was that they were always in good spirits, never irritable or cranky, and had a good outlook on life. Similarly, Maddox (1962), in a study of the elderly, found that perceived health was less positive among persons with a history of depression, who felt neglected by others, and whose morale was low. More recently, Palmore and Luikart (1972) have shown that among persons aged forty-five to sixty-four, self-rated health is the strongest correlate of life satisfaction, and Campbell et al. (1976) have shown, using a national probability sample, that people dissatisfied with their health are also less likely to have a strong sense of well-being.

This paper examines the association between social and psychological status and the judgments persons make of their health status, and shows that patients' concepts of their health are more global and experiential than traditional medical conceptions would suggest. In contrast to most prior research in this area, we will make efforts to control for indicators of physical health status in examining the associations between social and psychological factors and health perceptions. The central focus of this analysis is the relationship between psychological distress and perceptions. In a prior prospective study of physician utilization, Tessler et al. (1976) found that psychological distress was an important determinant of the use of medical care services. Here we examine the question of whether distress is also associated with the ways people view their health status.

Methods

Examination of the relationship between psychological distress and perceived health status requires a data set containing an objective measure of physical health status and a sample reasonably heterogeneous with respect to such background characteristics as age and education. A national probability sample containing measures of physical health status, psychological distress, and subjective health status would be ideal for this purpose. Unfortunately, available surveys based on national probability samples do not contain all of these variables in the same data set. The National Health Survey sponsored by the National Center for Health Statistics does not contain a measure of subjective health status, and the surveys conducted by the National Opinion Research Center of the University of Chicago, although they do contain measures of subjective health and psychological well-being, do not include adequate measures of physical health status. It is necessary, therefore, to consider other sources of data, drawing on health surveys of community and institutionalized populations which, although not representative of the general population, do meet other requirements for the necessary analyses.

In this paper we present data from four data sets. Three are based on survey interviews, and a fourth (the student survey) involves a self-administered questionnaire. The characteristics of the four samples contrast sharply among samples. They include a sample of persons participating in alternative health insurance plans in Milwaukee, Wisconsin; a sample of students at a large midwestern university; a sample of men in a state prison; and, finally, a sample of persons aged forty-five to sixty-nine in North Carolina. The particular measures of perceived health status, psychological distress, and physical health status also vary somewhat from survey to survey, and these variations will be presented in detail below. It is enough to note here our general belief that diversity with respect to sample characteristics and measures employed is an advantage in this type of analysis for, if the same result emerges across data sets in spite of their differences, we can have increased confidence in the generality of the basic phenomenon.

The Four Data Sets

Milwaukee Data

This sample was drawn from two large industrial firms in the city of Milwaukee. Sample members were participating in a prepaid group practice and in alternative insurance programs. Household interviews were carried out in the summer of 1973 as part of a family health survey. When possible, women (usually wives of employees) were interviewed. A total of 989 individuals, approximately 91% of eligible respondents, were successfully interviewed. Eighty-five percent were white; 83% were married. Fifty-six percent had completed high school, and another 19% had at least some college education. Approximately 55% of the sample were between the ages of thirty and forty-nine, and another 20% were over fifty years of age.

In order to measure perceived health status, each respondent was asked "How about your personal health . . . would you say that overall it is excellent, good, fair, or poor?" In this survey the measure of physical health status consisted of a list of thirty-four chronic physical conditions drawn from the national health survey. For example, respondents were asked if they had ever had hay fever, stomach ulcer, high blood pressure, arthritis, or diabetes. Affirmative responses were added to create a simple summated scale. It should be clear that this measure is not fully independent of respondents' subjective perceptions, because it is they who provide the information.

The measure of psychological distress drawn from this data set is composed of seven items commonly used in community surveys to measure negative affect.[1] Respondents were asked how often during the past year they had feelings corresponding to "loneliness," "nervousness," "depressed or blue," "didn't have the energy you needed," "so restless that you couldn't sit long in a chair," "you couldn't take care of things because you couldn't get going," or "you were going to have a nervous breakdown." Responses to individual items were scored on four-point scales and added together to create a summary index. Cronbach's alpha (a measure of internal consistency) for this index is .78.

Student Data

These data come from a random sample of the student population of the University of Wisconsin in Madison. A self-administered questionnaire was mailed to a random sample of this university's students (excluding foreign students) during the academic year 1972–73; with repeated follow-ups an 82% response rate was attained. Data on 1391 respondents, for whom complete information on all relevant variables was available, are used in the present analysis. Over 62% of the respondents were men. Approximately 26% were under twenty years of age; about 34% were between twenty and twenty-one, and the remainder (approximately 40%) were over twenty-one years of age. Twenty percent were married, and the vast majority were white (over 98%). Most of the students came from well-educated families. Fewer than 18% reported that their fathers had not graduated from high school; approximately 59% reported that their fathers had at least some college education.

The measure of perceived health status was similar to the measure used in the Milwaukee survey except that it explicitly included the word "physical." Respondents were asked, "Would you say your physical health this past year was excellent, good, fair, poor, or very poor?" Fewer than 1% of the respondents (six persons) checked "very poor," and, in order to make this question comparable to measures of perceived health status employed in the other data sets, the last two categories ("poor" and "very poor") were combined into a single category.

Two single-item measures of psychological distress from the student ques-

1. This item was adapted from an item on the Langner scale (Langner, 1962). Though available in full form in two of the data sets at issue here, and despite the fact that in each it was strongly associated with perceived health status, the entire Langner scale was intentionally not used as an indicator of psychological distress in any of the analyses because it contains many psychophysiological items, and thus may confound physical health status with psychological distress.

tionnaire are used in the present analysis. These are a measure of personal happiness ("Would you describe yourself as a very happy person, a happy person, a somewhat unhappy person, or a very unhappy person?") and a measure of nervousness ("Have you been bothered by nervousness, i.e., by being irritable, fidgety, and tense?"). The response alternatives offered for the nervousness item were "never," "sometimes," and "often."

To measure physical health status, respondents were simply asked if and to what extent they had been physically sick during the past three months, regardless of whether or not a physician had been consulted. A score of 0 was assigned if no sickness was reported, 1 if sickness occurred but it was not at all serious, 2 if it was not very serious, 3 if it was somewhat serious, and 4 if it was very serious. Although such reports of sickness may also be influenced by subjective psychological factors and thus may not be adequate measures of physical illness, the specific time reference makes it more likely that this question taps objective illness than would a more ambiguous item. In any case, to the extent that subjective factors are involved, the inclusion of this measure should weaken the influence of distress on the subjective evaluation of health.

Prison Data

These data are drawn from personal interviews with a random sample of men at Wisconsin State Prison in Waupun. The interviews were conducted in the spring of 1976. Interviews completed numbered 339, which represented a response rate of 77% of those men who were to be included in the sample. The analysis reported here is based on 301 men for whom data on all relevant variables are available. Fifty percent were nonwhite. Twenty-six percent were married. The mean age for these men was thirty-one years. Relative to other samples considered in this paper, this group had much less formal education; the mean number of years of school completed was 9.8.

To measure perceived health status, each man was asked, "At this time, how would you rate your physical health . . . Would you rate your physical health as excellent, good, fair, or poor?" Note that, like the measure of perceived health used in the student survey, this question explicitly includes the word "physical." The measure of psychological distress used in this survey is also very similar to one of the items used in the student survey. Each man was asked if in the last seven days he felt nervous (irritable, fidgety, or tense), and his response was coded as yes or no; 58% responded in the affirmative.

The measure of physical health status in the prison sample, in contrast to other samples described above, comes not from respondent self-reports but from a physician's judgment about the man's physical health at the admission physical.[2] The examining physician either judged the person to be in "normal and

2. Since the physicians' judgments concerning the men's health problems were made at varying points in time, some of the ratings are fairly old in relation to the occurrence of the survey interviews,

good" health or he indicated that the person had one or more health problems; 24% were found to have some health problem. These judgments, however, were unstandardized and unsystematic, and we have limited faith in them.

Duke Data

These data come from a large-scale longitudinal research project, designed and conducted by the Duke University Center for the Study of Aging and Human Development. The sample consisted of noninstitutionalized, ambulatory, white, middle-class and upper-class residents of Durham, North Carolina, between the ages of forty-five and sixty-nine. The data to be reported are based on the first wave of a sample of 379 persons who had participated in three waves of testing at approximately two-year intervals, beginning in 1968. The mean age for this group was fifty-eight years. Approximately 48% were women. Over 85% were married. On the average, participants in this study had completed twelve years of formal education.

The measure of perceived health status was similar to measures used in the other data sets. The specific question, which was asked as part of a medical history interview, reads as follows: "In general how is your health right now—poor, fair, good, or excellent?" The measure of psychological distress was based upon Bradburn's (1969) index of negative affect. This index includes the following five items: "very lonely or remote from other people," "depressed or very unhappy," "bored," "so restless you couldn't sit long in a chair," and "vaguely uneasy about something without knowing why." Respondents were asked whether they had had each of these feelings in the past week. Scores on the index could range from 0 (no negative feelings) to 5 (each negative feeling experienced). The alpha coefficient for this scale was .68. Four of the items included in this scale are very similar to items used in the Milwaukee survey to measure psychological distress.

The measure of physical health status consisted of three objective ratings by a physician, covering two major body systems (Nowlin, 1970) plus a rating of overall functional status (Karnofsky et al., 1948). The objective rating scales for the body systems require the examining physician to evaluate a combination of historical and physical findings in formulating his/her rating. These ratings are based almost entirely on evidence of disease or impairment rather than on the respondent's symptom reports. The Karnofsky scale calls for an overall objective assessment of health with emphasis on functional capacity. Scores on the composite index based on the three ratings could range from 1–7, with higher scores indicating the presence of more disease and/or functional impairment.

In summary, this paper draws on data from four different health surveys. The four surveys contrast sharply with one another in respect to the characteris-

while others are more recent. Approximately 85% of the admission physicals were conducted within the past three years.

tics of the populations studied. All four studies, however, include items tapping perceived health status, physical health status, and psychological distress. The adequacy of any one of these data sets to provide a definitive examination of the manner in which persons view their physical health can be questioned. Taken together, however, the four data sets provide a fuller and more adequate basis upon which to examine this issue.

Results

The distribution of perceived health status in the four samples is presented in columns 1–4 of table B—19. For purposes of comparison, we also present, in column 5, results derived from a recent national survey which included a comparable question on perceived health status (National Opinion Research Center, 1973). Examination of the percentage distributions reveals that, with the exception of the prison survey, the vast majority of respondents assess their health status as excellent or good.

Zero-order correlates. The guiding hypothesis in this paper is that perceived health status is associated with psychological distress, even after controlling for variation in physical health status. To examine this hypothesis, we turn first to zero-order correlations between psychological distress, physical health status, and subjective health status. Throughout, correlations are reported as significant when $p \leq .05$.

In the Milwaukee data, subjective health was significantly associated with the index of negative affect ($r = .24$) and with chronicity ($r = .40$). In the student data, subjective health status was significantly associated with each measure of psychological distress we considered (with being a happy person, $r = .21$ and with being nervous, $r = .23$), as well as with the measure of sickness within the past three months ($r = .44$). In the prison data, nervousness was also significantly correlated with perceived physical health ($r = .16$), but the association between being judged as having a health problem and subjective health status, although in the anticipated direction, did not attain the .05 level of probability ($r = .11$). Finally, with respect to the Duke data, perceptions of health were sig-

Table B—19. *Perceived health status in five samples (percentages).*

Perceived health status	Milwaukee sample ($N = 989$)		Student sample ($N = 1391$)		Prison sample ($N = 301$)		Duke sample ($N = 379$)		National sample (NORC) ($N = 1500$)	
Excellent	44	87	39	87	15	51	17	73	32	72
Good	43		48		36		56		40	
Fair	11		11		32		24		21	
Poor	1		3		17		3		7	

Note: Percentages may not add to 100 because of rounding.

nificantly correlated with the negative affect scale (r = .27) as well as the physician's rating (r = .35), as anticipated.

In two of the data sets, measures of psychological distress were also significantly associated in the expected direction with measures of physical health status. In the Milwaukee data, negative affect and chronicity were significantly correlated (r = .21). In the student data, each of the distress measures are significantly correlated with reports of sickness in the past three months (r = .13 for the happiness item and reported sickness, and r = .25 for the nervousness item and reported sickness). However, with respect to the prison and Duke data sets, neither of the measures of psychological distress was significantly associated with the measures of physical health status based on physician judgments. These findings support the more general assumption underlying this study, i.e., that respondents' reports of illness are influenced by their psychological state.

Multivariate analyses. A variety of sociodemographic factors have been associated with health status in different studies. In general, these studies indicate that morbidity is higher in older age groups, among those more poorly educated, among nonwhites, and among those who are not married. In addition, various studies indicate that women report more illness than men and use more medical services, although it is not clear whether these differences are primarily differences in reporting and behavior or actual differences in physical health status. In any case, we shall use all of the above variables in the analysis when they are included in the data set. Two of the surveys (the Milwaukee and student surveys) include all of these variables. In the student survey, however, father's education is used. The prison survey includes only men; the Duke survey includes only whites.

For each data set, the regression analysis had two stages. First, we regressed perceived health status simultaneously against physical health status, psychological distress, and various sociodemographic variables. Next, we recomputed the regression equations so as to include only the significant predictors. The results of these regressions are shown in tables B—20–B—23. Although the regression coefficients are presented in both standardized (B) and unstandardized (b) form, the unstandardized coefficients are not comparable across data sets, because the scales used to measure the independent variables differ from one survey to another.

Inspection of the data from the Milwaukee study (table B—20) indicates that poorer perceived health status is significantly affected by negative affect (B = .16), more chronic problems (B = .34), nonwhite status (B = .23), lower education (B = −.12), and older age (B = .11). These variables accounted for 28% of the variance in perceived health status.

Table B—21 indicates that self-rated health among college students is significantly affected by reported happiness, marital status, and physical health status. Health is rated more poorly by those who are relatively unhappy (B = .15), unmarried (B = −.08), and those who have experienced physical illness in their recent past (B = .42). Similar results are obtained when nervousness is sub-

Table B—20. *Multiple regression coefficients for perceived health status: Milwaukee data* (N = *989).*

Variable	b	B
Negative affect	.03	.16*
Chronicity	.13	.34*
Nonwhite status	.44	.23*
Education	−.09	−.12*
Age	.01	.11*
R^2 = .28		

*$p < .05$.

Coding: Perceived health status: 1 = excellent, 2 = good, 3 = fair, 4 = poor; Negative affect: higher scores = more negative affect; Chronicity: higher scores = more chronic problems; Race: 2 = nonwhite, 1 = white; Education: higher scores = more education; Age: in years (e.g., 18 = 18, 19 = 19, etc.).

Table B—21. *Multiple regression coefficients for perceived health status: student data* (N = *1391).*

Variable	b	B
	"Happiness" included	
Happiness	.18	.15*
Married	−.15	−.08*
Physical sickness	.36	.42*
R^2 = .22		
	"Nervousness" included	
Nervousness	.14	.13*
Married	−.16	−.09*
Physical sickness	.35	.41*
R^2 = .22		

*$p < .05$.

Coding: Perceived health status: 1 = excellent, 2 = good, 3 = fair, 4 = poor or very poor; Happiness: 1 = very happy, 2 = happy, 3 = somewhat unhappy, 4 = very unhappy; Nervousness: 1 = never, 2 = sometimes, 3 = often; Married: 1 = married, 0 = unmarried; Physical sickness: scores range from 1 to 5, higher scores = more serious illness in past three months.

stituted for happiness in the regression equation. In this equation the *Beta* for nervousness is equal to .13. Each of the regression equations shown in table B—21 accounts for approximately 22% of the variance in perceived health status.

The results of the regression analysis for the prison data appear in table B—22. Examination of this table shows that here, too, nervousness is predictive of perceived health status (B = .18), even when controlling for other variables. In this equation, perceived health status was also significantly affected by physical

Table B—22. *Multiple regression coefficients for perceived health status: prison data (*N = *301).*

Variable	*b*	*B*
Nervousness	.36	.18*
Physician's rating	.28	.12*
Race	−.23	−.11*
R^2 = .05		

*$p < .05$.

Coding: Perceived health status: 1 = excellent, 2 = good, 3 = fair, 4 = poor; Nervousness: 0 = not nervous in past 7 days, 1 = nervous in past 7 days; Physician's rating: 0 = no health problem, 1 = health problem; Race: 0 = nonwhite, 1 = white.

Table B—23. *Multiple regression coefficients for perceived health status: Duke data (*N = *379).*

Variable	*b*	*B*
Negative affect	.14	.24*
Physician's rating	.15	.30*
Education	.05	.29*
R^2 = .27		

*$p < .05$.

Coding: Perceived health status: 1 = excellent, 2 = good, 3 = fair, 4 = poor; Negative affect: higher scores = more negative affect; Physician's rating: higher scores = poorer health; Education: years of schooling completed.

health status and race; self-ratings of health tended to be poorer for those prisoners judged by a physician to have health problems of note (B = .12), and among blacks as compared with whites (B = −.11). The full model, however, accounted only for 5% of the variance in perceptions of health.

The final data set to be considered is the Duke study; results of the relevant multiple regression appear in table B—23. These results also show a significant effect for the measure of psychological distress (B = .24). In addition to the effect of the index of negative affect on perceptions of health, perceived health status was significantly affected by the physician's rating of the person's health (B = .30) and also by the person's educational attainment (B = .29). Consistent with the education effect observed in the Milwaukee data, we find that the more education a person has had, the more favorably the person tends to rate his or her health, even controlling for measured differences in objective health status and psychological distress. The full model accounted for 27% of the variance in perceived health among these North Carolina respondents.

Discussion

In this analysis we examined the relationship between various measures of psychological distress and perceived health status in four diverse samples involving different age groups, socioeconomic status levels, and regional and institutional settings. In these analyses we have controlled, as best we can with the data available, physical health status as well as various sociodemographic factors. In two cases, the measures of physical health status are suspect because they depend on the reports of respondents. In the other two cases, however, and particularly in the Duke data set, the measure of physical health status represents an independent, objective evaluation made by physicians.

The only "variable" that retains a statistically significant standardized *beta* coefficient in all four data sets, other than the measure of physical health status, is psychological distress. In every case, the measure used to capture this concept is associated with the ways people report their health status. Although obtaining this result with different measures of psychological distress in varying data sets might be viewed as a strength in this study, it also presents problems. To the extent that we use different measures of concepts from one data set to another, the analyses are not truly replications and, although the collection of measures has a certain face validity as indicators of distress, one can reasonably argue that they do not really tap the same conceptual dimension. The value of repeating the analysis in these diverse data sets depends in part on the reader's agreement that the measures of lack of happiness, nervousness, and negative affect all share a common domain, one that for convenience we have called psychological distress. The fact is that when these measures appear in the same data set they are significantly associated with one another, and this adds a certain rationale to the claim that they share some common features.

As we anticipated, physical health status has a larger influence on perceived health status than psychological distress, although this was not true in the case of the prison data, and the standardized *betas* were fairly close in the Duke data (.30 and .24). It is worthy of note that the physical health measures were less powerful in those two cases in which they were less contaminated by respondents' subjective perceptions and reports. This seems to support our basic contention that subjective reports of symptoms already reflect in some fashion the psychological state of the person providing the data.

Although the association between psychological distress and perceived health is consistent across data sets, the amount of variance explained in perceived health is small, as it is when all of the predictors are used as well. This is not particularly surprising, since both the distress measures and the physical health status measures are extremely crude and involve a good deal of measurement error. These data suggest, however, that the issue is an important one, and that it requires further careful exploration and specification. It also suggests that researchers who use perceived health status as a dependent variable in their analyses should be alert to the implications of its use and skeptical of the contention that it is an adequate proxy for a more objectively defined concept of health status.

Finally, it is important to emphasize that the association between psychological distress and perceived health status is, in all likelihood, reciprocal in character. It would probably be a mistake to assume that causality runs only from distress to perceived health. It seems very likely that lower perceived health status also causes psychological distress. Regardless of the reciprocal character of the relationship, however, the demonstration of a consistent association between distress and health perceptions in four different data sets provides further indication that patients experience physical symptoms and dysfunctions in a more global manner than traditional medical conceptions would suggest. Patients respond to their total sense of well-being, and their notions of physical health both affect and are affected by their sense of psychological vitality. If practitioners are to be responsive to patients' definitions and perceptions of their needs, they must give attention not only to tangible evidence of illness but also to patients' total life circumstances.

References

Apple, D. How laymen define illness. *Journal of Health and Human Behavior*, 1:219–22, 1960.

Baumann, B. Diversity in conceptions of health and physical fitness. *Journal of Health and Human Behavior*, 2:39–46, 1961.

Bradburn, N. M. *The structure of psychological well-being*. Chicago: Aldine, 1969.

Campbell, A., Converse, P. E., and Rodgers, W. L. *The quality of American life: Perceptions, evaluations, and satisfactions*. New York: Russell Sage Foundation, 1976.

DiCicco, L., and Apple, D. Health needs and opinions of older adults. *Public Health Reports*, 73:479–87, 1958.

Hennes, J. D., and Wharton, T. M. Criteria for measures of health. (Report No. 8). Columbia: University of Missouri School of Medicine, Section of Health Care Studies, 1970.

Karnofsky, D. A., et al. The use of nitrogen mustard in the palliative treatment of carcinoma. *Cancer*, 1:634–56, 1948.

Langner, T. S. A 22-item screening score of psychiatric symptoms indicating impairment. *Journal of Health and Human Behavior*, 3:269–76, 1962.

Maddox, G. L. Some correlates of differences in self-assessment of health status among the elderly. *Journal of Gerontology*, 17:180–5, 1962.

Mechanic, D. *Medical sociology*. New York: Free Press, 1968.

Mechanic, D. The design of medical care organization and responsiveness to patients. In D. Mechanic (Ed.), *The growth of bureaucratic medicine*. New York: Wiley, 1976, 99–118.

National Data Program for the Social Sciences. *Codebook for the spring 1973 general social survey*. Chicago: National Opinion Research Center, 1973.

Nowlin, J. B. Health rating forms, Longitudinal II. Mimeograph. Durham, N.C.: Duke University Center for the Study of Aging and Human Development, 1970.

Palmore, E. B., and Luikart, C. Health and social factors related to life satisfaction. *Journal of Health and Social Behavior*, 13:68–80, 1972.

Schulman, S., and Smith, A. M. The concept of "health" among Spanish-speaking villagers of New Mexico and Colorado. *Journal of Health and Human Behavior*, 4:226–34, 1963.

Svarstad, B. L. Physician-patient communication and patient conformity with medical advice. In D. Mechanic (Ed.), *The Growth of bureaucratic medicine*. New York: Wiley, 1976, 220–38.

Tessler, R., Mechanic, D., and Dimond, M. The effect of psychological distress on physician utilization: A prospective study. *Journal of Health and Social Behavior*, 17:353–64, 1976.
Twaddle, A. C. The concept of health status. *Social Science and Medicine*, 8:29–38, 1974.

Drowsiness and Driving

Daniel Gianturco, Dietolf Ramm, and Charles W. Erwin

Our main purpose in this study was to screen a population of middle aged and older drivers for physical problems or psychological traits which might predispose the individuals to alertness difficulties. Identification of such problems or traits would be an important step in future preventive efforts. Second, the driving questionnaire used in this study served an an important testing ground for the more extensive questionnaire used in the large population survey of drowsiness and driving as reported by Tilley (1973). As will be reported, many of the results of the population survey are similar to the results in this smaller study.

Method

A panel of volunteer subjects participating in the Duke Second Longitudinal Study were asked to complete a short questionnaire about their driving habits and propensity toward drowsiness while driving. The subjects were white, aged forty-five to seventy, and a slight majority of them were male. All subjects received a careful physical examination and extensive laboratory tests, including EEG, EKG blood chemistries, chest x ray, and urinalysis. The Cattell 16 PF was administered to all subjects to measure personality traits. This test was selected for its comprehensiveness and because it is grounded on an organized and integrated body of knowledge in clinical, industrial, and educational areas. Completion of the driving questionnaire took only several minutes and cooperation was excellent.

Results

A total of 347 subjects completed the questionnaire. Ninety-seven percent of the males and 82 percent of the females were current drivers. Drivers were asked, "Do you become drowsy when driving?" The possible responses were "yes,"

Reprinted by permission from paper 730123, presented at the Society of Automotive Engineers International Engineering Congress, New York, 1973.

"no," and "occasionally." Fifty-seven percent of the males and 30 percent of the females responded "yes." These percentages do not include the response "occasionally," so that those who answered "yes" did not themselves consider it a rare occurrence.

The subjects who admitted to drowsiness while driving were then asked, "Have you ever fallen asleep briefly while driving without being aware of it until later?" In this case, 11 percent of the males and 2 percent of the females admitted to such an episode.

The subjects were then asked, "Have you ever had an accident because of becoming drowsy or falling asleep?" Three percent of the males and 1 percent of the females said "yes." The proportion was markedly higher for "near accidents." The subjects were asked, "Have you ever had a near accident because of drowsiness?" Twenty percent of the males and 2 percent of the females said "yes" to this question. A substantial portion (15 percent of the males and 2 percent of the females) noted that when they become drowsy while driving, only sleeping for a period enables them to return to a fully alert state.

We suspected that at least part of the difference observed thus far between men and women can be accounted for by driving habits. We asked all subjects to estimate their yearly driving mileage on a five-point scale. The men averaged 12,000 miles yearly and the women averaged 7,000 miles. None of the male drivers said they drove less than 1,000 miles yearly, while 16 percent of the women said that was their limit. Only 7 percent of the males drove from 1,000–6,000 miles, whereas 54 percent of the females drove that distance. This distance (1,000–6,000 miles) was, by far, the most frequent distance estimate given by our female sample. Those who drove more than 15,000 miles include 30 percent of the men and only 3 percent of the women. Figure B—6 plots the percentage of drivers admitting drowsiness as a function of their estimated driving mileage.

Since we also suspected that long-trip driving was particularly fatiguing and conducive to drowsiness, we asked each subject in which of the following categories he belongs regarding long trips:

1. You do all the driving.
2. Someone occasionally helps you do the driving.
3. You share the driving equally with someone else.
4. You occasionally help someone else do the driving.
5. You never drive on long trips.

Figure B—7 plots the results. Seventy-eight percent of the men are in the category of doing all or almost all the long-trip driving; only 18 percent stated that they shared the driving equally with someone else. Only 14 percent of the females said that they did all the driving on long trips and almost 30 percent said that they rarely or never drive on long trips. This is, as suspected, almost an inverse ratio to the men. Figure B—8 plots the percentage admitting drowsiness while driving within the categories for long-trip driving. The figure demonstrates a significant drop for those who share the driving equally.

Figure B—9 plots the proportion admitting near accidents due to drow-

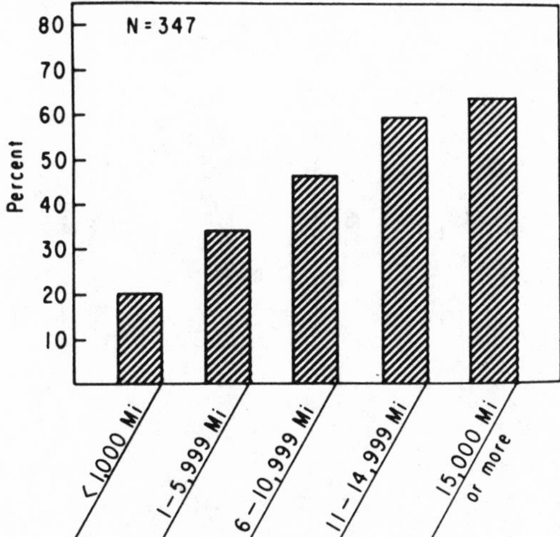

Figure B—6. *Percentage of drowsy drivers as function of mileage per year.*

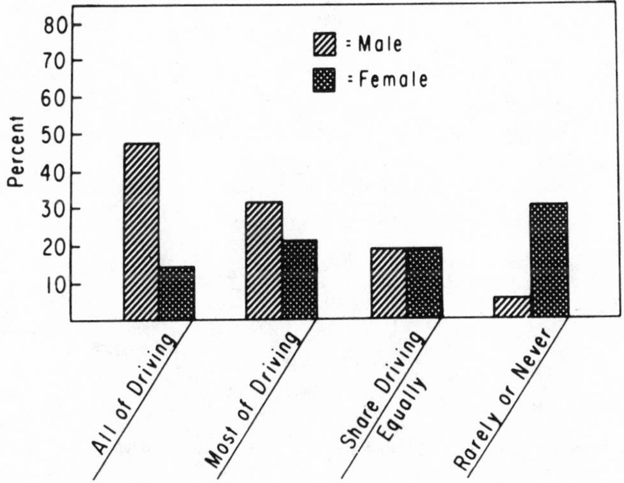

Figure B—7. *Long-trip driving.*

siness within the categories for long trip driving. Of the men and women who did all the driving on long trips or who received only occasional help, 28 percent admitted to near accidents due to drowsiness while, of the group who shared the driving equally, only 13 percent admitted to such near accidents.

All subjects took the Cattell 16 PF test of personality. We made an extensive series of profile comparisons of drivers who admitted drowsiness versus those who did not. Preliminary analysis indicated that it was safe to group our age range (forty-five to seventy) together. However, using general population stens it

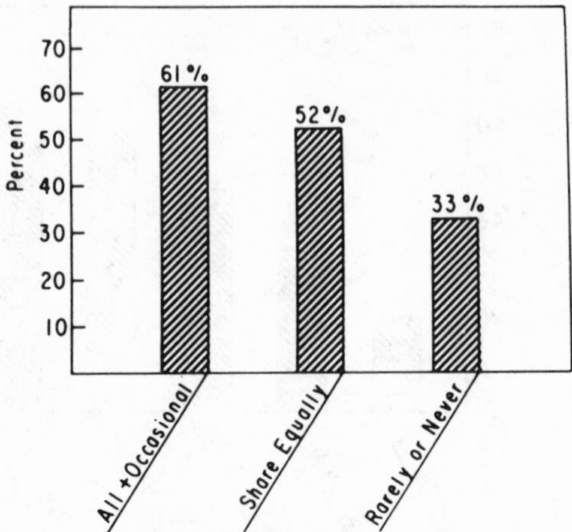

Figure B—8. *Percent of total who get drowsy while driving within long-trip categories.*

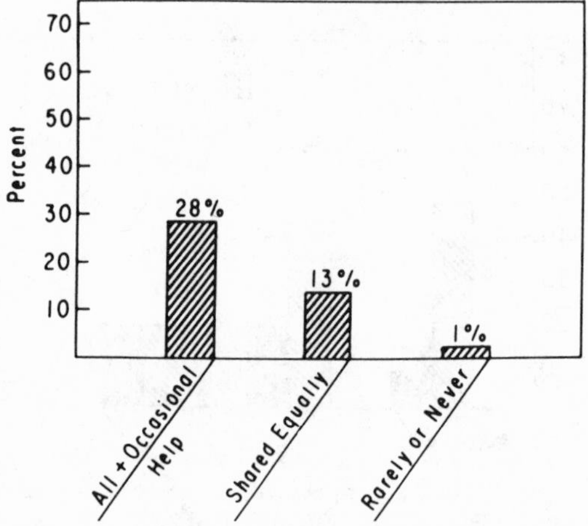

Figure B—9. *Percent of total who had near-accidents within trip-driving categories.*

was necessary to analyze men and women separately. Simple profile comparisons of drowsy and nondrowsy drivers showed no consistent distinguishing trait or pattern of traits that delineated the groups. This suggests that drowsiness while driving is more likely related to environmental factors than to peculiarities of individual personality. However, those individuals who seemed to have a more severe drowsiness problem, who by answering "yes" to such questions as "having near accidents because of drowsiness," "falling asleep behind the wheel," "driving many miles asleep," or "having difficulty making themselves alert again," manifested a small but consistent personality difference. This group that handled drowsiness poorly had a low score on factor C. Low C people are easily annoyed by things and people and tend to worry, give up, and evade responsibilities. They also tend to show a fatigue-worry response under situational stress. This factor has been implicated previously in accident research and, as indicated by Suhr, low C people have been regarded usually as accident prone.

We suspected eye strain or fatigue to be a factor, so visual acuity, both uncorrected and corrected, was carefully compared in both groups. Uncorrected visual acuity was only slightly worse in the drowsy group (between 20/30 to 20/40) as compared to the nondrowsy group (less than 20/30). However, both groups corrected to approximately 20/25 or better. Another important source of eye strain separate from visual activity is lenticular opacities (cataracts). These can produce glare problems particularly with oncoming headlights and are an important reason why older people often avoid driving at night. There were 11 percent (18 of 151) in the drowsy group with mild to moderate opacities and 12 percent of the nondrowsy group (22 to 190) with similar opacities.

A variety of blood determinations, including hemoglobin, calcium, phosphorous, fasting blood sugar, blood urea nitrogen, uric acid, cholesterol, total protein, and triglycerides gave us an assessment of many metabolic functions. All were similar in both groups. Twenty-seven percent of the drowsy group and 26 percent of the nondrowsy group had abnormal EKGs. Weight and blood pressure findings failed to discriminate the groups.

We also suspected chronic tiredness or fatigue to be a problem but, when the data were examined, 15 percent (26 of 173) of the drowsy group and 16 percent (31 of 192) of the nondrowsy group complained of tiredness or lack of pep. We also asked each subject to make a global assessment of his health. Again, 83 percent of the drowsy group and 81 percent of the nondrowsy group felt their health to be excellent or good.

Forty-six percent of the drowsy group and 39 percent of the nondrowsy group were smokers. Fifty-five percent of the drowsy group and 52 percent of the nondrowsy group admitted to taking alcohol. Thirteen percent of all subjects were taking tranquilizers, including 10 percent of the drowsy group and 16 percent of the nondrowsy group. Six percent of the subjects were taking sleeping pills including 8 percent of the drowsy group and 5 percent of the nondrowsy group. Among the women, 25 percent were taking female hormone pills. Fifteen percent were in the drowsy group, and 24 percent were in the nondrowsy group.

Discussion

Our data are by no means conclusive, but they are useful in this neglected area of driving safety research. Much more needs to be known about the relationship between driver alertness and an array of other factors in the driving environment. Thus far, the failure to identify a host factor in drowsiness (i.e., vision, metabolism, cardiac function, drugs, smoking, alcohol, psychological traits, and self-health assessment) leads one to pay increasing attention to this driving environment.

There is a malady called narcolepsy in which drowsiness and even deep sleep can occur suddenly at any time under almost any circumstance, including driving. Yoss (1969) of the Mayo Clinic has made a study of this fortunately small group. He has also reported objective tests utilizing the size of the pupils to identify such people. Stimulant drugs can help those who suffer this malady to lead more normal lives. However, the problem of the sleepy driver goes far beyond this small group, as indicated by our study results, with half the driving population affected.

There is no evidence in our study to support such speculation, but it is tempting to speculate that technologic advances, in the form of expertly built, straight, and smooth highways, with their sameness and monotony, the rhythmic hum of a powerful modern engine, and the luxurious interiors of automobiles today, with their comfortable seats, carpeting, and soundproofing, act to lull the driver into excessive relaxation, drowsiness, and even sleep.

It is common knowledge that tranquilizers, sedatives, and alcohol (alcohol is really not an eye opener) can act to promote drowsiness. We find it hard to explain the study findings of no difference in usage rates of these substances in drivers who report drowsiness and those who do not. The critical factor with these substances may not be usage but dose or quantity consumed over a short time period. It is well known that alcohol, in combination with tranquilizers, sedatives, or hypnotic drugs, acts synergistically; that is, the drowsiness induced is greater than the additive total drowsiness produced by each.

The findings that near misses happen to only 13 percent of our subject population who share long-trip driving equally and that the figure is more than twice that percentage in the subject population who do all or most of the long-trip driving have definite implications. Usually it is the husbands who take the wheel when the family goes on trips, while the wife tends to the children. Driving is frequently portrayed in our culture as a way for men to express their masculinity. The very names of many cars evoke images of rugged masculinity: Barracuda, Challenger, Charger, Cougar, Cutlass, Falcon, Fury, and Mustang are examples. This cultural connotation makes it hard for men to give up the wheel.

In this study dealing with people forty-five to seventy years of age, we are studying the survivors of twenty or more years of driving. They have coped. Those who had fatal accidents are no longer here to study. We do not know how many actual fatalities are caused by this problem. Of course this older population has a much lower incidence of drowsiness than the younger people reported in Tilley's paper. How does one explain their higher accident rate?

Older drivers have a number of accidents disproportionate to their yearly mileage totals. Since older people are less hardy, their accidents may have more serious consequences. Usually their driving accidents are caused by errors of omission rather than commission: incorrect turning or failing to keep a proper lookout rather than speeding or tailgating, for example. Vision deteriorates, particularly night vision and the ability to see while exposed to the glare of oncoming headlights. Older drivers often have difficulty in assessing a complex traffic situation and are inclined to concentrate on certain aspects only. Forgetting the traffic situation can be a fatal error. These difficulties make older people much more cautious in their approach to the driving task.

Unfortunately, we live in an age in which the style of living is largely shaped by the motor vehicle. Shopping facilities, friends, and even doctors have moved away from where old people live, making transportation essential to obtain the goods and services conducive to a happy life.

The loss of mobility, status, and power and the increasing dependence on others makes it particularly difficult for elderly males to give up driving or their cars. For example: "A 74-year-old man had several minor accidents. He was no longer a safe driver. He reluctantly agreed to stop road driving but absolutely refused to sell his car. For the next several years until his death he kept it in his garage. Every Saturday he would pull it out, run the engine for a while and then give the car a thorough cleaning inside and out." In this example, the symbolic equation of car and manhood was not hard to find.

Summary and Conclusion

The incidence of middle-aged and elderly drivers admitting drowsiness while driving is high. This appears related to maleness, yearly mileage logged, and long-trip driving. Cattell personality testing revealed no consistent group of personality traits which correlates with getting drowsy. Subjects who handled drowsiness especially poorly (that is, those who fell asleep) did show a low factor C which measures emotionality, tendency to worry, give up, and evade responsibilities. Many physical factors were examined, but all failed to reveal a consistent pattern of physical defect in the drowsiness group.

References

Suhr, V. W. The Cattell 16PF as a prognosticator of accident susceptibility. *Proceedings of the Iowa Academy of Science*, 60:558–561, 1953.

Tilley, D. H., Erwin, C. W., and Gianturco, D. T. Drowsiness and driving: Preliminary report of a population survey. Paper 730121, presented at the Society of Automotive Engineers Automotive Engineering Congress, Detroit, January 1973.

Yoss, R. E. The sleepy driver: A test to measure ability to maintain alertness. *Mayo Clinic Proceedings*, 44:769–783, 1969.

Section C: Psychological Aging

Introduction

Ilene C. Siegler

The papers in this section have been written over the past ten years (1973–83). They illustrate the extraordinary vitality of the data included in the psychological and social psychological sections of the longitudinal studies. This section of papers has been divided into those from the Duke First Longitudinal Study and those from the second study because the psychological variables were rather different between the first and the second studies. As I have discussed elsewhere (Siegler, 1983) it is important to consider each study from the historical perspective that shaped it. Main psychological findings from the first longitudinal study have been reported in *Normal Aging* (1971) and those from the second longitudinal study in *Normal Aging II* (1974).

The descriptions of all of the measures used in the psychological parts of both studies, as well as a review of published and unpublished papers pertaining primarily to psychological content, can be found in Siegler (1983). In that chapter, my purpose was to show how the longitudinal studies have made contributions to psychology using the psychological measures singly and in combination with measures from other disciplines.

In order to understand the differences between the first and second studies, it is useful to consider the time that the studies were designed. The first study started data collection in March 1955. Individuals were tested at Duke Hospital, and two days of testing were required to complete the full set of measurements taken. The psychological laboratory was under the direction of Carl Eisdorfer. Each subject was tested with the Wechsler Adult Intelligence Scale (Weschler, 1955), then a new measure of intelligence; the Rorschach test as an index of the organization of personality; and an audiogram for pure tones and a measure of speech perception. At the second time of measurement in 1960, the Weschler Memory Scale and a reaction time task were added to the measures. The Rorschach test was dropped after the fourth examination: otherwise the variables remained constant for the next ten examinations. Other areas assessed were psychiatric functioning (EEG and mental status measures); physical health (including medical history, physical examination, and blood and urine tests); ophthalmology; dermatology; and social functioning, including measures of morale, life satisfaction, activity and attitudes, and a complete social history.

The second longitudinal study was developed from the first study in 1966–67 and its first subject was tested in 1968. The two studies were run in sequence, as the same laboratory space and data technicians tested all the subjects in both studies. The decision was made to double the number of subjects in order to take advantage of the methodological revolution (Harris, 1963; Schaie, 1965) which encouraged the use of developmental designs. This decision was also related to cutting the time per subject in half and it resulted in short forms of many of the instruments. A major emphasis was placed on looking at stress from a variety of viewpoints. The major psychological measures were a continuous performance task, which assessed cognitive performance under timed (and somewhat stressful) conditions and had concomitant physiological monitoring; the Cattell 16 Personality Factors Questionnaire, four subtests to estimate WAIS performance, and a series of social psychological constructs measured in the social history.

The papers assigned to the Psychological Aging Section in this volume are those that in the First Longitudinal Study deal primarily with intellectual development, memory performance, and reaction time performance. Data from these tests appear in many papers in the two preceeding sections on Physical Aging and on Mental Health and Mental Illness; in this section, however, we are concerned with the variables themselves and how they look when assessed cross-sectionally (at a particular time of measurement) and longitudinally. This set of papers also raises methodological issues: the role of selective attrition in a long-term longitudinal study and the degree to which the number of years included in a cohort group and the intervals between measurements approach equality. Additional concerns are two theoretical questions: the relative competence of the "young-old" versus the "old-old" and the evaluation of distance from death as a variable in aging research. A final paper in this section considers whether these issues are reflected in structural changes in intellectual functioning when measured by factor analytic studies. The role of health, age, and intellectual performance and distance from death in aging research, as well as the implications of the terminal drop hypothesis, could be further enlightened with more work on these data. Work on new methods (Clive, Woodbury, and Siegler, 1983; Woodbury, Manton, and Siegler, 1982; Woodbury and Manton, 1983; Manton and Woodbury, 1983) and new ways of looking at distance from death (Hook and Siegler, 1983a; 1983b) hold out promise that the First Longitudinal Study has not yet yielded its final secrets.

The Second Longitudinal Study was a very different study. The focus was on stress and adaptation to life events. The psychological laboratory participated in the development of an experimental measure of stress, the vigilance or CPT (continuous performance task), (Harkins et al., 1974). In this section we have a fascinating set of papers that are concerned with (1) normative changes in personality functioning, (2) the role that personality plays as a predictor of dropout, and (3) the relative influence of personality and social status on the major indices of disengagement. These papers move from the realm of psychology to social psychological concerns, and thus deal with constructs that put individuals in the social context.

Two important indices here are self-concept and locus of control. Both constructs are attractive, intuitively meaningful, and the objects of large and often contradictory literatures. Problems inherent in these constructs grow even worse when questions of development and aging are added. The operationalization of these constructs are difficult and the Second Longitudinal Study had nonstandard measures of both constructs. The two papers on these constructs are similar in that both use the data in the Second Longitudinal Study as a way to learn important things about the behavior of these important constructs in later life.

Finally, the third set of papers report findings on the life graph, an open-ended technique which examines an individual's perceptions of the highs and lows of his life from two very different methodological perspectives: a traditional psychosocial analysis that relates these graphs to life events and a very sophisticated procedure, grade of membership (GOM) analysis, that explores methodological as well as theoretical frontiers.

The Second Longitudinal Study led to a third study, the Coping Study (Siegler et al., 1979; George and Siegler, 1980), because we wanted more insights into the individual's perceptions of the events in his life. These papers can be found in the section on mental health and illness; they are mentioned here to suggest that the Second Longitudinal Study, as well as the First, has a future as a rich source of archived data about the lives of middle-aged and older persons.

References

Clive, J., Woodbury, M. A., and Siegler, I. C. Fuzzy and crisp set-theoretic based classification of health and disease: A qualitative and quantitative comparison. *Journal of Medical Systems*, 7:317–332, 1983.

George, L. K., and Siegler, I. C. *Coping with stress and challenge: Older persons speak for themselves. Final Report*, American Association of Retired Persons-Andrus Foundation, December, 1980.

Harkins, S. W., Nowlin, J. B., Ramm, D., and Schroeder, S. Effects of age, sex and time-on-watch on a brief continuous performance task. In E. B. Palmore (Ed.), *Normal Aging II*. Durham, North Carolina: Duke University Press, 1974, 139–150.

Harris, C. (Ed.), *Problems in measuring change*. Madison: University of Wisconsin Press, 1963.

Hook, J. D., and Siegler, I. C. A WAIS regression model of years to death. Paper presented at the meeting of the Southeastern Psychological Association, Atlanta, Georgia, March, 1983 (a).

Hook, J. D., and Siegler, I. C. Regression models of years to death. Poster presented at the meeting of the American Psychological Association, Anaheim, California, August, 1983 (b).

Manton, K. G., and Woodbury, M. A. A mathematical model of the physiological dynamics of aging and correlated mortality selection: II. Application to the Duke longitudinal study. *Journal of Gerontology*, 38:406–413, 1983.

Schaie, K. W. A general model for the study of developmental problems. *Psychological Bulletin*, 64:92–108, 1965.

Siegler, I. C. Psychological aspects of the Duke longitudinal studies. In K. W. Schaie (Ed.), *Longitudinal studies of adult psychological development*. New York: Guilford Press, 1983, 136–190.

Siegler, I. C. *Aging competently. Final Report*. Washington, D.C.: U.S. Administration on Aging, April 1979.

Wechsler, D. *Wechsler Adult Intelligence Scale*. New York: Psychological Corp., 1955.

Woodbury, M. A., and Manton, K. G. A mathematical model of the physiological dynamics of aging and correlated mortality selection: I. Theoretical development and critiques. *Journal of Gerontology*, 38:398–405, 1983.

Woodbury, M. A., Manton, K. G., and Siegler, I. C. Markov network analysis: Suggestions for innovations in covariance structure analysis. *Experimental Aging Research*, 8:135–140, 1982.

Intellectual Changes

Frances Wilkie and Carl Eisdorfer

Considerable attention has been focused upon the discrepancy in results between the cross-sectional studies which show a marked intellectual loss with advancing age and longitudinal studies which show relatively little intellectual change. Some of the data question the standardization and generalizability of specific tests measuring intelligence among the very old. In addition, there is a need to identify some of the factors associated with differential rates of intellectual decline among the aged. Thus, there is some evidence to indicate that intellectual loss is not a function of normal aging but may be secondary to cardiovascular disease and hypertension. It is important, therefore, to consider a variety of factors, including sex differences, cohort differences, and the like in our attempts to understand differential rates of intellectual decline among the old.

The results to be reported here represent findings on intellectual functioning among a group of fifty participants in the Duke First Longitudinal Study who had seven evaluations over approximately a fifteen-year follow-up period.

This report focuses upon age and sex differences in intellectual functioning as measured by the Wechsler Adult Intelligence Scale (WAIS). Of the fifty subjects, thirty-five entered the program aged sixty to sixty-nine, with a mean age of sixty-four years and they were followed to a mean age of about seventy-nine years; twelve were males and twenty-three were females. The remaining fifteen entered the program aged seventy to seventy-nine with a mean age of about seventy-one years and they were followed to a mean age of about eighty-five years; nine were males and six were females.

The results have been derived from three separate analyses. The first analysis focused upon age and sex differences in the WAIS weighted scores across time. Also examined were the changes in the individual subtest scores between tests 1 and 7. The second analysis focused upon cohort differences. Thus, the two age groups (that is those initially in their sixties and those initially in their seventies) overlapped in age during the fifteen-year follow-up period, with the overlap in age occurring between ages seventy-one to about age seventy-nine.

Paper presented at the annual meeting of the Gerontological Society, Miami, Florida, 1973.

For purposes of this analysis, the sequence of evaluations (that is whether it was the first, second, third, etc. testing) was ignored. The third analysis compared the changes in full scale weighted scores (which are uncorrected for age) to the changes in the intelligence quotient (IQ) scores (which are corrected for age) over the fifteen-year period.

Results

Age and sex differences. The results of the first analysis indicated that there were no significant age or sex differences in the full scale, verbal or performance weighted scores for each evaluation. Because of this finding, and at the risk of oversimplification, figure C—1 shows the full scale, verbal, and performance weighted scores for the total group of subjects pooled on each evaluation. As the subjects aged from a mean of about sixty-eight years to a mean of about eighty-

Figure C—1. *WAIS scores by age.*

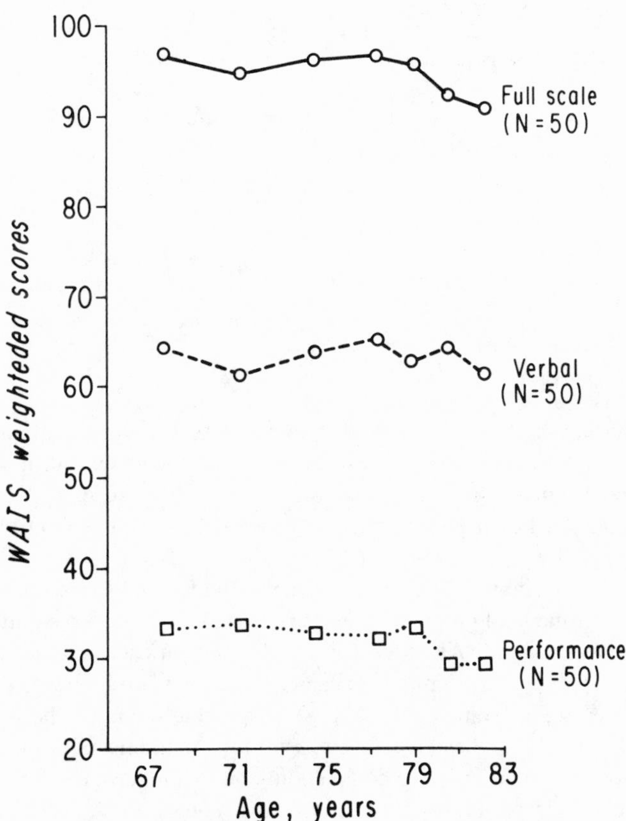

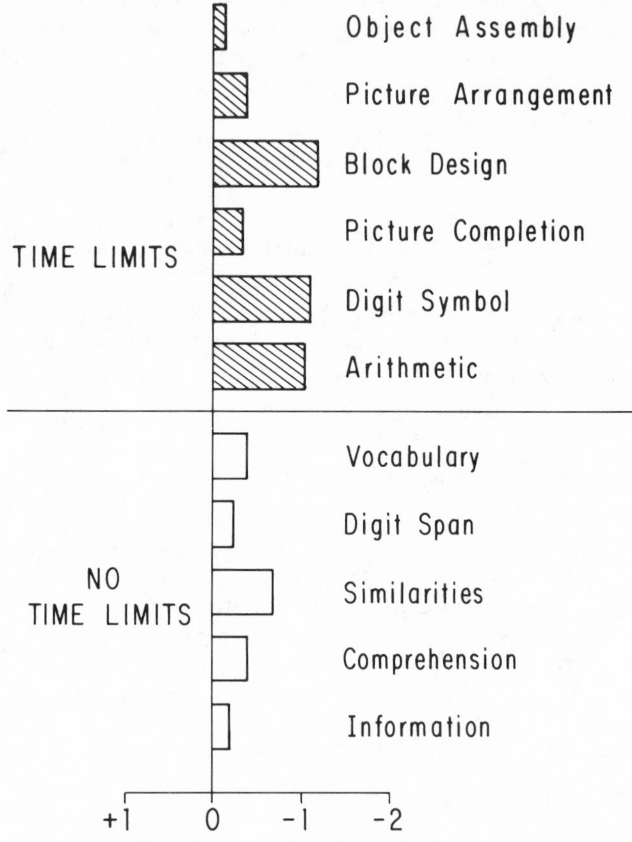

Figure C—2. *Change in WAIS scores.*

two years during the follow-up period, they had losses in the verbal and performance areas of 3.2 and 4.4 points, respectively, reflected as a 7.6 drop in the full scale weighted score, with these losses significant at the .01 level. However, it should be noted that their performance remained relatively stable until about the ninth decade of life.

Figure C—2 shows the changes in the individual subtest scores between tests 1 and 7 for the total group of subjects pooled. There were no significant age or sex differences noted. Although the mean losses on each individual subtest were less than two points, significant changes were found on six out of the eleven subtests. Thus, losses significant at the .01 level were found on the arithmetic, digit symbol, and block design subtests, with losses significant at the .05 level found on the vocabulary, picture completion, and picture arrangement subtests. As expected, the decrements were greater on the subtests administered with time limits than on the subtests where no time limits were imposed. Thus, the overall mean loss of 7.6 points on the WAIS was reflected as a 5.4 loss on the timed subtests and a mean 2.3 loss on the untimed subtests.

Thus, for the total group of subjects there is relatively little intellectual change until about the ninth decade of life, with the major portion of observed loss found in those tasks which involve a speed component. In contrast to previous findings of sex differences among younger age groups (Bayley, 1968), such differences were not found among these subjects. Our failure to find sex differences may in part be due to the fact that our sample was limited to the survivors of the fifteen-year study; in that respect they represented an elite group of older persons. In addition, as noted by Bieri (1968), one might expect at later stages in life that there would be a pattern of convergence of intellectual skills between the sexes.

Cohort differences. The next analysis focused upon cohort differences. There were two age groups, with one group entering the program in their sixties and another group entering the program in their seventies. During the fifteen-year follow-up period they overlapped in age between the age of seventy-one to about age seventy-nine. As reported above, the two age groups did not differ

Figure C—3. *WAIS scores by age and cohort.*

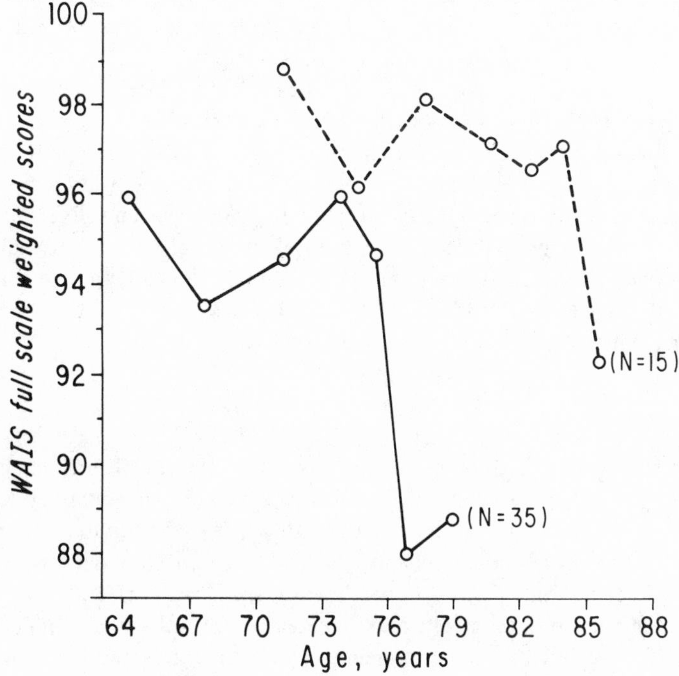

significantly across evaluations (that is, whether it was the first, second, third, etc. testing) nor did they differ in the magnitude of change which occurred between the initial and final testing over the fifteen-year period. This analysis differs from the previous one in that the sequence of evaluation is ignored.

Figure C—3 shows the full scale weighted scores for the two age groups according to their age at testing. Focus is upon that period when the subjects were aged seventy-one to about seventy-nine years of age. Those initially tested in their seventies tended to have slightly higher scores and were more stable between the ages of about seventy-one to seventy-nine than the group that entered the program in their sixties, with these differences also reflected in their verbal scores.

This finding of a significant cohort effect could in part be attributed to environmental differences. However, previous findings have also associated marked intellectual losses with nearness to death. One could speculate that the differential rates of decline observed among these subjects between the ages of seventy-one and seventy-nine could in part be attributed to some members of the initially younger group being closer to death, since they had their last evaluations during this period. The initially older group survived for an additional three evaluations, with a sharp decline noted on their last evaluation.

Weighted versus IQ changes. Figure C—4 shows a comparison of the full scale weighted scores and the full scale intelligence quotient (IQ) scores for the two age groups. In the weighted scores, both age groups had losses of about six to seven points over the fifteen-year period. In contrast in their IQ scores, the group followed from age sixty-four to seventy-nine had a gain of almost eight points, while the group followed from age seventy-one to age eighty-five had only a one point gain in IQ over the fifteen-year period. Since the upper age limit of Wechsler's (1955) IQ conversion table is age seventy-five, an examination was made of the changes in IQ before and after age 75 among these subjects. The group entering the program in their sixties had a gain in IQ of ten points before age seventy-five, followed by a one-point gain after age seventy-five. The group who entered the program in their seventies had a two-point gain in IQ before age seventy-five, followed by an approximately four-point loss after age seventy-five. These findings support Botwinick's (1967) and others' contention that Wechsler's norms are not adequate for describing the very old.

Summary

In contrast to previous findings, there were no significant differences between the sexes in intellectual functioning. Furthermore, there was relatively little intellectual change until about the ninth decade of life, and the major portion of observed loss was in those tasks which involve speed components. A cohort analysis indicated that nearness to death was more closely related to intellectual decline than was chronological age. A comparison of full scale weighted scores with the full scale intelligence quotient (IQ) scores indicates that Wechsler's

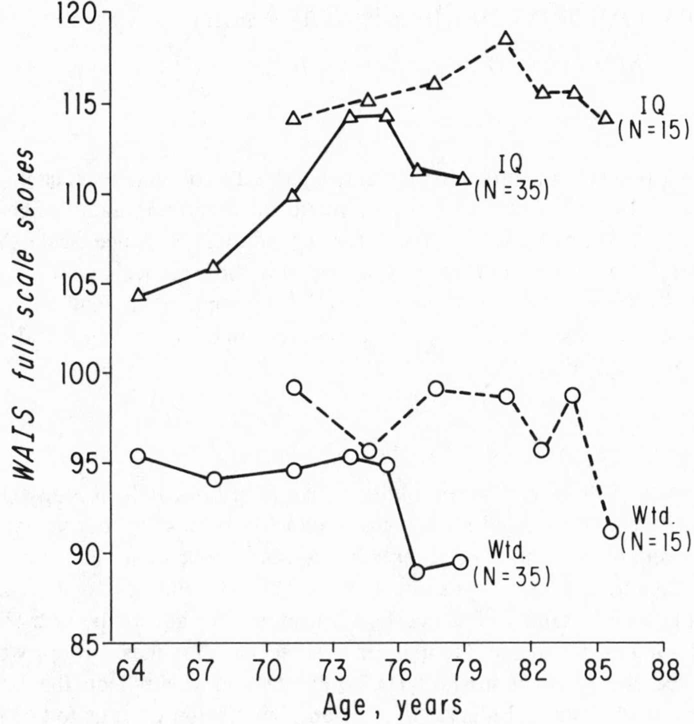

Figure C—4. *WAIS IQ and weighted scores by age and cohort.*

norms (on which the IQ scores are based) are not adequate for describing the very old.

References

Bayley, N. Cognition and aging. In K. W. Schaie (Ed.), *Theory and methods of research on aging*. Morgantown: West Virginia University, 1968.

Bierri, J. Sex differences in cognitive behavior: A response to Bayley's paper. In K. W. Schaie (Ed.), *Theory and methods of research on aging*. Morgantown: West Virginia University, 1968.

Botwinick, J. *Cognitive processes in maturity and old age*. New York: Springer, 1967.

Wechsler, D. *The Wechsler Adult Intelligence Scale*. New York: Psychological Corp., 1955.

Selective Attrition and Intellectual Ability

Ilene C. Siegler and Jack Botwinick

This paper points to the problem of selective subject attrition (Riegel et al., 1967; Riegel and Riegel, 1972) and how this relates to describing age changes. The present report charts scores on the Wechsler Adult Intelligence Scale (WAIS; Wechsler, 1955), across the test sessions for only those subjects who completed the WAIS during all the sessions prior to the one under examination. In other words, the present study was directed to the question of ability levels and subject attrition in longitudinal investigation.

Methods

The subjects of this study were from the Duke First Longitudinal Study (Busse, 1970) and were categorized in three age groups: sixty to sixty-four years, sixty-five to seventy-four years, and seventy-five to ninety-four years, in order to keep relationships between scores and attrition rates as independent of age as possible and still keep the number of subjects significantly large during the later test sessions. Table C—1 indicates the number of subjects (*N*) in these groups who had been tested at each prior session. The severe decline in *N* reflects the expected attrition due to death and illness. In addition, the attrition was due to two procedural requirements: that the whole WAIS had to be completed and, very importantly, that for a subject to be represented at any one time of measurement he or she must have been tested during each of the previous times of measurement.

The average time between the first and second longitudinal study observations was nearly three years; the intertest intervals from the second through the ninth longitudinal observation ranged from less than one year to three years. The tenth and eleventh test sessions were carried out after nine-month and eleven-month intervals, respectively.

Results and Discussion

Figure C—5 is of mean WAIS full scale scores *made at test 1* by only those subjects who remained in the study until the time represented by the abscissa values. Note the general pattern of increasingly higher test 1 scores as the number of subjects diminishes with greater number of test sessions. The same type of figure was drawn for both the verbal and the performance parts of the WAIS (not shown here) with essentially the same findings: differential subject dropout such

Reprinted and adapted by permission from *Journal of Gerontology*, 34:242–245, 1979.

Table C—1. *Dates of longitudinal testing, age of subjects at the start of testing, and number of subjects (N) completing the WAIS in all test sessions up to and including the session indicated.*

Test session (number)	Dates (month/year)	60–64 *N*	65–74 *N*	75–94 *N*	Total *N*
1	3/55–5/59	49	130	67	246
2	9/59–5/61	39	94	36	169
3	1/64–3/65	28	67	19	114
4	10/66–6/67	27	48	10	85
5	4/68–11/68	21	40	7	68
6	2/70–6/70	19	32	5	56
7	1/72–4/72	16	26	2	44
8	2/73–6/73	15	18	1	34
9	4/74–8/74	14	13	0	27
10	3/75–7/75	12	13	0	25
11	3/76–8/76	10	8	0	18

that, with each subsequent testing, the subjects who scored higher at test time 1 remained in the study.

Since subjects represented in the later longitudinal test sessions (number 11 in figure C—5, for example) are also represented in earlier sessions, appropriate statistical analyses comparing mean performance across sessions are not possible. Accordingly, two *t*-tests were carried out, bearing on only a small part of the selective attrition. Of those aged sixty to sixty-four, table C—1 shows that ten subjects dropped out of the study from test session 1 to test session 2. The mean WAIS full scale scores of these ten dropouts were compared to that of the ten subjects of this age who remained in the study throughout ($N = 10$, see session 11 of table C—1). The respective means ± one standard deviation were 84.8 ± 37.3 and 105.2 ± 40.5; with $t(18) = 1.17$, $p > .05$. The corresponding analysis of those aged sixty-five to seventy-four was M = 69.0 ± 28.8, $N = 36$; M = 114.0 ± 17.8, $N = 8$. The *t*-test (3.96, $df = 41$) was highly significant at less than the .0003 confidence level. This latter test indicated what is visually apparent in figure C—5, namely, the effect of selective subject attrition. The standard deviations, particularly those associated with the younger group, reflected the very large individual differences. It is noteworthy that among those in the younger group who dropped out after the first test session, two people (20 percent) were not tested again because they moved elsewhere. Only one person (2.8 percent) in the older group moved and so was not tested. Twenty percent of the younger group and 41.7 percent of the older group died after the first test session. These differences in moving and death percentages may account for the significant *t*-test associated with the older sample and not the younger one.

Effort was made to determine the nature of longitudinal age change in test

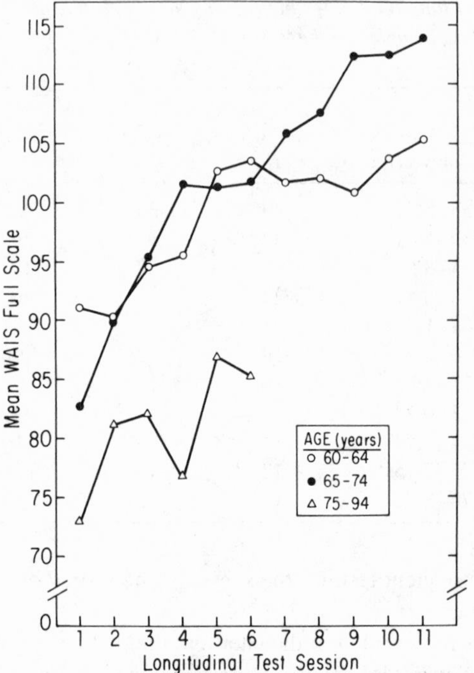

Figure C—5. *Mean intelligence test score* at the time of first testing *as a function of the number of longitudinal test sessions. Only subjects who were tested on all test sessions up to and including the abscissa test number are represented here. For example, subjects represented at test session 11 comprise only those who had been tested on ten previous occasions.*

score with each succeeding session of testing; that is, test scores were plotted of those subjects who completed the WAIS at the first two test sessions, those who completed the first three test sessions, and so on through the whole series of eleven test sessions. The mass of data plots made for visual confusion; to simplify presentation, only four longitudinal series of the eleven were selected. Figure C—6 presents the full scale WAIS scores for those subjects who completed three test sessions (an average of about seven years of longitudinal research), four test sessions (about ten years), seven sessions (about fifteen years), and eleven test sessions (about twenty years). The respective *N*s may be seen in table C—1. The data of the oldest group, aged seventy-five to ninety-four years, are not represented here because of severe attrition over the course of years of longitudinal testing.

In the main, the figure reflects two main points. One, except in very old age, the fall in score is not very great. Two, as longitudinal research progresses and the initially less able drop out from the study, the decline in scores over time decreases. This is seen more clearly in the age group sixty to sixty-four years. Note the relatively flat functions for at least the first twelve years of the fifteen-year and twenty-year curves as compared to the declines seen during the briefer seven-year and ten-year periods of research (that is, compare the first six points of the upper two curves with all the points of the two lower curves). In the older group, sixty-five to seventy-four years, the massive drop from test session 1 to test session 2 in the twenty-year curve obscures the stability in score seen from the second session (early seventies) to the late eighties.

While continued longitudinal testing can thus obfuscate findings of age decline seen earlier in longitudinal investigation, figure C—6 does highlight a most important fact: there is a sizable proportion of old people, identified by their initial test superiority in intellectual ability and by their continued presence as subjects in longitudinal study, who decline very little as old age advances or decline not at all except perhaps in extreme old age.

Not shown here are plots similar to that seen in figure C—6, drawn for both the WAIS verbal and performance sections. The verbal plots, as expected, reflect little or no age decline in any of the functions represented in figure C—6. The performance scores do reflect decline, but continued longitudinal testing seemingly has lesser obfuscating character. That is, continued longitudinal testing

Figure C—6. *Subjects aged sixty to sixty-four (left half of figure) and sixty-five to seventy-four years (right half of figure) at the start of the study were tested over the course of approximately twenty years. The first seven, ten, and fifteen years of longitudinal research are represented by solid circles; twenty years of longitudinal research is represented by dashed lines. Table C—1 shows the* Ns *for each of the curves.*

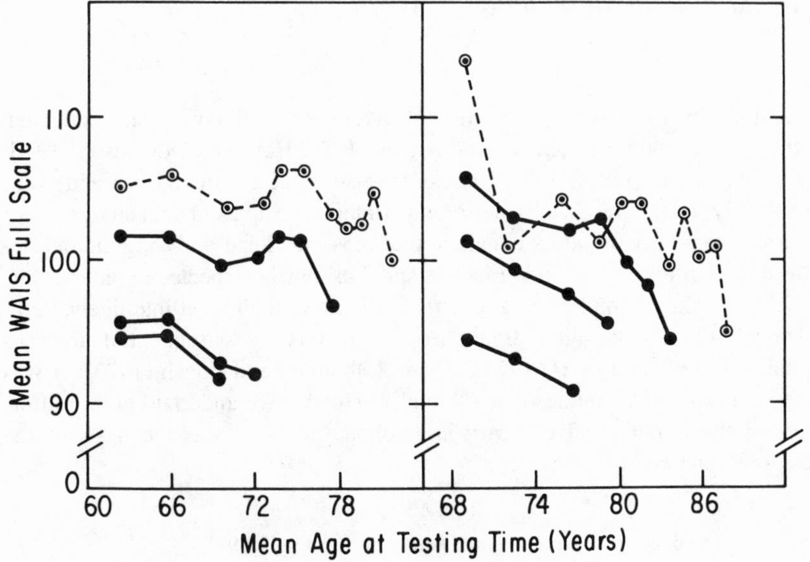

over fifteen and twenty years reflects decline mainly during the first ten years of testing.

Overall, the data of this study point to the importance of distinguishing between subjects selected to begin longitudinal investigation and subjects who remain in the study after a long time: subjects who show up to be tested at every test session. It would seem that the more stringent the testing demands are on the subject, the more it is mainly the intellectually, and perhaps physically, superior who live up to those demands.

References

Busse, E. W. A physiological, psychological and sociological study of aging. In E. B. Palmore (Ed.), *Normal aging*. Durham, N.C.: Duke University Press, 1970.

Riegel, K. F., and Riegel, R. M. Development, drop, and death. *Developmental Psychology*, 6:306–319, 1972.

Riegel, K. F., Riegel, R. M., and Meyer, G. A study of the dropout rates in longitudinal research in aging and the prediction of death. *Journal of Personality and Social Psychology*, 5:342–348, 1967.

Wechsler, D. A. *Manual for the Wechsler Adult Intelligence Scale*. New York: Psychological Corp., 1955.

Cross-Sectional and Longitudinal Patterns of Intellectual Ability

Jack Botwinick and Ilene C. Siegler

There are substantive reasons for the controversy concerning whether intellectual ability declines with age (Baltes and Schaie, 1976; Horn and Donaldson, 1976, 1977; Schaie and Baltes, 1977). There are also value considerations and, very importantly, methodological issues of experimental design and data analysis. For example, some investigators conclude that cross-sectional and longitudinal designs reflect different underlying factors and thus may be expected to yield different results. This is implicit in two often referenced studies on intelligence employing both these designs simultaneously, that is, cross-sequential analyses (Schaie and Labouvie-Vief, 1974; Schaie, Labouvie, and Buech, 1973). It was believed in these two studies that although age may have underlaid group differences in the longitudinal comparisons, cohort, not age, was the basis of the cross-sectional comparisons.

Reprinted by permission from *Developmental Psychology*, 16:49–53, 1980.

This conclusion is far from universally accepted, even though the findings reported in these two studies are typically seen as generalizable; that is, cross-sectional group differences were found to be greater than longitudinal differences. This may be an appropriate generalization, but there is inadequate evidence for it, because proper tests have not been made. For a meaningful comparison between cross-sectional and longitudinal results, the age ranges within the two designs should be identical (Botwinick and Arenberg, 1976). In other words, comparing a forty-year to fifty-year difference in cross-sectional research with a much briefer time difference in longitudinal research (e.g., seven years, as in the study of Schaie and Strother, 1968 or fourteen years, as in the study of Schaie and Labouvie-Vief, 1974) does not permit statements regarding whether one or the other design reflects greater change.

The present study on intellectual ability in old age is based on cross-sequential analysis employing nearly identical cross-sectional and longitudinal age ranges (about twelve years). With this analysis the question, is the cross-sectional group difference greater than the longitudinal group difference? can be answered. Is there a significant interaction between cross-sectional and longitudinal group comparisons so that older subjects show more decline over time than younger ones, as previous reports would suggest? These questions will be answered, but the subject pool will be limited to people aged sixty and over.

Method

Subjects. The subjects were drawn from the Duke First Longitudinal Study population. There were seventy subjects distributed among four age groups: sixty to sixty-three, sixty-four to sixty-seven, sixty-eight to seventy-one, and seventy-two to seventy-five. Twenty were in the younger group, twenty-one were in the next, eighteen were in the sixty-eight- to seventy-one-year group, and eleven were in the oldest group. The groups included thirty-one male and thirty-nine female and fifty-one white and nineteen black subjects. The mean education level was 11.9 years (SD = 5.6); statistical tests of significance did not reflect significant education differences as related to age, sex, or race. The means (and ranges) of formal education level from youngest to oldest age group were 11.4 (1–19), 12.2 (3–20), 11.6 (0–20), and 12.2 (3–19). The corresponding SDs were 5.5, 4.9, 6.9, and 5.4.

Procedure. The first longitudinal study was started in 1959 and ended in 1976. The Wechsler Adult Intelligence Scale (WAIS), including all eleven subtests, was given to subjects who initially ranged in age from sixty to ninety-four. As the times between testing were variable, the actual times between examinations were calculated, and subjects and tests sessions were selected so that the age groups in the cross-sectional comparisons corresponded as closely as possible to the age groups in the longitudinal measurements. In this way, there were four test sessions with approximately four-year intervals between them. The time between the first testing and the second was approximately three and a half years,

Table C—2. *Cross-sequential design: means and standard deviations of Wechsler Adult Intelligence Scale scores.*

	Longitudinal test session									
Cross-sectional	1		2		3		4		M	
test comparisons	M	SD	M	SD	M	SD	M	SD	M	SD
Age (N = 20)	62.2		65.7		69.5		73.6		67.8	
Full	100.5	33.8	100.8	34.4	98.1	32.2	96.2	37.7	98.9	33.9
verbal	64.2	21.3	64.4	21.6	63.9	19.6	62.9	23.2	63.8	21.5
performance	35.0	15.0	36.3	13.8	34.2	13.8	33.4	15.5	34.7	14.5
Age (N = 21)	66.3		69.6		73.7		77.7		71.8	
Full	101.7	19.6	101.4	19.5	98.1	21.0	95.7	22.9	99.2	20.8
verbal	67.2	13.3	66.6	13.5	65.0	14.5	65.2	14.2	66.0	13.9
performance	34.4	7.9	34.8	7.7	33.0	8.5	30.5	10.5	33.2	8.7
Age (N = 18)	70.0		73.5		77.5		81.6		75.6	
Full	94.6	29.4	95.4	28.2	92.0	30.4	85.3	32.0	91.8	30.0
verbal	61.6	19.0	63.2	19.1	61.3	19.3	56.3	21.7	60.6	19.8
performance	33.1	11.4	32.3	11.2	30.3	11.8	29.0	11.6	31.2	11.5
Age (N = 11)	73.4		77.0		81.2		85.2		79.2	
Full	98.7	25.5	99.7	25.1	98.4	27.0	95.7	29.2	98.2	26.8
verbal	65.9	17.6	65.6	17.3	66.6	18.7	65.3	19.3	65.8	18.3
performance	32.8	8.7	34.2	8.7	31.9	8.9	30.4	11.4	32.3	9.5
M (N = 70)	67.2		70.6		74.7		78.7			
Full	99.1	27.2	99.4	27.0	96.6	27.5	93.2	30.7	97.1	28.1
verbal	64.7	17.8	65.0	17.8	64.0	17.7	62.3	19.7	64.0	18.3
performance	34.0	11.1	34.5	10.7	32.5	11.0	30.9	12.4	33.0	11.3

the time between the other testings was approximately four years. The age groupings were also kept to four-year intervals as indicated above (i.e., sixty to sixty-three, sixty-four to sixty-seven, sixty-eight to seventy-one, and seventy-two to seventy-five), with mean ages at time of testing shown in table C—2.

Thus, each subject had to survive the length of the study and be available for all four test sessions to remain in it. While the age groupings were in four-year intervals (i.e., sixty to sixty-three through seventy-two to seventy-five) and the length of the study averaged about twelve years, the actual time between the first and the last test sessions ranged from 9.2 to 13.2 years. Note that as subjects are recruited to survive multiple test sessions, it is mainly the initially high test-scoring subjects who remain in the study, not the others. This was true in the present study (Siegler and Botwinick, 1979).

Results

A repeated-measures analysis of variance (ANOVA) was performed with the cross-sequential data so that there were four (between) age groups in the cross-sectional component of the analysis and four (within) times of testing in the longitudinal component. This type of analysis was performed with the verbal, performance, and full scale scores of the WAIS, with the results essentially the same for each. The analyses of all three scores showed no significant cross-sectional age differences (Fs < 1) but significant longitudinal changes. The ratio of the longitudinal group comparisons were $F(3, 198) = 11.62$, 4.99, and 13.59 ($p < .001$ in each case) for the full, verbal, and performance scale scores, respectively. There were no significant interactions between the cross-sectional and longitudinal aspects.

Table C—2 presents the mean full scale, verbal, and performance scaled scores. This table shows that the longitudinal test score differences, although statistically significant, are small. Decline with time is seen in all age groups. It is noteworthy that although there was significant longitudinal decline overall and no significant cross-sectional decline, the cross-sectional and longitudinal functions were similar in overall magnitude of change, that is, the combined average performance of the two older ages was similar in cross-sectional and longitudinal comparisons, as in the two younger ages. Figure C—7, which shows the mean full scale cross-sectional and longitudinal functions, illustrates this. The com-

Figure C—7. *Mean Wechsler Adult Intelligence Scale full-scale scores as a function of age. (Each of four age groups [60–63, 64–67, 68–71, and 72–75 years] was tested four times, each time approximately four years after the previous testing. This figure represents the mean of the four age groups in the cross-sectional comparison [C] and the mean of the four test sessions in the longitudinal comparison [L].*

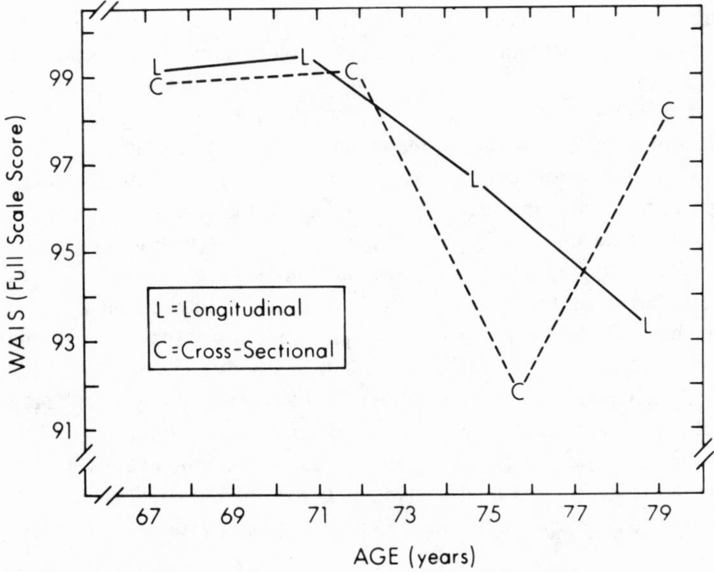

parable figures of verbal and performance scores are not shown, but they may be drawn from table C—2.

The subjects in each of the age groups were of wide educational range. They were of both sexes and of two races. Accordingly, two analyses of covariance were also carried out, one with both race and sex as covariates and the other with educational level as a covariate. The results were similar to the ANOVA. In addition, an ANOVA was carried out with white subjects only. Again, the results were similar.

Post hoc comparisons of mean scores between age groups within the significant longitudinal component (of the ANOVA described in detail) were made by Scheffe tests. The full scale scores were significantly different between the oldest group and each of the three younger groups ($p < .05$). The verbal scores were different between the oldest group and each of the two youngest ones ($p < .05$). The performance score differences were the same as the verbal, with the addition that the two middle groups were significantly different ($p < .05$).

Figure C—7 might suggest that the significant longitudinal results, and not significant cross-sectional results, are due to the fourth longitudinal test sessions and the oldest age group in the cross-sectional component. Accordingly, the ANOVA was repeated, this time disregarding the data of the oldest age group and the fourth longitudinal test point. The results were similar except for the verbal scores; i.e., there were no significant cross-sectional or interaction effects ($p > .05$) but significant longitudinal effects ($p < .004$). With verbal scores, neither the cross-sectional nor the longitudinal differences were significant.

Discussion

Generalizations based on the results of this study are necessarily limited by the following three procedural issues: First, only older adults were examined; their age range was about twelve years, from sixty to sixty-three to seventy-two to seventy-five at the start of the study. Second, the different age groups were similar in levels of education. Third, the demands on each subject were great; each had to be available for four testings over a period of about twelve years to be included in the study. In regard to the first issue, therefore, conclusions of this study cannot bear on issues of maintenance or decline in function prior to age sixty. In regard to the second issue, generalizations must not be based on random or representative sampling. The conclusions regarding intellectual ability in later life must be limited to highly selected subjects in terms of survival and long-term attendance in the study. While the subjects of this study were of average IQ at the start, as determined by the WAIS norms (Wechsler, 1955), they must be regarded as select in terms of health, motivation, and perseverance to remain in the study.

The problem of selective subject dropout in longitudinal research is well documented (e.g., Siegler and Botwinick, 1979): the more able subjects tend to remain in a study over time and the less able ones tend to drop out. The problem of selective subject dropout is not nearly so well documented in cross-sectional research. The present data suggest that when the same or similar requirements for subject selection are imposed on both cross-sectional and longitudinal comparisons, the results of the two types of analyses convey similar results. In other words, the selection of only those subjects who survive and persevere through approximately twelve years of longitudinal testing may allow mainly for subjects who are hardy, able, and motivated. Moreover, it would seem that this subject selectivity increases as we go from the youngest to the oldest subjects in the cross-sectional comparisons. Such subject selectivity might explain the significant age differences in the cross-sectional analyses that are seen so often in the literature of less stringently selected subjects (e.g., Doppelt and Wallace, 1955). This emphasis on subject selectivity suggests that practice effects in longitudinal research, if any, do not account for the usual discrepancy with cross-sectional research.

Given the nonsignificant cross-sectional results, plus the frequent observation that subjects tested longitudinally tend to show maintenance of functions, the significant longitudinal declines in this study appear surprising. Similarly, the lack of significant interaction between cross-sectional and longitudinal comparisons in the full, verbal, and performance scales may come as a surprise. Such interactions have been reported (Schaie et al., 1973; Schaie and Labouvie-Vief, 1974). It would seem that the significant longitudinal effects and nonsignificant interactions are less important than the fact that the longitudinal group differences are of relatively small magnitudes.

The significant longitudinal effect and nonsignificant cross-sectional effect might best be evaluated not only in regard to F ratios but also in regard to the magnitude of mean age levels and change. Figure C—7 shows the cross-sectional and longitudinal functions as similar in level and overall change. Perhaps the most conservative conclusion of this study is that little, if any, meaningful decline with age in intellectual ability was seen either cross-sectionally or longitudinally with these very select subjects. This is compatible with the conclusion of a recent review that cross-sectional data do not always reflect greater decline than longitudinal data, particularly if allowances are made for sampling differences (Botwinick, 1977).

When the results of this study are compared to those of the often-referenced studies of Schaie et al. (1973) and Schaie and Labouvie-Vief (1974), it becomes even more obvious that it is crucial to keep age ranges as identical as possible and subject selection characteristics similar when comparing cross-sectional and longitudinal test effects. Otherwise, spurious conclusions can be drawn. In this study, in which there were nearly identical age ranges, education levels were similar among age groups, and subject selection was limited to only those who were healthy and motivated enough to persevere through four test sessions over an approximate twelve-year period, the cross-sectional and longitudinal results can be regarded as similar. This selection factor is typically present in longitudinal research but not in cross-sectional. Here, it was present in both. In the present study, it was seen that from age sixty on, many older adults maintain their intellectual skills or decline only marginally at least until the end of the seventh decade.

References

Baltes, P. B., and Schaie, K. W. On the plasticity of intelligence in adulthood and old age: Where Horn and Donaldson fail. *American Psychologist*, 31:720–725, 1976.

Botwinick, J. Intellectual abilities. In J. E. Birren and K. W. Schaie (Eds.), *Handbook of the psychology of aging*. New York: Van Nostrand Reinhold, 1977.

Botwinick, J., and Arenberg, D. Disparate time spans in sequential studies of aging. *Experimental Aging Research*, 2:55–61, 1976.

Doppelt, J., and Wallace, W. L. Standardization of the WAIS for older persons. *Journal of Abnormal and Social Psychology*, 51:312–330, 1955.

Horn, J. L., and Donaldson, G. On the myth of intellectual decline in adulthood. *American Psychologist*, 30:701–719, 1976.

Horn, J. L., and Donaldson, G. Faith is not enough: A response to the Baltes-Schaie claim that intelligence does not wane. *American Psychologist*, 32:369–373, 1977.

Schaie, K. W., and Baltes, P. B. Some faith helps to see the forest: A final comment on the Horn and Donaldson myth of the Baltes-Schaie position on adult intelligence. *American Psychologist*, 32:1118–1120, 1977.

Schaie, K. W., and Labouvie-Vief, G. Generational versus ontogenetic components of change in adult cognitive behavior: A fourteen-year cross-sequential study. *Developmental Psychology*, 10:305–320, 1974.

Schaie, K. W., Labouvie, G. V., and Buech, B. U. Generational and cohort specific differences in adult cognitive functioning: A fourteen-year study of independent samples. *Developmental Psychology*, 9:151–166, 1973.

Schaie, K. W., and Strother, C. R. A cross-sequential study of age changes in cognitive behavior. *Psychological Bulletin*, 70:671–680, 1968.

Siegler, I. C., and Botwinick, J. A long-term longitudinal study of intellectual ability of older adults: The matter of selective subject attrition. *Journal of Gerontology*, 34:242–245, 1979.

Wechsler, D. *Wechsler Adult Intelligence Scale*. New York: Psychological Corp., 1955.

Memory and Blood Pressure

Frances L. Wilkie, Carl Eisdorfer, and John B. Nowlin

The incidence of hypertension increases with age and is frequently complicated by cardiovascular disease and strokes (Grover, 1948; Pickering, 1961; Masters, Garfield, and Walters, 1952). Among the middle-aged and the aged, hyperten-

Reprinted by permission from *Experimental Aging Research*, 2:3–16, 1976.

sion has been associated with psychomotor slowing (Birren et al., 1963; Birren and Spieth, 1962; King, 1956; Spieth, 1962, 1964, 1965; Light, 1975; Wilkie and Eisdorfer, 1971), lowered flicker fusion threshold (Enzer, Simonson, and Blankstein, 1942), organic brain impairment (Apter, Halstead, and Heinburger, 1951; Reitan, 1954), and intellectual loss (Spieth, 1965; Wilkie and Eisdorfer, 1972).

The relationship between hypertension and cognitive functioning is complex and its underlying mechanisms are not clear at this time. In hypertension associated with atherosclerosis and heart disease, cerebral vascular insufficiency may in part account for poor performance (Spieth, 1965; Eisdorfer and Wilkie, 1977). It is not known, however, whether hypertension in old age is associated with a generalized behavioral decrement or whether specific skills may be more affected than others. As noted above, hypertensives show a slowing in psychomotor response speed. In a ten-year follow-up study of individuals initially in their sixties, Wilkie and Eisdorfer (1971) found that subjects with diastolic hypertension had a greater loss in overall intellectual ability, based upon the Wechsler Adult Intelligence Scale (WAIS), than their counterparts with normotensive or mild elevations of blood pressure and that these differences were primarily reflected in the performance subtest scores. There was little change in verbal ability among these subjects during the follow-up period. Spieth (1965) found that hypertensives performed poorly on the digit symbol and block design subtests on the WAIS performance section. These findings could be interpreted to indicate that hypertensives would perform most poorly on memory tasks that involve a psychomotor component, time limits, and complex nonverbal material. On the other hand, blood pressure does not appear to be related to memory for highly meaningful verbal material.

This report examines the relationship between blood pressure (BP) and memory, as measured by the Wechsler Memory Scale (Stone and Wechsler, 1945; Wechsler, 1945) in aged individuals over approximately a 6.5-year follow-up period. This memory test primarily consists of tasks involving meaningful verbal material but does include a visual reproductions task that involves drawing from memory somewhat meaningless designs that have been presented visually under timed conditions. It was hypothesized that the hypertensives would perform more poorly than their counterparts with normal and mild elevations of blood pressure on the visual reproductions task. It was also hypothesized that memory for the highly meaningful verbal material would not be related to blood pressure.

Method

The results reported here stem from the Duke First Longitudinal Study. The study was not designed specifically to investigate the relation between BP and memory, but BP values were obtained during the programmed physical examination, and the Wechsler Memory Scale was one of several psychological tests administered.

Subjects

Although there were initially 256 subjects in the sixty to ninety-six age range, the focus in this report is upon those initially in the sixty to sixty-nine age range since none of the older hypertensives completed the follow-up program (Wilkie and Eisdorfer, 1971). The size of the present sample of forty-two subjects was determined by the number of individuals for whom Wechsler Memory Scale (WMS) measurements were available on two evaluations separated by about a 6.5-year period. Although there were initially 122 subjects in the sixty to sixty-nine age range, the WMS was first administered at the second examination, by which time twenty-six subjects had dropped out of the study. The data for fifty additional subjects could not be included in this report, since they were unavailable for testing at either the second or fourth examination. Four subjects with diagnosed cerebrovascular disease were also excluded.

Procedure

Blood pressure (BP). The BP values in this report were obtained by standard auscultation technique with the person in a recumbent position. Diastolic rather than systolic pressure was used since the measures were highly correlated ($p < 0.01$) and diastolic pressure is less sensitive to minor fluctuations. The physician rounded the BP values to the nearest 10 mm-Hg. Approximating Master, Garfield, and Walter's classification (1952), the subjects were divided into a normal group with diastolic pressures between 66 and 95 mm-Hg, a borderline elevated group with pressures between 96 and 105 mm-Hg, or a high group with pressures of over 105 mm-Hg. Subjects were divided into these BP groups based upon their BP levels at the initial testing. All the subjects with high BP had evidence of end-organ change (that is, a cardiac-thoracic ratio of more than 50 percent on the basis of measurements taken from x-ray photographs and clinical signs of eyeground changes of grade II or III). Approximately 35 percent of those with mildly elevated BP and 10 percent of the normotensives had eyeground changes of grade II, with heightened cardiac-thoracic ratio occurring significantly less often ($p < 0.02$) than in the high BP group. Because of the nature of the study, antihypertensive drug usage could not be controlled. It is not clear at this time to what extent antihypertensive drugs affect performance. Spieth (1965) reported evidence that suggests that such drugs would tend to attenuate rather than exaggerate any difference in performance between our subjects. The complexity of the relationship between antihypertensive drugs and performance, however, is illustrated in Light's (1975) observation that humoral influences may play an important role. Light found that medicated patients with renin levels showed improvement in their performance while their counterparts with low and normal renin levels performed more poorly than unmedicated hypertensive and normal control patients.

Test Materials

Memory as measured by the Wechsler Memory Scale (WMS) included the following tasks adopted from forms I and II (Stone and Wechsler, 1945; Wechsler, 1945): (1) logical memory; (2) paired associate learning; and (3) visual reproductions. The instructions, administration, and scoring procedures were those described by Wechsler. A brief description of each task follows.

Logical memory (form I). This task involves the recall of new learning based upon meaningful material. There were two passages of about four or five lines each. Following the presentation of the first passage there was an immediate recall which was followed by the presentation of the second passage and an immediate recall. The immediate and delayed recalls were separated by a twenty-minute interval, with a hearing test for pure tones administered during that period. Subjects were not informed that there would be a delayed recall.

Paired associate learning (form I). This task involves memory/learning, especially short-term memory involving registration (Botwinick and Storandt, 1974). The list consisted of ten pairs, six of which involved easy associations or items that appear to go together (e.g., baby cries) and four hard or low association value pairs (e.g., obey-inch). There were three presentation trials, with each stimulus pair presented every 2 seconds. Test trials followed each presentation of the list, allowing a maximum of 5 seconds for response. For purposes of this report the easy and hard association items were treated separately, using the total number of correct responses on the three trials.

Visual reproductions (form II). This procedure involved the presentation of three designs consisting of geometrical figures. Each design was presented for 10 seconds, with the subject allowed unlimited time for reproducing the designs. The focus in this report is upon the total number of correct reproductions of the three designs.

On test times 1 and 3, univariate analyses of variance were completed to evaluate the hypothesis that the three BP groups would differ on the visual reproductions task which involves a visual motor component. On both tests 1 and 3, multivariate analyses (MANOVA) were completed to confirm the hypothesis that the three BP groups would not differ significantly on the four memory tasks involving highly meaningful verbal material.

Results

Table C—3 presents the number of subjects in each of the three BP groups as well as their socioeconomic level (SES) and mean ages at the initial and third testing on the WMS. SES was based upon a 1–10 point scale, with a score of one representing the highest SES level. SES was examined rather than educational level, since earlier unpublished findings from this subject population indicated a discrepancy between some subjects' initial and subsequent reporting of educa-

Table C—3. *Subject characteristics.*

Blood pressure group	*N*	Mean age Test 1	Mean age Test 3	Socioeconomic level
Normotensive	23	67.8	74.5	3.43
Borderline high	10	67.8	74.4	3.10
High	9	67.1	73.7	4.00

Table C—4. *Wechsler Memory Scale (WMS) mean scores and standard deviations on test 1 (T_1) and test 3 (T_3) for the normotensive (N), borderline high (BH), and high (H) diastolic blood pressure (BP) groups.*

		Logical memory				Paired associate learning				Visual reproductions	
		Immediate recall		Delayed recall		Easy associations		Hard associations			
BP groups		T_1	T_3	T_1	T_3	T_1	T_3	T_1	T_3	T_1	T_3
N	x̄	8.43	9.00	5.59	6.78	16.22	16.70	5.91	4.70	10.39	9.30
	SD	3.21	2.69	3.61	3.32	2.15	1.61	3.29	3.14	2.86	3.50
BH	x̄	7.45	8.35	5.05	6.05	16.50	16.70	6.20	5.50	9.20	8.60
	SD	2.66	2.75	2.89	3.24	1.78	2.45	3.55	3.98	3.88	3.34
H	x̄	7.72	5.56	4.94	3.78	15.89	14.11	5.78	3.89	8.44	4.67
	SD	4.99	4.50	3.16	4.36	1.69	3.15	4.63	3.44	3.78	4.27

tional level. During the 6.5-year follow-up period, the subjects aged from about 67.7 years to 74.3 years. Analyses of variance indicated that the BP groups did not differ significantly in age or in SES.

The focus in this report is upon (1) memory scores on test 1, and (2) memory scores on the third evaluation.

Test 1

On the initial testing, the high BP group did not differ significantly from their age peers with normotensive or borderline high elevations of pressure on the visual reproductions task ($p = 0.296$) nor on the four verbal memory tasks ($p = 0.992$).

As shown in table C—4, independence of BP, the logical memory task (maximum possible score = 22) was difficult for these elderly subjects with their immediate recall (overall mean = 7.9) superior ($p < 0.01$) to their delayed recall (overall mean = 5.2). Although the paired associate easy learning task (maximum possible score = 18) was no special problem for these subjects (overall mean = 16.20) they had considerably more difficulty recalling the hard associations (overall mean = 6.0 out of a possible 12 correct). Independent of BP, the overall mean was 9.3 out of a possible correct score of 14 on the visual reproductions task.

Test 3

On the third testing, the high BP group correctly reproduced only about half the number of details on the visual reproductions task in comparison with the normotensive and borderline elevated BP groups ($p = 0.009$). The BP groups did not differ significantly on the four verbal memory tasks ($p = 0.209$). It should be noted, however, that the high BP group tended to score lower on each of the verbal tasks than did the remaining BP groups.

As indicated in table C—4, the normotensive and borderline high BP groups showed slight gains in their scores between tests 1 and 3 on the immediate and delayed recall on the logical memory task as well as on the easy paired associate learning task. The high BP groups experienced some decline on these tasks. All BP groups had a loss in memory for the hard paired associates during the follow-up period. The visual reproductions task was the most difficult for the subjects in this sample, with 83 percent experiencing some decline on the follow-up evaluation.

The results described above were based upon the total scores obtained on each task. In order to determine the extent to which the significant relationship found on test 3 between BP and visual reproductions was related to item difficulty, the three designs were examined separately. Of interest was the finding that the high BP group performed more poorly on the second design (the first design presented with two figures) than did the normotensive and borderline high BP groups ($p < 0.01$), while no differences were found on the initial design (which had only one figure) or on the third design (which had two figures). It should be noted, however, that on all of the visual reproduction designs the high BP group performed more poorly than the remaining BP groups, accounting for the significant difference found on the total score noted earlier. The finding that the high BP group was able to draw from memory the second but not the first design involving two nonmeaningful figures may indicate that their difficulty was not related to item complexity alone, but perhaps to the shift between designs involving one figure to those involving two figures. To examine this possibility further, the verbal material was examined by item rather than solely according to total scores. Although, as noted earlier, the multivariate analysis indicated that on test 3 there was no significant difference between the BP groups on the four verbal tasks, univariate ANOVA indicated that the BP groups did differ on the immediate recall of the logical memory task ($p = 0.029$). For purposes of generating hypotheses, the immediate recall for the two stories was examined as a function of BP. The results indicated that the high BP group had a significantly greater inability to recall the first passage of the logical memory ($p < 0.05$) but did not differ from the normotensive and borderline elevated groups on the second passage on the third testing.

As noted earlier, hypertension among these subjects was already reflected in end-organ change (i.e., eyeground changes and cardiac-thoracic ratio). Since it could be speculated that changes in retinal vessels could account in part for poor performance on the visual reproductions task, this was examined. No significant difference in performance was found between groups classified according to eyeground changes ($p = 0.225$).

The results indicate that BP was not related to memory on the initial testing, but on the follow-up evaluation BP was related to performance on the visual reproductions task involving a visual motor component and nonmeaningful material. The poorer performance observed among the hypertensives, however, was found only on specific subtask items.

Discussion

Two hypotheses were tested in this investigation. The first was that hypertensives would perform more poorly than normotensives or those with mild elevations of BP on tasks such as visual reproduction, which involves memory of nonmeaningful material and a visual motor component. The results of the 6.5-year follow-up evaluation supported this hypothesis although it did not appear on the initial testing. Our data support previous findings which have suggested that hypertenives perform most poorly on tasks involving time limits, less meaningful material, and a psychomotor component. The finding that the groups differed on the follow-up but not on the initial evaluation suggests that increasing central nervous system involvement may be the consequence of length of hypertensive illness as well as severity of physical pathology.

The results also supported the second hypothesis that BP would not be related to short-term memory for highly meaningful verbal material. It should be noted, however, that the discrepancy between the BP groups in memory for meaningful verbal material was greater (albeit nonsignificant) at the follow-up evaluation than at the initial testing, again suggesting that duration of cardiovascular disease may be an important factor.

Independent of BP, these elderly subjects performed poorly on the immediate as well as the delayed recall of meaningful material, which supports previous findings (Botwinick and Storandt, 1974; Gordon and Clark, 1974). Although the subjects in the present investigation recalled less on the delayed than on the immediate recall, the difference was not as great as that observed by Gordon and Clark (1974) among their subjects. However, this may in part be due to different test material as well as to the short time interval (of twenty minutes) between immediate and delayed recalls used in this investigation compared to the one-week delay used by Gordon and Clark. As a group, the subjects in the present investigation performed relatively well on the paired associate easy task but had more difficulty with the hard associations, which also supports Botwinick and Storandt's (1974) observations among their aged sample. During the 6.5-year follow-up period, our normotensive and borderline high BP groups had little change in their memory for meaningful verbal material, with only a slight decline noted on the less meaningful tasks.

These findings suggest that the hypertensives' poorer performance on some memory tasks on the follow-up evaluation may be related more to performance factors than to memory deficits. Thus, their poor performance on the visual reproductions total score was primarily reflected in poor performance on one design (involving two figures). Their performance was not different from the remaining BP groups on the initial design (involving one figure) or on the third design (which also involved two figures). On the logical memory task, the hypertensives at the follow-up evaluation had difficulty recalling the first, but not the second, passage read to them. These findings tend to suggest that their difficulty was not due to memory impairment or item difficulty but instead to performance factors such as "learning to learn," a change in set, or to state anxiety associated with the testing situation. It is, of course, not clear from these findings what intervening factors may have been related to the poorer performance found among the hypertensives on specific subtask items. In this instance, the Wechsler Memory Scale was the first of a number of psychological tests administered to these subjects in their two day evaluation. As noted by Spieth (1965) and in a review by Eisdorfer and Wilkie (1977), young hypertensives appear to be more stressed in the laboratory testing situation than those in lower blood pressure levels, and this in turn could affect their performance. State anxiety has been associated with impaired memory among the young in free recall learning situations (Butter, 1970; Corteen, 1969; Kaplan and Kaplan, 1969; Kleinsmith and Kaplan, 1964; Maltzman, Kantor, and Langdon, 1966; Walker and Tarte, 1963; Warren and Harris, 1975) although habituation of autonomic nervous system activity may be a confounding variable in many of these studies (Zelinski, Walsh, and Thompson, 1975). Another possible explanation for the apparent memory impairment noted among the hypertensives in this investigation may have been suggested by Spieth (1965) when he noted that his hypertensives appeared to have more difficulty in deciding what to do than in doing. Thus, on the logical memory task which was difficult for the subjects in the present investigation, the hypertensives showed some decrement on the follow-up evaluation in the immediate recall of the first but not the second passage, which suggests that they may have a better understanding of what was expected of them or in some way profited from the experience associated with the first passage. On the visual reproductions task, the hypertensives had their greatest difficulty when the design shifted from that of one figure to designs involving two figures, but again appeared to profit from their experience and were able to reproduce the third design that also involved two figures. Performance on the visual reproductions task was not related to retinal changes associated with sustained elevations of blood pressure. Whatever the appropriate explanation may be for these findings, it appears that it represents a change that occurred only within the hypertensive group during the 6.5-year follow-up period, since on the initial testing their memory was not markedly different from the memory of their counterparts with normotensive or mild elevations of blood pressure. These findings suggest that the impairment in cognitive functioning associated with hypertension may in part be due to performance factors such as test instructions, strategy, or anxiety related to the test situation.

References

Apter, N. S., Halstead, W. C., and Heinburger, R. F. Impaired cerebral functions in essential hypertension. *American Journal of Psychiatry*, 107:808–813, 1951.

Birren, J. E., et al. Interdisciplinary relationships: Interrelations of physiological, psychological, and psychiatric findings in healthy elderly men. In J. E. Birren et al. (Eds.), *Human aging: A biological and behavioral study*. PHS Pub. No. 986. Washington, D.C.: U.S. Government Printing Office, 1963, 283–305.

Birren, J. E., and Spieth, W. Age, response speed and cardiovascular functions. *Journal of Gerontology*, 17:390–391, 1962.

Botwinick, J., and Storandt, M. *Memory, related functions, and age*. Springfield, Ill.: Charles C. Thomas, 1974.

Butter, M. J. Differential recall of paired associates as a function of arousal and concreteness-imagery levels. *Journal of Experimental Psychology*, 84:252–256, 1970.

Corteen, R. S. Skin conductance changes and word recall. *British Journal of Psychology*, 60:81–84, 1969.

Eisdorfer, C., and Wilkie, F. Stress, disease, aging, and behavior. In J. E. Birren and K. W. Schaie (Eds.), *Handbook of the psychology of aging*. New York: Van Nostrand Reinhold, 1977.

Enzer, N., Simonson, E., and Blankstein, S. S. Fatigue of patients with circulatory insufficiency, investigated by means of fusion frequency of flicker. *Annals of Internal Medicine*, 1942, 16:701–707, 1942.

Gilbert, J. G., and Leveer, R. F. Patterns of declining memory. *Journal of Gerontology*, 26:70–75, 1971.

Goldman, H., et al. Correlation of diastolic blood pressure and signs of cognitive dysfunction in essential hypertension. *Diseases of the Nervous System*, 35:571–572, 1974.

Gordon, S. K., and Clark, W. C. Adult age differences in word and nonsense syllable recognition memory and response criterion. *Journal of Gerontology*, 29:659–665, 1974.

Grover, M. Physical impairments of members of low-income farm families—11,490 persons in 2,477 rural families examined by the Farm Security Administration, 1940. VII. Variation of blood pressure and heart disease with age, and the correlation of blood pressure and heart disease with age, and the correlation of blood pressure with height and weight. *Public Health Reports*, 63:1083–1101, 1948.

Heyman, D. K., and Jeffers, F. C. Study of relative influences of race and socio-economic status upon the activities and attitudes of a southern aged population. *Journal of Gerontology*, 19:225–229, 1964.

Kaplan, R., and Kaplan, S. The arousal-retention interval interaction revisited: the effects of some procedural changes. *Psychonomics Science*, 15:84–85, 1969.

King, H. E. Comparison of fine psychomotor movement by hypertensive and hypotensive subjects. *Perceptual Motor Skills*, 6:199–204, 1956.

Kleinsmith, L. J., and Kaplan, S. The interaction of arousal and recall interval in nonsense syllable paired-associate learning. *Journal of Experimental Psychology*, 67:124–126, 1964.

Light, K. C. Slowing of response time in young and middle-aged hypertensive patients. *Special Review of Experimental Aging Research*, 1:209–227, 1975.

Maltzman, I. W., Kantor, W., and Langdon, B. Immediate and delayed retention, arousal, and the orienting and defensive reflexes. *Psychonomics Science*, 6:445–446, 1966.

Master, A. M., Garfield, C. I., and Walters, M. B. *Normal blood pressure and hypertension*. Philadelphia: Lea & Febiger, 1952.

Pickering, G. W. *The nature of essential hypertension*. New York: Grune & Stratton, 1961.
Reitan, R. M. Intellectual and affective changes in essential hypertension. *American Journal of Psychiatry*, 110:817–824, 1954.
Spieth, W. Abnormally slow perceptual-motor task performances in individuals with stable, mild to moderate heart disease. (Abstract.) *Aerospace Medicine*, 33:270, 1962.
Spieth, W. Cardiovascular health status, age, and psychological performance. *Journal of Gerontology*, 19:277–284, 1964.
Spieth, W. Slowness of task performance and cardiovascular disease. In A. T. Welford and J. E. Birren (Eds.), *Behavior, aging and the nervous system*. Springfield, Ill.: Charles C. Thomas, 1965, 366–400.
Stone, C. P., and Wechsler, D. *Wechsler Memory Scale. Form II*. New York: Psychological Corp., 1945.
Walker, E. L., and Tarte, R. D. Memory storage as a function of arousal and time with homogeneous and heterogeneous lists. *Journal of Verbal Learning and Verbal Behavior*, 2:113–119, 1963.
Warren, L. R., and Harris, L. J. Arousal and memory: Phasic measures of arousal in a free recall task. *Acta Psychologica*, 39:303–310, 1975.
Wechsler, D. A standardized memory scale for clinical use. *Journal of Psychology*, 19:87–95, 1945.
Wilkie, F., and Eisdorfer, C. Intelligence and blood pressure in the aged. *Science*, 172:959–962, 1971.
Wilkie, F. L., and Eisdorfer, C. Blood pressure and behavioral correlates to the aged. Paper presented at the meeting of the International Gerontological Society, Kiev, Russia, 1972.
Zelinski, E., Walsh, D. A., and Thompson, L. W. Relation of electrodermal response to the effects of level of information processing on immediate and delayed recall. Paper presented at the meeting of the Society for Psychophysiological Research, Toronto, Canada, 1975.

Cross-Sectional and Longitudinal Patterns of Memory Scores

Sarah M. McCarty, Ilene C. Siegler, and Patrick E. Logue

The Wechsler Memory Scale (WMS) (Stone et al., 1946; Wechsler, 1945) is used widely in clinical practice. Although it does not have the sophistication of many experimental tasks, Prigantano (1978) has presented evidence that it has reasonable construct validity and reliability. There have been few studies which describe the WMS performance of healthy older persons cross-sectionally or longitudinally. Declines in memory function are among the most commonly reported symptoms of aging, and it is important that patterns of change in normal older persons be made available for use as a reference point.

The Duke First Longitudinal Study provides an opportunity to examine WMS scores in such a population. Three WMS subtests were administered beginning at wave 2 in 1959–1960: logical memory, visual reproduction, and associate learning. These subtests have been reported to be the most suceptible

Reprinted by permission from *Journal of Gerontology*, 37:169–175, 1982.

to decline with age (Kear-Colwell and Heller, 1978; Klonoff and Kennedy, 1965, 1966).

Cross-sectional studies of WMS scores (Bak and Greene, 1980; Hulicka, 1966; Kear-Colwell and Heller, 1978; McCarty et al., 1980) indicate that decreases in memory performance may begin around or even before age fifty. It is therefore likely that declines in performance on memory tests occurred in the Duke sample prior to their inclusion in the study. The question addressed here is whether age-related changes can be observed in the later years.

Botwinick (1977) suggested that lower performance than verbal subtest scores on the WAIS constitutes a classic aging pattern. There is some indication, from cross-sectional studies of the WMS, that nonverbal visuospatial memory tasks such as the visual reproduction subtest also show a more pronounced decline than verbal memory tasks such as logical memory or associate learning (Bak and Greene, 1980; Hulicka, 1966; Logue and Wyrick, 1979). The data examined in the present study are expected to show a similar pattern.

Furthermore, the impact of selective attrition and repeated participation observed with the WAIS (Siegler and Botwinick, 1979) will affect patterns of test performance on the WMS as well, so that those who complete the study can be expected to have higher initial scores and a better maintenance of function.

Method

Participants. Of the original 270 participants in the first longitudinal study, 172 had complete data on logical memory, visual reproduction, and associate learning at wave 2 when the WMS was first administered. These 172 people made up the cross-sectional sample, although they had all been present for wave 1 approximately four years previously. This was an unavoidable departure from the usual procedure for cross-sectional designs in which participants are evaluated only once.

Three subsets of participants were used in the longitudinal analyses: those with complete data at waves 2 and 3, waves 2–6, and waves 2–11. The number of participants was not sufficient for mutually exclusive groups.

The longitudinal groups were divided into two cohorts: those aged seventy or less and those aged seventy-one or more at wave 2. The number of "older" participants present through wave 11 was too small to permit division into cohorts for purposes of statistical analysis, but mean scores for the two cohorts are shown in figure C—8.

Table C—5 contains the number of subjects and mean ages and educational levels of the longitudinal subgroups and the cross-sectional group. There were no significant differences in education between younger and older cohorts for those present at waves 2–3 and 2–6. Greatly unequal numbers precluded testing the difference for those present at waves 2–11. However, it should be noted that there was a difference in education that may have been meaningful for the wave 2–11 participants.

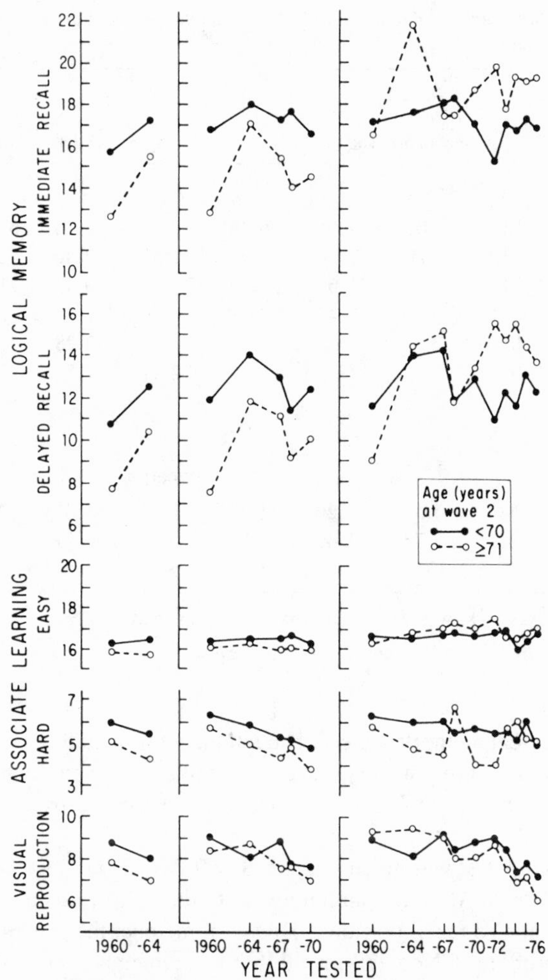

Figure C—8. *Longitudinal Wechsler Memory Scale subtest curves for participants present at waves 2–3 (left), 2–6 (middle), and 2–11 (right).*

The cross-sectional participants included eighty-five males and eighty-seven females; 109 were white and sixty-three were black. Longitudinally, the proportion of black participants varied from 34 percent for the wave 2–3 group to 46 percent for the wave 2–11 group. The proportion of females ranged from 50 percent for the wave 2–3 group to 65 percent for the wave 2–11 group.

Procedure. The items adapted from the WMS included logical memory, form I; associate learning, form I (Wechsler, 1945); and visual reproduction, form II (Stone et al., 1946). A twenty-minute delayed recall procedure was

Table C—5. *Mean age and educational levels of participants in cross-sectional and longitudinal analyses.*

Wave	Dates		At Wave 2 (Cross-sectional)	Waves 2–3 Younger[b]	Waves 2–3 Older	Waves 2–6 Younger	Waves 2–6 Older	Waves 2–11[a] Younger	Waves 2–11[a] Older
						Age			
2	9/59–	M	73.09	67.61	76.16	67.76	75.30	67.38	74.09
	5/61	SD	6.29	2.36	3.73	2.39	2.46	2.43	2.46
3	1/64–	M		71.62	80.25	71.73	79.45	71.41	78.30
	3/65	SD		2.43	3.69	2.50	2.46	2.68	2.40
6	2/70–	M				77.35	85.28	77.05	84.00
	8/70	SD				2.52	2.53	2.76	2.40
11	3/76–	M						83.08	90.10
	8/76	SD						2.72	2.44
						Education			
		M	10.57	11.26	11.21	11.95	11.65	12.00	13.68
		SD	5.76	5.49	5;97	5.55	6.71	5.57	4.78
N			172	54	62	39	23	19	7

[a]Participants at waves 2–11 were not divided into cohorts for analyses.

[b]Younger = 63 to 70 at wave 2; older = 71 to 87 at wave 2.

added to the logical memory subtest. The rationale for including form II of visual reproduction was that this subtest was the most likely to be confounded by previous exposure. Since form I is usually used clinically, the use of form II was preferable.

An audiology test was given immediately following the logical memory immediate recall test. After the audiology test, the following instructions were given for the delayed recall portion: ''Do you remember the stories I read to you before the hearing test? Now tell me all that you remember about the first story. [Story recalled.] Now tell me all that you remember about the second story. [Story recalled.]'' Associate learning and visual reproduction were then administered in that order as directed by Wechsler (1945) and Stone et al. (1946). Scoring criteria were relatively stringent, although credit was given for close paraphrases of the stories. All test forms were scored by the examiner and then rescored by a second examiner. Any discrepancies were resolved before the data were keypunched. After completion of the data collection in 1976, all of the original forms were rescored to assess any criterion changes during the study. Interrater reliability coefficients were not calculated; however, we have a high degree of confidence that the scoring criteria were maintained across time. The review of the raw data forms found only a few arithmetic and keypunch errors, which were corrected prior to the analyses presented below. All procedures used in the psychological laboratory of the Duke longitudinal studies can be found in Siegler (1983).

Analyses. Questions concerning age-related differences in test scores after age sixty and the relative differences in performance on verbal versus nonverbal tasks are appropriately addressed by both cross-sectional and longitudinal data. Scores were examined for immediate and delayed recall of logical memory, easy and hard associates of associate learning, and visual reproduction. Univariate rather than multivariate tests are reported in order to assess the patterns in each of the tests; however, in all cases multivariate tests were also calculated and they confirmed the univariate results. It was thought appropriate in the cross-sectional analyses to explore not only the influence of age but also those of sex, race, and education. The number of participants did not permit analysis of variance with all four independent variables; consequently, simultaneous multiple regression analyses (SYSREG, SAS Institute, Inc., 1979) were used. For the longitudinal analyses, repeated-measures ANOVA was used. Orthogonal contrasts were applied to determine whether significant time effects were linear. The data were analyzed with BMDP2V (UCLA, 1977). This program allows unequal spacing in the calculation of the orthogonal polynominals.

The Duke First Longitudinal Study was designed in 1954 and was a traditional longitudinal design; however the cohort range was broad (1866–1899), allowing for the assessment of multiple cohort groups. While age and cohort cannot be disentangled logically in the present design, the duplication of patterns across time would argue for an age rather than a period effect. These time effects represent both age/cohort and the effects of repeated testing.

Results

Cross-sectional analyses. Table C—6 presents means and standard deviations for WMS scores at wave 2. The results of the simultaneous multiple regression analyses of age, sex, race, and level of education on WMS scores are summarized in table C—7.

Education had the highest standardized *B* values for all WMS variables; it was the only variable which produced consistently significant effects. The relationship of the remaining variables to memory scores was less consistent. Age appeared related to performance on immediate but not delayed logical memory and to visual reproduction. Sex was related only to hard associates, with women performing better than men. Race appeared related to associate learning and visual reproduction; whites scored higher than blacks on these subtests.

Age, sex, race, and educational level, when taken together, accounted for 20 percent to 35 percent of the variance in memory test scores. Education was a more important predictor of performance than age, sex, or race. Thus, cross-sectionally, there was evidence for a linear age-related difference after age sixty only for immediate recall of logical memory and for visual reproduction. The

Table C—6. *Means and standard deviations for Wechsler Memory Scale subtests at first time measurement (wave 2).*

	M	SD
Logical memory[a]		
Immediate recall	13.35	7.07
Delayed recall	8.39	6.88
Associate learning		
Easy associates	15.57	2.94
Hard associates	5.12	3.39
Visual reproduction	7.56	3.18
N = 172.		

[a]Immediate and delayed recall scores for logical memory are the sums of the two stories as suggested by Russell (1975), rather than their average as suggested by Wechsler (1945).

Table C—7. *Simultaneous regression of age, sex, race, and education on Wechsler Memory Scale variables at wave 2.*

	Standardized *B*				
	Age	Sex	Race	Education	R^2
Logical memory[a]					
Immediate recall	−.17*	.00	−.11	.44***	.25
Delayed recall	−.12	.03	−.04	.42***	.20
Associate learning					
Easy associations	−.13	.11	−.19**	.33***	.20
Hard associations	−.13	.20**	−.14*	.41***	.29
Visual reproduction	−.26***	.01	−.23***	.45***	.35
N = 172, ages 63 to 87.					

[a]Immediate and delayed recall scores for logical memory are the sums of the two stories as suggested by Russell (1975), rather than their average as suggested by Wechsler (1945).

*$p < .05$.

**$p < .01$.

***$p < .001$.

relationship between age and visual reproduction was the strongest. The education variable is typically seen as a major explanatory variable in accounting for cohort effects. However, as can be seen in table C—5, the younger and older cohorts in this study have equivalent levels of formal education.

Longitudinal analyses. Table C—8 presents repeated-measures ANOVAs of memory scores for the three sets of longitudinal curves; figure C—8 shows corresponding longitudinal curves.

Cohort was significant only for the group present at waves 2–3 for immediate and delayed logical memory, although the means in figure C—8 indicate that the younger cohort scored higher than the older cohort on the majority of subtests for both waves 2–3 and 2–6. However, the younger cohorts generally did not score significantly better over time than the older cohorts.

Time was significant for all subtests except easy associates for participants present at waves 2–3 and 2–6. As can be seen in figure C—8, logical memory scores actually increased significantly over time for those present at waves 2–3, whereas hard associates and visual reproduction scores decreased significantly over time for this group. Time was significant only for visual reproduction for those who were present at waves 2–11. The percentage of variance accounted for, as indicated by ω^2, was quite small for all significant effects.

Orthogonal contrasts on the time factor for waves 2–6 and 2–11 were used to determine whether there was a linear decrease in test scores across time or whether a higher-order polynomial best describes each curve. For waves 2–6, only hard associates and visual reproduction had significant linear trends, $F(1,60) = 24.33$, $p < .001$, and $F(1,60) = 12.73$, $p < .001$, respectively. There was also a significant linear component to the wave 2–11 curve for visual reproduction, $F(1,25) = 11.78$, $p < .002$. It is not surprising that immediate and delayed recall of logical memory had significant quadratic and cubic components, given the large initial increase and subsequent variability in mean scores.

In sum, only scores on hard associates and visual reproduction showed evidence of decline with time. Easy associates did not change significantly; immediate and delayed logical memory either increased or they lack a linear downward trend. Further, only visual reproduction showed significant decreases for all three longitudinal periods.

Selective attrition. Figure C—8 also illustrates the selective attrition phenomenon: participants who remained in the study longer and were present at all waves tended to score higher than those who dropped out earlier in the study. This is true even given the fact that the WMS was not added to the study until the second time of measurement, after a significant dropout had already occurred. Since the groups represented by the three sets of curves were not mutually exclusive, statistical analysis of these differences was not possible. However, this phenomenon was especially clear for the older cohort. Older participants present for waves 2–11 often not only scored higher than older participants who dropped out earlier; they also frequently scored higher than the younger participants present throughout the study. Except for visual reproduction, both younger and older participants present throughout failed to show significant declines in test performance. This was not the case for those present only through wave 6; these participants showed significant declines on hard associates as well as visual reproduction, and they appeared to decline somewhat on logical memory after wave 3. Siegler and Botwinick (1979) reported similar effects of selective attrition on WAIS scores.

Table C—8. *Longitudinal analyses of variance.*

Source	Waves 2–3				Waves 2–6				Waves 2–11			
	df	MS	*F*	ω^2(%)	*df*	MS	*F*	ω^2(%)	*df*	MS	*F*	ω^2(%)
					Logical memory, immediate recall							
Cohort	1	334.38	4.70*	4.45	1	455.88	2.86	—	—	—	—	—
Error	114	71.21	—	—	60	159.66	—	—	—	—	—	—
Time	1	263.27	19.95***	4.21	4	60.40	5.58***	1.32	9	10.34	1.03	—
C × T	1	35.46	2.69	—	4	24.74	2.29	—	—	—	—	—
Error	114	13.20	—	—	240	10.82	—	—	225	10.03	—	—
					Logical memory, delayed recall							
Cohort	1	382.92	4.90*	—	1	492.88	2.77	—	—	—	—	—
Error	114	78.12	—	—	60	177.68	—	—	—	—	—	—
Time	1	302.40	13.95***	4.57	4	103.18	6.89***	2.76	9	28.72	1.87	—
C × T	1	11.02	0.51	—	4	15.99	1.07	—	—	—	—	—
Error	114	21.67	—	—	240	14.98	—	—	225	15.33	—	—
					Associate learning, easy associates							
Cohort	1	16.93	2.15	—	1	8.26	0.72	—	—	—	—	—
Error	114	7.89	—	—	60	11.53	—	—	—	—	—	—
Time	1	0.35	0.23	—	4	0.92	0.55	—	9	1.42	0.81	—
C × T	1	0.92	0.60	—	4	0.50	0.30	—	—	—	—	—
Error	114	1.52	—	—	240	1.66	—	—	225	1.75	—	—

					Associate learning, hard associates							
Cohort	1	56.63	3.12	—	1	44.28	1.08	—	—	—	—	—
Error	114	18.14	—	—	60	40.88	—	—	—	—	—	—
Time	1	25.24	6.02*	1.75	4	24.54	6.97***	3.02	9	2.96	0.77	—
C × T	1	1.50	0.36	—	4	0.96	0.27	—	—	—	—	—
Error	114	4.20	—	—	240	3.52	—	—	225	3.86	—	—
					Visual reproduction							
Cohort	1	59.92	3.23	—	1	11.82	0.27	—	—	—	—	—
Error	114	18.53	—	—	60	44.33	—	—	—	—	—	—
Time	1	37.18	9.48***	6.75	4	18.93	4.98***	1.67	9	15.85	4.01***	11.32
C × T	1	0.01	0.00	—	4	6.54	1.72	—	—	—	—	—
Error	114	3.92	—	—	240	3.80	—	—	225	3.95	—	—

*$p < .05$.

**$p < .001$.

Discussion

The results of the current study of WMS performance was generally consistent with studies of performance on intelligence tests: (1) age-related differences were not great; (2) nonverbal test scores appeared to decrease more than verbal test scores; and (3) longitudinal results were confounded by the effects of selective attrition.

The amount of change in memory scores after age sixty suggested by both the cross-sectional and longitudinal results were generally small. Cross-sectionally, only immediate recall and visual reproduction showed relationships to age. Longitudinally, the younger cohort showed significantly superior performance only for immediate and delayed logical memory. Hard associates showed decreases with time across waves 2–3 and 2–6; visual reproduction showed declines for all three longitudinal periods. The ω^2 values were rather small for all these effects. Greater differences would probably occur in studies with larger age ranges (e.g., twenties through nineties) judging by comparisons with norms for younger groups. Even the younger longitudinal cohorts had borderline-to-mild impairment at wave 2 on immediate and delayed logical memory and visual reproduction according to Russell's (1975) norms. The younger cohorts also performed below Wechsler's (1945) twenty- to twenty-nine-year-old normative groups on all subtests except delayed logical memory, for which he provided no norms. The current groups did not perform consistently below Wechsler's forty- to forty-nine-year-old group, however, so that many were functioning on a par with the average person in his or her forties, despite probable prior decreases in memory performance.

The present findings supported previous reports of the relative vulnerability of nonverbal as compared with verbal test performance for measures of both intelligence (Botwinick, 1977) and memory (Hulicka, 1966; Logue and Wyrick, 1979). Among cross-sectional WMS studies, significant age differences were consistently reported for visual reproduction, whereas findings for logical memory and associate learning have been more variable (Bak and Greene, 1980; Kear-Colwell and Heller, 1978; Klonoff and Kennedy, 1965; McCarty et al., 1980). Similarly, the findings with respect to visual reproduction were more consistent within the current study. It is not known whether the greater decreases on nonverbal memory and intelligence tests are attributable to a relative inability to process visuospatial information or to other age-related changes such as slowing of cognitive and motor processes.

Selective attrition produced biases similar to those reported for intelligence test scores (Botwinick, 1977; Jarvick, 1973; Schaie, 1979; Siegler and Botwinick, 1979). Performance was better for longitudinal participants who remained in the study longer.

The longitudinal curves no doubt provided an overestimate of memory scores and an underestimate of expected declines. Our longitudinal sample may have not only scored higher than the normal elderly population but also benefitted more from repeated testings than the average person, thus minimizing changes with time. "True" rates of decline in test scores are probably higher and level of performance lower than those of the wave 2–11 longitudinal group. However, age as a predictor of test performance surely does not exceed the cross-sectional estimate of R^2 at 20 percent to 35 percent for age, sex, race, and education taken together. It appears that changes in test performance after age sixty are a function of other variables, some of which become more salient in old age.

References

Bak, J. S., and Greene, R. L. Change in neuropsychological functioning in an aging population. *Journal of Consulting and Clinical Pathology*. 48:395–399, 1980.

Botwinick, J. Intellectual abilities. In J. E. Birren and K. W. Schaie (Eds.), *Handbook of the psychology of aging*. New York: Van Nostrand Reinhold, 1977.

Hulicka, I. M. Age differences in Wechsler Memory Scale scores. *Journal of Psychology*, 109:135–145, 1966.

Jarvik, L. F. Discussion: Patterns of intellectual functioning in the later years. In L. F. Jarvik, C. Eisdorfer, and J. E. Blum (Eds.), *Intellectual functioning in adults*. New York: Springer, 1973.

Kear-Colwell, J. J., and Heller, M. A normative study of Wechsler Memory Scale. *Journal of Clinical Psychology*, 34:437–442, 1978.

Klonoff, H., and Kennedy, M. Memory and perceptual functioning in octogenarians and nonagenarians in the community. *Journal of Gerontology*, 20:328–333, 1965.

Klonoff, H., and Kennedy, M. A comparative study of cognitive functioning in old age. *Journal of Gerontology*, 21:239–243, 1966.

Logue, P. E., and Wyrick, L. Initial validation of Russell's Revised Wechsler Memory Scale: A comparison of normal aging vs. dementia. *Journal of Consulting and Clinical Psychology*. 47: 176–178, 1979.

McCarty, S. M., et al. Alternate-form feliability and age-related scores for Russell's Revised Wechsler Memory Scale. *Journal of Consulting and Clinical Psychology*, 48:296–298, 1980.

Prigantano, G. P. Wechsler Memory Scale: A selective review of the literature. *Journal of Clinical Psychology*, 34:816–832, 1978.

Russell, E. W. A multiple scoring method for the assessment of complex memory functions. *Journal of Consulting and Clinical Psychology*. 43:800–809, 1975.

SAS Institute, Inc. *SAS user's guide*. Raleigh, N.C.: SAS Institute, 1979.

Schaie, K. W. A general model for the study of developmental problems. *Psychological Bulletin*, 64:92–107, 1965.

Schaie, K. W. The primary mental abilities in adulthood: An exploration in the development of psychometric intelligence. In P. B. Baltes and O. G. Brim (Eds.), *Life-span development and behavior*, Vol. 2. New York: Academic, 1979.

Siegler, I. C. Psychological aspects of the Duke longitudinal studies. In K. W. Schaie (Ed.), *Longitudinal studies of psychological development in adulthood*. New York: Guilford Press, 1983.

Siegler, I. C., and Botwinick, J. A long-term longitudinal study of intellectual ability of older adults: The matter of selective subject attrition. *Journal of Gerontology*, 34:242–245, 1979.

Stone, C. P., Girdner, J., and Albrecht, R. An alternate form of the Wechsler Memory Scale. *Journal of Psychology*, 22:199–206, 1946.

University of California, Los Angeles. *Biomedical computer programs*. Berkeley: University of California Press, 1977.

Wechsler, D. A standardized memory scale for clinical use. *Journal of Psychology*, 19:87–95, 1945.

Memory, Attrition, and Distance from Death

Ilene C. Siegler, Sarah M. McCarty, and Patrick E. Logue

The problem of selective subject attrition or dropout from longitudinal study populations is a serious one. As a longitudinal study continues, participants are lost due to death and to refusal, typically such that the remaining participants become increasingly less representative of the initial longitudinal study population. These effects have been reported for many longitudinal studies including the Hamburg studies (Riegel and Riegel, 1972; Riegel et al., 1967, 1968), Schaie's longitudinal study (Baltes et al., 1971; Schaie, 1979), and previously in the Duke studies (Siegler, 1983; Siegler and Botwinick, 1979). In general, selective subject attrition leads to an underestimate of developmental change in longitudinal studies, because participants who are generally less able on cognitive and intellectual measures are those who drop out of the study. To the extent that the dropout is due primarily to death of the participants, then performance of those closer to death may be impaired in relation to that of their longer-lived counterparts (Siegler, 1975). Baltes (1968) makes a distinction between selective survival and selective dropout. Selective survival refers both to the populations of cohorts under study and the particular sample in any longitudinal investigation, whereas selective dropout applies only to the particular longitudinal sample of interest. Selective survival becomes particularly problematical if there is reason to believe that successive cohorts are subject to different underlying mechanisms that would lead to differential survival, as may be the case in the modification of risk factors for cardiovascular disease. Selective dropout may represent factors related to the willingness of individuals to participate in a study which generally has a positive selection bias; it may also be related to factors in the experimental situation and management of a particular longitudinal study that make it unlikely that continued participation rates will be high. In the Duke First Longitudinal Study, care was taken to reduce experimental mortality due to factors within the laboratory or because of problems in transportation or scheduling.

As Horn and Donaldson (1980) illustrate, pure longitudinal designs are most likely to be affected by such biases. Thus, in the following report, the initial group of participants were evaluated in terms of their repeated participation in order to assess selective attrition and in terms of their initial scores as a function of distance from death. Terminal drop is not evaluated in this paper, since a majority of the individuals in the third distance from death group (≥ fourteen years) are still alive.

Kaszniak et al. (1978) evaluated the relationships among neuropsychological test performance, cerebral atrophy, and electroencephalograph (EEG) abnor-

Reprinted with adaptations by permission from *Journal of Gerontology*, 37:176–181, 1982.

malities in a group of forty-seven older patients (aged 52 to 88, M = 71.5) with dementia. The neuropsychological test battery was extensive and included form I of the WMS. At the end of one year, nineteen patients were still alive, sixteen had died and twelve were lost to follow-up. Neither demographic variables (age, education, sex, and race), CAT-scan measures of cerebral atrophy, nor historical data about the length of the dementing disorder discriminated between survivors and nonsurvivors. In addition, the demographic variables did not discriminate among survivors, nonsurvivors, and those lost to follow-up. Only the categorical rating of the EEG and neuropsychological test performance significantly discriminated between survivors and nonsurvivors. The survivors had primarily normal or mild diffuse slow EEG patterns, while the nonsurvivors had predominately severe diffuse slowing or left-temporal slowing. Visual reproduction and paired associate learning, but not logical memory, significantly discriminated survivors from nonsurvivors. The neuropsychological test variables were then included in a discriminant analysis in order to predict survival status. All three WMS variables made significant contributions to the discriminant function, which correctly classified 97.14 percent of the patients. While the Kaszniak et al. (1978) patients were all demented, they were similar to the longitudinal study population in demographic categories (age, race, and sex); the interesting comparison is, then, whether the WMS is related to distance from death in a nondemented sample.

Method

The participants and general procedures used in the administration of the WMS are described in the preceding paper. In the analysis presented in this paper, a verbal memory score was calculated by summing individual performance on the logical memory subtests (immediate/delayed) and on the paired associates (easy/hard) subtest. This verbal memory score was calculated to provide a comparison with the verbal section of the Wechsler Adult Intelligence Scale (WAIS) verbal score.

A subset of 160 participants was used in the analyses that looked at distance from death at the first time of measurement. Only individuals with complete data on the WMS and complete data on the WAIS were used in this analysis. Because of the importance of the level of formal education, as shown in the preceding paper, the known importance of level of formal education on the WAIS (Birren and Morrison, 1961), had the relationship between age and probability of survival, the age and educational levels of groups of subjects within seven years of death, were evaluated first, then those within eight to thirteen years of death, and then those within fourteen or more years of death. The distances from death were so categorized as to provide for approximately equal numbers of individuals in each group. An analysis of variance was then performed in order to test group differences.

Results

Two issues are of importance descriptively about the first longitudinal study sample population: the degree of dementia in the study population and the participation patterns. As the longitudinal study was multidisciplinary, data are available about the psychiatric status of the participants. For a fuller explanation of the psychiatric profile of the sample see Gianturco and Busse (1978). All study participants were seen individually by a psychiatrist, and their mental status was rated on the basis of a structured interview. While the coding scheme changed slightly across examinations, all participants could be rated as not demented or mild, moderate, or severe dementia at each examination. Of the twenty-six who were tested for the full sixteen years and who had complete data at each testing, one individual was rated as mildly demented at the tenth examination only; of the fifty-three individuals who were tested through the ten-year period, two received ratings of dementia, one at the first examination, and one at the fourth examination; of the 116 individuals seen over a four-year period, two were rated mildly demented at the first examination. In no case did the ratings of dementia persist for more than one examination. At the second examination, 172 of the 183 who were seen had completed WMS scores. All 183 were evaluated for presence of dementia; eighteen individuals had ratings of at least mild dementia. Of these, eleven did not have complete data on the WMS and seven did. Thus, it is reasonable to conclude that the sample evaluated in this study was reasonably free of dementia.

The WMS was added to the longitudinal test battery at the second examination in 1960, approximately five years after the start of the study. The degree of attrition from the sample was large, especially in the psychological area, as these tests were the most difficult. In 1955, at the start of the study, the original panel included 270 individuals. Of these, 267 had psychological data and 246 had complete data on the WAIS. At the second examination in 1960, 195 were seen; 184 had complete WAIS data, 172 had complete WMS data, and 160 had complete data on both WMS and WAIS. Of those not seen at the second examination, 44 percent ($N = 33$) refused and 56 percent died ($N = 42$). Over the course of the study, the percentage of those alive but not seen ranged from 15 percent to 20 percent of the sample (including those who had moved away). The proportion of deaths increased linearly, so that at the final measurement point in 1976, 95 percent (212) of those not seen were due to deaths with 5 percent (eleven) alive but not seen. These patterns reflect considerable attrition leading to the initial sample for the current analysis.

Selective attrition. In order to evaluate the impact of repeated participation, the initial scores for individuals tested at the first measurement point for the WMS (wave 2) were plotted as a function of the number of times of sequential participation. These results are presented in figure C—9.

As can be seen from figure C—9, the impact of selective attrition is particularly severe for the older cohort of individuals for the verbal memory scores

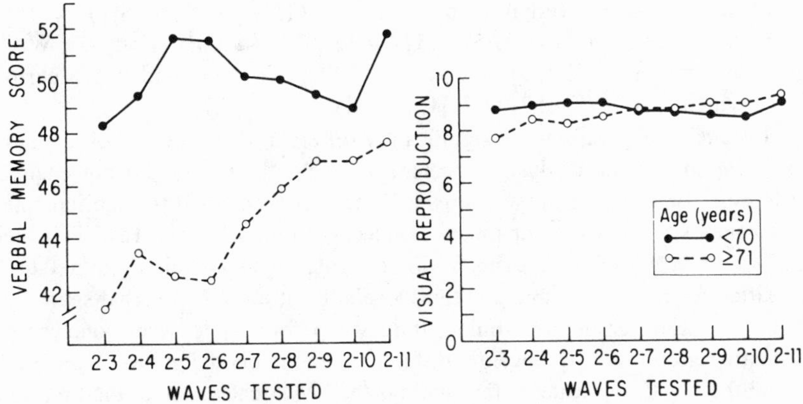

Figure C—9. *Wechsler Memory Scale scores at wave 2 as a function of survival in the study. (The verbal memory score is the sum of logical memory and associate learning.)*

throughout the study and for the young cohort for the first ten years of the study. This attrition would suggest that some of the observed change in performance in the verbal memory subtests may be underestimated, given that those who remain are among the higher scoring ones initially. An examination of the visual reproduction graph indicates that this measure appears not to be affected by selective attrition. Thus, the changes seen with time in visual reproduction are more accurate reflections of the performance of the total initial sample.

Distance from death. In order to evaluate distance from death, the 160 individuals with data on both WMS and WAIS in 1960 were categorized into three groups on the basis of the distance from death at that measurement point. The intervals were chosen to be of approximately equal width and to include approximately equal numbers of individuals. Group 1 included fifty-nine individuals with a mean age of 75.63 (SD = 7.04) and a mean level of formal education of 9.56 years (SD = 5.75); 42 percent of the group was black. The individuals in group 1 died within seven years of testing. Group 2, which was eight to thirteen years from death, included fifty persons. The mean age was 78.13 (SD = 4.92) and the educational attainment mean was 10.40 (SD = 2.82); 44 percent of this group was black. The third group included fifty-one individuals, whose mean age was 69.33 (SD = 4.23). The mean level of education was 11.35 years (SD = 5.56); 43 percent of the group was black. These individuals either died fourteen or more years after testing or were alive in 1981, with a range of fourteen to twenty-one years. The groups were balanced as to size and as to racial composition. The age and education distributions were tested by ANOVA. The age effect was significant, $F(2,157) = 17.28$, $p < .001$, $\omega^2 = .16$, while the education effect was not, $F(2,157) = 1.35$, $p > .05$. Scores for the years-to-death groups on the WMS and the WAIS are shown in table C—9 and figure C—10. The results of the ANOVAs indicated that distance from death was significantly related to all four variables: verbal memory score, $F(2,157) = 8.68$, $p < .001$, $\omega^2 = .08$; visual reproduction, $F(2,157) = 12.37$, $p < .001$, $\omega^2 = .07$; WAIS verbal scaled score, $F(2,157) = 4.97$, $p < .001$, $\omega^2 = .04$; and WAIS performance scaled score, $F(2,157) = 7.34$, $p < .001$, $\omega^2 = .07$.

Because the groups were significantly different as a function of age, age was covaried and the analyses repeated; however, the results did not change. MANOVAs on both the initial scores and the scores covaried for age indicated significant *F*s. Post-hoc comparisons (Duncan's Multiple Range Test) indicated that for both WMS scores and the WAIS performance only the first group (0 to 7) was different from the second and third levels (8+); for WAIS verbal score, the first group was different only from the third group (fourteen to twenty-one years), and neither group was significantly different from the middle group. These findings on the WAIS replicate earlier findings the WAIS calculated at the first time of measurement (Siegler, 1983) and also indicate that the WMS scores are reliable indicators of distance from death. Thus in a healthy nondemented group of older persons, the WMS appears to be related to distance from death, indicating the initial superiority of the scores of those who are the longer-term survivors.

Selective survival and distance from death vary as a function of the type of memory assessed. For verbal memory, continued, repeated participation was shown to be related to initially higher levels of verbal memory as seen in table C—9, which was the case with distance-from-death picture for verbal memory, as seen in figure C—10. The pattern for visual reproduction was discrepant. Initial scores were not related to repeated, continued participation, whereas there was a significant relationship between visual reproduction and distance from death.

The differences may also reflect the underlying patterns of change reported by McCarty et al. (1982) for these data. The verbal memory score is the sum of logical memory and paired associate learning. As indicated in the preceding

Table C—9. *Mean memory scores as a function of years to death.*

		WAIS		WMS	
Years to death	*N*	Verbal score	Performance score	Verbal score[a]	Visual reproduction
0 to 7	59	50.66	24.41	35.51	6.10
		(20.38)	(12.73)	(17.59)	(3.04)
8 to 13	50	57.88	29.30	43.44	8.04
		(18.43)	(11.65)	(14.07)	(2.76)
14 or more	51	62.67	33.22	48.41	8.84
		(21.51)	(11.74)	(17.1[illegible])	(3.13)

Note: Standard deviations are in parentheses.

[a]The verbal memory score is the sum of logical memory and associate learning.

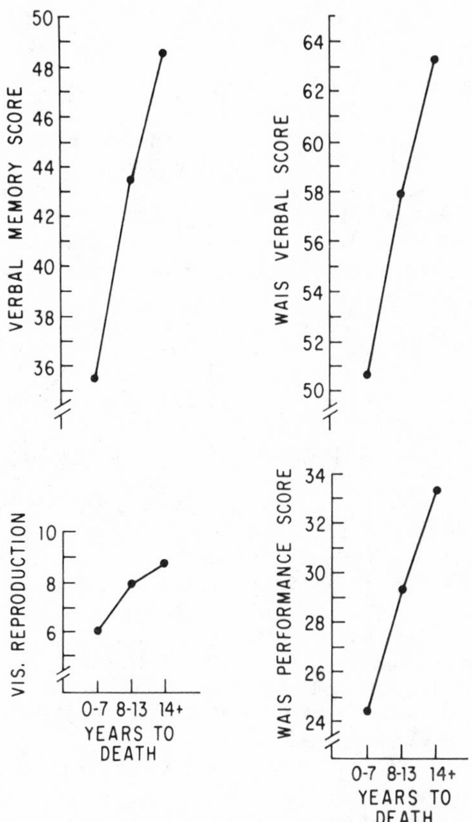

Figure C—10. *Mean Wechsler Memory Scale and WAIS scores by years to death at wave 2. (The verbal memory score is the sum of logical memory and associate learning.)*

paper, there were no significant changes over the course of the study on immediate recall, delayed recall, and easy paired associates. Furthermore, when assessed through the sixth time of measurement, there were significant increases in performance on both components of logical memory. This suggests that through the first ten years of testing, a practice effect may have been operative for logical memory. It is, however, difficult to argue that if this were causal that it would not also operate to reduce the significant declines on hard paired associates, which were observed in the same individuals at the same times of measurement. The pattern for visual reproduction declined consistently across the entire study, with a pattern similar to that observed for hard paired associates.

The results of this study, in conjunction with the preceding paper, argue for the potential use of the WMS scale as a predictor of survival in normal as well as demented populations.

References

Baltes, P. B. Longitudinal and cross-sectional sequences in the study of age and generation effects. *Human Development*, 11:145–171, 1968.

Baltes, P. B., Schaie, K. W., and Nardi, A. H. Age and experimental mentality in a seven-year longitudinal study of cognitive behavior. *Developmental Psychology*, 5:18–26, 1971.

Birren, J. E., and Morrison, D. F. Analysis of the WAIS subtests in relation to age and education. *Journal of Gerontology*, 16:363–369, 1961.

Gianturco, D. T., and Busse, E. W. Psychiatric problems encountered during a long-term study of normal aging volunteers. In A. D. Isaacs and F. Post (Eds.), *Studies in geriatric psychiatry*. New York: Wiley, 1978.

Horn, J. L., and Donaldson, G. Cognitive development in adulthood. In O. G. Brim and J. Kagan (Eds.), *Constancy and change in human development*. Cambridge, Mass.: Harvard University Press, 1980.

Kaszniak, A. W., et al. Predictors of mortality in presenile and senile dementia. *Annals of Neurology*, 3:246–252, 1978.

McCarty, S. M., Siegler, I. C., and Logue, P. E. Cross-sectional and longitudinal patterns of three Wechsler Memory Scale subtests. *Journal of Gerontology*, 37:169–175, 1982.

Riegel, K. F., and Riegel, R. M. Development, drop, and death. *Developmental Psychology*, 6: 309–316, 1972.

Riegel, K. F., Riegel, R. M., and Meyer, G. A study of the drop-out rates in longitudinal research on aging and the prediction of death. *Journal of Personality and Social Psychology*, 4:342–348, 1967.

Riegel, K. F., Riegel, R. M., and Meyer, G. The prediction of retest-resisters in longitudinal research on aging. *Journal of Gerontology*, 23:370–374, 1968.

Schaie, K. W. The primary mental abilities in adulthood: An exploration in the development of psychometric intelligence. In P. B. Baltes and O. G. Brim (Eds.), *Life-span development and behavior*, Vol. 2. New York: Academic, 1979.

Siegler, I. C. The terminal drop hypothesis: Fact or artifact? *Experimental Aging Research*. 1:169–185, 1975.

Siegler, I. C. Psychological aspects of the Duke longitudinal studies. In K. W. Schaie (Ed.), *Longitudinal studies of psychological development in adulthood*. New York: Guilford Press, 1983, 136–189.

Siegler, I. C., and Botwinick, J. A. A long-term longitudinal study of intellectual ability of older adults: The matter of selective attrition. *Journal of Gerontology*, 34:242–245, 1979.

Mental Performance in the Young-Old versus the Old-Old

Ilene C. Siegler

Neugarten (1975) introduced the concept of thinking of older persons as young-old versus old-old as particularly helpful for policy reasons. In this paper we are

Paper presented in a symposium at the XIIth International Congress of Gerontology, Hamburg, Federal Republic of Germany, July 1981.

concerned with consistency and change in cognitive performance within these two large groups of older persons. Those in cohorts currently aged fifty-five to seventy-four and those aged seventy-five and older *do* form distinct groups on the basis of sociodemographic and health characteristics. For example, Uhlenberg (1979) evaluated the characteristics of cohorts becoming elderly. In the United States in 1975, the mean number of years of schooling for those over age sixty-five who died in 1975 was 8.9 years, while the mean level of education for those who became sixty-five was 10.5 years. Changes in the level of formal education of older cohorts should have an impact on their measured levels of cognitive and intellectual performance as well.

With random samples of older persons from the general population, we would expect that similar findings would occur, that is that the young-old group would be expected to score higher and have a better maintenance of functioning than the old-old group. However, when we switch to a consideration of data from longitudinal aging studies, the predictions need to be modified to take into account some of the special characteristics of older persons who participate in experimental research, especially the long-term surviving participants.

Data from a variety of studies in the United States and in Germany (e.g., Lehr and Schmitz-Scherzer, 1976; Riegel and Riegel, 1972; Schaie, 1979) indicates that there is a positive bias toward enhanced performance for those individuals who participate in longitudinal research which may underestimate the decline assumed to be occurring in the general population. As the requirements for continued participation become more stringent, this pattern can be seen to intensify (Siegler and Botwinick, 1979). The retest and sequential participation effects can be controlled with designs, such as those suggested by Schaie, which use random samples from the same cohorts. Such analyses suggest that declines in intellectual abilities are generally more severe, although different for different component abilities.

However, within the context of traditional longitudinal studies, some interesting comments can be made about the cognitive abilities of the young-old and the old-old, as long as the special nature of these study populations is taken into consideration. The analyses presented here look at the observed stability and change in three different measures of cognitive performance.

Methods

At the first time of measurement, the Wechsler Adult Intelligence Scale (WAIS) was the only measure of cognitive functioning. At the second examination, 1959–61, three subtests from the Wechsler Memory Scale and a reaction time task were added. Three measures from each test are used in the analyses presented here:

WAIS	*Wechsler memory*	*Reaction time*
Verbal scaled score	Paired associate language	Decision (lift)
Performance scaled score	Logical memory	Motor (press)
Total scaled score	Visual reproduction	Total time

While these are not "cognitive" measures in the sense of experimental cognitive psychology research traditions, they do represent a sampling of intellectual and cognitive processes that allowed a meaningful examination of the issues.

Individuals were aged fifty-nine to ninety-six at the first time of measurement. While the data are somewhat "old" for the young-old group, three groups were identified for analysis.

Young-old$_1$: Subjects initially aged 59–69, seen waves 1–5 (1955–68)
Old-old$_1$: Subjects initially aged 70–96, seen waves 1–5
Old-old$_2$: Subjects from the initial young-old cohort, seen waves 6–11 (1970–76)

On the basis of the identification described above, the resulting groups formed the basis for the analysis:

Group	*Mean ages across measurement interval*	*N*
YO$_1$	65.5—76.9 (Waves 1–5)/69.1—77.3 (Waves 2–5)	46/38
OO$_1$	74.0—85.6 (Waves 1–5)/77.4—85.9 (Waves 2–5)	26/23
OO$_2$	78.4—85.6 (Waves 6–11)	19

Of particular interest are comparisons of the two OO groups. While they cover the same age range, the OO$_2$ group contains individuals from later birth cohorts, who also had full participation in the study across an additional five waves of measurement.

Review of Findings

When the young-old were compared to the old-old cohorts at the same time of measurement, of the nine different indices of cognitive performance, the only significant difference was for logical memory. The logical memory subtest required that the individual remember "thought units" from a paragraph. This is the sum of their performance immediately after hearing each of two paragraphs, and then recalling the paragraphs after a delay of half an hour, in which their hearing was tested. There was not a significant age by time of measurement interaction.

The second consideration is the change observed over time, which was thirteen years for the WAIS measures and eight years for the memory and reaction time measures. When the young-old and the old-old cohorts are analyzed across the first five times of measurements, we find significant time differences for all three WAIS components, where the trend was for declines in all three components over the thirteen year (figure C—11) period. For the logical memory subtest of the WMS, memory for the paragraphs increased at the second time of measurement then declined thereafter, with the final measurement point at about the same as the starting performance, suggesting a significant curvilinear trend across time. Total (RT) reaction time was stable across the eight-year time pe-

Table C—10. *Summary of effects.*

Variable	YO vs. OO[a]	Time	AC × T	Educ. cov.[b]	Trends	Time-lag[c]	"Age"	T × A
Verb SS (1–5)	—	*	—	$B = 2.52$*	1,q,–	—	—	—
Verb SS (6–11)	na	*	na		–,q,c			
Perf SS (1–5)	—	*	—	$B = 1.33$*	1,–,c	—	*	—
Perf SS (6–11)	na	*	—		1,–,–			
Tot SS (1–5)	—	*	—	$B = 3.85$*	1,–,–	—	*	—
Tot SS (6–11)	na	*	—		1,q,c			
Stor. (2–5)	*	*	—	$B = .79$*	–,q,c	—	—	*
Stor. (6–11)	na	*	na					
PAL (2–5)	—	—	—	$B = .27$*		—	—	—
PAL (6–11)	na	—	na					
PIC (2–5)	—	—	—	$B = .30$*		—	*	—
PIC (6–11)	na	*	na		1,–,–,q			
LiftRT (2–5)	—	*	—	$B = -.700$*	1,–,–	—	—	*
LiftRT (6–11)	na	*			1,q,–			
PressRT (2–5)	—	*	—	$B = -.806$*	1,q,c	—	—	—
PressRT (6–11)	na	—	—					
RT (2–5)	—	—	—	$B = -1.567$*		—	—	—
RT (6–11)	na	*	na		1,–,–			

[a] YO = cohort 1 time 1, 2–5 vs. OO_1 cohort 2 time 1, 2–5. OO_2 = Cohort 2, time 6–11.

[b] Covariate always statistically significant relationship to variable. Never changed results analysis.

[c] Age constant at 81, 84, 86 years with $cohort_2$ (OO_1) times 3, 4, 5 and $cohort_2$ (OO_2) times 7, 9, 11.

riod. This is because the decision time significantly decreased, while the motor time significantly increased, over the times of measurement.

The initial survivors of the younger cohort, who completed the remaining six visits of the study, were then evaluated across time. These measurement intervals were approximately one year apart and covered 1970–76. The mean ages of this group of nineteen subjects went from 78.4 years to 84.6 years of age. This is of course a very select group from within the already select longitudinal study population. Here we see the greatest change on six of the nine indices. On the WAIS, for the verbal and the full scale scaled scores, the level of maintenance of function was maintained until the final measurement point and then it declined precipitously (figure C—11). The change on the performance subtests was more linear. Stability was maintained on logical memory and paired associate learning on the WMS, with a decline in performance on the visual reproduction subtests of the WMS. The decision RT significantly increased at the final measurement point, as did the total RT. While a trend was apparent for the motor RT, it was not large enough to reach statistical significance.

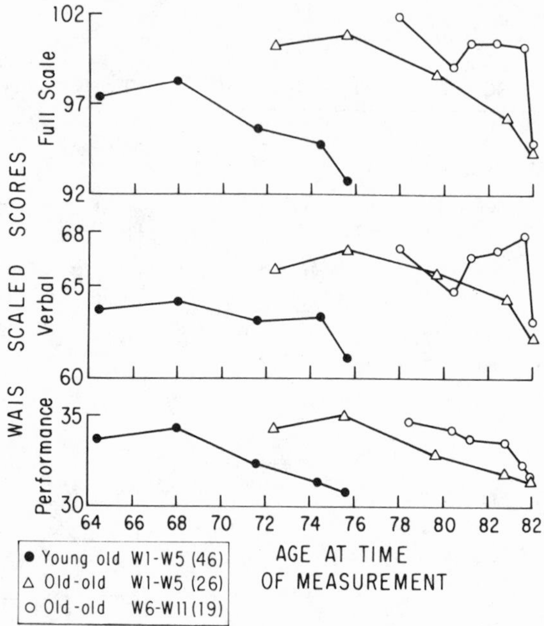

Figure C—11. *WAIS scaled scores by age and cohort.*

Although the study was not designed with the cross-sequential model in mind, it is possible to make some additional comparisons which hold age constant by varying cohort and time of measurement (time lag). The between-subject factor then becomes a combination of cohort/time of measurement. The younger cohort, initially aged sixty to sixty-nine has values in the analysis from the seventh, ninth, and eleventh times of measurement. The older cohort initially aged over seventy, has values in the analysis from the third, fourth, and fifth times of measurement. For both groups, the mean ages of observation are eighty-one, eighty-four, and eighty-six years of age.

None of the between-subject differences (cohorts and different times of measurement) was significant. However, there were significant differences observed, which replicated across the cohorts and times of measurement for performance and total IQ and for visual reproduction. In all cases, the trend was towards higher performance among the younger cohort (those with additional practice by the same age). Verbal IQ, paired associate learning, motor, and total RT were all stable in these analyses.

On two of the variables there were significant interactions: recall of the stories and decision reaction time. On the stories, the older cohort tested at the waves 3–5 had a decline, whereas the younger cohort at the later waves had an increase. The pattern was reversed for decision RT.

Thus, even when holding age constant, superior performance was found in the group which has had more practice on the tests and is more "elite" in terms of participation survival but equivalent in terms of survival in years since birth.

Summary

When we put this set of analyses together, what then can we say about constancy and change in cognitive performance in the young-old versus the old-old? First, that when dealing with select longitudinal subjects, the type of distinction proposed by Neugarten, which suggests better performance in the young-old than the old-old, does not hold up. These results suggest that in our study group the old-old are by and large not significantly different from their young-old counterparts. In general, the mean levels of the old-old groups at the same times of measurement are higher, though not significantly so. Second, that, when controlling for actual age in the time-lag analysis, those individuals who have greater participation survival, and with it increased practice on the measures used, also do better than their similarly aged peers. Third, that when the cognitive variables in the longitudinal study are looked at as a set, they show differential patterns of stability and change. Fourth, that when educational attainment was used as a covariate in the analyses, the *beta* weights indicated that the relationship between level of formal education and the score on each measure was statistically significant, which suggests that future cohorts of older persons may perform at predictably higher levels, as the level of formal education of future elderly increases.

References

Lehr, U., and Schmitz-Scherzer, R. Survivors and non-survivors. Two fundamental patterns of aging. In H. Thomae (Ed.), *Patterns of aging*. Basel: S. Karger, 1976.

Neugarten, B. L. The future and the young old. *Gerontologist*, 15:4–9, 1975.

Riegel, K. F., and Riegel, R. M. Development, drop, and death. *Developmental Psychology*, 6:306–319, 1972.

Schaie, K. W. The primary mental ability in adulthood: An exploration in the development of psychometric intelligence. In P. B. Baltes and O. G. Brim (Eds.), *Lifespan development and behavior*. Vol. 2. New York: Academic, 1979.

Siegler, I. C., and Botwinick, J. A long-term longitudinal study of intellectual ability of older adults: The matter of selective attrition. *Journal of Gerontology*, 34:242–245, 1979.

Uhlenberg, P. Demographic changes in problems of the aged. In M. W. Riley (Ed.), *Aging from birth to death*. Boulder, Colo.: Westview, 1979.

Longitudinal Comparisons of WAIS Factor Analyses

Ilene C. Siegler and Jack Botwinick

Introduction

A variety of factor analytic studies of the WAIS have appeared over the years that have suggested multidimensionality in the WAIS performances. Matarazzo (1972) summarized this literature, indicating that most studies report a large general first factor representing general intelligence (or Spearman's "g") and three additional factors with small loadings of a few of the subtests. The three small factors are named variants of verbal comprehension, perceptual organization, and memory/freedom from distractibility.

Cross-sectional studies indicate a similarity in the factor structure across the age ranges of eighteen–nineteen to sixty–seventy-five years. Similar findings have been replicated with confirmatory factor analysis (Spiro, 1979). In a now classic study, Birren and Morrison (1961) reported four similar factors with the WAIS standardization group (Dopplet and Wallace, 1955) and pointed to the importance of education, rather than age, as a major explanatory variable.

In the present study, effort is made to determine whether the WAIS factor structure is also invariant when examined longitudinally. The subjects tested were select in that: (1) their age range was sixty–eighty years, (2) their education levels were not related to age of the subject and (3) they were survivors in the longitudinal study, both in terms of life and health and in being examined up to five times over a fourteen-year period. Note that such survivors constitute an unrepresentative sample in that they are intellectually superior at the start of the study (see Siegler and Botwinick, 1979).

Would the WAIS factor structure based on these select survivors in longitudinal studies be the same as cross-sectional studies of more randomly selected subjects? Would the WAIS factor structure in longitudinal age comparison be the same when information of time before death is part of the analysis? Time before death is known to be related to WAIS performance (see Siegler, McCarty, and Logue, 1982).

Method

Subjects. All were participants in the Duke First Longitudinal Study. Individuals were selected so that their test data were complete at the following three times of measurement: time 1 (1955–59), time 2 (1960), and time 3 (1968). Time 3 represents the fifth time of measurement for these subjects, as detailed below.

Analyses. A series of principal components analyses was carried out with

Table C—11. *Results of analyses with various subsets of the data.*

Subtest	Time 1 1957 *N* = 253	Time 2 1960 *N* = 173	Time 2 1960 *N* = 76	Time 3 1968 *N* = 76	Time 3 1968 *N* = 89
Information	.905	.901	.897	.888	.891
Comprehension	.878	.877	.860	.848	.852
Arithmetic	.854	.836	.804	.847	.853
Similarities	.880	.874	.879	.907	.902
Digit span	.696	.674	.606	.766	.752
Vocabulary	.903	.884	.874	.910	.917
Digit symbol	.857	.877	.878	.867	.882
Picture compl	.869	.848	.833	.849	.865
Block design	.801	.815	.814	.796	.822
Picture arr	.819	.809	.764	.813	.796
Object assemb	.768	.698	.660	.758	.767
Lambda	7.780	7.574	7.240	7.804	7.890
Variance	70.8%	68.6%	65.8%	70.9%	71.7%

the eigenvalue criterion set to 1.0. All eigenvalues that met the criterion were rotated with varimax rotation and were calculated according to the program FACTOR in SAS (SAS Institute, 1979). Such analyses were carried out with the data of testing times 1, 2, and 3.

Variables. The factor analyses were carried out with the following different variables in combination: (1) the eleven WAIS subtests only; (2) eleven WAIS subtests plus age, sex, and race; (3) eleven WAIS subtests plus age, sex, race, and education; and (4) eleven subtests, age, sex, and race plus time before death (TBD) (see Siegler, McCarty, and Logue, 1982).

Results

The WAIS Alone

When the eleven subtests alone were factor analyzed, only one factor emerged. This was true for the analyses which included all subjects with complete data at the first time of testing (*N* = 253), complete data at the second test period (*N* = 173), complete data at the third test period (*N* = 89), and for the special subset of respondents who had complete data at both the second and third testings (*N* = 76 at each measurement point). In these five analyses the eigenvalues ranged from 7.24 to 7.89; the proportion of total variance accounted for by the single factor ranged from 65.8 percent of variance to 71.7 percent of variance; and the loadings ranged from a low of .61 to a high of .95. These results, shown in table C—11, are different from most of the studies reported by Matarazzo in that the three smaller factors were not indicated in the present data.

The WAIS and Sociodemographic Variables

When sociodemographic variables were added, a two-factor solution resulted but a unifactor structure of the WAIS was indicated nevertheless. The main variables added to the analyses were age, sex, race, and education. These variables formed their own second factor. Those subtests which were represented on this factor were more highly represented on the first one. As seen in table C—12, age was not represented on the first general cognitive factor, only on the second demographic factor. Table C—12 shows the results of this analysis, based on all of the subjects with complete data at the first time of measurement. The second factor, while having seven loadings that were larger than .20, nonetheless adds less than 1 percent to the variance explained.

The WAIS and Time Before Death

Table C—13 shows the same analysis as table C—12 for all subjects at time 1 who had died by 1979, replacing education with time before death. As the various analyses in table C—11 indicated, there were few differences due to subject selection, dropout, or survival and repeated measures.

The analyses with time before death resulted in a three-factor solution. The first factor once again was a "g" factor; neither age nor sex was associated with g. Age was represented, along with time before death, on a second factor. Only

Table C—12. *Factor analysis of the WAIS subtests and demographic factors. (Time 1,* N = *252)*

	Factor 1	Factor 2
Age		−.623
Sex		.773
Race	−.465	.260
Educ	.813	
Info	.920	
Comp	.878	
Arith	.865	
Sim	.871	
Dig sp	.661	.335
Vocab	.906	
Dig sym	.847	.219
Pic com	.869	
B ds	.783	.223
Pic arr	.814	
Obj ass	.746	.209
Lambda	8.59	1.37
Cum var	66.28%	66.42%

Table C—13. *Factor analysis of the WAIS subtests and demographic factors with time before death. (Time 1,* N = *213, all dead by 1979)*

	Factor 1	Factor 2	Factor 3
Age		−.885	
Sex	.950		
Race	−.534		
Educ	na	na	na
TBD	.200	.712	.205
Info	.918		
Comp	.856		
Arith	.829		−.265
Sim	.858		
Dig sp	.619	.296	
Vocab	.906		
Dig sym	.792	.370	
Pic com	.856		
B ds	.775		.254
Pic arr	.808		
Obj ass	.733	.219	
Lambda	7.68	1.67	1.62
Cum var	70.23%	70.25%	70.80%

three subtests loaded on this factor, with digit symbol showing the highest contribution and with arithmetic and block design showing less. Even here, however, digit symbol had a loading of only .37 when the loading was .79 on the first factor. Sex of subject was the only variable on the third factor whose loading was greater than on the first two factors. With each of the two factors accounting for less than 1 percent of the variance, these results suggest that the unifactor solution is for all practical purposes correct.

These results together, based on very select subjects, are not in agreement with a part of the literature of the WAIS factor structure. These results show a strong single general intelligence factor with no specific factors such as verbal comprehension and memory. These results are compatible, however, with the literature showing invariant factor structures over time. In this study, time was a longitudinal comparison; in the literature, time was a cross-sectional comparison. Also compatible with the literature (supporting the results of Birren and Morrison) is our finding that age was not important in regard to the general intelligence factor, but that education was very important.

References

Birren, J. E., and Morrison, D. F. Analysis of the WAIS subtests in relation to age and education. *Journal of Gerontology*, 16:363–369, 1961.

Dopplet, J. E., and Wallace, W. L. Standardization of the Wechsler Adult Intelligence Scale for older persons. *Journal of Abnormal and Social Psychology*, 51:312–330, 1955.
Matarazzo, J. *Wecshler's measurement and appraisal of adult intelligence*. 5th Ed. New York: Oxford University Press, 1972.
SAS Institute, *SAS User's Guide*. Raleigh, N.C.: SAS Institute, 1979.
Siegler, I. C., and Botwinick, J. A long-term study of intellectual ability of older adults: The matter of selective subject attrition. *Journal of Gerontology*, 34:242–245, 1979.
Siegler, I. C., McCarty, S. M., and Logue, P. E. Wecshler memory scale scores, selective attrition and distance from death. *Journal of Gerontology*, 37:176–181, 1982.
Spiro, A. Age differences in ability structure: A confirmatory factor analysis of the WAIS. Paper presented at the meeting of the Gerontological Society, Washington, D.C., November 1979.

Personality, Dropout, and Death

Michele J. Rusin and Ilene C. Siegler

Longitudinal studies are the major way in which developmental change can be assessed. However, as subject dropout by death and refusal is not a random process, it is important to understand its effects. Studies of cognitive and attitudinal variables have shown that those who refuse to continue as research subjects tend to be less intelligent and more rigid than those who do continue to participate (Riegel, Riegel, and Meyer, 1968; Baltes, Schaie, and Nardi, 1971). Riegel and Riegel (1972) observed that refusers were more likely to die within the following five-year period when compared to continuing participants.

When sociological dimensions are examined, it is found that refusers from longitudinal aging studies are less likely to be married (Maddox, 1962), members of the lower social class (Streib, 1966; Atchley, 1969), in poorer health (Maddox, 1962; Atchley, 1969), and more socially isolated (Cumming and Henry, 1961; Atchley, 1969) than continuing participants. A high self-esteem accompanied by a denial of old age is also noted among refusers. Siegler (1973) found that those who refused to participate in the second wave of a national survey were similar to participants on measures of life satisfaction, morale, and health but were low on measures of social interaction.

Personality measures have been examined in a longitudinal study of adolescents. It was found that refusers were more independent than participants; no other factors were significant in discriminating the two groups (Nesselroade and Baltes, 1973). Since so little is known about personality factors involved in dropout among older subjects, the following study was undertaken to detect and examine personality differences between participants and dropouts, both refusals and deaths, in a middle-aged sample.

Paper presented at the annual meeting of the Gerontological Society, Louisville, Ky., 1975.

Method

Subjects. The Duke Second Longitudinal Study began in 1968 with 261 male and 241 female subjects ranging in age from forty-five to sixty-nine years. Of the 502 subjects who were originally seen, 443 subjects returned for retesting in round 2. In round 3, 392 subjects were seen, leaving a group of 110 dropouts six years after the study began. Personality data were available for 381 participants and 104 dropouts.

Measure. Personality was assessed by form C of the Cattell Sixteen Personality Factor Inventory. Except for cases of extreme reading difficulty, the test was self-administered. Analyses were based upon the round 1 sten scores for the combined population for the sixteen primary- and four second-order factors.

Analysis. When the 16 PF sten scores of participants and dropouts were compared, several significant differences were noted. We felt it would be appropriate to examine the dropout group more closely to determine whether reason for dropout was being reflected in the personality factors. After turning to notes of telephone conversations with the subjects at the time they decided to withdraw from the study, we classified the subjects into one of four groups, based upon the stated reason for dropout. Thus we had the following groups: (1) those who were too busy; (2) those who felt some negative affect toward the center or were uninterested; (3) those who were sick; and (4) those who had died. A comparison of the 16 PF sten scores for these groups by MANOVA failed to yield a significant overall multivariate *F*. Therefore, we placed all dropouts, regardless of reason for dropout, into one group. The data were analyzed by MANOVA for main effects for participation and sex and their interaction.

Results

To understand clearly what is occurring as subjects drop out of our original sample, it is necessary to obtain a picture of our total round 1 sample in terms of the twenty personality factors, to note the distribution of the dropout by age and sex, and, finally, to see what the dropout group looked like in comparison to the participants on the personality dimensions which were measured.

The total second longitudinal study group obtained a mean score within normal limits on fifteen of the twenty factors measured. They differed slightly (0.5 to 1 standard deviation from the mean) from the general population in the following ways: they were less intelligent, relatively sober, apprehensive, self-sufficient, and introverted (B^-, F^-, O^+, Q_2^+, Q_I^-). Our subjects also fit some sex stereotypes. The male subjects tended to be reserved, apprehensive, tough-minded, and self-sufficient (A^-, O^+, I^-, Q_2^+). Our females were more conforming, sensitive, forthright, dependent, and ruled by emotions (E^-, I^+, N^-, Q_{III}^+, Q_{IV}^-). Although the females also tended toward apprehension and self-sufficiency (O^+, Q_2^+), their scores were significantly lower than those of the males.

An examination of dropouts according to age and sex shows that they were

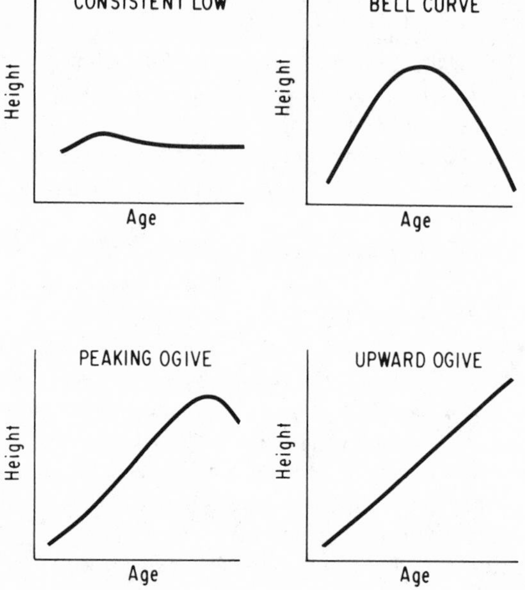

Figure C—12. *Personality differences between dropouts and participants.*

evenly distributed between the sexes and that dropout increased linearly with age. When the dropouts were separated into deaths and refusals, a different pattern is seen. Refusals distributed evenly across both ages and sexes. Deaths, however, increased linearly with age, and 75 percent of the deaths were males. The high number of deaths of the older subjects is responsible for the finding that the average dropout was older than the average participant.

Bearing in mind the previous baseline information on the total sample, let us proceed to a consideration of the personality differences between dropouts and participants. The main results are shown in figure C—12.

For both males and females we find that our subjects who dropped out were significantly ($p < .05$) more emotional, apprehensive, and tense (C^-, O^+, Q_4^+) than those who continued to participate. These factors cluster together to describe a dropout group which was more anxious ($p < .01$) than the participants. The sex/dropout interactions define more sharply the dropout profile. Males who dropped out tend to be aloof and self-sufficient. On the other hand, we find that the female dropouts tend to be even less intelligent than the sample population and they are conscientious and rule-bound. In a capsule, the male dropouts tended to be anxious and aloofly independent; the female dropouts tended to be anxious, dull, and inflexible.

Notice, however, that a large set of variables are unrelated to dropouts: nine primary, and three second-order factors. The personality constellations of introversion, ability to respond quickly, and independence (Q_I, Q_{III}, Q_{IV}), and the primary factors of assertiveness, seriousness, timidity, tender sensitivity, suspiciousness, practicality, shrewdness, conservativism, and self-control (E, F, H, I, L, M, N, Q_1, and Q_3) were not at all involved in the distinction of participants from dropouts.

Discussion

In relating our findings to the previous research in this area, we have found several discrepancies.

1. The dropout has characteristically been considered low in intelligence and high in rigidity. For this sample, this image is true only for the females, although the strong aloofness of the males may indicate a defensive sort of rigidity.

2. The Riegels have pointed to refusal as an indicator of imminent death; refusal does not predict death with our sample. Up to the present time, there have been forty-two deaths; of these, only six subjects (that is, 14 percent) ever refused to participate. This figure is similar to the overall refusal rate of 16 percent, that is, seventy-eight out of the original 502.

3. Siegler found cognitive and emotional differences between deaths and refusals. We could not make any distinction between deaths and refusals in the second longitudinal study. It is possible that such differences do exist but that they are not evident because there have not been enough deaths. Also, in the current analysis we are using scores from 1968, and many of the deaths occurred several years later.

The three discrepancies noted above may be due to differences between the samples which were studied. The earlier research focused upon death and refusal in a group which included some very old individuals, whereas the second longitudinal study sample is composed of middle-aged and "young-old" individuals. It is reasonable to expect that the fifty-year-old may respond differently from the eighty-year-old when death is near.

This study has more immediate implications for longitudinal research. Dropout is a serious complication in the search for developmental trends. For example, if we examined the scores on intelligence from round 1 to round 3, we would see that the mean group scores were increasing. One might be tempted to say that the subjects were growing more intelligent as they grew older if one did not realize that the less intelligent subjects were dropping out. One could, of course, examine the scores of subjects who had participated for all rounds of the study in order to search for trends. However, in this case the external validity is threatened, for the participants are representative of neither the original sample nor of the population.

The major finding of our study was that of significant anxiety among the dropouts. This anxiety was higher than the population norm, but not so high as to keep the subjects from participating in the first round and certainly not high enough to interfere with normal activities. Possibly the testing situation interacted with the anxiety proneness of these subjects, making the experience so unpleasant that they decided to drop out. The study format calls for neutral or slightly positive feedback to the subjects who inquire about their performance. Subjects often seemed dissatisfied with this feedback, however, and were seldom convinced that their performance was indeed good. Given the strain of the intellectual tests and the ambiguity of feedback, our anxious subjects may have suspected the worst and decided to withdraw.

References

Atchley, R. C. Respondents vs. refusers in an interview study of retired women: An analysis of selected characteristics. *Journal of Gerontology*, 24:42–47, 1969.

Baltes, P. B., Schaie, K. W., and Nardie, A. H. Age and experimental mortality in a seven-year longitudinal study of cognitive behavior. *Developmental Psychology*, 5:18–26, 1971.

Cumming, M. E., and Henry, W. E. *Growing old*. New York: Basic Books, 1961.

Maddox, G. L. A longitudinal multidisciplinary study of human aging: Selected methodological issues. *Proceedings, American Statistical Association, Social Statistics Section*, 1962, 280–285.

Nesselroade, J. R., and Baltes, P. B. A study of ontogenetic and generational change in adolescent personality by means of multivariate longitudinal sequences: Phase II: Final Report, USDHEW Grant #OEG-3-71-0113, Morgantown: West Virignia University, May 1973.

Riegel, K. F., and Riegel, R. M. Development, drop, and death. *Developmental Psychology*, 6: 306–309, 1972.

Riegel, K. F., Riegel, R. M., and Meyer, G. The prediction of retest-resistance in longitudinal research. *Journal of Gerontology*, 23:370–374, 1968.

Siegler, I. C. Threats to external validity: The effects of selective drop-out on health, morale, social relations and environmental circumstances in the elderly. Ph.D. diss., Syracuse University, 1973.

Streib, G. F. Participants and drop-outs in a longitudinal study. *Journal of Gerontology*, 21:200–209, 1966.

Cross-Sequential Analysis of Adult Personality

Ilene C. Siegler, Linda K. George, and Morris A. Okun

Longitudinal studies of adult personality suggest that both continuities and discontinuities are observed. Much of this work has focused upon the separation of age from cohort effects. Previous research suggests that cohort effects, the effects of the differential socialization of successive birth cohorts, account for more of the differences in adult personality than do changes with age (cf. Costa and McCrae, 1978; Schaie and Parham, 1976). These results have been based on

Reprinted by permission from *Developmental Psychology*, 15:350–351, 1979.

only two measurement points. Previous research also suggests that men and women exhibit somewhat different patterns of personality change (e.g., Maas and Kuypers, 1974; Schaie and Parham, 1976). The purpose of the present study is to evaluate cohort and time effects in personality in a longitudinal study with four measurement points and to determine whether these effects are equivalent for men and women.

Methods

The data in this study are part of the Duke Second Longitudinal Study. The analysis reported here is based on the 331 adults who had complete data on the personality measure.

Cohorts born between 1899 and 1922 were assessed four times over an eight-year period (1968–76). Data collection required about eighteen months for each wave. The majority of the adults were seen in 1969, 1971, 1973, and 1975. There were twelve two-year age cohorts. The youngest cohort was aged forty-six to forty-seven and the oldest cohort sixty-eight to sixty-nine in 1969. The study design does not permit the separation of age from cohort over all of the cohorts and ages of interest, as new samples from the cohorts were not taken at subsequent waves (see Schaie, 1977); thus the terms are used jointly.

Personality was assessed with form C, a shortened version of Cattell's 16 PF (Cattell, Eber, and Tatsouka, 1970; Institute for Personality and Ability, 1962). There are 105 items, and each factor is estimated on the responses to six items. The factors are measured in stens, a standard score with a mean of 5.5 and a standard deviation of 2. The reliability of form C, assessed by a one week retest, ranges on the sixteen scales from .32–.61 with an average scale reliability of .48. Thus, the relatively low test-retest correlation makes the separation of unreliability from true change more difficult.

The data were analyzed with a repeated measures analysis of variance design with twelve age cohorts, two sexes, and four times of measurement. Due to the large number of analyses, only F values significant beyond the .01 level are reported.

Results

Before presenting the results of the ANOVAs, it is important to consider two general measures of stability: the average cross-wave correlations and the standard deviations of the sample. The average cross-wave correlations were $r_{12} = .503$, $r_{23} = .501$, and $r_{34} = .510$. Thus these stability coefficients are at the same level as the short-term (one week) stabilities of the test. The average standard deviations across the four measurements were 1.91, 1.93, 1.95, and 1.94, slightly higher than the test but consistent across measurement intervals.

Significant main effects for cohort and for time were observed for factor B (intelligence). The oldest cohort had the lowest ($\bar{x} = 4.2$) and the youngest cohort had the highest ($\bar{x} = 5.6$). Across time, there was an increase in mean levels of factor *B* through the third measurement ($\bar{x}_{1-3} = 4.52, 4.74, 4.86$), with the fourth measurement ($\bar{x}_4 = 4.70$) at the same level as the second.

There were two significant interaction terms. There was a cohort by sex interaction for factor Q_1 (liberal versus conservative thinking). The greatest sex differences were observed for the oldest cohort (males, $\bar{x} = 5.9$; females, $\bar{x} = 5.6$). There was also a sex-by-time interaction observed for factor O (guilt-prone vs. confident). Over time, the mean level decreased for males (time 1, $\bar{x} = 6.6$; time 4, $\bar{x} = 6.2$) while the level increased for females (time 1, $\bar{x} = 6.3$; time 4, $\bar{x} = 6.6$).

Significant main effects for sex were observed on five factors: A (reserved versus outgoing), E (submissive versus dominant), I (toughminded versus tenderminded), N (naive versus shrewd), and Q_4 (relaxed versus tense). These sex differences were consistent across cohorts and time. Thus the females were relatively less reserved ($\bar{x} = 5.3$ versus 4.9), more submissive ($\bar{x} = 4.8$ versus 5.5), more tenderminded ($\bar{x} = 7.3$ vs. 4.2), more naive ($\bar{x} = 4.8$ versus 5.4), and more tense ($\bar{x} = 5.8$ versus 5.5).

Discussion

Overall, the results indicate little evidence of significant differences across cohorts, change over time, or their interaction. The strongest effects in the data were main effects for sex. The only main effects for cohort and time were on factor *B*. This is consistent with research in adult intelligence (cf., Botwinick, 1977), with other results on form C of the 16 PF with middle-aged and older adults (Botwinick and Storandt, 1974), and with data on more than 2,000 men aged twenty to eighty using forms A and B of the 16 PF (Costa and McCrae, 1978).

Gutmann (1975), on the basis of data from projective tests, argues that personality change in adulthood is mediated by sex differences. Here, only one trait, O, displayed a sex-by-time interaction; and only one trait, Q_1, a cohort-by-sex interaction. Five traits had significant main effects for sex, which tended to be in the sex-stereotyped direction and stable over time.

Schaie and Parham (1976) studied personality change in adults from twenty to eighty years of age using a trait approach, reporting more cohort effects than observed in the present study. They also reported consistent sex differences without interactions.

To date, the literature in adult personality makes it difficult to draw conclusions due to: (1) differences in instruments, (2) lack of replicability between paper-and-pencil and projective measures, and (3) the constraints in designing studies where age, cohort, and time of measurement can be estimated separately and replicated across both repeated measures and independent sample designs. The findings presented here suggest that there is, as yet, little evidence for age-related changes in personality in the adult years.

References

Botwinick, J. Intellectual functioning. In J. E. Birren and K. W. Schaie (Eds.), *Handbook of the psychology of aging*. New York: Van Nostrand, Reinhold, 1977.

Botwinick, J., and Storandt, M. *Memory related functions and age*. Springfield, Ill.: Charles C. Thomas, 1974.

Cattell, R. B., Eber, H. W., and Tatsouka, M. M. *Handbook for the sixteen personality factor questionnaire (16PF)*. Champaign, Ill.: Institute for Personality and Ability Testing, 1970.

Cattell, R. B. *Handbook for the sixteen personality factor questionnaire (16PF) . . . Supplement . . .* Champaign, Ill.: Institute for Personality and Ability Tesing, 1962.

Costa, P. T., Jr., and McCrae, R. R. Objective personality assessment. In M. Storandt, I. C. Siegler, and M. F. Elias (Eds.), *The clinical psychology of aging*. New York: Plenum, 1978.

Gutmann, D. Parenthood: A key to the comparative study of the life cycle. In N. Datan and L. Ginsberg (Eds.), *Life-span developmental psychology: Normative life crises*. New York: Academic, 1975.

Maas, H. S., and Kuypers, J. A. *From thirty to seventy*. San Francisco: Jossey-Bass, 1974.

Schaie, K. W. Quasi-experimental designs in the psychology of aging. In J. E. Birren and K. W. Schaie (Eds.), *Handbook of the psychology of aging*. New York: Van Nostrand Reinhold, 1977.

Schaie, K. W., and Parham, I. A. Stability of adult personality: Fact and fable? *Journal of Personality and Social Psychology*, 34:146–158, 1976.

The Impact of Personality and Social Status upon Activity and Psychological Well-being

Linda K. George

It is, by now, widely acknowledged that the disengagement versus activity theory debate is a specious argument. Historically, both perspectives focused upon the relationship between levels of activity and psychological well-being in late life and viewed that relationship as the criterion for a theory of optimal aging. Subsequent empirical evidence precluded the conclusion that a simple and straightforward relationship exists between activity levels and psychological well-being. That evidence, along with findings from longitudinal studies of persistence in levels of activity and life satisfaction over the course of adulthood (cf. Maddox, 1968; Williams and Wirths, 1965), led to the development and general acceptance of continuity theory.

While evidence of continuity in levels of activity and psychological well-being in adulthood is persuasive, these variables are of more than historical interest. Explanation of individual differences in levels of activity and psychological

Reprinted by permission from *Journal of Gerontology*, 33:840–847, 1978.

well-being remains a salient theoretical and substantive issue, as demonstrated by the large number of recent studies which address this issue (cf., Bell, 1975; Bull and Aucoin, 1975; Cutler, 1976, 1977; George and Maddox, 1977). In order to be applied usefully to the issue of psychological well-being or activity levels in late life, suggested theoretical explanations must meet two criteria: first, the theoretical perspectives must be able to account for individual stability in behavior over time; and second, the theory must also be able to account for differences across individuals. Two major theoretical perspectives appear to meet both of these criteria. From a psychological perspective, personality has been suggested as the major explanatory factor which accounts for both individual differences in levels of activity and psychological well-being and of behavioral continuity over time. Using a sociological framework, other theorists have suggested that both individual differences in activity levels and psychological well-being and individual stability in these behaviors primarily reflect the impact of social status variables.

Personality is typically conceptualized as a stable configuration of cognitive-emotional characteristics which operates to produce consistent behavioral outcomes (Mischel, 1969). The presumed stability of personality makes it a theoretically attractive explanation for behavioral continuity over the course of adulthood. In addition, personality theorists suggest that individual differences in behavior reflect personality differences across individuals.

Social status variables index the social roles that pattern behavior and the social context within which behavior is conducted. This perspective also has been used to explain both behavioral continuity and individual differences in behavior. Most social status variables (e.g., sex, race, and social class) are relatively enduring individual characteristics, and they thus provide a stable context for social interaction and foster behavioral continuity. Individual differences in behavior presumably reflect individual differences in relevant social status factors. Our social status factors, however, are more mutable (e.g., some married persons lose their spouses by death or divorce, and working people may retire). In contrast to the typical pattern of stability and consequent behavioral continuity, changes or shifts in these social status variables would be expected to generate changes in relevant behavioral outcomes.

Both personality factors and social status variables previously have been related to levels of activity and psychological well-being in adulthood. Neugarten et al. (1968) observed a variety of activity and morale patterns in their study of older persons and suggested that the particular pattern evidenced reflects stable underlying personality factors. Similarly, Reichard et al. (1962) suggested that patterns of adjustment to retirement (measured in part by level of activity and satisfaction with life) exhibited in their sample of older men were due to personality factors. In both studies, measures of personality were derived from detailed semistructured interviews. A test of the ability of standardized personality measures to predict levels of activity and psychological well-being remains empirically unaddressed. Further, in these studies, the possible influence of social status factors was not examined.

Social status variables also have been examined as predictors of both behavioral continuity and individual differences in levels of activity and psychological well-being in middle and late life. Using the same sample as Neugarten and associates, Williams and Wirths (1965) concluded that patterns of activity and life satisfaction reflect stable life-style characteristics. Maddox (1968), using longitudinal data, also suggested that behavioral persistence is related to patterns of life-style. Recently, social status has been related to individual differences in life satisfaction (cf. Adams, 1971; Beiser, 1974; Edwards and Klemmack, 1973; Spreitzer and Snyder, 1974) and social participation or activity (cf. Bell, 1975; Bull and Aucoin, 1975; Cutler, 1973). These studies have neglected, however, the possible impact of personality factors upon levels of activity and psychological well-being.

The purpose of the present study is to examine the relative impact of both personality factors and social status variables upon levels of activity and psychological well-being in a sample of middle-aged and older persons. The joint impact of personality and social status factors upon levels of activity and psychological well-being has not been examined previously.

Methods

Sample

The data used in this study are part of the Duke Second Longitudinal Study. Data used in this analysis were obtained at the third test date, (1972–74), since the age range at that time proved an optimal span of late adulthood. The sample at the third test date consisted of 197 white males and 183 white females, aged fifty to seventy-six. The sample was designed to include approximately equal numbers of males and females in five-year age groups. At the third test date, the ten age-sex cells range in size from thirty-five to forty-four. Data collected at other test dates are selectively included to illustrate the stability and change of relevant variables over time.

Measures

The present study requires four sets of variables. There are two sets of independent variables: personality factors and measures of social status. The two dependent variables are measures of psychological well-being and activity level.

Personality factors. Personality factors are measures using form C of the Cattell 16 PF (Cattell et al., 1970), a standardized instrument which yields sten scores for sixteen primary and four secondary personality traits. In this analysis, scores were calculated using normative standards for the general adult population, regardless of gender. It is necessary to use this scoring system, since gender is one of the social variables included in the analysis, and gender comparisons must be based on sten scores calculated using the same metric.

Social status measures. Several social status variables were included in the analysis to index social roles or social resources available to the individual. Sex was included as a dummy variable, with 0 representing males and 1 the code for females. Age was coded directly as years since birth. Both gender and age are important social characteristics, related to a wide array of behavioral outcomes.

Socioeconomic status has been related previously to social roles and lifestyle characteristics. Education and occupational prestige were included as measures of socioeconomic status. Education was coded simply as years of formal education. Occupational prestige, based upon major lifetime occupation, was classified into three broad categories: (1) farm laborers, semiskilled workers, and unskilled workers; (2) skilled workers, craftsmen, clerical sales workers; and (3) professional, managerial, and technical workers. The original nine categories were collapsed to three in order to increase the reliability of the measure. (Cronbach's *alpha* with nine categories was .39; with three categories, alpha increased to .89.) Females who had devoted their adult years to homemaking were assigned the occupational prestige of their spouse.

Employment status and marital status are important social roles in adulthood. Employment status was a dummy variable, where 0 represented no employment and 1 indicated being currently employed. Marital status was also dichotomized, with 0 representing being currently unmarried and 1 indicating that the subject was currently married and living with his or her spouse. Checks were conducted to determine whether being retired should be distinguished from other kinds of unemployment and whether the divorced or widowed should be distinguished from the never-married. The results indicated that the dichotomized variables resulted in no significant information loss or distortion.

Health status is also an important social characteristic in late life. A measure of objective (i.e., clinically assessed) health impairment was included. The range of this variable was zero to nine, with higher scores representing increased impairment.

Activity levels. The activities measure consisted of time spent, on a weekly basis, in: church attendance, religious organizations, volunteer work, clubs and voluntary organizations, and informal socializing. Self-reports of these activities were summed to yield a single score representing general activity level. The intercorrelations among the activities ranged from .49 to .67. Cronbach's *alpha* was used to determine the internal consistency of the activity measure, and the coefficient was acceptable ($a = .78$). Checks were conducted to determine that summing the activities did not result in information loss or distortion.

Psychological well-being. The Affect Balance Scale was used to measure psychological well-being (Bradburn and Caplovitz, 1965). This measure is an attractive indicator of psychological well-being as it appears to be a sensitive measure, reactive to intrapsychic changes (Lawton, 1977), and its relationship to mental health has been empirically documented (Bradburn, 1969).

Analyses

Multiple regression was used to examine the separate and joint effects of personality traits and social status measures upon levels of activity and psychological well-being. For each dependent variable, three regression equations were calculated. In the first equation, model 1, the independent variables were the personality traits of the 16 PF; in the second equation, model 2, the measure of social status were the independent variables; and in the third equation, model 3, the joint impact of the personality and social status measures were examined. The independent variables are intercorrelated to some degree; however, multiple regression yields net coefficients, thus the effect of each variable is assessed with all other independent variables statistically controlled. Standardized regression coefficients (*B*s) are used to determine the impact of a predictor relative to other predictors in the same equation. Unstandardized regression coefficients (*b*s) are used to assess the impact of a given predictor across equations.

Results

Table C—14 presents the ranges, means, and standard deviations of the variables used in this analysis. The means of the dependent variables are reported at all four test dates and are quite stable, indicating continuity in both activity and psychological well-being for the sample over the course of the study. This evidence of behavioral continuity supports the conclusion of previous studies (cf., Maddox, 1968; Williams and Wirths, 1965). Since the phenomena of interest are stable over time, the choice of a cross-sectional or longitudinal regression model is largely irrelevant. In fact, a series of cross-sectional and longitudinal regression equations were calculated, yielding essentially the same results and thus confirming that the presentation of cross-sectional data results in no significant information loss or distortion. The regression equations presented below are based on cross-sectional data, since the emphasis in this paper is on explaining individual difference rather than changes within individuals over time.

It is interesting to note that the correlation between the activity measure and the Affect Balance Scale is relatively weak ($r = .18$). This supports the findings in previous studies (cf. Bull and Aucoin, 1975; Cutler, 1973), that there is not a significant, predictable relationship between activity and psychological well-being in late life.

Table C—15 presents the three regression equations which predict individual differences in activity levels. The equation for model 1 indicates that the personality traits of the Cattell 16 PF explain 10.4 percent of the variance in activity levels. Only one factor, sense of trust, is by itself, however, a significant predictor. Model 2 indicates that five of the seven social status measures are significant predictors of activity levels. As a group, the social status variables explain 11.2 percent of the variance in activity levels. Finally, model 3 shows the joint impact of the personality and social status measures upon activity levels. The results

Table C—14. *Ranges, means, and standard deviations of variables used in analysis.*

	Range	Mean	Standard deviations
Social status variables			
Sex	0–1	.48	.50
Age	50–75	62.36	7.16
Education	1–27	12.15	3.92
Occupational prestige	1–3	2.05	.82
Health impairment	0–19	2.15	2.65
Marital status	0–1	.79	.41
Employment status	0–1	.56	.50
Personality factors[a]			
(A) Outgoing	1–10	5.11	1.92
(B) Intelligence	1–9	4.84	2.00
(C) Emotional stability	1–10	5.18	2.14
(E) Dominance	1–10	5.22	1.98
(F) Soberness	1–10	4.41	2.02
(G) Conscientiousness	1–10	5.60	1.84
(H) Social boldness	1–10	4.88	1.92
(I) Tough mindedness	1–10	5.87	2.15
(L) Sense of trust	1–10	5.35	1.99
(M) Practicality	1–10	4.75	1.81
(N) Naivete	1–10	5.13	2.07
(O) Security	1–10	6.34	1.83
(Q1) Conservation	1–10	5.22	1.96
(Q2) Self-sufficiency	1–10	6.18	1.83
(Q3) Control	1–10	5.81	1.99
(Q4) Tenseness	1–10	5.66	1.97
(QI) Extroversion	1–9	4.10	1.50
(QII) Anxiety	1–10	5.46	1.58
(QIII) Cortical arousal	1–10	4.52	1.73
(QIV) Independence	1–9	4.53	1.63
Activity hours (per week)			
Round 1	0–42	14.66	7.89
Round 2	0–66	16.89	10.10
Round 3	0–42	13.57	7.62
Round 4	1–58	14.71	9.24
Affect Balance Scale[b]			
Round 1	11–30	21.04	2.94
Round 2	0–32	23.30	4.26
Round 3	0–31	22.63	4.44
Round 4	5–32	22.77	3.78

[a]The labels of the personality factors have been simplified to a key word. The alphabetical labels are those used by Cattell (1970).

[b]A constant of 30 was added to all Affect Balance Scale scores in order to yield positive numbers.

Table C—15. *Regression equations of personality factors and social status variables predicting activity levels.*

Independent variables	Model 1 *b*	Model 1 *B*	Model 2 *b*	Model 2 *B*	Model 3 *b*	Model 3 *B*
Sex			1.50*	.10*	1.62**	.11**
Age			−.11**	−.11**	−.10**	−.10**
Education			.19**	.10**	.17**	.09**
Occupational prestige			1.12**	.10**	1.02**	.09**
Health impairment			−.16	−.05	−.17*	−.06*
Marital status			−.69	−.04	−.81	−.04
Employment status			−3.76**	−.25**	−3.70**	−.24**
(A) Outgoing	.53	.13			.40	.10
(B) Intelligence	−.22	−.06			−.32**	−.08**
(C) Emotional stability	.03	.01			−.08	−.02
(E) Dominance	.13	.03			.14	.04
(F) Soberness	.05	.01			.23	.06
(G) Conscientiousness	.30	.07			.38	.09
(H) Social boldness	−.25	−.06			−.22	−.06
(I) Tough mindedness	.00	.00			.45	.13
(L) Sense of trust	1.10**	.31**			.08	.02
(M) Practicality	−.10	−.02			−.21	−.05
(N) Naivete	.09	.02			.09	.02
(O) Security	.18	.04			.28	.07
(Q1) Conservation	.19	.05			.19	.05
(Q2) Self-sufficiency	−.36	−.09			−.53*	−.13*
(Q3) Control	.26	.07			.18	.05
(Q4) Tenseness	.33	.09			.38	.10
(QI) Extroversion	.42	.08			.25	.05
(QII) Anxiety	−.77	−.16			−.89	−.19
(QIII) Cortical arousal	1.06	.24			.78	.18
(QIV) Independence	−.24	−.05			−.11	−.02
Constant	12.55		23.70		15.63	
Total R^2	.104		.112		.188	

*$p \leq .05$.

**$p \leq .01$.

indicate that the two sets of variables explain 18.8 percent of the variance. Comparison of the regression coefficients across models indicates that the social status variables are the more significant predictors of activity levels in the joint equation (i.e., the impact of the personality factors is very small, once the social status variables are controlled).

Model 3 suggests that six of the seven social status measures are significant predictors of activity levels. Females, relatively younger subjects, persons of higher educational attainment and occupational prestige, individuals in better

Table C—16. *Regression equations of personality factors and social status variables predicting psychological well-being.*

Independent variables	Model 1		Model 2		Model 3	
	b	*B*	*b*	*B*	*b*	*B*
Sex			−.26	−.03	−.08	−.01
Age			−.03	−.05	−.01	−.02
Education			.11**	.10**	.07*	.06*
Occupational prestige			−.26	−.04	−.37	−.06
Health impairment			−.21**	−.13**	−.19**	2**
Marital status			1.36**	.14**	1.31**	.13**
Employment status			−.76	−.09	−.59*	−.07*
(A) Outgoing	.41*	.19*			.37	.17
(B) Intelligence	.00	.00			−.06	.03
(C) Emotional stability	.12	.06			.10	.05
(E) Dominance	−.31	−.15			−.29	−.14
(F) Soberness	.07	.03			.08	.04
(G) Conscientiousness	.30**	.13**			.32**	.14**
(H) Social boldness	−.20	−.09			−.16	−.07
(I) Tough mindedness	.38*	.20*			.41*	.21*
(L) Sense of trust	−.16	−.08			−.12	−.06
(M) Practicality	−.35**	−.16**			−.34**	−.15**
(N) Naivete	.15	.07			.14	.07
(O) Security	.06	.03			.02	.01
(Q1) Conservation	.11	.05			.13	.06
(Q2) Self-sufficiency	−.32*	−.14*			−.31*	−.14*
(Q3) Control	.05	.02			.06	.03
(Q4) Tenseness	−.47**	−.23**			−.52**	.25**
(QI) Extroversion	−.04	−.02			−.07	−.03
(QII) Anxiety	−.06	−.02			.07	.03
(QIII) Cortical arousal	.88**	.38**			.85**	.36**
(QIV) Independence	.47	.19			.38	.15
Constant	11.86		17.90		12.57	
Total R^2	.183		.057		.218	

*$p \leq .05$.

**$p \leq .01$.

physical health, and persons who are not currently employed devote greater time to activities. Two personality traits—intelligence and self-sufficiency—significantly predict activity levels, with persons scoring lower on these factors reporting higher activity levels. The negative impact of intelligence is somewhat surprising. The regression coefficients, however, indicate the impact of an independent variable with all other independent variables in the equation statistically controlled. The zero-order correlation between intelligence and activity is small, but positive (r = .12). It is only with the impact of all the other independent variables statistically controlled that intelligence is inversely related to activity levels.

Table C—16 presents the three regression equations that predict individual differences in psychological well-being in this sample. The first model indicates that, by themselves, the personality variables explain 18.3 percent of the variance in affect balance scores, with seven factors operating as significant predictors. The social status measures, as a set, explain only 5.7 percent of the variance in psychological well-being. Finally, examined jointly, personality factors and social status measures explain 21.8 percent of the variance in affect balance scores.

The results suggest that personality traits are better predictors of psychological well-being than are the social status measures. Six of the sixteen factors of the Cattell 16 PF are significant predictors of affect balance scores. Persons who score as relatively more conscientious, tender-minded, practical, group-dependent, relaxed, and high in arousal score more positively on the Affect Balance Scale. Examining the social status measures, education, good physical health, being married, and being unemployed (in this sample, retired or a housewife) are significantly related to psychological well-being.

Discussion and Summary

The concepts of activity and psychological well-being have long been wedded in gerontological thinking, reflecting the pervasive influences of disengagement and activity theory perspectives. The results of this study support the conclusion of previous studies (cf. Bull and Aucoin, 1975; Cutler, 1973) which question the presence of a significant and predictable relationship between levels of activity and psychological well-being. The findings indicate a weak correlation between levels of activity and psychological well-being and further suggest that the two phenomena are best predicted by different variables. Personality factors were better predictors of psychological well-being than were social status factors, while activity levels were better predicted by social status variables. In addition, psychological well-being and activity were best predicted by different personality and social status factors.

Perhaps the most striking finding in the present study is the substantial power of presumably stable personality factors to significantly predict psychological well-being as measured by what has been suggested as a transitory and situationally reactive measure of intrapsychic affect. These results suggest the potential importance of personality factors as predictors of individual differences in psychological well-being in adulthood. It appears that earlier suggestions that psychological well-being in adulthood reflects long-term personality styles were at least partially correct. In addition, these results suggest that intrapsychic affect may be a more stable characteristic, as in Murray's early (1938) discussions of temperament as a personality trait, than has been recently conceptualized. Considering the plethora of life-satisfaction related studies in social gerontology, the fact that previous studies have neglected to examine the impact of personality factors is noteworthy.

The social status factors examined in this analysis have been included in previous studies of activity and psychological well-being in adulthood. The results generally support the findings reported in previous studies. In regard to activity levels, the findings are consistent with previous studies which report higher levels of activity, particularly voluntary association participation, among females (Cutler, 1977), persons of higher socioeconomic status (Babchuck and Booth, 1969; Cutler, 1976). In addition, data in the present study suggest that retired persons and housewives exhibit higher activity levels than persons in the labor force, undoubtedly reflecting higher amounts of leisure time among the unemployed. The findings also support previous studies of psychological well-being which report that higher levels of well-being are associated with higher socioeconomic status (Edwards and Klemmack, 1973; George and Maddox, 1977; Spreitzer and Snyder, 1974), good health (Edwards and Klemmack, 1973; Spreitzer and Snyder, 1974), and being married (Campbell et al., 1976; Edwards and Klemmack, 1973; George and Maddox, 1977).

Many of these social status variables previously were examined as bivariate correlates of levels of activity or psychological well-being. In the regression analyses, these variables remained satistically significant predictors of activity and psychological well-being when the impact of the other independent variables was statistically controlled. This provides considerably stronger evidence that these variables are indeed important predictors of individual differences in levels of activity and psychological well-being and not merely spurious relationships which result from intercorrelations among various personality and social status factors.

References

Adams, D. L. Correlates of satisfaction among the elderly. *Gerontologist*, 11:64–68, 1971.

Babchuck, N., and Booth, A. Voluntary association membership: A longitudinal analysis. *American Sociological Review*, 34:31–45, 1969.

Beiser, M. Components and correlates of mental well-being. *Journal of Health and Social Behavior*, 15:320–327, 1974.

Bell, B. D. The limitations of crises theory as an explanatory mechanism in social gerontology. *International Journal of Aging & Human Development*, 6:153–168, 1975.

Bradburn, N. M. *The structure of psychological well-being*. Chicago: Aldine, 1969.

Bradburn, N. M., and Caplowitz, D. *Reports on happiness*. Chicago: Aldine, 1965.

Bull, C. N., and Aucoin, J. B. Voluntary association participation and life satisfaction: A replication note. *Journal of Gerontology*, 30:73–76, 1975.

Campbell, A., Converse, P. E., and Rodgers, W. L. *Quality of American life*. New York: Russell Sage Foundation, 1976.

Cattell, R. B., Eber, H. W., and Tatsuoka, M. M. *Handbook for the 16 personality factor questionnaire (16PF)*. Champaign, Ill.: Institute for Personality and Ability Testing, 1970.

Cutler, S. J. Voluntary association participation and life satisfaction: A cautionary research note. *Journal of Gerontology*, 28:96–100, 1973.

Cutler, S. J. Membership in different types of voluntary associations and psychological well-being. *Gerontologist*, 16:335–339, 1976.
Cutler, S. J. Aging and voluntary association participation. *Journal of Gerontology*, 32:470–479, 1977.
Edwards, J. N., and Klemmack, D. L. Correlates of life satisfaction: A reexamination. *Journal of Gerontology*, 28:497–502, 1973.
George, L. K., and Maddox, G. L. Subjective adaptation to loss of the workrole: A longitudinal study. *Journal of Gerontology*, 32:456–462, 1977.
Lawton, M. P. Morale: What are we measuring? In C. N. Nydegger (Ed.), *Measuring morale: A guide to effective assessment*. Washington, D.C.: Gerontological Society, 1977.
Maddox, G. L. Persistence of life-style among the elderly. In B. L. Neugarten (Ed.), *Middle age and aging*. Chicago: University of Chicago Press, 1968.
Mischel, W. Continuity and change in personality. *American Psychologist*, 24:1012–1018, 1969.
Murray, H. A. *Explorations in personality*. New York: Oxford University Press, 1938.
Neugarten, B. L., Havighurst, R. J., and Tobin, S. S. Personality and patterns of aging. In B. L. Neugarten (Ed.), *Middle age and aging*. Chicago: University of Chicago Press, 1968.
Palmore, E. B. Appendix A: Adaptation study design. In E. B. Palmore (Ed.), *Normal aging II*. Durham, N.C.: Duke University Press, 1974.
Reichard, S., Livson, F., and Peterson, P. G. *Aging and personality*. New York: Wiley, 1962.
Spreitzer, E., and Snyder, E. E. Correlates of life satisfaction among the aged. *Journal of Gerontology*, 29:454–458, 1974.
Williams, R. H., and Wirths, C. G. *Lives through the years*. New York: Atherton, 1965.

Age Patterns in Locus of Control

Ilene C. Siegler and Margaret Gatz

This paper brings together a series of analyses which are concerned with understanding the construct of locus of control. The sense of personal control has been viewed as an important individual-differences variable for the past fifteen years (Rotter, 1966, 1975; Lefcourt, 1976, 1981; Phares, 1973). Personal control refers to an individual's beliefs that he exercises influence over outcomes in his own life (an internal locus of control), versus a feeling that chance or powerful others determine consequences (an external locus of control). Research has tended to indicate that a heightened sense of personal or internal control is related to psychological well-being and physical health, while a diminished sense of control is related to negative effects (Rodin, 1982). In older adults, internality, more often than externality, has been related to a variety of behaviors and personal constructs including activity, involvement, positive adjustment, and life satisfaction

Based on a set of earlier presentations and manuscripts: Bielby & Siegler (1977); and Gatz & Siegler (1981). We would like to acknowledge support from NIA (AG00364) and from AoA (90-A-1022).

(Kuypers, 1972; Palmore and Luikart, 1972; Wolk and Kurtz, 1975; Ziegler and Reid, 1979). On the other hand, it has been suggested that in certain situations such as living in a restricted environment or when severely ill, externality may be adaptive (Felton and Kahana, 1974; Levenson, 1974). As well, there has been considerable conceptual and empirical interest in studying the relationships between age and locus of control. However, investigations to date have raised a number of methodological problems and have generated some apparently contradictory results, and the normative nature of internality/externality (I-E) across the life cycle remains unclear.

Most of the previous studies have been cross-sectional. Using Potter's I-E Scale (1966), Nehrke, Hulicka, and Morganti (1980) found no significant age differences among those in their fifties, sixties, and seventies, while both Lao (1974) and Staats (1974) found middle-aged adults to be more internal than young adults. Ryckman and Malikiosi (1975) used Levenson's I-E Scale (1974), which provides separate subscale scores for personal control, control by chance, and control by powerful others. They found no significant age differences from the twenties to the seventies on personal control. On the other two subscales, there were significant age differences but no unidirectional trends: those in their thirties indicated the least belief in chance control and those in their fifties, the most belief in control by powerful others. Brim (1974) postulated erosion and giving up of the sense of control during the later years. In one of the few longitudinal studies, Lachman (in press) analyzed three personal efficacy items. There was essentially no change in mean score levels at three times of measurement over a total of four years. However, correlational stability, which indicates interindividual differences in change, was lower for those in their sixties than for middle-aged cohorts.

It is not only with respect to I-E that age-related patterns are unclear. Many scholars in the field of adult development have focused on the debate between stability and change of personality (Costa and McCrae, 1980; Bengtson, Reedy, and Gordon, 1977). This paper used data from the Duke Second Longitudinal Study, in conjunction with data from other sources, to examine ways of clarifying the relationship between age and locus of control. We apply two methods of evaluating patterns of stability and change—correlation coefficients and mean levels—to exploration of three issues: (1) when looked at longitudinally, what is the underlying nature of the construct? does it behave like a stable personal characteristic or is it responsive to environmental and situational pressures? The answer to this question is essential to interpreting patterns of change in the variable. (2) longitudinally, what are the patterns of individual change seen in middle-aged and older persons? and (3) when middle aged and older persons are compared to younger persons, what type of age differences are seen, both overall and on different dimensions of control?

Respondents used in these analyses are the same set of 375 persons used in the larger analysis of adaptation to life events (Palmore et al., 1979; reprinted on pps. 341–56 infra). Aged forty-six to sixty-nine at the start of the study, the panel was evaluated four times at approximately two-year intervals. A subset of 300 individuals had complete locus of control data at all four times of measurement.

In the second longitudinal study, locus of control was assessed with the Jessor I-E Scale (Jessor et al., 1968). The construct of locus of control has been operationalized with a number of paper and pencil scales. Indeed, one of the problems in making sense of the literature has been the differences among the scales (cf. Lefcourt, 1981). By far the most often used scale has been the one originally developed by Rotter (1966) for college students. Those who study adults have used a variety of revisions or adaptations including: dropping items such as those concerned with school work (Gurin et al., 1978); developing new formats based on interview techniques (Gatz, 1979; Felton and Kahana, 1974); and developing new paper and pencil scales (e.g., Jessor et al., 1968; Levenson, 1974; Ziegler and Reid, 1979). While the choice of a particular scale to measure a construct is an important decision, one of the issues involved in longitudinal research is the understanding and recognition of the point in time or the historical context in which the study was designed (see Siegler, 1983). Rotter's monograph was published about the time that the second longitudinal study was being designed. Jessor et al. (1968) was one of the first groups to use the scale with non-college age populations, therefore the Jessor scale was adapted for use in the second longitudinal study. The scale used is an eleven-item forced choice inventory. When the Rotter and the Jessor scales were both given to groups of college students, the two scales correlated .60 (see cross-sectional analyses, infra); in two samples of older persons, correlations of .58 and .65 were found (Siegler et al., 1979). Thus the Jessor scale and the Rotter scale, while sharing only 36 percent common variance, nonetheless do have a significant relationship. It is important to remember that the findings in the following analyses need to be interpreted with reference to the particular scale used. The eleven-item Jessor scale items are found in table C—17.

Correlational Analyses

In personality theory, it is common to speak about personality traits as opposed to states (Speilberger, 1966). The term trait refers to a stable, enduring characteristic of an individual. Traits are assumed to develop on the basis of significant early experience and to be modified only by the types of events in later life that would be related to a major personality reorganization. The term state, by contrast, may be conceptualized as a response that varies across situations and over time. These variables have the characteristics of mood states. They relate to whatever is happening in the proximate environment and are thus reflective of the current life-space around the individual. The question of age-related change versus stability for locus of control thus may be addressed by asking which type of variable we are dealing with, a trait or a state. If locus of control is a traitlike variable, then we would predict stability in adulthood and later life unless there were massive changes in the individual's life situation. If, on the other hand,

Table C—17. *Dimensions of the Jessor locus of control scale.*

Item	Scale	Rxx	$F(2,305)$
1. If you've got the ability you can always get a good job. Versus: Getting a good job depends on being in the right place at the right time.	Exper.	100.0%	62.60
2. Some of the good and some of the bad things in my life have happened by chance. Versus: What's happened to me has been my own doing.	Philo.	87.5%	2.73
3. Sometimes, no matter how clearly you've thought something out, other people just don't get it. Versus: If you know what's on your mind, you can get it across to other people.	Exper.	87.5%	6.98
4. When I make plans, I am most certain that I can make them work. Versus: I have usually found that what is going to happen will happen regardless of my plans.	Philo.	87.5%	2.42
5. I like to do things on the spur of the moment. Versus: I prefer to have things planned out in advance.	Philo.	100.0%	2.00
6. Working hard and steady is the way to get ahead in a job. Versus: Getting ahead in a job depends on what kind of boss you happen to have.	Exper.	100.0%	6.62
7. No matter how hard a person tries, some people just don't like him. Versus: When a person isn't liked, it's because of the way he does things.	Exper.	87.5%	5.01
8. It's very important to have your life laid out pretty far in advance. Versus: It's really not possible to see your life more than a year ahead.	Philo.	75.0%	6.24
9. Sometimes family troubles just can't be avoided. Versus: A family will be happy only if everyone does his part.	Exper.	100.0%	7.85
10. Most people who get in trouble start out looking for it. Versus: Often trouble starts because a person happened to be in the wrong place at the wrong time.	Exper.	100.0%	6.99
11. Often, I seem to have little influence over what other people believe. Versus: When I'm right I can usually convince others.	Philo.	87.5%	.74

locus of control has more statelike qualities, then we would expect that the construct would be sensitive to some of the subtle changes we associate with aging, and we would predict significant change as a function of normal life events.

Consequently, in this first set of analyses, we compared the correlational stability of locus of control to two other constructs, one with known traitlike characteristics and the other with known statelike characteristics. Verbal intelligence was selected as the traitlike construct and happiness as the statelike. Verbal intelligence was estimated from subscale scores on the information and vocabulary subtests of the WAIS. Verbal intelligence is known to be extremely stable, particularly during the age range covered in the study (forty-six to seventy) and over a six-year period. Happiness was assessed with the Affect Balance Scale (Bradburn and Caplovitz, 1965). Affect balance was designed to be a mood state measure, using a time referent of positive and negative feelings experienced during the previous week.

We calculated three indices of relationships (according to the formulae given in Heise, 1969) which can be compared for these variables: (1) cross-wave correlation coefficients; (2) stability coefficients; and (3) reliability coefficients. For affect balance, the cross-wave correlations were 0.40 (waves 1 and 2), 0.53 (waves 2 and 3), and 0.55 (waves 3 and 4); stability coefficients were 0.76, 1.01, and 0.77 with a reliability of 0.52. For verbal intelligence, the cross-wave coefficients were 0.96, 0.96. and 0.95; the stability coefficients were 0.99, 0.99, and 0.98; and the reliability was 0.95. The locus of control scale had the following values: cross-wave coefficients 0.60, 0.60, and 0.61; stability coefficients 0.94, 0.94, and 0.89, and the reliability was 0.63. The cross-wave correlations appeared mid-range; however the stability coefficients were closer to verbal intelligence. These comparisons suggest that locus of control appears more stable than affect balance and thus more traitlike.

Longitudinal Analyses of Mean Levels

In this next set of analyses, we used repeated measures analysis of variance to evaluate change over the four times of measurement on the same three variables: verbal intelligence, affect balance and locus of control. Between-subjects factors included: age, sex, and the occurrence of five major life events during the study period: retirement of self or spouse, widowhood, empty nest, or a medical event requiring hospitalization (see Siegler, infra, pp. 335–41, and Palmore et al., 1979, pp. 341–56, infra). Response to the life events studies were predicted for statelike rather than traitlike constructs. The group was divided into two age groups resulting in a younger group aged forty-six to fifty-seven and an older group aged fifty-eight to sixty-nine at the start of the study. Over the six years of observation, 63 percent of the sample experienced at least one event.

The results of the repeated measures multivariate analysis of variance indicated that all three variables changed significantly over time: verbal intelligence improved with practice (F = 81.53), affect balance became more positive (F = 100.00), and the total group became somewhat more external (F = 7.00). Most of the largest changes were between the first two waves. Significant time interactions with both age and sex were seen only with verbal intelligence.

For the between-subjects factors of age, sex, and occurrence of events, affect balance showed a significant age effect (F = 4.95), with middle-aged respondents reporting a more positive balance than older respondents; and a significant event-by-sex interaction (F = 10.18). The most positive affect balance was reported by males who experienced life events during the six years and by females who did not experience events. Locus of control differed only by sex, with men consistently more internal than women (F = 38.70). There were no between-subjects effects for verbal intelligence.

Finally, the patterns of individual change seen over the six-year period were classified by the shape of the curve and the direction of the change. The results indicated that, of the 300 individuals with complete I-E data whose patterns could be characterized, 229 or fully 76 percent were stable (defined as changing three or fewer points). The other seventy-one showed changes in the range of four or more points, shifting them to another third of the score distribution. For this group, however, no single pattern or direction of change predominated.

To summarize, these findings further document the traitlike nature of the construct in middle and later life. Only affect balance was responsive to the individual's life situation. While there was a small change towards externality in the total group, locus of control did not vary as a function of differential life experience.

Cross-Sectional Analyses of Mean Levels

In order to evaluate age differences across a broader range of the life cycle, young adult data were collected from undergraduates at the University of Maryland to be compared to data from middle-aged and older respondents randomly selected from the second longitudinal study. One hundred and one middle-aged (mean age = 49.88, SD = 2.63) and 106 older persons (mean age = 66.59, SD = 2.21) were selected from the total sample of 502 at the first time of measurement in such a way that they were comparable in formal education to the group of university undergraduates aged seventeen to twenty-six (mean age = 20.95, SD = 1.74). The levels of education were 15.29 years for the young, 13.70 years for the middle, and 14.97 years for the oldest group. The three groups had equivalent sex ratios.

There is discrepancy in the literature regarding age differences in locus of control. One of the major reasons for this discrepancy may be related to the multidimensionality of various scales and the related problem of multiple scales. A variety of factor analytic studies have been done with the Rotter scale (Gurin, Gurin, and Morrison, 1978; Gatz, 1979). Gurin et al. reported finding five factors with national data. Three of the factors replicated across samples of white men and women and blacks: personal control (first person items), control ideology (third person items about what determines an individual's reinforcements in this culture), and political control. Other investigators interested in expectancy or attribution have proposed other relevant conceptual distinctions (e.g., Bandura, 1977; Weisz and Stipek, 1982; de Charmes, 1981). When we examined the content of the eleven Jessor items, we identified two types of items which appear to reflect a major distinction which recurs in the literature. We called the dimensions experiential (reflecting types of items that vary with adult experience) and philosophical (reflective of traitlike beliefs).

On the one hand there are beliefs about the control or predictability of reinforcements (Rotter, 1966), similar to what Bandura (1977) called outcome expectancies, what Weisz and Stipek (1982) called perceived contingency of outcomes, what Gatz called attributions about the world, and the control ideology of Gurin et al. (1978). With the Jessor scale we called these experiential items. The most salient aspect is whether effort and ability or luck and chance determine individual attainment of goals.

On the other hand, there are beliefs about causation, what Bandura (1977) calld efficacy expectations, what Weisz and Stipek (1982) called perceived competence of self, Gatz's attributions about self (1979), Gurin et al.'s personal control (1978), and similar to de Charms' notion of the experience of personal causation. We labeled these items philosophical items, as they concern the individual's belief system. These items reflect the role that fate plays in the universe. Most of these items are phrased in the first person.

We hypothesized that if we compared individuals across the full adult age range there would be age differences on the experiential dimension but not the philosophical dimension. Items were classified by the two authors and three additional raters. The items, their scale assignments, the interrater agreements, and the *F*'s for the one-way age group ANOVA are given in table C—17.

With a single I-E score, the young adult group was significantly more external than the two older groups. However, when the two subscales were analyzed, the predicted pattern of age differences was found. At the item level, all six experiential items showed predicted age differences, while four of the five philosophical items did not. The item that did not work as predicted, item 8, was judged philosophical because the item content included planning.

Conclusion

Cross-sectionally, the oldest cohorts were the most internal, consistent with other cross-sectional and between-cohort comparisons (Lao, 1976; Staats, 1974; Lachman, in press) and the students were the most external, consistent with Rotter's (1975) observation about a historical shift toward externality among college students. Interestingly, longitudinally our older subjects, while more internal than the younger subjects, became slightly more external over the six years of observation, although this did not vary with the occurrence of the life events we studied. Our attention to dimensions of the locus of control construct also appeared useful. Experiential items were related to age differences, while philosophical items were stable over the age range studied. This system appears to be a useful way to help organize many of the findings in the literature, by predicting differential developmental patterns for the dimensions of locus of control.

References

Bandura, A. Self-efficacy: Toward a unifying theory of behavioral change. *Psychological Review*, 84:191–215, 1977.

Bengtson, V. L., Reedy, M. N., and Gordon, C. R. Aging and self-conceptions: Personality processes and social contexts. In J. E. Birren and K. W. Schaie (Eds.), *Handbook of the psychology of aging*. New York: Van Nostrand Reinhold, 1977.

Bielby, D. D., and Siegler I. C. Internal-external locus of control in middle and late life: The search for construct validation. Paper presented at the meeting of the Gerontological Society, San Francisco, November 1977.

Bradburn, N. M., and Caplovitz, D. *Reports on happiness*. Chicago: Aldine, 1965.

Brim, O. G., Jr. The sense of personal control over one's life. Paper presented at the meeting of the American Psychological Association, New Orleans, August 1974.

Costa, P. T., Jr., and McCrae, R. R. Still stable after all these years: Personality as a key to some issues in adulthood and old age. In P. B. Baltes and O. G. Brim, Jr. (Eds.), *Life-span development and behavior*. [Vol. 3]. New York: Academic, 1980.

de Charms, R. Personal causation and locus of control: Two different traditions and two uncorrelated measures. In H. M. Lefcourt (Ed.), *Research with the locus of control construct. Vol. 1. Assessment methods*. New York: Academic, 1981.

Felton, B., and Kahana, E. Adjustment and situationally-bound locus of control among institutionalized aged. *Journal of Gerontology*, 29:295–301, 1974.

Gatz, M. Ready or not: Solicited and unsolicited life events. Paper presented at the meeting of the Gerontological Society, Washington, D.C., November 1979.

Gatz, M., and Siegler, I. C. Locus of control: A retrospective. Paper presented at the meeting of the American Psychological Association, Los Angeles, August 1981.

Gurin, P., Gurin, G., and Morrison, B. M. Personal and ideological aspects of internal and external control. *Social psychology*, 41:275–296, 1978.

Heise, D. R. Separating reliability and stability in the test-retest correlation. *American Sociological Review*, 34:93–101, 1969.

Jessor, R., et al. *Society, personality and deviant behavior*. New York: Holt, Reinhart and Winston, 1968.

Kuypers, J. A. Internal-external locus of control, ego functioning, and personality characteristics in old age. *Gerontologist*, 12:168–173, 1972.

Lachman, M. E. Personal efficacy in middle and old age: Differential and normative patterns of change. In G. H. Elder (Ed.), *Life course dynamics: From 1968 to the 80's.*, in press.

Lao, R. C. The developmental trend of the locus of control. *Personality and social psychology bulletin*, 1974, 1:348–350.

Lefcourt, H. M. *Locus of control: Current trends in theory and research*. Hillsdale, N.J.: Erlbaum, 1976.

Lefcourt, H. M. (Ed.), *Research with the locus of control construct. Vol. 1, Assessment methods*. New York: Academic, 1981.

Levenson, H. Activism and powerful others: Distinctions within the concept of internal-external locus of control, *Journal of Personality Assessment*, 38:377–383, 1974.

Levenson, H. Differentiating among internality, powerful others and choice. In H. M. Lefcourt

(Ed.), *Research with the locus of control construct. Vol. 1. Assessment methods*. New York: Academic, 1981.

Nehrke, M. F., Hulicka, I. M., and Morganti, J. Age differences in life satisfaction, locus of control, and self-concept. *International Journal of Aging and Human Development*, 11:25–33, 1980.

Nesselroade, J. R. Implications of the trait-state distinction for the study of aging. Address given at the meeting of the American Psychological Association, Anaheim, Calif., 1983.

Palmore, E. B., et al. Stress and adaptation in later life. *Journal of Gerontology*, 34:841–851, 1979.

Palmore, E. B., and Luikart, C. Health and social factors related to life satisfaction. *Journal of Health and Social Behavior*, 13:68–79, 1972.

Phares, E. J. *Locus of control: A personality determinant of behavior*. Morristown, N.J.: General Learning Press, 1973.

Rodin, J. Personal control through the life course. Paper presented at the meeting of the American Psychological Association, Washinton, D.C., August 1982.

Rotter, J. B. Generalized expectancies for internal versus external control of reinforcement. *Psychological Monographs*, 80, whole no. 609, 1966.

Rotter, J. B. Some problems and misconceptions related to the construct of internal versus external control of reinforcement. *Journal of Clinical and Consulting Psychology*, 43:56–67, 1975.

Ryckman, R. M., and Malikiosi, M. X. Relationship between locus of control and chronological age. *Psychological Reports*, 36:655–658, 1975.

Siegler, I. C. Psychological aspects of the Duke longitudinal studies. In K. W. Schaie (Ed.), *Longitudinal studies of adult psychological development*. New York: Guilford Press, 1983.

Siegler, I. C., et al. *Aging competently*. Final Report. Washington, D.C.: U.S. Administration on Aging, April 1979.

Speilberger, C. (Ed.), Anxiety and behavior. New York: Academic Press, 1966.

Staats, S., et al. Internal versus external locus of control for three age groups. *International Journal of Aging and Human Development*, 5:7–10, 1974.

Weisz, J. R., and Stipek, D. J. Competence, contingency, and the development of perceived control. *Human Development*, 25:250–281, 1982.

Wolk, S., and Kurtz, J. Positive adjustment and involvement during aging and expectancy for internal control. *Journal of Consulting and Clinical Psychology*, 43:173–178, 1975.

Ziegler, M., and Reid, D. W. Correlates of locus of desired control in two samples of elderly persons: Community residents and hospitalized patients. *Journal of Consulting and Clinical Psychology*, 47:977–979, 1979.

Self-Concept Content

Linda K. George and Morris A. Okun

The topic of self-concept has great potential and numerous problems. The potential of self-concept lies primarily in its role as a mechanism by which social phenomena influence individual attitudes and behavior. The identification and understanding of such mechanisms remains a major challenge for the social sciences. To be sure, previous research has not completely delineated the process by which self-concept serves as a mediating variable between social interaction and individual experience; nonetheless, previous theory and research have been sufficiently compelling to foster continued interest in the nature, antecedents, and consequences of self-perception.

The problems in the self-concept literature also must be acknowledged. The study of self-concept has been characterized by theoretical and methodological disagreement, and progress in understanding the nature and dynamics of self-perception has been concomitantly sluggish. Theoretical dissensus is perhaps the major obstacle to unified and programmatic examinations of self-concept (cf. Breytspraak and George, 1982; Wells and Marwell, 1976; Wylie, 1974). As a direct result of the multiple theoretical perspectives which address self-concept, instrumentation for measuring self-concept and related constructs (e.g., self-esteem and self-regard) is heterogeneous, with little evidence that the measures tap the same underlying phenomena (Breytspraak and George, 1982; Crandall, 1973). Consequently, communication and cumulation of results are hindered.

Theoretical Background and Rationale

This paper builds directly upon an emerging theme in the self-concept literature: the distinction between and the importance of self-concept content and structure. Self-concept content refers to the specific elements of self-perception that the individual has about himself or herself. Perceptions of oneself as good with figures, disliking crowds, and having a cheerful disposition are examples of elements of self-concept content. Self-concept structure refers to the way in which the individual organizes his or her self-concept contents into an overall configuration.

A number of theoretical perspectives interface well with the distinction between self-concept content and structure. For example, sociologists frequently focus on the links between role occupancy and self-concept (cf. Burke and Tully, 1977; George, et al., 1980). Role theory thus provides fertile ground for the development of hypotheses about the relationships between social structure and self-concept content. Role theory also is potentially important for examination of the dynamics of self-perception in that one would expect role changes to be accompanied by changes in self-concept content. Role occupancy also may be related to the structure of self-concept. Role loss and role gain may trigger changes in the structure (as well as the content) of self-concept. Although previous self-research based on role theory has focused primarily upon issues of self-concept content, the theoretical perspective appears well suited to the development of testable hypotheses concerning both self-concept content and structure.

Self-concept structure has received less theoretical and empirical attention than self-concept content. Stryker (1968) suggests that self-concept content is organized along a salience hierarchy, reflecting the differential importance that the individual attaches to self-concept elements. Other theorists suggest, from a role theory perspective, that social roles vary in their pervasiveness and that this affects the organization of the self (George, 1980; Linton, 1936). The roles associated with broad, ascribed statuses such as sex roles, for example, are viewed as highly pervasive and thus expected to be more central components of the self-concept structure than roles with narrow behavioral boundaries.

Perhaps the most intriguing perspective on self-concept structure is provided by Epstein, who suggests that self-concept is a theory about oneself. "It is a theory that the individual has unwittingly constructed about himself as an experiencing, functioning individual; and it is part of a broader theory which he holds with respect to his entire range of significant experience" (1973: 407). Epstein contends that the self-concept can be evaluated using general criteria applicable to scientific theories. "All theories can be evaluated by the degree to which they are extensive, parsimonious, empirically valid, internally consistent, testable, and useful. Accordingly, it should be of interest to examine the self-theories of individuals with respect to each of these attributes" (Epstein, 1973: 408). Epstein's work is a creative and stimulating approach to identifying aspects of self-concept structure that impact on individual adaptation and behavior.

Although brief, this discussion demonstrates that the distinction between self-concept content and structure is valuable. It interfaces well with previous theoretical perspectives and is a fertile area for generating testable hypotheses. This paper focuses exclusively upon self-concept content, an appropriate point of departure in that measurement of self-concept structure presupposes the ability to identify the contents of the self.

Measuring Self-Concept Content

Several reference works provide detailed descriptions and evaluations of standardized measures of self-concept content (Breytspraak and George, 1982; Crandall, 1973; Wells and Marwell, 1976; Wylie, 1974). These measures can be classified into six types of instruments: Likert scales, dichotomous forced-choice instruments, adjective checklists, semantic differential scales, Q-sorts, and semiprojective/open-ended measures (Breytspraak and George, 1982).

For the purposes of this paper, the most relevant difference in the various measurement approaches is the degree to which the respondent versus the investigator determines and defines the self-perceptions about which information is gathered. In semiprojective/open-ended measures, the respondent defines the relevant self-perceptions reported. According to phenomenological and symbolic interactionist perspectives, subjective determinations are crucial in that the individual's self-concept cannot be understood apart from his or her definitions. The other five measurement strategies are variations of forced-choice measures (Selltiz et al., 1976). The investigator determines the elements of self-concept which are examined, and the respondent's role in data collection is restricted to reports of the degree to which each element included in the measure is true of himself or herself.

In terms of psychometric and statistical issues, forced-choice self-concept measures clearly are more attractive than open-ended instruments. Forced-choice instruments ensure that comparable data are obtained from all respondents (comparable in both content and amount), permit the application of standard psychometric assessment techniques, and generate quantitative data which increase analytic flexibility. Open-ended measures are limited in the psychometric and statistical techniques that can be applied and typically generate nominal data which vary in scope and content across respondents.

Conceptually, however, open-ended measures have some attractive features that are not characteristic of forced-choice instruments. At the broadest level, self-concept is a subjective phenomenon, available only to the individual. The most attractive measures are those which permit the respondent to provide information about his or her self-concept contents in a natural manner. It is difficult to justify the more quantitative approaches simply because they better fit the standard statistical tools used by social scientists. Moreover, self-concept typically is conceptualized as a changeable phenomenon that is modified on the basis of experience and, according to at least some theorists, also may be affected by more transitory situational factors. From this perspective, many standard psychometric assessment techniques, such as test-retest reliability procedures, may be inappropriate methods of determining the adequacy of self-concept measures.

Our purpose is not to condemn forced-choice self-concept measures and praise open-ended instruments. Instead, we urge a more balanced perspective in which the potential benefits of both measurement strategies are recognized. There is nothing inherently difficult or invalid in the use of forced-choice instruments. Considerable experience suggests that respondents can respond to forced-choice mesaures in a meaningful way. When using forced-choice measures, however, it becomes encumbent upon the investigator to document that the self-concept elements included in the measures are representative of the entire universe of relevant self-concept elements. Unless this assumption can be made with confidence, the investigator runs a great risk of missing self-concept content that is important to at least some study participants. The neglect of relevant self-concept elements would not only render measurement of self-concept content incomplete; it also would greatly hinder efforts to elucidate the structure of the self-concept. The organization of the self-concept cannot be accurately specified if essential content elements are not collected.

Increased attention should be devoted to the potential utility of open-ended measures in general and the degree to which forced-choice and open-ended self-concept measures generate similar—or at least compatible—information. In this paper, we examine responses to one of the best-known open-ended self-concept measures (the Who Are You?) in a heterogeneous sample of middle-aged and older adults and we correlate responses from the open-ended measure with those from a forced-choice self-concept measure included in the same study.

Self-Concept in Middle and Later Life

Because this examination utilizes a sample of middle-aged and older adults, a few comments about the relevance of self-concept to the broader concerns of the aging and adult development literatures are merited. Self-concept has been featured in a number of previous sociological perspectives on the aging process. Kuypers and Bengtson (1973), for example, suggest that the aging process can be characterized as a "social breakdown syndrome" in which older persons are systematically deprived of valued attachments to the social structure, labeled an incompetent, internalize those negative labels into their self-perceptions, and experience atrophy of skills as a result of the labeling process and its internalization. The atrophy of skills then becomes evidence that seemingly justifies the negative labeling, thus perpetuating the vicious cycle of the social breakdown syndrome. Rosow (1974) makes a similar argument, suggesting that the social structure systematically deprives older people of fundamental and meaningful attachments to the social order and that this is a form of structural alienation which impacts negatively upon self-concept and self-esteem in later life.

Adult development theorists also attach substantial significance to the self-concept. Levinson (1978) places perhaps the greatest emphasis upon the self-concept, viewing it as the central arena within which developmental processes can be observed. Other developmental theorists view adulthood as characterized by identifiable maturational changes, but with less crisis and discontinuity than suggested by Levinson. Haan, for example, concludes that adult development is primarily a process of increased individuation over time, with the patterns of individuation consisting primarily of a refining and strengthening of preexistent personality traits and intrapsychic commitments (1981). She views self-concept as one of the psychological phenomena exhibiting this type of gradual development.

On yet another front, a number of social scientists have focused their attention upon the major life events and role transitions characteristic of adulthood and the effects of such transitions upon self-concept and subjective well-being. Events such as widowhood (Glick et al., 1974; Lopata, 1973), retirement (Back and Guptill, 1966), and departure of children from the parental home (Harkins, 1978) are examples of transitions which can lead to major reorganizations of self-concept and social identity. The work of Fiske and colleagues comprises the most detailed examination of the relationship between self-concept and life events during adulthood. The focus of their work is the self-concept, which is viewed as the "wellsprings of choice and behavior" during adulthood (Fiske, 1980: 245). Their research suggests four important dimensions of adult self-concept content: an interpersonal dimension that focuses upon social relationships; an altruistic dimension that incorporates ethical, religious, and philosophical concerns; a mastery dimension that encompasses competence and a sense of efficacy; and self-protectiveness which includes concerns about economic, physical, and subjective well-being. People differ with respect to the amount of commitment invested in the four dimensions of self-concept, generating different hierarchies of commitment. In addition to differences across persons, an individual's hierarchy of commitment changes over time. The central focus of Fiske's research is documentation of the degree to which significant life events trigger changes in individuals' hierarchies of commitment and the patterns of change typical of specific types of life events. Fiske's work has been a major contribution to the life events literature and one of the few research efforts to examine both the content and structure of self-concept in a theoretically grounded manner.

Methods

Sample

The analyses reported in this paper are restricted to respondents who participated in the first round of the Duke Second Longitudinal Study. Cross-sectional analyses were necessary because the Who Are You (WAY) was administered only at the first time of measurement. Further, the analyses are based on the subset of respondents with complete information on all the variables of interest, resulting in an analytic sample of 316 respondents—163 men and 153 women, ranging in age from forty-six to seventy-one. Empirical comparisons indicate that the respondents omitted from analyses did not differ significantly from those with complete information in age, sex, education, income, marital status, self-rated health, and physician-rated health.

Instruments

The Who Are You. The Who Are You? (WAY) was introduced by Bugental and Zelen in 1950 as a measure of self-concept content. The instrument was specifically designed to permit respondents to define the aspects of self-concept most salient to personal identity. In original form, the WAY elicited three responses to the stimulus question: Who Are You? In 1954, Kuhn and McPartland introduced the Twenty Statements Test (TST), which used the same stimulus question as the WAY, but required respondents to report twenty self-descriptors. Clearly, the TST generates more data about self-concept content than the WAY.

Although administration of the WAY (and TST) is simple and straightforward, coding the heterogeneous responses elicited by the stimulus has proven to be complex. Over the past thirty years, a variety of coding schemes have been developed for the WAY and TST. The WAY data reported in this paper were coded four ways.

Kuhn and McPartland (1954), in a classic study of self-concept content, applied a simple dichotomous coding scheme to TST data, classifying responses as consensual or subconsensual. In their words, consensual references refer to groups, statuses, and roles "whose limits and conditions of membership are matters of common knowledge" and subconsensual references include groups, attributes, and traits "which would require interpretation by the respondents to be precise or to place him relative to other people'' (Kuhn and McPartland, 1954: 70). The ratio of consensual to subconsensual references then provides a measure of the degree to which personal identity is based on social attachments. It is interesting to note that the few previous studies which examined age differences in self-concept using the WAY or TST indicate that older adults report significantly fewer consensual self-references than younger adults (Kuhn and McPartland, 1954; Mulford and Salisbury, 1964).

Epstein classifies self-concept content into what he calls three major ''empirical selves'': the physical self, the social self, and the psychological self (1973). Compatible with this orientation, responses to the WAY and TST can be coded into three categories: physical and material references, social references, and psychological references. In addition to categorizing self-descriptors in three broad categories, this coding scheme orders the self-references along a continuum of increasing abstraction.

The most detailed and theoretically grounded coding scheme for the WAY and TST is that developed by Gordon (1968). This coding scheme, depicted in table C—18, includes thirty detailed categories which can be aggregated into eight more general aspects of the self. The data were coded into the thirty detailed categories and also aggregated into the eight broader categories of the Gordon classification system. We used the detailed system to detect the most specific patterns in the data; the aggregated coding scheme was used to permit examina-

Table C—18. *Gordon's coding scheme for WAY or TST data.*

A. Ascribed characteristics
   1. Sex
   2. Age
   3. Name
   4. Racial or national heritage
   5. Religious categorization

B. Roles and memberships
   6. Kinship roles
   7. Occupational roles
   8. Student roles
   9. Political affiliation
   10. Social status
   11. Territoriality, citizenship
   12. Membership in actual interacting group

C. Abstract identification
   13. Existential, individuating
   14. Membership in an abstract category
   15. Ideological and belief references

D. Interests and activities
   16. Judgments, tastes, likes
   17. Intellectual concerns
   18. Artistic activities
   19. Other activities

E. Material references
   20. Possessions, resources
   21. Physical self, body image

F. Four systemic senses of self
   22. Sense of moral worth
   23. Sense of self-determination
   24. Sense of unity
   25. Sense of competence

G. Personal characteristics
   26. Interpersonal style
   27. Psychic style, personality

H. External meanings
   28. Judgments imputed to others
   29. Situational references
   30. Uncodable responses

tion of broader patterns and to maximize category size for comparisons across subgroups.

Duke Semantic Differential Self-Concept Measure. The forced-choice self-concept measure included in the study was one of the many semantic differential measures which have been developed to elicit respondents' self-ratings. This semantic differential measure is very brief, including seven bipolar adjectives which respondents rate in terms of the referent "what I really am." The seven adjective pairs are: inactivity/busy, not free to do things/free to do things, useless/useful, look to the past/look to the future, ineffective/effective, dissatisfied/satisfied, and disregarded/respected.

In spite of the small number of items, factor analysis confirms that the items comprise three distinct dimensions (Back, 1971, Back and Guptill, 1966). The first factor taps perceptions of usefulness and includes three adjective pairs: inactive/busy, useless/useful, and ineffective/effective. The second factor, also comprised of three items, appears to represent a well-being dimension. The adjective pairs loading on the second factor are: not free to do things/free to do things, dissatisfied/satisfied, and disregarded/respected. The remaining item, look to the future/look to the past, does not load on either of the first two factors and is analyzed separately.

Results

Table C—19 presents the percentages of the sample reporting one or more self-representations in the categories of the Kuhn and McPartland and Epstein schemes, and major categories of the Gordon coding schemes. Percentages are presented for the whole sample, for males and females, and for three age groups that roughly correspond to ten-year cohorts. Univariate tests of statistical significance were used to determine if differences across categories for the whole sample, sex differences in proportions of reporting within categories, and age differences within categories were statistically significant. Because of the multiple types of statistical significance testing, significant results are not noted on the table. Any significant results are highlighted in the text, however.

In terms of consensual versus subconsensual references, the vast majority (95 percent) of the respondents report at least one subconsensual reference. A much smaller, but nonetheless sizeable, 44 percent of the respondents mention at least one consensual self-reference. The difference between these two proportions is statistically significant. There is not a significant sex difference in the likelihood of reporting either type of reference. There also are no significant age differences in reports of subconsensual references. The age groups significantly differ in reports of consensual references, however, with fifty-five to sixty-four year olds reporting the fewest consensual referents and forty-five to fifty-four year olds reporting the most consensual references. These age differences do not support earlier findings (Kuhn and McPartland, 1954; Mulford and Salisbury, 1964) of a monotonic decrease in reports of consensual references across successively older age groups.

Table C—19. *Percentages of respondents reporting categories of self-concept content, using Kuhn and McPartland, Epstein, and Gordon major categories coding schemes.*

Self-concept content	Whole sample N=316	Gender Male N=163	Female N=153	Age 45–54 N=98	55–64 N=128	65+ N=90
Gordon's major categories						
Ascribed characteristics	.06	.08	.05	.08	.06	.06
Roles and memberships	.21	.25	.17	.22	.20	.21
Abstract identification	.07	.08	.05	.04	.07	.09
Interests and activities	.37	.40	.35	.36	.34	.43
Material references	.28	.22	.33	.34	.23	.28
Four systemic senses of self	.77	.77	.78	.77	.82	.71
Personal characteristics	.45	.43	.47	.41	.45	.50
External meanings	.04	.06	.02	.03	.05	.03
Epstein's system						
Physical self	.24	.19	.30	.30	.20	.26
Social self	.29	.37	.20	.29	.30	.28
Psychological self	.94	.92	.96	.92	.95	.94
Kuhn and McPartland system						
Consensual referents	.44	.45	.42	.49	.39	.44
Subconsensual referents	.95	.94	.96	.93	.97	.94

The Epstein classification scheme exhibits similar patterns. Again, the vast majority of respondents reported one or more psychological self-descriptions. Smaller and nearly equal proportions of respondents reported physical and social references. The differences in proportions of respondents reporting types of self-references is statistically significant. There also are significant sex differences for two of the three categories. A significantly greater percentage of men than women report social self-references. Women were significantly more likely than men to report physical references. One of the three age comparisons was statistically significant. Again, a nonlinear trend emerged, with those aged fifty-five to sixty-four least likely and those aged forty-five to fifty-four most likely to report physical references.

Turning to the eight major categories of the Gordon classification system, the largest differences occur across categories. Very few respondents report ascribed characteristics, abstract identifications, or external meanings. In contrast, 20–45 percent of the respondents reported roles and memberships, interests and activities, material references, and personal characteristics. The most popular type of self-description was systemic sense of self, reported by over 75 percent of the sample. Analysis of variance indicated that the differences across categories were highly statistically significant. Only one of the eight categories differed

Table C—20. *Percentages of respondents reporting categories of self-concept content, using Gordon detailed categories.*

Self-concept content	Whole sample $N=316$	Gender Male $N=163$	Female $N=153$	Age 45–54 $N=98$	55–64 $N=128$	65+ $N=90$
1. Sex	0	0	0	0	0	0
2. Age	.03	.04	.02	.02	.04	.03
3. Name	0	0	0	0	0	0
4. Race, national heritage	0	0	0	0	0	0
5. Religion	.03	.04	.02	.06	.01	.02
6. Kinship roles	.13	.18	.07	.15	.11	.13
7. Occupational roles	0	0	0	0	0	0
8. Student role	0	0	0	0	0	0
9. Political affiliation	0	0	0	0	0	0
10. Social status	.01	.01	.01	.01	.01	0
11. Territoriality, citizenship	.10	.10	.12	.08	.11	.02
12. Membership in group	.01	.01	0	.02	0	0
13. Existential, individuating	0	0	0	0	0	0
14. Abstract category	0	0	0	0	0	0
15. Ideology and belief	.07	.08	.06	.04	.08	.09
16. Judgments, tastes, likes	.34	.39	.35	.31	.37	.41
17. Intellectual concerns	0	0	0	0	0	0
18. Artistic activities	0	0	0	0	0	0
19. Other activities	.04	.06	.01	.05	.03	.02
20. Possessions, resources	.06	.08	.05	.05	.08	.06
21. Physical self, body image	.22	.15	.29	.30	.16	.23
22. Sense of moral worth	.44	.37	.51	.44	.47	.40
23. Sense of self-determination	.30	.29	.31	.36	.31	.23
24. Sense of unity	.23	.29	.18	.24	.23	.23
25. Sense of competence	.04	.05	.02	.03	.02	.08
26. Interpersonal style	.45	.43	.47	.41	.45	.50
27. Psychic style	0	0	0	0	0	0
28. Judgments imputed to others	.03	.04	.01	.02	.03	.03
29. Situational references	0	0	0	0	0	0
30. Uncodable responses	.01	.01	.01	.01	.02	0

significantly by gender: a higher proportion of women than men reported material references. None of the age comparisons was significant.

Table C—20 presents the percentages of respondents reporting one or more self-references in the thirty detailed categories of the Gordon classification system. Again, results are reported for the whole sample, for men and women, and for the three age groups. Because of the complexity of this table, description of results will be restricted to major patterns. First, fully twelve of the thirty categories were empty (i.e., less than half of one percent reported a relevant self-description). An additional ten categories were reported by less than 10 percent of the respondents. Thus, only eight categories were reported by 11 percent or more of the sample. The categories reported with considerable frequency included kinship roles, citizenship, judgments and tastes, physical references, moral worth, self-determination, unity, and interpersonal references.

Because of the large number of empty cells, tests of significance were limited. Analysis of variance was applied to the eighteen categories with non-empty cells for the whole sample. The results were statistically significant, indicating that the differences among rates of self-description were greater than would be expected by chance. Four of the eighteen gender comparisons within categories were statistically significant. Men were significantly more likely than women to report kinship roles and references concerning unity. Women were significantly

Table C—21. *Relationships between WAY self-concept measures and dimensions of the semantic differential self-concept measure.*

WAY self-concept content	Usefulness	Satisfaction
Gordon's major categories		
Ascribed characteristics	−.10	−.10
Roles and memberships		
Abstract identification		
Interests and activities		
Material references	−.13	
Four systemic senses of self	.18	.15
Personal characteristics		
External meanings		
Epstein's system		
Physical self	−.10	
Social self		
Psychological self	.09	.11
Kuhn and McPartland system		
Consensual references	.11	−.13
Subconsensual references	−.11	.13

Note: There were no significant correlations between the "look to the future" dimension of the semantic differential and the WAY variables.

more likely than men to make physical and moral references. Again, age was nonlinearly related to a self-concept category. Specifically, respondents aged fifty-five to sixty-four were least likely and those aged forty-five to fifty-four were most likely to report a physical reference. Age differences in rates of report for the other seventeen categories were not statistically significant.

In examining the relationships between the WAY and the semantic differential, the eight superordinate categories of Gordon's classification system were used. By using the eight-category system in lieu of the thirty-category system, the problem of small or empty cells is partially alleviated. Obviously the eight- and thirty-category systems overlap considerably, resulting in little information loss.

Table C—21 presents the significant correlations between the WAY as coded in three ways with the dimensions of the semantic differential self-concept measure. The most striking aspect of the table is that few relationships between the WAY and the semantic differential responses are significant. Moreover, the few correlations that achieve statistical significance are quite weak (highest $r = .18$). These results suggest that the two self-concept measures did not share much variance.

Discussion

There are several issues which we wish to address in this section of the paper. We will summarize the results of the study, briefly discuss what we believe to be the substantive and methodological implications of the findings, describe the limitations of the study, and conclude with a recommended agenda for future efforts to effectively measure self-concept content.

In this sample, the majority of responses to the WAY were relatively abstract personality traits, psychological characteristics, and subconsensual attributes. The smaller proportion of consensual and more concrete self-descriptions were nearly equally divided between physical or material references and social references. We were surprised at the low percentage of respondents who reported social roles and group memberships. The proportion of social references was low both in absolute terms and in comparison to those reported in previous studies of older adults (cf. Coe, 1965; Kahana and Coe, 1969; Smith, 1966). Other analyses based on these data indicate that this is an active group of adults who are engaged in many social roles and embedded in supportive social structures (cf. George, 1978; Palmore and Luikart, 1972). We do not have an explanation for the sample's focus upon personal as opposed to social characteristics, but we find it an intriguing pattern.

Our examination of possible gender and age differences among types of self-references revealed few systematic patterns. Two findings, however, are worth reiteration and replication in future studies. First, in terms of gender, a relatively strong pattern emerged across coding schemes in which women were more likely than men to report physical and material self-references and men were more likely to report aspects of identity linked to social roles and group memberships. Second, although few significant age differences were identified in the types of self-references reported, those which emerged were consistently nonlinear. In each of the significant age differences, the major contrast was between respondents aged fifty-five to sixty-four and those aged forty-five to fifty-four, with the group of respondents aged sixty-five and older intermediate. This pattern suggests that age should not be used as a continuous variable in studies of self-concept unless possible deviations from linearity have been considered. Moreover, this pattern of findings is more compatible with an interpretation of cohort differences than of developmental change—although the latter point should be interpreted only as a hypothesis in need of longitudinal examination.

Based on the results of this study, we do not prefer a particular coding scheme for the WAY (or TST). The more detailed classification systems developed by Gordon retain the most information and do not preclude aggregating the data into broader categories during data analysis. Therefore, from a practical perspective, the more detailed coding schemes seem to be worthwhile investments that maximize the information available and the opportunities for data analysis. Conceptually, however, all of the coding schemes offer ways of organizing the data that permit the testing of useful hypotheses.

Interpreting the relationships between the WAY data and the dimensions of the sematic differential measure is the most difficult aspect of the paper. The difficulty stems from the results that indicate only a few significant (and very modest) correlations. If one considers these correlations to be convergent validity coefficients, one would be disappointed by their magnitude. We do not feel, however, that the correlations reported in this paper represent an adequate test of convergent validity. Neither of the self-concept measures is sufficiently comprehensive to permit conclusions about convergent validity. Both measures may elicit valid data about self-concept content, but they may fail to overlap because they tap different elements of content.

If we do not view the relationships among the WAY and semantic differential as convergent validity coefficients, however, the question remains: what does this analysis tell us? We suggest that the two measures can best be viewed as alternate methods of eliciting information about a limited number of self-concept elements. Our conclusion, based on the results, is that the two measures generate information about different elements of the self-concept.

This study had two major limitations which merit explicit comment. The most consequential limitation of the study was the brevity of the two self-concept measures. We would have preferred the TST to the WAY and a longer forced-choice measure. We were particularly hindered by the low frequencies for many of the categories in the more complex coding schemes of the WAY. The second major limitation builds directly upon the first: because the data were very sparse, we were limited in the types of statistical analysis that could be employed. It should be noted that the statistical limitations were more a reflection of the number of responses made to the WAY than to the qualitative nature of the responses. Gordon's experience with the TST is informative. Because he had a much greater number of responses per respondent, he was able to develop more quantitative measures of self-concept content (e.g., sums of the number of times each category was reported) and to utilize more sophisticated statistical techniques to examine patterns of content and their relationships to other variables.

We believe that the measurement of self-concept is an important issue which merits increased attention. Development of a more comprehensive measure of self-concept content is perhaps the most important task awaiting effort. We also believe that the development of such an instrument would render the differences between open-ended and forced-choice measures nearly irrelevant.

A giant step forward would be the development of a forced-choice measure that is based on a representative sampling of the full range of self-concept elements. The first step in the development of such an instrument would be assembling the universe of self-concept elements. Such a procedure might involve collating the items from all extant measures and, more importantly, eliciting reports of all possible self-concept elements from broad and representative samples. Various forms of qualitative and open-ended measurement would be the only method available for obtaining such information. Obviously a measure cannot be developed which would require respondents to rate all possible elements of self-concept content. But one sample, chosen to be sufficiently representative to generate adequate population norms, could be asked to do so—and the results from that sample could be used to determine the number and nature of the dimensions that characterize the universe of elements. Ultimately, a comprehensive measure of reasonable length could be developed by appropriately sampling items within dimensions.

The plan we have outlined for the development of a more comprehensive measure of self-concept content also includes attention to self-concept structure. Statistical analyses that could identify the dimensions of self-concept content would in fact generate information about the structure of the self-concept. This is an important component of the overall development of the instrument. If one of the goals of measuring self-concept content is to permit us to also explore self-concept structure, it is crucial that the sampling of elements be performed in such a way that important dimensions of the self not be inadvertently omitted or sampled inadequately.

Undoubtedly some originators of self-control measures already believe that they have implemented our general plan outlined. The work of Fitts (1965), who originated the Tennessee Self-Concept Scale (TSCS), is similar in some ways to our general plan, but there also are important differences. Fitts reports that the TSCS was developed by selecting the ninety items which comprise the scale from a "large pool" of potential items. The ninety items included in the scale were chosen on the basis of recommendations of relevance made by seven psychologists, and the dimensional structure of the scale was determined by factor analysis. (The TSCS is usually described as a 100-item measure. Ten of the scale's items are the MMPI L-Scale and they are used to adjust TSCS scores for social desirability. The remaining ninety items are self-descriptions of self-concept content.) Although the TSCS is a sophisticated and lengthy self-concept measure, relative to others available it is not based on the type of development plan outlined above. First, a broad sample of respondents was not tested with respect to their self-concept elements in order to generate an item pool. Second, the dimensions were identified after selection of the items, whereas we suggest that determination of the dimensional structure precede the selection of items. Until the dimensions are identified, one cannot sample items in a way to ensure that an adequate number of items from each dimension are included in the instrument. In short, we are confident that what we are suggesting has not been done previously—and that it is worth doing.

The relevance of the self-concept for the social sciences in general and the study of aging and adult development in particular cannot be questioned. At this point, theories about the self outstrip our ability to effectively measure the content and structure of self-concept. Self-concept research has much potential. Without attention to measurement problems, however, progress will be considerably slower.

References

Back, K. W. Transition to aging and the self-image. *Aging and Human Development*, 2:296–304, 1971.

Back, K. W., and Guptill, C. S. Retirement and self-ratings. In I. H. Simpson and J. C. McKinney (Eds.), *Social aspects of aging*. Durham, N.C.: Duke University Press, 1966.

Breytspraak, L. M., and George, L. K. Self-concept and self-esteem. In D. J. Mangen and W. A. Peterson (Eds.), *Research instruments in social gerontology. Volume 1. Clinical and social psychology*. Minneapolis: University of Minnesota Press, 1982.

Bugental, J., and Zelen, S. Investigations into the self-concept. I: The WAY technique. *Journal of Personality*, 18:483–498, 1950.

Burke, P. J., and Tully, J. C. The measurement of role identity. *Social Forces*, 55:881–897, 1977.

Coe, R. Self-conceptions and institutionalization. In A. M. Rose and W. A. Peterson (Eds.), *Older people and their social world*. Philadelphia: F. A. Davis, 1965.

Crandall, R. C. The measurement of self-esteem and related constructs. In J. Robinson and P. Shaver (Eds.), *Measures of social psychological attitudes*. Ann Arbor, Mich.: Survey Research Center, Institute for Social Research, 1973.

Epstein, S. The self-concept revisited: Or a theory of a theory. *American Psychologist*, 28:404–416, 1973.

Fiske, M. Changing hierarchies of commitment in adulthood. In N. J. Smelser and E. H. Erikson (Eds.), *Themes of work and love in adulthood*. Cambridge, Mass.: Harvard University Press, 1980.

Fitts, W. H. *Tennessee Self-Concept Scale: Manual*. Nashville: Counselor Recordings and Tests, 1965.

George, L. K. The impact of personality and social status factors upon levels of activity and psychological well-being. *Journal of Gerontology*, 33:840–847, 1978.

George, L. K. *Role transitions in later life*. Monterey, Calif.: Brooks/Cole, 1980.

George, L. K., Mutran, E., and Pennybacker, M., The meaning and measurement of age identity. *Experimental Aging Research*, 6:283–298, 1980.

Glick, I. O., Weiss, R. S., and Parkes, C. M. *The first year of bereavement*. New York: Wiley, 1974.

Gordon, C. Configurations of content. In C. Gordon and K. J. Gergen (Eds.), *The self in social interaction*. New York: Wiley, 1968.

Haan, N. Common dimensions of personality development: Early adolescence to middle life. In D. H. Eichorn et al. (Eds.), *Present and past in middle life*. New York: Academic, 1981.

Harkins, E. B. Effects of empty-nest transition on self-report of psychological and physical well-being. *Journal of Marriage and the Family*, 40:459–556, 1978.

Kahana, E., and Coe, R. M. Self and staff conceptions of institutionalized aged. *Gerontologist*, 9:264–267, 1969.

Kuhn, M. H., and McPartland, T. S. An empirical investigation of self-attitudes. *American Sociological Review*, 19:68–76, 1954.

Kuypers, J. A., and Bengtson, V. L. Social breakdown and competence. *Human Development*, 16:181–201, 1973.

Levinson, D. J., et al. *The seasons of a man's life*. New York: Knopf, 1978.

Linton, R. *A study of man*. New York: Appleton-Century, 1936.

Lopata, H. Z. Self-identity in marriage and widowhood. *Sociological Quarterly*, 14:407–418, 1973.

Mulford, H. A., and Salisbury, II, W. W. Self-conceptions in a general population. *Sociological Quarterly*, 5:35–46, 1964.

Palmore, E. B., and Luikart, C. Health and social factors related to life satisfaction. *Journal of Health and Social Behavior*, 13:68–80, 1972.

Rosow, I. *Socialization to old age*. Berkeley: University of California Press, 1974.

Selltiz, C., Wrightsman, L. W., and Cook, S. W. *Research methods in social relations*. 3d Ed. New York: Holt, Rinehart and Winston, 1976.

Smith, J. The narrowing social world of the aged. In I. H. Simpson and J. C. McKinney (Eds.), *Social aspects of aging*. Durham, N.C.: Duke University Press, 1966.

Stryker, S. Identity salience and role performance. *Journal of Marriage and the Family*, 4:558–564, 1968.

Wells, L. E., and Marwell, G. *Self-esteem: Its conceptualization and measurement*. Beverly Hills, Calif.: Sage, 1976.

Wylie, R. C. *The self concept*, Vol. 1. Lincoln: University of Nebraska Press, 1974.

Life Graphs and Life Events

Linda Bookover Bourque and Kurt W. Back

In earlier papers we reported the characteristics of a projective technique, the life graph, which simultaneously investigates aspects of the society in which the aging individual lives and the aging individual's perception of his own unique passage through that society (Back and Bourque, 1970; Bourque and Back, 1969). The data showed that the majority of respondents had a picture of their whole lives, past and future, and could visualize it in the form of a curve. The data reported in earlier papers were collected in a single, national, cross-sectional survey of adults over the age of twenty-one.

The current paper asks specific questions about the use of graphs. The principal question is how many people have a relatively constant picture of their lives

Reprinted by permission from *Journal of Gerontology*, 32:669–674, 1977.

and how it is changed by potentially stressful events. For this purpose we are using a study based on a special population to which the life graphs were administered several times over a span of four years. Data about stressful events which occurred to respondents during this same period are also available. In this further analysis of changes in life graphs, our intention is threefold. First, we ascertain whether the pattern of life graphs described in the earlier work is repeated in this ad hoc sample. Second, we describe different procedures which can be used in analyzing the patterns and possible changes. Third, we explore the effect various potentially stressful life events have on the graphs that are drawn.

The life graph method conforms to a conceptual orientation which sees the self as essentially stable but adapting in different guises to changing life conditions. This theory has been stated by Marris (1974, 1978–79) and applied by one of the present authors to a model of human development (Back, 1976). In essence, the theory suggests that individuals look at their life as a unit, consider themselves consistent, and anticipate and accept many events without appreciably changing their picture of their whole lives. Thus, people may expect that certain events will make them happy or unhappy, but these events are taken as part of the nature of things and do not upset the whole image of one's life. Some events, which may be called catastrophes, do upset the whole life image. These events will cause a reevaluation of one's whole life, and it is these events that should be reflected in the life graphs as changes over time.

We are studying, therefore, two kinds of events: fluctuations in life graphs which occur as a function of events which may be already anticipated on the graph and fluctuations which occur because of unanticipated events and which lead to a complete restructuring of the graph.

Method

Sample. The data reported in this paper were collected as part of the Duke Second Longitudinal Study. We are concerned only with data collected during time 1, August 1968 through April 1970, and time 3, August 1972 through April 1974. Complete data were obtained from 371 of 380 panel members.

Measuring techniques. The dependent variable is measured using the life graph, and it is operationalized as either the graph characteristics in 1972 or the change in graph characteristics that occurs within the age interval described for a subject between 1968 and 1972.

During each collection period, each subject was presented with a blank grid and was asked: "Imagine how your life could be put in a graph. That is, ups and downs, level periods and so forth. Assuming you live up until at least 80 years of age, how do you think a graph of your life would look? Indicate this by making the graph on this page." Height at five-year intervals is measured in eighths of an inch. Though a number of techniques have been used, the broadest perspective of the life cycle is given by comparing the respondent's present position on the life graph to the graph peak. Is the peak still to come; is it past; how far away is it? Thus, the difference between current age in 1972 and age at peak can also be used as a measure of subjective feelings.

The schedule used during the third testing period included a modified version of Holmes and Rahe's Social Readjustment Rating Scale (Holmes and Masuda, 1974; Holmes and Rahe, 1967). Subjects were asked, "Have any of the following happened to you in the past 12 months, or since the first of 1968?" Items from the SRRS were used as self-reported indicators of social experiences. In contrast to traditional usage, they were not considered as part of a ratio scale designed to measure stress and to predict the occurrence of morbidity and mortality (Goldberg and Comstock, 1976; Hough et al., 1976; Rabkin and Struening, 1976).

In order to generate subsamples that were large enough for analysis, it was necessary to combine the events reported in the last twelve months with those reported since the beginning of 1968. This combination causes a conceptual problem in that life events are an intervening variable and, by going back to the beginning of 1968, we may be including events prior to the collection of the first set of life graphs. There is no way, given the data, that we can determine how many of the reported events happened prior to, or simultaneously with, the drawing of the first graph. We do know that approximately one-third occurred within the past twelve months.

On the basis of substantive interest, we selected four general types of life events to investigate: (1) movement of a child out of the household due to marriage, attending college, etc.; (2) retirement of self or spouse or major change in employment characteristics; (3) major illness of self or family member; and (4) death of spouse or close family member. Because of the rarity of some events, some composite variables combining a series of related questions were created. Questions were combined because of substantive similarity and in order to obtain a sufficient number of subjects to make statistical analysis meaningful. Questions can be raised about the extent to which composite measures obscure the relative importance of the items combined. It is probable that people react somewhat differently to their own retirement and to that of their spouse. Ideally, we would investigate these experiences independently; however, cell size does not allow for that luxury and, since our major objective is to ascertain whether patterns of graphs respond to life-span relevant experiences, we do not consider our inability to make such analyses a major problem at this time.

Analyses. Three-way analyses of variance in which three variables, age, sex, and whether or not the respondent has experienced one of the four categories of life events, were considered as independent variables. A fixed-effect or linear hypothesis model and a classical experimental approach were employed (Nie et al., 1975).

Results

Although mean height at each age was lower, the general shape of the graphs remained as it was reported in earlier papers. Mean height of the graph for the entire sample peaked at age fifty-five. This pattern remained stable through all three measurement periods. Females' graphs were higher at younger ages and showed their highest point at a somewhat earlier age than males. Older subjects drew graphs that were consistently lower. Further, a comparison with previous studies (Back and Bourque, 1970; Bourque and Back, 1969) showed that graphs drawn by subjects in this study were consistently lower for all age groups than those drawn by subjects under forty-five. However, when repeated graphs are drawn by the same individual over intervals of years, the height of the graph is more frequently expanded than constricted.

It is reassuring to learn that the life graph technique appears to have some reliability over both time and different data sets. This consistency very likely reflects the stability of the general view individuals have of their lives; the general perspective is quite lasting and pervasive. However, embedded in this com-

Table C—22. *Multiple classification analysis between difference in height at peak and current age (time 3) and age, sex, and departure of children from the household.*

Variable and category	Unadjusted deviation	*Eta*	Adjusted for independent deviation	*Beta*
Age at time 1				
45–49	−11.6		−10.4	
50–54	− 6.3		− 5.6	
55–59	− 1.0		− 0.4	
60–64[a]	7.4		6.3	
		.34		.30
Sex				
Male	− 4.2		− 3.8	
Female	4.5		4.1	
		.21		.19
Departure of a child				
Yes	− 7.5		− 2.6	
No	3.0		1.0	
		.23		.08
Grand mean = 7.8				
R = .40				
R^2 = .16				

[a]The age cohort which was 65–70 in time 1 was merged with those 60–64 because few respondents in that cohort reported at time 3 the departure of a child within the past four years.

Table C—23. *Multiple classification analysis between difference in height at peak and current age (time 3) and age, sex, and change in work status.*

Variable and category	Unadjusted deviation	*Eta*	Adjusted for independent deviation	*Beta*
Age at time 1				
50–54[a]	−8.5		−8.4	
55–59	−0.9		0.3	
60–64	4.8		3.6	
65–70	9.2		9.1	
		.34		.33
Sex				
Male	−4.2		−4.1	
Female	4.5		4.4	
		.21		.20
Change in work status				
Yes	2.8		1.0	
No	−1.3		−0.5	
		.09		0.3
Grand mean = 7.8				
R = .39				
R^2 = .16				

[a]The age cohort which was 45–49 in time 1 was merged with those 50–54 since respondents in that cohort reported few changes in work status during the past four years in time 3.

munality, we do find differences among people which are, in part, dependent on varied experiences. We expect, therefore, that important experiences may change the picture of the pattern of life. Although in this small sample we cannot expect too many substantial disruptions, the schedule of recent events suggests some areas of life in which the occurrence of important events might make a difference in the ways people look at the total pattern of their lives.

After considering several alternative procedures for measuring the characteristics of the life graph, we decided on a measure which represents the general shape of the curve but is quite easy to compute. This is the horizontal distance between the respondent's own age and the age at the maximum height of the graph. Is the peak still to come? Is it past? How far away is it? And does the distance between peak age and current age change for our respondents between 1968 and 1972?

Subjects, particularly women, were quite consistent in the age at which their graphs peak. This consistency persisted over time (i.e., from 1968 to 1972) and over age cohorts (i.e., persons aged fifty-five in 1968 and persons sixty-five in 1968). Since the choice of peak year was fairly stable over time and type of subject, it exhibited basic stability and has the ability to convert what was, with other analytical techniques, a curvilinear dependent variable into a linear function.

Effect of events. Using the difference between current age and peak age as the procedure for measuring the dependent variable, we found that the events selected generally affected younger and older respondents in different ways. Departure of children from the household had its greatest impact on persons aged forty-five to forty-nine and those sixty and over (table C—22; $F = 9.7$; $p < .001$). It had more impact on females than males ($F = 14.9$; $p < .001$). Work change and retirement had its greatest impact on the pattern of the life graph during the interval immediately prior to the normal time of retirement, sixty to sixty-four years of age, and was more pronounced for males than for females (table C—23; $F = 14.1$ and 16.8; $p < .001$). Experiencing a death had an impact for all ages ($F = 11.9$; $p < .001$) and both sexes ($F = 16.9$; $p < .001$); its impact was possibly slightly more likely to change the normal pattern of the graph in younger subjects than in older ones, but its effect was more consistent across age and sex cohorts than were any of the other events investigated (table C—24). In contrast, there was some indication that illness was differen-

Table C—24. *Multiple classification analysis between difference in height at peak and current age (time 3) and age, sex, and death.*

Variable and category	Unadjusted deviation	*Eta*	Adjusted for independent deviation	*Beta*
Age at time 1				
45–49	−11.6		−11.5	
50–54	− 6.3		− 6.4	
55–59	1.0		− 0.4	
60–64	4.8		3.9	
65–70	9.2		9.2	
		.35		.34
Sex				
Male	− 4.2		− 4.0	
Female	4.5		4.4	
		.21		.20
Death				
Yes	0.8		− 0.5	
No	− 0.7		0.5	
		.04		.02

Grand mean = 7.8
R = .40
R^2 = .16

Table C—25. *Multiple classification analysis between difference in height at peak and current age (time 3) and age, sex, and illness.*

Variable and category	Unadjusted deviation	*Eta*	Adjusted for independent deviation	*Beta*
Age at time 1				
45–49	−11.6		−11.6	
50–54	− 6.3		− 6.4	
55–59	1.0		− 0.3	
60–64	4.8		3.9	
65–71	9.2		9.2	
		.35		.34
Sex				
Male	− 4.2		− 4.0	
Female	4.5		4.4	
		.21		.20
Illness				
Yes	0.4		0.4	
No	− 0.1		− 0.1	
		.01		.01
Grand mean = 7.8				
R = .40				
R^2 = .16				

tially experienced by sex as well as by age. In table C—25 we see that age and sex were the significant determinants of the graph pattern. Once age and sex were eliminated, little power remains for the illness event itself.

Discussion

Several points have emerged from the data. Our experience with peak age is similar to the findings of Lowenthal et al., (1975). Our finding that the height of the graphs at a given age rose slightly between 1968 and 1972 is similar to the observation of Lowenthal et al. that there is some tendency for subjects to view the stage of life currently being experienced as the more favorable.

Life events have some influence on the life perspective as measured by the life graph. This is true even in the oldest age group. Our results do not support the observation of Lowenthal et al. that the number of life-course events or stressors declined across stages. However, this finding does not disagree with their hypothesis of decreased density with greater age. Our findings may reflect the fact that we looked at only four major life change events which all subjects sooner or later must experience. Where we asked respondents about prespecified events, Lowenthal et al. (1975) asked respondents to voluntarily report events.

The events which we selected are particularly relevant to our age group; they are also appropriate to certain ages within it and they are expected to occur at particular times. They are perceived most strongly if they occur at the wrong time: children leaving is least traumatic during the fifties—perhaps the "normal" age for such departures; retirement is worst if it happens just before the conventional age, during the sixty to sixty-four period. Death experience is a shock at any age. In contrast, Lowenthal et al. solicited information on a much broader range of roles and events and used more numerous sources for that information.

To the extent that our data are similar to those of other writers on four events—departure of children, retirement, illness, and death—we get comparable results. Children leave home at times that are normatively predictable. The impact of that departure on women is not as severe as one might predict (cf. Lowenthal et al., 1975). Retirement occurs at a predictable time, but its impact is not significantly greater on men than on women. Retirement does appear to have more of an anticipatory impact on men than an actual or postretirement impact. Riley et al. (1972) have suggested that satisfaction with retirement is related to, or dependent upon, income, health, and one's perception of whether one perceives that retirement was voluntary or coerced. Lowenthal et al. (1975) suggest that women react more to stresses involving persons around them, while men react to events involving their own work. Our findings on the impact which retirement has on self-perceived satisfaction support these prior findings.

Death events impact on all ages and both sexes and generally have the power to generate a turning point or change in the graph. As Lowenthal et al. suggest, any period of crisis or transition can initiate a life review process or change. Such processes are not limited to old age (Butler, 1963). Our data suggest that exposure to death has a power to do this at all ages; one need not be immediately approaching one's own death.

In contrast, exposure to illness is more selective. Differential reactions to illness of self or family member apparently relate to both age and sex. The basic pattern of the graph supports Neugarten's (1963) suggestion that different theories of aging need to be generated for males and females. We find that younger women and older men often perceive their immediate future as better after they have experienced illness. Whereas the other events either impact at what can be considered normatively appropriate times and in normatively appropriate ways (departure of children and retirement) or have constant effects over all groups (death), illness affects persons differentially.

Use of the life graph. The principal value of the life graph lies in its ability to inform us about life-span or a whole life perspective. Graphs are useful for assessing the current emotional state, comparing perceived emotional states between groups and over time periods, and determining the conditions under which heights and patterns of graphs change. Few respondents draw graphs in such detail that small changes at their current age can be detected or meaningfully analyzed. Thus, detailed inferences should not be made from minute changes. The rough form of the usual graph is, in itself, advantageous in that it forces both the respondent and the investigator to focus on the meaning of the whole pattern of the graph.

References

Back, K. W. Personal characteristics and social behavior theory and method. In R. H. Binstock and E. Shanas (Eds.), *Handbook of aging and the social sciences*. New York: Van Nostrand Reinhold, 1976.

Back, K. W., and Bourque, L. Life graphs: Aging and cohort. *Journal of Gerontology*, 25, 249–255, 1970.

Bourque, L., and Back, K. W. The middle years as seen through the life graph. *Sociological Symposium*, 1:19–29, 1969.

Butler, R. N. The life review: An interpretation of reminiscence in the aged. *Psychiatry*, 26:65–76, 1963.

Goldberg, E. L., and Comstock, G. W. Life events and subsequent illness. *American Journal of Epidemiology*, 104:146–158, 1976.

Holmes, T. H., and Masuda, M. Life change and illness susceptibility. In B. S. Dohrenwend and B. P. Dohrenwend (Eds.), *Stressful life events*. New York: Wiley, 1974.

Holmes, T. H., and Rahe, R. H. The social readjustment rating scale. *Journal of Psychosomatic Research*, 11:213–218, 1967.

Hough, R. L., Fairbank, D. T., and Garcia, A. M. Problems in the ratio measurement of life stress. *Journal of Health and Social Behavior*, 17:70–82, 1976.

Lowenthal, M. F., Thurnher, J., and Chiriboga, D. *Four stages of life*. San Francisco: Jossey-Bass, 1975.

Marris, P. *Loss and change*. London: Routledge & Kegan Paul, 1974.

Marris, P. Conservation, innovation and old age. *International Journal of Aging and Human Development*, 9:127–135, 1978–79.

Neugarten, B. L. Personality changes during the adult years. In R. G. Kuhlen, (Ed.), *Psychological backgrounds of adult education*. Chicago: Center for the Study of Liberal Education for Adults, 1963.

Nie, N. H., et al. *SPSS Primer: Statistical package for the social sciences*. New York: McGraw-Hill, 1975.

Palmore, E. B. Appendix A. Design of the adaptation study. In E. B. Palmore (Ed.), *Normal aging II*, Durham, N.C.: Duke University Press, 1974.

Rabkin, J. G., and Struening, E. L. Life events, stresses, and illness. *Science*, 194:1013–1020, 1976.

Riley, M. W., and Foner, A. (Eds.), *Aging and society*. Vol. 3. *A sociology of age stratification*. New York: The Russell Sage Foundation, 1972.

Stability and Change in Life Graph Types

Kurt W. Back and Chris P. Averett

The perception of one's whole life is an important aspect of a person's current condition. This perception is complex; at the minimum it consists of assessments of satisfaction at different ages. Complex configurations are recalcitrant to conventional measurement techniques; in consequence, many types of interesting data of this kind which could be collected are neglected or insufficiently exploited. A number of variables are needed to describe sample data, and their arrangement and relationships are inadequately summarized into simple indices for further analysis. Forcing the data into one or two linear dimensions is sometimes possible, but frequently too much information is lost. In this paper we demonstrate a set-theoretic technique of fuzzy partitions (Grade of Membership Technique), which allows simple characterizations of complex data, and apply it to a problem of curves obtained in a panel study.

The measure of life course perception to be discussed is the so-called life graph (Back and Bourque, 1970; Bourque and Back, 1977). Subjects are presented with a blank grid on which the abscissa is gradated from zero to eighty years, and then given the following instructions: "Imagine how your life would be if put into a graph. That is, ups and downs, level periods and so forth. Assuming that you live up to at least eighty years of age, how do you think a graph of your life would look? Indicate this by marking the graph on this table."

Graphs obtained in this way differ, of course, in many ways. A preliminary characterization of the curves can be obtained by measuring the height of the curve at five-year intervals, counting the number of peaks, and ascertaining the age of the highest peak (the high point of life). From these data the mean height of the curve and the standard deviation of the measuring points can be obtained. Based on these figures one can obtain ipsatively standardized values (i.e., standardized by mean and SD of each individual) for each age. Thus we have two types of data: those that give a general shape and response tendency (mean, SD, and the peak measures) and those that show variations within these individual patterns (the standardized heights).

It is possible to use these measures and similar ones for important analyses. However, given the free-form nature of the task itself, individual variation in the whole form of the curve is necessarily lost. An attempt was made using factor analysis of selected measures to establish some types of graphs which would give a general picture (Back, 1982). Although this exercise yielded interesting results, it had some drawbacks. Chief among them was the degree of arbitrariness in establishing the types, the fact that respondents represented these types to varying degrees, and the fact that even the best representation of each type could not be ascertained. Measurement also suffers from spurious precision; although the heights are measured to the nearest millimeter and are continuous variables, it is likely that respondents do not discriminate finely and look at the graph in rough units.

In order to overcome these difficulties, a method was selected which determines the best set of pure types which fit the data and assigns a degree of membership in these types to each respondent. This method was based on Zadeh's (1965) theory of fuzzy sets and was developed by Woodbury (Woodbury and Clive, 1974; Woodbury et al., 1978; Woodbury and Manton, 1982) as the grade of membership (GOM) algorithm of fuzzy partitions. The unique contribution of the GOM technique is that it yields a characterization of a group data space (the pure types) as well as how individuals relate to the emergent types (the grades of membership). A goodness of fit measure, the log likelihood ratio statistic, is available for each fitted model.

Mathematically, the concept "fuzzy" signifies that an element is a member of a set only in an uncertain fashion. Normally in mathematics we understand that an element either is or is not in a set. Zadeh went beyond standard mathematics by introducing the notion of weighted membership. An element can belong more or less to a subset. In ordinary set theory, a characteristic function is used to indicate whether or not an object is a member of a set. This function takes on the values of either 0 or 1. In the algebra of ordinary sets, the characteristic functions are multiplied or added to determine the intersection or union of sets respectively. Fuzzy subset theory requires a redefinition of membership and the simple operations of combining subsets. Grade of membership can be represented by any number in the range 0 to 1. These numbers stand for the concepts "not belonging," and "belonging a little," all the way to "belonging a lot," and "belonging completely." We emphasize, however, that these numbers are unlike probabilities; there is not uncertainty in the degree or grade of membership. It simply represents the extent to which the object belongs; it is a physical property. The calculus or ordinary subsets had to be redefined and expanded to account for the fuzziness factor.

The obvious question which arises now is: How is the theory of fuzzy subsets to be applied to problems in the real world? How are the fuzzy groups to be defined and the grades of membership calculated? In most mathematical treatises in the field, the assignment of the fuzzy membership weights is made intuitively (Kaufman, 1975). In applying the theory we need some system which can analyze data to isolate the natural fuzzy subsets and estimate grade of membership coefficients. To this end, Woodbury (Woodbury and Clive, 1974; Woodbury et al., 1978) developed a mathematical typology algorithm called the grade of membership technique (GOM).

To summarize the procedure briefly:

1. The researcher begins by predetermining an appropriate number of groups. Individuals are then assigned uniquely to these groups. This assignment can be made in any meaningful way, whether empirically by some method of ordinary (or what Woodbury calls "crisp") clustering or by some measure of proximity to predefined groups. At this point each individual has a GOM score of 1 in one group and 0 in all the others.

2. The GOM program then estimates the probabilities that the manifest characteristics of the individuals (the choices on the set of categorical variables input to the program), relate to the initial partition. These sets of probabilities characterize the initial classification statistically.

3. The next step is to use the probabilities to improve the estimates of the GOMs. The new GOMs are then used to improve the estimates of the probabilities. This iterative procedure continues until no significant improvement is made in an appropriate likelihood function.

The results then define the pure types which yield the best fit, the contribution of each variable to this definition, and the grade of membership of all individuals in each class; subjects can then be assigned to their class of highest membership.

The GOM technique allows us to not only characterize life graphs into rough types which are likely to represent the perceptual processes of the respondents and to determine the characteristics of respondents exhibiting each pattern but also to estimate the stability of life graph types over the four waves and describe individual stages and changes. We will be able to answer several questions: Do the pure types themselves vary over the eight-year period? Do individuals alter their graphs of their lives in significant ways from wave to wave, i.e., do their GOMs change? What distinguishes individuals who are consistent in their descriptions of their whole lives from those who reevaluate and change their pattern? Significant changes in grades of membership may represent significant life course transitions.

Method

Sample

The life graph data were collected during the Duke Second Longitudinal Study in which 330 respondents completed life graphs in all four waves.

Instrument

Subjects were presented with a blank grid and instructed to: "Imagine how your life could be put in a graph. That is, ups and downs, level periods and so forth. Assuming you live up until at least 80 years of age, how do you think a graph of your life would look? Indicate this by marking the graph on this page." Height at five-year intervals was measured in millimeters. The technical features are described in Back and Bourque (1970) and Hagestad (1982).

Data

Twelve variables, constructed from each graph, were used as internal variables to determine the types of graphs: mean height (the average of all five-year interval heights); standard deviation (the standard deviation of all five-year interval heights); number of peaks; age at highest peak; standardized height at fifteen, thirty-five, fifty-five, and seventy-five years (height of the graph at these years standardized by subject's own mean and standard deviation); and slope at fifteen, thirty-five, fifty-five, and seventy-five years (the difference between standardized height at that year and the height five years previous). Twenty-year, rather than five-year, intervals were selected to ensure some independence of the measures.

Several measures were chosen as external variables in the GOM analysis to help interpret the resulting types: sex; age (forty-six to fifty, fifty-one to fifty-four, fifty-five to fifty-nine, sixty to sixty-four, and over sixty-five years); education (less than high school, high school, some college, college degree, and more than college degree); annual income (less than $4,000, $4,000–$6,999, $7,000–$9,999, $10,000–$14,999, and $15,000 or more); subjective social class (upper/upper middle, middle, working/lower class); marital status (divorced/separated/spouse absent, widowed, never-married, married); current life satisfaction (measured by a ladder, the bottom representing lowest and the top greatest satisfaction); subjective age identification (young, middle-aged, elderly/old/aged); and whether or not the subject has children. Life satisfaction over the life course, as depicted by the graphs, may vary with other social-psychological characteristics such as current life satisfaction, subjective age identification, and social circumstances, as indicated by such variables as education and income. Also, persons of varying ages may view their life courses differently, as they are looking either toward the future or the past.

For some additional analyses, two health-related interpretive factors—subjective health status and how close the subject felt to death (measured by a ladder, the bottom of which stood for birth, the top for death)—were added. Persons may view their whole lives differently from relative health or illness. Also, for these analyses, marital status was collapsed to married/not married.

GOM Analysis Strategy

The GOM procedure was used on each wave of data separately. Internal variables determine the pure types. In order to determine the number of pure types appropriate for these life graph data, the variables from the initial wave (479 subjects) were analyzed with both five and four pure types. Subsequent waves were analyzed with only four pure types. The number of subjects completing graphs in each wave were 419, 356, and 359 for the second, third, and fourth, respectively.

Regression Analyses

While the GOM technique provides hypothetical pure types, one can also classify subjects into observed types based on their largest GOM. For example, a subject can be assigned to a particular observed type if his or her GOM for that type is larger than for any other type. Examining characteristics of these observed types differs from that of pure types in that each type includes subjects who may or may not be perfectly aligned with the type assignment, i.e., the subject may partially belong to other types.

Subjects in each wave were classified as such and then four variables were created which order the subjects by their consistency in type assignment across waves. For instance, each pattern variable orders subjects from one to four based on how many waves the subject exhibited a particular pure type. These observed patterns were used as dependent variables in regression analyses which predict, therefore, consistency of graph type across time from the external variables described above plus subjectivê health status and subjective distance from death.

Results

Types of Life Graphs

Using the first wave, chi-squares were obtained for both the four and five pure type models ($x^2 = 4812.5$, $df = 1629/x^2 = 5415$, $df = 2168$); the difference in x^2s indicated the addition of the fifth type did not contribute significantly to explaining variation in the data.

Table C—26 contains the standardized coefficients, interpretable as probabilities, relating the life graph variables to the four pure types. These coefficients allow us to characterize the four pure types as follows: (1) Low and flat with a small peak at early age (CONSISTENT LOW). (2) Bell-shaped with a peak in middle age (BELL CURVE). (3) Increase with decrease in late life (PEAKING OGIVE). (4) Continuous increase throughout life (UPWARD OGIVE). (These patterns are depicted in figure C—13.) For example, examining the coefficients for "mean height" one can see that a CONSISTENT LOW pure type life graph has a high probability, relative to the original proportions, of being less than 8 mm in height while UPWARD OGIVE graphs are more likely to have a greater than 20 mm average height. Also, the "age at highest point" clearly differentiates the pure types quite well: CONSISTENT LOWs peak before age forty, BELL CURVEs between ages forty-five and fifty-five, PEAKING OGIVEs between sixty and seventy, and UPWARD OGIVE at age seventy-five or eighty. The QRFs reflect the relative importance of questions in determining types. Here the "age at highest point" and the "standardized height at age 75" measures contribute the most while the "number of peaks" contributes the least. It appears that the number of peaks a graph has varies quite a lot within types, thus not contributing to differentiation between types.

GOM analyses of the subsequent three waves of data resulted in four similar pure types. The x^2 values for each of these waves was wave 2: $x^2 = 3586$ with 1449 *df*; wave 3: $x^2 = 2952$ with 1260 *df*; wave 4: $x^2 = 3188$ with 1269 *df*. Again, in all three waves the additional three pure types significantly improve the fit over a one pure type model. More importantly, coefficients relating the variables to pure types are quite similar to those in wave 1, indicating that the characterization of the four pure types described above is appropriate for all four panels. Thus, the structure of life graph types appears to be stable across at least an eight-year time span.

External Characteristics of Pure Types

Gom analyses. In addition to relating the internal variables to pure types, the GOM technique also produces coefficients for variables external to the

Table C—26. *Coefficients relating four pure types to life graph variables in round 1,* N = *479.*

Variables	Proportion of sample with graphs possessing attribute	Consistent low P_{1jl}	Bell curve P_{2jl}	Peaking ogive P_{3jl}	Upward ogive P_{4jl}
Mean height					
<4 mm.	.07	0.22	0.00	0.00	0.00
≥4 and <8 mm.	.25	0.78	0.00	0.00	0.00
≥8 and <14 mm.	.31	0.00	0.58	0.43	0.29
≥14 and <20 mm.	.24	0.00	0.29	0.57	0.21
≥20 mm.	.13	0.00	0.13	0.00	0.50
		(1.14)[a]	(0.94)	(0.92)	(0.98)
Standard deviation of heights					
<2 mm.	.15	0.38	0.00	0.00	0.00
≥2 and <3.5 mm.	.24	0.62	0.00	0.00	0.00
≥3.5 and <6 mm.	.27	0.00	0.68	0.17	0.48
≥6 and <10 mm.	.27	0.00	0.32	0.83	0.00
≥10 mm.	.07	0.00	0.00	0.00	0.52
		(1.38)	(0.85)	(0.94)	(0.74)
Standardized height at age 15					
<−1	.34	0.00	0.00	1.00	0.63
≥−1 and <0	.37	0.26	0.81	0.00	0.37
0	.01	0.05	0.00	0.00	0.00
>0 and ≤1	.23	0.56	0.19	0.00	0.00
>1	.04	0.13	0.00	0.00	0.00
		(1.11)	(0.95)	(0.95)	(0.97)
Standardized height at age 35					
<−1	.11	0.42	0.00	0.00	0.14
≥−1 and <0	.33	0.32	0.00	0.46	0.86
0	.02	0.09	0.00	0.00	0.00
>0 and ≤1	.38	0.00	0.67	0.54	0.00
>1	.16	0.17	0.33	0.00	0.00
		(0.76)	(1.24)	(1.04)	(0.93)
Standardized height at age 55					
<−1	.05	0.16	0.04	0.00	0.00
≥−1 and <0	.21	0.77	0.00	0.00	0.00
0	.02	0.07	0.00	0.00	0.00
>0 and ≤1	.46	0.00	0.42	0.60	1.00
>1	.26	0.00	0.54	0.40	0.00
		(0.99)	(0.95)	(1.13)	(0.94)

Table C—26. *(Continued)*

Variables	Proportion of sample with graphs possessing attribute	Consistent low P_{1jl}	Bell curve P_{2jl}	Peaking ogive P_{3jl}	Upward ogive P_{4jl}
Standardized height at age 75					
<−1	.14	0.20	0.34	0.00	0.00
≥−1 and <0	.31	0.65	0.66	0.00	0.00
0	.02	0.15	0.00	0.00	0.00
>0 and ≤1	.32	0.00	0.00	1.00	0.00
>1	.21	0.00	0.00	0.00	1.00
		(0.45)	(1.16)	(1.31)	(1.16)
Slope at age 15					
<−1	.05	0.16	0.00	0.00	0.00
≥−1 and <0	.11	0.00	0.00	0.30	0.21
0	.27	0.62	0.00	0.19	0.15
>0 and ≤1	.49	0.00	0.94	0.51	0.63
>1	.08	0.21	0.06	0.00	0.00
		(1.10)	(0.92)	(1.02)	(0.95)
Slope at age 35					
<−1	.11	0.31	0.00	0.00	0.00
≥−1 and <0	.15	0.14	0.14	0.02	0.34
0	.21	0.43	0.00	0.24	0.00
>0 and ≤1	.45	0.00	0.86	0.54	0.66
>1	.08	0.12	0.00	0.20	0.00
		(1.29)	(0.87)	(0.85)	(0.96)
Slope at age 55					
<−1	.08	0.22	0.06	0.00	0.00
≥−1 and <0	.17	0.00	0.52	0.00	0.00
0	.25	0.57	0.08	0.28	0.00
>0 and ≤1	.41	0.00	0.27	0.72	1.00
>1	.48	0.21	0.06	0.00	0.00
		(1.03)	(1.12)	(0.94)	(0.85)
Slope at age 75					
<−1	.05	0.09	0.05	0.04	0.00
≥−1 and <0	.40	0.00	0.96	0.67	0.00
0	.36	0.84	0.00	0.28	0.20
>0 and ≤1	.17	0.00	0.00	0.00	0.80
>1	.02	0.07	0.00	0.00	0.00
		(1.06)	(0.88)	(0.94)	(1.18)
Number of peaks					
0	.05	0.13	0.00	0.00	0.10
1	.28	0.10	0.55	0.16	0.34

Table C—26. *(Continued)*

Variables	Proportion of sample with graphs possessing attribute	Consistent low P_{1jl}	Bell curve P_{2jl}	Peaking ogive P_{3jl}	Upward ogive P_{4jl}
Number of peaks					
2	.39	0.39	0.35	0.54	0.21
3	.18	0.24	0.10	0.20	0.20
≥4	.09	0.14	0.00	0.10	0.15
		(1.04)	(0.94)	(1.07)	(0.95)
Age at highest point					
≤25	.12	0.67	0.00	0.00	0.00
≥30 and ≤40	.17	0.33	0.32	0.00	0.00
≥45 and ≤55	.23	0.00	0.68	0.00	0.00
≥60 and ≤70	.22	0.00	0.00	1.00	0.00
≥75	.26	0.00	0.00	0.00	1.00
		(0.65)	(1.17)	(0.89)	(1.39)
	Log likelihood = 2406.25, x^2 = 4812.5, *df* = 1629				

[a]Numbers in parentheses are question relevance factors. These are the sums of the unstandardized weights, and they show the relative importance of the item in defining a particular type.

model, i.e., variables which do not contribute to defining the life graph types or to the fit but which may characterize hypothetical persons who draw different pure type graphs. The pure types differed somewhat in external characteristics in all four waves; the first type was the most depressed by demographic indicators, characterized by lower social status, while the third and fourth types were more elevated. A hypothetical pure type person drawing a CONSISTENT LOW graph is more likely to be female, less educated, have less income and lower subjective social class, be divorced, separated, widowed or never married, and have no children, while hypothetical persons drawing the latter two graphs were more likely to be male, have more education and more income, and identify with the upper and upper-middle class. Also, comparing the types with measure of current life satisfaction, the groups showed ascending satisfaction in the indicated order.

Regression analyses. Four pattern variables order subjects by consistency in graph type across waves. For instance, variable PATTERN 1 has the following values: (1) CONSISTENT LOW in only 1 wave; (2) CONSISTENT LOW in 2 waves; (3) CONSISTENT LOW in 3 waves; (4) CONSISTENT LOW in 4 waves. Patterns 2, 3, and 4 describe consistency in BELL CURVE, PEAKING OGIVE, and UPWARD OGIVE, respectively.

Each of these pattern variables was regressed on the nine external variables plus subjective health status and how close the subject felt to death, all as measured in the first wave. The results of these four regressions appear in table C—27.

As can be seen, although only a few variables are statistically significant in each model, the R^2s are moderately high for all but the BELL CURVE pattern. In the bivariate pure type analysis described above, the external characteristics also had their least differentiating power for the BELL CURVE type. Net of other variables in the model, subjects who more consistently drew CONSISTENT LOW graphs were more likely to be female, less educated, and have no children. Also, subjects with more education and subjects with children were more likely to draw more PEAKING OGIVE graphs. Males and subjects who subjectively felt they were younger drew more UPWARD OGIVE graphs.

The life satisfaction, health, and income variables may not have had an impact in these models because they change across waves, and here we included only their measure at time 1. As will be seen later, changes in these three variables are related to changes in graph type.

Stability of Life Graph Types

In spite of the free-form nature of the task, not only were the same four types as apparent in each wave, but the subjects were quite consistent in their drawings

Table C—27. *Unstandardized coefficients for predicting consistency of life graph types across waves from characteristics of subjects measured in wave 1.*

	Consistency of life graph types			
Predictors	Consistent low Pattern 1	Bell curve Pattern 2	Peaking ogive Pattern 3	Upward ogive Pattern 4
Constant	1.25	.97	2.21	−.43
Sex[a]	.37*[b]	.13	−.41*	−.08
Age	.06	−.08	.05	−.02
Education	−.14*	−.04	−.04	.21*
Income	−.07	.02	.05	.00
Class	.00	.01	.04	−.04
Marital status	.17	.00	.10	−.27
Life satisfaction	−.03	−.08	.10	.01
Subjective age iden.	.06	.16	−.37*	−.16
Children	−.31*	.01	−.22	.52*
Subjective health	−.04	−.05	.05	.04
Distance from death	.01	.06	−.06	.00
R^2	.17	.04	.08	.16

[a]Higher values for variables were female, older, higher education, more income, upper class identification, not married, higher life satisfaction, older subjective age identification, has children, better subjective health, and subjectively feels closer to death.

[b]Starred coefficients are two or more times their standard errors.

across waves. As above, subjects were classified into types on the basis of their largest GOM. The percentages of subjects assigned to the same type in wave 1 and wave 2, wave 2 and wave 3, and wave 3 and wave 4 were 39.4 percent, 43.2 percent, and 40.7 percent, respectively (see table C—28). As the time span increased from wave 1, the percentage of subjects drawing the same type decreased.

One tenth of the subjects remained in the same type for all four waves (see table C—29). Assigned to the same type three out of four times were 33.9 percent of the subjects; thus, 44.3 percent were consistent across at least three waves; 62.1 percent drew only two different types of graphs. Only 3.3 percent of the subjects changed types each wave.

Table C—30 contains coefficients relating assignment in a particular type in wave 1 to the hypothetical pure types in the subsequent three waves. As can be seen, hypothetical CONSISTENT LOW and UPWARD OGIVE pure types in wave 1 were twice as likely to draw the same type as would be expected by chance alone (the original proportions) for each of the following waves, while

Table C—28. *Percent of subjects who drew same type of graph in a successive wave.*

Time span	Stable	Change	*N*
Wave 1 to wave 2	39.4	60.6	419
Wave 1 to wave 3	35.7	64.3	356
Wave 1 to wave 4	32.9	67.1	359
Wave 2 to wave 3	43.2	56.8	352
Wave 2 to wave 4	43.1	56.9	353
Wave 3 to wave 4	40.7	59.3	332

Table C—29. *Number of subjects with various patterns of stability and change across all four waves (*N = *330).*

Number of subjects	Number of waves in which type was the same
34 (10.4%)	4
112 (33.9%)	3
173 (52.4%)	2
11 (3.3%)	1
146 (44.3%)	at least 3
319 (96.7%)	at least 2
61 (18.5%)	2 and 2[a]
207 (62.1%)	at least 3 or 2 and 2[b]

[a]These subjects drew two of one type and two of another type.

[b]These subjects drew only one or two types of graphs in all.

Table C—30. *Coefficients relating four pure types in waves 2, 3, and 4 to pure type assignment from wave 1.*

		Pure types, wave 2 (N = 419)			
Type in wave 1	Proportion	Consistent low	Bell curve	Peaking ogive	Upward ogive
Consistent low	.29	.65	.28	.22	.16
Bell curve	.31	.08	.52	.33	.24
Peaking ogive	.22	.17	.17	.32	.20
Upward ogive	.19	.10	.03	.15	.40
		Pure types, wave 3 (N = 356)			
Type in wave 1	Proportion	Consistent low	Bell curve	Peaking ogive	Upward ogive
Consistent low	.28	.62	.26	.12	.20
Bell curve	.31	.32	.43	.31	.20
Peaking ogive	.22	.06	.21	.34	.24
Upward ogive	.18	.00	.10	.23	.36
		Pure types, wave 4 (N = 359)			
Type in wave 1	Proportion	Consistent low	Bell curve	Peaking ogive	Upward ogive
Consistent low	.29	.64	.26	.13	.20
Bell curve	.31	.25	.39	.45	.11
Peaking ogive	.21	.10	.19	.25	.28
Upward ogive	.18	.00	.15	.17	.40

only two-thirds more likely for the hypothetical BELL CURVE and PEAKING OGIVE types.

Change in Life Graph Types

While the pure types refer to hypothetical persons who would draw a perfect CONSISTENT LOW, BELL CURVE, PEAKING OGIVE, or UPWARD OGIVE graph, i.e., would have a GOM of 1 in one type and 0 otherwise, subjects actually received GOMs reflecting their degree of membership in the pure type categories. One would expect subjects who were more crisply classified, that is, have large GOMs in one type and small otherwise, to be least likely to change to a different type in subsequent waves. In fact, change in membership is significantly related to the degree of fuzziness of initial classification. Subjects with larger GOM weights were more likely to remain in the same type across waves than were those less crisply classified (see table C—31). Actually, less than one-fifth of respondents could be very crisply classified, i.e., had GOMs greater than .975 in one group, demonstrating the usefulness of a fuzzy technique for highly variable data such as these.

The life graph pure types can be ordered by degree of optimism about later

Table C—31. *Relationship between size of GOM weight and stability of life graph type across four waves.*

	GOM weight, wave 1			
Wave 1 to wave 2	<.50	≥.50 and <.75	≥.75	Total
No change	26.2% (16)	34.5% (70)	51.0% (79)	39.4% (165)
Change	73.8% (45)	65.5% (133)	49.0% (76)	60.6% (254)
	$x^2 = 15.18$, $df = 2$, $p \leq .001$			

	GOM weight, wave 1			
Wave 1 to wave 3	<.50	≥.50 and <.75	≥.75	Total
No change	17.3% (9)	34.1% (61)	45.6% (57)	35.7% (127)
Change	82.7% (43)	65.9% (118)	54.4% (68)	64.3% (229)
	$x^2 = 13.21$, $df = 2$, $p \leq .001$			

	GOM weight, wave 1			
Wave 1 to wave 4	<.50	≥.50 and <.75	≥.75	Total
No change	23.6% (13)	32.4% (56)	37.4% (49)	32.9% (118)
Change	76.4% (42)	67.6% (117)	62.6% (82)	67.1% (241)
	$x^2 = 3.37$, $df = 2$, n.s.			

	GOM weight, wave 2			
Wave 2 to wave 3	<.50	≥.50 and <.75	≥.75	Total
No change	22.2% (10)	41.1% (62)	51.3% (80)	43.2% (152)
Change	77.8% (35)	58.9% (89)	48.7% (76)	56.8% (200)
	$x^2 = 12.51$, $df = 2$, $p \leq .01$			

	GOM weight, wave 2			
Wave 2 to wave 4	<.50	≥.50 and <.75	≥.75	Total
No change	36.7% (18)	42.3% (63)	45.8% (71)	43.1% (152)
Change	63.3% (31)	57.7% (86)	54.2% (84)	56.9% (201)
	$x^2 = 1.31$, $df = 2$, n.s.			

	GOM weight, wave 3			
Wave 3 to wave 4	<.50	≥.50 and <.75	≥.75	Total
No change	38.9% (21)	33.6% (47)	48.6% (67)	40.7% (135)
Change	61.1% (33)	66.4% (93)	51.4% (71)	59.3% (197)
	$x^2 = 6.55$, $df = 2$, $p \leq .05$			

life as follows; CONSISTENT LOW, BELL CURVE, PEAKING OGIVE, UPWARD OGIVE. Note that this ordering reflects an order based on preference by those lower in current life satisfaction and more depressed in demographic characteristics. Let us consider those respondents whose patterns did change consistently. Of 206 who did so, 63.1 percent drew consistently less optimistic graphs in later waves and 36.9 percent drew consistently more optimistic graphs. Thirty-seven percent (124) of the subjects either remained in the same type or moved up and down this scale of types over waves. Over the eight-year span of the study, in which all subjects aged, subjects were more likely to reevaluate downward than upward.

This pattern of change upward or downward in optimism is highly related to changes in income, life satisfaction, and subjective health (see tables C—32 through C—34). Subjects whose status on each of these variables decreased over

Table C—32. *Relationship between change in life satisfaction between wave 1 and wave 4 and consistent change in life graph optimism across four waves (*N = *206).*

Change in life graph type	Change in life satisfaction, wave 1 to wave 4			
	Less satisfied	No change	More satisfied	Total
Less optimistic	76.5% (104)	39.4% (13)	35.1% (13)	63.1% (130)
More optimistic	23.5% (32)	60.6% (20)	64.9% (24)	36.9% (76)
Total	66.0% (136)	16.0% (33)	18.0% (37)	100.0% (206)

$x^2 = 10.84$, $df = 2$, $p = <.001$.

Table C—33. *Relationship between change in household income between wave 1 and wave 4 and consistent change in life graph optimism across four waves (*N = *206).*

Change in life graph type	Change in income, wave 1 to wave 4			
	Less income	No change	More income	Total
Less optimistic	92.2% (94)	43.6% (24)	24.5% (12)	63.1% (130)
More optimistic	7.8% (8)	56.4% (31)	75.5% (37)	36.9% (76)
Total	49.5% (102)	26.7% (55)	23.8% (49)	100.0% (206)

$x^2 = 77.31$, $df = 2$, $p <.0001$.

Table C—34. *Relationship between change in subjective health status between wave 1 and wave 4 and consistent change in life graph optimism across four waves (*N = *206).*

Change in life graph type	Change in subjective health status, wave 1 to wave 4			
	Poorer health	No change	Better health	Total
Less optimistic	84.3% (107)	28.6% (14)	30.0% (9)	63.1% (130)
More optimistic	15.7% (20)	71.4% (35)	70.0% (21)	36.9% (76)
Total	61.6% (127)	23.8% (49)	14.6% (30)	100.0% (206)

$x^2 = 63.61$, $df = 2$, $p <.0001$.

the eight years drew less positive graphs in later than in earlier waves, while those whose status increased drew more optimistic graphs in later waves.

Conclusion

In sum, this example demonstrates that the GOM technique can yield a simple classification scheme of rather complex data which is stable over time. Essential individual variation is preserved in the grades of membership, which prove to relate to a real "commitment" to life graph types: stability in assignment of individuals to pure types is related to how crisply they were originally classified. In addition, by producing coefficients relating pure types to external characteristics, GOM concomitantly allows a description of hypothetical pure type persons in a fashion similar to a discriminant function. Likelihood function chi-square values aid in decisions about the appropriate number of types for different sets of data. It allows the construction of theoretical classifications as well as an assessment of the empirical distribution of cases. Also, since subjects can be classified into what we have called observed types on the basis of relative GOM size, many other kinds of analysis posterior to GOM processing can be accomplished. For example, here we found that change in type up or down a scale reflecting optimism about later life is related in predictable ways to changes in income, life satisfaction, and subjective health.

As Zadeh, the originator of the theory of fuzzy set, has indicated, this type of analysis is extremely well fitted to social science data, which is often characterized by only a fuzzy idea of who should and who should not be classified in a certain manner.

We can consider the types as different perceptions of the life course which are ordered according to optimism about life. In general, types with later peak will represent more optimism and a more favorable outlook on life. The types stayed remarkably consistent over the eight years of the study; a third showed the same type three or four times in different waves. This can be taken as a measure of reliability, especially as two kinds of conditions were conducive to change: (1) the less similar the drawing was to a pure type, the more likely the change and (2) people who changed to a less optimistic type were more likely to have decreased their life satisfaction, lost income, or deteriorated in their subjective health ratings.

References

Back, K. W. Types of life course and gerontology. *Academic Psychology Bulletin*, 4:9–16, 1982.

Back, K. W., and Bourque, L. B. Life graphs: Aging and cohort effects. *Journal of Gerontology*, 25:249–255, 1970.

Bourque, L. B., and Back, K. W. Life graphs and life events. *Journal of Gerontology*, 32:669–674, 1977. (also this volume pp. 282–290).

Hagestad, G. O. Life-phase analysis. In D. J. Mangen and W. A. Peterson (Eds.), *Clinical and social psychology*, Vol. 1 of *Research instruments in social gerontology*. Minneapolis: University of Minnesota Press, 1982.

Kaufman, A. *The theory of fuzzy subsets*. Vol. 1. New York: Academic, 1975.

Palmore, E. B. (Ed.), *Normal aging II*, Durham, N.C.: Duke University Press, 1974.

Woodbury, M. A., and Clive, J. Clinical pure types as a fuzzy partition. *Journal of Cybernetics*, 4:111–121, 1974.

Woodbury, M. A., Clive, J., and Garson, A., Jr. Mathematical typology: A grade of membership technique for obtaining disease definition. *Computers and Biomedical Research*, 3:277–298, 1978.

Woodbury, M. A., and Manton, K. G. A new procedure for the analysis of medical classification. *Methods of Information in Medicine*, 21:210–220, 1982.

Zadeh, L. A. Fuzzy sets. *Information and Control*, 8:338–353, 1965.

Section D. Social Aging

Introduction

George L. Maddox

Individuals age in the context of societies which share different cultural expectations about the timing and meaning of the transition into old age and about the allocation of societal resources in later life. Societies therefore constitute natural experiments which affect the processes of aging and the experience of being old. Comparative research has documented considerable variation both between and within societies in regard to survival, adaptation, and well-being in later life. Life expectancy at birth is observed to vary as much as thirty years between less developed and more developed countries. And within a developed country such as the United States rates of morbidity and death rates vary significantly by sex, ethnicity, and socioeconomic status among older adults, with the result that the probabilities of functional incapacity and death increase, not just with age, but with the social location of older people in society. Similarly, the probabilities of and responses to widowhood, involuntary retirement, and economic impoverishment are not simply a matter of being older but are affected by the location of older adults in the structure of society.

Observed variations in the outcomes of processes of aging and the experience of aging have important theoretical and practical implications. First, at the theoretical level, identification of *primary* processes of aging (i.e., universal age-related changes) must take into consideration observed variations in these processes which reflect environmental factors. The interaction of individuals with their environments over the life course ensure that they will learn and respond to different social expectations about aging; will develop different conceptions of self, behavior, coping skills, and life-styles which constitute the personal resources for adaptation in later life; and will have access to more or less of the societal resources essential for achieving and maintaining well-being (e.g., income, services, and health care). These interactions constitute the *secondary* aging processes which affect *primary* aging processes in ways which are, at present, only partially understood. At any rate, observed variation among older adults is a warning against making sweeping generalizations about intrinsic, and hence inevitable and universal, processes of aging and the experience of aging.

Second, observed variations in aging processes and experiences have an important practical implication. Processes and experiences related to aging are clearly not immutable. We do not know the limits of their modifiability, but the natural experiments of societies that produce different outcomes for older adults are a reminder that we do not know the boundaries of longevity, of maintenance of functional capacity, of successful adaptation to changing personal or social circumstances, or of the capacities of individuals and societies to ensure well-being in the later years. The willingness of social groups to undertake purposive interventions to change the processes and the experience of aging in beneficial ways reflects social values. Social groups have different preferences and different assumptions about the desirability and feasibility of testing the modifiability of aging processes.

Consideration of purposive intervention in aging processes raises ethical and legal questions about what change is desired and under what circumstances. There are serious questions which require thoughtful answers, but there is no longer any question about the possibility of modifying aging processes that just a few years ago were considered immutable. Some of the correlates of later life such as poverty, lack of education, and social isolation are largely socially and politically determined and clearly are modifiable through social action. Largely biologically determined processes reflected in age-related patterns of disease, functional impairment, and longevity, however, also are modifiable.

The Duke longitudinal studies document a broad range of variations in the social processes of aging and in the experience of aging in two samples of older adults who live in the community. These studies demonstrate that this variation reflects, in part, both the social location of individuals in society and the interaction of older adults with existing social institutions and cultural values.

The opening chapter of this section by Maddox and Douglass, for example, demonstrates variability in a wide range of biological, psychological, and social characteristics of a panel of subjects studied longitudinally. Measures of central tendency such as averages, they concluded, mask observed variation. In general, variance in the characterization of aging processes and the experience of older adults does not decrease with age. This is the case even when the long-run longitudinal trend for these processes and experiences indicates, on average, declining function. Further, this chapter documents the relative stability of individual characteristics over time. When individuals are compared with their age peers, they tend to maintain a consistent position. For example, those in the best health, who are functioning best cognitively, and who are adapting most adequately initially—and, correspondingly, those who do less well—tend to maintain their position in relation to others over time even when, on average, they are experiencing decline.

The article by Linda George illustrates one of the ways in which individuals are taught and learn to think of themselves as old and to identify themselves that way. She documents longitudinally the stability of personal identification as old or not old but she also notes the reality orientation of most older adults. By age seventy, 75 percent of the older people studied identified themselves as old and the probability of this identification was affected not only by chronological age but also by the imputed evaluation of others, by the age of friends, by assessment of health, and by the experience of functional impairment.

A decade ago, age-related declines in personal competence and in social resources were assumed to make older adults particularly vulnerable to the inevitable role losses and transitions associated with later life. Change was expected to produce crises. In the past decade, social scientific research has focused less on imputed crises and increasingly on stress associated with age-related life events (e.g., retirement, widowhood, the last child leaving home, and serious illness) and has stressed three important considerations in understanding stress and responses to stress in later life. First, the probability of experiencing potentially stressful life events is not the same for all older persons; second, life events are potentially, not inevitably, stressful; and, third, whether an event is stressful and how an individual responds to the challenge of an event are mediated by the availability of personal and social resources. Three articles in this section address these issues.

The article by Ilene Siegler documents that over a period of six years, in a longitudinal study of older adults, five age-related life events were, in fact, relatively rare and that the individuals studied were quite varied in the health, cognitive, and social resources available for responding. Then an article by Palmore and colleagues documents the differential success with which older individuals adapt to life events; the availability of personal and social resources make a difference. Major medical events were found to have the greatest impact on subsequent physical adaptation but little impact on social-psychological adaptation. Retirement had some initial negative impact on subjective adaptation but little impact on physical adaptation. Retirement of spouse, widowhood, and departure of the last child had relatively little lasting impact on adaptation. Also, the availability of resources tended to mitigate beneficially the potential negative impact of all the life events studied. Rosemary Wade Wilson reviews some of the persistent methodological problems associated with research on life events and responses to them. In her article she comments, as Siegler does, on the low incidence of events observed in random samples of older adults. Further, Wade argues for assessing the impact of each event separately, as Palmore and his colleagues do, and against developing a composite measure which summarizes a number of events collectively.

Measures of life satisfaction tap an important subjective dimension of adaptation in later life. In their article on change in life satisfaction in later life, Palmore and Kivett document relatively high and sustained levels of satisfaction in the longitudinal study of older adults. The best single predictor of life satisfaction over time, they found, is the initial level of an individual's reported satisfaction. Maintenance of the satisfaction level observed initially is the rule, not the exception. Further, as might be anticipated from the evidence in the previous chapters in this section, the predictors of stable, high levels of satisfaction are personal social resources such as health, socioeconomic status, and maintenance of active social involvement.

The article by Judith Fox on continuities in the experience on aging notes and discusses some problems in the conceptualization and measurement of continuity in the behavior of older individuals. Standardized, reliable measures of continuity do not currently exist, but one important implication of research on continuity, she concludes, is the importance of maintaining flexibility to permit alternative responses when change is required. Maintenance of personal flexibility is not the whole story, however, as the article by Janet Lowry indicates.

An event such as mandatory retirement, Lowry concludes, may present a requirement to adapt to a significant role change regardless of the preferences or the resources available to an individual. This article also makes two additional important points. Retirement is not just an event; it is a process. Therefore, it is important to know not only that an individual is retired but for how long and with what resources. The experience of retirement is variable. Further, Lowry found in her analysis that one successful response to retirement is to become reemployed. Those who returned to work following retirement appeared to adapt most successfully to later life.

Judith Fox notes in her article, also on retirement but focused specifically on that of women, how social expectations and opportunities regarding work affect the work experience of women and their experience of retirement. Significantly, research on retirement has generated models of retirement adaptation for men but not for women. Fox documents from her research that retired women tend to be more economically dependent, in poorer health, and more dependent on social support than either women who were still in the workforce or those who were housewives most of their lives. Research on the retirement of women is long overdue, and Fox outlines some of the information that is most urgently needed about the experience of retirement by women as an increasing proportion of women enter the work force with commitments to continuous employment and to careers.

Maintenance of active social involvement, which has been noted in the articles above as an important contributor to life satisfaction, is explored in Stephen Cutler's article on participation in voluntary associations. One indication of the tendency of older persons to disengage socially, Cutler comments, would be whether active ties with formal organizations are maintained. He documents, both from the Duke longitudinal studies and from a special comparative study, that stability of involvement over time is the rule, not the exception. In a study of involvement in a particular institution—religion—Blazer and Palmore also document that, while religious participation does not predict longevity, participation in religious organizations and related religious attitudes are positively correlated with life satisfaction and with a sense of personal usefulness. They caution that their conclusions were based on a study sample drawn from an area of the country described as the Bible Belt.

Jacquelyne Jackson's article on longitudinal patterns of activity and happiness provides a relatively rare characterization of the experience of aging among older black adults. Among blacks, as among older whites, continuities in patterns of activity and the positive relationship of activity to reported happiness are observed. Social integration and characteristics of social status (such as occupation and education) are important predictors of happiness. Whether the experience of aging for blacks is significantly different from that of whites (once socioeconomic status is controlled) remains to be demonstrated by research which is designed to explore possible differences in ethnic values and in the quantity and quality of social support networks.

In the final article of this section, Palmore reviews evidence from the first longitudinal study regarding the lifetime prevalence of institutionalization. The point prevalence of institutionalization of older adults is suggested by a commonly quoted statistic: at any point in time about 5 percent of persons aged sixty-five and older are institutionalized. This estimate, Palmore documents from longitudinal evidence, significantly underestimates the probability of institutionalization of older individuals during their lifetime. The lifetime prevalence, he estimates is above 20 percent. The probability of institutionalization increases with age after sixty-five (2 percent for those sixty-five to sixty-nine to 14 percent for those eighty-five and over). However, the lifetime chances of institutionalization are higher for the never-married or separated and those with more income and education. Palmore also notes that older blacks who, given the factors known to be related to institutionalization, might be expected to have high rates of institutionalization, in fact have relatively low rates. The extent to which this outcome reflects societal discrimination or special characteristics of supportive social networks among blacks remains to be clarified.

The processes of aging and the experience of aging are, in sum, quite variable. The observed variation clearly is related to the location of older adults in the structure and culture of social groups which share definitions of what it means to be old and which distribute resources and opportunities differentially to males and females, to black and whites, and to those with higher and lower socioeconomic status. Social structure and cultural understandings change, sometimes as a result of purposive action. Social change, we believe the evidence suggests, has as its probable consequences change in the processes and experience of aging.

Aging and Individual Differences

George L. Maddox and Elizabeth B. Douglass

This paper explores the relationship between age and individual differences. The nature of this relationship is important for understanding the later years of life and for developing methodologies appropriate for investigation of the human life-span.

Reprinted and adapted by permission from *Journal of Gerontology*, 29:555–563, 1974.

Differentiation increases with age. Literature on human development repeatedly suggests this is generally the case (Neugarten, 1973; Sarbin, 1954), but the applicability of this generalization to the middle and late years of life is debatable, and the literature reflects uncertainty on the issue. The uncertainty persists not only because of substantive differences in theory about human development and change but also because reliable data are not available to test adequately the competing hypotheses.

One encounters, on the one hand, the claim derived from a life-span perspective that individual differences in life-style and intellectual functioning observed in the middle years are accentuated in late life (Bromley, 1966; Havighurst, 1957; Riegel, 1971; Riegel et al., 1967). As Neugarten (1964) has argued, "Within the social and cultural realms, we can expect differences between individuals to be accentuated with time, as educational, vocational, and social events accumulate one after another to create more and more differentiated sets of experiences from one person to the next." Disengagement theorists have reinforced the argument for social variability. They argue that in the later years of life, for a variety of reasons, social constraints weaken. The observed variability in social and psychological functioning can in fact be accentuated at least at the beginning of old age, as the individual activates preferred but suppressed conceptions of the self (Cumming and Henry, 1961). The literature on physiological functioning in late life also suggests that individual differences increase (Botwinick and Thompson, 1968; Comfort, 1968; Obrist, 1953). Dispersion of scores on a variety of physiological indicators increases over time for a cohort of older individuals, apparently because some persons have maintained their earlier performance level while others have declined because of disease or decremental aging effects.

On the other hand, one also encounters arguments for de-differentiation in the later years. Proponents of this view in the literature on social, psychological, and physiological functioning typically argue that mean performance on a variety of parameters decreases in the later years (Kelly, 1955; Malmo and Shagass, 1949; Riegel et al., 1967). With death being the end point of life, it is implied, individuals become increasingly alike as they approach this common denominator. Mean performance among the elderly decreases, and there is an apparent regression toward a progressively lower mean. Such de-differentiation would presumably result from both selective mortality, which removes individuals who function least well, and increased morbidity, which limits the physiological functioning of survivors. Increased morbidity, in turn, constrains social and psychological functioning. In fact, then, there is not a regression toward the mean, in the statistical meaning of that term, but rather a narrowing of the range, with the less able person dying from the population.

The available literature thus offers contradictory conclusions, and assessment of the comparative strengths of the competing arguments has been difficult because adequate data often have not been available. Whether heterogeneity in populations remains stable or decreases in the later years of life and whether the hypothesized differentiation applies equally to social, psychological, and physiological phenomena remain unresolved issues in the absence of reliable data. This paper presents data relevant to resolving these issues.

Some Methodological Considerations

Whether or not aging cohorts become more homogeneous or heterogeneous over time will not be adequately resolved as long as several important methodological problems persist. In the succeeding paragraphs, six problems which are important in the analysis of relevant data are discussed briefly.

1. *Cross-sectional data sets*. Most of the studies that have explicitly examined age and variability have used cross-sectional data and have not made a clear distinction between age differences and age changes. Sequential observation of individual differences in particular cohorts is adequate for definitive tests of hypotheses regarding variability in the later years of life.

2. *Selective survival*. Selective mortality confounds tests of variability over time. The effects of subject loss due to death on the composition of any panel must be taken into account in studies of the relationship between aging and individual differences. It is reasonable to assume that subjects with extreme values (''outlayers'') would most probably disappear from a cohort. If so, the effect would be to reduce observed variance.

3. *Sampling bias*. Related to selective survival is the problem of sampling bias. Less able persons in a population tend to refuse retesting as well as initial testing, particularly among the elderly. Such bias can produce artifactual differences in observed variability (Riegel et al., 1967) but, again, the general effect would be to reduce variability, not increase it.

4. *Terminal drop*. A terminal drop (i.e., rapid change) in social, psychological, and physiological functioning immediately prior to death has been suggested by several writers as a possible source of individual differences in late life (see Riegel and Riegel, 1972, for further citations). In studying elderly persons, it is argued, investigators are in fact studying samples which include both elite survivors and an undetermined proportion of individuals who experience rapid decline in functional capacity prior to death. The proportion of individuals in this terminal phase presumably would affect observed variability, although the extent of the effect remains a matter of conjecture.

5. *Intraindividual versus interindividual variability*. The effect of intraindividual variability in functioning on observed interindividual variability among elderly persons remains speculative. For example, increased personal as well as group variability in auditory reaction time appears to be related to aging, although the data for this conclusion are largely cross-sectional (Botwinick and Thompson, 1968; Obrist, 1953). However, the precise effect of such intraindividual variability on the assessment of individual differences within a group is unknown, since relevant data are scarce.

6. *Sex and age differences*. Whether differentiation by sex increases with age has been debated in social-psychological literature (Cameron, 1968; Neu-

garten, 1964; Palmore, 1968). It is, therefore, important in any discussion of individual differences in relation to age to anticipate that males and females may exhibit dissimilar patterns. Moreover, research evidence suggests the utility of distinguishing between the "younger aged" and the "older aged" (Riegel et al., 1967; Spieth, 1965). Perhaps it is the "very old" among whom individual differences disappear rather than among "the old" in general. In any case, research on human variability must consider possible sex differences and the special effects of advanced old age. In our initial analyses of data, for example, we studied separately males and females, and relatively old and young aged. Clear evidence for either sex or age differences with respect to variability was not found. There were only a few isolated instances suggesting that differences might exist.

Among these six considerations, this paper addresses items 1, 2, and 5 most directly.

In the balance, our reading of the inconclusive published evidence on variability in individual differences in late life leads us to propose two hypotheses:

(1) *Individual differences do not decrease with age*. Variability on a variety of indicators is at least maintained, if not increased, in late life. Reduction of variance in functioning with age has not been adequately demonstrated and, when observed, is probably artifactual rather than substantive; that is, any observed reduction is most likely to be due to selective survival and/or sampling bias rather than to decreases in the individual differences among cohorts of persons who survive to old age.

(2) *Individuals tend to maintain the same rank on a variety of indicators in relation to age peers throughout the later years of life*. Maintenance of individual differences in late life is not due, we argue, to "dynamic equilibrium" within a specific population, whereby there is random individual crossover and movement throughout the range of relevant scores (cf. Kelly, 1955, for an opposing argument). We reaffirm that maintenance of differentiation in late life is not artifactual but substantive. Even if social activities are on average curtailed in an aged group, for example, those who earlier in life were the most active of their cohort remain, relatively speaking, the most active; less socially active old persons become the less socially active very old persons. This hypothesis is based on evidence of a persistence of life-style throughout the late adult years.

A major implication of these hypotheses is that any generalization about the aged which implies increasing homogeneity with age should be viewed with the same skepticism as generalizations made about other highly diverse social categories: e.g., adolescents, adults, females, blacks, or Americans. Selective mortality does create a social, psychological, physiological elite among the older cohorts and less diversity among the aged than among younger age groups is possible, though not demonstrated. What we seek to demonstrate in this paper, however, is a different point: in an identified cohort, the range of individual differences among survivors is maintained. These persons continue to grow, develop, and change; in short, they maintain individual differences in the face of any presumed or demonstrated decrements of aging. As more and more individuals survive to old age, we conjecture, the range of individual differences among the aged in the future will be increasingly like that observed in younger age groups.

Research Design

We have employed data from a continuing longitudinal investigation of human functioning at the Duke University Center for the Study of Aging and Human Development. From this broader study we have concentrated on specific indicators of variability in individual differences over time observed in the first longitudinal study. Our sample is composed of 106 current survivors of an original panel of 271 persons initially ranging in age from sixty to ninety-four; the mean age initially was seventy. Panelists were drawn from the area in and around Durham, North Carolina, and their social and economic characteristics reflect those of the area. Repeated measures of functioning in terms of a wide range of social, psychological, and physiological parameters in this multidisciplinary study have enabled us to test the two hypotheses in a defined sample.

Six rounds of observation are available (1974), spanning an average of thirteen years from observation 1 to observation 6. At each observation we have been able to measure and compare the variability on a variety of variables observed among nonsurvivors as well as survivors in the original panel of 271.

We tested the first hypothesis using Pitman's (1939) test for correlated variances. In this test, if one assumes that the measures X_1 and X_2 follow a bivariate normal distribution, then $D = X_1 - X_2$ and $S = X_1 + X_2$ are bivariate normal also. The correlations r_{DS} between D and S is computed finally by the formula: $r_{DS} = (F - 1)/\sqrt{[(F + 1)^2 - 4r^2F]}$, where $F = S_1^2/S_2^2$ and r is the correlation between X_1 and X_2. R has the same distribution as for independent normal samples if X_1 and X_2 have equal variances. Hypothesis 2 is tested by the Spearman Rank Order Correlation.

For convenience in presenting data, we have concentrated primarily on comparisons of surviving panelists at the first and sixth observations, though some information is presented on observations at times 2–5.

From a battery of hundreds of measures covering a wide range of biological, behavioral, and social variables, we selected nineteen measures as illustrative for our purposes. Complete information on the nineteen variables is not uniformly available for all six observations, so at any particular observation there may be less than nineteen variables for comparison. Only at time 6 are all nineteen variables available. There are fifteen variables with observations both at times 1 and 6. When times 3 and 6 are compared, on the other hand, there are eighteen variables available.

The number of subjects available for specific analysis varies. This is because any given individual in our study sample of 106 may have missed one or more rounds of observation during the approximately thirteen years. Moreover, some of the very old subjects who are unable to come to the center are seen at home, where certain procedures and tests are omitted.

These particular nineteen variables were selected for the following reasons: They were either ordinal or interval; they gave a broad spectrum of fairly representative social, psychological, and physiological functioning; and the physiological and psychological measures were generally objective measures relatively independent of subjective judgments of investigators. A brief description of the measures appears below.

We were also able to test variability of intraindividual differences with respect to one variable, visual reaction time. This is important because it enabled us to assess the effect of personal variability in response, as related to interindividual differences. As noted below, an individual's reaction time score used for interindividual comparisons was the grand mean of four reaction time mean subscores. An individual's reaction time variability score was the standard deviation of these four reaction time means around the grand mean of that individual's RT scores. Individual reaction time variability scores were assessed by Pitman's test of correlated variances to determine whether the dispersion of the variability of scores changed significantly over time. A paired *t*-test was made to test whether mean individual variability changed from time 1 to time 6.

Description of Variables

Life satisfaction and level of social activity. Morale and activity are defined in terms of scores based on the activity and attitude inventories developed by Havighurst and associates (Cavan et al., 1949). The activity inventory score cumulatively assesses differences in physical vitality, in intimate social contacts with family and friends, in use of leisure time, in organizational membership and participation, and in work role maintenance. Possible scores range from a low of 0 to a high of 50.

The attitude inventory includes items which, cumulatively, assess what might be called an individual's master definition of self in relation to others and environment: items such as feelings about health, friends, work, economic security, religion, personal usefulness, happiness, and family relationships. Possible scores range from a low of 0 to a high of 48.

Self-health assessment. Classification of subjects by self-assessment of health status was based on answers to the question, "How do you rate your health at the present time?" The basic response categories were *excellent*, *good*, *fair*, and *poor*. A subject could in fact qualify his response by selecting "excellent for my age," "good for my age," and so on. Possible scores range from 1 (very poor) to 8 (excellent).

Concern about health. Self-health concern was measured on a four-point scale in response to the question, "How concerned do you feel about your health troubles?'' Answers ranged from 0 (not concerned) to 3 (chief problem at present).

Depression. Subjects were rated by a psychiatrist as to presence and degree of depressive affect (not according to diagnosis of depression) after an extensive psychiatric examination. The scale was from 1 (none) to 5 (severe).

WAIS. The psychological measure included was the Wechsler Adult Intelligence Scale score. The WAIS weighted scores uncorrected for age were used rather than intelligence quotients. The WAIS full scale weighted score is the sum of the verbal and performance weighted scores, which are based upon six and five subtest scores, respectively.

Reaction time. At the beginning of a visual reaction time task, the subject was instructed to keep his finger on a start button until a signal light came on, and then as quickly as possible he was to lift his finger from the start button and press the response button under the appropriate right or left light. There were twenty practice trials, ten of which involved only the right signal and ten involved the left signal. Following the practice trials there were sixty-four trials interspersed with four ''conflict'' trials when both signal lights came on simultaneously. For our purposes we studied lift times (the amount of time it took for the subject to raise his finger from the start button in responding to the signal light). We did not study press time (the amount of time it then took the subjects to press the appropriate button under the signal light). Further, we studied only the first forty measures, before any conflict situations were presented. The first forty life-time scores were averaged into four mean scores: the first ten right signals, first ten left signals, second ten right signals, and second ten left signals. For purposes of this study we computed a grand mean of these four mean scores, which we call the individual's reaction time score. In order to obtain several reaction time scores for each person, we were forced, because of the coding procedures, to use both right and left, early and late mean scores. A multiple analysis of variance (MANOVA) test indicated that there were significant right and left effects ($p < .0001$) and significant early and late effects ($p < .0001$) in the four RT means. Therefore, in averaging these four mean scores we have a right/left, early/late confound. We cannot be sure the extent to which change in variability is partially a result of these confounds. We considered the confounding to be relatively unimportant in this particular analysis because we assumed that the confounding occurred systematically for all subjects. Reaction time was measured in milliseconds.

Physician's functional rating. Objective health status was measured on a six-point scale of physical functioning following an extensive medical and psychiatric evaluation by a project physician. This rating was the physician's estimate of the subject's capacity to function effectively in daily living, and it was determined after comprehensive examinations which included a medical history, physical and neurological examination, and ophthalmological and dermatological examinations. The tests also included an audiogram, chest x ray, electroencephalogram, electrocardiogram, ballistocardiogram, and routine blood and urine studies. The physician indicated the existence of physical impairment in the subject and assessed on a rating scale the degree of limitation of function in everyday life situations. Possible range of scores was from 0 (no pathology) to 5 (total disability).

Performance status. Performance status was measured by the subject's ability to carry on his normal activities or, alternatively, his degree of dependence on help and nursing care, as assessed by a project social worker. The score was expressed in terms of percentage disability (from Karnofsky, 1948). Subjects were rated on this scale beginning at the third observation. Possible range of scores was from 100 percent (normal) to 10 percent (moribund).

Weight. Weight was recorded in pounds and was coded in terms of the nearest 10 pounds. A score of 13, therefore, referred to 130 pounds, or specifically, any weight between 125 and 134 pounds.

Cardiovascular status. The presence or absence of cardiovascular disease was clinically assessed from EKG interpretations, estimates of heart size, extent of calcification, and evidence of peripheral arteriosclerosis hypertension, or cardiac decompensation. The subjects were rated on a nine-point scale according to the number and severity of their symptoms and the limitations these posed on their activities. Scores could range from 1 (none, or equivocal heart disease) to 9 (definite heart disease, severe symptoms).

Visual acuity, right and left eyes. Visual acuity for both eyes was assessed on a far distance vision test with correction. The possible range of scores was from 0 (20/15 vision) to 12 (can discern hand movements with good light projection).

Hearing loss, binaural. Binaural hearing loss was measured in terms of percentage hearing loss by a pure form (MAICO) audiometric study. Measurement of hearing loss is stated as percentage of hearing lost.

Diastolic and systolic blood pressure. The blood pressure values were obtained by cuff measures with the subject in a recumbent position. The physician rounded the blood pressure values to the nearest 10 mm/Hg.

Blood cholesterol. Total serum cholesterol determinations were made on blood drawn between 8 a.m. and 9 a.m. Analyses were made according to Bloor's method, adapted to photoelectric colorimeter. The Liebermann-Burchard reaction was used. Measures were rounded to the nearest 10 mg. percent.

Findings

Table D—1 reports changes in variability of individual differences for the series of social, psychological, and physiological measures considered in this study. We will concentrate on comparing observations 1 and 6 in this summary of findings. Fifteen variables are available for comparison in testing the first hypothesis.

1. For eight out of fifteen variables there was no significant change in vari-

Table D—1. *Changes in variability: observations 1 and 6, 3 and 6, for selected parameters of functioning.*

Parameter	N[a]	Test for correlated variances[b] 1 and 6	Test for correlated variances[b] 3 and 6
Social/Social-psychological			
Life satisfaction	69	−.26[d]	−.20
Level of social activity	71	−.07	.05
Self-health assessment	72	.23[d]	−.03
Concern about health	64	−.37[e]	.04
Depression	60	[c]	.02
Psychological			
WAIS, full scale	59	−.10	−.15
WAIS, verbal weighted	63	−.09	−.12
WAIS, performance weighted	59	−.02	−.12
Reaction time	56	[c]	−.15
Physiological			
Physician's functional rating	55	.12	.07
Performance status	80	[c]	−.38[c]
Weight	63	−.07	[c]
Cardiovascular state	51	−.31[d]	.01
Visual acuity, right	55	−.46[e]	−.03
Visual acuity, left	53	−.45[e]	.06
Hearing loss, binaural	59	−.14	−.30[d]
Diastolic blood pressure	62	.30[d]	.22
Systolic blood pressure	62	−.04	.04
Blood cholesterol	33	[c]	−.18

[a]The basic sample size for this study was 106. For specific analyses the number of subjects varies because there were missing data at various points of measurement for many subjects. For each measure of functioning, only persons who had all completed data for that one measure were included. No systematic bias appeared to operate in the omission of particular items. Some subjects were not available for study at a particular time of observation. Others were housebound at the time of observation and some tests or observations were omitted.

[b]A negative correlation indicates an increase in variance through time. A positive correlation indicates a decrease in variance through time.

[c]No data were collected for this variable at the times indicated.

[d]$p < .05$.

[e]$p < .01$.

ances between times 1 and 6. Existing differentiation was maintained.

2. For five out of fifteen variables there was a statistically significant increase in variance from the first to the last observation.

3. For two out of fifteen variables there was a significant decrease in variance. A brief discussion of these two deviant variables is appropriate. The first

Table D—2. *Group variances: observations 1 through 6 for selected parameters of functioning.*

Parameter	*N*[a]	Time 1[a]	Time 2	Time 3	Time 4	Time 5	Time 6
Social/Social-psychological							
Life satisfaction	69	20.5[c]	23.9	22.5	23.5	26.2	31.1[d]
Level of social activity	71	37.3	38.5	44.8[d]	31.2[c]	32.3	41.7
Self-health assessment	72	3.2[d]	2.3	1.9	1.6[c]	2.2	2.0
Concern about health	64	.3[c]	.6	.7[d]	.6	.6	.6
Depression	60	[b]	1.1[d]	1.0	.6[c]	.9	.9
Psychological							
WAIS, full scale	59	869.4	813.4[c]	844.4	876.8	967.8[d]	942.0
WAIS, verbal weighted	63	378.7	369.4[c]	369.9	393.5	426.7[d]	403.9
WAIS, performance weighted	59	138.1	123.9[c]	128.5	130.7	141.8[d]	141.3
Reaction time	56	[b]	109.3[c]	247.1	131.7	160.2	305.2[d]
Physiological							
Physician's functional rating	55	1.0[d]	.8	.9	.5[c]	.8	.8
Performance status	80	[b]	[b]	118.8	95.4[c]	175.7	239.1[d]
Weight	63	8.6[c]	8.9	[b]	[b]	[b]	9.1[d]
Cardiovascular state	51	1.3[c]	1.6	2.4	2.5[d]	1.6	2.4
Visual acuity, right	55	1.5[c]	3.4	3.6	2.9	2.2	3.8[d]
Visual acuity, left	53	1.2[c]	1.5	3.1[d]	2.9	2.1	2.8
Hearing loss, binaural	59	139.3	128.1[c]	129.4	150.5	162.3	167.6[d]
Diastolic blood pressure	62	1.7	1.0[c]	1.5	1.5	2.3[d]	1.0
Systolic blood pressure	62	5.3	4.4[c]	6.1	5.7	6.8[d]	5.6
Blood cholesterol	33	[b]	[b]	16.2	16.1[c]	16.5	21.8[d]

[a]See table D—1 for explanation of sample size.

[b]No data were collected for this variable at times indicated.

[c]Smallest variance in the six observations.

[d]Largest variance in the six observations.

[e]Years between times of observation vary. In the early years of the study, subjects were interviewed every four to five years. Later observations have been made at intervals of two to three years as the sample decreased in size and subjects became very old.

variable showing a decrease in variance through time was self-health assessment. We know from previous longitudinal research that elderly subjects tend to overestimate their health status as they age (Maddox and Douglass, 1973). While most subjects are realistic in self-evaluation of health, those who differ with a physician's assessment of their health are much more likely to deny than to stress poor health inappropriately. In this sense, they become more alike as they age; regardless of their objective physical condition, they tend to report good health. This measure, therefore, does not support our initial hypothesis.

The only other variable which contradicts our hypothesis is diastolic blood pressure. We offer an explanation for this contradiction because it alerts us to a problem in longitudinal research on older subjects. The observed pattern of blood pressure is quite probably a treatment effect. No detailed data are available on prescribed drugs being taken by the subjects at the time of each observation. We do know, however, that if a subject was found to have high blood pressure in the early observations of the study, the subject's personal physician was notified and the subject would normally be treated for the reported condition. Consequently, blood pressure (usually a relatively simple problem for medical management) would tend to be brought into normal range over time. Such intervention would logically result in the observed decrease in variance. While this interpretation is speculative, it alerts us to the importance of treatment effects when studying longitudinal change in physiological variables.

4. Table D—2 presents the group variances for all measures for all observations. For six out of fifteen variables, the time 1 variance was the smallest of the six variances. For six out of the nineteen measures available at the last observation, the time 6 variance was the largest of the six. However, there was no linear, monotonic change in variance (except for weight) from times 1–6.

5. This lack of a linear, monotonic change in variance over time led us to test the difference in variance between times 3 and 6 to insure that our earlier findings were not an artifact of the particular observations selected. When times 3 and 6 were compared, there were eighteen variables available. Sixteen of the eighteen showed a maintenance of variability. Two variables showed a significant increase in variance; there were no significant decreases in variance for any variable. This led us to reaffirm the hypothesized maintenance of variability with age.

6. Table D—3 presents average variances over adjacent time periods. These averages provide additional information about the pattern of variance over the six observations. In columns 1 and 2, for fifteen out of nineteen measures the average of times 1, 2, and 3 variance was smaller than the average of times 4, 5, and 6 variance, indicating a general trend toward increase in variance through time.

7. Mortality was controlled in this study by concentrating on subjects known to have survived through the last time of observation. Therefore, in reporting observations from times 1–5, subjects who were not to survive have been removed. When mortality is controlled in this way, the basic study sample numbers 106. However, in a separate analysis of these longitudinal data, we did not control for mortality and, thus, were essentially observing two different groups at times 1 and 6 in much the same way as one would in a cross-sectional design. In columns 3 and 4 of table D—3, one observes that when mortality is not controlled, variance does decrease in ten of nineteen instances. From this we infer that reported decrease in variance with age is in most cases an artifact of sampling.

8. Intraindividual variability of reaction time showed no clear pattern of change through time. Personal variability was analyzed in two ways: (*a*) For each subject a grand mean of individual 4 RT mean scores was computed at each time of observation. The mean RT scores plotted in the first graph of figure D—1

Table D—3. *Changes in variability: observations 1–3 and 4–6 for selected parameters of functioning, mortality controlled and not controlled.*

Parameter	Mortality controlled[b] Average variances		Mortality not controlled[c] Average variances	
	Times 1–3	Times 4–6	Times 1–3	Times 4–6
Social/Social-psychological				
Life satisfaction	22.3	26.9[a]	31.8[a]	31.2
Level of social activity	40.2[a]	35.1	42.9[a]	42.6
Self-health assessment	2.5[a]	1.9	3.0[a]	2.4
Concern about health	.5	.6[a]	.7	.8[a]
Depression	1.0[a]	.8	1.1[a]	.8
Psychological				
WAIS, full scale	842.4	928.9[a]	1007.5	1054.5[a]
WAIS, verbal weighted	372.7	408.0[a]	416.5	434.3[a]
WAIS, performance weighted	130.2	137.9[a]	159.8	165.9[a]
Reaction time	178.2	199.0[a]	195.1	531.6[a]
Physiological				
Physician's functional rating	.9[a]	.7	1.2[a]	.8
Performance status	118.8	170.1[a]	194.7	203.7[a]
Weight	8.8	9.1[a]	9.2[a]	8.7
Cardiovascular state	1.8	2.2[a]	2.5[a]	2.1
Visual acuity, right	2.8	3.0[a]	3.3	3.3
Visual acuity, left	1.9	2.6[a]	3.0	3.0
Hearing loss, binaural	132.2	160.1[a]	231.3[a]	206.7
Diastolic blood pressure	1.4	1.6[a]	1.8[a]	1.6
Systolic blood pressure	5.2	6.0[a]	7.6[a]	6.0
Blood cholesterol	16.2	18.1[a]	16.4	18.0[a]

[a]Larger of the two variance averages.

[b]Basic sample $N = 106$.

[c]Basic sample $N = 271$.

(solid line) represent the group mean of these individual grand RT mean scores. The standard deviations are represented by the dotted lines. Neither the RT mean scores for each of 5 observations nor the associated standard deviations show significant change over time. (*b*) The standard deviation of the 4 RT means around the grand mean of each subject at each observation became his RT variability score. The second graph of figure 1 presents the mean RT variability scores (solid line) for all subjects; the dotted lines represent the standard deviations from these mean scores.

The sample variability (of individual variability in subtests) was subjected to the Pitman test for correlated variances. There was a fluctuation of variance through time, though no clear trend. Time 3 variability was the largest of the six

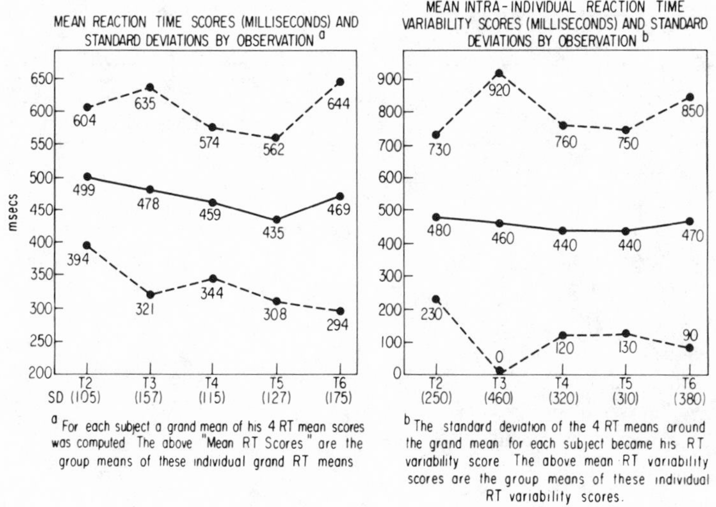

Figure D—1. *Grand mean of individual 4 RT mean scores.*

observations; time 2 was the smallest. There was a significant increase in variance ($p < .01$) between times 2 and 6, but no significant change between times 3 and 6.

A paired *t*-test, comparing mean intraindividual variability for times 2 and 6 ($t = .05$) and for times 3 and 6 ($t = .15$) showed no significant difference. We conclude that stability in intraindividual variability in RT measures characterizes these subjects in late life.

9. Finally, table D—4 presents the rank order correlations for the fifteen variables at times 1 and 6 and the eighteen variables at times 3 and 6. Rank order is clearly maintained in most measures of functioning. The maintenance of group variability is not simply due to "dynamic equilibrium" of persons fluctuating within the group without disturbing the appearance or stability of group variability. Those who score high on a particular variable in earlier observations tend to score high later; low scorers tend to remain low scorers.

Conclusions

Our conclusions are straightforward. When mortality and other losses within a defined sample are controlled, the observed variability of a number of social, psychological, and physiological measures tend to remain stable through time. In some instances, there is a significant increase in individual differences. Increased variability of individual differences, moreover, is not due simply to increased personal variability or instability. On the contrary, there is stability through time

Table D—4. *Persistence of rank order: observations 1 and 6 and observations 3 and 6 for selected parameters of functioning.*

Parameter	N^a	Spearman Rho, 1 and 6	Spearman Rho, 3 and 6
Social/Social-psychological			
Life satisfaction	69	.65[d]	.60[d]
Level of social activity	71	.55[d]	.67[d]
Self-health assessment	72	−.02	.17
Concern about health	64	.35[d]	.29[c]
Depression	60	[b]	.02
Psychological			
WAIS, full scale	59	.92[d]	.94[d]
WAIS, verbal weighted	63	.93[d]	.93[d]
WAIS, performance weighted	59	.85[d]	.91[d]
Reaction time	60	[b]	.64[d]
Physiological			
Physician's functional rating	55	.12	.31[c]
Performance status	80	[b]	.48[d]
Weight	63	.89[d]	[b]
Cardiovascular state	51	.15	.44[d]
Visual acuity, right	55	.41[d]	.43[d]
Visual acuity, left	53	.36[d]	.53[d]
Hearing loss, binaural	59	.76[d]	.91[d]
Diastolic blood pressure	62	.45[d]	.44[d]
Systolic blood pressure	62	.51[d]	.43[d]
Blood cholesterol	33	[b]	.57[d]

[a] See table D—1 for explanation of sample size.

[b] Data were not collected for this variable at the times indicated.

[c] $p < .05$.

[d] $p < .01$.

in individual variability in at least the case of visual reaction time. Rarely is there a decrease in group differentiation through time. Our first hypothesis is confirmed.

The range of observed individual differences is maintained, and within that range the individual's rank ordering is relatively constant. The second hypothesis is also confirmed.

There are several ramifications of the questions raised in this study which are beyond the scope of this paper. Although we have dealt exclusively here with variance, we recognize the significance of the mean, the range, and the distribution of scores (Comfort, 1968; Spieth, 1965). For a complete characterization of human performance, changes of distribution and patterns of performance are important. Our investigation in no sense assumes a simple, unchanging relationship between age and performance as measured by a variety of indicators. Our objective has been to demonstrate that, in a defined sample of aged persons, individual differences are maintained.

We have not in this paper dealt with the hypothesized terminal drop in scores prior to death. Insofar as terminal drop is a beginning of the death process, it is distinct from the gradual decrement of functioning within normal aging. Terminal drop would presumably be found prior to any disease-related death, regardless of age. The phenomenon warrants further longitudinal study.

This study challenges the generalization that, while children and adolescents become more differentiated through their development, adults become less differentiated in the later years of life. The data presented here provide evidence that development, change, and growth continue through the later years of the life-span in spite of the decrement of social, psychological, and physiological functioning which typically accompanies the aging process.

References

Botwinick, J., and Thompson, L. W. Individual differences in reaction time in relation to age. *Journal of Genetic Psychology*, 112:73–75, 1968.

Bromley, D. B. *The psychology of human aging*. Baltimore: Penguin Books, 1966.

Cameron, P. Masculinity-femininity in the aged. *Journal of Gerontology*, 10:63–65, 1968.

Cavan, R. S., et al. *Personal adjustment in old age*. Chicago: Science Research Associates, 1949.

Comfort, A. Physiology, homeostasis and aging. *Gerontologia*, 14:224–234, 1968.

Cumming, E., and Henry, W. E. *Growing old: The process of disengagement*. New York: Basic Books, 1961.

Havighurst, R. J. The social competence of middleaged people. *Genetic Psychological Monographs*, 56:297–375, 1957.

Karnofsky, D. A. The use of nitrogen mustards in the palliative treatment of carcinoma. *Cancer*, 1:634–656, 1948.

Kelly, E. L. Consistency of the adult personality. *American Psychologist*, 10:659–681, 1955.

Maddox, G. L., and Douglass, E. B. Self-assessment of health: A longitudinal study of elderly subjects. *Journal of Health and Social Behavior*, 14:87–93, 1973.

Malmo, R. B., and Shagass, C. Variability of heart rate in relation to age, sex, and stress. *Journal of Applied Physiology*, 2:181–184, 1949.

Neugarten, B. L. A developmental view of adult personality. In J. E. Birren (Ed.), *Relations of development and aging*. Springfield, Ill.: Charles C. Thomas, 1964.

Neugarten, B. L. Personality change in late life: A developmental perspective. In E. Eisdorfer and M. P. Lawton (Eds.), *The psychology of adult development and aging*. Washington, D.C.: American Psychological Association, 1973.

Obrist, W. D. Simple auditory reaction time in aged adults. *Journal of Psychology*, 35:259–266, 1953.

Palmore, E. B. The effects of aging on activities and attitudes. *Gerontologist*, 8:259–263, 1968.

Palmore, E. B. (Ed.), *Normal aging*. Durham, N.C.: Duke University Press, 1970.

Palmore, E. B. (Ed.), *Normal aging II*. Durham, N.C.: Duke University Press, 1974.

Pitman, E. J. G. A note on normal correlation. *Biometrika*, 31:9–12, 1939; summarized in G. W. Snedecor and W. G. Cochran, *Statistical methods*. 6th Ed. Ames: Iowa State University Press, 1967, 195–197.

Riegel, K. F. The prediction of death and longevity in longitudinal research. In E. B. Palmore and

F. C. Jeffers (Eds.), *Prediction of life span: Recent findings*. Lexington, Mass.: Heath Lexington Books, 1971.

Riegel, K. F., and Riegel, R. M. Development, drop, and death. *Developmental Psychology*, 6:306–319, 1972.

Riegel, K. F., Riegel, R. M., and Meyer, G. Socio-psychological factors of aging: A cohort-sequential analysis. *Human Development*, 10:27–56, 1967.

Sarbin, T. R. Role theory. In G. Lindzey (Ed.), *Handbook of social psychology*, Vol. 1. Cambridge, Mass.: Addison-Wesley, 1954.

Spieth, W. Slowness of task performance and cardiovascular disease. In A. T. Welford and J. E. Birren (Eds.), *Behavior, aging and the nervous system*. Springfield, Ill.: Charles C. Thomas, 1965.

Socialization to Old Age

Linda K. George

The topic of socialization to age and sex roles is enmeshed in both theoretical and empirical controversy. There appears to be general consensus that socialization consists of preparations for particular roles. The bone of contention is whether or not age and sex statuses are in fact accompanied by discernible social roles. One perspective posits that they are not. According to this viewpoint, age and sex categories cannot be linked with sufficient specific behavioral, attitudinal, or value patterns to meet the criteria as distinct social roles. An opposite point of view contends that persons of different ages and/or genders do behave, think, and believe differently to a significant degree and that, although they are broad in scope, age and sex roles certainly exist.

Empirically, the same lines of evidence have been used to support both perspectives. Proponents of age and sex roles point to the significant attitudinal and behavioral differences typically observed between age groups or genders and view this as evidence for normatively-governed roles. The opposite perspective focuses upon the substantial variation within age and sex groups as evidence that there are not corresponding social roles. Thus, using the same evidence, one perspective emphasizes the variation explained by group membership and the other stresses the unexplained within-group variation.

In this paper socialization to a particular age role is examined in a more narrow sense. We do not examine differences between age groups and attribute them to differing normative expectations. Rather, a path model is used to describe the process of socialization to old age. The dependent variable is a criterion measure which indicates whether or not socialization has taken place. The independent variables represent a variety of events and processes which one would theoretically expect to influence the socialization outcome.

Theoretical Rationale and Model

Traditionally, two kinds of criterion variables have been used as indications of the outcome of socialization: self-concept and role-relevant behaviors (Rosow, 1974). Thus, in their study of the socialization of medical students, Merton and his associates (1957) examined behavioral outcomes. For their purposes, medical students had become doctors when they were able to treat patients, prescribe medication, and so forth. In another study, Becker and associates (1961) defined socialization outcome as the self-definition of medical students as physician. One would expect these two types of criteria to be highly correlated, although evidence bearing on this issue remains unavailable.

Self-concept is the criterion variable for socialization used in this study. Specifically, the process of age identification during middle and late life is traced. Subjects identify themselves as either middle-aged or old, and this response is interpreted as their conception of themselves in terms of age. The choice of self-concept is not intended to negate the usefulness of examining behavioral outcomes. Indeed, in this sample, age identity was significantly associated with a variety of attitudinal and behavioral measures including life satisfaction, participation in voluntary organizations, amount of contact with significant others, and feelings of anomie. Furthermore, the relationships remained highly significant with the impact of chronological age statistically controlled, indicating a close relationship between self-concept and behavior.

Self-concept was used as the criterion variable for both practical and theoretical reasons. Pragmatically, the self-concept measure seemed preferable to either choosing a single behavioral variable or to constructing an index of several of them. Theoretically, the use of self-concept provided an available body of literature from which to choose potentially significant independent variables. Moreover, self-concept might be usefully conceptualized as an intervening variable between the independent variables and behavioral outcomes. In fact, we have some empirical support for this: controlling on age identity, the relationships between the independent variables and the behavioral measures were observed to be severely attenuated.

The path model employed seven independent variables. These predictors are intended to identify sources of evaluation and types of referents used by individuals in assessment of their age identities. *Source of evaluation* refers to a distinction between internal and external standards. Broadly speaking, individuals may compare themselves to internalized images of what persons of various social locations are like or they may assess themselves in terms of evaluations of and treatments they receive from significant others. *Type of referent* refers to the particular characteristics used in the self-assessment process. We posit three broad categories of referents in the transition from self-conception as middle-aged to old: chronological age, social situations and events, and physical health.

The path model used in this analysis is presented in figure D—2. Chronological age, a baseline measure of age identity, and events are the exogenous

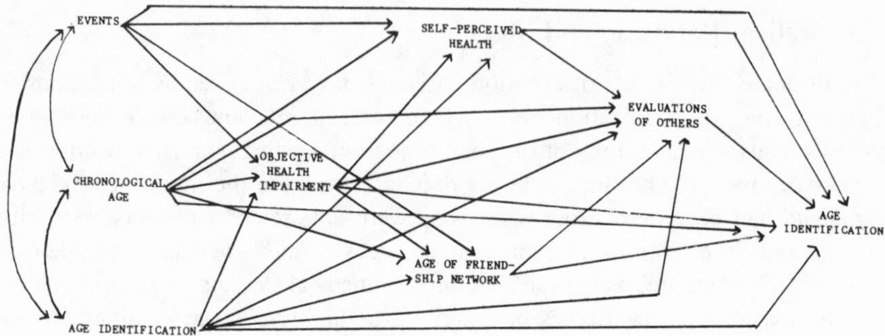

Figure D—2. *Generic path model describing process of age identity.*

variables. The relationship between chronological age and age identity may seem patently obvious, but it is not. Although our society imposes chronological criteria on the incumbency of certain roles and activities, age-based eligibility for role occupancy is quite rare and the relevant roles are narrow in scope. This society is not characterized by rigid and formalized age grades. Although chronological age is expected to be significantly related to age identity, the most interesting aspect of its impact will be its relative importance as compared to the other types of referents that serve as culturally available alternative standards for self-appraisal.

The baseline measure of age identity is included in order that *changes* in age identity over time can be examined. This residualized change analysis involves entering the baseline measure of age identity into the first stage of the equation and permitting other variables to predict the residualized outcome measure of age identity.

The measure of events is a sum of the number of events such as retirement, widowhood, and the empty nest (i.e., departure of the last child from the parental home) which occurred during the previous year. These events are fairly common during later life and might be expected to lead individuals to perceive themselves as old.

The second stage of the path model consists of an objective measure of physical health status. The measure is objective in that it is based on a physician's assessment of the respondent's physical health status. Declines in health are common in later life and they may trigger a change in age identity from middle-aged to old.

The third stage of the path model includes two variables: self-rated health and the age composition of the respondent's friendship network. Self-rated health consists of respondents' perceptions of their health as poor, fair, good, or excellent. Again, a decline in health is expected to increase the likelihood of self-identification as old. Age composition of the respondent's friendship network refers to the proportion of the respondent's friends who are age sixty-five or older. Because people tend to define themselves as similar to their friends, we expected that, the higher the proportion of older friends, the more likely the respondent would identify as old rather than middle-aged.

The final predictor in the path model is a measure of the individual's perceptions of how others view him or her in terms of age (i.e., as middle-aged or old). This variable taps the degree to which individuals' perceptions of the evaluations of others influence their own self-conceptions. We expected that those respondents who believed that others believed that they were old also would be most likely to identify themselves as old. This independent variable addresses the source of the individual's evaluative standards.

Path analysis is a useful analytic technique for the present problem since it forces the researcher to specify an ordering of the variables which clarifies both the theoretical linkages among variables and interpretation of results. Path analysis also permits decomposition of the effects of predictors into their total, direct, and indirect effects. This will be particularly useful for understanding the effects of chronological age. All of the other variables were expected to—and did—correlate significantly with chronological age. The decomposition procedure permitted examination of the direct and indirect effects of chronological age—that is, to assess the degree to which chronological age per se operated upon age identity and the degree to which it operated through a variety of age-related variables.

Sample

The data used in this analysis are from the Duke Second Longitudinal Study. The sample consists of the 345 white men and women who had completed all three relevant rounds of data collection. The respondents were age forty-six to seventy at time 1 and fifty to seventy-five at the third test date.

Because the path model was designed to represent a dynamic process of change in age identification over time, measures were used from three data collection dates. The exogenous variables were measured at time 1, the endogenous variables were measured at time 2, and the outcome measure of age identification was obtained at time 3.

One further issue complicated the analysis somewhat. A check for interactions indicated that age interacted significantly with several of the other independent variables in the model and had a nonlinear relationship with the outcome measure of age identification. Examination of relevant bivariate distributions indicated that the significant difference was between respondents age sixty-nine and younger and those age seventy and older at the third test date. Thus, the sample was split into two age groups: those aged fifty to sixty-nine (N = 295), and those age seventy and older (N = 50) at the third test date. The path model then was calculated separately for the two groups.

Results

Table D—5 provides the means, ranges, and standard deviations of the major variables for the total sample. As the means indicate, 10 percent of the sample experienced a change in age identification during the five years between the first and third test dates. Virtually all of the changes were from self-identification as middle-aged to age identification as old. Both health measures suggest that the majority of respondents are in good physical health. Twenty-two percent of the respondents' friends, on average, were age sixty-five or older. Most respondents experienced very few of the normative events in the year prior to the first interview. Finally, 34 percent of the respondents reported that others view them as old; this is almost identical to the proportion of participants who described themselves as old.

Table D—6 presents the structural and reduced form equations for the respondents aged fifty to sixty-nine. Table D—7 presents comparable equations for the respondents age seventy and older. Both sets of equations correspond to the path model presented in figure D—2.

In the following discussion, both standardized and unstandardized coefficients are examined. The standardized coefficients are used *within* groups to assess the relative importance of the independent variables for that group. When examining *cross-group* comparisons, however, the metric or unstandardized coefficients are examined. The age split resulted in different variances for the two groups (i.e., the younger group had an age range of twenty years and the older group had an age range of six years). These differences in variances affect the standardized, but not the unstandardized, coefficients.

As tables D—6 and D—7 indicate, the path model operated much differently for the two groups in terms of both the impact of particular predictors and the overall fit in terms of explained variance. For the younger group, chronological age, the perceived evaluations of others, and the health variables all were

Table D—5. *Means, ranges, and standard deviations of variables.*

Variable	Potential range	Actual range	Mean	SD
Baseline age identification (time 1)	0–1	0–1	.26	.44
Chronological age (time 1)	NA	41–70	58.06	7.06
Number of events (time 1)	0–6	0–5	.48	.67
Objective health impairment (time 2)	1–10	1–9	1.85	2.49
Self-rated health (time 2)	1–4	2–4	3.05	.65
Age composition of friendship network (time 2)	0–1	0–1	.22	.29
Perceived evaluations of others (time 2)	0–1	0–1	.34	.48
Outcome age identification (time 3)	0–1	0–1	.36	.48

Table D—6. *Coefficients in structural and reduced form equations for model of age identification, standardized (top) and unstandardized (bottom) coefficients, respondents aged 50–69.*

Dependent variable	Baseline age identification	Age	Events	Objective health impairment	Age of friendship network	Self-rated health	Evaluation of others	R^2
Objective health impairment	.06*	.13*	.14*					.05*
Age of friendship network	.10*	.44*	−.03					.24*
	.10*	.44*	−.03	.00				.24*
Self-rated health	−.25*	.05	−.09*					.06*
	−.23*	.08*	−.06	−.22*				.11*
Evaluation of others	.35*	.26*	.08*					.28*
	.34*	.25*	.07*	.07*				.28*
	.33*	.27*	.06	.05	−.05	−.07*		.29*
Outcome age identification	.42*	.35*	.06					.44*
	.42*	.34*	.05	.08*				.45*
	.39*	.34*	.05	.05	.02	−.13*		.47*
	.30*	.27*	.03	.04	.03	−.11*	.28*	.52*
Objective health impairment	.36*	.05*	.33*					.05*
Age of friendship network	.06*	.02*	−.01					.24*
	.06*	.02*	−.01	.00				.24*
Self-rated health	−.41*	.01	−.06*					.06*
	−.39*	.01*	−.04*	−.06*				.11*
Evaluation of others	.39*	.02*	.03*					.28*
	.39*	.02*	.03*	.01*				.28*
	.37*	.02*	.03	.01	−.08	−.05*		.29*
Outcome age identification	.49*	.03*	.03					.44*
	.48*	.03*	.02	.02*				.45*
	.44*	.03*	.02	.01	.03	−.09*		.47*
	.34*	.02*	.01	.01	.06	−.08*	.28*	.52*

* $p \leq .05$.

Table D—7. *Coefficients in structural and reduced form equations for model of age identification, standardized (top) and unstandardized (bottom) coefficients, respondents aged 70 and older.*

Dependent variable	Baseline age identification	Age	Events	Objective health impairment	Age of friendship network	Self-rated health	Evaluation of others	R^2
Objective health impairment	−.36*	.15*	.04					.03
Age of friendship network	−.06	−.05	.17*					.03
	−.03	−.09	.16*	.23*				.08*
Self-rated health	−.22*	.03	.21*					.07
	−.29*	.10	.23*	−.48*				.29*
Evaluation of others	.34*	.18*	−.03					.16*
	.35*	.16*	−.04	.10*				.17*
	.30*	.19*	−.02	−.01	.12*	−.16*		.20*
Outcome age identification	.56*	−.05	−.02					.29*
	.58*	−.08	−.03	.14*				.31*
	.59*	−.06	−.07*	.11*	.20*	.03		.35*
	.53*	−.10	−.07*	.11*	.18*	.06	.20*	.38*
Objective health impairment	−.78*	.46*	.29					.03
Age of friendship network	−.04	−.02	.06*					.03
	−.02	−.03	.06*	.02*				.08*
Self-rated health	−.30*	.02	.17*					.07
	−.38*	.07	.18*	−.11*				.29*
Evaluation of others	.30*	.08*	−.02					.16*
	.31*	.08*	−.02	.01*				.17*
	.27*	.09*	−.01	−.01	.17*	−.11*		.20*
Outcome age identification	.50*	−.03	−.01					.29*
	.52*	−.04	−.02	.02*				.31*
	.53*	−.03	−.04*	.02*	.30*	.02		.35*
	.47*	−.05	−.04*	.02*	.26*	.04	.20*	.38*

*$p \leq .05$.

significant predictors of age identity. The baseline measure of age identity had highly significant direct and total effects in the model, indicating relative stability in this measure over time in this sample. Chronological age also had significant total and direct effects upon age identification; about one-third of the impact of chronological age was indirect via other age-related variables in the model. The path coefficients for both of the health variables achieves statistical significance and, as would be expected, much of the total impact of objective health operated indirectly via its impact upon self-rated health. Neither the events measure nor the proportion of friends age sixty-five and older were significant predictors of changes in age identification. Finally, the measure of the perceived evaluations of others was a very important predictor of the dependent variable. The overall fit of the model was quite good for the fifty to sixty-nine year olds, accounting for about 52 percent of the variance.

The older group exhibited quite different patterns. Chronological age was not a significant predictor of age identification in this group. Objectively assessed physical health, self-rated health, perceived evaluations of others, events measure, and age composition of the friendship network, however, all were significant predictors of age identification changes among the age seventy and older subsample. The model fits this group less well, as it accounted for about 38 percent of the variance in age identification.

Discussion

The path model proved to be useful for tracing the transition in age identification from middle-aged to old. The difference in the two age groups suggested that there are essentially two sets of mechanisms whereby an individual can come to perceive himself or herself as old. The model better fit the younger group (i.e., age fifty to sixty-nine) and chronological age and health were the most important predictors of coming to identify oneself as old. For the older group, (i.e., age seventy and older), chronological age was not a significant predictor—although the other predictors in the model all were important. For both age groups, the perceived evaluations of significant others were highly predictive of the individuals' own self-appraisals. Had we used cross-sectional data, this relationship would have been interpretatively problematic; do individuals see themselves as others see them or do individuals perceive that others see them as they see themselves? The combination of longitudinal data (in which perceptions of the opinions of others was measured prior to self-perception) and residualized change analysis (in which we predicted only changes in self-perception from middle-aged to old) clarified the interpretation. In this analysis, we have strong evidence that individuals changed their self-perceptions to match their perceptions of others' appraisals.

Conventional chronological standards inform individuals that old age begins somewhere around the age of sixty-five. For most people approaching this transition, the chronological referent is highly salient. In the present analysis this was seen in the importance of chronological age in the model for the younger group. By the age of seventy, about 75 percent of the sample defined themselves as old, again attesting to the impact of chronological age. About 25 percent of the group, however, did not define themselves as old by the age of seventy. Obviously, chronological age per se had not been a sufficiently salient referent to lead those individuals to change their age identification. In effect, the cultural messages concerning the significance of chronological age for age identification had lost their relevance; they had been available but were not heeded. Changes in age identification after age seventy were best explained by personal and situational variables (e.g., normative events, health, and age composition of the friendship network) which serve as culturally available alternatives to chronological referents. Thus there seems to be a group of people who ignored the chronological referent and did not change their age identification unless and until other circumstances suggested the need or appropriateness of doing so.

The results also suggest that it is the social definition of chronological age, rather than any intrinsic aspect of chronological age, that is important in changing age identification from middle-aged to old. If there were an inherent aging process at work, we would expect chronological age to have a linear, unidirectional impact upon age identification. Such was not the case in this sample. Chronological age had a nonlinear relationship with age identification, increasing the probability of self-perception as old until about age seventy and having no significant impact on later ages. Chronological age was a significant referent only for that period of the life span that society has designated as the beginning of old age. Moreover, this social definition of age-related life stages is salient to some persons but not to others. The fact that about three-quarters of the sample were affected by chronological age testifies to the importance of social definitions. The fact that such norms are ignored by one-quarter of the sample, however, indicates that the phenomenon is a socially defined appendage to age rather than an intrinsic component of the aging process.

In summary, this paper is based upon a path model of the hypothesized predictors of changes in age identification. The process depicted is compatible with socialization theory because of its emphasis upon self-conception as the outcome and the additional evidence that self-conception is related to relevant behavioral outcomes. Rather than debate whether or not old age constitutes a social role, we examined the degree to which we could identify the social and personal factors which lead to a change in age identity. The results suggest that the process of identity change is a complex one—but one that can be understood in part by this kind of predictive analysis.

References

Becker, H. S., et al. *Boys in white*. Chicago: University of Chicago Press, 1961.

Merton, R. K., Reader, G., and Kendall, P. (Eds.), *The student-physician*. Cambridge, Mass.: Harvard University Press, 1957.

Palmore, E. B. (Ed.), *Normal aging II*. Durham, N.C.: Duke University Press, 1974.
Rosow, I., *Socialization to old age*. Berkeley: University of California Press, 1974.

Distribution of Life Events and Resources

Ilene C. Siegler

This is the first of two related studies (see the following paper) which investigated stress and adaptation in the Duke Second Longitudinal Study. The shared conceptual framework in these studies was an event-response paradigm, characterized by relating five significant life events (retirement of self and of spouse, widowhood, last child leaving home, and major medical event requiring hospitalization). The occurrence and pattern of events were observed over a six-year period and so were responses to such events. Then the role of the individual's resources (in health, psychological, and social domains), as they related to the occurrence or mediation of response to the events, was considered.

The purposes of this investigation were to document the actual number and distribution of the events that were observed in a small but randomly selected sample of older adults, to document the distribution of resources, and to explore how resources are related to the occurrence of and response to events.

The 502 respondents in the second longitudinal study were aged between forty-six and sixty-nine at the first time of measurement in 1968–70; it was assumed that in this age range the probability of experiencing major events we associate with later middle life would be high. Thus in terms of events this was a prospective study. As we will see, random sampling of adults in this age range does not insure the observation of a large number of events.

Method

Subjects. Subjects were 375 individuals from the second longitudinal study who were seen at both the first (1968–70) and the last (1974–76) times of measurement.

Operationalization of variables. The five events studied were chosen because they were common, expectable transitions for individuals aged forty-six to seventy. All of the events studied had reasonably straightforward definitions: retirement of self and spouse, widowhood, last child leaving home, and illness requiring hospitalization. The interval within which the event occurred, but not

Paper presented at the meeting of the Gerontological Society, San Francisco, California, November 1977.

the exact timing of events, was known. In order to be considered, events had to be experienced during the period between observations. For example, those who were already retired, or widowed, or whose children had already left home did not contribute to the analysis. Hindsight suggests that addition of the actual date of occurrence of the life event of interest woud have been simple as well as useful. For most respondents, this would have added minimally to the time required for data collection and it would have extended considerably the types of data analyses we were able to do.

Resources were defined by a single indicator each for health, psychological functioning, and social functioning measured initially in 1968–70, before any of the events we studied had occurred. *Health resources* was indexed by a physician's rating of overall functional capacity. This rating was made upon completion of the physical examination and indicated the degree to which the individual was disabled because of physical or mental health problems. *Psychological resources* was indexed by a variable which combined an individual's level of intellectual functioning with his or her score on a personality factor representing the dimension of neuroticism/adjustment. *Social resources* was indexed by a variable which summed income, educational attainment and the density of the social network to which the individual related.

Results

Distribution of Resources

The distributions of resources within the sample is presented in table D—8. The observed distributions provide a profile of the characteristics of the sample at the start of the study.

A consideration of the procedures for locating subjects on the continuum of resource availability for each type of resource provides a useful characterization of sample characteristics. The sample as a whole was quite healthy at the first time of measurement. This is perhaps not so surprising, given that the subjects were aged forty-six to seventy and all had to be capable of getting themselves to the lab for a full day of testing. As a result, the range of functioning differentiating subjects was relatively small.

The cut points for differentiating psychological resources were chosen so that those with highest intelligence were quite bright; those in the middle category normal and above average; and those in the low category below average. The score for the personality factor was a standard ten-point score scaled to range from 0 to 9 and divided in thirds. The joint distribution of intelligence and adjustment classified 42 percent of the sample at the high end and 16 percent at the low end of the psychological resources continuum.

Regarding social resources, a very large range in income and education was found, and individuals tended to have extensive social networks. While the variation in social resources is impressive, it is also important to note that the panel

Table D—8. *Definitions and distributions of resources.*

Health resources		*N*	%
Physical functioning rating, High	100% functioning	142	37.9%
	90% functioning	188	50.1%
	80% functioning	43	11.5%
Middle	70% functioning	2	0.6%
	< 60% functioning	0	

Psychological resources

		Anxiety/adjustment low	Anxiety/adjustment middle	Anxiety/adjustment high	Totals	%
Intelligence	low	43	86	8	137	36.5%
	middle	30	142	23	195	52.0%
	high	4	27	12	43	11.5%
	Totals	77	255	43	375	
	%	20.5%	68.0%	11.5%		

Cut points:
Intelligence: < 91; 92–134; > 135.
Anxiety/Adjustment: 1–3; 4–6; 7–9.

Psychological resources:
Low—upper left triangle (N = 159, 42.4%),
middle—on the diagonal (N = 154, 41.1%),
high—lower right triangle (N = 62, 16.5%).

Social resources

Income	*N*	%	Education	*N*	%	Social network	*N*	%
<$ 4,000	60	16.0%	< 7	49	13.1%	9–10 assoc.	7	1.9%
$ 4–$ 7,000	67	17.9%	8–11	89	27.7%	11–12 assoc.	32	8.5%
$ 7–$10,000	82	21.9%	12	86	22.9%	13–14 assoc.	92	24.5%
$10–$15,000	84	22.4%	13–15	74	19.7%	15–16 assoc.	148	39.4%
>$15,000	82	21.9%	>16	77	20.5%	17–18 assoc.	96	25.6%

Social network was the sum of three levels of association with spouse, children, confidant, relations, friends, and neighbors.

Social resources scale = Income + Education + Social network
0–9 0–9 6–18

Cut points: 0–13—*low* (0%); 14–29—*middle* (62%); > 29—*high* (38%).

was relatively secure economically and more highly educated than the general population of age peers (see e.g., Murrell, Norris, and Hutchins, in press). This was reflected in our decision to classify none of the respondents as low in social resources. Overall, our subjects can be characterized as resource-rich in health and social functioning and average in psychological resources.

Distribution of events. The prevalence of the events observed is interesting for several reasons. The initial population included 502 subjects, of whom 375

(74.7 percent) were examined on the average six years later (each wave of the study took about two years, so the total study took eight years to complete). Given the events which we chose, some members of the study group were not eligible for the event. That is, one needed to be married at the start of the study in order to be widowed or to experience the retirement of a spouse. One needed to have a child living at home at the start of the study in order to enter the phase of the empty nest, and one needed to be working to experience retirement. All individuals were eligible for a medical event. The percentages of individuals eligible for the events and the percent of those eligible who had the events during the study are given in table D—9.

Widowhood was the rarest event (7.9 percent experienced); a major medical event was more probable (26.1 percent); then retirement (33.7 percent), spouse's retirement (46.1 percent), and "empty nest," which was the most probable (50.9 percent). Thus, the frequencies with which specific events were experienced varied by event and, overall, were relatively low. Obviously, unless one has a large population study, it is difficult to insure that significant numbers of a particular type of event will be observed in a prospective study.

Table D—9. *Number eligible for specific events, percentage eligible, and percentage of eligibles with the event.*

Event	*N*	Percentage eligible	Percentage of eligibles with event
Retirement	231	61.6	33.7
Spouse retirement	169	45.0	46.1
Empty nest	112	29.8	50.9
Widowhood	318	84.8	7.9
Illness	375	100.0	26.1

Table D—10. *Matrix of 2 × 2 event combinations.*

	Retire	Spouse retire	Widow-hood	Empty nest	MM1	MM2	MM3
Retire	33**	9	3	6	6	4	5
Spouse retire		40	4	4	3	4	1
Widowhood			11	—	2	—	—
Empty nest				36	8	1	—
MM1*					21	—	—
MM2						20	—
MM3							11

*MM1, 2, 3 denotes the interval in which a major medical event occurred.

**Numbers on the diagonal represent single events.

Table D—11. *Three-way event combinations.*

MM1*	MM2	MM3	Retire	Spouse retirement	Widowhood	Empty nest	*N*
**			**	**			4
**				**	**		3
**			**			**	2
	**		**	**			3
	**			**	**		1
		**	**	**			2
		**	**		**		1
Total three-way combinations							16

*MM1, 2, 3 denotes the interval in which a major medical event occurred.

**The three events starred in each row indicate the three-way type of combination.

Table D—12. *The timing and distribution of events by interval.*

Number of events per person	Number of persons			Total number of events
	R1–R2*	R2–R3	R3–R4	
0	328	327	328	0
1	28	18	24	70
2	10	6	9	50
3	2	2	4	24
4	1	—	5	24
5	—	—	—	0
6	—	—	1	6
7	—	—	—	0
8	—	—	—	0
9	—	—	2	18
Total number of events	58	36	98	192

*R refers to round of observation over the study.

Event combinations. Overall, 238 individuals (63.4 percent) of the 375 in the sample experienced one or more events. Of the 127 who did not complete the study, 18.9 percent experienced one or more events during the time they participated. Twenty-one different event combinations were observed with frequencies of 1–9 per event combination. The pairs of events are shown in table D—9. The three-way combinations are shown in table D—11. Multiple event combinations were rare in the panel.

All major medical events were counted, even though some persons had more than one medical event in the same interval. However, the maximum number of different events observed was nine. The events and their time of occurrence are given in table D—12.

These distributions in table D—12 have been given in great detail in order to illustrate what was observed. We did not sample in such a way as to increase the observation of events. The sample came from the community, and a major objective of the sampling was an even age distribution across the age range forty-six to seventy. While many interesting event combinations were observed, even with a sample of 375 persons, most of the patterns were more idiosyncratic than common.

Impact of Resources on Events

We postulated that resources influenced the adaptive process before events occurred and, subsequently, response to events. A series of chi-square analyses were done in order to evaluate the relationship between resources and events for each event separately. Overall, only psychological resources were related to the occurrence of events during the six years of the study. Those who were lowest in resources experienced more events. For each event, those who experienced the event were contrasted with those who were eligible for, but did not experience the event. Each event was evaluated for each type of resource variable. This resulted in twenty-five contingency tables; seven were statistically significant beyond the 1 percent level. These findings are summarized below.

The relationships among resources and events are not surprising. Age and lower health resources were related to retirement and being older related to having a spouse retire. Being female and having lower social resources were related to becoming a widow; men were more likely to have their last child leave home; and lower health resources were related to more medical events.

Discussion

About two-thirds of the panelists experienced at least one putatively significant event over the six-year course of the study. These events were not randomly distributed, but were related to the resources of individuals at the start of the study. Our findings raise an interesting practical as well as theoretical issue. A relatively low frequency of events was observed in the randomly selected sample. If we add the numbers eligible for the first four events (which could occur only once) to three times the 375 eligible for a major medical event (since there were three intervals), we find that there was a total of 1,955 possible events. The panelists actually experienced only about 10 percent (192) of these potential events.

A recent study by Murrell et al. (in press), confirms that, while the events analyzed in our study are commonly associated with later life, they are not commonly experienced events in a representative sample. In Murrell's study the distribution of fifty-four life events was explored in a sample of 1,102 men and 1,758 women of all ages over a one-year period. Their fifty-four events included three of the events examined in our study. In terms of frequency of occurrence, retirement ranked forty-second for females and fortieth for males; only 1.9 percent of females and 3.3 percent of males experienced the event. Three percent of the women and 1.6 percent of the men became widowed, ranking widowhood forty-first and forty-sixth, respectively. Spouse's retirement was experienced by 1.5 percent of the women and 1.3 percent of the men, ranking spouse's retirement forty-fifth and forty-seventh. These results reinforce the conclusion that events commonly associated with later life are, in fact, relatively rare events in randomly drawn populations (Hughes, 1983; Pearlin and Lieberman, 1979).

Other sampling strategies are possible and are required if the objective is to explore the occurrence and consequence of life events. For example, Lowenthal et al. (1975), sampled in four specific age bands and life situations so that individuals who were eligible for specific events would form the group for study.

Overall, the data from various studies suggest that while major events are rare, research can appropriately focus on strains (Pearlin and Lieberman, 1979), hassles (Lazarus and DeLongis, 1983), and respondent defined content of events (George and Siegler, 1984; Siegler and George, 1984), in exploration of stress and coping in adult life.

References

George, L. K., and Siegler, I. C. Stress and coping in later life. In Palmore, E. B. et al. (Eds.), *Normal aging III*. Durham, N.C.: Duke University Press, 1984.

Hughes, D. C. Personal communication, August, 11, 1983.

Lazarus, R. S., and DeLongis, A. Psychological stress and coping in aging. *American Psychologist*, 38:245–254, 1983.

Lowenthal, M. F., Thurner, M., and Chiriboga, D. A. *The Four Stages of Life*. San Francisco: Jossey-Bass, 1975.

Murrell, S. A., Norris, F. A., and Hutchins, G. L. Distribution and desirability of life events in older adults: Population and policy implications. *Journal of Community Psychology*, in press.

Pearlin, L., and Lieberman, M. A. Social sources of emotional distress. *Research in Community and Mental Health*, 1:217–248, 1979.

Siegler, I. C., and George, L. K. Sex differences in coping and perceptions of life events. In Palmore, E. B. et al. (Eds.), *Normal aging III*. Durham, N.C.: Duke University Press, 1984.

Stress and Adaptation in Later Life

Erdman B. Palmore, William P. Cleveland, Jr., John B. Nowlin, Dietolf Ramm, and Ilene C. Siegler

There is now a vast multidisciplinary literature concerned with stress research. The work of Cannon, Meyer, and Selye has led to an interest in life events as potential stresses in the development of physical and mental illness (Dohrenwend

Reprinted and adapted by permission from *Journal of Gerontology*, 34:841–851, 1979.

and Dohrenwend, 1974; Hultsch and Plemons, 1979; Lowenthal et al., 1975; Timiras, 1972). Many studies have focused on the response to particular events, for example, retirement (Sheppard, 1976; Streib and Schneider, 1971); widowhood (Lopata, 1975); and the empty nest (Lowenthal and Chiriboga, 1972). Major medical and psychiatric events have been studied, both as events which require adaptation (Hamburg, et al., 1976; House, 1974; Pearlin and Schooler, 1978), and as indices of adaptation in response to combinations of other major life events (Rabkin and Struening, 1976).

Various models of adaptation in late life have been proposed (House, 1974; Kuhlen, 1959; Lieberman, 1975; Lowenthal et al., 1975; Pearlin and Schooler, 1978). The various models have in common an emphasis on the multiple determinants of adaptation to stress and the importance of physical, psychological, and social resources as mediating variables which affect the level of adaptation to the stressful event. We will view adaptation as the outcome of attempts to use various resources to cope with the stresses of life events.

Evaluation of stress-illness association has been, of necessity, piecemeal, since data sets which purport to examine the relationship usually are not sufficiently broad-based to include all relevant individual attributes and responses to life events (Eisdorfer and Wilkie, 1977). Coronary heart disease has been associated with stress in several studies (Rosenman et al., 1970; Rosenman, 1974). While there have been attempts to link numerous other illnesses with stress, definitive work to substantiate these impressions is largely lacking. Multiple life events have been correlated with the advent of illness (Holmes and Masuda, 1974). However, the association is not strong, and the life event scale itself provides a host of methodological problems (Rabkin and Streuning, 1976).

Much of previous research and writing about life events and social-psychological adaptation has had a crisis orientation. This orientation assumes that major life events in later life, such as retirement, widowhood, and serious illness, usually produce great stress and often, if not typically, result in negative outcomes such as unhappiness, loss of self-esteem, withdrawal, and general decline (Butler, 1975; Datan and Ginsberg, 1975; Rosow, 1973, 1974). On the other hand, some have viewed these life events as potentially stressful but typically resulting in positive readjustment and new growth (Gould, 1978; Maas and Kuypers, 1974). Since studies of social-psychological adaptation have typically been tied to one particular event, we will briefly consider the literature on each event separately.

Most of the crisis orientation literature has emphasized the problems of adapting to retirement and its negative effects on satisfaction, self-esteem, and activity (Atchley, 1971). On the other hand, Streib and Schneider (1971) found little or no evidence of such detrimental effects.

As for spouse's retirement, the Duke First Longitudinal Study found that more than one-half of the wives of retirees were sorry that their husbands retired, especially if they were from the lower socioeconomic group (Heyman and Jeffers,

1968). An earlier Duke study also found that wives of retirees report less satisfaction than their retiring husbands (Kerckhoff, 1964).

Previous research relevant to medical events has shown that health is strongly related to life satisfaction and to other measures of adaptation in later life (Palmore, 1974). Therefore, it seemed reasonable to hypothesize that the occurrence of major illness would cause substantial declines in our indicators of adaptation.

Many people believe that widowhood is the most disruptive of life events (Parkes, 1973). The Holmes and Rahe schedule of life events (1967) rates death of spouse as having a higher score than any other event in terms of seriousness of effect. However, the first longitudinal study found little or no long-term detrimental effects on those widowed during the study (Heyman and Gianturco, 1973).

Departure of last child from home is so often believed to be problematic by the public, clinicians, and some researchers that there is a common term for these problems: the "empty nest" syndrome (Lowenthal and Chiriboga, 1972). However, Glenn (1975) concluded that the departure of children from home does not typically have an enduring negative effect.

This paper analyzes the physical, psychological, and social adaptation to five common life events in later life: retirement, spouse's retirement, major medical events, widowhood, and departure of last child from home. These events were chosen because they are so common and because there is considerable controversy about the difficulty of adapting to them. The paper also analyzes physical, psychological, and social resources as potential mediators which facilitate adaptation to these life events. The second longitudinal study provides a unique opportunity to analyze such problems because it has measures of adaptation before and after the occurrence of these events as well as the same measures for comparable groups who did not experience the events.

Method

Sample. The data were collected as part of the second longitudinal study, conducted by the Duke Center for the Study of Aging and Human Development (Palmore, 1974). A probability sample, stratified by age and sex, was drawn from the membership list of the major health insurance association in Durham County, North Carolina. Ten age-sex cohorts were defined of approximately equal size and representing five-year intervals between the ages of forty-five and seventy in 1968. The membership list from which the sample was drawn included a majority of white and middle and upper income level Durham residents. Black, as well as disabled, illiterate, and institutionalized persons were excluded. Lower socioeconomic persons were significantly under-represented. There was a refusal rate of 52 percent, but an analysis of differences between the refusers and participants found little significant difference in terms of demographic characteristics, socioeconomic status, and health (Palmore, 1974). Data were collected at four points in time between 1968 and 1976 (with two years between each round of examinations). There were 502 subjects at the beginning of the study, but the present analysis is based on the 375 who returned for the fourth and final round of examinations. An analysis of dropouts indicates that they tended to have somewhat lower health, psychological, and social resources than the 375 who did not drop out but that there was otherwise little significant difference between the dropouts and the returners.

Events. The events chosen for study were five major events commonly related to transitions in middle and later life: subject's retirement, spouse's retirement, widowhood, departure of last child from home, and major medical event (occurrence of an illness severe enough to require hospitalization). All event variables were dichotomous except for medical events, which could range from 0 to 3, depending on how many periods contained a medical event. Thus, total events could range from 0 to 7. The number of persons who experienced each event during the study were: retirement, 78; spouse's retirement, 78; widowhood, 25; departure of last child, 57; and major medical event, 92. The number of persons eligible for each event who did not experience the event were: retirement, 154; spouse's retirement, 170; widowhood, 293; departure of last child, 55; and major medical event, 283. There were a total of 238 persons who experienced one or more events during the study.

Resources. Because of space limitations, the conceptualization and measurement of the resources analyzed will be described briefly. More information on details of measurement and scoring may be obtained from the authors on request.

Health resources were defined in terms of functional ability and they were measured by a single overall medical rating made during the first examination by the examining physician; the rating could range from 1 (normal functional ability) to 9 (totally disabled). However, no one received a rating of more than 4, because no one in this sample was severely disabled. Thirty-eight percent were rated 1 (high health rsources); 50 percent were rated 2; and 12 percent were rated 3 or 4 (low health resources).

Psychological resources were defined as a combination of level of intellectual functioning measured by four subtests of the Wechsler Adult Intelligence Scale: information, vocabulary, digit symbol, and picture arrangement (Wechsler, 1955) and a personality factor (anxiety versus adjustment) derived from the Cattell 16 PF Scale (Cattell et al., 1970). This combination resulted in a score classification of low psychological resources (42 percent); middle psychological resources (41 percent), and high psychological resources (17 percent).

Social resources were defined as a combination of income, educational attainment, and the density of the available social network such as spouse, children, relatives, friends, neighbors, and confidants. The two socioeconomic measures (income and education) were each scored to range from 1 to 9. Each of the six types of role partners were scored on a three-point scale with 3 representing greatest availability. Thus, the combined social resources scale could range from

8 (one for each of two SES measures and one for each of six role partners) to 36 (nine for each of two SES measures and three for each of six role partners), and it gives equal weight to the socioeconomic variables and to the social network variables. The median social resources score was 28.

Adaptation Measures

Table D—13 presents the means and standard deviations for all adaptation measures at rounds one and four, to indicate their levels and overall stability over time.

Physical. The first category of physical adaptation measures included three health ratings. The cardiovascular system rating was based upon history taking, physical examination, and laboratory data; the examining physician rated each study participant on a 0 to 9 scale for the extent of cardiovascular disease (0 representing no cardiovascular disease and 9 a near terminal state). The musculoskeletal system rating used a similar procedure for rating the extent of a disease or injury-related joint and muscle incapacity. The self-rated health was the participant's own rating of his health, ranging from one for "poor health" to 4 for "excellent health."

Table D—13. *Means and standard deviations for adaptation measures, rounds 1 and 4 (N = 375).*

	Means (SD)			
Physical measures	Round 1		Round 4	
1. Cardiovascular system (CVR)	0.46	(0.83)	0.43	(0.77)
2. Musculoskeletal system (MSR)	0.50	(0.86)	0.67	(0.93)
3. Self-rated health (SRH)	2.8	(0.71)	2.9	(0.67)
4. Weight (WT)	71.0	(13.0)	71.0	(13.0)
5. Systolic blood pressure (SBP)	140.0	(22.0)	127.0	(18.0)
6. Diastolic blood pressure (DBP)	84.0	(11.0)	71.0	(12.0)
7. Physician visits/year (MD visits)	2.1	(2.3)	2.7	(2.7)
8. Regular medications (Meds)	0.80	(1.1)	1.1	(1.3)
9. Weeks in bed/year (Sick time)	0.65	(1.5)	0.67	(1.7)
10. Symptoms checked (Ck-list)	2.2	(2.0)	2.0	(2.0)
Social-psychological measures				
1. Life satisfaction	7.0	(1.4)	7.0	(1.4)
2. Affect balance	1.1	(2.8)	2.9	(3.5)
3. Psychosomatic symptoms	3.7	(3.8)	3.1	(3.6)
4. Feeling useful	5.5	(0.95)	5.4	(1.0)
5. Feeling respected	2.1	(0.97)	1.9	(0.96)
6. Social hours/week	9.8	(6.0)	9.3	(7.3)
7. Active hours/week	64.0	(17.0)	56.0	(20.0)

A second category included the direct measures of weight, systolic blood pressure, and diastolic blood pressure. The third category might be called illness behavior. This included number of physician visits per year, number of medications taken on a regular basis, number of weeks spent in bed with illness per year, and number of responses on a thirty-item symptom checklist.

Social-psychological. There is considerable agreement among researchers about the essential dimensions of social-psychological adaptation to stress. For example, Hamburg (1974) identified four requirements of adaptation to stress: containment of distress within tolerable limits, maintenance of self-esteem, preservation of interpersonal relations, and meeting the conditions of the new environment. Our measures of satisfaction, self-esteem, and social activity are indicators of the first three of these adaptation requirements. All of the subjects in this analysis met the fourth requirement in that they survived and were able to participate in the fourth round of examinations.

The general area of satisfaction is of primary importance in social-psychological adaptation. We used three different indicators of satisfaction: life satisfaction, affect balance, and psychosomatic symptoms. Life satisfaction was measured by the "Cantril Ladder," a ten-point scale ranging from 0 ("worst possible life") to 9 ("best possible life") (Cantril, 1965). In contrast to this global measure of life satisfaction, the Affect Balance Scale focuses on four positive and four negative emotions experienced during the past week (Bradburn and Caplovitz, 1965). The third measure of satisfaction was an indirect one, based on the frequency during the last week of nine psychosomatic symptoms such as headaches, nervousness, and sleeplessness (Leighton, 1963).

Self-esteem. Self-esteem was measured by two sets of adjectives from the semantic differential scale, respect, nonrespect and useful, nonuseful. This scale permits respondents to describe how they really are by marking a point on a seven-point scale between two polar opposites: "respected" versus "not respected," "useful" versus "useless" (Palmore, 1974).

Activity. Measured by the number of leisure social hours and the number of active hours engaged in during the latest typical week, the variable *social hours* is an indicator of interpersonal relations and the *active hours* is an indicator of general activity.

A correlation matrix of these seven social-psychological measures of adaptation (not shown) demonstrated that, on the one hand, each appeared to measure a separate aspect of adaptation because none of the correlations is high (none over .43); on the other hand, the measures within each of the three areas tended to be more highly correlated with each other than with the measure in the other two areas. A factor analysis confirmed that there were indeed three factors corresponding to these three areas, and that these factors accounted for 65 percent of the total variance.

About 2 percent of the values on the adaptation variables were missing due to incomplete questionnaires or examinations. These missing values were estimated by a program which predicts the most likely value obtained from recursive linear regression on all the other variables (Orchard and Woodbury, 1972).

Analyses

Two types of analysis were used for this investigation: (1) regression of residualized change scores and (2) repeated measures analysis of variance. Each method has distinctive advantages. Further, the use of alternative statistical procedures provides a formal of replication of findings which can be compared.

A dominant feature of any longitudinal study is that subjects tend to preserve their rank order on any measure. It is the deviations from this expectation, or the residual change, which requires explanation. Not so evident is the fact that changes tend to be negatively correlated with initial values. Since all data contain some noise, or unexplainable random variation, persons with initially low values will tend to show larger than average increases, while those with initially high values will tend to show larger than average decreases; this tendency is known as "regression toward the mean." To control for this tendency, residual change analysis uses a special form of a regression model to analyze the factors related to change after initial scores are controlled. It nullifies the negative correlation of changes with initial values (regression toward the mean) by entering the initial score on an outcome variable as the first independent variable, leaving only residual change to be explained by the other variables. A discussion of this method appears in Cronbach and Furby (1970).

The presence of a control group, who were eligible for an event but did not experience it, means that the effects of the event on the residual changes are relative to changes in an event-free group. The main question answered by residual change analysis is, what are the effects of the events and the mediating effects of resources on adaptation when initial level of adaptation is taken into account?

In repeated measures analysis, in contrast, the values for the dependent variable at each of the four rounds were treated as the response. Since more than one measure might occur before or after an event, a more precise measure of responses surrounding an event for each subject was available. However, it was necessary to adjust for secular time effects. Our analysis differed from traditional repeated measures analysis of variance in that occurrence of an event was represented by a step function occurring in the interval in which the event occurred (Winter, 1971). Adjustment for resource levels was accomplished by dividing the population into groups with different kinds and amounts of resources. Adjustment for the pattern of adaptation which would have occurred in the absence of an event was made by estimating a time effect for all subjects, with and without events.

The advantage of this method was that it used all the available data at four points in time, which include the measures immediately before and after an event. More subjects were measured during or near the unstable period marked by events. If an event had no effect, then all four points would follow the time effect. If an event had an effect, then the multiple measures before and after the event would show the level and direction of effect. The disadvantage of this method was that it did not control for regression toward the mean effects noted above.

Analysis of both physical adaptation and social-psychological adaptation with both the residual change analysis and the repeated measures analysis produced basically similar results. Since the physical adaptation measures are less likely to be biased by regression toward the mean, we will present the results of the repeated measures analysis for the physical adaptation. This allows fuller use of all the data. However, for the social-psychological measures we will present the residual change analysis which nullifies the substantial regression toward the mean present in these measures.

Results

Physical adaptation. The influence of the life events upon physical adaptation, as well as modification of this influence by resources, is presented in table D—14. This table shows the significant association ($p < .05$) found in the fifty separate analyses of variance required for the five events and ten outcomes. For the significant associations between events and outcomes, a plus sign (+) indicates that event occurrence was associated with an increase in variable score, a minus sign (−) indicates a decrease. For the significant interaction effects of resources and events, a plus sign (+) indicates that the presence of *high* resources of the indicated type accompanying the event was accompanied by a higher variable score; conversely, a minus sign (−) indicates a lower variable value with high resources in conjunction with an event.

A review of table D—14 indicates that major medical events were the events most likely to be followed by statistically significant change toward poor health, as might be expected. However, it is noteworthy that participants with high resources tended to have less change following such an event. For example, the self-rated health tended to show a significant decrease after a major medical event, yet those persons with high resources had a smaller decrease than did those with low resources. This moderating effect was observed not only for health resources but also for psychological and social resources.

One would expect that occurrence of a major medical event would be followed by decline in physical adaptation; of greater interest are declines in physical adaptation following nonmedical events. Although significant physical changes were less frequent following nonmedical events, they were more frequent than would be expected by chance alone.

The two retirement events were followed by more significant declines in physical adaptation than were departure of last child or widowhood. However, when events were followed by significant declines, they tended to be ameliorated

Table D—14. *Effects of life events, resources upon selected health variables—results of repeated measures analysis.*

	CVR	MSR	SRH	WT	SBP	DPB	MD visits	Meds	Sick time	Symptom ch-list
Major medical event										
Event	+(**)	+(**)	−(**)		+(**)		+(***)	+(***)	+(***)	+(***)
Event-HR interaction	−(**)	−(*)	+(**)				−(*)	+(***)	−(***)	−(***)
Event-SR interaction		−(***)	+(*)					−(*)		
Event-PR interaction	−(**)	−(**)	+(*)		−(*)	−(*)	−(**)	−(***)		
Last child leaves home										
Event										
Event-HR interaction					−(*)		−(*)			
Event-SR interaction		−(**)								
Event-PR interaction		−(*)				+(**)				
Widowhood										
Event							+(*)			+(*)
Event-HR interaction										
Event-SR interaction							−(**)	−(**)		
Event-PR interaction								−(**)		
Retirement										
Event		−(*)						+(***)		+(***)
Event-HR interaction	−(**)		+(**)	−(*)					−(***)	
Event-SR interaction										
Event-PR interaction	−(*)							−(*)		
Spouse retirement										
Event	+(*)						+(*)			
Event-HR interaction	−(***)	−(**)	+(**)	−(*)		−(**)				
Event-SR interaction						−(*)	−(**)			
Event-PR interaction		−(*)								

* = $p < .05$ ** = $p < .01$ *** = $p < .001$.

"+" = Increase in variable score.

"−" = Decrease in variable score.

Event-HR interaction = Interaction between event and health resources.

Event-SR interaction = Interaction between event and social resources.

Event-PR interaction = Interaction between event and psychologic resources.

by high resources. Separate analyses by age and sex groups revealed no statistically significant differences in these patterns between groups.

Social-Psychological Adaptation

Effects of individual events. Table D—15 presents the results of the residual change analyses in terms of the *b* coefficients (unstandardized) for the significant effects of the five events (separately) on the seven social-psychological measure of adaptation. Thus, table D—15 represents thirty-five separate regression equations, one for each of the event and adaptation measure combinations (5 × 7). The *control groups* in each analysis were those who were subject to occurrence of the event (in the retirement analysis, for example, those who were employed full-time at the beginning of the study) but did not experience the event (retirement). Table D—15 represents the total group, but men and women were also analyzed separately.

These analyses show that retirement was followed by more negative changes than any other life event. After retirement, life satisfaction decreased slightly; affect balance declined by more than a point; psychosomatic symptoms increased by one point; feeling useful declined about one-half point; and the number of active hours declined by twenty, because of the decrease in working hours. On the other hand, the number of social hours increased by two points, as a partial compensation for the decrease in working hours. However, the decreases in satisfaction measures were all less than one-third of a standard deviation. Also, when

Table D—15. *Residual change analysis, rounds 1 to 4:* b *weights*[a] *for significant effects.*

	Measures of adaptation[b]						
Events	Life satisfaction	Affect balance	Psychosomatic symptoms	Useful	Respect	Social hours	Active hours
Retirement ($N = 232$)	−0.3*	−1.0*	−1.1**	−0.4**		+2.3**	−20.1**
Spouse retired ($N = 170$)							
Major medical ($N = 375$)			−0.9**	−0.2*			− 4.6**
Widowhood ($N = 317$)	−0.6*		−1.2*				
Child leaves ($N = 112$)	+0.5*	+1.3*					

[a]Unstandardized *b* coefficients.

[b]All measures scored so that negative *b* indicates negative effect.

* = $p < .05$.

** = $p < .01$.

women were analyzed separately, no significant declines in satisfaction or self-esteem measures followed retirement. Apparently work and retirement were less important to the working women than to the men.

The analyses showed no significant effects of spouse's retirement on any of these measures of adaptation, either in the total group or in men or women separately. There did appear to be a small decline in life satisfaction (− 0.4) and in affect balance (− 0.8), but the probabilities of this occurring by chance were greater than .05. Apparently, most of the problems of adaptation which occurred when the spouse retired were resolved during the period of this study.

Since illness so clearly affects physical adaptation, we were surprised to find that the small declines in life satisfaction and affect balance after illness were not quite large enough to be statistically significant. Among the satisfaction measures, only psychosomatic symptoms showed a significant negative change, and this may have resulted from some symptoms actually being part of the illness itself rather than indicating increased tension or anxiety. The self-esteem measure, usefulness, went down slightly and the number of active hours declined some, but these declines were not significant among the women. Thus, overall, most participants seemed to have adapted rather well by the end of the study to the occurrence of major illness. If we had measured adaptation shortly after the illness, we possibly would have found stronger, and temporary, effects.

The analysis of adaptation to widowhood found few lasting negative effects. There were two significant but relatively small negative changes following widowhood: (1) a decline of about one-half a point in life satisfaction (one-third of a standard deviation) and (2) a decline of one point on psychosomatic symptoms (one-fourth of a standard deviation). Affect balance also showed a small decrement, mainly among women, but it was not statistically significant. None of the other measures declined significantly and, in fact, social hours increased somewhat, especially among men. Apparently widows and widowers tended to increase their social interaction outside the household to compensate partially for their loss of spouse.

Finally, we found no negative effects of last child leaving and, instead, found two significant positive effects: life satisfaction and affect balance increased significantly. Thus, rather than calling this state the empty nest, it might be more appropriate to call it the child-free home.

Effects of multiple events. Since we found so few negative outcomes of individual events other than retirement, we analyzed the data to determine whether events might have a cumulative effect, such that there would be more negative outcomes for those experiencing two, three, or more of them. Holmes and Masuda (1974), for example, reported such cumulative effects. We first performed a residual change analysis counting each event as one, so that a person could have experienced up to seven events (there were three possible medical events, one for each of the three two-year intervals in the study). The number of events experienced showed more significant effects on adaptation measures than the occurrence of any single event. However, since spouse retirement and departure of last

Table D—16. *Residual change analysis of number of events and resources, rounds 1 to 4:* b *weights*[a] *for significant effects* (N = *375*).

Independent variables	Measures of adaptation[b]						
	Life satisfaction	Affect balance	Psychosomatic symptoms	Useful	Respect	Social hours	Active hours
Number events	−0.2*	−0.5**	−0.6**	−0.2**			−7.4**
Health resources			−0.4*			+1.2*	
Psychological resources	+0.2**	+0.5**					
Social resources	+0.1**	+0.1*	+0.1*				

[a]Unstandardized *b* coefficients.

[b]All measures scored so that negative *b* indicates negative effect.

* = $p < .05$ at entry.

** = $p < .01$ at entry.

child had no significant negative effects, they were omitted from a second analysis, which reduced the total possible number of events to five. This resulted in even stronger effects, as shown in table D—16.

The first line of table D—16 (*b* coefficient for number of events) shows how much change was related to the occurrence of one event (nonsignificant changes are omitted). It is clear that all three measures of satisfaction were substantially reduced by the occurrence of multiple events. The feeling of usefulness was also reduced by the number of events, but not the feeling of respect. As for activity, the number of active hours was substantially reduced, but not the number of social hours.

To assess whether there were some other shorter term effects which disappeared by the end of the study, we repeated the analysis (not shown) presented in table D—16 for each of the three possible two-year intervals, and found no differences from the patterns shown in table D—16.

Effects of resources. Finally, we investigated whether the existence of better health, psychological, and social resources tended to reduce any negative effects of these life events. That is, does being healthier, more intelligent, less anxious, having higher socioeconomic status (SES), and a larger social network tend to facilitate social-psychological adaptation to these potentially stressful events? For this analysis, resources were scored as continuous variables. In table D—16, each of the seven columns represents a separate multiple regression analysis of the effects of events and resources on an adaptation measure.

Table D—16 shows that both psychological and social resources help to maintain most of the measures of satisfaction, but having better health resources did not help significantly. In fact, those with better health appeared to develop more psychosomatic symptoms than they had at the beginning of the study. This finding may be a result of residual "ceiling" effects in our method of analysis. However, in terms of self-esteem and activity, none of these resources seems to provide significant help, except that health resources provide some help in maintaining social hours.

These analyses were repeated, using the components of psychological and social resources separately (for example, SES separate from social network), and we found a pattern of positive effects, except that fewer of the associations between components and adaptation reached statistical significance. We also tried the interaction terms for number of events by resources and found little significant interaction effects. In other words, better resources were related to better adaptation, regardless of the occurrence of events.

Discussion

Before we discuss the theoretical and practical implications of these results, a few caveats are in order. First, the sample was limited to white, mostly middle-class, relatively healthy residents of a southern city. Thus, our findings may not be generalizable to other groups. Second, our measures were limited to those we could get during a one-day visit to our medical center. There were no observations of behavior in the "real world." Many of the measures were based on self-reports whose validity is difficult to establish. On the other hand, we have generally used well-established measures whose reliability has been found acceptable in other studies as well as ours. Third, in doing so many tests of a significance on the same data we run the risk of finding a sizable number of "significant" relations by chance alone (one in twenty at the .05 level, and one in 100 at the .01 level). However, it should be clear that there were many more statistically significant relations than would be expected by chance alone.

One major advantage of this study is its longitudinal nature. We can be sure that, if there is any causal relationship, the events caused the adaptation rather than the other way around. Also the use of before and after measures allowed control of initial level of adaptation, and the use of comparable control groups who did not experience the event strengthens a causal interpretation of the relationships.

The major theoretical implications seem to be the following. Major medical events have the expected negative effects on physical adaptation, but little effect on social-psychological adaptation. This seems to indicate that most seriously ill persons manage to limit any social-psychological reactions to a short period after the illness and tend to return to baseline within a few months. Retirement appears to be the most serious of the nonmedical events, and yet even its negative effects tended to be small related to the overall variability among individuals and subgroups. These small effects do not support the crisis orientation toward retirement which assumes severe stress and long-term negative outcomes. Similarly, the fact that all the other events had even less negative effects on either physical or social-psychological adaptation challenges the literature which has emphasized the problems created by these "crises."

On the other hand, there was evidence that when several of these events occurred to the same individual during this study they tended to cumulate in their impact, most clearly on the measures of satisfaction. Furthermore, those with less resources, especially those with poorer psychological and social resources, appeared to have more difficulty adapting to these events. Thus, the implication appears to be that while most people with resources normally available can adapt fairly well to any one of these events within a short time, the occurrence of several events simultaneously or consecutively tends to have some long-term effects, especially for those with less resources.

One practical implication would be that it is the "frail" or "at risk" older person who needs the concentrated services of social and welfare agencies in adapting to these events rather than the average elder. The "at risk" elders may be defined in our terms as those who have experienced several of these events within a short time and the "frail" elders as those who have poor physical, psychological, and social resources for coping with such events. A corollary implication would be that most persons with average or better resources need not fear long-term negative effects of these events unless too many happen too fast.

Summary

The effects of five major life events (retirement, spouse's retirement, major medical event, widowhood, and departure of last child from home), and of three types of resources (physical, psychological, and social) on the physical and social-psychological adaptation of 375 participants in a longitudinal study were examined. When the effects of the events were examined separately, major medical events, as expected, had the most impact on physical adaptation, but they had surprisingly little impact on social-psychological adaptation.

Retirement had the most negative social-psychological effects, but had little overall effect on physical adaptation. Retirement's negative effects on physical adaptation tended to be limited to those with lower resources. Furthermore, retirement's negative social-psychological effects were small and there was considerable variability in patterns among subgroups.

The other events (spouse's retirement, widowhood, and departure of last child) had even less pronounced effects on either physical or social-psychological adaptation. In fact, departure of child produced two significant positive effects. However, multiple events tended to cumulate in their impact, most clearly on the measures of satisfaction.

On the other hand, better resources tended to mitigate the negative effects of these events. Health resources were most beneficial in physical adaptation to events. However, health resources had almost no significant effects on social-psychological adaptation. Better psychological and social resources helped to maintain all the measures of satisfaction and had some scattered advantages for physical adaptation but no other significant effects.

In summary, it appears that many of these potentially stressful events have less serious long-term outcomes than a "crisis orientation" would suggest and those with good physical, psychological, and social resources have even less to fear from these "fearful" events.

References

Atchley, R. Retirement and leisure participation: Continuity or crises? *Gerontologist*, 11:13–17, 1971.

Bradburn, N., and Caplovitz, D. *Reports on happiness*. Chicago: Aldine, 1965.

Butler, R. N. *Why survive?* New York: Harper and Row, 1975.

Cantril, H. *The pattern of human concerns*. New Brunswick, N.J.: Rutgers University Press, 1965.

Cattell, R., Eber, H., and Tatsuoka, M. *Handbook for the 16 Personality Factor Questionnaire*, 4th Ed. Champaign, Ill.: Institute for Personality and Ability Testing, 1970.

Cronbach, L., and Furby, L. How should we measure "change"—or should we? *Psychological Bulletin*, 74:68–80, 1970.

Datan, N., and Ginsberg, L. H. *Life-span developmental psychology: Normative life crises*. New York: Academic, 1975.

Dohrenwend, B. S., and Dohrenwend, B. P. *Stressful life events*. New York: Wiley, 1974.

Eisdorfer, C., and Wilkie, F. Stress, disease, aging and behavior. In J. E. Birren and K. W. Schaie (Eds.), *Handbook of the psychology of aging*. New York: Van Nostrand Reinhold, 1977.

Engel, G. L. *Psychologic development in health and disease*. Philadelphia: W. B. Saunders, 1962.

Glenn, N. Psychological well-being in the post-parental stage. *Journal of Marriage and the Family*, 37:105–110, 1975.

Gould, R. L. *Transformations*. New York: Simon and Schuster, 1978.

Hamburg, D. Coping behavior in life-threatening circumstances. *Psychotherapy and Psychosomatics*, 23:13–25, 1974.

Hamburg, D. A., Adams, J. E., and Brodie, H. K. H. Coping behavior in stressful circumstances: Some implications for social psychiatry. In B. H. Kaplan, R. N. Wilson, and A. H. Leighton (Eds.), *Further explorations in social psychiatry*. New York: Basic Books, 1976.

Heyman, D., and Jeffers, F. Wives and retirement. *Journal of Gerontology*, 23:488–496, 1968.

Heyman, D., and Gianturco, D. Long-term adaptation by the elderly to bereavement. *Journal of Gerontology*, 28:359–362, 1973.

Holmes, T., and Masuda, M. Life change and illness susceptibility. In B. S. Dohrenwend and B. P. Dohrenwend (Eds.), *Stressful life events*, New York: Wiley, 1974.

Holmes, T., and Rahe, R. The social readjustment scale. *Journal of Psychosomatic Research*, 11:213–218, 1967.

House, J. Occupational stress and coronary heart disease: A review and theoretical integration. *Journal of Health and Social Behavior*, 15:12–27, 1974.

Hultsch, D., and Plemons, J. Life events and life span development. In P. Baltes and O. Brim (Eds.), *Life span development and behavior, Vol. II*. New York: Academic, 1979.

Kerckhoff, A. Husband-wife expectations and reactions to retirement. *Journal of Gerontology*, 19:510–516, 1964.

Kuhlen, R. G. Aging and life adjustment. In J. E. Birren (Ed.), *Handbook of aging and the individual*. Chicago: University of Chicago Press, 1959.

Leighton, D. *The character of danger*. New York: Basic Books, 1963.

Lieberman, M. A. Adaptative procession in late life. In N. Datan and L. H. Ginsberg (Eds.), *Life-span developmental psychology: Normative life crises*. New York: Academic, 1975.

Lopata, H. Z. Widowhood: Societal factors in life span disruptions and alternatives. In N. Datan and

L. H. Ginsberg (Eds.), *Lifespan developmental psychology: Normative life crises*. New York: Academic, 1975.

Lowenthal, M. F., and Chiriboga, D. Transition to empty nest: Crisis, challenge or relief? *Archives of General Psychiatry*, 26:8–14, 1972.

Lowenthal, M., Thurner, M., and Chiriboga, D. *Four stages of life*. San Francisco: Jossey-Bass, 1975.

Maas, H. S., and Kuypers, J. A. *From thirty to seventy*. San Francisco: Jossey-Bass, 1974.

Orchard, T., and Woodbury, M. A missing information principle. *Proceedings of the Sixth Berkeley Symposium on Mathematical Statistics and Probability*. Berkeley: University of California Press, 1972.

Palmore, E. B. (Ed.), *Normal aging II*. Durham, N.C.: Duke University Press, 1974.

Parkes, C. M. *Bereavement*. London: Tavistock, 1973.

Pearlin, L. I., and Schooler, C. The structure of coping. *Journal of Health and Social Behavior*, 19:2–21, 1978.

Rabkin, J. G., and Struening, E. L. Life events, stress and illness. *Science*, 194:1013–1020, 1976.

Rosenman, R. H., et al. Coronary heart disease in the Western Collaborative Group Study: A follow-up experience of 4½ years. *Journal of Chronic Disease*, 23:177–190, 1970.

Rosenman, R. H. The role of behavior patterns and neurotenic factors in the pathogenesis of coronary heart disease. In R. S. Eliot (Ed.), *Stress and the heart*. Mt. Kisco, N.Y.: Futura, 1974.

Rosow, I. Social contacts of the aging self. *Gerontologist*, 13:82–87, 1973.

Rosow, I. *Socialization to old age*. Berkeley: University of California Press, 1974.

Selye, H. *The physiology and pathology of exposure to stress*. Montreal: Acta, 1950.

Selye, H. *The stress of life*. New York: McGraw-Hill, 1956.

Selye, H. *Stress without distress*. Philadelphia: Lippincott, 1974.

Sheppard, H. L. Work and retirement. In R. H. Binstock and E. Shanas (Eds.), *Handbook of aging and the social sciences*. New York: Van Nostrand Reinhold, 1976.

Streib, G. F., and Schneider, C. J. *Retirement in American society*. Ithaca, N.Y.: Cornell University Press, 1971.

Timiras, P. S. *Developmental physiology and aging*. New York: Macmillan, 1972.

Wechsler, D. *Manual for the Wechsler Adult Intelligence Scale*. New York: Psychological Corp., 1955.

Winer, B. J. *Statistical principles in experimental design*. 2d Ed. New York: McGraw-Hill, 1971.

Assessing the Impact of Life Change Events

Rosemary Wade Wilson

This research can best be viewed within the continuing debate regarding useful approaches to studying the influence of life events and stress on various dimensions of psychological and physical health. Careful review of the literature on life events research calls into clear focus a variety of theoretical and methodological shortcomings to date which severely limit current understanding of the link between experience of life change events and health-related outcomes (Cleary, 1974; Radkin and Struening, 1976; Sarason et al., 1975). In combination, such problems in life events studies have resulted in very equivocal empirical evidence about the impact of events or their etiological role in health and illness (Dohrenwend and Dohrenwend, 1974a, 1974b; Rabkin and Struening, 1976).

Essentially, the current study was designed with two objectives in mind. The first objective was to try to improve the overall design features of prior research on life events, stress, and illness so that the impact of events could be assessed as unambiguously as possible. To this end, a longitudinal model for evaluating the impact of life events on a variety of psychological and physical well-being outcomes has been proposed (Dohrenwend, 1974c; Dohrenwend and Dohrenwend, 1975; Gersten et al., 1977; Hinkle, 1974; Kellam, 1974). In addition, the proposed model calls for the inclusion of several social status indicators which life events literature has suggested as fundamental in assessing accurately the influence of events (Hough et al., 1976; Gersten et al., 1977; Myers et al., 1974; Nelson, 1974; Rabkin and Struening, 1976). Overall, the basic features and relationships represented by the conceptual model are as follows: (1) a baseline as well as an outcome measure of psychological or physical condition must be specified so that stability of condition and any influence of initial condition on events occurrence can be taken into account; (2) social status characteristics which might influence exposure to events and also represent differential abilities for coping with events experience must be specified; and (3) the key question of the model is: once the influence of initial condition and social status factors are taken into account, do life events adversely affect one's psychological and physical well-being?

Within the context of this conceptual model, the second purpose of this research was to address directly some important unresolved issues regarding measurement of the key variable—the experience of life events (cf. Rabkin and Struening, 1976). Set within the overall paradigm of research in life events, stress, and illness, the research tradition being examined here has proposed the need for broad measurement of recent life experiences, with emphasis on the cumulative impact of any recent life changes. Although there is variation in the life events measures used by investigators (see Dohrenwend, 1974), many researchers have adopted the original or a modified form of the instruments developed by Holmes and Rahe (1967) and their colleagues. Some investigators use the original instrument, the schedule of recent events (SRE), or variants, in which scores consist of the sum of responses to events experienced during a specified time period. Other researchers use the Social Readjustment Rating Scale (SRRS), or variants, in which a weight is assigned to each event checked as having occurred. As Cleary (1974) has observed, the summary scores on such life events measures are intended to be indices of the cumulative life stress in the period under investigation. This paper presents some of the basic arguments and findings of a larger methodological critique and empirical examination of this widely used approach to assessing the influence of life events on psychological and physical well-being.

Data and Methods

Data for this study were drawn from the second and third rounds of the Duke Second Longitudinal Study. Analyses were based on data for the 317 men and women who had complete information on all of the study variables described below. This reduced sample did not differ significantly from the full group of 380 persons who completed testing through the third round of the study.

Dependent Variables

Numerous psychological and physical conditions from reports of minor symptomatology to psychiatric disturbance to major debilitating physical illness have been posited as possible outcomes of life events experienced (Dohrenwend and Dohrenwend, 1974a; Holmes and Masuda, 1974; Rabkin and Struening, 1976; Rahe, 1972). To some degree, the specific measures described below span the range of relevant outcomes and are generally well grounded in prior research on life events, stress, and illness. On the whole, they provide the opportunity to examine questions about the effects of events on a variety of psychological and physical outcomes.

Psychophysiological symptoms. The first dependent variable was a nine-item index of psychophysiological symptomatology adapted from Bradburn (1969). Respondents were asked to indicate how often in the previous week they had experienced each of the following: dizziness, general aches and pains, headaches, muscle twitches or trembling, nervousness or tenseness, rapid heart beat, sleeplessness, loss of appetite, and constipation. For the present analyses, each of the nine symptom items was coded so that 0 indicated that the symptom was not experienced at all and 1 indicated that the symptom was experienced. The summed responses to these nine symptom items produced the measure of reported psychophysiological symptomatology experienced during the preceding week. Scores could range from 0 (no symptom reported) to 9 (all symptoms reported). The baseline measure (SYMPSB) was drawn from round 2; the outcome measure (SYMPSO) came from round 3.

Affect. Another dependent variable was affect, measured by the Bradburn and Caplovitz Index of Psychological Well-Being (Bradburn and Caplovitz, 1965; Bradburn, 1969). Respondents were presented with a list of items describing "some of the ways people feel at different times" and were asked how often during the preceding week they had felt that way. For the present analyses, each of the affect items was coded so that 0 indicated that the feeling had not been experienced; 1 that the feeling had been experienced.

Following Bradburn's schema (1969), the nine affect items were ranged in three different ways. First, responses to the following four items were summed to provide an index of *positive affect*: On top of the world; particularly excited or interested in something; pleased about having accomplished something; and proud because someone complimented you on something you had done. Scores on the positive affect measure (POSAFFB) could range from 0 (no positive feelings experienced) to 4 (all positive feelings experienced).

The remaining five items—very lonely or remote, depressed or unhappy, bored, restless, and vaguely uneasy—made up the *negative affect* measure (NEGAFFB). Scores could range from 0 (no negative feelings) to 5 (all negative feelings) experienced.

Subtracting negative affect from positive affect yielded an *affect balance* score (ABS). According to Bradburn (1969), an individual is considered high in overall psychological well-being to the degree that he has an excess of positive affect over negative affect. Scores on this measure could range from −5 to +4. For ease in further computations, a constant was added to eliminate negative values. The resulting range of scores was 0 to 9, with higher scores indicating more pronounced psychological well-being.

Baseline measures (POSAFFB, NEGAFFB, ABSB) come from round 2; outcome measures of positive affect (POSAFFO), negative affect (NEGAFFO), and affect balance (ABSO) were taken from round 3.

Physical health status. Physical health status was measured by an index composed of ratings by a physician of two major body systems plus a rating of overall functional status as follows: (1) Musculoskeletal system—objective rating scale (Nowlin, 1970); (2) Cardiovascular system—objective rating scale (Nowlin, 1970); and (3) Karnofsky Performance Status—overall functional status rating by a physician (Karnofsky et al., 1949).

Each of the three components was first recoded into a trichotomy. For the two body system rating scales, 0 indicated no evidence of disease; 1 indicated minimal evidence; and 2 indicated moderate evidence. The Karnofsky was recoded so that 1 corresponded to no complaint or evidence of disease, 2 to minor symptoms or signs of disease, and 3 to moderate signs or symptoms of disease. Scores on the composite built from these three ratings could range from 1 to 7, with higher scores indicating more disease and/or impairment present; this is poorer physical health status. The baseline health measure (PHINDEXB) came from round 2; the outcome measure (PHINDEXO) was drawn from round 3.

Independent Variables

Social status variables. As previous research has indicated, a variety of sociocultural or social status variables show relationships with life events scores as well as with measures of psychological and physical outcomes. Therefore, it is important to control for the possible effects of these social factors when assessing the impact of life events occurrence on psychological and physical condition over time. The variables described below are among those most commonly cited as correlates of the measures of symptoms, affect, physical status, and life events used in this study.

Age. The chronological age of the respondent was recorded in years. Ages at round 2 ranged from forty-eight to seventy-three.

Sex. The respondent's sex was coded 0 for males and 1 for female.

Education (EDUC). Respondents were asked: "What is the highest grade of regular school (college) you ever attended?" Years of education ranged from 0 to 27.

Income. The respondent was asked about how much his and his spouse's total income from all sources was during the preceding twelve months. The ten response categories ranged from 0 for income under $1,000 to 9 for income of $15,000 and over.

Marital status (MARST). The respondent's marital status was recorded as married and living with spouse, married but spouse absent, divorced or separated, widowed, or never-married. For these analyses the variable was coded so that 0 indicated that the person was not currently married; 1 indicated the respondent was currently married. Over 75 percent of the respondents in the 0 category were widowed.

Work status (WORKST). The respondent was asked if he (she) had a job or business (paid employment) at the present time. "No" was recorded as 0, "Yes" as 1.

All social status measures came from round 2 of the adaptation study with the exception of sex and education which were recorded only at round 1. Therefore, the respondent's standing on the above six variables was tapped at the point at which his baseline standing on symptoms, affect, and physical health were assessed in round 1.

Life events. The events list included in the Duke study is actually a slight modification of the Holmes and Rahe (1967) original SRE. Respondents were asked to indicate which of the thirty-nine events listed in table D—17 they had experienced during the preceding twelve months. Since the SRE was not included until round 3 of the adaptation study, the life events questions tap a time period falling between the baseline and outcome assessments of symptoms, affect, and physical health rating.

As table D—17 shows, the frequencies of the life events vary widely. In fact, three events—being fired, divorce, and marital reconciliation—were not experienced at all in the time period under study. A comparison of these event distributions with those of several other studies (Dohrenwend and Dohrenwend, 1975; Smith, 1971) indicates that the infrequent occurrence of various events is in no way limited to this study.

A final issue involves the scoring of the life events information provided by the schedule of recent events checklist. The standard approach to scoring life events information involves summing the events experienced by the respondent in the twelve-month period covered. Based on methodological arguments presented in the next section, this study will deviate from the standard approach and present an alternative scoring method.

Table D—17. *The schedule of recent events, with the frequency of each life event (N = 317).*

Frequency	Event
271	Vacation
10	Retirement from work
19	Changing to a new type of work
27	Major change in working hours or conditions
25	Major change in responsibilities at work (promotion, demotion, transfer, etc.)
10	Major business readjustment (merger, reorganization, etc.)
0	Being fired or laid off from work
6	Troubles with boss
27	Major change in living conditions (build new home, remodeling, deterioration of home or neighborhood)
24	Major change in financial state
24	Taking on a mortgage or loan of less than $10,000
4	Taking on a mortgage or loan of more than $10,000
1	Foreclosure on a mortgage or loan
4	Marriage
11	Change in residence
16	Spouse beginning or stopping work (outside home)
33	Son or daughter leaving home (marriage, attending college, etc.)
12	Gaining new family member (birth, adoption, or relative moving in)
22	Major change in the number of family get-togethers
30	Major change in the health or behavior of a family member
5	In-law troubles (sponse's parents or your children's in-laws)
6	Major change in number of arguments with spouse
3	Marital separation from mate
0	Divorce
0	Marital reconciliation with mate
5	Sexual difficulties
7	Death of spouse
36	Death of a close family member
8	Outstanding personal achievement
11	Major change in social activities (clubs, visiting, etc.)
15	Major change in usual type or amount of recreation
18	Major change in church activities
16	Major personal illness or injury
11	Major change in sleeping habits (number of hours or hours you sleep)
15	Major change in eating habits (amount of food, different times)
9	Change in personal habits (dress, interests, friends, etc.)
12	Minor violations of the law (traffic ticket, jaywalking, etc.)
2	Detention in jail or prison
46	Death of a close friend

Selected Problems in Life Events Measurement

A starting point in addressing issues in life events measures is identification of an explicit measurement model. This study adopts a model using empirical rather than factor analytic, or rational scaling (Edwards, 1970; Guilford, 1965). That is, while events information is typically summed to measure the theoretical construct "stress," the event items are best viewed as relatively independent determinants of, rather than reflections of, the construct of interest. Therefore, internal consistency and factorial structure of events measures are not relevant issues. This break with the factor analytic view, endorsed by some reviewers of life events research (e.g., Rabkin and Struening, 1976), indicates the need for closer examination of potential problems with the use of events summary scores.

In the following paragraphs, some of the potential problems of using events summary scores such as the SRE or SRRS are presented. The implications of summing event items to arrive at a summary score of all events or of categories of events (e.g., "undesirable events," "desirable events") can best be understood with reference to the statistical formulae which express the correlation of events sums with some criterion variable. While a full technical discussion of these formulae is beyond the scope of this paper, a few summary remarks can highlight several critical issues, specifically: the correlations of individual events with the criterion, the standard deviations of the individual events, and the intercorrelations among the individual events. The use of differential weightings (e.g., life change unit weightings) for the event items is simply a logical extension of the basic formula (Guilford, 1965).

Specifically, the correlation of events summary scores with some outcome variable has a number of potentially confounding features. The major problems include the following. First, while use of an SRE summary score assumes that all events will have the same *direction* of effect on the outcome, it is possible that some included events actually have positive effects on the dependent variable while other events have negative effects. Such a situation of opposite effects could reduce the size of the correlation of events sum with the dependent variable to virtually zero. Second, the *strength of the relationships* of individual events with the dependent variable of interest could vary widely; that is, the assumption that all effects are equal may not be legitimate. Third, although an observed correlation between an events sum and different dependent variables may be similar in size, the basis for the correlations may be very different. More specifically, this problematic feature implies that different life events could be predictive of some outcomes but not of others. Finally, there is the problem of substantive interpretation of the overall relationship between the events sum and the outcome variable. Recall that most researchers conclude that it is solely the *number* of events or amount of life change experienced that accounts for the observed correlation of SRE scores with an outcome variable. In effect, the correlation of an events sum with some dependent variable results from the aggregation of individual events effects while controlling for any lack of independence among the included events. Therefore, it is theoretically possible that only one or two *particular* events account for the overall correlation. Stated somewhat differently, a few particular life events may be as predictive of an outcome condition as the sum of thirty, forty, or more life events.

Analyses and Results

In light of the problematic features of events sums and their implications for interpretation of results, the present study approaches the scoring of life events information somewhat differently. That is, each life event is entered as a separate dummy-coded variable into the multiple regression equation estimating the effect of life event experience on psychological or physical well-being. This approach allows examination of the effect of a specific event, net of the effect of any other life events and social status variables included. It can also be used to determine the effects of combinations of life events on change in the psychological or physical condition of interest. In brief, the approach can retain any valuable information that might be lost in analyses involving only event summary scores.

A simple initial approach to the questions about life events measurement presented earlier centers on the correlations of each of the thirty-six life events with each of the five outcome measures used in this study. Since tabular presentation of the relevant correlation matrix is very unwieldy, the major features of this matrix will be summarized in the text.

The correlation matrix for all thirty-six SRE events and the five measures of physical and psychological conditions reveals the following: (1) the direction of observed correlations of the life events with any given outcome measure are very mixed; for each outcome condition, roughly half of the event correlations are positive in sign and half are negative. (2) For any given outcome condition, the strength of association with the individual life events varies widely. The vast majority of the life events show no statistically significant correlation with any outcome examined, i.e., most correlations are not statistically different from zero.

Single event models. While the above findings are useful, a look at zero-order correlations can take us only so far. Recall that in this study the criterion variable of concern is actually "change" in psychological or physical condition. This "change" is estimated by the regression of the outcome measure on the baseline measure (Bohrenstedt, 1969; Cronbach and Furby, 1970). To identify life events related to this criterion, the thirty-six dummy-coded life events were examined one at a time to determine which ones have statistically significant ($p \leq .05$) effects on one or more of the five psychological or physical conditions under investigation. The twelve life events which met this requirement are presented in the first column of table D—18.

Before turning to a full report of the results of these single event models, several points should be made about the selected events. First, in terms of frequency of occurrence, these twelve events span the entire range found in this

Table D—18. *Zero-order correlations and regression estimates of effects of twelve selected life events on psychophysiological, psychological, and physical health outcomes.*

Events	Condition	r (with outcome)	Simple model B	Simple model b	Complete model B	Complete model b
E1. Death of a close friend	SYMPS	.135	.089	.366	.088	.359
E2. Major change in living conditions	SYMPS	.157	.112	.580	.118	.611
	NEGAFF	.160	.125	.518	.122	.508
E3. Major change in financial state	NEGAFF	.122	.085	.375	.100	.439
E4. Marriage	NEGAFF	.117	.096	1.000	.103	1.068
	PHINDEX	−.090*	−.088	−1.106	−.083	−1.047
E5. Major change in the number of arguments with spouse	NEGAFF	.184	.094	.803	.105	.893
E6. Death of spouse	SYMPS	.114	.110	1.080	.126	1.230
	NEGAFF	.156	.137	1.083	.146	1.152
	ABS	−.163	−.123	−1.488	−.126	−1.530
E7. Outstanding personal achievement	POSAFF	.151	.113	.913	.098	.791
E8. Major change in social activities	PHINDEX	.126	.108	.826	.107	.821
E9. Major personal illness or injury	PHINDEX	.145	.114	.731	.116	.744
E10. Major change in sleeping habits	NEGAFF	.152	.107	.680	.107	.682
E11. Major change in eating habits	SYMPS	.227	.146	.987	.145	.986
	NEGAFF	.128	.104	.567	.101	.554
E12. Change in personal habits	NEGAFF	.128	.089	.619	.101	.703

Notes: Simple model controls for BASELINE only. Complete model controls for BASELINE and 6 SOCIAL STATUS variables. B = standardized regression coefficient. b = metric coefficient. All nonstarred coefficients are significant at $p \leq .05$.

$^{*}p > .05$.

sample except zero. Therefore, there is no particular reason to believe that these twelve events met the requirement of statistical significance simply because their potential maximal correlations with the criterion variables were the highest (Carroll, 1961; Cleary, 1974). Second, these events were chosen because of their effects on one or more of the measures of "change" in condition. This selection process made no attempt to take possible intercorrelations among life events into account at this time.

At this point we know that only twelve of the original thirty-six SRE events predict change in any of the physical or psychological conditions. The remaining columns of table D—18 provide more complete data on these effects and allow closer examination of the key questions raised in the discussion of issues guiding this analysis. One primary question is whether life events are predictive of some outcomes but not of others. Looking down the column headed "condition," one can see that eight of the twelve events have an effect on only *one* condition. Three of the twelve events—change in living conditions, marriage, and change in eating habits—are predictive of change in two conditions. The remaining event, death of spouse, has an impact on three different conditions. Therefore, within this reduced focus on only twelve life events, the event effects appear to be fairly specific.

These specific effects can perhaps be seen more clearly by shifting focus to examine the five conditions (SYMPS, NEGAFF, POSAFF, ABS, and PHINDEX) separately to summarize the life event affects that emerged for each. The last two columns of table D—18 present estimates of the impact of a particular life event on the psychological or physical outcome measure, controlling for the influence of baseline and the six social status variables. In light of the highly skewed distributions for individual life events, the metric regression coefficient (b) in the last column provides the best information about impact of the event.

Consider the four individual life events that are predictive of change in symptomatology (SYMPS), net of the influence of social status variables. These are EI, death of a close friend; E2, major change in living conditions; E6, death of spouse; and E11, major change in eating habits. For each of these events, the regression coefficient indicates that persons who experience the event are expected to have higher SYMPSO scores than those persons who do not experience the event. The most notable effect is that of death of spouse: $b = 1.23$, or the difference of just over one point on SYMPSO. The effect of E11, a major change in eating habits, is also of interest since it may represent some conceptual confounding with the dependent variable.

The largest number of individual event effects can be seen for outcomes with negative affect. These eight events are: E2, major change in living conditions; E3, major change in financial state; E4, marriage; E5, major change in number of arguments with spouse; E6, death of spouse; E10, major change in sleeping habits; E11, major change in eating habits; and E12, change in personal habits. In each case, those experiencing these life events are expected to have higher NEGAFFO scores, controlling for baseline and social status variables. Death of spouse, E6, had the greatest impact on negative affect over time ($b = 1.152$). Marriage also showed a sizable effect ($b = 1.068$).

The pictures for positive affect and affect balance are much less complex. Only one event, E7, outstanding personal achievement, is predictive of change in positive affect level. As the metric coefficient indicates, those experiencing this particular event are expected to have higher POSAFFO scores ($b = .791$) than those not experiencing the event. Death of spouse, E6, is the only event which impacts affect balance. Those experiencing this event would be expected to have lower scores ($b = 1.53$) on the affect balance outcome measure (ABSO).

The final condition of interest is physical health status (PHINDEX), where higher scores indicate poorer physical condition. The following three events were predictive of change in physical condition: E4, marriage; E8, major change in social activities; and E9, major personal illness or injury. Each of these events deserves some comment since their impacts are not in the same direction. The effect of marriage, E4, on PHINDEXO scores is negative controlling for baseline and social status variables ($b = -1.047$). In other words, marriage is predictive of improved physical health status. The impact of both E8, major change in social activities, and E9, major personal illness or injury, are opposite in sign to that of marriage. Given the coding direction of the physical health status measure, each of these two events is predictive of poorer physical condition.

Events subset models. The preceding analyses focused on estimation of life events effects when examined singly. Overall, the preceding analyses indicated that a few individual life events are predictive of change in well-being. However, recall that a guiding premise in standard life events research (Dohrenwend and Dohrenwend, 1974; Rahe, 1974c) holds that a broader measurement of events experience, or more events information, may yield even better predictions of health-related outcomes. The present segment of analysis explores this issue by examining the implications of combining information provided by the individual life events identified earlier. The primary question of interest throughout is: are life change events in combination predictive of "change" in condition? That is, do events make an additive contribution to explaining variance in the outcome measure, once the influence of initial standing and social status factors are taken into account?

Table D—19 directs attention to the first indicator of well-being, psychophysiological symptomatology (SYMPS). The upper half of the table shows the effects of baseline and the six social status variables on SYMPSO. Taken together, these seven variables, which enter the equation first, explain 33 percent of the variance in SYMPSO (Adjusted R^2). The lower half of the table identifies the events subset under examination. Note that these are the four life events which were significantly predictive of change in symptomatology in the individual life events models (table D—18). The current question is how predictive this *set* of life events information is of change in symptomatology. Entry of the events set does in fact result in a significant increment in R^2. The events set accounts for an additional 3 percent of the variance in SYMPSO. Since the event set is significant, one can now ask if any event makes a significant, unique contribution to R^2. Only one of the four events survives this test (Cohen and Cohen, 1975:109). Although it is not highly unusual, this latest finding requires closer attention. In general, the situation of significant R^2 for a set of independent variables, with failure of the individual variables to reach statistical significance, occurs when the variables which correlate with the dependent variable are substantially redundant so that unique effects are not large enough to emerge (Cohen and Cohen, 1975). In the case at hand, this finding calls attention to the intercorrelations among the four life events in the set. The relevant correlation matrix for

Table D—19. *Regression of outcome measure of psychophysiological symptoms (SYMPSO) on baseline, social status variables, and a subset of four selected life events.*

Independent variables		Dependent variable: SYMPSO *b*	*B*
SYMPSB		.413*	.484*
AGE		.019	.092
SEX		.028	.010
EDUC		−.038*	−.101*
INCOME		−.038	−.060
MARST		−.019	−.005
WORKST		−.174	−.056
MR	.58656		
R^2	.34405		
Adj. R^2	.32919		
E1. Death of close friend		.298	.073
E2. Major change in living conditions		.349	.068
E6. Death of spouse		.817	.083
E11. Major change in eating habits		.789*	.116*
MR	.62009		
R^2	.38451		
Adj. R^2	.36231		
Constant	.23466		

Notes: *b* = metric coefficient. *B* = standardized coefficient. All regression coefficients and the constant are from the complete equation containing BASELINE, SOCIAL STATUS VARIABLES, and the indicated LIFE EVENTS.

$^*p \leq .05$.

events and outcomes reveals a number of moderate-sized correlations among these dichotomously coded life events. In some cases, the strength of correlations among events exceeds the correlations of events with the dependent variable. In brief, there are substantial intercorrelations among the events which significantly predicted change in symptomatology in the single event models. In the events subset model, these intercorrelations among events keep three of the unique event effects from reaching significance.

Table D—20 presents results of the equation for the second indicator of well-being, negative affect (NEGAFF). In this case, the baseline measure and social status variables explain about 19 percent of the variance in NEGAFFO. Next, the eight events which were predictive of change in negative affect in the single event models (table D—18) enter as a set. Addition of the event set increases the variance explanation by just over 2 percent. Here the situation of significant event set, but *no* significant unique event effects, is even more striking

Table D—20. *Regression of outcome measure of negative affect (NEGAFFO) on baseline, social status variables, and a subset of eight selected life events.*

Independent variables		Dependent variable: NEGAFFO *b*	*B*
NEGAFFB		.358*	.403*
AGE		.003	.017
SEX		.052	.022
EDUC		−.006	−.019
INCOME		−.014	−.028
MARST		−.012	−.004
WORKST		−.167	−.067
MR	.45708		
R^2	.20893		
Adj. R^2	.19101		
E2. Major change in living conditions		.250	.060
E3. Major change in financial state		.198	.045
E4. Marriage		.646	.062
E5. Major change in number of arguments with spouse		.878	.103
E6. Death of spouse		.776	.098
E10. Major change in sleeping habits		.254	.040
E11. Major change in eating habits		.264	.048
E12. Change in personal habits		.026	.004
MR	.51002		
R^2	.26012		
Adj. R^2	.22325		
Constant	.36947		

Notes: *b* = metric coefficient. *B* = standardized coefficient. All regression coefficients and the constant are from the complete equation containing BASELINE, SOCIAL STATUS VARIABLES, and the indicated LIFE EVENTS.

*$p \leq .05$.

than it was for SYMPS. The disappearance of significant event effects for E4, marriage, E6, death of spouse, and E12, change in personal habits, are particularly notable since these events were among the best single event predictors of change in negative affect. Again, intercorrelations among the eight subset events have come into play. The sizeable correlations of E6 with E2, E3, and E4; of E4 with E12; and among E10, E11, and E12 are especially noteworthy.

Table D—21 focuses on physical health status (PHINDEX). This is the only remaining indicator of well-being that was predicted by more than one event in the single event models. For this condition, the baseline measure and social status variables explain over 46 percent of the variance in PHINDEXO. The set of three life events accounts for an additional 3 percent of the variance in physical health outcome.

The problem of redundant life events information is not present for PHINDEX; that is, each of the three life events makes a single unique contribution to R^2 for this condition. The only significant intercorrelation among these events is between E4, marriage, and E8, major change in social activities; even this correlation is small.

In brief, the occurrence of some events does appear to be related to occurrence of other life events. At this point, speculation about the basis for the observed correlations among some life events may be worthwhile. Within the framework of the empirical measurement model for life events, one does not

Table D—21. *Regression of outcome measure of physical health status (PHINDEXO) on baseline, social status variables, and a subset of three selected life events.*

Independent variables		Dependent variable: PHINDEXO *b*	*B*
PHINDEXB		.646*	.638*
AGE		.026*	.132*
SEX		.000	.000
EDUC		.010	.029
INCOME		.000	.001
MARST		.054	.014
WORKST		.154	.051
MR	.68878		
R^2	.47442		
Adj. R^2	.46252		
E4. Marriage		−1.190*	−.095*
E8. Major change in social activities		.888*	.116*
E9. Major personal illness or injury		.699*	.109*
MR	.71187		
R^2	.50675		
Adj. R^2	.49063		
Constant	−.88816		

Notes: b = metric coefficient. B = standardized coefficient. All regression coefficients and the constant are from the complete equation containing BASELINE, SOCIAL STATUS VARIABLES, and the indicated LIFE EVENTS.

$*p \leq .05$.

have to assume that correlations among events are spurious; that is, that they result from common dependence on an underlying construct. Rather, it is possible that some of the events intercorrelations observed in these data may reflect causal relationships among the life experiences. For example, it is reasonable to propose that the event "death of spouse" could be the first in a sequence of events such as "change in living conditions," "change in financial state," or "change in habits." Unfortunately, effective exploration of any causal sequences among events was not possible with the data at hand, since information on timing of the life events was not available.

Summary and Conclusions

The findings presented here have implications in at least two directions: implications for the conceptual model of the study and implications for issues in life events measurement.

One notable finding of the regression analyses in this study was the relative stability of psychological and physical well-being during the time period under study. In all of the models estimated, there was considerable stability of the psychological or physical condition over the two-year period covered by the present study. Negative affect level was least stable; physical status was the most stable.

The most striking results were in answer to the key question of the model: do life events adversely affect physical and psychological well-being? The two major segments of analyses designed to explore this question were based on arguments against the use of standard approaches to scoring life events information, since they may result in loss of valuable substantive information and in erroneous conclusions about the impact of life events on well-being over time. These two phases of analyses centered on examination of correlations between the thirty-six SRE events and the five outcome measures and examination of effects of events in individual event models. The results indicated that important information would indeed have been lost had these events been simply summed. Most notable was the finding that *most* of the life events were *not* predictive of change in any of the psychological or physical conditions examined. Moreover, the few significant event effects that did emerge were quite specific in their influence on outcome measures.

Results from the analyses of life events subsets shed some light on the often asked question: does combining events information improve the ability to predict health and illness outcomes? The answer can be viewed from two perspectives. In comparison with any single life event model, events subsets did account for more explained variance in the outcome measure being examined. However, this is not surprising since the subsets were composed only of those events which were predictive singly. From another perspective, the findings would suggest that the argument about gathering more and more events information may not be the right issue; a more appropriate concern may be about the nature of the information provided by the life events under consideration. This revised focus directs attention toward trying to increase understanding of the relationship between individual life events and outcomes and the relationships among life events themselves.

At least one possible course for future research follows rather directly from the results of the present study; are the reported findings about the effects of specific events unique to the study population of middle class, white community residents in middle and late life? In one sense, yes. That is, as with any analyses involving empirical identification of single events or sets of events, the results can best be termed "exploratory" rather than "confirmatory." Ideally one would want to cross-validate these findings with other samples from the same population and with samples from other kinds of populations. By conducting similar series of events analyses one could ask what effects any specific events or even subsets of events have. Interpretation of metric regression coefficients would of course be necessary for making such comparisons across study populations.

Further, the findings from this study should alert researchers to examine the rationale and practical implications of constructing longer and longer events checklists and deriving increasingly complex summary measures of events experience. As Hauser (1972:16) noted, researchers too often separate index construction from other aspects of analysis and interpretation of data; that is, they often create composite measures to represent some theoretical construct and then enter only these composites in subsequent analyses of the data. This approach can all too easily lead to loss of information which could be obtained from the index components. Even more important is the fact that this approach can result in misinterpretation of the impact of life events on various physical and psychological outcomes.

References

Bohrnstedt, G. W. Observations on the measurement of change. In E. F. Borgatta and G. W. Bohrnstedt (Eds.), *Sociological methodology*. San Francisco: Jossey-Bass, 1969, 111–133.

Bradburn, N. M. *The structure of psychological well-being*. Chicago: Aldine, 1969.

Bradburn, N. M., and Caplovitz, D. *Reports on happiness*. Chicago: Aldine, 1965.

Carroll, J. B. The nature of the data or how to choose a correction coefficient. *Psychometrika*, 26:347–372, 1961.

Cleary, P. J. *Life events and disease: A review of methodology and findings*. Stockholm, Sweden: Laboratory for Clinical Stress Research, Karolenska Institute, 1974.

Cohen, J., and Cohen, P. *Applied multiple regression/correlation analysis for the behavioral sciences*. Hillsdale, N.J.: Lawrence Erlbaum, 1975.

Cronback, L. J., and Furby, L. How should we measure "change"—or should we? *Psychological Bulletin*, 74:68–80, 1970.

Dohrenwend, B. P., and Dohrenwend, B. S. The conceptualization and measurement of stressful life events: An overview of the issues. Paper presented at the Conference of the Society for Life History Research in Rochester, New York, 1975.

Dohrenwend, B. S., and Dohrenwend, B. P. A brief historical introduction to research on stressful life events. In B. S. Dohrenwend and B. P. Dohrenwend (Eds.), *Stressful life events: Their nature and effects*. New York: Wiley, 1974a, 1–5.

Dohrenwend, B. S., and Dohrenwend, B. P. Overview and prospects for research on stressful life events. In B. S. Dohrenwend and B. P. Dohrenwend (Eds.), *Stressful life events: Their nature and effects*. New York: Wiley, 1974b, 313–331.

Dohrenwend, B. S., and Dohrenwend, B. P. Problems in defining and sampling the relevant population of stressful life events. In B. S. Dohrenwend and B. P. Dohrenwend (Eds.), *Stressful life events: Their nature and effects*. New York: Wiley, 1974c, 215–312.

Edwards, A. L. *The measurement of personality traits by scales and inventories*. New York: Holt, Rinehart, and Winston, 1970.

Gersten, J. C., et al. An evaluation of the etiologic role of stressful life-change events in psychological disorders. *Journal of Health and Social Behavior*, 18:228–244, 1977.

Guilford, J. P. *Fundamental statistics in psychology and education*. 4th Ed. New York: McGraw-Hill, 1965.

Hauser, R. M. Disaggregating a social-psychological model of educational attainment. *Social Sciences Research*, 1:159–188, 1972.

Hinkle, L. E., Jr. The effect of exposure to culture change, social change, and changes in interpersonal relationships on health. In B. S. Dohrenwend and B. P. Dohrenwend (Eds.), *Stressful life events: Their nature and effects*. New York: Wiley, 1974, 9–44.

Holmes, T. H., and Masuda, M. Life change and illness susceptibility. In B. S. Dohrenwend and B. P. Dohrenwend (Eds.), *Stressful life events: Their nature and effects*. New York: Wiley, 1974, 45–72.

Holmes, T. H., and Rahe, R. H. The Social Readjustment Rating Scale. *Journal of Psychosomatic Medicine*, 11:213–218, 1967.

Hough, R. L., Fairbank, D. T., and Garcia, A. M. Problems in the ratio measurement of life stress. *Journal of Health and Social Behavior*, 17:70–82, 1976.

Karnofsky, D. A., et al. The use of nitrogen mustard in the palliative treatment of carcinoma. *Cancer*, 1:634–656, 1949.

Kellam, S. G. Stressful life events and illness: A research area in need of conceptual development. In B. S. Dohrenwend and B. P. Dohrenwend (Eds.), *Stressful life events: Their nature and effects*. New York: Wiley, 1974, 207–214.

Myers, J. K., Lindenthal, J. J., and Pepper, M. P. Social class, life events, and psychiatric symptoms: A longitudinal study. In B. S. Dohrenwend and B. P. Dohrenwend (Eds.), *Stressful life events: Their nature and effects*. New York: Wiley, 1974, 191–206.

Nelson, P. D. Comment. In E. K. E. Gunderson and R. H. Rahe (Eds.), *Life stress and illness*. Springfield, Ill.: Charles C. Thomas, 1974.

Nowlin, J. B. Health rating forms, Longitudinal II. Mimeographed. Durham, N.C.: Duke University Center for the Study of Aging and Human Development, 1970.

Rabkin, J. G., and Struening, E. L. Life events, stress and illness. *Science*, 194:1013–1020, 1976.

Rahe, R. H. Subjects' recent life changes and their near-future illness reports. *Annals of Clinical Research*, 4:250–265, 1972.

Rahe, R. H. The pathway between subjects' recent life changes and their near-future illness reports: Representative results and methodological issues. In B. S. Dohrenwend and B. P. Dohrenwend (Eds.), *Stressful life events: Their measure and effects*. New York: Wiley, 1974.

Sarason, I. G., Monchaux, C. de, and Hunt, T. Methodological issues in the assessment of life stress. In L. Levi (Ed.), *Emotions—their parameters and measurement*. New York: Raven Press, 1975, 499–505.

Smith, W. G. Critical life-events and prevention strategies in mental health. *Archives of General Psychiatry*, 25:103–109, 1971.

Change in Life Satisfaction

Erdman B. Palmore and Vira R. Kivett

There is a large body of literature reporting the correlates of life satisfaction and a few recent attempts to analyze the relative importance of factors influencing life satisfaction (Edwards and Klemmack, 1973; Palmore and Luikart, 1972; Spreitzer and Snyder, 1974). Most of this research indicates that the strongest factors related to life satisfaction are health, socioeconomic status, and social activity. There is less agreement about the importance of such background factors as age, sex, and marital status. A weakness of most of this research is that it is cross-sectional and does not attempt to predict future life satisfaction or the factors related to change in life satisfaction.

This paper reports the results of a longitudinal analysis of life satisfaction among the middle-aged and the "young-old," those aged forty-six to seventy. Specifically, this paper attempts to answer three questions: (1) are there significant differences between age cohorts and sex in life satisfaction changes? (2) what variables measured at initial testing are significant in predicting life satisfactions at a later time? and (3) what variables are significant in predicting changes in life satisfaction?

Methods

Subjects. The data came from an initial sample of 502 adults, forty-six to seventy years of age, who constituted the panel for the Duke Second Longitudinal Study. This analysis is based on the first three rounds of longitudinal data, with two years between each round. Attrition between round 1 and 3 was 25% and due mainly to death or inconvenience of the timing of the interviews. This rate was about 5 percent higher than originally anticipated, but it is not a major problem for comparison of change among the 378 who returned for the third round. All analyses were performed only with those who returned, so that overall change cannot be attributed to difference in the sample at different points in time. Returners, in comparison to dropouts, do tend to have somewhat better health, higher socioeconomic status, more social activity, and higher life satisfaction.

Measures

The dependent variable, life satisfaction, was measured by the Cantril ladder technique (Cantril, 1965). The respondent was first asked to describe "your

Reprinted by permission from *Journal of Gerontology*, 32:311–316, 1977.

wishes and hopes for your future'' and then to describe ''your fears and worries about your future.'' The respondent was then presented with a picture of a ladder numbered from 0 on the bottom rung to 9 on the top rung. The respondent was asked to suppose ''that the top of the ladder represents the best possible life for you and the bottom represents the worst possible life for you. Where on the ladder do you feel you stand at the present time?'' This measure is self-anchoring in the sense that it is relative to each person's own conception of maximum and minimum life satisfaction. The measure is also fairly reliable; its crosswave reliability coefficient was .65, which compares favorably with those generally reported for social-psychological variables (Heise, 1969). The face validity of this measure is fairly obvious, and its construct validity is demonstrated by its significant correlations with variables with which it theoretically should be correlated (table D—23). Finally, this measure of life satisfaction requires no judgment by the investigator as to what the important dimensions of life satisfaction are, but rather allows each individual respondent to rate his or her life in terms of his or her own important values (Bloom, 1975). The most frequent values or concerns expressed by Americans in relation to life satisfaction have been in the areas of health, standard of living, and family (Cantril, 1965).

In order to determine which variables were related to life satisfaction at the beginning of the study, seventeen variables were tested for zero-order correlations with life satisfaction at round 1 on the basis of their potential theoretical relevance. They included: self-rated health, organizational activity, social activity hours, productive hours, sexual enjoyment, age, sex, income, education, physical functioning, number of social contacts, employment, career anchorage, having a confidant, marital status, number of moves, and intelligence. The first five of these variables were found to have significant zero-order correlations with round 1 satisfaction (at the .05 level of significance used in this analysis, less than one of the seventeen correlations would be expected to be ''significant'' by chance alone). We decided to retain only these five significant variables for predictive purposes because we believe that if a variable is not significantly related to life satisfaction on a cross-sectional basis it is unlikely to be truly predictive on a longitudinal basis. This is based on the fact that future values of these variables are highly related to present values. We did not want to increase the chances of finding spurious ''predictive'' variables by including all seventeen variables in a multiple prediction equation analysis. Furthermore, an earlier analysis (Palmore and Luikart, 1972), which included all seventeen variables in a cross-sectional multiple regression, revealed only two other variables to be significantly related to life satisfaction. One (physical function) was of borderline significance and one (internal-external locus of control) was dropped from this analysis because of uncertainty about its validity and reliability. The five significant variables were measured as follows:

(1) *Self-rated health* was also measured by the Cantril ladder, with the bottom of the ladder (0) representing the most serious illness and the top of the ladder (9) representing perfect health. The mean score for the first testing was

6.8. An objective rating by the examining physician was also analyzed, but revealed nonsignificant correlations with life satisfaction which were smaller than the relationships obtained with the self-rated measure. The objective rating is not included in tables D—23 through D—25. For discussion of the differences between the subjective and objective measures, see Palmore and Luikart (1972).

(2) *Organizational activity* was measured by the sum of the number of religious services and meetings of other groups such as clubs, unions, or associations which the respondent reported usually attending each month. There was a maximum of nine religious services and a maximum of nine other meetings coded, giving a possible range of 0 through 18 (mean for the first round = 5.2).

(3) *Social activity hours* were measured by summing the number of hours spent during the last typical week "attending a sports event such as baseball or football games; attending church or other meetings, lectures, or concerts; doing volunteer work for church, other organizations, or relatives; visiting, telephoning, or writing friends or relatives; parties, eating out, or entertaining" (mean of first round = 9.9).

(4) *Productive hours* were measured by summing the number of hours spent during the last typical week working or doing housework and doing volunteer work for church, other organizations, or relatives; and doing yard care, gardening, repairing, building, mending, sewing, and other such activities (mean of first round = 41.3).

(5) *Sexual enjoyment* was based on responses to the following question: "How much pleasure or enjoyment do you have during sex relations at the present time: None, mild, moderate, or very much pleasure and enjoyment?" The coded responses range from 0 for none up to 3 for "very much pleasure and enjoyment" (mean of first round = 1.4). Most nonmarried persons responded "none." We did not ask about enjoyment from masturbation.

Analysis

Mean life satisfaction scores by age, sex, and round are presented in table D—22. The significance of change in these scores was tested by the related *t*-test and differences among age cohorts and between males and females tested by the independent *t*-test. Multiple regressions between significant round 1 variables and life satisfaction at rounds 1, 2, and 3 are presented in table D—23.

Sixteen percent of the 378 persons returning for round 3 did not have a usable score on one or more variables. In order to save these cases for the multiple regression analysis, we inserted an estimated value for each missing score, based on the individual's score on that variable in the previous (or subsequent) round and the regression equation for those two sets of scores. The procedure used does not attenuate the resulting correlation coefficients as do some other methods, such as the substitution of sample means for missing scores.

In order to test which varIables might be significant predictors of change in life satisfaction, we used the technique of analyzing residual changes (tables

Table D—22. *Mean life satisfaction at two-year intervals by age and sex.*

Age at round 1	*N*	Round 1	Round 2	Round 3	Change from round 1 to 3*
		Men			
46–50	36	7.1	7.6	7.3	+.2
51–55	35	6.9	6.8	7.1	+.2
56–60	49	7.2	7.3	7.2	.0
61–65	38	7.3	7.2	6.9	−.4
66–70	39	7.2	7.3	7.1	−.2
Total men	197	7.2	7.3	7.1	−.1
		Women			
46–50	37	7.1	7.2	6.9	−.2
51–55	30	7.2	7.5	7.1	−.1
56–60	35	7.5	7.3	7.3	−.2
61–65	36	6.7	6.9	6.8	+.1
66–70	43	6.8	7.2	7.0	+.1
Total women	181	7.0	7.2	7.0	.0
Grand total	378	7.1	7.2	7.0	−.1

*No changes from round 1 to 3 in any cohort are significant at .05 level (related *t*-test). No differences between cohort or sexes at any one round are significant at .05 level (independent *t*-test).

D—24 and D—25); that is, we used round 3 life satisfaction as the dependent variable and entered round 1 life satisfaction as the first independent variable. This has the effect of controlling for initial level of life satisfaction and leaving only the residual change to be explained by the other variables. The residual change is the change which occurs independently of the change that could be predicted on the basis of initial score on the variable. This technique avoids the problem of regression to the mean, because residual change is uncorrelated with initial score and it avoids the compounding of measurement error inherent in raw change analysis (Cronback and Furby, 1970).

Findings and Discussion

Overall stability. There were no significant changes in mean life satisfaction for the total group or for any of the ten age-sex cohorts from round 1 to round 3 (table D—22). Also, there were no significant cross-sectional differences between the means of the ten age-sex cohorts at any one round.

This stability of means is contrary to much existing theory about aging which postulates general crisis periods (such as retirement for men and menopause for women) during which life satisfaction is assumed to decline. It is also contrary to most cross-sectional research which tends to find less life satisfaction in the later years (Bradburn and Caplovitz, 1965; Edwards and Klemmack, 1973;

Gurin et al., 1960; Kutner et al., 1956). Possible reasons for this discrepancy between our findings and the previous research are (1) ours is a true longitudinal study which measures actual change over time in the same cohorts, while the previous studies have been cross-sectional and (2) our measure of life satisfaction is self-anchoring, or relative to the individual's own values and expectations. Most of the other measures of life satisfaction depend on the investigator's judgment about the relevant dimensions of life satisfaction and their relative importance. Thus, we conclude that, relative to a person's own expectations, there was no overall decline in life satisfaction in this forty-six to seventy age range.

Table D—22 also shows that there were no significant differences between men and women in life satisfaction. This is similar to the findings of Bradburn and Caplowitz (1965), Cantril (1965), and Edwards and Klemmack (1973), but contrary to those of Kutner et al. (1956) and Spreitzer and Snyder (1974). Again, the difference in findings may be due to differences in the measures used.

Despite the overall stability and lack of difference between age and sex groups, there were some individual changes: three-fourths of the individuals had changes in life satisfaction of at least one point up or down (comparing rounds 1 and 3), including about one-fourth who changed by two or more points. The next steps in the analysis, therefore, were attempts to predict future life satisfaction and the changes that did take place.

Predicting life satisfaction. Previous cross-sectional studies have shown that life satisfaction at one point in time is strongly related to the following factors at the same point in time: health, socioeconomic status, and social activity. Furthermore, when analyzed with multiple regressions, these factors generally show substantial independent associations with life satisfaction, even when the other factors are simultaneously controlled. However, no previous study has been able to analyze longitudinally whether these factors are able to predict life satisfaction at a later point in time.

Our study found that three of the round 1 variables which had significant zero-order correlations with round 1 life satisfaction also had significant correlations with round 3 life satisfaction: self-rated health, sexual enjoyment, and social activity hours (table D—23). Round 1 self-rated health had by far the strongest relationship with life satisfaction at each round, in terms of both zero-order correlations and *betas*. This suggests that subjective health is the most important factor influencing future life satisfaction. Reported sexual enjoyment was the only other variable that retained significant predictive power in the multiple regression, but its contribution to variance explained was small.

Attempt to predict change in life satisfaction. Our next step was to use the procedure for predicting residual change discussed in the analysis section to see if any of the independent variables adds to the predictive power of a multiple regression equation which already contains round 1 life satisfaction. In addition to round 1 life satisfaction, we tested the five independent variables by entering them in a multiple regression analysis with round 3 life satisfaction as the dependent variable (order specified as in table D—23). We also did this separately for

Table D—23. *Multiple regression of independent variables from round 1 with life satisfaction at rounds 1, 2, and 3 as the dependent variable.*

Round 1 variables	Life satisfaction at Round One *r*	*R*	*Beta*	Round Two *r*	*R*	*Beta*	Round Three *r*	*R*	*Beta*
Self-rated health	.42**	.42	.39**	.30**	.30	.27**	.25**	.25	.25**
Sexual enjoyment	.14*	.43	.07	.16**	.32	.11*	.13**	.27	.10*
Social activity hours	.11*	.44	.06	.09	.33	.08	.12*	.29	.09
Organizational activity	.18**	.46	.15**	.07	.33	.04	.10	.30	.06
Productive hours	.10*	.46	.05	.09	.34	.04	.03	.30	.01

Notes: *r* = Zero order Pearsonian correlation. *R* = Multiple correlation coefficient. *Beta* = Standardized regression coefficient.

* = Statistically significant at .05 level.

** = Statistically significant at .01 level.

Table D—24. *Multiple regression with round 1 life satisfaction and self-rated health as the independent variables and round 3 life satisfaction as the dependent variable.*

Independent variable	*r*	*R*	*Beta*
Round 1 life satisfaction	.40	.40	.36*
Round 1 self-rated health	.25	.41	.10*

*Increase in variance explained by each variable is statistically significant at .05 level.

men, women, those under sixty, those over sixty, and those with lower and those with higher life satisfaction at round 1, but the results were generally similar to those found in the total group (table D—24).

As expected, life satisfaction at round 1 was by far the strongest predictor of life satisfaction at round 3 (table D—24). In other words, the best single predictor of a person's life satisfaction at a later time was simply his life satisfaction level at an earlier time.

Less expected was the fact that only self-rated health was significantly related to the residual change in life satisfaction and it increased the variance explained by only 1 percent. Several of the other variables had *F* values that approached significance at the .05 level, but their contribution to increased variance was even smaller than that of self-rated health, and so they are not included in table D—24. It appears that the initial levels of these variables are not useful in predicting change in life satisfaction.

Attempt to use change in predictor variables. Since the initial levels of these

Table D—25. *Multiple regression with significant round 1 and 2 independent variables and round 3 life satisfaction as the dependent variable.*

Independent variable	*r*	*R*	*Beta*
Round 2 life satisfaction	.56	.56	.45*
Round 2 self-rated health	.32	.57	.11*
Round 1 life satisfaction	.40	.59	.14*

*Increase in variance explained by each variable is statistically significant at .05 level.

variables did not seem to add much in prediction of change in life satisfaction, we attempted to see if previous change in the predictor variables might help. We did this by using round 3 life satisfaction as the dependent variable, entering round 2 life satisfaction as the first variable (in order to analyze the residual change in life satisfaction between rounds 2 and 3), entering the round 2 values of the five independent variables in the second stage, and finally entering the round 1 values of life satisfaction and the five independent variables. If the changes in these independent variables between rounds 1 and 2 were significantly related to the subsequent change in life satisfaction, the addition of the round 1 values should significantly increase the variance explained. Only the addition of round 1 life satisfaction added a significant increase to the variance explained, and the increase was only 1.4 percent (table D—25). Thus, neither the initial levels of the independent variables nor their previous change in values were substantially related to future change in life satisfaction.

This is additional evidence for the overall stability of life satisfaction during the middle and later years. The best predictor of future life satisfaction appears to be the person's life satisfaction in the past, and the relatively small changes which occur appear to be largely unrelated to initial values or changes in values of other variables that are related to life satisfaction in cross-sectional analyses. Changes in life satisfaction appear to be complex and elusive phenomena whose prediction has largely escaped our available data and methods of analysis.

Summary

Most previous research on life satisfaction among older persons has been limited to cross-sectional analysis of the correlates of life satisfaction at one point in time. There has been little or no attempt to measure changes in life satisfaction or to account for these changes.

This study measures the changes in life satisfaction over a four-year period among a sample of 378 community residents aged forty-six to seventy and attempts to answer three basic questions about these changes: (1) are there significant differences between age and sex categories in life satisfaction changes, (2) what variables measured at the beginning are significant predictors of life satisfaction at the end, and (3) what variables are significant in predicting changes in life satisfaction?

The results showed that there were no significant differences in average life satisfaction changes between any age and sex categories. This indicates that the overall picture seems to be one of basic stability in life satisfaction throughout this age range for both sexes. However, there were some individuals (about one-fourth) who did report substantial changes, up or down, in their life satisfaction. Significant predictors of life satisfaction were, primarily, self-rated health and, to a much lesser extent, sexual enjoyment and social activity hours. Attempts to predict changes in life satisfaction were mostly unsuccessful both in terms of initial scores and in terms of changes in the scores of other variables. In terms of practical implications for maintaining life satisfaction during these years, this analysis does give some support for the theory that the most important thing is to maintain good health and to remain socially and sexually active.

References

Bloom, M. Discontent with contentment scales. *Gerontologist*, 15:99, 1975.

Bradburn, N. M., and Caplovitz, D. *Reports on happiness*. Chicago: Aldine, 1965.

Cantril, H. *The pattern of human concerns*. New Brunswick: Rutgers University Press, 1965.

Cronbach, L., and Furby, L. How we should measure "change"—or should we? *Psychological Bulletin*, 74:68–80, 1970.

Edwards, J., and Klemmack, L. Correlates of life satisfaction: A reexamination. *Journal of Gerontology*, 28:297–502, 1973.

Gurin, G., Veroff, J., and Feld, S. *Americans view their mental health*. New York: Basic Books, 1960.

Heise, D. Separating reliability and stability in test-retest correlations. *American Sociological Review*, 34:93–101, 1969.

Kutner, B., et al. *Five hundred over sixty*. New York: Russell Sage Foundation, 1956.

Palmore, E. B. (Ed.), *Normal aging II*. Durham, N.C.: Duke University Press, 1974.

Palmore, E., and Luikart, C. Health and social factors related to life satisfaction. *Journal of Health and Social Behavior*, 13:68–80, 1972.

Spreitzer, E., and Snyder, E. Correlates of life satisfaction among the aged. *Journal of Gerontology*, 29:454–458, 1974.

Continuities in the Experience of Aging

Judith Huff Fox

The purpose of this study is threefold: to identify the degree to which continuity is characteristic of a six-year span in the lives of older men and women; to identify conditions under which social and solitary activities of older persons can be characterized as more or less continuous over time; and to test the hypothesis that continuity of activity is positively related to psychological well-being.

Background

As the gerontological research literature has grown in sophistication and volume, both of the two leading social-psychological perspectives on aging—the disengagement and the activity perspectives—have been called into question. While some aging persons find satisfaction from disengaging from many major adult roles and activities, others do not. Conversely, certain aging persons depend on high levels of social activity to maintain feelings of psychological well-being and others do not. In the place of both disengagement and activities perspectives, the concept of continuity has been offered as a more adequate characterization of the aging process and as an explanation of why neither the disengagement nor activity perspective seems to be satisfactory.

Although continuity appears generally to refer to connectedness of one's present to one's past, the concept of continuity has in fact been used in a number of different ways. Thus Atchley (1971) uses the concept to argue that individuals do not typically suffer a crisis of identity upon retirement by pointing to the continuation of familial and friendship roles into later life. Both Lemon et al. (1972) and Keith-Ross (1977) use continuity as an explanation for why neither high nor low activity levels are associated with life satisfaction in their samples. Cutler (1977) uses the concept synonomously with "stability" to show lack of decline over time in participation in formal organizations. Maddox argues that while social activity may decline somewhat with age, those people who are relatively active initially remain more active than others over time (1968). Many others have also argued for the relative life-span stability of general activity level, preferences for particular activities, and life satisfaction itself (e.g., George and Maddox, 1977; Havighurst and Feigenbaum, 1959; Palmore and Kivett, 1977; Peppers, 1976; Simpson and McKinney, 1966).

While the concept of continuity has found widespread acceptance, lack of comparability of usage and less than adequate data sources upon which to test its implications have hampered the formulation of a coherent theory of continuity. In most instances in which the concept is used, little attempt is made to make clear what it means. If defined broadly enough, the concept refers to a careerlike relationship of activities or stages to each other or, as Rosow (1963) puts it, to a "continuity of self" over time. Such definitions imply not lack of change but order and connectedness of experience. At the other extreme is the connotation of nonchange or a rigid sameness of activities and attitudes. Some investigators use continuity to simply mean "lack of decline" (e.g., Cutler, 1977).

"Continuity of what?" is a second ambiguity. Does continuity refer simply to *level* of activity, to *kind* of activity, to roles and role content, to self-definitions, or worldview? The concept has been applied to each of these domains, but with little attention paid to their relationship to each other. Can one radically alter one's life-style but maintain a continuous image of self? Is a change in activity from business executive to volunteer leader continuous or discontinuous? How does the element of individual choice enter into the definition of any change as continuous or discontinuous?

Related to and dependent upon clarification of definition is the problem of measurement. To date, most attempts to measure continuity have been by necessity fairly unrefined and have focused primarily on similarity of activity level at two points in time. Thus, for example, Cutler (1977) uses "percent with stable or higher organization attendance"; Maddox (1968) uses "above or below median level of activity" at two points in time; and Pepper (1976) uses aggregate rankings of preferred leisure activities before and after retirement. Such measures potentially mask a great deal of individual change and cannot reflect the subtleties of shifts in specific activities, in the content of roles, or the relative salience of various activities to the individual. Moreover, the fact that data are collected at only two points in time makes the inference of trend or direction a risky one. Differences between any two times of measurement may reflect idiosyncratic deviations from a stable state rather than actual trends. In short, the degree to which continuity, however defined, is in fact characteristic of the aging process is simply not currently known.

Also implicit in the continuity perspective is the idea that continuity is positively related to psychological well-being in old age. The concept has been used as a post hoc explanation for the lack of a clear-cut correlation between activity level and morale in old age (Lemon, et al., 1972; Keith-Ross, 1977). The argument goes that if people can have high morale doing and thinking different things it is because they are doing what they have always done and possibly what they prefer. They were not all alike in earlier life and they are equally diverse in old age. It is an easy and logical leap to conclude that continuity has a direct and positive effect on adaptation in old age and that, therefore, the more continuity the better.

Whether in fact the behavior or attitude the investigator observes within a study sample in a correlational cross-sectional study is in fact a reflection of continuity with earlier times is of course open to question. Furthermore, there is increasing evidence that continuity, at least if it takes the form of "lack of change," may be negatively related to subjective well-being in late life. Snow and Havighurst (1977), for example, report that men whose retirement life-styles were a radical break from their former lives ("transformers") were less bored, less lonely, and less likely to find "no advantages" in retirement than those who held on to their professional activities ("maintainers"). Graney (1975) reports that increases in activity were more highly associated with happiness in old age than was continuity of activity, and that changes in activity may be even more important for morale among the very old. Peppers (1976) reports significantly higher life satisfaction among retirees whose activity level increased than among those for whom it remained constant or decreased. While some of these reports make it difficult to determine whether increases or changes are in fact logical extensions of former life-styles or are radical alterations, it appears that those who increase activity seem more satisfied in old age than those who maintain the status quo. If continuity is a requisite of positive adaptation in later life, we would not necessarily expect people to choose to do anything new. No one would seek changes, and in fact everyone would instead attempt to avoid disruptions of any kind (cf. Riegel, 1976, for presentation of a dialectical model of development).

In sum, there are many unanswered questions about what continuity means, about the degree to which it is in fact characteristic of the aging process, and whether continuity is related to psychological well-being in late life.

Methods

Data to answer these questions were taken from the Duke Second Longitudinal Study, specifically information for the sixty-nine men and eighty women aged sixty and over at time 1 who participated in all four rounds of interviews. Vari-

Figure D—3. *Key variables in the assessment of continuities in the experience of aging.*

Variable	*Question/responses*
Church attendance	"How many times a month do you attend religious services?" (Code 0–9 or more times)
"Other group" attendance	"How many times a month do you attend meetings of other groups such as clubs, unions, or associations?" (Code 0–9 or more times)
Freetime companion	"With whom do you spend most of your free time?" 1. by myself 2. spouse, children 3. friends, relatives 4. self and spouse, children
Daily social contact	"Some people talk to a lot of people each day. Others do not. Look at these (concentric) circles and imagine that the center (1) stands for very few people. The largest circle (9) stands for very many people. Which circle describes how many people you talk to on an average day?"
	"During the last typical week, how many hours did you spend:
Hours TV	Watching TV or listening to radio?
Hours meetings	Attending church or other meetings?
Hours social activities	Visiting, telephoning, or writing friends or relatives, parties, eating out, or entertaining?
Hours hobbies	Playing a sport or working on a hobby (Code 0–9)?
Health	"Here is a picture of a ladder. Suppose we say that the top of the ladder (pointing) represents perfect health, and the bottom (pointing) represents the most serious illness. Where on the ladder (moving finger up and down) would you say your health is at the *present time*?" (Code step on ladder 0–9)

ables included in this analysis were selected on the basis of their face validity of measurement of social or solitary activity and on their reliability as reported by the other investigators of the Duke research team. Exact wording of these items and their responses are contained in figure D—3.

Three measures of continuity were constructed:

An index of *persistence of activity level* measures the extent to which level of activity at time 1, whether high or low, is stable over time (the degree to which persons with relatively high or low activity levels remain higher or lower relative to the rest of the sample over time). Distributions of scores on interval level variables were broken into quartiles separately for each of the four waves of data. Individuals received a score of 1 on the persistence variable if their scores fell into the same quartile in each of the four waves, and a 0 if they did not. The one nominal level variable was coded so that individuals whose responses were identical on all four rounds received a score of 1. This measure allows for changes within age cohort over time and also some individual changes, but it suffers from the same limitations as do median splits, in that scores may in fact be very similar but fall into different quartiles.

The second index of continuity is a *sum of first differences* score, which measures degree of variation in scores. To obtain this measure, the sum of absolute values of the differences between consecutive scores for the four waves of data is divided by the possible range of that item. The possible range for this measure is 0–3.

A measure of *directionality of change*, or trend, was constructed by correlating time of measurement (time 1 = 1; time 4 = 4) with interval level scores over the four waves. Possible range is −1.0 (perfect negative trend) over four times of measurement to +1.0 (perfect positive trend).

Results

Table D—26 presents the distribution of scores for each of the three measures of continuity. For the persistence of activity scores in column 1, there appears to be stability over the four waves, and degree of stability varies with the activity in question. Thus, while about half of the sample remained in the same quartile in frequency of church attendance for all four waves, and almost as many remained in the same quartile in frequency of attending other organizational meetings, less than a quarter remained in the same relative quartile for number of hours they devoted to church and organizational meetings. Only 15 percent of the sample remained stable in their reports of the number of people to whom they speak on an average day. Among activities which may be either social or solitary (that is, hours spent on hobbies or watching television), only 28 percent and 16 percent, respectively, remained in the same relative quartile over the eight-year span. On the average, respondents remained in the same quartile for 2.6 of the eight activities.

Turning to the sum of first differences measure, one finds that the measure

Table D—26. *Continuity scores on activity variables, total sample (N = 149).*

Activity variables[a]	Persistence of activity level[b] (%)	of First differences[c] ($\bar{X}$)	Directionality[d] (r)
Church attendance	49.0	.39	.062
"Other group" attendance	43.6	.38	.045
Free-time companion	40.3	N.A.	N.A.
Daily social contact	15.4	.47	.037
Hours TV	16.1	.24	.024
Hours meetings	23.5	.05	−.075
Hours social activities	14.8	.12	.334*
Hours hobbies	28.2	.14	.030

[a]Questions associated with variables are reproduced in figure D—3.

[b]Percentage falling into the same quartile on all 4 waves of data.

[c]Sum of absolute values of the differences between consecutive scores divided by the range for that variable. Possible range for this measure is 0–3.

[d]Correlation of individual scores with time of measurement.

*$p < .05$.

which is used influences the degree of continuity. Thus, while church and voluntary organization attendance are the most stable variables in terms of persistence of activity level, they also show greater variability than most of the others. Clearly there is variation in individual scores over time which is not sufficient to explain changes in quartile rankings. In general, however, overall variation among waves is not very great, considering the possible maximum value of 3.0.

Finally, there is almost no pattern, in either a positive or a negative direction, to changes which do occur over time. Only one of the correlation coefficients relating time of measurement to scores on each of the four waves is statistically significant: that between number of hours devoted to social activities and time of measurement. The relationship is positive, offering little evidence of disengagement from social activities over time.

Table D—27 presents the results of an attempt to predict persistence of activity level, sum of first differences, and directionality from several time 1 variables. Only statistically significant results are indicated.

Column 1 shows that sex is not very useful in predicting directionality and is associated significantly only with the persistence of activity level variables. Men are more likely than women to have spent their free time with the same person over the four waves of interviews. This sex difference is a reflection of the fact that women were more likely than men to have been widowed during the eight-year period. Sex is the most useful of the variables examined in table D—26 in predicting sum of first difference scores on five of the eight activity measures. In all cases, there is greater variability for women than for men.

Table D—27. *Association of time 1 predictors with activity continuity* (N = *149).*

Activity variables[a] by continuity measure	Sex		Age	Income	Health	Job status		Marital status	
	M	F				Yes	No	Yes	No
Persistence of activity level[b]									
Church attendance				.16*					
"Other group" attendance									
Freetime companion	49.**	32.		.30**				45.**	.24
Daily social contact					.14*				
Hours TV									
Hours meetings									
Hours social activities									
Hours hobbies				.17*					
Sum of 1st Differences[c]									
Church attendance	.33**	.51		−.26**	−.18*			.35*	.52
"Other group" attendance	.30*	.45							
Daily social contact									
Hours TV	.16*	.20				.20**	.27	.21*	.31
Hours meetings	.41**	.70							
Hours social activities	.08**	.17				.11**	.16	.11**	.16
Hours hobbies						.10**	.17	.12**	.19
Directionality[d]									
Church attendance			−.33**			.36**	−.04		
"Other group" attendance									
Daily social contact									
Hours TV									

Table D—27. *(Continued)*

Activity variables[a] by continuity measure	Sex		Age	Income	Health	Job status		Marital status	
	M	F				Yes	No	Yes	No
Hours meetings									
Hours social activities			−.17*	.19**	.14*				
Hours hobbies						.12*	−.05		

[a]Questions associated with variables are reproduced in figure D—3.

[b]Percentage falling into the same quartile on all 4 waves of data.

[c]Sum of absolute values of the differences between consecutive scores divided by the range for that variable. Possible range for this measure is 0–3.

[d]Correlation of individual scores with time of measurement.

*$p < .05$.

**$p < .01$.

Age is significantly related to only two of the twenty-two dependent variables; in both of these cases, the older the individual was at time 1, the more likely there is to be a negative trend over time.

Income at time 1 is related to four of the persistence variables, and in all cases is positively related to maintenance of the same relative level over time. Income is negatively associated with fluctuation in church attendance and associated with an increase over time of the number of hours devoted to social activities.

Like age, subjective health rating at time 1 has modest predictive power. Correlations are weak, but in the expected direction.

Employment status at time 1, which is unrelated to any of the "persistence" variables, does predict three of the sum of first difference scores, with those who were not employed at time 1 showing greatest variation. Employment status also affects the direction of change over time in both church attendance and time devoted to hobbies. For those who were working at time 1, there were increases in these activities over time, whereas those who were unemployed show a slight negative trend.

Finally, marital status at time 1 (here defined as "married, spouse present" versus all others) shows only a scattering of significant associations with the dependent variables. Those who were married at time 1 were more likely to maintain the same free-time companion, to show less fluctuation in church attendance and in time devoted to social activities, hobbies, and television watching.

In addition to time 1 variables, four measures of change over time were correlated with the three kinds of continuity indices. Table D—28 examines the effects of change in marital and employment status over the course of data collection and the effects of directional changes in income and subjective health status. Again, only significant results are shown.

The only variable correlated with decline in subjective health rating over time is a small but significant decline in the number of hours devoted weekly to hobbies. Health status changes are associated with none of the persistence of activity level measures and with none of the trend measures.

Declines in income present a complicated pattern of associations. A decrease in income over time appears to stabilize the persistence of relative level of church attendance and the respondent's free-time companion and to decrease variation in the number of people the respondent sees on the average day. On the other hand, income decline is associated with declines in this same variable of daily social contact and with declines in attendance of voluntary organization meetings. Income drops are associated with increased fluctuation in time spent viewing television. Taken together, these correlations suggest that with decreasing financial resources, individuals may become locked into certain less expensive activities as they drop others and, in the process, experience a net decline in their social interaction.

To control for changes in marital status over the data collection period, respondents were classified as "stable married," "stable not married" (widows, divorcees, and those never-married), and "other" (all but one of whom was widowed during this period). In column 3 of table D—28, marital status changes are associated with three of the continuity variables. Not surprisingly, those who remained married throughout the period were most likely to name the same free-time companion in all four interviews. "Stable marrieds" also show significantly less fluctuation over time in their church attendance. An unexpected finding is that those who remained unmarried throughout the time period show a slight negative trend in daily social contact, while those who were widowed actually

Table D—28. *Correlates of activity continuity.*

Activity variables by continuity measure[a]	Directionality[d] in income	Directionality[d] in health	Marital stability[e]			Job stability[f]		
			SM	other	SNM	SW	other	SNW
Persistence of activity level[b]								
Church attendance	−.18*							
"Other group" attendance						35.*	42.	48.
Free-time companion	−.25**		49.*	16.	23.			
Daily social contact								
Hours TV								

Table D—28. *(Continued)*

Activity variables by continuity measure[a]	Directionality[d] in income	Directionality[d] in health	Marital stability[e] SM	other	SNM	Job stability[f] SW	other	SNW
Hours meetings						38.*	17.	23.
Hours social activities								
Hours hobbies								
Sum of 1st differences[c]								
Church attendance			.34**	.66	.61			
"Other group" attendance								
Daily social contact	.15*							
Hours TV	−.26**							
Hours meetings								
Hours social activities						.08	.10	.17**
Hours hobbies		.17*						
Directionality[d]								
Church attendance						.23	.27	−.09**
"Other group" attendance	.14*							
Daily social contact	.22**		.06	.26	−.13*	.23**	−.13	.10*
Hours TV								
Hours meetings						.14	.01	−.23**
Hours social activities						.26	.45	.26*
Hours hobbies						.25*	.02	−.05

[a]Questions associated with variables are reproduced in figure D—3.

[b]Percentage falling into the same quartile on all 4 waves of data.

[c]Sum of absolute values of the differences between consecutive scores divided by the range for that variable. Possible range for this measure is 0–3.

[d]Correlation of individual scores with time of measurement.

[e]SM = stable married, SNM = stable not married, other = those who changed marital status during study. Differences are expressed as differences from "other" category.

[f]SW = stable working, SNW = stable retired, other = those who changed job status during study. Differences are expressed as differences from "other" category.

*$p < .05$.

**$p < .01$.

tended to increase overall social interaction. We can only hypothesize that this increase was a result of the response of relatives and friends to the respondents' widowhood.

Change in employment status is by far the most effective predictor of changes in activity levels, showing significant distinctions in five of the "directionality" indices. The direction of these effects, however, are by no means uniform, suggesting that retirement does bring about activity changes which may be either increases or decreases in activity level.

Table D—29. *Regression of time 4 affect balance on activity continuity measures.*

Activity variables by continuity measures[a]	*Beta* (*r*)	*Beta* (net time 1 affect balance)
Persistence of activity level[b]		
Church attendance	−.033	(−.050)
"Other group" attendance	−.178*	(−.174*)
Freetime companion	−.014	(−.010)
Daily social contact	−.016	(−.021)
Hours TV	−.133	(−.115)
Hours meetings	−.058	(−.054)
Hours social activities	−.010	(−.003)
Hours hobbies	−.017	(−.017)
Sum of 1st differences[c]		
Church attendance	.061	(.068)
"Other group" attendance	.226**	(.222**)
Daily social contact	−.165	(−.153)
Hours TV	.002	(.019)
Hours meetings	.100	(.068)
Hours social activities	.052	(.034)
Hours hobbies	.179*	(.150)
Directionality[d]		
Church attendance	.046	(.053)
"Other group" attendance	.006	(.010)
Daily social contact	−.066	(−.013)
Hours TV	−.099	(.119)
Hours meetings	.037	(.061)
Hours social activities	.024	(.028)
Hours hobbies	−.034	(−.023)

[a]Questions associated with variables are reproduced in figure D—3.

[b]Percentage falling into the same quartile on all 4 waves of data.

[c]Sum of absolute values of the differences between consecutive scores divided by the range for that variable. Possible range for this measure is 0–3.

[d]Correlation of individual scores with time of measurement.

*$p < .05$.

**$p < .01$.

The third objective of this study was to test the hypothesis that continuity is positively related to psychological well-being in late life. Table D—29 presents the zero-order correlations between time 4 scores on Bradburn's Affect Balance Scale (Bradburn, 1969) and each of the continuity measures. In addition, in order to control for stability of affect balance itself, standardized regression coefficients net of time 1 affect balance are shown in parentheses. The correlation between time 1 and time 4 affect balance in this sample is .230, considerably less than the stability of the Kutner Morale Scale scores reported by George and Maddox (1977).

Considering first the effects of the persistence of activity level measures, we see that only one variable is significantly related to affect balance, and the relationship is negative. Individuals who maintained the same relative frequency of "other group" attendance scored lower on time 4 affect balance than those who were less constant over time. The same relationship is expressed in the sum of first difference scores: The more variability in reported meeting attendance, the higher the positive affect of time 4. Only one other relationship is statistically significant and again that association is positive: the more variation in the number of hours devoted weekly to hobbies, the higher the relative positive affect at time 4. The coefficient drops to statistical insignificance, however, controlling for the effects of time 1 affect balance.

Discussion

Let us review the data just presented in light of each of the study's three objectives in order to determine the extent to which we were able to accomplish its goals.

With few guidelines regarding how best to measure continuity or how much stability in fact constitutes evidence of continuity, we can only reiterate that the measurement is the message. In no case did more than half of the respondents remain in the same quartile of relative frequency of activity level over the four waves of data collection, and in some cases fewer than 20 percent indicated such stability. On the other hand, fluctuation between scores, as measured by "sum of first differences," was low and there was evidence of little positive or negative direction of change over time. Variables in the larger data set known to be unreliable over time were not included in the analysis; however, the degree to which the variables used are reliable is not known. In other words, we do not know whether score "differences" between waves are reflections of "true" differences or random error, and we can only hope that such error is normally distributed throughout the sample. Nor were the available indices of activity as finely honed as we would wish in a study of activity continuity. The variable "frequency of attending 'other groups'" does not capture shifts or continuities in the particular organizations of which the individuals are members, changes or continuities in intensity, or personal salience of organization memberships. "Time devoted to engagement in hobbies" tells us little about what those hobbies are. "Time devoted to 'social activities'" is even more obscure. A considered definition of "continuity" and an acceptable measure of concept that individuals' activities over an eight-year period are characterized as being relatively "continuous," if the concept is conceived broadly, but the extent of continuity varies with the activity in question.

The second objective of the analysis was to identify conditions under which activities were more or less continuous. Of the six time 1 predictors, sex and marital status were the most effect predictors, with women and those who were not married at time 1 showing more variation than others in scores over time. Not surprisingly, being employed at time 1 predicted greater fluctuation in years to come, and a likelihood to increase church attendance and time spent on hobbies. Of greater interest was the relative lack of predictive power of either age or health status at time 1.

The lack of an influence of health is also evident in the fact that the decline in perceived health status is associated with only one of the continuity measures. While job stability over time showed significant relationships with some of the activity measures, no consistent patterns emerged to indicate how alterations in employment status affect activity level. Downward trends in income are associated with declines in only two of the social activities.

Considering the number of possible associations tested for and the likelihood that a certain proportion will be statistically significant by chance alone, little success was achieved in identifying strong predictors of activity continuity, however it is measured. All of the relationships presented in tables D—27 and D—28 are zero-order, however, and it may be that controlling for certain confounding factors would allow other relationships to emerge.

The final objective of the study was to determine the extent to which activity continuity was associated with psychological well-being (affect balance). We found little evidence that continuity over an eight-year period predicts affect balance at the end of that period. Indeed, the only two relationships that were statistically significant indicated that change was *positively* related to time 4 affect balance. The latter finding, in combination with the lack of significant positive associations between continuity and well-being, contradicts suggestions in the literature that continuity is a desirable commodity. Like Snow and Havighurst's "transformers" (1977), and like Williams and Wirths' "Living Life Fully" types (1965), our data suggest that it may be those who seek out changes and whose lives are not characterized by "sameness" but by role flexibility (Kline, 1975; Sinnott, 1977) who adapt best to the exigencies of late life. On the other hand, it may simply be that the activity variables at our disposal are not the most salient ones for maintenance of positive affect among older people. Unfortunately we have no data to address the issues of the importance of volition in the meaning of discontinuities for older persons or of which spheres of activity continuity may be more or less salient to the individual.

Conclusion

To counter charges that activity levels decline with advancing age and to explain the fact that neither high nor low levels of activity can predict life satisfaction among older people, the concept of continuity has been posited. Little systematic investigation of its appropriateness has been undertaken, however, and at most continuity and discontinuity have been inferred from data collected at only two points in time.

It may be that, when the right data are available and analyzed, the fact that older people are as heterogeneous as younger ones is best attributed to the fact that they are doing and thinking what they have been doing and thinking all their lives. It may be that the extremes of both continuity and discontinuity indicate responses that are less adaptive than some middle ground where "continuity of self" is accompanied by flexible growth, change, and new experiences.

In the meantime, the preliminary analysis presented here may serve to stimulate thought as well as analysis of the continuity perspective. What do we really mean by the concept? How can we best measure it? Until we can answer these questions, we should avoid the trap of assuming that continuity is a final solution to our questions about adaptation to, and in, old age.

References

Atchley, R. C. Retirement and leisure participation: Continuity or crises? *Gerontologist*, 11:13–17, 1971.

Bradburn, N. M. *The structure of psychological well-being*. Chicago: Aldine, 1969.

Cutler, S. J. Aging and voluntary association participation. *Journal of Gerontology*, 32:470–479, 1977.

George, L., and Maddox, G. L. Subjective adaptation to loss of the work role: A longitudinal study. *Journal of Gerontology*, 32:456–462, 1977.

Graney, M. Happiness and social participation in aging. *Journal of Gerontology*, 30:701–706, 1975.

Havighurst, R. J., and Feigenbaum, K. Leisure and life-style. *American Journal of Sociology*, 64:396–404, 1959.

Keith-Ross, J. *Old people, new lives*. Chicago: University of Chicago Press, 1977.

Kline, C. The socialization process of women. *Gerontologist*, 15:486–492, 1975.

Lemon, B., Bengtson, V., and Peterson, J. An exploration of the activity theory of aging. *Journal of Gerontology*, 27:511–523, 1972.

Maddox, G. L. Persistence of life style among the elderly: A longitudinal study of patterns of social activity in relation to life satisfaction. In B. L. Neugarten (Ed.), *Middle age and aging*. Chicago: University of Chicago Press, 1968.

Palmore, E. B. Appendix A. Design of the adaptation study. In E. B. Palmore (Ed.), *Normal aging II*. Durham, N.C.: Duke University Press, 1974, 291–296.

Palmore, E. B., and Kivett, V. Change in life satisfaction: A longitudinal study of persons aged 46–70. *Journal of Gerontology*, 32:311–316, 1977.

Peppers, L. G. Patterns of leisure and adjustment to retirement. *Gerontologist*, 16:441–446, 1976.

Reigel, K. F. The dialectics of human development. *American Psychologist*, 31:679–700, 1976.

Rosow, I. Adjustment of normal aged. In R. H. Williams et al. (Eds.), *Processes of aging*, Vol. 2. New York: Atherton, 1963.

Simpson, I. H., and McKinney, J. C. (Eds.), *Social aspects of aging*. Durham, N.C.: Duke University Press, 1966.

Sinnot, J. D. Sex-role inconstancy, biology, and successful aging. *Gerontologist*, 17:459–463, 1977.
Snow, R. B., and Havighurst, R. J. Life style types and patterns of retirement of educators. *Gerontologist*, 17:545–552, 1977.
Williams, R. H., and Wirths, C. G. *Lives through the years*. New York: Atherton, 1965.

Predictors of Successful Aging in Retirement

Janet Huber Lowry

The incidence of mandatory retirement was high in the 1940s, 1950s, and 1960s. Usually assumed to have a negative impact on retirees, mandatory retirement has been blamed for the general problems of many older citizens. Did mandatory retirement typically have a negative impact on retirees? Did those who reentered the labor force age more successfully than those who did not? These are the major questions which guided this investigation. Several other concerns were also prominent. Understanding patterns of response at various stages of retirement requires longitudinal rather than cross-sectional data. Since processes of biological aging affect retirement decisions and responses, control for sex and health is required. Since retirement is a social process, controls for race, family relations, and socioeconomic status are also required.

Literature Review

Controversy in the literature about successful aging centers around the different answers proposed to three questions. First, what are the criteria for successful aging? Second, who determines these criteria (Dean et al., 1961)? Third, how do these identified criteria in fact explain observed responses to retirement? While this research deals specifically with personal adjustments during retirement, the broader concept of successful aging provides the starting point for the research design. The selection of dependent variables is guided by answers to these three questions.

Successful aging as discussed by Atchley (1972, 1976) involves both the specific feelings about facts of life for the elderly and the general orientation of the older person toward life, both past and present. Havighurst et al. (1964) have demonstrated the importance of this broader perspective. Rosow's discussion of socialization to old age (1974) also supports the argument for multiple criteria for successful aging. The criteria for successful aging should include the individual's self evaluation as well as external indicators established by social theory and empirical research.

This research addresses these concerns for assessing successful aging by utilizing three indicators of adaptation: (1) activity level, sometimes identified as a causal factor and sometimes used to assess continuity of life-style; (2) general satisfaction, a summary of the individual's response to attitude items; and (3) adjustment rating, an interviewer's rating of individual adaptation following an extensive interview. These dependent variables provide a variety of criteria and both internal and external views of the impact of retirement on successful aging.

Other studies demonstrate important factors which must be controlled. These include health, both objectively and subjectively defined (Jeffers and Nichols, 1961), sex (Palmore, 1968), race, socioeconomic differences (Heyman and Jeffers, 1964), and occupational status (Simpson et al., 1966; Havighurst and Devries, 1969).

Continuity of life-style is a major finding in research on retirement as well as an important criterion in several hypotheses of successful aging. Atchley's 1971 article focused on the continuity/crisis debate. Maddox (1966) identified the "persistence of life-style" in old age. Palmore (1968) demonstrated this persistence in the Duke panel through increasing homogeneity of activity and attitude scores over time. Parnes and Nestel (1981) emphasized the importance of causes of retirement which include factors of timing, mandatory retirement policies, subjective evaluation of events, and health considerations.

Study Design and Method

This research uses data from the Duke First Longitudinal Study of Aging. A major difficulty in studies of adaptation to retirement is the lack of a clear definition of retirement. Questions about employment history, subjective identification as retired, and, as a last recource, age were utilized in this study to assign each case individually to one of five approximately five-year retirement cohorts. In this report *round* refers to the times panelists were studied while *stage* refers to sequences in the retirement process. The relation of these two different timing factors is summarized in figure D—4. Here the data are located historically in columns as collected from round 1, which began in 1955 and covered four years, through round 6 in 1970, which covered five months. The intervals between examinations were irregular, ranging from 1.6 to 4.3 years on the average, and the standard deviations for these intervals ranged from .3 to .9 years. Once the retirement cohorts were identified (based on year retired), the retirement timing—a social rather than an historical definition of time—was established by stages within each cohort. Stage A, *still working*, precedes retirement by more than five years and stage B, *preretirement*, precedes retirement by less than five years. The event of retirement occurs between stages B and C, *just retired*. Stage D, *settling in*, is four or more years after retirement. Stage E, *established*, is about twelve years postretirement. Stage F, *later retirement*, is about twelve years postretirement, and stage G, *the last stage*, is around fifteen years postretirement. Cohorts in the same stage are illustrated in diagonals of figure D—4 (adopted from Riley et al., 1972). The letters in figure D—4 indicate the stages in relation to retirement sequence (social time); the numbers indicate the rounds in relation to panel participation (historical time). The average intervals between stages of retirement are

Figure D—4. *Relation between panel rounds, retirement cohorts, and retirement stages with duration statistics.*

		Panel Round					
	Dates:	5/55–5/59	9/59–5/61	1/64–3/65	10/66–1/67	4/68–11/68	2/70–6/70
	Round #:	1	2	3	4	5	6
	Interval:						
	Mean years		3.2	4.3	2.4	1.6	1.7
	Standard deviation		.9	.6	.7	.5	.3
Retirement cohort	(Ns)	(263)	(192)	(173)	(134)	(108)	(105)
year retired I 1940–46	(36)	1 E	2 F	3 G			
II 1947–51	(61)	1 D	2 E	3 F	4 G		
III 1952–56	(98)	1 C	2 D	3 E	4 F	5 G	
IV 1957–61	(38)	1 B	2 C	3 D	4 E	5 F	6 G
V 1962–64	(39)	1 A	2 B	3 C	4 D	5 E	6 F

Retirement stage (totals):	A (39)	B (73)	C (148)	D (186)	E (188)	F (137)	G (96)
Stage interval:							
Mean years	3.2	3.7	3.2	3.3	2.7	1.9	
Standard deviation	.8	.9	1.0	1.2	1.1	.8	

Cell entries indicate the round number and the stage letter.

more uniform in length than those between rounds, but they have greater variance than the latter. This analysis is organized by social time, so panelists are grouped by retirement stages.

The variables utilized were collected from the social history questionnaires, except for the physician's functional rating of health, here employed as an objective measure of health. The primary variables of interest are those which measure activity level (Chicago Activity Inventory developed by Cavan et al., 1949), satisfaction (Chicago Attitude Inventory), and adjustment (Cavan Adjustment Rating Scale). These provide for continuity of measurement over time, individual responses to the inventories, and a general objective indication of successful aging (interviewer adjustment rating). Each of these scores was used as a dependent variable in a regression analysis. Table D—30 reports descriptive statistics for all variables.

In this study we investigated the three indicators of successful aging in relation to the sequences of stages in retirement. For women who were housewives, the location in a stage is based on retirement of husband. While age is an important variable generally, it is not analyzed directly in this research because the extent of retirement around age sixty-five during the period of the Duke panel study assures that age closely corresponds to the retirement stages. When retirement stage is controlled, age has minimal variance. This analysis covers approximately fifteen years, most of which immediately followed the retirement event for these subjects.

Other independent variables include background information (measured once) and current marital and health status (measured at each visit). The background information, with initial frequencies, included sex (male, 127; female, 141); women's work experience (housewives, 68; employed, 73); race (black, 95; white, 172); and occupational class, dichotomized with manual and clerical/sales versus other nonmanual workers considered indicative of low (134) or

Table D—30. *Descriptive statistics—round 1 and by retirement stage.*

Variables	1	A	B	C	D	E	F	G
Successful aging: (means)								
Activity level	28.0	32.2	31.3	28.4	28.1	26.7	26.5	25.9
Attitudinal satisfaction	34.3	37.4	36.4	34.7	34.5	33.3	33.9	33.1
Adjustment rating	4.7	5.3	5.2	4.8	5.0	4.7	4.6	4.4
Background characteristics: (percentages)								
Sex MALE	47	39	43	57	50	40	42	40
Work HSWIFE	25	33	30	21	23	30	29	30
Race BLACK	35	39	37	35	34	35	36	33
Occup. HIGHSES	49	51	55	50	51	51	53	52
Current characteristics: (percentages)								
MARITAL	58	64	62	64	55	45	42	41
SELFHLTH[a]	63	74	70	71	71	61	61	62
PFRATING[b]	49	67	56	49	43	37	31	39
Retirement characteristics: (percentages)								
MANDATORY RET[c]	13	NA	8	18	18	15	18	18
FEEL SORRY RET[d]	18	15	12	20	18	18	20	21
PART-TIME WORK[e]	33	23	27	32	31	33	33	35
FULL-TIME WORK[e]	19	49	38	26	22	19	24	19
Subjects (*N*)	272	39	73	148	186	188	137	96

[a]Subjective self-health rating: percent good or excellent.

[b]Objective health rating by physicians: no functional disability.

[c]Round 2 retirement questionnaire supplement (only males were asked why they retired).

[d]Round 1 opinion, whether glad or sorry about retirement.

[e]Labor force participation after initial retirement.

high (132) socioeconomic status, respectively. Other current information included a self-health rating (dichotomized from eight responses into good to excellent, 169 categories, and fair to poor, 99 categories); a physician's functional health rating (dichotomized as no disability, 128 or mild to severe disability, 130); and marital status (dichotomized as married, 157 and not married, 111).

This research was particularly interested in four special subgroups in this panel: (1) Those retired because of mandatory retirement; (2) those who expressed regret that they had retired; (3) part-time workers; and (4) full-time returners to the labor force. Unfortunately only men were asked why they retired. Half of the retired men in round 2 (36 of 71) said they had to retire because of age. Married women were asked about their husband's reason for retirement (15 mandatory of 44), not about their own retirement. How subjects felt about retirement was assessed in round 1. Their answers permitted a distinction between those who were sorry or ambivalent and those who were glad about retirement. The other two special subgroups, full-time (51) and part-time (79) returners to the labor force, were identified by inspection of the data on employment experience subsequent to retirement.

These four retirement subgroups were not mutually exclusive, since six full-time and fourteen part-time returners were among the mandatorily retired. However, the reason for retirement and subsequent return to the labor force were not related. In addition, none of these subgroups is significantly related to the background variables except, as noted, for the restriction by sex for questions about the reason for retirement.

Regression analyses, both simple and stepwise, were used to investigate the contribution of these retirement characteristics to the explanation of successful aging. The initial model for each retirement stage used the background and current characteristics variables of sex, women's work experience, race, socioeconomic (occupational) status, marital status, subjective health, and physician's rating of health to explain variance in the three dependent variables: activity level, satisfaction, and adjustment rating. The full model added the retirement characteristics outlined above. Each model for each dependent variable at each stage was also investigated with stepwise regression to establish the most significant predictor variables. The criteria employed in stepwise regression included a maximum of .25 probability of entry by chance for each independent variable included in the equation and a maximum of six steps. Given the relatively small sample size in some stages, the adjusted R^2 is reported, along with significance levels for the F ratio. The change in adjusted R^2 between the initial and full models provides a test of the importance to successful aging of cohort, mandatory retirement, feelings about retirement, and full or part-time labor force reentry.

Results

Descriptive statistics in table D—30 show both initial panel composition and variations over retirement stages. The indicators of successful aging all dropped somewhat immediately following retirement (stage C), the largest decline for any of the consecutive stages. However, none of the changes was statistically significant.

Though men made up less than half of the sample, they are in the majority for the stage immediately following retirement. Women are split rather evenly between primary homemakers and those who have had significant labor force participation. Blacks constitute a bit more than one-third of each stage. Those with higher socioeconomic status were about one-half of each stage. The porportion of those who were married declined, as did the proportion who reported good to excellent health and the proportion with no disability.

With regard to retirement characteristics, there was little change across the stages. The mandatory retirees were about one out of every six subjects. Those who felt sorry about retirement were about one out of five. The part-time re-

Table D—31. *Stepwise regression analyses for activity level with independent variables listed by step of entry (unstandardized regression coefficients at entry, and change in adjusted* R^2 *in parentheses).*

	Postretirement stages				
Step	C	D	E	F	G
1st	MALE	SLFHLTH	SLFHLTH	SLFHLTH	PFRATING
	−4.11***	4.03***	3.33***	4.77***	4.27**
	(.089)	(.092)	(.061)	(.138)	(.101)
2nd	MARITAL	PFRATING	MALE	PFRATING	MALE
	5.03***	3.18***	−2.58**	3.93***	−3.49**
	(.097)	(.063)	(.035)	(.067)	(.070)
3rd	PFRATING	HIGHSES	MARITAL	MALE	MARITAL
	3.03**	2.17**	4.10***	−2.87**	3.97**
	(.047)	(.029)	(.059)	(.049)	(.063)
4th	COHORT	BLACK	COHORT	FEELRET	SLFHLTH
	1.59*	1.78*	.83*	−2.20	3.75**
	(.031)	(.015)	(.022)	(.015)	(.077)
5th	FULLWORK	FEELRET	PARTWORK	MARITAL	MANDRET
	2.25*	−2.02	2.32*	2.12	−2.45
	(.016)	(.013)	(.026)	(.013)	(.009)
6th	PARTWORK	COHORT	FEELRET	BLACK	
	2.43*	.61	−2.08	1.65	
	(.019)	(.007)	(.012)	(.012)	
adj. R^2	.299	.219	.215	.294	.320
chng[a]	.040	.001	.038	.004	.086
N	137	180	178	133	93

[a]Change in adj. R^2 from model without retirement characteristics.

$*p < .05$.

$**p < .01$.

$***p < .001$.

Table D—32. *Stepwise regression analyses for satisfaction with independent variables listed by step of entry (unstandardized regression coefficients at entry, and change in adjusted* R^2 *in parentheses).*

	Postretirement stages				
Step	C	D	E	F	G
1st	SELHLTH	SLFHLTH	SLFHLTH	SLFHLTH	PFRATING
	3.88***	4.78***	5.26***	5.59***	4.77***
	(.114)	(.156)	(.181)	(.187)	(.184)
2nd	COHORT	COHORT	COHORT	FEELRET	SLFHLTH
	1.32**	.90*	.90**	−3.53**	2.87**
	(.039)	(.024)	(.031)	(.047)	(.061)
3rd	PFRATING	PARTWORK	FEELRET	PFRATING	BLACK
	1.99*	1.82*	−2.20*	2.93**	2.37*
	(.027)	(.019)	(.017)	(.034)	(.037)
4th	PARTWORK	FULLWORK	BLACK	MANDRET	MANDRET
	1.48	1.72	1.12	−2.55*	−1.73
	(.012)	(.009)	(.004)	(.020)	(.009)
5th	MANDRET	FEELRET	FULLWORK	FULLWORK	PARTWORK
	−1.31	−1.37	1.61	2.03	1.26
	(.003)	(.004)	(.005)	(.014)	(.006)
6th	MARITAL	BLACK		PARTWORK	FULLWORK
	1.36	1.32		1.56	1.47
	(.008)	(.008)		(.006)	(.003)
adj. R^2	.203	.220	.238	.308	.300
chng[a]	.050	.052	.055	.080	.018
N	137	180	178	133	93

[a]Change in adj. R^2 from model without retirement characteristics.

*$p < .05$.

**$p < .01$.

***$p < .001$.

turners were about one out of three, and the full-time returners were about one out of four or five. Altogether, about half of the subjects reentered the labor force at some time after retirement.

Tables D—30 through D—32 contain results from the stepwise regression models for postretirement stages. These tables also report the total adjusted R^2 for the full regression models and the change attributed to adding the retirement characteristics variables.

The *N*s of the two preretirement stages, A (still working) and B (preretirement), were too small to support reliable conclusions. The only significant equation was that which predicted activity level at stage A. Noticeably lower activity level was characteristic for men, people with disability, those sorry about retirement, and those who eventually reentered the labor force with part-time employment. Noticeably higher activity level was exhibited by women, however, those in good to excellent health and those with higher socioeconomic status.

The best predictors of activity level in postretirement stages are found in table D—31. Sex, health, and marital status were the most important. Being female, married, able-bodied, and with good to excellent health meant a significantly higher activity level. Later retirement cohorts (younger persons) had higher activity levels. Those who returned to work were more active in early retirement. Those who felt sorry about retirement had lower activity levels in the middle stages. Higher socioeconomic status and race were significantly related to higher activity level in stage D, about four years after retirement. The total adjusted R^2 shows that the regression models explained 22–32 percent of the variance in activity level. The retirement characteristics added 0–9 percent of this explanation, primarily in early or late retirement.

Table D—33. *Stepwise regression analyses for adjustment rating with independent variables listed by step of entry (unstandardized regression coefficients at entry, and change in adjusted* R^2 *in parentheses).*

	Postretirement stages				
Step	C	D	E	F	G
1st	SELHLTH	SLFHLTH	SLFHLTH	SLFHLTH	HIGHSES
	1.13**	1.13***	1.20***	1.35***	1.03**
	(.062)	(.074)	(.101)	(.121)	(.090)
2nd	COHORT	HIGHSES	FULLWORK	PFRATING	PFRATING
	.45*	.83**	1.04**	1.14**	.70
	(.027)	(.045)	(.048)	(.063)	(.028)
3rd	PFRATING	BLACK	HIGHSES	FEELRET	MALE
	.66	.55*	.44	−.82*	−.61
	(.018)	(.015)	(.010)	(.027)	(.024)
4th	MALE		PFRATING	FULLWORK	SLFHLTH
	−.54		−.36	.75*	.47
	(.010)		(.004)	(.023)	(.008)
5th	HIGHSES		MARITAL	HIGHSES	FEELRET
	.42		.34	.51	−.51
	(.005)		(.002)	(.014)	(.007)
6th	BLACK			MANDRET	
	.46			−.57	
	(.005)			(.008)	
adj. R^2	.127	.134	.166	.256	.157
chng[a]	.013	0	.048	.054	.007
N	137	180	178	133	93

[a]Change in adj. R^2 from model without retirement characteristics.

*$p < .05$.

**$p < .01$.

***$p < .001$.

Table D—32 shows the best predictors for the satisfaction indicator of successful aging in the postretirement stages. Health is very important again but, in the early and middle stages, so are being in a recent cohort, working part-time after retiring, not being mandatorily retired, and feeling glad about retirement. Race was also relevant; blacks reported higher satisfaction, particularly in later retirement. The total adjusted R^2 shows that the models explained 19–32 percent of the variance in satisfaction during retirement. The retirement characteristics contributed 5–8 percent of this explanation, except for the last stage.

The adjustment rating predictors are shown in table D—33. The models were considerably less helpful in predicting this indicator of successful aging. Only 13–26 percent of the variance in adjustment was explained. However, health and high socioeconomic status were consistently important to good adjustment. Returning to full-time work also produced higher adjustment ratings in later retirement.

Summary

Differences in successful aging by type of retirement experience were detectable and significant. Those who felt sorry or ambivalent about retirement and those who reentered the labor force part-time had remarkably lower activity levels initially—foreshadowing their later reentry into the labor force. Negative evaluation of retirement was always negatively related to successful aging indicators. Mandatory retirement due to age had no effect or a small negative impact on successful aging. Retirement cohort was related to successful aging in the early stages: those who retired after the mid-1950s had more satisfaction, higher activity level, and better adjustment in their first decade of retirement. Labor force reentry had a strong positive impact on successful aging.

The relationship of background variables to successful aging indicators changed across the stages. Males had significantly lower activity levels at all stages. Housewives were better adjusted before their husbands retired. Blacks reported more satisfaction than whites at most stages. Those with higher socioeconomic status were more active before retirement and better adjusted throughout retirement.

Health and marital status were related to successful aging in a consistent way. The married always had higher activity levels. Their attitude in early retirement was also more positive. Higher self-health ratings were generally predictors of successful aging. The physician's assessment of disability was important to successful aging for those just retired and increasingly critical in the last two stages.

The models in this analysis did explain 10–32 percent of the variance in successful aging in retirement. The retirement characteristics became less important over time for predicting activity level but more important for predicting satisfaction after retirement.

In summary, health subjectively and/or objectively defined was the primary predictor of successful aging. Sex and marital status were important in predicting activity level. Race affected satisfaction. Socioeconomic status predicted adjustment. Being mandatorily retired had some detrimental effects on satisfaction in later retirement, as well as immediately following the event. Far more pervasive was the negative impact on successful aging of feeling sorry or ambivalent about retirement. A cohort or period effect distinguished those who retired before the first round (1955–59) from those who retired after it. The latter group adapted more successfully in early retirement. The growing acceptance of retirement as a legitimate stage of life after the mid-1950s probably helps explain this significant cohort difference. In addition, labor force reentry contributed to the successful aging of many panelists. Both full-time and part-time return to work enhanced indicators of successful aging.

Thus, background, current, and retirement characteristics were all significant predictors of successful aging in retirement.

References

Atchley, R. C. Retirement and leisure participation: Continuity or crisis? *Gerontologist*, 11:13–17, 1971.

Atchley, R. C. *The social forces in later life: An introduction to social gerontology*. Belmont, Calif.: Wadsworth, 1972.

Atchley, R. C. *The sociology of retirement*. Cambridge, Mass.: Schenkman, 1976.

Busse, E. W. A physiological, psychological, and sociological study of aging. In E. B. Palmore (Ed.), *Normal aging*. Durham, N.C.: Duke University Press, 1970, 3–6.

Cavan, R. S., et al. *Personal adjustment in old age*. Chicago: Science Research Associates, 1949.

Cumming, E., and Henry, W. E. *Growing old*. New York: Basic Books, 1961.

Dean, L. R., McCaffrey, I., and Cassetta, R. The issue of successful aging. In E. Cumming and W. E. Henry, *Growing old*. Chapter 8. New York: Basic Books, 1961.

Havighurst, R. J. Successful aging. In R. H. Williams, C. Tibbits, and W. Donahue (Eds.), *Processes of aging*, Vol. I. New York: Atherton, 1963, 299–311.

Havighurst, R. J., and DeVries, A. Life style and free time activities of retired men. *Human Development*, 12:34–54, 1969.

Havighurst, R. J., Neugarten, B. L., and Tobin, S. S. Disengagement, personality and life satisfaction in the later years. In P. F. Hansen (Ed.), *Age with a future; Proceedings of the Sixth International Congress of Gerontology, Markaryd, Sweden, 1963*. Copenhagen: Munksgaard, 1964, 419–425.

Heyman, D. K., and Jeffers, F. C. The influence of race and socio-economic status upon the activities and attitudes of the aged. *Journal of Gerontology*, 19:225–229, 1964.

Hochschild, A. R. Disengagement theory: A critique and proposal. *American Sociological Review*, 40:553–569, 1975.

Jeffers, F. C., and Nichols, C. R. The relationship of activities and attitudes to physical well-being in older people. *Journal of Gerontology*, 16:67–70, 1961.

Maddox, G. L. Disengagement theory: A critical evaluation. *Gerontologist*, 4:40–42+, 1965a.

Maddox, G. L. Fact and artifact: Evidence bearing on disengagement theory from the Duke geriatrics project. *Human Development*, 8:117–130, 1965b.

Maddox, G. L. Persistence of life style among the elderly. *Proceedings, Seventh International Congress of Gerontology*, 1966, 309–311.

Maddox, G. L. Selected methodological issues. In E. B. Palmore (Ed.), *Normal aging*. Durham, N.C.: Duke University Press, 1970, 22–27.

Palmore, E. B. The effects of aging on activities and attitudes. *Gerontologist*, 8:259–263, 1968.

Palmore, E. B. When can age, period, and cohort be separated? *Social Forces*, 57:282–295, 1978.

Palmore, E. B. (Ed.), *Normal aging*. Durham, N.C.: Duke University Press, 1970.

Palmore, E. B. *Normal aging II*. Durham, N.C.: Duke University Press, 1974.

Parnes, H. S., and Nestel, G. The retirement experience. In Parnes et al., *Work and retirement data: A longitudinal study of men*. Chapter 6. Cambridge, Mass.: MIT Press, 1981.

Riley, M. W., et al. *Aging and society*, Vol. 3. New York: Russell Sage Foundation, 1972.

Rose, A. M. A current theoretical issue in social gerontology. *Gerontologist*, 4:45–50, 1964.

Rosow, I. *Socialization to old age*. Berkeley: University of California Press, 1974.

Simpson, I. H., Back, K. W., and McKinney, J. C. Continuity of work and retirement activity. In I. H. Simpson and J. C. McKinney (Eds.), *Social aspects of aging*. Durham, N.C.: Duke University Press, 1966, 106–119.

Effects of Retirement and Former Work Life on Women's Adaptation

Judith Huff Fox

Growing numbers of older women in the labor force and indications that women will be spending larger portions of their adult lives employed outside the home suggest that occupational retirement, once an experience primarily of males only, is becoming increasingly relevant to women as well.

Three major arguments may be cited to explain the lack of attention paid to women's retirement in the past. Each of them points to a need to rethink prevailing assumptions about the relationship between women and work.

1. For men, the work role is seen as a major source of self-identity. Their occupations occupy a major portion of their adult lives and are linked to the family roles of husband and father by their capacities as economic providers. The cessation of the work role, therefore, is thought to leave men's lives unstructured and their self-identities undermined (see for example, Cavan, 1962; Miller, 1965). For women, on the other hand, work is seen as a secondary role (Donahue et al., 1960; Palmore, 1965), with family roles assuming prominence in priority and salience. Cessation of work, therefore, would not affect their primary sources of self-identity.

Such a gender role distinction, however, does not take into account several characteristics of working women. First, only 57 percent of working women are married with spouses present; many of the rest are themselves heads of household (U.S. Bureau of the Census, 1973a, table 5). Work for these women is

Reprinted by permission from *Journal of Gerontology*, 32:196–202, 1977.

hardly a secondary activity. Second, women today have finished childbearing, on the average, by the age of thirty-one (U.S. Bureau of the Census, 1971); the secondary nature of work, therefore, may well be limited to a relatively restricted period of the life cycle, if limited at all. Third, for many middle-class women, work is a matter of individual preference. They may pursue work or careers precisely because their primary roles within the home are not personally fulfilling or they may work because they need the income. For women who choose to work, we might expect even greater adverse reaction to retirement than for men who never had the choice.

2. In addition to providing a sense of self-identity, men's occupations are seen to tie the individual to the larger social structure. Such perquisites of the work role as income and power locate men within a status hierarchy in their communities and in society. Being cut off from active participation in the work place upon retirement, men supposedly lose status in the eyes of society (Miller, 1965). Women, on the other hand, are assumed to derive their social status from their husbands, and their occupational retirement cannot be interpreted as status demeaning since they still perform their "primary" family roles. Despite the facts that many women are the only workers in their families and that as many as a third of married working wives exceed their husbands in occupational status (Haug, 1973), almost no attention has been paid to the wider effects of women's employment. For example, women who retire from occupations may be at a disadvantage in relation to those who have not been employed. While work itself is a tie to the larger community, employment may have necessitated the curtailment of other activities. Given the fact that working women usually continue to have primary responsibility for childcare and housekeeping, engagement in the work role may preclude extrafamilial social interaction. Booth (1972), for example, shows that working women participate in formal organizations less frequently than those who are not employed.

3. A third possible reason for the lack of female retirement studies is the problem of operationalizing occupational retirement for women. To retire, one has to have been employed, but for how long? and, especially important for women, how continuously? The answers to these questions are open to debate. The criteria most often used to classify male retirement status self-reporting of retirement—objective standards such as number of hours worked per week, and eligibility for pension or Social Security—all have problems associated with them, even for men. For example, is a career military man who begins another career at age forty or a man who says he is retired but is working part-time really retired?

The problem of defining women's retirement status is even more difficult because of the variety of career paths their work lives may take. While the distinction between "retired" and "working" (whatever the criteria used) covers almost all men, a third category of "never or rarely worked" must be included when one considers women. In addition, the effects among older women of occupational retirement must be separated from those attributable to their having been employed for much of their adult lives.

The few studies which have focused specifically on women's retirement do suggest that it is not necessarily a smooth, trouble-free transition. Atchley (1976), comparing men and women retired from schoolteaching or from a telephone company, found that women report taking longer to get used to retirement than do men and that women retirees are lonelier and more depressed than men. Jaslow (1976) demonstrated the persistence of a significant negative effect of retirement on morale among older females after controlling for differences between working and retired women in age, income, health, and physical incapacity.

The literature on male retirement has focused most heavily on two components of adaptation: that having to do with disruptions and continuities in social activities and that of reported psychological well-being (e.g., Atchley, 1976; Simpson and McKinney, 1966; Streib and Schneider, 1971; Thompson, 1973). The concept of "social and personal resources" has been employed to explain the ease or difficulty with which individuals are able to maintain a positive sense of well-being in retirement. For example, Stokes and Maddox (1967) hypothesize that higher-status individuals come to retirement with "relatively superior community involvement, interpersonal competence, personal . . . as well as financial resources . . . which should be related to successful aging in the long run." More generally, it is assumed that the more social and personal resources available to the male retiree, the wider number of options he has to choose from in order to develop and maintain a personally satisfying life-style. These options in turn facilitate maintenance of high morale in retirement (Loether, 1964; Shanas, 1972).

The following analysis will examine the effects of retirement and of having been employed for much of one's life on both the resources at the disposal of retired women and their reported sense of psychological well-being in relation to women who are still employed and those who have been housewives for most of their lives.

Method

Sample. The sample consists of 212 white, middle-class women interviewed in 1970–72 as participants in the Duke Second Longitudinal Study of Aging. Women who responded affirmatively to the interview question, "Are you retired from full-time work in your lifetime occupation?" were classified as "retirees"; those who responded negatively as "workers"; and those who said that they had been housewives most of their lives as "housewives." This classification yielded groupings of fifty-six retirees, eighty-seven workers, and sixty-nine housewives.

The mean age of the total sample is 60.7, although retirees are significantly older (mean age = 65.8; range from 51 to 72) than either the workers (mean age, 56.7; range 48 to 66) or housewives (mean age, 61.5; range 49 to 73). Retirees had been retired for an average of 5.96 years. Seventy percent of all the women in the sample were married with spouse present; half of the married respondents had husbands employed in professions or management. The women in this study were slightly better off financially and better educated and more likely to be currently married and to have held high status, nonmanual jobs than women in the United States as a whole (cf. U.S. Bureau of the Census, 1973b).

Measures

Retirement status. A self-report of retirement status was used as our index of retirement status. Such a measure does not control for length or continuity of work history but it does identify women who consider themselves "retirees" as opposed to merely having worked at some point in their lives. In fact, all but twenty of those who call themselves housewives had also worked outside their homes at some time during their adult lives.

Social and personal resources. Eight items were used to measure "social resources" and four to measure "personal resources." More precisely, four questions tapped the actual existence of social resources, or options, and four more indexed the utilization of social resources. Measures of social resources were the number of relatives within an hour's travel of the subject's residence (#Rel), the number of close friends in the area (#Frnd), the number of neighbors known (#Nbs), and a subjective judgment of the number of people talked to on an average day (GenCont). The first three variables have a possible range of 0–9; the fourth ranges from 1, "very few," to 9, "very many." The resource utilization variables included the average number of visits or telephone conversations per month with relatives, friends, and neighbors (ContRel, ContFrnd, and ContNbr, respectively, each with possible ranges of 0–9), and the average monthly attendance of nonreligious association meetings (FreqOrg, ranging from 0–9). The four "personal resources" refer to individual characteristics brought to retirement that are also considered to facilitate adaptation in old age. They were levels of education, graded in single years of schooling; total annual family income, an index ranging from 0–9; subjective assessment of health, ranging from 0, "very serious illness," to 9, "perfect health"; and marital status, where currently married women are coded 1 and widows, divorcees, and never-marrieds are coded 0. This latter classification, while it lumps together diverse elements of the "not currently married" category, is based on the assumption that having a spouse present in the home is an additional "resource." Preliminary analysis indicated no significant differences within this category on any of the major variables to be considered.

Psychological well-being. The Affect Balance Scale (Bradburn and Caplovitz, 1965) was used to measure psychological well-being. Respondents were asked to report the frequency in the past week with which they have had four "positive" and five "negative" feelings or mood states: "often," "several times," "once," or "not at all." Positive and negative responses were summed separately, and the score on the negative scale was subtracted from the score on the positive scale. A highly positive score thus indicates a preponderance of positive over negative feelings and a highly negative score indicates the reverse.

Results

Focusing first on the resources at the disposal of retirees, table D—34 presents group means for retirees, workers, and housewives on the eight social and four personal resources. In terms of "personal resources," although there is little difference in the educational attainments of the three groups, the retirees had significantly lower family incomes than either housewives or women who are still employed. In addition, retirees saw their health as significantly worse than did workers and slightly worse than housewives, and they were less likely to currently have spouses than the other groups. Among the "social resources," retirees had significantly fewer relatives in the Durham area and said that they talk to significantly fewer people on an average day than do women who were still in the labor force. On the other hand, they knew more of their neighbors and had slightly more close friends living locally than workers did. Retirees had significantly more contact with their neighbors and somewhat more contact with friends and relatives and they attended voluntary association meetings slightly more frequently than did workers.

It was suggested above that, compared to women who had not been in the

Table D—34. *Mean social and personal resources by retirement status.*

Resources	Retirees	Workers	Housewives
Personal resources			
Education	11.80	11.95	12.36
Income	4.42	6.73**	5.88**
Health	6.76	7.33*	7.10
Marital status	59.0[a]	72.0[a]	75.0[a]
Social resources			
# Rel	3.13	5.23**	3.17
# Nbr	4.96	4.28**	4.75
# Frnd	5.63	5.26	5.78
GenCont	4.16	5.42**	3.46*
ContRel	22.49	19.08	15.58
ContNbr	31.43	21.79*	26.74
ContFrnd	36.07	31.47	33.55
FreqOrg	2.04	1.61	3.12*
N	56	87	69

[a]Percentage currently married.

*Significantly differs from retirees at $p < .05$ level.

**Significantly differs from retirees at $p < .01$ level.

Table D—35. *Regression of affect balance on retirement status[a] and selected resources for retirees and workers, understandardized regression coefficients.*

Control variable	*B* (Retirement status net control variable)
	1.330[b]
Age	1.934**
Income	.593
Health	.824
Number of Rel	1.717**
GenCont	.744
Income and health	.273
Income, health, and GenCont	−.044

[a] Workers = 1, retirees = 0.

[b] Mean affect balance for workers is 3.437; for retirees, 2.107.

*$p < .05$.

labor force, retired women might have few nonwork social resources to draw upon. According to our data, however, this is not the case. Retirees say that they talk with significantly more people on an average day than do housewives, and there is almost no difference between these groups on the other social resources available to them. Although they attend voluntary association meetings less often than do housewives, retirees appear to utilize informal social resources somewhat more frequently. Far from being disadvantaged by having been employed for much of their lives, the retirees in our sample have social resources similar to those of women who have been housewives much of their lives. Despite greater age, poorer perceived health, and lower income, retirees appear somewhat more involved in informal visiting with friends and neighbors than do workers. Although the total number of people women report seeing on an average day may decrease following retirement (we of course have no way of knowing whether it is merely retirees' perception of decreased overall interaction or an actual decline in numbers), this figure remains higher than it does for those who have not worked.

Table D—35 indicates that women who are still employed have more positive affect balance than retirees. To test the hypothesis that differences between groups in social and personal resources explain differences in psychological well-being in old age, we entered each of the resources on which workers were higher than retirees (see table D—34) into regression equations along with a 0–1 dummy variable to control for employment status. In addition, we tested for effects of the age differences between groups. Results of this analysis show that differences in age between groups actually mask the extent of their differences on affect balance; a similar suppressor effect is found when #Rel is entered into the equation. However, workers' superior incomes, health status, and general level of social contact each independently account for some of the group differences on affect balance. When income and health are both controlled, the unstandardized regression coefficient (*B*) for workers is only .273 and, when GenCont is included as well, workers in fact have a slightly lower affect balance than retirees. Even avoiding the controversy over whether perceived poor health is more cause than effect of retirement, we may conclude that, for women in this sample, retirement negatively affects psychological well-being in that it reduces income and perceived general level of social contact.

Table D—35 indicates that retirees had significantly lower affect balance than housewives and that only income, among those resources on which housewives scored significantly higher, appreciably reduced these differences on affect balance, although *B* dropped to statistical nonsignificance when any of the control variables were included. Housewives continued to exhibit a higher proportion of positive to negative affect.

To explore the possibility that group differences in affect balance result from their having different sources of psychological well-being, Pearson product-moment correlations between the social and personal resources and affect balance are presented separately in table D—37 for each of the three groups. The retirees are the only group in which there is a positive correlation of affect balance with the number of friends one has, the number of neighbors known, and the amount of contact with each. In addition, retirees' correlation of affect balance with GenCont is highest of the three groups. For the working women, only one social resource, FreqOrg, is significantly associated with affect balance and, among housewives only GenCont, of the social resources, is a significant correlation.

When all of the significant zero-order correlates of affect balance for each group were entered simultaneously into stepwise free entry regression equations, it was found that, for retirees, four resources—ContNbr, GenCont, Education and #Frnd—made statistically significant independent contributions. For work-

Table D—36. *Regression of affect balance on retirement status[a] and selected resources for retirees and housewives, understandardized regression coefficients.*

Control variable	*B* (Retirement status net control variable)
	1.490[b]*
Age	1.246
Income	.861
FreqOrg	1.243

[a]Housewives = 1, retirees = 0.

[b]Mean affect balance for workers is 3.597; for retirees, 2.107.

$*p < .05$.

Table D—37. *Correlation between affect balance and social and personal resources for retirees, workers, and housewives.*

Resources	Retirees	Workers	Housewives
Education	.388**	.254*	.161
Income	.126	.146	.236**
Health	.306**	.297*	.185
Marital status	−.134	.094	.146
# Rel	−.147	−.166	−.054
# NBR	.391**	−.063	.177
# Frnd	.331**	.099	−.039
GenCont	.407**	.125	.293*
ContRel	−.064	−.199*	−.020
ContNbr	.368**	.114	−.010
ContFrnd	.329**	.016	−.065
FreqOrg	.266**	.250*	.023
N	56	87	69

*$p < .05$.

**$p < .01$.

ers, only health status had an independent effect on affect balance and, among housewives, GenCont was the only independently significant predictor.

For retirees, then, both specific kinds of informal social interaction and the overall level of social contact is of much more importance than it is for either workers or housewives. It is as if women who have left the workplace and its broad exposure to other people are attempting to make up for that loss by maintaining or developing interaction with friends and neighbors. In turn, such interaction is positively relayed to their balance of affect. Although housewives too depend on a high general level of social contact for maintenance of positive affect balance, they apparently do not rely specifically on neighbors and close friends or their organizational commitments.

Discussion

Our comparison of older women who report that they are retired to women still in the labor force and those who have been housewives much of their lives suggests that, while women may curtail their social involvement while they are working, they make up for this deficit after retirement by utilizing their social resources more. Retirement appears to lower feelings of psychological well-being by reducing income level and the overall number of people to whom women talk on an average day. Perception of poorer health also accounts for less positive affect balance among retirees. For women who have worked for much of their lives, extrafamilial social contact is more highly linked to positive affect balance than it is for housewives.

The hypothesis emerges that women who have spent a greal deal of their adult lives in the labor force may be more dependent on social contact outside the home than are women who have been housewives. While they are in the labor force, the job itself serves to satisfy the desire of women workers for such exposure, as suggested by the lack of correlation between extrawork social resources and affect balance among workers. Following retirement, such women turn to informal social activities with friends and neighbors. To the extent that women who have been housewives most of their lives are more dependent on interpersonal activities which occur within the home as sources of psychological well-being, they are less vulnerable than retirees to changes in their environment which affect level of nonhome centered social interaction. Thus, despite apparent increased informal social activity following retirement, formerly employed women may still not receive a sufficient amount of such contact to compensate for the shrinking of their social circles.

Our data support Atchley's general contention (1976) that women may have as much difficulty as or more difficulty than men in adapting to retirement. Our data suggest that, upon retirement, working women increase their engagement in formal friendship and neighbor roles.

This research both partly confirms and disagrees with Jaslow's (1976) conclusions. We are in agreement on the positive effects of health and income level on differences in psychological well-being between employed and retired women. However, our results differ from his evidence of a positive effect of former work experience on psychological well-being as compared with those with no work experience. These differences may be due to differences in either our well-being measures or our operationalizations of retirement status. Such discrepancies point to the need for further study and refinement of the concept of occupational retirement among women.

The research reported here has gone further than previous studies in explaining female worker/retiree differences in psychological well-being by the inclusion of our measure of the number of people talked to in an average day (GenCont). We have shown that retirement has real consequences for women in terms of reduction of income; general level of social contact; and, possibly, perception of health. It appears that the losses incurred by retirement have to do with what work has previously provided, i.e., social contact and income, as much as with intrinsic aspects of work itself. Had retirees severely missed intrinsic aspects of their jobs, we might expect worker/retiree differences in affect balance to persist. We have further indicated that retirees' less positive affect balance relative to housewives' may be due, in addition to differences in income, to the fact that retired women do not receive sufficient rewards from their present social contacts to compensate for the reduction of involvement since their working days. In effect, we are arguing from one end of the adult life-span what researchers who study "career-oriented" college women argue at the other: women for whom the occupational role was, or is intended to become, an integral part of their lives have different values, opinions, and interpersonal needs than others (cf., Almquist and Angrist, 1971; Gybers, 1968). Other investigators base their conclusions on the slightly greater likelihood of men to take up new employment following retirement and the small tendency for women to report less participation in organizations after retirement. Whether retired women in our sample attended meetings somewhat less and therefore sought employment or whether employment accustomed them to high levels of social involvement is an issue for life-span research beyond the scope of the present research. The retirees studied, however, are reminiscent of Rosow's (1967) "insatiables"—individuals who, even with relatively high levels of social contact in old age, desire still more.

Limitations of the present analysis, including the middle-class bias of the sample and the failure of certain "resources" to have any effect on psychological well-being among these women, indicate the direction which future research on women's retirement must address. Missing from this report is any exploration of occupational status or social class differences in adaptation within the group of retirees studied. Do women who have held professional jobs and have careers or are married to professional men bring superior social and personal resources to retirement and therefore adapt to their retirement role with greater ease than do former manual workers? Or do the demands of a professional career, coupled with presumably stronger commitment to work, leave the professional women without meaningful alternatives in retirement? Atchley's (1976) work suggests that the latter might be the case, although the author (1975) has found a positive relationship between status of former occupation and positive affect balance in retirement. Had we been able to control for type, length and continuity of work history, other differences among retirees might have emerged.

The fact that level of family income, among the "personal" resources studied here, and both number of local kin and amount of contact with them were unrelated to affect balance among retirees in this sample indicates a need for further specification of those "resources" which are important in the maintenance of high morale in old age. Similarly, the lack of a clear effect of marital status, as it is here defined, argues against a simple, monolithic relationship between "resources" and psychological well-being.

Finally, there is an obvious need for research on, and discussion of, what constitutes occupational retirement among women. Do those who call themselves retirees differ from women who do not in terms of the length of work history, its continuity, status of former job, or self-identification with work role? What objective criteria of retirement status would be most appropriate for women? Would eligibility for pension or social security exclude too many "retired" women from consideration?

The present research only begins to explore these issues concerning women's retirement. It does, however, record the impact of women's occupational histories on their social and psychological adaptation in later life. Occupational retirement has real consequences for women in terms of their social lives, and the fact of their having been employed distinguishes them from others in their experience of the aging process.

Summary

The sociological literature suggests that, for many women, the work role is a large and salient component of their adult lives. Retirement from that role may leave them with few nonwork-related social supports relative to women who have not been employed. Women's adaptation to retirement was investigated in terms of social and personal resources at their disposal and their reported sense of psychological well-being. Two hundred and twelve white, primarily middle-class women who were participants in the second longitudinal study were classified as "still working," "retired," or "housewives most of their lives" according to self-report. Mean age of the sample was sixty-one years. Results of analysis show that women who have worked much of their lives have no fewer social resources and, in fact, appear to be more socially involved than lifelong housewives. Compared to women still in the labor force, retirees have a lower perceived level of social contact but are more involved in informal interaction with friends and neighbors. The less positive balance of affect of retirees relative to workers is attributable to lower income, subjective health status, and perceived level of social contact. Only income differentials appear to explain the fact that the retirees' affect balance is significantly less positive than housewives'. Comparison of zero-order correlations between social involvement and affect balance for each of the three groups reveals that social contact is much more highly related to psychological well-being for retirees than for the others. The hypothesis is presented that retirees are more dependent on extrafamilial social contact than are housewives, and that failure to maintain a sufficient level of interaction accounts for the less positive affect balance of retirees.

References

Almquist, E., and Angrist, S. Role model influences on college women's career aspirations. *Merrill-Palmer Quarterly*, 17:273–279, 1971.

Atchley, R. Selected social and psychological differences between men and women in later life. *Journal of Gerontology*, 31:204–211, 1976.

Booth, A. Sex and social participation. *American Sociological Review*, 37:183–193, 1972.

Bradburn, N. M., and Caplovitz, D. *Reports on happiness*. Chicago: Aldine, 1965.

Cavan, R. Self and role in adjustment during old age. In A. M. Rose (Ed.), *Human behavior and social processes*. Boston: Houghton Mifflin, 1962.

Donahue, W., Orbach, H. L., and Pollak, O. Retirement: The emerging social pattern. In C. Tibbitts (Ed.), *Handbook of social gerontology*. Chicago: University of Chicago Press, 1960.

Fox, J. H. Women, work and retirement. Ph.D. diss., Duke University, 1975.

Gybers, M. C. Characteristics of homemaker- and career-oriented women. *Journal of Counseling Psychology*, 15:541–546, 1968.

Haug, M. Social class measurement and women's occupational roles. *Social Forces*, 52:85–97, 1973.

Jaslow, P. Employment, retirement, and morale among older women. *Journal of Gerontology*, 31:212–218, 1976.

Loether, H. J. The meaning of work and adjustment to retirement. In A. B. Shostak and W. Gomberg (Eds.), *Blue-collar world*. Englewood Cliffs, N.J.: Prentice-Hall, 1964.

Miller, S. J. The social dilemma of the aging leisure participant. In A. M. Rose and W. A. Peterson (Eds.), *Older people and their social world*. Philadelphia: F. A. Davis, 1965.

Palmore, E. B. Differences in the retirement patterns of men and women. *Gerontologist*, 5:4–8, 1965.

Palmore, E. B. (Ed.), *Normal aging II*. Durham, N.C.: Duke University Press, 1974.

Parsons, T. *Essays in sociological theory*. Glencoe, Ill.: Free Press, 1954.

Rosow, I. *Social integration of the aged*. New York: Free Press, 1967.

Shanas, E. Adjustment to retirement: Substitution or accommodation? In F. M. Carp (Ed.), *Retirement*. New York: Behavioral Publications, 1972.

Simpson, I. H., and McKinney, J. C. *Social aspects of aging*. Durham, N.C.: Duke University Press, 1966.

Stokes, R., and Maddox, G. L. Some social factors in retirement adaptation. *Journal of Gerontology*, 22:329–333, 1967.

Streib, G. F., and Schneider, C. *Retirement in American society*. Ithaca, N.Y.: Cornell University Press, 1971.

Thompson, G. Work vs. leisure roles: An investigation of morale among employed and retired men. *Journal of Gerontology*, 28:339–344, 1973.

U.S. Bureau of the Census. Population characteristics. *Current population reports*. P-20, #263. Washington, D.C.: U.S. Government Printing Office, 1971.

U.S. Bureau of the Census. Marital status. *1970 Census of the population*. Subject Report PC(2)-4C. Washington, D.C.: U.S. Government Printing Office, 1973a.

U.S. Bureau of the Census. Detailed characteristics of the U.S. *1970 Census of the population*. PC(1)DO1. Washington, D.C.: U.S. Government Printing Office, 1973b.

Aging and Voluntary Association Participation

Stephen J. Cutler

Social scientists in the pluralist tradition (e.g., Kornhauser, 1959; Rose, 1960) typically view voluntary associations from a functionalist perspective. According to this point of view, decision makers are more accessible to organized groups of individuals with salient interests than to uninvolved individuals. Associations, then, can promote the goals of their members, resist changes inimical to their members' interests, and heighten feelings of efficacy to the extent that goals are met. Associations are also said to reduce isolation by fostering social interaction and by striving to meet the socioemotional needs of their members. If these and a host of other functions (Amis and Stern, 1974; Taietz, 1976; Trela, 1976) may be seen as services or resources which benefit association participants, it is of some importance to understand differentials in who has access to such services and resources. Of primary interest in this paper is a facet of this

Reprinted by permission from *Journal of Gerontology*, 32:470–479, 1977.

question that has received relatively little empirical consideration: is aging, as is often thought, accompanied by decreasing membership and involvement in associations? As persons age, in other words, are voluntary association resources and services available to a lesser extent than at earlier stages of the life cycle because of declining participation?

Background

Cross-sectional analyses of age differences in voluntary association participation have consistently found curvilinear patterns. Both membership and involvement levels are relatively low for persons in their twenties, rise to a peak somewhere in the age range thirty-five to forty-four, and then show progressively lower levels for persons after age forty-five. The form of this relationship has led some (e.g., Hausknecht, 1962) to conclude that the observed age differences are attributable to age changes. These findings have also been taken as support for disengagement theory, a major postulate of which is that declining levels of social interaction and activity accompany aging at the later stages of the life cycle.

There are now, however, some data which call into question the inference that age differences in voluntary association participation reflect age changes. A number of studies (Bell and Force, 1956; Cutler, 1976; Foskett, 1955; Nie et al., 1974; Taietz and Larson, 1956; Verba and Nie, 1972) have recognized that association membership and involvement are related to socioeconomic status, that the socioeconomic levels of older persons are lower than those of other age groups, and that the curvilinear pattern may stem largely from these compositional differences in socioeconomic status rather than from age changes. When socioeconomic differences between age groups are controlled, the resulting pattern is generally one of relatively stable or increasing levels of membership and participation after age forty-five through at least ages seventy-five to eighty. Only toward the very late stages of the life cycle does the increasing prevalence of infirmities and mobility limitations begin to lower association activity levels appreciably.

Other studies yield additional evidence which contradicts the notion that voluntary association activity decreases after age forty-five. Videbeck and Knox (1965), for example, found very little change in a sample of persons fifty to sixty-nine years of age who were asked to compare their present levels of association participation with those five years earlier. Among retired teachers and retirees from a telephone company, Atchley (1976) found that the proportion reporting higher levels of present association participation compared to most of their adult life exceeded the proportion reporting lower levels. In a cohort analysis spanning seven years, Johnson (1975) also notes increasing proportions of older persons both belonging to one or more associations and belonging to several specific types of associations.

What is perhaps the best evidence to date on the nature of age changes in voluntary association participation is found in Babchuk and Booth's (1969) four-year longitudinal study of persons twenty-one to sixty-nine years of age. Among their major findings are the following: Sixty-one percent of the respondents forty to fifty-nine years of age had either a stable or increasing number of association memberships over the four-year period and only 28 percent had a net loss; among those sixty years of age and older, the majority (51 percent) again had a stable or increasing number of memberships and only 22 percent had fewer memberships after four years. Based on these and other results, Babchuk and Booth conclude that "membership remains stable over time," and that "the aged do not become disengaged from voluntary associations until they approach the age of seventy and, even after this age, many continue to remain affiliated." Similarly, Bell (1975) found no significant change in the mean number of hours spent per month in voluntary association activities during the year long interval between preretirement and postretirement interviews with a sample of nonwhite males fifty-three to seventy-two years of age.

The weight of these findings would seem to favor the interpretation that aging is not generally accompanied by declining levels of membership and activity in voluntary associations. However, the above review also indicates that direct, supporting evidence for this conclusion is not extensive. In the present study, therefore, longitudinal data on association participation levels are presented for a sample of persons ages forty-six to seventy who were followed over a four-year period and for a sample of persons sixty-five to ninety years of age who were followed over a two-and-a-half-year period. At least three advantages accrue from using the two samples: (1) a broader age range is available; (2) a more diverse, yet partially overlapping, set of association participation measures can be examined; and (3) the degree to which the results for each sample are comparable can be evaluated. In fact, both sets of findings are consistent in providing additional support for the conclusion that stability and continuity in levels of voluntary association participation accompany aging more often than declining levels of participation among middle age and elderly persons.

Samples

The first set of data comes from the Duke Second Longitudinal Study. At the start of the research in 1968, the panel consisted of 502 persons between the ages of forty-six and seventy. The subjects were randomly selected from a list, stratified by age and sex, of the members of the local health insurance association and are thus primarily representative of the middle and upper socioeconomic levels (for detailed information on the design of the adaptation study, see Palmore [1974]). The 374 respondents in the present analysis are those who participated in the study at rounds 1, 2, and 3 and on whom voluntary association participation data are available at all three times. Death accounted for approximately 29 percent of the 128 dropouts; illness accounted for about 17 percent; subjects who were too busy, had moved, or were unlocatable comprised an additional 25 percent; and the remaining 28 percent refused for other reasons (Rusin and Siegler, 1975). At round 1, the mean age of the 374 respondents was 58.4, 41 percent had completed one or more years beyond high school, 86 percent were married and living with their spouse, 46 percent had a total family income for the previous twelve months of over $10,000, and 48 percent were women.

The second set of data comes from a longitudinal study of older persons in Oberlin, Ohio. In fall 1970, interviews were conducted with a randomly selected sample of 170 noninstitutionalized persons age sixty-five and over. In spring 1973, 106 of the original respondents were reinterviewed. Among the sixty-four persons who did not participate in the study at round 2, the reasons for dropping out were distributed as follows: 23 percent refused to be interviewed, 22 percent could not be interviewed because of illness, 20 percent had moved from the community, 14 percent had died, 11 percent could not be contacted after several attempts, and 9 percent were residing in nursing homes at the time of the follow-up. At the initial interview, the mean age of the 106 respondents was 72.8 (range = 65–90), 42 percent were married and living with their spouse, 52 percent of the sample had completed one or more years of education beyond high school, 62 percent had an expected total family income for 1970 of under $4,000, 70 percent of the sample were women, and 80 percent were whites. After missing data are excluded, responses from 104 of the 106 respondents are examined in the analysis.

Variables

Several measures of voluntary association membership and participation are available. Following a question on the frequency of attendance at religious services, respondents in the Duke adaptation study were asked "How many times a month do you attend meetings of other groups such as clubs, unions, or associations?" Responses were coded 0 for those attending no meetings up through 9 for those who reported attending nine or more times per month. In the Oberlin surveys, there are three measures of membership and participation. First, respondents were read a list of sixteen types of associations and were asked to indicate "which of these kinds of organizations you belong to, if any?" For each type of association in which the respondent indicated membership, the second question asked "Would you say you are very involved in or not very involved in [that type of organization or club]?" From these two questions, summary indices were computed for the number of associations to which the respondent belonged and for the number of associations in which the respondent was very involved. For respondents indicating membership in one or more associations, a third item was asked to determine overall frequency of attendance: "All in all, how often do you attend meetings of (this/these) organization(s)?" Responses to this item were recorded along the following scale with scores ranging from 0 to 5: never, a few times a year or less, once a month, two or three times a month, once a week, or more than once a week.

From these basic variables, five measures of association membership and participation were developed for the analysis. Each of these will be described in detail in the following section.

Results

Findings from the Duke Adaptation Study

Extent of attendance. In the total sample of middle-aged persons in the Duke adaptation study, 57 percent reported attending one or more meetings of clubs, associations or unions per month at round 1, 61 percent at round 2, and 56 percent at round 3. While it is clear from these data that the majority of respondents were affiliated with and attended meetings of some association at any one round, the fact that persons shift from being nonattenders to being attenders and vice versa understates the total extent of attendance at some time during the study (cf. Babchuk and Booth, 1969). Thus, the data in the first row of table D—37 show the proportion of respondents who reported attending one or more meetings per month at one or more of the three measurement times. For the total sample, slightly more than three-fourths of the respondents were attending association meetings at least once a month at some point during the four-year period. This figure is somewhat greater for females than for males and is somewhat lower for older persons than for younger persons, findings which are in agreement with Booth (1972). Although lower socioeconomic groups are underrepresented in the Duke sample, when it is recalled that attendance is a more stringent criterion of association participation than mere membership and that this is generally an older sample, the 76 percent attendance figure compares favorably with the 84 percent figure reported by Babchuck and Booth (1969) for the proportion belonging to one or more associations at some point during the four-year period covered by their study.

Changes in attendance. The data presented above, however, do not bear directly on the issue of change in voluntary association participation. In order to address that question, four additional measures are presented in table D—38. The data in row 2 give the mean number of times per month respondents reported attending meetings of associations at rounds 1 and 3. With one exception, mean monthly attendance remained essentially stable over the four years. The only significant change is among those who are fifty-two to fifty-seven years of age whose mean monthly attendance has declined from 2.1 to 1.7 times per month ($p < .05$). Further analysis of the data (not presented here) showed that the decline within this age group was more pronounced among females than among males and was significant only for females. Because this decline coincides roughly with the onset of the "empty nest" period, at which point some of these women may have entered the labor force, it was thought that the competition of family, domestic, and occupational responsibilities for a limited time may have reduced freedom to participate in associations. Additional analysis provided little support for this hypothesis, however, as women fifty-two to fifty-seven years of age were less likely than women in the other three age groups to have entered the labor force during the four-year period. Similarly, the notion that this decline in association participation may have resulted from the disruptive effects of a higher occurrence of widowhood among women fifty-two to fifty-seven years of age was also not supported, given that the greatest proportion of women who became widows over the four-year period was among those fifty-eight to sixty-three years of age. Thus, it is still not clear why women fifty-two to fifty-seven years of age depart from the general pattern of stability in voluntary association attendance.

Although mean monthly attendance levels were fairly stable, there was a considerable amount of individual change. For the total sample, 24 percent of the respondents were attending more often at round 3 than at round 1, 29 percent were attending less often, and 16 percent were attending at neither time. However, because cross-sectional data have shown lower levels of participation after age forty-five and because disengagement theory would predict declining levels of social activity especially among older respondents, data will be presented on the proportion of respondents whose monthly association attendance at round 3 was the same as or higher than at round 1.

It should be noted that there are at least three ways to calculate this proportion. Consider a 10 × 10 table with round 1 monthly attendance (0–9) in the columns and round 3 monthly attendance (0–9) in the rows. The first method would consider those respondents falling in the diagonal cells as being at the same level of attendance, those below the diagonal as having higher levels of attendance at round 3, and those above the diagonal as having lower levels of attendance. By this method, 70 percent of the respondents in the total sample were attending at the same or higher levels after four years. However, it is misleading to say that 70 percent of the respondents were attending at the same frequency or more frequently, because a certain proportion of those included within the category of stable attendance were, in fact, not attending at both rounds 1 and 3. Moreover, because respondents who did not attend at round 1 can only be at the same or higher levels at round 3, this procedure is intrinsically biased against diengagement theory. (Although the same problem occurs among those at the highest attendance level at round 1—their frequency of attendance can stay the same or decrease, but it cannot increase—the actual effect is minimal because there are very few respondents at the highest attendance level.) An alternative method of calculating the proportion whose attendance levels remained the same or increased, which is biased in favor of disengagement theory, would be to exclude those who were nonattenders at round 1. The rationale for this procedure would be that respondents whose attendance levels cannot decrease are removed. By this method, 48 percent of the respondents have the same or higher attendance levels after four years. The difficulty with this method, however, is that by excluding persons who were nonattenders at round 1, a number of respondents whose attendance levels have increased from initial nonattendance to attendance one or more times a month at round 3 are also excluded. The third method, which will be used in this analysis, excludes those respondents who were nonattenders at both rounds 1 and 3. Because this procedure still includes those who were attending one or more times a month at either round 1 or round 3, it allows nonattenders at round 1 to show up as having higher attendance levels at round 3 and allows attenders at round 1 to be nonattenders at round 3. Furthermore, it would appear to be a more precise method in a substantive sense in that persons with the same frequency of attendance at rounds 1 and 3 are, in fact, attenders, thus avoiding a source of confusion in the first method.

From the data in row 3 of table D—38, it is evident that the proportion (57 percent) of respondents who were attending one or more association meetings per month at either round 1 or round 3 and who maintained or increased their frequency of association attendance exceeded the proportion who decreased their frequency of attendance (43 percent). The proportion with stable or increasing attendance is higher for females than for males, but it is especially interesting to

Table D—38. *Measures of voluntary association attendance over a four-year period.*

			Sex		Age			
		Total	Males	Females	46–51	52–57	58–63	64–70
1. Total % attending one or more times per month at T1 or T3:		76%	72%	80%	85%	74%	76%	69%
2. Mean monthly attendance:	T1	1.8	1.6	2.1	1.9	2.1	1.7	1.6
	T3	1.8	1.6	2.0	1.9	1.7	1.7	1.8
	p[a]	NS	NS	NS	NS	$p<.05$	NS	NS
(*N*: Rows 1–2)		(374)	(196)	(178)	(82)	(97)	(84)	(111)
3. % with stable or higher attendance among those attending one or more times per month at T1 or T3:		57%	54%	60%	59%	49%	53%	67%
(*N*)		(258)	(126)	(132)	(61)	(70)	(55)	(72)
4. % of those not attending at T1 who were still not attending at T3:		73%	71%	74%	57%	82%	92%	75%
(*N*)		(160)	(98)	(62)	(37)	(33)	(38)	(52)
5. % of those attending one or more times per month at T1 who were still attending one or more times per month at T3:		77%	69%	84%	76%	77%	72%	83%
(*N*)		(214)	(98)	(116)	(45)	(64)	(46)	(59)

Source: Duke application study.

[a]Two-tailed *t*-test for paired comparisons.

note that the highest proportion with stable or increasing attendance (67 percent) is found precisely among those respondents (i.e., the oldest) for whom disengagement theory would have predicted a preponderancy with declining attendance. Furthermore, for only one of the groups examined in the analysis—those fifty-two to fifty-seven years of age—does the proportion with stable or increasing attendance fall below 50 percent. Thus, these data provide no support for the notion that a pattern of declining association attendance predominates after age forty-five.

The extent to which continuity in previous participation levels prevails can be examined with two additional sets of findings. Among respondents who did not attend association meetings at the time of the first interview, the data in the fourth row of table D—37 give the proportion who were still nonattenders at round 3, while the data in row 5 show the proportion of those who attended one or more meetings per month at round 1 who still attended one or more meetings per month at round 3.

The major conclusion to be drawn from these results is that respondents tended to maintain their general association attendance levels over time. Close to three-fourths (73 percent) of the respondents who were not attending any association meetings at round 1 reported not attending any at round 3. Men and women did not differ greatly in this regard, although somewhat less continuity is in evidence for the youngest group of respondents. In no instance, however, does the proportion of initial nonattenders who continued to be nonattenders fall below one-half. Similarly, among those attending one or more times per month at round 1, 77 percent were still attending at least once a month at round 3. Women were more likely than men to attend continuously, and persons in the oldest age group were more likely to be continuous attenders than those in the other three age groups.

In sum, then, the data from the Duke adaptation study show that most (76 percent) of the respondents attended association meetings once a month or more at some time over the four-year period; that aggregate levels of attendance have for the most part remained the same; that the proportion attending as often or more often at round 3 as compared to round 1 exceeded the proportion with declining attendance levels; that most of those (73 percent) not attending initially did not attend later; and that most of those (77 percent) attending one or more times per month at the first interview were attending at the same level at the time of the third interview.

Because the Duke data contain only one measure of association participation and because the sample is comprised mainly of middle-aged persons, it would be desirable to compare the findings discussed above with results based on other measures of voluntary association participation and to test the assumptions of disengagement theory with longitudinal data on older persons. Thus, we turn to a similar analysis using data from the Oberlin longitudinal survey.

Findings from the Oberlin Longitudinal Survey

Extent of participation. The data in row 1 of table D—39 show that the great majority (87 percent) of the persons sixty-five years of age and older in the Oberlin sample reported belonging to one or more associations at one of the two measurement times and that there were no appreciable differences by sex or by age. Not only did most of the respondents belong to at least one voluntary association, but most (69 percent) reported being very involved in one or more associations (row 2, table D—38). Females were more likely than males to report being very involved, and persons sixty-five to seventy-two years of age were slightly more likely than respondents seventy-three and over to be very involved in one or more associations (cf., Booth, 1972). Furthermore, 74 percent of the total sample attended association meetings once a month or more frequently at one of the two measurement times (row 3, table D—39). Again, females were more likely than males to be frequent attenders, although the difference by age was slight. Therefore, voluntary association participation was also widespread for the respondents in this sample.

Changes in participation. Contrary to what one would expect based on hypotheses derived from disengagement theory, the findings presented in rows 4, 5, and 6 of table D—39 show considerable stability in mean levels of voluntary association participation. For all respondents categories, the mean number of association memberships increased slightly over the two-and-a-half-year period, although none of the changes was of sufficient magnitude to be statistically significant. The mean number of associations in which respondents were very involved also increased slightly but not significantly. Finally, on the six-point frequency of attendance scale, the mean scores show increases over the period of the study, although in no instance were the changes significant.

As with the findings from the Duke adaptation study, a good deal of individual change is masked by these aggregate level data. In regard to the number of voluntary association memberships, for example, 27 percent of the respondents belonged to fewer associations at round 2 than at round 1, 40 percent belonged to more, 20 percent belonged to the same number, and 13 percent belonged to none at both times. Again, because disengagement theory would lead us to expect declining levels of participation, data are presented in terms of the proportion of participants at round 1 or round 2 whose participation levels have remained constant or increased over the two-and-a-half-year period. From this perspective, it is evident from the data in rows 7, 8, and 9 of table D—39 that respondents who have either maintained or increased their levels of voluntary association participation outnumber those with declining levels on all measures and for all sex and age groups. While there is some variability between males and females and between those sixty-five to seventy-two and those seventy-three years of age and older across the three measures, in no instance do the proportions with stable or increasing levels of participation fall below 50 percent. In fact, over half are above 67 percent, which indicates that the proportion of respondents with stable

Table D—39. *Measures of voluntary association participation over a two-and-a-half-year period.*

			Sex		Age	
		Total	Males	Females	52–57	58–63
1. Total % belonging to one or more associations at T1 or T2:		87%	84%	88%	86%	87%
2. Total % very involved in one or more associations at T1 or T2:		69%	44%	79%	70%	66%
3. Total % attending once a month or more often at T1 or T2:		74%	58%	81%	75%	72%
4. Mean number of memberships[a]:	T1	2.5	2.0	2.6	2.5	2.4
	T2	2.7	2.5	2.8	2.8	2.6
5. Mean number of associations in which very involved[a]:	T1	1.0	.5	1.2	1.0	1.0
	T2	1.2	.7	1.4	1.3	1.1
6. Mean attendance score[a]:	T1	2.2	1.4	2.5	2.3	2.1
	T2	2.5	1.9	2.7	2.5	2.4
(*N*: rows 1–6)		(104)	(32)	(72)	(57)	(47)
7. % with stable or more memberships among those belonging to one or more associations at T1 or T2:		69%	78%	66%	63%	76%
(*N*)		(91)	(27)	(64)	(49)	(42)
8. % involved in the same or more associations among those very involved in one or more at T1 or T2:		64%	64%	64%	68%	58%
(*N*)		(72)	(58)	(14)	(40)	(32)
9. % with stable or more frequent attendance among those ever attending at T1 or T2:		70%	74%	68%	65%	75%
(*N*)		(86)	(23)	(63)	(49)	(37)
10. % of those not belonging at T1 who still did not belong at T2:		61%	63%	60%	57%	67%
(*N*)		(22)	(8)	(14)	(13)	(9)
11. % of those not very involved in any at T1 who were still not involved in any at T2:		64%	78%	52%	65%	64%
(*N*)		(51)	(23)	(28)	(26)	(25)
12. % attending less than once a month at T1 who still attended less than once a month at T2:		61%	65%	58%	58%	68%
(*N*)		(44)	(20)	(24)	(24)	(20)
13. % belonging to one or more associations at T1 who still belonged to one or more at T2:		98%	100%	97%	98%	97%
(*N*)		(82)	(24)	(58)	(44)	(38)

Table D—39. *(Continued)*

	Total	Sex Males	Females	Age 52–57	58–63
14. % very involved in one or more associations at T1 who were still involved in one or more at T2:	75%	67%	77%	77%	73%
(*N*)	(53)	(9)	(44)	(31)	(22)
15. % attending one or more times per month at T1 who still attended as frequently at T2:	85%	75%	88%	82%	89%
(*N*)	(60)	(12)	(48)	(33)	(27)

Source: Oberlin longitudinal survey.

[a]None of the T2–T1 differences is significant by the two-tailed *t*-test for paired comparisons.

or increasing participation levels is more than twice as great as the proportion with declining levels.

The final two measures bear more directly on the question of continuity. Rows 10, 11, and 12 of table D—39 present data on the proportion of respondents with low association participation levels at round 1 who still had low participation levels at round 2. Thus, 61 percent of the respondents who did not belong to any associations at the time of the initial interview still belonged to none at the time of the second interview (see row 10). While males and females did not differ greatly in this regard, the older respondents were more persistent in their nonmembership than the younger respondents. Similarly, 64 percent of those who were not very involved in any association at the time of the first interview remained uninvolved at the time of the second interview, although males were more likely than females to stay uninvolved (see row 11). Again, a majority (61 percent) of the respondents who attended less than once a month at round 1 were also attending at this level at round 2 (see row 12). On this measure, both males and the older respondents were more likely than females and the younger respondents to persist in their low attendance levels.

Finally, nearly all (98 percent) of the respondents who belonged to one or more associations initially reported belonging to one or more at round 2 (row 13, table D—38), 75 percent of those who were very involved in one or more associations at the initial interview reported being very involved in one or more after two and a half-years (row 14), and 85 percent of those who were attending once a month or more frequently at round 1 were still attending as frequently at round 2 (row 15). Females tended to maintain their involvement and attendance levels to a greater extent than males, although the age differences are similar and more variable.

Summary and Discussion

The results of this analysis have several theoretical, methodological, and substantive implications. First, one of the enduring debates in the sociological literature has been over the question of the extent of voluntary association participation among American adults. While the results of some studies (e.g., Wright and Hyman, 1958) have been used to refute Tocqueville's observation that America is a "nation of joiners," other findings have been taken as evidence supporting that contention (e.g., Babchuk and Booth, 1969). The results of this study clearly support the latter position. Although both of the samples used in the analysis are above average in their socioeconomic composition, which tends to lead to higher levels of voluntary association participation, it must also be recalled that cross-sectional data have consistently shown lower levels of membership and involvement among those forty-five years of age and older compared to persons between the ages of thirty and forty-four. That 76 percent of the Duke sample had attended association meetings at least once a month at some point during the four-year period, that 87 percent of the Oberlin respondents belonged to at least one association, that 69 percent reported being very involved in one or more associations, and that 74 percent were attending meetings at least once a month at one or both of the measurement times are compelling indications that voluntary association membership and participation are widespread.

Second, these findings may be taken as one more illustration of the fallacious interpretations that can be drawn when cross-sectional data are used to make conclusions about aging. When middle-aged and older persons are used as their own controls and followed over time, there is no support for the position that decreasing levels of association participation are the norm. Rather, these findings give further, indirect, support to the conclusion that the lower levels of voluntary association membership and participation among older adults compared to younger adults are probably largely attributable to socioeconomic compositional differences between the age groups (Cutler, 1976).

Third, these results provide no support for disengagement theory as a general characterization of aging. The modal pattern is not withdrawal from or declining levels of social activity and interaction but one of continuity and stability. That previous life-styles and participation levels are carried through time is perhaps best indicated by the findings that the majority of members and participants maintained their membership and participation levels while the nonmembers and nonparticipants did likewise. These data, in other words, provide additional evidence for the position that behavior patterns in middle and old age cannot be considered in isolation from those existing at earlier stages of the life cycle (Maas and Kuypers, 1974; Maddox, 1970; Palmore, 1970; Videbeck and Knox, 1965).

However, one possible qualification to the conclusions presented above relates to the general issue of how dropouts differ from continuing panelists.

Would the conclusions have differed if data on association participation rates were available for the dropouts? Put another way, can continued involvement in a longitudinal study itself be construed as a measure of participation such that the dropouts may be those who have also disengaged in other spheres of participation? Several bits of evidence bearing on this issue can be presented, although none provides definitive answers.

Compared with the dropouts, the continuing panelists in the Duke study differ significantly in the following ways: they are younger, have higher levels of educational attainment and income, are more likely to be employed, perceive their health to be better, and report spending less time in bed during the previous year because of illness or health conditions. Differences in marital status are not significant. The continuing panelists in the Oberlin study differ from the dropouts in that they are significantly more likely to be married, to report their health as excellent or good, and to be younger. Differences on education, income, and employment status are not significant. However, in neither study are there significant differences between the continuing panelists and the dropouts on any of the round 1 measures of voluntary association participation. Thus, the round 1 levels of association involvement do not appear to be inflated as a result of exclusion of the dropouts from the analysis.

Still, it might be argued that nonresponse at the later rounds owing to reasons such as institutionalization and illness would be accompanied by decreasing levels of voluntary association participation. The high levels of participation and continuity disclosed in the analysis, therefore, may stem to some extent from the continuing panelists being an engaged elite. While this assertion is undoubtedly valid, it is also probable that these effects are offset to an unknowable degree by stable or increasing association participation among dropouts who were unlocatable, who had moved to a different community, who were too busy to be interviewed, or whose refusal is unrelated to declining levels of participation. Whether these various effects cancel out one another is indeterminable for the data available but, as should be clear from this discussion, the general issue warrants consideration in assessing the findings and conclusion of the study.

Finally, although overall continuity in levels of voluntary association participation does seem to prevail among the continuing panelists in the two studies, it should be reiterated that changing participation levels characterized the majority of respondents in both samples. Some of these changes may have stemmed from errors in reporting and recording. Others may be attributable to the disappearance or emergence of organizations. Still other changes may result from any number of transitional situations in the life course of the respondents. Retirement may be associated with withdrawal from occupation related associations and subsequent participation in other types of associations. Changes in health, in economic status, in marital status, in residence, and in access to transportation may also be related to individual variability in participation levels over time. Thus, while this analysis has been primarily concerned with determining whether declining levels of voluntary association participation accompany aging, additional research is needed to examine the factors related to individual changes in participation levels.

References

Amis, W. D., and Stern, S. E. A critical examination of theory and functions of voluntary associations. *Journal of Voluntary Action Research*, 3:91–99, 1974.

Atchely, R. C. Selected social and psychological differences between men and women in later life. *Journal of Gerontology*, 31:204–211, 1976.

Babchuk, N., and Booth, A. Voluntary association membership: A longitudinal analysis. *American Sociological Review*, 34:31–45, 1969.

Bell, B. D. The limitations of crisis theory as an explanatory mechanism in social gerontology. *International Journal of Aging and Human Development*, 6:153–168, 1975.

Bell, W., and Force, M. Urban neighborhood types and participation in formal association. *American Sociological Review*, 21:25–34, 1956.

Booth, A. Sex and social participation. *American Sociological Review*, 37:183–192, 1972.

Cutler, S. J. Age differences in voluntary association memberships. *Social Forces*, 55:43–58, 1976.

Foskett, J. M. Social structure and social participation. *American Sociological Review*, 20:431–438, 1955.

Hausknecht, M. *The joiners*. New York: Bedminster Press, 1962.

Johnson, M. Voluntary affiliation: Changing age patterns? (Abstract). *Annual Proceedings of the American Sociological Association*, 1975, 209–210.

Kornhauser, W. *The politics of mass society*. Glencoe, Ill.: Free Press, 1959.

Maas, H. S., and Kuypers, J. A. *From thirty to seventy*. San Francisco: Jossey-Bass, 1974.

Maddox, G. L. Persistence of life style among the elderly. In E. B. Palmore (Ed.), *Normal aging*. Durham, N.C.: Duke University Press, 1970.

Nie, N. H., Verba, S., and Kim, J. Political participation and the life cycle. *Comparative Politics*, 6:319–340, 1974.

Palmore, E. B. The effects of aging on activities and attitudes. In E. B. Palmore (Ed.), *Normal aging*. Durham, N.C.: Duke University Press, 1970.

Palmore, E. B. Design of the adaptation study. In E. B. Palmore (Ed.), *Normal aging II*. Durham, N.C.: Duke University Press, 1974.

Rose, A. M. The impact of aging on voluntary associations. In C. Tibbetts (Ed.), *Handbook of social gerontology*. Chicago: University of Chicago Press, 1960.

Rusin, M. J., and Siegler, I. C. Personality differences between participants and drop-outs in a longitudinal aging study. (Abstract.) *Gerontologist*, (no. 5, pt. 2), 15: (no. 5, pt. 2), p. 55. 1975.

Taietz, P. Two conceptual models of the senior center. *Journal of Gerontology*, 31:219–222, 1976.

Taietz, P., and Larson, O. F. Social participation and old age. *Rural Sociology*, 21:229–238, 1956.

Trela, J. E. Social class and association membership: An analysis of age-graded and non-age-graded voluntary participation. *Journal of Gerontology*, 31:198–203, 1976.

Verba, S., and Nie, N. H. *Participation in America: Political democracy and social equality*. New York: Harper & Row, 1972.

Videbeck, R., and Knox, A. B. Alternative participatory responses to aging. In A. M. Rose and W. A. Peterson (Eds.), *Older people and their social world*. Philadelphia: F. A. Davis, 1965.

Wright, C. R., and Hyman, H. H. Voluntary association memberships of American adults: Evidence from national sample surveys. *American Sociological Review*, 23:284–294, 1958.

Religion and Aging

Dan Blazer and Erdman B. Palmore

Religion is thought to become increasingly important with the onset of late life and the inevitable approach of death. For instance, a conversation was overheard between two children. The first asked, "Why is Grandma spending so much time reading the Bible these days?" "I guess she is cramming for final exams," the second replied. This exemplifies the stereotyped view that the primary concern of the elderly in our society is religion and preparation for death. Mathiasen (1955) has asserted that religion is "the key to a happy life in old age. A sense of the all-encompassing love of God is the basic emotional security and firm spiritual foundation for people who face the end of life."

Investigators who have studied religious activity and attitudes of the elderly have been limited to cross-sectional analysis (Havighurst, 1953; Orbach, 1961) with the exception of two limited longitudinal studies (Streib, 1965; Wingrove, 1971). The general impression from the existing literature is that church attendance is generally at a high level among men and women in their sixties, but it becomes less regular in advanced old age (Riley and Foner, 1968). On the other hand, Orbach (1961) found no consistent age trends in church attendance when he controlled for other related factors. Private religious activities (devotional practices) have been shown to be greater in older age categories in one denomination (Fukuyama, 1961) and, again in cross-sectional analysis, such activities as Bible reading and prayer are reported in a greater percentage of the elderly than in younger age groups (Erskine, 1965). One study indicates that these private activities increase with advancing age (Cavan et al., 1949). There have been no longitudinal studies over an extended period of time to substantiate these conclusions. The cross-sectional differences by age groups may be due to waning religious activities in younger cohorts rather than to increasing activities with older age.

The general hypothesis that churchgoing and religious interests are significantly correlated with old age adjustment is stated by many authors (Barron, 1958; Mathiasen, 1955; Moberg, 1970). Edwards and Klemmach (1973), Scott (1955), Shanas (1962), and Spreitzer and Snyder (1974) have shown a significant correlation between life satisfaction and church attendance and church-related activities. On the other hand, Havighurst and Albrecht (1953) found little relationship between professed attitudes toward religion and personal adjustment.

The Duke First Longitudinal Study of Aging provides the first opportunity to examine the amount and patterns of decline or increase in religious activities and attitudes over time. The purpose of this paper is to analyze these patterns and

Reprinted by permission from *Gerontologist*, 16:82–85, 1976.

to examine the correlates of religion with happiness, usefulness, personal adjustment, and longevity.

Longitudinal Study of Aging

The data examined in this study were collected as a part of the First Longitudinal Study of Aging at Duke University (Palmore, 1970, 1974). Survivors have been followed for nine rounds of examinations over the past twenty years. Ninety percent were Protestant and 94 percent said they were church members. This is a somewhat higher proportion than the 78 percent of all persons in the United States over age fifty who reported that they are members of a church (Erskine, 1964).

The Chicago Inventory of Activities and Attitudes has been administered in each of the nine rounds to date (Burgess et al., 1948). The religion subscale of the activity inventory, which includes measures of church attendance, listening to church services on radio and TV, and reading the Bible and/or devotional books, was used as an indicator of religious activity at a given point in time. Data were coded on a 0–10 scale (10 indicating the highest level of religious activity). The religion subscale of the attitude inventory, which is based on agreement or disagreement with such statements as "religion is a great comfort," and "religion is the most important thing to me," was used as a rating of positive religious attitudes at a given point in time and was coded on a 0–6 scale, 6 indicating the most positive religious attitude.

The "happiness" and "usefulness" subscales of the attitude inventory were examined for correlations with the religion subscales. The Cavan Adjustment Scale, a rating of social and emotional adjustment by the interviewing social worker, was used as a measure of personal adjustment (Cavan et al., 1949). A longevity quotient (LQ) was also tabulated for each panelist, which controls for the effects of age, race, and sex (Palmore, 1974). The LQ is the observed number of years survived after initial examination divided by the actuarially expected number of years to be survived after examination based on the person's age, sex, and race. For those who were still living (about one-fifth of the panel), an estimate was made of how many years they will have lived since initial testing, by adding the present number of years survived since initial testing to the expected number of years now remaining according to actuarial tables.

Religious activity and religious attitude were then correlated with happiness, usefulness, personal adjustment, and longevity. Controls were also introduced for sex, age, and occupation. These correlations were computed for rounds 1 and 7 to see if the relationships changed as the panel aged.

Some questions which were asked only in round 1 were also analyzed. These included questions concerning religious activity at age twelve, amount and type of prayer life, frequency of church attendance, frequency of listening to religious programs on radio and TV, and frequency of Bible and devotional reading.

Frequency of Religious Activity

Religious activities were relatively frequent in this sample compared to national samples of persons over sixty-five. For example, 61 percent of our sample reported in round 1 that they attended church at least once a week compared to only 37 percent of a national sample (*Catholic Digest*, 1953). In addition, 59 percent listened to religious programs on radio or TV at least once a week, and 79 percent read the Bible or a devotional book at least once a week. Also, 43 percent reported that they prayed at a regular time during the day and 31 percent said that they "prayed continuously during the day," whereas only 3 percent said they did not pray at all.

Background Factors

The women were significantly more religious than men in activities (about .7 higher on the religious activity subscale, *t*-test significant at .02 level), and in attitudes (about .3 higher on the religious attitudes subscale, *t*-test significant at .05 level). This supports the general finding that women tend to be more religious than men (Orbach, 1961; Riley and Foner, 1968).

Persons from nonmanual occupations also tended to be more active in religion than those from manual occupations. The nonmanual group had a mean religious activity score of 7.2 compared to 6.1 for the manual group (*t*-test significant at .01 level). The mean religious attitude score for nonmanual group was 5.7 compared to 5.1 for the manual group (*t*-test significant at the .001 level).

However, church attendance at age twelve had no significant relationship to present church attendance. This is contrary to the idea that childhood training determines religious practices for the rest of life. Substantial proportions of those who attended church regularly as a child now attend rarely. There was a general decline in church attendance from age twelve; 80 percent attended once a week or more at age twelve compared to 61 percent at round 1.

Changes Over Time

In order to analyze change over time in religious activities and attitudes, we plotted for the survivors to that round the differences in mean scores between each round and the initial round. Thus, these differences represent true longitudinal changes and cannot be attributed to attrition in the sample, because each comparison between the initial and later round is based on the scores of the same persons in the initial and later rounds. These analyses were also controlled for sex, socioeconomic status, and age. Religious activity did show a gradual but definite decrease over time (figure D—5). This decrease from round 1 was significant at the .02 level in rounds 3, 5, 6, 7, 8, and 9. The decrease became steadily greater after round 5 (about ten years after round 1). Religious activity among females remained significantly higher than that for males over time but

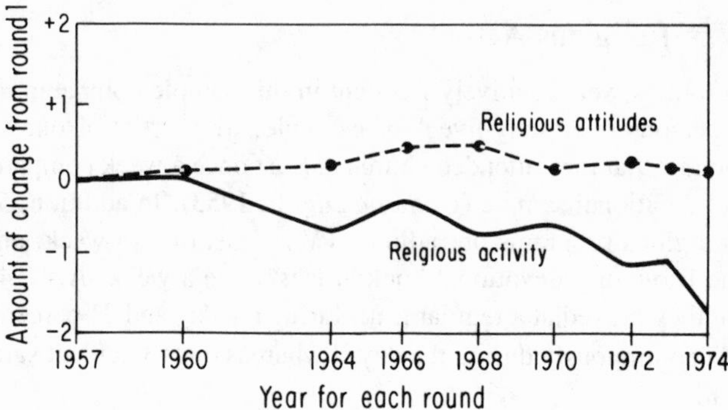

Figure D—5. *Religious attitudes and activity over time.*

declined in a similar manner. There was a greater decrease in religious activities among persons from nonmanual occupations than those from manual occupations, perhaps because those from nonmanual occupations started from a higher level of religious activity. There was also more decline among those over age seventy at round 1, probably because of a greater decline in health, vision, and hearing.

In contrast, average religious attitudes remained quite stable over time, with almost identical levels at the early and the last rounds (figure D—5). There was a slight, but temporary, increase in positive religious attitudes during the middle rounds (1964–68). When separated for age, sex, and manual versus nonmanual, no significant variation from this stable pattern was noted. Thus it appears that, when measured longitudinally, religious activities tend to gradually decline in late old age, but religious attitudes and satisfactions tend to remain fairly level, neither increasing nor decreasing substantially.

Correlates

Because our earlier analysis of longevity (Palmore, 1971) had found significant correlations between total activity and the longevity quotient ($r = .15$) as well as between total attitudes and the longevity quotient ($r = .26$), we expected that there would be substantial correlations of religious activities and attitudes with the longevity quotient. These expectations were contradicted by the data. There was almost no correlation between religious activities and the longevity quotient ($r = .01$) or between religious attitudes and longevity ($r = -.06$). Thus, in this sample, religion was clearly unrelated to a longer life.

On the other hand, many of the correlations of religious attitudes and activities with happiness, feelings of usefulness, and personal adjustment were significant (.01 level) and moderately strong, as expected. Religious attitudes were not significantly related to happiness, but they were significantly related to feelings of usefulness ($r = .16$), especially among those from manual occupations

(r = .24). Religious attitudes also had a small correlation with adjustment (r = .13), which reached significance among those from nonmanual occupations (r = .24).

Religious activities generally had even stronger relationships to happiness, usefulness, and adjustment. Religious activities were significantly related to happiness (r = .16), especially among men (r = .26), and persons over age seventy at round 1 (r = .25). Religious activities were most strongly related to feelings of usefulness (r = .25), especially among those from manual occupations (r = .34), and those over age seventy (r = .32). Similarly, religious activities were significantly related to personal adjustment (r = .16), especially among those from manual occupations (r = .33) and among males (r = .28). These stronger correlations between religious activities and various measures of adjustment, compared to religious attitudes and adjustment, suggest that religious behavior was more important than attitudes in influencing adjustment.

The fact that these correlations were generally higher among the older persons is similar to the fact that the correlations tended to increase between rounds 1 and 7. These facts support the theory that religion tends to become increasingly important in the adjustment of older persons as they age, despite the decline in religious activities such as church attendance.

Importance of Religion

In this Bible Belt community, most of the elderly who were studied reported relatively high levels of religious activity and positive attitudes toward religion. Women and persons from nonmanual occupations tended to be more religious in activity and attitudes. There was a general shift from more church attendance in childhood to less in old age. Part of this shift may reflect the general shift toward less church attendance in our society over the past half century.

Longitudinal analysis over a period of eighteen years showed that positive religious attitudes remained stable despite a general decline in religious activities. This supports the cross-sectional findings of decline in religious activities in old age but contradicts the theory of increasing interest in religion among aging persons.

There was no correlation of religious activity or attitude with longevity, but they were correlated with happiness, feelings of usefulness, and personal adjustment, especially among men, those from manual occupations, and those over seventy. It was also observed that these correlations tended to increase over time. The greater correlations at older ages and in later rounds support the theory that religion becomes increasingly important for personal adjustment in the later years.

The stronger correlations between religious activities and various measures of adjustment, compared to the correlations between religious attitudes and adjustment, suggest that religious behavior was more important than attitudes. When interpreting these results, several cautions should be borne in mind: the sample was composed of volunteers from a limited area, those who respond positively on one item tend to respond positively on others, correlation does not prove causation, etc. Nevertheless, limited as they are, these findings do support the theory that, despite declines in religious activities, religion plays a significant and increasingly important role in the personal adjustment of many older persons. One implication is that churches need to give special attention to their elderly members in order to compensate for their generally declining religious activities and to maximize the benefits of their religious experience.

References

Barron, M. L. The role of religion and religious institutions in creating the milieu of older people. In D. L. Scudder (Ed.), *Organized religion and the older person*. Gainesville: University of Florida Press, 1958.

Burgess, E. W., Cavan, R. S., and Havighurst, R. J. *Your attitude and activities*. Chicago: Science Research Associates, 1948.

Catholic Digest. How important religion is to Americans. 17:7–12, 1953.

Cavan, R. S., et al. *Personal adjustment in old age*. Chicago: Science Research Associates, 1949.

Edwards, J. N., and Klemmach, D. L. Correlates of life satisfaction: A reexamination. *Journal of Gerontology*, 28:497–502, 1973.

Erskine, H. G. The polls. *Public Opinion Quarterly*, 29:679, 1964; 29:154, 1965.

Fukuyama, Y. The major dimensions of church membership. *Review of Religious Research*, 2:154–161, 1961.

Havighurst, R. J., and Albrecht, R. *Older people*. New York: Longmans, 1953.

Mathiasen, G. The role of religion in the lives of older people. In Governor's Conference on Problems of the Aging, Albany, 1955. *Charter for the aging*. Albany, New York, 1956.

Moberg, D. O. Religion in the later years. In A. M. Hoffman (Ed.), *The daily needs and interests of older people*. Springfield, Ill.: Charles C. Thomas, 1970.

Orbach, H. L. Age and religion: A study of church attendance in the Detroit metropolitan area. *Geriatrics*, 16:530–540, 1961.

Palmore, E. B. *Normal aging*. Durham, N.C.: Duke University Press, 1970.

Palmore, E. B. The relative importance of social factors in predicting longevity. In E. B. Palmore and F. Jeffers (Eds.), *Prediction of life-span*. Lexington, Mass.: Heath Lexington Books, 1971.

Palmore, E. B. *Normal aging II*. Durham, N.C.: Duke University Press, 1974.

Riley, M. W., and Foner, A. *Aging and society*. New York: Russell Sage Foundation, 1968.

Scott, F. G. Factors in the personal adjustment of institutionalized and noninstitutionalized aged. *American Sociological Review*, 20:538–540, 1955.

Shanas, E. The personal adjustment of recipients of old age assistance. In R. M. Gray and D. O. Moberg (Eds.), *The church and the older person*. Grand Rapids, Mich.: Eerdmans, 1962.

Spreitzer, E., and Snyder, E. E. Correlates of life satisfaction among the aged. *Journal of Gerontology*, 29:454–458, 1974.

Streib, G. *Longitudinal study of retirement*. Final Report. Washington, D.C.: U.S. Social Security Administration, 1965.

Wingrove, C. R., and Alston, J. P. Age, aging and church attendance. *Gerontologist*, 11:356–358, 1971.

Activity and Happiness among Aged Blacks

Jacquelyne Jackson

Unfortunately, almost no longitudinal data about predictors of life satisfaction or satisfactory adjustment to old age are available for black men and women. However, the Duke data do permit the description of a black sample and some limited inferences. Table D—40 contains some background data by sex about the blacks in round 1 in the Duke First Longitudinal Study. Those data were collected between 1955 and 1961.

Characteristics of Older Blacks

Few sex differences are found among the variables reported in table D—40. The women, significantly younger than the men in the subsample, were less likely to have a living spouse. There were more men than women at the extremes of the educational distribution; men were more likely to have a college education, women to have less than a high school education. Tobacco use was also more common among the men. Marital status differed by sex, with women more likely to be never-married, separated, or widowed. Women reported themselves generally in better health than did the men. In rounds 1, 3, and 5, differences by sex were present but small for total positive attitudes scores. The total activity scores were significantly higher at rounds 1, 3, and 5 for the females.

There were fifty-four black women in round 1, thirty-three in round 3, and twenty-one in round 5. By round 3, 28 percent of those in round 1 had died; an additional 9 percent were dropouts. By round 5, 44 percent were dead and 17 percent were dropouts. There were forty-one black men in round 1, twenty-six in round 3, and twelve in round 5. By Round 3, 32 percent of the men were dead; 5 percent were dropouts. By Round 5, 61 percent were dead; 10 percent were dropouts. Attrition was obviously most often caused by death.

Among the women between rounds 1 and 3, those who died were most likely to have identified themselves as previous or current users of alcohol at round 1, while the dropouts were among those least likely to have identified themselves in that manner.

Distinguishing characteristics over the same time for the men in this sample were that the dead and the dropouts reported initially the least number of friends and the physical functioning rating (medical) was worst at round 1 for those who were dead by round 3. Among the women between rounds 1 and 5, survivorship was greater among the better educated, those whose major lifetime occupations were more prestigious, those spending most or all of their lives in urban areas,

Reprinted by permission from *Black Aging*, 1:18–29, 1976.

Table D—40. *Background and related social history characteristics of blacks by sex (initial observation).*

Characteristic (in percentages)	Females N = 54	Males N = 41
Under 65 years of age	38.9	14.6
Between 65 and 69 years of age	14.8	31.7
Between 70 and 74 years of age	22.2	26.8
75 or more years of age	24.1	26.8
With less than 11 years of formal education	59.3	70.7
With 11 to 12 years of formal education	7.4	0.0
With 13 to 15 years of formal education	22.2	4.9
With 16 or more years of formal education	11.1	24.4
Never married	5.6	0.0
Married, living with spouse	22.2	73.2
Separated	7.4	4.9
Widowed	64.8	22.0
Whose major lifetime occupations were nonmanual	35.2	22.3
With no living children	27.8	14.6
With no living grandchildren	37.2	22.3
Reporting no new friends during past two years	42.5	36.8
Rating marital happiness below average	15.7	4.8
Who never used tobacco	49.1	24.4
Who never used alcohol	29.4	16.7
With no disease present or disease present, no limitation	13.2	10.0
Whose self-health ratings were good or excellent	57.4	61.0
Whose health was worse compared w/that when 55 years old	48.2	56.1
With no concern about their health	59.3	37.8
Spending majority of lifetime in urban area	83.3	87.5
Residing in own home, apartment	68.5	82.9
Living only with spouse	13.0	53.7
Living alone or with roomers	33.3	17.1
Living with children only	29.6	7.3
Whose present living arrangements were by choice only	66.7	55.0
Wishing to retain their present residential dwelling	46.2	59.0
Wishing to retain their present household composition	56.1	72.2
Liking present neighborhood less than that when 55 years old	27.8	12.5
With ten or more friends	83.3	80.0
Mean, total attitude score	34.8	34.4
Standard deviation	5.7	6.0
Mean, total activities score	29.6	26.5
Standard deviation	7.2	7.3

those not changing residences since they were fifty-five years of age, and those who, while not childless, had few children. The physical functioning rating was also worse for those dead by round 5 at round 1, a finding also true for the males.

Widowhood increased among both sexes between rounds 1 and 5. The self-health rating for the males decreased between rounds 1 and 3; the self-health rating for the females decreased between both rounds 1 and 3 and 3 and 5. Their concern about health also increased over time, while their living arrangements shifted. The physical functioning rating for black females was lower at round 5 than at round 3.

Only tentative characterizations and findings are possible about these blacks, due largely to the small sample size, especially among the men. In addition, specific data for each subject on the items relevant to the proposed investigation were not always available. No estimated scores were assigned for missing data; therefore the number of subjects in the analyses reported in tables D—41 through D—46 will be found to vary, depending on the availability of data. Nevertheless, some hypotheses about aging among older blacks can be generated from their data.

With that aim in mind, then, and using data drawn largely from the social history items, stepwise multiple regression analyses were used to determine separately by sex the best descriptors among available variables of total attitudes scores (a measure of sense of well-being), happiness subscale scores, and total activities scores. All these scores are from the Cavan Adjustment Scale. Independent variables were entered without specifying order. Dependent variables were drawn from round 3 (1964–65) for both sexes and from round 5 (1968–69) for the women. Putting in the initial score on the dependent variable as the first independent variable has the effect of leaving only residual change to be explained. Thus, tables D—43 through D—45 are analyses of factors related to change.

Due to the extremely small number of men by round 5, regression analyses were performed for them by using dependent variables in round 3 and independent variables in round 1 only. Although the sample size in round 5 was somewhat larger for the women, the analyses were not restricted to women who were in rounds 1, 3, and 5. Instead, analyses were performed for women with relevant data in rounds 1 and 3, 1 and 5, and 3 and 5. Therefore, the reported results should not be interpreted as longitudinal data for precisely the same women over the entire time period between rounds 1 and 5.

Some of the independent variables were true continuous variables. Those set up as dummy variables were marital status, economic position, and living arrangements. Major lifetime occupation, scored by traditional broad census categories, was also coded, with the highest value assigned to the lowest occupational category, but the signs have been reversed to facilitate interpretation by the reader.

Table D—41. *Zero-order Pearsonian correlations of selected variables from rounds 1 or 3 with total attitudes scores at rounds 1 and 3 (both sexes) and 5 (women).*

Variable	Total attitudes scores	
Round 1 variables Males (N = 21)	Round 1	Round 3
Total attitudes score	—	.6282*
Education	.2486	.1788
Age	−.4091	−.3425
Occupation	.3691	.2168
Marital status	.2272	.0445
Self-health rating	.0649	.4633*
Number of living children	−.3243	.0600
Number of new friends	.1346	.2013
Total activity score	.7198*	.4832*
WAIS full-scale weighted score	.1092	.2194
Physical functioning rating	−.1352	−.2252
Number of friends	−.0823	.1554

Variable	Total attitudes scores	
Round 1 variables Females (N = 18)	Round 1	Round 5
Total attitudes score	—	.4283
Number of relatives seen monthly	.2847	−.0496
Economic position	.2235	.2116
Major lifetime occupation	.1444	.0564
Marital status	.3289	.5938*
Education	.2765	.5938*
Self-health rating	.6804*	.3903
Number of living children	.0272	−.3827
Living arrangements	−.2761	−.1593
Number of membership organizations	.0664	.0306
Age	−.0620	−.2187

Variable	Total attitudes scores	
Round 3 variables Females (N = 28)	Round 1	Round 3
Total attitudes score	—	.6861*
Number of relatives seen monthly	.1178	.0135
Economic position	.4588*	.5342*
Major lifetime occupation	.3850*	.2984*
Marital status	.2762	.1534
Education	.5533*	.4672*
Self-health rating	.3137	.4090*
Number of living children	−.2591	−.3372
Living arrangements	−.1036	−.0452
Number of membership organizations	.2863	.1964
Age	−.0378	−.3325

Table D—41. *(Continued)*

Variable	Total attitudes scores	
Round 3 variables Females (N = 18)	Round 3	Round 5
Total attitudes score	—	.7915*
Number of relatives seen monthly	−.0926	−.0496
Economic position	−.0866	.2116
Major lifetime occupation	.1030	.0564
Marital status	.1537	.1857
Education	.5364*	.5938*
Self-health rating	.3014	.3581
Number of living children	−.5440*	−.3827
Living arrangements	.0108	−.1593
Economic position	.0709	.0306
Age	−.3277	−.3715

*Significant at least at the .05 level.

Correlates of Attitudes, Happiness, and Activities

The zero-order Pearsonian correlations between the independent variables entered into the multiple regression analyses by sex and by rounds for each dependent variable are shown in tables D—40 through D—42. In general, the strength and magnitude of the relationships between the various independent and dependent variable changes between rounds. Consider, for example, table D—41, where, among both males and females in rounds 1 and 3, the strengths of the relationships between each independent variable and attitudes shifted.

In table D—41, round 1, the only strong correlation with attitudes among the males was with activity. Economic position, occupation, and education were all significantly correlated with attitudes among the women. Aside from attitudes in rounds 1 and 3 being significantly correlated for both sexes, self-health rating was significantly correlated with attitudes for the men. Self-health rating, economic position, and education were significantly correlated with attitudes for women.

In table D—42, round 1, happiness was correlated significantly with attitudes and activities for both sexes. Education, number of new friends, and intelligence were also significantly correlated with happiness among women. In round 3, happiness in round 1 and attitudes correlated significantly with happiness for both sexes. Age was negatively correlated with happiness significantly among women.

In table D—43, round 1, attitudes, economic position, occupation, and education were significantly correlated with activity for both sexes. A strong negative relationship existed between age and activities among the males. Self-health rating and the number of membership organizations were significantly

Table D—42. *Zero-order Pearsonian correlations of selected variables from rounds 1 or 3 with happiness subscores at rounds 1 and 3 (both sexes) and 5 (women).*

Variable	Happiness subscale scores	
Round 1 variables		
Males (N = 22)	Round 1	Round 3
Happiness subscale score	—	.6711*
Total attitudes score	.8170 *	.5063*
Education	.1807	.2692
Age	−.3563	−.4548
Major lifetime occupation	.3259	.1939
Marital status	.1103	.0149
Self-health rating	−.1385	.4101
Number of living children	−.1385	−.0533
Number of new friends	.1168	.1450
Total activity score	.6500 *	.4045
WAIS full-scale weighted score	.0766	.3323
Number of friends	.0072	.1409

Variable	Happiness subscale scores	
Round 1 variables		
Females (N = 25)		
Happiness subscale score	—	.5146*
Total attitudes score	.7729 *	.4684*
Education	.4748 *	.3788
Age	−.0314	−.4941*
Major lifetime occupation	.3443	.2297
Marital status	.2222	.1074
Self-health rating	.3424	.2948
Number of living children	−.2240	−.2806
Number of new friends	−.4654	−.1886
Total activity score	.4912	−.1954
WAIS full-scale weighted score	.3842	.3254
Total number of friends	.1719	.1480

Variable	Happiness subscale scores	
Round 3 variables		
Females (N = 17)	Round 3	Round 5
Happiness subscale score	—	.5684*
Marital status	.2667	.6650*
Number of new friends	−.4998 *	−.2790
Number of friends	−.3071	−.2988
Education	.6223 *	.6055*

*Significant at least at the .05 level.

Table D—43. *Zero-order Pearsonian correlations of selected variables from rounds 1 or 3 with total activity scores at rounds 1 and 3 (both sexes) and 5 (women).*

Variable	Total activity scores	
Round 1 variables Males (N = 26)	Round 1	Round 3
Total activity score	—	.6965*
Total attitudes score	.6480*	.5871*
Economic position	.4146	.3637
Life expectancy	.3760	.5197*
Self-health rating	.1583	.4424*
Age	−.3966*	−.5307*
Number of living children	.0895	−.0004
Marital status	.2009	−.0209
Major lifetime occupation	.5404*	.2030
Education	.5325*	.3861*

Variable	Total activity scores	
Round 1 variables Females (N = 21)	Round 1	Round 5
Total activity score	—	.4292*
Total attitudes score	.6045*	.2599
Number of membership organizations	.3822	.5647*
Major lifetime occupation	.1540	.3480
Marital status	.0570	.2331
Self-health rating	−.0489	.7727*
Number of living children	−.0489	−.2019
Education	.2547	.5211*
Economic position	.2488	.2385
Living arrangements	−.1232	−.2905
Age	−.0408	−.4190

Variable	Total activity scores	
Round 3 variables Females (N = 25)	Round 1	Round 3
Total activity score	—	.7474*
Total attitudes score	.6666*	.6071*
Number of membership organizations	.3711*	.2915
Major lifetime occupation	.3598*	.5933*
Marital status	.1352	.1901
Self-health rating	.4234*	.3510*
Number of living children	−.1284	−.1378
Education	.4633*	.5788*
Economic position	.3745*	.4317*
Living arrangements	−.0964	−.1081
Age	−.0484	−.2316

Table D—43. *(Continued)*

Variable	Total activity scores	
Round 3 variables Females (N = 21)	Round 3	Round 5
Total activity score	—	.6040*
Total attitudes score	.4491 *	.5273*
Number of membership organizations	.3438	.5647*
Major lifetime occupation	.5613 *	.3480
Marital status	.1032	.3164
Self-health rating	.1951	.3157
Number of living children	−.1348	−.2019
Education	.4114	.5211*
Economic position	.1670	.2385
Living arrangements	.0568	−.2905
Age	−.0792	−.4190

*Significant at least at the .05 level.

correlated with activity among the women. In round 3, activity at round 1, attitudes, self-health rating, and education correlated significantly with activity for both sexes. Additionally, variables correlated significantly characteristically were life expectancy (a variable not entered for the women) and age among the men and occupation and economic position for the women.

Perhaps socioeconomic status is an important determinant of psychological adjustment to aging among the women, but not among the men. Increasing age and unhappiness were related strongly among the women, but not among the men. Socioeconomic status, perceived health status, and aging attitudes were related strongly to activity among both sexes, but the magnitude of those variables differed by sex, with some of the changes explained by widowhood among females.

Increasing age may operate more effectively and swiftly in reducing male activity. The number of membership organizations seems more critically related to female activities among the elderly. This is plausible since black men more often belong to professional (or work-related) organizations than do black women, or at least they have in the past. These black women more often belonged to social organizations where continuing participation was generally independent of employment.

Predictors of Attitudes, Happiness, and Activities

Consider table D—44, which summarizes a multiple regression analysis of the determinants of observed attitudes and scores. About 39 percent of the variance in total attitudes scores in round 3 among the men can be explained by their round 1 attitudes scores. Adding self-health rating, number of living children,

Table D—44. *Multiple regression analysis results with total attitudes score as the dependent variable for rounds 3 (both sexes) and 5 (women).**

Variable and group	*r*	*R*	*F*	*Beta*	SE *Beta*
Dependent variable, round 3					
Males, independent variables, round 1					
Total attitudes score	.6282*	.6282	31.1100*	1.1386	0.2041
Self-health rating	.4633*	.7576	24.0450*	0.6071	0.1238
Number of living children	.0600	.8439	16.8239*	0.5960	0.1453
Total activity score	.4832*	.8906	6.2587*	−0.493	0.1979
Females, independent variables, round 1					
Total attitude score	.6861*	.6861	26.1130*	0.6745	0.1320
Age	−.3325	.7516	5.4102*	−0.3070	0.1320
Dependent variable, round 5					
Females, independent variables, round 1					
Education	.5938*	.5938	10.2016*	0.7290	0.2282
Total attitudes score	.4283	.6543	3.9136	0.4829	0.2441
Number of living children	−.3827	.6864	5.5368*	−0.5156	0.2191
Marital status	.1600	.7197	5.8223*	0.5659	0.2345
Self-health rating	.3903	.7703	3.8315	−0.5957	0.3043
Number of membership organizations	.0306	.8274	3.1799	−0.3462	0.1942
Females, independent variables, round 3					
Total attitudes score	.7915*	.7915	26.8503*	0.79158	0.1527

*All of the independent variables above increased the explained variation within the respective groups at a statistically significant level of at least .05. With the exception of one group, only the variables which themselves were significant at entry in influencing the dependent variable are shown. The one exception is for females in rounds 1 and 5, where three of the independent variables helped increase greatly the power of the overall descriptors, but were not themselves significant independently. All of the variables which were used are shown in table D—45. Order of entry was not specified.

and activity accounts for about 79 percent of that variance. About 47 percent of the variance in attitudes scores in round 3 for women could be accounted for by their attitudes scores in round 1. With age added, about 56 percent of the variance could be explained. Also for the women, with attitudes scores in round 5 as the dependent variable, education appeared first as an explanatory variable, accounting for about 35 percent of the variance. Then, attitudes scores, number of living children, marital status, self-health rating, and number of membership organizations increased the explained variance to about 68 percent. Of the round 3 independent variables, when attitudes scores in round 5 was the dependent variable, only attitudes, accounting for about 63 percent of the variance, appeared significant in the analysis.

Table D—45 shows that about 45 percent of the variance in happiness subscale scores among men in round 3 was explained by happiness in round 1. Self-

Table D—45. *Multiple regression analysis results with happiness subscale score as the dependent variable for rounds 3 (both sexes) and 5 (women).**

Variable and group	*r*	*R*	*F*	*Beta*	SE *Beta*
Dependent variable, round 3					
Males, independent variables, round 1					
Happiness subscale score	.6711*	.6711	20.5601*	0.6578	0.1450
Self-health rating	.4101	.7749	7.1367*	0.3876	0.1450
Females, independent variables, round 1					
Happiness subscale score	.5146*	.5146	10.8327*	0.4996	0.1517
Age	−.4941*	.7025	9.9351*	−0.4784	0.1517
Dependent variable, round 5					
Females, independent variables, round 3					
Marital status	.6650*	.6650	9.9685*	0.5356	0.1696
Education	.6055*	.7937	7.1076*	0.4522	0.1696

*All of the independent variables above increased the explained variation within the respective groups at a statistically significant level of at least .05. Only the variables which themselves were significant at entry in influencing the dependent variable are shown. All of the variables that were used are shown in table D—47. Order of entry was not specified.

Table D—46. *Multiple regression analysis results with total activity score as the dependent variable for rounds 3 (both sexes) and 5 (women).**

Variable and group	*r*	*R*	*F*	*Beta*	SE *Beta*
Dependent variable, round 3					
Males, independent variables, round 1					
Total activity score	.6965*	.6965	15.5089*	0.5338	0.1355
Self-health rating	.4424*	.7735	6.7141*	0.3247	0.1253
Age	−.5307*	.8151	4.3312*	−0.2805	0.1347
Females, independent variables, round 1					
Total activity score	.7474*	.7474	28.6161*	0.6133	0.1146
Major lifetime occupation	.5933*	.8243	10.5642*	−0.3726	0.1146
Dependent variable, round 5					
Females, independent variables, round 1					
Self-health rating	.7727*	.7727	29.5304*	0.6725	0.1237
Number of membership organizations	.5647*	.8614	10.1199	0.3937	0.1237
Females, independent variables, round 3					
Total activity score	.6040*	.6040	6.9897*	0.4647	0.1758
Number of membership organizations	.5647*	.7137	5.3061*	0.4049	0.1758

*All of the independent variables above increased the explained variation within the respective groups at a statistically significant level of at least .05. Only the variables which themselves were significant at entry in influencing the dependent variable are shown. All of the variables that were used are shown in table D—47. Order of entry was not specified.

health increased the explained variance to about 60 percent. About 26 percent of the variance in happiness in round 3 among the women was explainable by happiness in round 1, with age increasing the explained variance to about 49 percent. The relationship between age and happiness was negative. The explanatory variables when happiness in round 5 was the dependent variable were different. Then marital status and education at round 3 explained about 63 percent of the variance in the happiness subscale scores at round 5.

Table D—46 shows that the independent variables in round 1 of activity and self-health rating accounted for about 66 percent of the score variation in the round 3 activity scores for the men. Self-health rating was strongly related to activity score. For women, activity and occupation as independent variables from round 1 explained about 67 percent of the variation in the round 3 dependent variable of total activity score. Between rounds 1 and 5, the most powerful descriptors of activity scores in round 5 were self-health rating and number of membership organizations, which explained about 74 percent of the variance in the dependent variable. Using activity in round 5 as the dependent variable and independent variables from round 3, then the independent variables of activity and number of membership organizations explained about 51 percent of the variance.

Summary

To summarize information for the first longitudinal study about the older blacks, the results reconfirm among blacks the well-established observation about persistent relationships between prior and future attitudes and activities (see, e.g., Palmore, 1970). The results also suggest some sex variability in the major predictors of longitudinal changes in those attitudes and activities. Socioeconomic status and chronological age may be more significant predictors of psychological adjustment to aging among black women than among black men, while perceived health status and activity level are more significant for the men. In comparison with childless men, fathers in this sample appeared to make better psychological adjustments to growing old. However, among aged women, as they continued to grow old the number of offspring was inversely related to good psychological adjustment. We do not know why, but note the high proportion of widows in this sample of older black women. I suspect that relationships between adult children and their aged parents, and especially between such children and their mothers, are more fraught with maternal anxiety about discrepancies in desired and real child-parent role interactions when a spouse is absent. The presence of a spouse can lessen emotional dependency upon children or, perhaps, reduce the need to depend upon children for companionship. Women with a relatively large number of offspring may also be handicapped by conflicting negotiations between the children about the assumption, or lack of assumption, of "responsibility for mother." In any case, these data reinforce earlier findings about sex variations in black adult child/aged parent relationships (Jackson, 1971).

Age, inversely related to activity among the men, is more powerful in predicting activities among the men than among the women. The number of organizational memberships remains important for the women. Although both black women and men who have spent most of their adult lives gainfully employed within the labor force are affected by retirement, men may well be more cut off by retirement from their customary nonfamilial activities. This is not to contend, of course, that work is not a primary orientation throughout their working careers for many black professional women but, perhaps, to emphasize the different meanings of their careers.

Conclusion

Following Durkheim (1951), a key explanatory concept for good social and psychological adjustment in growing older, for both black women and black men, may well be that of social integration. The greater the integration into social units meaningful to the individual and the greater the individual's satisfaction with that integration, the greater is her or his successful adjustment to aging. Growing older is generally more successful when individuals share that continued aging with intimate others, and especially with satisfactory spouses who still believe that "the best is yet to be." Thus, principally because most older black women are bereft of spouses and an increasing number of such women will be bereft of spouses in their old age in the future, they are less likely to adjust satisfactorily to old age than are their male counterparts blessed with spouses, as well as their female counterparts similarly blessed. Therefore, it is important now to examine carefully and develop, where needed, social subsystems which promote increased social integration among aging blacks, and particularly among aging black women. It is time, in short, to follow through with Frazier's (1939) concerns about the adverse effects of rapid urbanization upon blacks by helping them to develop and maintain customary or alternative social structures which promote social integration among the individual members, including those who would otherwise be lonely during the menopause or unhappy in their old age. Fragmented structures such as elderly nutrition programs fall short of this goal.

References

Bart, P. B. *Depression in middle-aged women; Some sociocultural factors*. Ph.D. diss., University of California, Los Angeles, 1967.

Bart, P. B., and Grossman, M. Menopause. In M. T. Notman and C. C. Nadelson (Eds.), *The Woman Patient*. New York: Plenum, 1978.

Coppen, A., and Kessel, N. Menstruation and personality. *British Journal of Psychiatry*, 109:711–721, 1963.

Durkheim, E. *Suicide*. Glencoe, Ill: Free Press, 1951.

Frank, R. T. The hormonal causes of premenstrual tension. *Archives of Neurology and Psychiatry*, 26:1053–1057, 1931.

Frazier, E. F. *The Negro family in the United States*. Chicago: University of Chicago Press, 1939.

Jackson, J. J. Social gerontology and the Negro: A review. *Gerontologist*, 7:168–178, 1967.

Jackson, J. J. The blacklands of gerontology. *Aging and Human Development*, 2:156–171, 1971.
Multinovich, J. S. A comparative study of work attitudes of black and white workers. In D. L. Ford, Jr., (Ed.), *Readings in minority-group relations*. La Jolla, Calif.: University Associates, 1976, 133–155.
Neugarten, B. L. A new look at menopause. *Psychology Today*, 1:42–45, 67–69, 1967.
Neugarten, B. L., and Kraines, R. Menopausal symptoms in women of various ages. *Psychosomatic Medicine*, 27:266–273, 1965.
Neugarten, B. L., et al., Women's attitudes toward the menopause. In B. L. Neugarten (Ed.), *Middle age and aging*. Chicago: University of Chicago Press, 1968, 195–200.
Palmore, E. B. (Ed.), *Normal Aging*. Durham, N.C.: Duke University Press, 1970.
Stadel, B. V., and Weiss, N. Characteristics of menopausal women: A survey of King and Pierce counties in Washington, 1973–1974. *American Journal of Epidemiology*, 102:209–216, 1975.
Time. Estrogen and Cancer. *Time*, 14 June 1976, p. 65.
U.S. Public Health Service. National Center for Health Statistics. *Age at menopause*. Series 11, No. 19. Washington, D.C.: U.S. Government Printing Office, 1966.

Total Chance of Institutionalization

Erdman B. Palmore

The growing importance of institutionalization among older Americans is clear. The percentage of persons over age sixty-five who are residents of institutions increased by more than one-fourth between 1960 and 1970 (3.8 percent in 1960; 4.8 percent in 1970) (U.S. Bureau of the Census, 1970). The rising costs of institutionalization are putting enormous strains on public and private resources. One of the major fears of many older persons is that they will become so dependent on personal care that they will have to be institutionalized.

Yet we have no estimates of the chances of an older person's being institutionalized at some time and no information on the factors associated with these chances. We know that about 5 percent of persons over age sixty-five are residents of institutions at any one point in time, but this prevalence rate is of no use in estimating the total or cumulative chance over the years before death. Kastenbaum and Candy (1973), as well as Wershow (1976), have pointed out the "four percent fallacy" of assuming that the figure of 4 percent of aged in nursing homes can be used as an estimate of their cumulative chances.

Similarly, we know that, at any point in time, women, whites, those who live alone, and the very old are more likely to be institutionalized than are men, blacks, those who live with others, and the "young-old" (Riley, 1968). These and other correlates may not be associated in the same way with total chances of in-

Reprinted by permission from *Gerontologist*, 16:504–507, 1976.

stitutionalization, however, because of differential life expectancy, length of stay, and admission rates among these groups.

Thus, when a person tries to plan for his or her old age and asks "what are my chances of being institutionalized?" we cannot even give a general estimate, much less a specific answer based on his or her age, sex, race, and other relevant factors. This article is a first attempt to provide such estimates, based on a longitudinal study of normal aged persons over a twenty-year period.

Longitudinal Study of Institutionalization

There were 207 persons in the Duke First Longitudinal Study of Aging who were followed until their deaths prior to spring 1976. All were community residents at the beginning of the study in 1955. About one-half were men and one-half women; one-third were blacks and, at the beginning of the study, about three-fifths were aged sixty to sixty-nine and two-fifths were aged seventy or over. An additional sixty-four survivors were not included in this analysis. This study panel was not a probability sample; instead, participants were chosen from a large pool of community volunteers so as to approximate the age, sex, race, and socioeconomic distribution of older persons in the Piedmont area of North Carolina. For further description of the study sample and methods, see Palmore (1970).

Information on institutionalization was derived from two sources: questions in the social history (repeated in each of the eleven rounds of examinations) as to whether the participant had ever been in a long-term care institution and, if so, how long (all but one of those who had been institutionalized stayed for six months or more) and the death certificates which list the place of death. If the place of death was a chronic disease hospital, a nursing home, or a home for the aged, the person was categorized as having been institutionalized, regardless of length of stay, because length of stay information was often not available. Thus, our analysis includes as institutionalized a few persons who may have been in a long-term care institution for only a few days before death. This procedure results in a somewhat higher estimate than if one defined institutionalization as stays of at least one month (or six months) in a long-term institution. However, institutionalization is usually defined to include all persons in long-term institutions (regardless of the individual's length of stay), as distinct from hospitalization that includes persons in short-term institutions. On the other hand, we may have missed a few cases in which a person was institutionalized after our last examination but returned home before death. We believe that such cases were rare.

Total Chances

Using these procedures we found that fifty-four of the 207 persons (26 percent in the longitudinal panel had been institutionalized one or more times before death. Forty-five had died in an institution, and only nine had returned home prior to death. Thus, our general estimate of the total chance (lifetime prevalence) of institutionalization before death among normal aged persons living in the community would be about one in four. Or to put it the other way around, we would estimate that three out of four aged persons will never be institutionalized. It should be understood that this is only a rough estimate of population probability, because of possible inaccuracies in our data, sample bias, and the variation by region and type of locality. However, this estimate is compatible with Kastenbaum and Candy's (1973) estimate that 23 percent of aged deaths in Detroit occurred in extended care facilities. If one added an estimate of those who returned home before death (4 percent in our study) to their 23 percent, the resulting 27 percent would be about identical to our estimate.

Factors Related to Total Chances

The factors we found to be related to total chance of institutionalization may be grouped into those which indicate a greater need for institutionalization and those which indicate better access to institutions.

The significant *need* factors include living arrangements, marital status,

Table D—47. *Percentage ever-institutionalized in selected categories.*

Variable	Category All persons	(*N*) (207)	% Ever institu-tionalized 26	% Not 74	*p**
Living arrangement	Alone	(42)	33	67	.10
	With spouse	(119)	24	76	
	With others	(46)	24	76	
Marital status	Never-married	(13)	54	46	.001
	Separated	(10)	40	60	
	Spouse present	(119)	24	76	
	Widowed	(66)	20	80	
Children living	None	(38)	34	66	.05
	1 or 2	(74)	27	73	
	3 +	(95)	22	78	
Sex	Women	(97)	33	67	.01
	Men	(110)	20	80	
Finances	Enough or better	(180)	28	72	.10
	Cannot make ends meet	(23)	13	87	
Education	7 years +	(123)	30	70	.05
	0–6 years	(84)	20	80	
Race	White	(139)	32	68	.001
	Black	(68)	15	85	

*Probability of occurring by chance using Kendall's Tau C.

number of living children, and sex (table D—47). Those who live alone had a higher rate (33 percent institutionalized compared to 24 percent of those not living alone) probably because they are less able to arrange for someone to care for them outside an institution when they become physically or mentally incapacitated. Those never-married (54 percent institutionalized) and those separated from spouse (40 percent) had higher rates because there was no spouse to care for them. Those with no living children (38 percent) and those with only one or two (27 percent) had higher rates than those with several children (22 percent), which seems to indicate that the presence of several children to care for a person tends to reduce the chance of institutionalization. The final factor we considered as indicating greater need was sex: women had a higher risk of institutionalization (33 percent) than men (20 percent). However, most of this higher rate for women was explained by sex-related characteristics: women more often lived alone, were never-married or were separated, and had fewer living children. In a stepwise regression, when sex was entered in the equation after these three other factors, this variable accounted for only a small (and statistically insignificant) increase in the multiple correlation (table D—48). Thus, it is probably unnecessary to search for other explanations, such as that women may more readily accept the dependent role of being institutionalized.

The significant *access* factors included finances, education, and race (table D—47). Adequacy of finances was indicated by the responses to the question "How would you describe your present financial position in life? 1. Cannot make ends meet. 2. Enough to get along. 3. Comfortable. 4. Well-to-do. 5. Wealthy."

Table D—48. *Stepwise multiple regression of variables related to institutionalization (N = 204).*

Variable	Zero-order correlation	Multiple correlation	*F* value
Living alone[a]	.10	.10	2.0
Marital status[b]	.18	.19	5.2*
Number of children living	.11	.19	0.6
Sex[c]	.14	.21	1.6
Finances[d]	.10	.24	2.8
Education[e]	.11	.25	0.5
Race[f]	.19	.29	5.4*

[a]Coded as 0 for living with spouse or others and 1 for living alone.

[b]Coded as 0 for spouse present or widowed and 1 for never-married or separated.

[c]Coded as 0 for men and 1 for women.

[d]Coded as 0 for "cannot make ends meet" and 1 for "enough or better" reponses.

[e]Coded 0 for 0–6 years of education and 1 for 7 or more.

[f]Coded 0 for blacks and 1 for whites.

*Increase in variance explained at entry was statistically significant at .05 level.

Those who responded that they "cannot make ends meet" had a much lower rate of institutionalization (13 percent) than all the other categories (28 percent). Apparently, lack of money reduced the low income group's access to institutionalization. Those with less education (six years or less) also had lower rates of institutionalization (20 percent) than those with more education (30 percent). However, when entered into the multiple regression equation after finances (and the need factors), education made only a very small and statistically insignificant increase in the multiple correlation (table D—48). Therefore, the educational difference in institutionalization appears to be mainly explained by its association with lack of income to afford institutionalization. Finally, whites appeared to have much more access than blacks because the white rate of institutionalization was more than twice as high as the black rate. Furthermore, when race was entered into the equation after all other factors, it still made a substantial and statistically significant increase in the multiple correlation (table D—48). Thus, the greater access of whites cannot be explained entirely by their higher educational and financial resources. This appears to indicate that in this region of the country, even after need factors and other access factors are taken into account, blacks were less likely to be institutionalized because they had less access to institutions than whites.

Comparisons with Factors Related to Prevalence

In many ways, the factors related to total chance are similar to those known to be related to the prevalence of institutionalization among various groups. Several studies (Riley, 1968) have shown that, at any given point in time, there are higher rates of institutionalization among those who were living alone (prior to institutionalization), those without a spouse present, those without living children, women, and whites, just as indicated in this study.

However, there are two important differences. First, previous studies have found that "old people in institutions are comparatively disadvantaged financially" (Riley, 1968), while we found a lower chance of ever being institutionalized among the financially disadvantaged. This paradox may be resolved if one recalls that ours was a longitudinal study with a measure of financial adequacy that usually occurred years before institutionalization, while the previous studies were cross-sectional, and financial adequacy was measured after institutionalization. It may well be that financial adequacy provides greater access to institutions but that institutionalization itself soon depletes financial reserves, so that most persons in institutions rapidly become financially disadvantaged.

Second, the prevalence rate goes up dramatically with age from 2 percent institutionalized at ages sixty-five to sixty-nine to 14 percent institutionalized at ages over eighty-five (U.S. Bureau of the Census, 1960). However, we found little or no difference in total chance of institutionalization between persons who were older and those who were younger at the beginning of our study. Our explanation of this paradox is that as persons age their increased annual risk of institutionalization is balanced by decreased remaining years before death. Thus, the younger persons in our study had lower annual risks of institutionalization but more years ahead to be at risk; the older persons had higher annual risks but fewer years ahead.

On the other hand, since the sixty-four survivors who were not included in this analysis tended to be younger than the 207 who had died, we may find that their ultimate inclusion in the analysis may change this finding of no difference in lifetime prevalence of institutionalization between the older and younger persons. However, if this finding and interpretation are confirmed by other studies, it would mean that older persons need not fear that their total chances of institutionalization will increase as they age.

It should be clear that these findings need replication with larger samples from other areas in order to find out how representative they are. Furthermore, admission and discharge rates for various groups need to be studied in order to understand better the various factors which affect institutionalization. This understanding would help us to both increase access for those who need institutionalization and decrease unnecessary institutionalization.

References

Kastenbaum, R., and Candy, S. The four percent fallacy. *Aging and Human Development*, 4:15–21, 1973.

Palmore, E. B. (Ed.), *Normal aging*. Durham, N.C.: Duke University Press, 1970.

Riley, M. *Aging and society. Vol. 1*. New York: Russell Sage, 1968.

U.S. Bureau of the Census. *Inmates in institutions*. Washington, D.C.: U.S. Government Printing Office, 1960, 1970.

Wershow, H. The four percent fallacy. *Gerontologist*, 16:52–55, 1976.

Summary and the Future

Erdman B. Palmore

Before summarizing the findings of this volume, it may be worthwhile to repeat some of the standard cautions one should bear in mind when evaluating such data. First, the samples studied are somewhat unrepresentative of the universe from which they were drawn. The Duke First Longitudinal Study was drawn from a pool of volunteers to approximate the demographic composition of Durham, North Carolina, but they were volunteers nevertheless, and they therefore differed in various ways from a strict cross-section of the population of Durham. The second longitudinal study was based on a probability sample of members of the local health insurance association, but we were able to get the participation of only half of those eligible. While the participants appear similar to nonparticipants in basic characteristics, they undoubtedly differ in some ways. In general, the two samples appear to underrepresent the poorer, sicker, and less able members of the community. We can only guess how our findings might change if we were able to get samples which are more representative.

Second, the universe from which the samples were drawn was limited to fairly normal middle-aged and older persons living in the Durham area. We do not know how well our findings might apply to other areas or to other groups such as the institutionalized, although some of the reports discuss this through comparison with other studies.

Third, there are usually errors of measurement, coding, and processing which creep into the data despite our best efforts to catch and correct them (see Palmore, 1974, appendix B). There is also the problem of interpreting some chance fluctuation as significant or, on the other hand, of ignoring an important finding because the numbers are small.

A last caution is the old maxim: "Association does not prove causation." We had no classical experiments in these studies, because we wanted to study the aging process in its natural state. On the other hand, it is true that associations which persist with proper controls do provide evidence that a causal relationship probably exists. Furthermore, in the longitudinal analyses, the time order of events helps support a causal interpretation.

Propositions

Keeping in mind these cautions, we will summarize the major findings of these reports in the form of sixty-eight propositions about normal aging among persons over forty-five who live in the community. For summaries of previous findings, see Palmore, 1970, 1974, and 1981.

A. Physical aging

1. Older persons who are more insecure, unhappy, negative, or dissatisfied with themselves or who readily adopt the sick role use more medical drugs.

2. Older women report less sexual activity and interest than older men.

3. Among most married couples, sexual activity tends to remain stable over middle and later life.

4. While a few older couples decrease or stop sexual activity, a few others increase or resume sexual activity after a period of inactivity.

5. Both men and women usually say that the male partner was responsible for any cessation of sexual activity.

6. The predictors of longevity include health, nonsmoking, intelligence, education, work satisfaction, usefulness, secondary group activities, nongroup activities, happiness, better finances, and frequency and enjoyment of intercourse.

7. The predictors of successful aging include secondary group activities, physical activity, work satisfaction, more education, better cardiovascular function, and lower serum cholesterol.

8. Cardiovascular disease impairs psychomotor performance, especially the number of correct responses and the response time.

9. Cardiovascular disease also impairs performance intelligence, but not verbal intelligence.

10. Vibratory threshold increases with age.

11. Women have lower vibratory thresholds than men.

12. Vibratory threshold is increased by cardiovascular disease, mental disease, and generally poor health.

13. Serum B_{1A} antigen concentrations increase from the third to the seventh decade of life. The C3 component of the complement system tends to be maintained at adequate levels throughout adult life.

B. Mental health and mental illness

1. There is little or no difference in the longevity of those with organic brain disease when compared to normal aged when age and sex are controlled.

2. The prevalence of organic brain disease increases with age.

3. Over one-half of the elderly have one or more episodes of brain impairment before death.

4. Objective observations of depression do not increase with age, despite subjective reports of increasing frequency.

5. Hypochondriasis tends to decline in severity and frequency over time.

6. Over half of the elderly experience one or more periods of hypochondriasis.

7. About one-third of the elderly have focal EEG abnormalities, predominantly over the temporal area of the brain.

8. When these focal EEG abnormalities are confined to the anterior temporal area, there is no impairment of mental processes; however, when they involve adjacent areas of the brain or are associated with diffuse slowing of the brain waves, organic brain impairment is probable.

9. Cerebral blood flow decreases with age.

10. Demented older patients have lower cerebral blood flow than normal aged.

11. Normal aged with lower cerebral blood flow have greater deterioration in mental abilities than those with higher blood flow.

12. The elderly sleep patterns (compared to those of younger persons) are characterized by more wakefulness while in bed, more awakenings during the night, longer periods of awakening, less stage 4 (deep) sleep, and less REM sleep (sleep with rapid eye movements).

13. Elderly people with more REM sleep have high performance intelligence.

14. Vibratory thresholds tend to increase with age, especially among those with various diseases and inadequate diets and among smokers.

15. Vitamin B_{12} can lower vibratory thresholds.

16. Stresses which result from health problems are most frequent, followed in order of frequency by stresses from the family, self, economics, and work.

17. Coping is more effective when: (a) the individual feels in control of how the event is managed and (b) both instrumental and palliative coping strategies are used.

18. Men are more likely than women to experience personal work or health events as most important in their lives, while women are more likely to experience interpersonal health or family events as most important.

19. Major historical events had little impact upon the important events in this cohort's life course (second longitudinal study cohort).

20. Psychological distress reduces perceived health; lower perceived health increases psychological distress.

21. Drowsiness while driving is most frequent among males, those driving more miles per year, and those who do all or most of the driving on long trips.

C. Psychological aging

1. There is little intellectual change among normal elderly until the eighth or ninth decade of life.

2. Those who die early or drop out of a longitudinal study have lower intellectual ability than those who remain in the study.

3. Results of cross-sectional and longitudinal analysis of intelligence are similar when the subjects are similar in age range, education, and perseverance.

4. High blood pressure is related to greater decline in certain kinds of memory: visual reproduction, nonmeaningful material, and delayed recall.

5. The average decline in memory after age sixty is generally small and is restricted to certain kinds of memory (hard associates and visual reproduction).

6. Higher memory and intelligence scores predict greater longevity.

7. Age is a poor predictor of general intelligence; education is the best predictor of intelligence.

8. In a longitudinal study, male dropouts tend to be more anxious, aloof, and independent than male returners; female dropouts tend to be more anxious, dull, and inflexible than female returners.

9. There are little or no personality differences between cohorts or over time; the main personality differences are between men and women.

10. There is a weak correlation between activity levels and psychological well-being; activity levels are better predicted by social status, while psychological well-being is better predicted by personality factors.

11. Older cohorts are more internally oriented than young adult cohorts, but there is little longitudinal change in this orientation.

12. There are few significant differences between age groups in self-concept, and these few are not linearly related to age.

13. Life satisfaction tends to peak around age fifty-five.

14. Anticipated events such as departure of children and change in work status have little effect on life satisfaction; unanticipated events such as illness and death of relatives have strong effects.

15. Persons with more optimistic views of their life course are more likely to be male, to be better educated, to have children, and to feel younger.

16. Change to a more pessimistic view of one's life course is related to decreased life satisfaction, decreased income, and deteriorated health.

D. Social aging

1. Differences between individuals tend to remain the same or increase as individuals age.

2. Individuals tend to maintain a consistent position relative to their peers as they age, despite average declines in function.

3. Persons who identify themselves as "old" tend to be chronologically older and to have older friends, poorer health, and more functional impairment.

4. Among persons aged forty-five to sixty-nine, the most frequent of five major life events is last child departure; major medical events are much less frequent; and widowhood is the rarest event.

5. Persons with lower psychological resources are more likely to experience major life events than are persons with higher resources.

6. Of the major life events, medical events have the most impact on physical adaptation but little impact on social-psychological adaptation.

7. Retirement has some initial negative effects on subjective adaptation but little effect on physical adaptation.

8. Retirement of spouse, widowhood, and departure of last child had little lasting effect on adaptation; in fact, departure of last child tends to have positive effects.

9. Multiple events tend to have cumulative negative effects, especially on satisfaction.

10. Better resources tend to mitigate the negative effects of these major life events.

11. Life satisfaction tends to be stable for both men and women during middle and old age; the best predictor of later life satisfaction is earlier life satisfaction.

12. High life satisfaction is explained primarily by better health and, to a lesser extent, by sexual enjoyment and social activity.

13. Continuity in activities is *not* associated with psychological well-being.

14. Good health is the primary predictor of successful aging in retirement; mandatory retirement and negative attitudes toward retirement predict less successful aging; and return to work tends to enhance successful aging.

15. Retired women tend to be more economically dependent, in poorer health, and more dependent on social support than either women still employed or women who were housewives for most of their lives.

16. About three-fourths of older adults are active in one or more than one voluntary association.

17. Most older adults tend to maintain their levels of activity in voluntary associations as they age.

18. Religious attitudes remain stable as persons age but religious activities tend to decline.

19. Religious activity and attitudes are correlated with happiness, feeling useful, and personal adjustment.

20. Among older blacks, as among whites, patterns of activity tend to be stable over time and better psychological adjustment is predicted by higher socioeconomic status, better health, and more activity.

21. Above one-fourth of all older adults are institutionalized one or more times.

22. Older adults who were never married or are separated, who have higher incomes, who have more education, or who are white have higher chances of institutionalization at some time.

Themes

When we review these specific findings on normal aging, some general themes emerge which tie together findings from several substantive areas. The summary chapters of the first two normal aging volumes pointed out five such themes. The same themes are echoed and extended in this volume:

1. *Advantages of longitudinal and interdisciplinary study of aging.* The longitudinal method analyzed changes in the same persons over time in the following: sexual activity and interest, the predictors of longevity and successful aging, the effects of cardiovascular disease on psychomotor and intellectual performance, vibratory thresholds, the effects of organic brain disease on longevity, the prevalence of organic brain disease, depression, and hypochondriasis; EEG abnormalities, cerebral blood flow, intellectual change, blood pressure and memory, characteristics of dropouts, predictors of activity and psychological well-being, internal orientation, self-concepts, life satisfaction, predictors of life satisfaction, views of life course, homogeneity and heterogeneity, consistency and continuity, life events and the predictors of life events, the effects of life events and resources, predictors of successful aging, activity in voluntary associations, religious activity and attitudes, racial differences, and institutionalization.

Since aging is by definition a change over time in an individual, the advantages of the longitudinal method over the cross-section method of studying these changes are obvious.

The advantages of interdisciplinary collaboration is reflected in the fact that most of these reports involve the joint analysis of variables from two or more areas: biology, psychiatry, psychology, and sociology. Aging is a complex process with causes and consequences in all areas of life. Any analysis that is limited to just one area of discipline is necessarily of limited usefulness and, at best, provides only a partial understanding of aging; at worst it may provide a distorted or mistaken view of aging.

2. *Patterns of declining health and physical functioning*. This theme is repeated with some variations in the overall declines in sexual activity and in increasing cardiovascular disease, vibratory thresholds, organic brain disease, EEG abnormalities, impairment of cerebral blood flow, and sleep disturbances. This confirms the expected pattern of normal aging.

3. *Exceptions to physical decline*. Despite the overall declines as measured by averages or group percentages, substantial minorities show no decline and may even have improvement in sexual activity, especially among married couples; cardiovascular function; hypertension; brain function; depression; hypochondriasis; EEG abnormalities; vibratory thresholds; and serum antigens. Thus the process of physical aging is not necessarily an irresistible and irreversible force. Health and function can and do improve for some older persons, just as they do for younger persons.

4. *Little or no decline in social and psychological functioning*. This theme is in direct contrast to the theme of declining physical functioning. *Normal aging I* presented several findings which show little or no decline in activities, attitudes, cautiousness, recall, or general adjustment. *Normal aging II* reported only small overall declines in intelligence scores (especially among those aged sixty to sixty-nine and those free of hypertension), reaction times, correct signal detections, and EEG frequencies. The present reports show little or no declines in most measures of mental health—coping with stressful events, intellectual ability on untimed tests until the eighth or ninth decade, general intelligence, personality, internal orientation, self-concept, heterogeneity, life satisfaction, activity in voluntary associations, and religious attitudes—and in activity among blacks, as well as among whites. It is impressive how many of the normal aged are able to compensate for their growing physical handicaps and maintain fairly stable levels of social and psychological functioning. This evidence tends to refute the disengagement theory that social and psychological decline are typical, inevitable, and normal.

5. *Wide variation in aging patterns*. This theme takes two forms: (1) documenting the persistence (or increase) of individual variation which group averages obscure and (2) attempting to account for individual and group differences. These reports attempt to account for the individual variations by analyzing differences by sex, race, socioeconomic group, health practices, chronic and acute illness, retirement, occurrence of stressful events, coping styles, and religious activity and attitudes.

Assuming that these samples approximate in general the universe of older people in the United States, the above findings and themes represent significant advances in our understanding of normal aging in this country.

The Future

Although data collection for the first and second longitudinal studies of aging is finished, longitudinal studies continue at the Duke University Center for the Study of Aging and Human Development in two ways. First, we have made the data tapes for the first and second longitudinal studies available to any investigator who wishes to analyze the data further. We hope this will produce much additional useful analysis, because our present analyses have by no means exhausted the rich possibilities for scientific discovery contained in the millions of scores and measures recorded on these tapes. We estimate that the tapes for each study contain about two million pieces of information.

Second, we recently (1984) completed the data collection for a third longitudinal study of aging titled "Mental illness and social support among the very old." This is a ten-year follow-up study of 300 survivors from the 1972 Durham Community Survey. Most of these survivors were aged seventy-five or older at the time of the follow-up examinations. As in the first two longitudinal studies, the participants were brought to the center for comprehensive physical, mental, and social examinations; however, this third study emphasized the measurement and diagnosis of mental illness as well as the type and degree of social support available for the participants. Two additional annual reexaminations were also given to most of the participants. Analysis of these data is under way, and we expect it will continue for several years.

Thus, the complex and difficult enterprise of exploring and charting the territory of aging continues. We believe this enterprise will eventually allow more older people to safely reach the promised land of a better and longer life.

References

Palmore, E. B. (Ed.), *Normal aging*. Durham, N.C.: Duke University Press, 1970.
Palmore, E. B. (Ed.), *Normal aging II*. Durham, N.C.: Duke University Press, 1974.
Palmore, E. B. (Ed.), *Social patterns of normal aging*. Durham, N.C.: Duke University Press, 1981.

Index